# GEOGRAPHY
## OF THE WORLD

The Friday Mosque at Mopti in Mali

Street scene in Tokyo, Japan

Chinese boy writing characters

Black pepper plant and peppercorns from the Pacific Islands

Traditional house built by the Tswana people from Botswana

High, windswept plains, called the altiplano, in Bolivia

Aymará Indians from the altiplano in Bolivia

A variety of different crops grown on small farms in Italy

Copper from Namibia

Street market in Lausanne, Switzerland

Wine and cheeses from Germany

UNITED KINGDOM

PHILIPPINES

ARGENTINA

NEW ZEALAND

CANADA

BRUNEI

PARAGUAY

KAZAKHSTAN

BAHAMAS

SUDAN

UNITED STATES OF AMERICA

JAPAN

BHUTAN

ITALY

SWEDEN

GHANA

IVORY COAST

BRAZIL

MEXICO

NORWAY

INDIA

SAUDI ARABIA

GERMANY

FRANCE

SOUTH AFRICA

SENEGAL

AUSTRALIA

AZERBAIJAN

TUVALU

# GEOGRAPHY
# OF
# THE WORLD

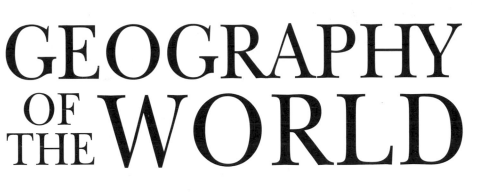

CHINA

RUSSIAN FEDERATION

VENEZUELA

PANAMA

PORTUGAL

BELGIUM

KENYA

SPAIN

IRAQ

CHILE

NETHERLANDS

JAMAICA

GREECE

INDONESIA

THAILAND

KIRIBATI

MALAYSIA

MONGOLIA

DK

**DK**

LONDON, NEW YORK,
MELBOURNE, MUNICH, and DELHI

**Senior Art Editor**
Rachael Foster

**Senior Editor**
Susan Peach

**Art Editors**
Marcus James, Tina Robinson,
Gillian Shaw, Jane Tetzlaff

**Editors**
Marie Greenwood, Fran Jones,
Nic Kynaston, Veronica Pennycook

**Deputy Art Director** Miranda Kennedy
**Deputy Editorial Director** Sophie Mitchell
**Senior DTP designer** Mathew Birch
**DTP designer** Almudena Díaz
**Cartography** Jan Clark, Robin Giddings
**Picture research** Rachel Leach, Jo Haddon
**Research** Robert Graham
**Special photography** Andy Crawford
**Production** Catherine Semark, Louise Barratt

**Chief consultant** Dr David Green

**Consultants**

Dr Kathy Baker, Professor Mark Blacksell, Dr Tanya Bowyer-Bower, Dr Robert Bradnock,
Dr Edward Brown, Dr Brian Chalkley, Professor Roman Cybriwsky, Professor Dennis Dwyer,
Professor Alan Gilbert, St John Gould, Professor Ian Hamilton, Robert Headland, Dr Michael Heffernan,
Professor Eleanore Kofman, Keith Lye, Professor Robert Mason, Professor Bill Mead, Professor William
Morgan, Susan Murrell, Jenny Nemko, Dr Rewi Newnham, Professor Robert Potter, Dr Jonathan Rigg,
Dr David Simon, Dr David Turnock, John Wright and Nicholas Awde, Dr Ted Yates

**Authors** Simon Adams, Anita Ganeri, Ann Kay
Additional text by Ann Kramer, Claire Watts

First published in Great Britain in 1996
This edition published in Great Britain in 2006
by Dorling Kindersley Limited,
80 Strand, London WC2R 0RL

Copyright © 1996 Dorling Kindersley Limited, London
Reprinted with revisions 1998, 2003, 2006
A Penguin Company

2 4 6 8 10 9 7 5 3 1

A CIP catalogue record for this book is available from the British Library.

ISBN-10 14053 1628 4
ISBN-13 978 1 4053 1628 6

Colour reproduction by Colourscan, Singapore
Printed and bound in Slovakia by Neografia

Discover more at
**www.dk.com**

# CONTENTS

# HOW TO USE THIS BOOK

THIS BOOK IS DIVIDED INTO six continental sections – North America, Central and South America, Europe, Asia, Africa, and Australasia and Oceania. At the start of each section there is a map showing the whole area, as well as pages that describe the peoples who live there. Each country, or group of countries, then has an individual map that shows its cities, towns, and main geographical features. This is followed by the country pages that go into detail about life in that country. The reference section can be used to find out more about subjects of general interest, such as world religions or political systems. There is also a glossary, a gazetteer, and an index. The pages here explain the information and symbols that you will come across in the book.

## COUNTRY PAGES

The country pages, like this one for Japan, have been designed to give you as much information as possible about the way of life in a country – its people, their traditions, politics, and the economy. All the countries of the world are featured in the book.

### FACT BOXES

Each country page has a box with important statistics about that country, such as its area, the size of its population, the capital city, and the currency. The notes below explain some other entries that appear in most fact boxes.

### COLOUR BORDERS

Each continental section has a different colour border to help you locate that section easily. This page on Japan has the colour used for all the countries in Asia.

### HEADING

Every page in the book has a heading that tells you the name of the section followed by the name of the country featured on that page.

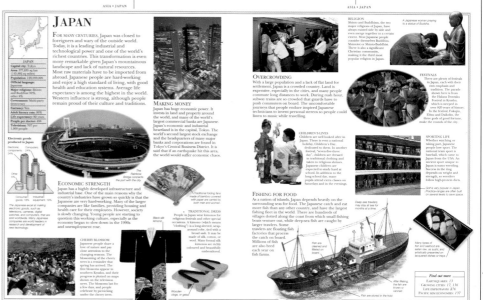

**Locator map**
*This shows the position of a country, or countries, in relation to its neighbours. This locator map shows where Japan lies off the coast of mainland Asia.*

| JAPAN | |
|---|---|
| **Capital city:** Tokyo | |
| **Area:** 377,835 sq km (145,882 sq miles) | |
| **Population:** 128,000,000 | |
| **Official language:** Japanese | |
| **Major religions:** Shinto and Buddhist 92%, other 8% | |
| **Government:** Multi-party democracy | |
| **Currency:** Yen | |
| **Adult literacy rate:** 99% | |
| **Life expectancy:** 82 years | |
| **People per doctor:** 496 | |
| **Televisions:** 707 per 1,000 people | |

**Major religions**
*The figures provide a breakdown of the religious beliefs of the people. All the main religions are explained in detail on pages 274–275.*

**Government**
*This describes how a country is ruled, or governed. The main types of government are explained on pages 270–271.*

**Adult literacy rate**
*This is the percentage of people who can read and write. Literacy rates are based on the ability of people aged 15 or over to read and write a simple sentence. Find out more about literacy rates on page 277.*

**People per doctor**
*This figure shows how many people there are for every one doctor. It gives a rough guide about whether people have easy access to medical attention. Find out more on page 276.*

**Life expectancy**
*The number shows how long the average person in a country can expect to live. Figures are a combination of the average life expectancy for men and women. There is more about life expectancy on page 276.*

### Abbreviations used in the book:

**Metric**

| m | metres |
|---|---|
| mm | millimetres |
| cm | centimetres |
| km | kilometres |
| sq km | square kilometres |
| km/h | kilometres per hour |
| °C | degrees Centigrade |

**Imperial**

| ft | feet |
|---|---|
| in | inches |
| sq miles | square miles |
| mph | miles per hour |
| °F | degrees Fahrenheit |

**Other abbreviations**

| BC | Before Christ |
|---|---|
| AD | Anno Domini |
| USA | United States of America |
| UK | United Kingdom |

### FIND OUT MORE BOXES

At the end of each country entry there is a Find out more box. This directs you to other pages in the book where you can discover more about a particular subject. For example, one of the pages on Japan explains how the country suffers from hundreds of earthquakes a year. You can then find out more about earthquakes and why they occur by turning to page 13 in the book.

# MAP PAGES

Each country appears on one of the regional maps, like the one of Southern Africa shown below. These maps show many geographical features, such as mountain ranges, deserts, rivers, and lakes, along with capital cities and other major towns. The key on the far right shows you what these features look like on the maps. A compass point fixes the direction of the region in relation to North (N).

*This figure is the page number.*

*This figure gives the grid reference on the map.*

**Durango** *Town* Mexico 39 E5
**Durban** *Town* South Africa 247 I10
**Dushanbe** *Town* Tajikistan 161 G8
**Düsseldorf** *Town* Germany 95 D6
**Dvina (Northern, Western)** *River* Russian Federation 78 I8, L6, 109 G6, J8, 138 E5
**Dzhugdzhur Range** *Mountain range* Russian Federation 133 O6, 139 Q8

## E

**East China Sea** China 10 K6, 133 L10, 265 A3
**East Frisian Islands** Germany 95 E3

## USING THE GRID

The grid around the outside of the page helps you to find places on the map. For example, to find the city of Durban, look up its name in the gazetteer on pages 284–295. Next to the word Durban are the reference numbers 247 I10. The first number shows that Durban is on page 247. The second number shows it is in square I10 of the grid. Turn to page 247. Trace down from the letter I on the grid and then across from the number 10. You will find Durban situated in the square where the number and the letter meet.

### Key to features on the maps

International border

Disputed border

State or province border

River

Wadi

Lake

Seasonal lake

Waterfall

Dam

Capital city

Major town

Special feature

Volcanic mountain

Mountain

---

## SCALE

Each map features a scale which shows how distances on the map relate to kilometres and miles. The scale can be used to see how big a country is, or how far it is from one place to another. Not all maps in the book are drawn to the same scale.

## LOCATOR MAP

This map shows the position of the country, or countries, within the continental section. It also shows how near the country is to the Equator, the Tropics of Cancer and Capricorn, or the Arctic or Antarctic Circle. This gives an indication of how hot or cold a country is. Find out more about climate on pages 14–15.

*Angola*   *Namibia*

## COUNTRY FLAGS

The national flag for each country or territory appears around the edge of the map. The designs often reflect the culture or religion of the country.

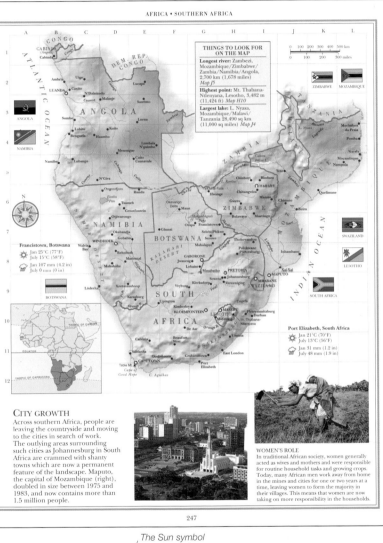

AFRICA • SOUTHERN AFRICA

**THINGS TO LOOK FOR ON THE MAP**
**Longest river:** Zambezi, Mozambique/Zimbabwe/ Zambia/Namibia/Angola, 2,700 km (1,678 miles) *Map J5*
**Highest point:** Mt. Thabana-Ntlenyana, Lesotho, 3,482 m (11,424 ft) *Map H10*
**Largest lake:** L. Nyasa, Mozambique/Malawi/ Tanzania 28,490 sq km (11,000 sq miles) *Map J4*

Francistown, Botswana
Jan 25°C (77°F)
July 15°C (58°F)
Jan 107 mm (4.2 in)
July 0 mm (0 in)

Port Elizabeth, South Africa
Jan 21°C (70°F)
July 13°C (56°F)
Jan 31 mm (1.2 in)
July 48 mm (1.9 in)

### CITY GROWTH

Across southern Africa, people are leaving the countryside and moving to the cities in search of work. The outlying areas surrounding such cities as Johannesburg in South Africa are crammed with shanty towns which are now a permanent feature of the landscape. Maputo, the capital of Mozambique (right), doubled in size between 1975 and 1983, and now contains more than 1.5 million people.

### WOMEN'S ROLE

In traditional African society, women generally acted as wives and mothers and were responsible for routine household tasks and growing crops. Today, many African men work away from home in the mines and cities for one or two years at a time, leaving women to form the majority in their villages. This means that women are now taking on more responsibility in the households.

247

---

## WEATHER FACTS

The average temperature and amount of rainfall recorded in January and July are shown around the main map. Weather facts are given for several places on the map to show how temperature and rainfall can vary within an area. The weather inland, for example, will generally be hotter than it is near the coast.

*The Sun symbol represents the average temperature.*

**Francistown, Botswana**
Jan 25°C (77°F)
July 15°C (58°F)
Jan 107 mm (4.2 in)
July 0 mm (0 in)

*The cloud symbol represents the average rainfall.*

### Abbreviations used on maps

| | |
|---|---|
| L. | Lake |
| I. or Is. | Island (s) |
| R. | River |
| Mt. or Mts. | Mountain (s) |
| St | Saint |
| C. | Cape |
| Res. | Reservoir |

# THE PHYSICAL WORLD

THE EARTH, OUR HOME in the universe, is one of the nine planets that circles around the Sun. It is the only place scientists know that can support life because it has oxygen in its atmosphere and water in its oceans – both essential for life. More than two-thirds of the Earth is covered with water in the form of oceans, seas, rivers, and lakes. The remainder is made up of seven vast expanses of land, called continents, whose physical features are remarkably varied. Among the most notable features are the mountain ranges, rivers, and deserts, which can be found on this world map.

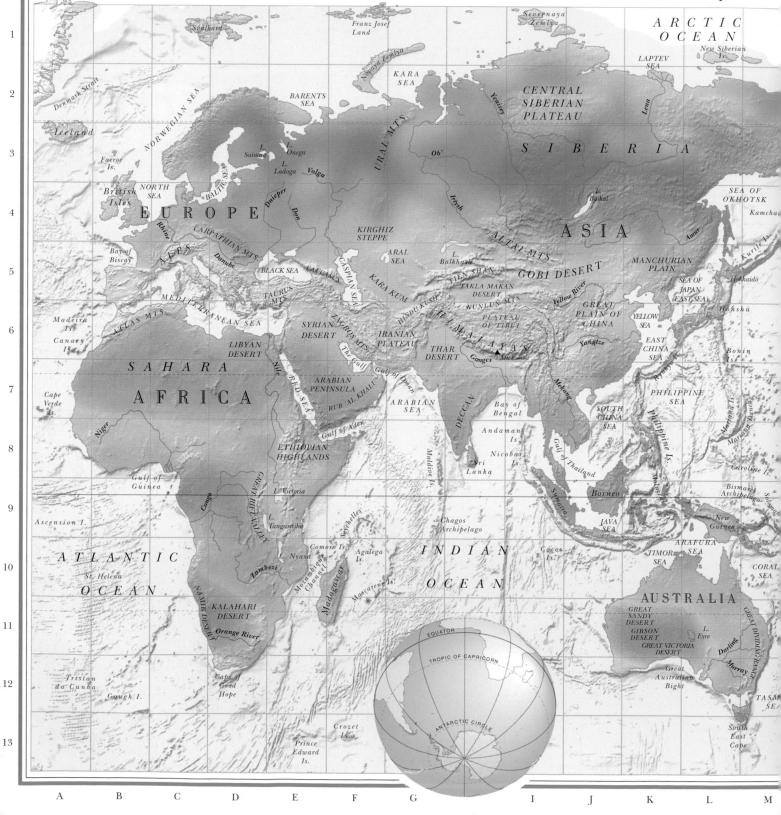

## CONTINENTS

The seven continents that make up the world's land mass are, from largest to smallest: Asia, Africa, North America, South America, Antarctica, Europe, and Australia. The Polar regions, not completely visible on the flat map, surround the North and South Poles and are shown on the globes, left and below.

Only 29 per cent of the Earth's surface is land. The percentage area of each continent is shown here

**Earth's surface**
Water: 71%
Land: 29%

Australia: 5%
Europe: 7%

Asia: 30%
Africa: 20%
North America: 16.5%
South America: 12%
Antarctica: 9.5%

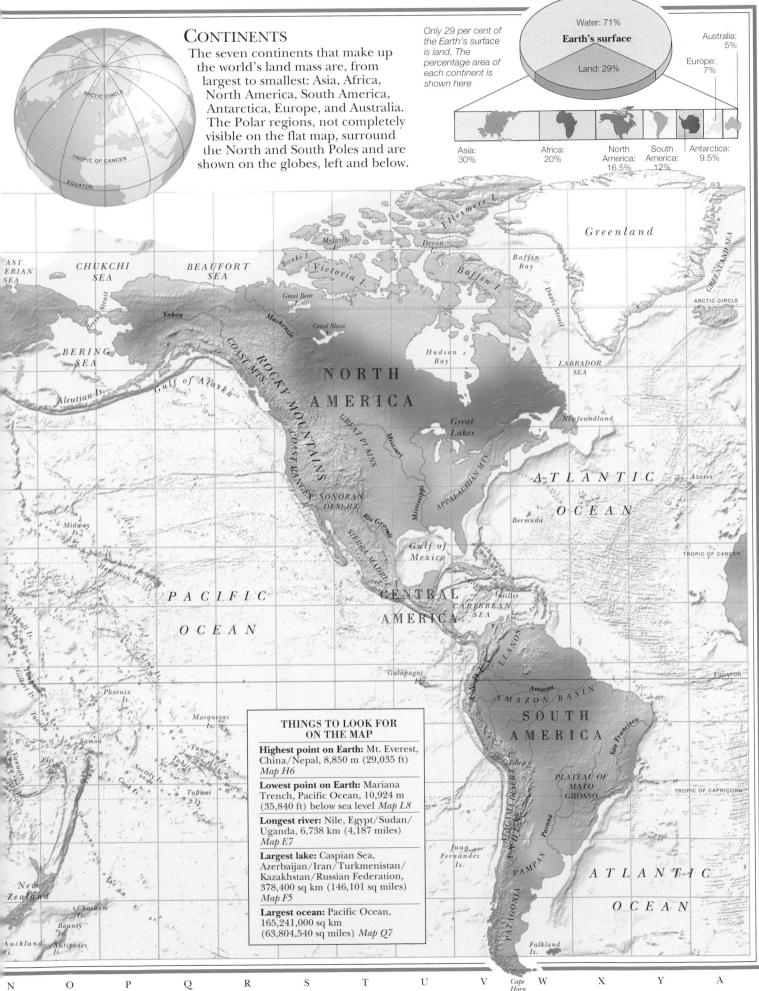

**THINGS TO LOOK FOR ON THE MAP**

**Highest point on Earth:** Mt. Everest, China/Nepal, 8,850 m (29,035 ft) *Map H6*

**Lowest point on Earth:** Mariana Trench, Pacific Ocean, 10,924 m (35,840 ft) below sea level *Map L8*

**Longest river:** Nile, Egypt/Sudan/Uganda, 6,738 km (4,187 miles) *Map E7*

**Largest lake:** Caspian Sea, Azerbaijan/Iran/Turkmenistan/Kazakhstan/Russian Federation, 378,400 sq km (146,101 sq miles) *Map F5*

**Largest ocean:** Pacific Ocean, 165,241,000 sq km (63,804,540 sq miles) *Map Q7*

# MOVING CONTINENTS

THE CONTINENTS THAT MAKE UP most of the Earth's land surface are always on the move, shifted around by forces deep inside the Earth. This is known as continental drift. Movement, or drift, takes place because the inside of the planet is hot and turbulent. The intense heat generated within the Earth is carried upwards where it disturbs the cool, rocky surface and forces the plates of crust that make up the continents to move. Each year the continents drift about a centimetre (nearly half an inch), some getting closer together, others moving further apart, some grinding past each other. When this happens, many of the Earth's natural features are created or changed.

## IN THE BEGINNING

Scientists believe that, some 300 million years ago, all the land on Earth was joined together in one "supercontinent", called Pangaea. It was surrounded by a giant ocean, Panthalassa. About 200 million years ago, as the plates moved, Pangaea began to split into two great landmasses, Laurasia in the north, and Gondwanaland in the south. These were separated by the Tethys Sea. As the plates continued to move, the two landmasses split and moved further apart, eventually forming the continents on the map below.

*200 million years ago*

PANTHALASSA — PANGAEA — PANTHALASSA

*180 million years ago*

LAURASIA — TETHYS SEA — GONDWANALAND

*65 million years ago*

NORTH AMERICA — EUROPE — ASIA — SOUTH AMERICA — AFRICA — INDIA — AUSTRALIA — ANTARCTICA

### INSIDE THE EARTH

The hot inner core is solid. — Liquid outer core — Earth's crust — Upper mantle — Lower mantle

The Earth is not a solid ball, but is made up of many different layers. The crust that forms the continents and the ocean floor is a thin layer of rock that covers the Earth like a shell. The mantle beneath is 3,000 km (1,864 miles) thick and made of hot rock, some of which is molten (liquid). At the centre is the core, the hot metallic centre of the Earth. This is liquid on the outside and solid on the inside.

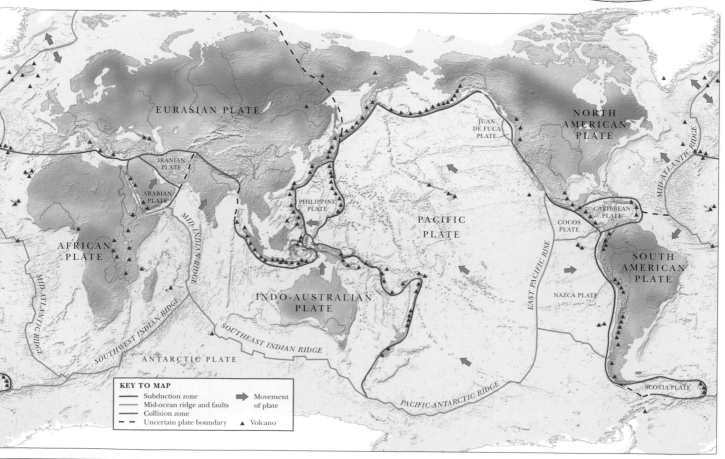

EURASIAN PLATE — JUAN DE FUCA PLATE — NORTH AMERICAN PLATE — IRANIAN PLATE — ARABIAN PLATE — PHILIPPINE PLATE — CARIBBEAN PLATE — COCOS PLATE — MID-ATLANTIC RIDGE — PACIFIC PLATE — AFRICAN PLATE — MID-INDIAN RIDGE — EAST PACIFIC RISE — SOUTH AMERICAN PLATE — INDO-AUSTRALIAN PLATE — NAZCA PLATE — SOUTHWEST INDIAN RIDGE — SOUTHEAST INDIAN RIDGE — ANTARCTIC PLATE — MID-ATLANTIC RIDGE — SCOTIA PLATE — PACIFIC-ANTARCTIC RIDGE

**KEY TO MAP**
- Subduction zone
- Mid-ocean ridge and faults
- Collision zone
- Uncertain plate boundary
- Movement of plate
- ▲ Volcano

# RESTLESS EARTH

Because the Earth appears to stand still, it is difficult to imagine that the crust is moving. However, there are three main ways in which plates move, and these are known as spreading ridges, subduction zones, and transform faults, all shown on the artwork below. It is possible to see the effect this activity has had on the landscape. The Rocky Mountains in North America were formed when two plates collided, while the Great Rift Valley in Africa is the result of plates pulling apart. Volcanoes and earthquakes are also dramatic reminders that the plates are still moving.

*At Thingvellir, Iceland, the spreading ridge between the North American and Eurasian plates appears as a long gash in the landscape.*

## SPREADING RIDGES

A spreading ridge occurs where two plates start to pull apart and molten rocks from the Earth's mantle well up to fill the gap. If this happens along the ocean floor, it creates an underwater mountain chain such as the Mid-Atlantic Ridge. Sometimes the peaks of these mountains break the surface as volcanic islands, as happened with Iceland. When a spreading ridge occurs on land it creates a steep-sided rift valley.

*Chains of volcanoes are often found along subduction zones.*

*A mid-ocean ridge where two plates are pulling apart.*

*Plates slide past each other along a transform fault.*

*When plates collide the crust buckles and folds and may be pushed up to form mountains.*

*At a subduction zone, the crust is forced down into the mantle, where it melts.*

## TRANSFORM FAULT

A transform fault is where two plates grind past each other in opposite directions, or in the same direction but at different speeds. No crust is made or destroyed in the process, but the movement creates deep cracks in the ground. The sliding movement often occurs in short bursts which are felt on the surface as earthquakes. The San Andreas fault in California, USA, is an active earthquake zone.

*The San Andreas fault is the point where the Pacific and North American plates meet.*

## SUBDUCTION ZONE

When two plates meet, the edge of one can be pushed down (subducted) under the other and into the mantle below. The rocks from the crust melt in the mantle. Often these molten rocks force their way to the surface as a volcano. The many volcanoes around the edge of the Pacific plate, such as Mt Mihara, Japan, were formed this way. Sometimes when plates collide, rocks are forced up to form great mountain ranges.

## LOOKING AT THE EVIDENCE

When the German scientist Alfred Wegener first put forward his theory of moving plates in 1923, people dismissed his ideas as nonsense. Since then, evidence had proved him correct. Fossils of the fern, *Glossopteris*, for example, have been found in rocks as far apart as India, Australia, and Africa. All these places were once joined together as Gondwanaland. Further proof comes from matching types of rock that have been found in Australia, Antartica, and South America.

*Today's continents fit together like a jigsaw, and show that they were once joined.*

*Fossil finds*

*Matching rock*

*The Glossopteris fern*

# CLIMATE AND VEGETATION

CLIMATE IS THE AVERAGE PATTERN of weather and temperature in a particular area over a long period of time. Similar types of climate are found in different places around the world. For example, there are regions of hot, dry desert in Africa and North America, as well as across central Australia. It is a region's climate, together with its physical landscape, that determines the sort of vegetation, or plant life, which is usually found there. Cold areas near the Poles, or icy mountain peaks, will support little, or no, vegetation. Hot, wet rainforests near the Equator, however, will encourage the fast growth of a variety of plants.

March:
Spring begins in the northern hemisphere.

December:
Summer in the southern hemisphere.

Sun

June:
Summer in the northern hemisphere

September:
Spring in the southern hemisphere.

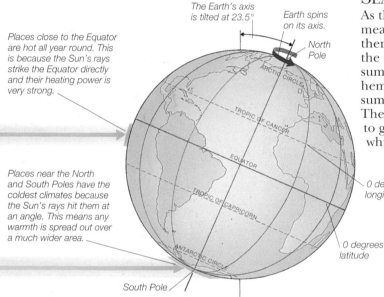

The Earth's axis is tilted at 23.5°

Earth spins on its axis.

North Pole

Places close to the Equator are hot all year round. This is because the Sun's rays strike the Equator directly and their heating power is very strong.

ARCTIC CIRCLE

TROPIC OF CANCER

EQUATOR

Places near the North and South Poles have the coldest climates because the Sun's rays hit them at an angle. This means any warmth is spread out over a much wider area.

TROPIC OF CAPRICORN

0 degrees longitude

ANTARCTIC CIRCLE

0 degrees latitude

South Pole

## LATITUDE AND LONGITUDE

A region's climate is influenced by how far to the north or south of the Equator it lies. This is called its latitude. The Equator, an imaginary line running round the Earth, lies at 0 degrees latitude. Other lines of latitude include the Tropics of Cancer and Capricorn. Regions around the Equator are the hottest in the world, while the closer to the Poles you go, the colder it gets. There are also lines which run from north to south, known as longitude.

## SEASONS OF THE YEAR

As the Earth travels around the Sun, the tilt on its axis means that each place leans gradually nearer the Sun, and then farther away from it. This causes the seasons. When the northern hemisphere leans towards the Sun it has summer. When it tilts away it has winter. In the southern hemisphere this is reversed. In between the warm days of summer and the cold of winter come spring and autumn. The Earth also spins on its axis, turning once every 24 hours to give us day and night. The side facing the Sun has day, while the other side has night.

RAINFALL
The amount of rainfall a place receives during the year greatly affects its vegetation as well as its climate. Plants need water to make their own food and will thrive in the warm, wet climate of a tropical rainforest, as shown here in Costa Rica. Where rainfall is very low, in deserts or Polar regions, only a few plants manage to survive. In other places, the amount of rainfall varies with the seasons.

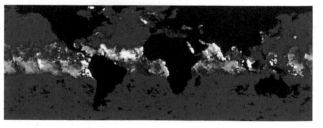

CHANGES IN WORLD CLIMATE
The world's climate can be changed by both natural as well as human events. When Mt Pinatubo, a volcano in the Philippines, erupted in 1991, it threw ash and dust high into the atmosphere. Locally, this caused dark skies, heavy rainfall, and high winds. The distance the ash was carried can be seen from this satellite photo. Equally, events such as the massive oil fires in Kuwait, started during the Gulf War, can have a damaging effect on climate.

LAND AND SEA
The climate of a region is affected by altitude – how high a place is above sea-level. The higher a place, the colder its climate, even if it lies near the Equator or the Tropics like these Atlas Mountains in Morocco. Another important influence is how close a place is to the sea. The sea warms and cools slower than land, so coastal areas usually have fewer extremes of temperature.

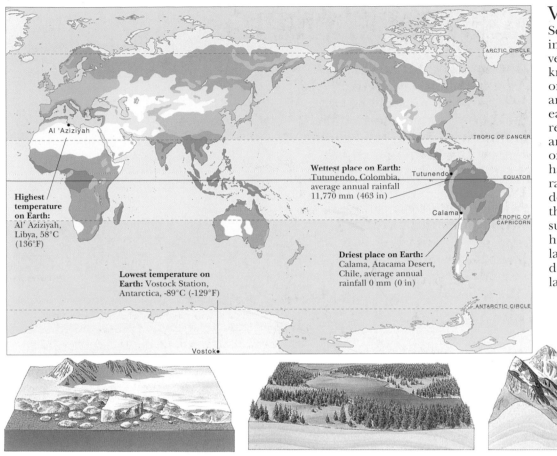

**Highest temperature on Earth:** Al' Aziziyah, Libya, 58°C (136°F)

**Lowest temperature on Earth:** Vostock Station, Antarctica, -89°C (-129°F)

**Wettest place on Earth:** Tutunendo, Colombia, average annual rainfall 11,770 mm (463 in)

**Driest place on Earth:** Calama, Atacama Desert, Chile, average annual rainfall 0 mm (0 in)

## VEGETATION ZONES

Scientists divide the Earth into a number of different vegetation zones, also known as "biomes", shown on the map left. The plant and animal life found in each zone depends on the region's climate, landscape, and latitude. Over millions of years, plants and animals have adapted to life in this range of climates, often developing special features that have helped them to survive. The map also highlights how similar landscapes, such as taiga or deserts, occur at the same latitude across the world.

### POLAR AND TUNDRA

The areas around the North and South Poles are freezing cold and covered in ice. South of the North Pole lies a region called the tundra, where the lower layers of soil are permanently frozen. Hardy mosses, lichens, and shrubs are the only plants that can survive here.

### TAIGA

In Russian, the word taiga means "cold forest". It describes the vast evergreen forests that stretch across northern Canada, Scandinavia, and the Russian Federation. Evergreen trees, such as fir, spruce, and pine, are well-adapted to the long, snowy winters.

### MOUNTAIN REGIONS

The higher up a mountain you go, the colder it gets. Trees and plants grow on the lower slopes of many mountains. But, above a certain level, called the tree line, it is too cold and windy for plants to survive. High mountain peaks are often covered in snow all year round.

### TEMPERATE FOREST

Much of the land in northern Europe and North America was once covered by deciduous forests (trees that lose their leaves in winter). Most of these have now been cut down. Deciduous trees grow well in temperate climates where it is never very hot or very cold.

### MEDITERRANEAN

Areas with a Mediterranean climate have hot, dry summers and cool, wet winters. They include land around the Mediterranean Sea and other similar places, such as California in the USA. Plants and trees, such as olives, have adapted to survive the lack of water in summer.

### DRY GRASSLAND

Vast grasslands cover the centre of some of the continents. They include the South American pampas and the North American prairies. They have hot, dry summers and very cold winters. Large parts of these grasslands are now ploughed for wheat or used to raise cattle.

### TROPICAL RAINFOREST

Around the Equator, the climate is hot and wet all year round, and provides ideal conditions for lush, green tropical forests to thrive. The world's rainforests may contain 50,000 different types of tree, as well as millions of other species of plants and animals.

### HOT DESERT

Deserts are the hottest, driest places on Earth. Temperatures are often very hot during the day but may plunge below freezing at night. Some deserts have no rain for several years. Deserts often contain sandy soil that can only support plants such as cacti.

### TROPICAL GRASSLAND

Between the hot deserts and tropical rainforests lie tropical grasslands, such as the African savanna. The climate here is always hot, but the year is divided into a wet and a dry season. Tall grasses, as well as low trees and shrubs, grow in these hot areas.

# WORLD POPULATION

PEOPLE HAVE LIVED ON EARTH for at least 2 million years. For most of that time, the population remained small, because the number of people born was roughly the same as the number who died. Disease and famine ensured that the size of the population did not overtake the supplies of food and other resources. However, as farming methods became more efficient and medical knowledge improved, the population rapidly began to grow. It now stands in excess of 6 billion people, with more than one million babies born every four days. In many parts of the world, rapid population growth can create serious problems, such as shortage of food or overcrowding in cities.

## WHERE PEOPLE LIVE

People are not evenly distributed among the world's continents. The fact that a continent is large, such as North America, does not necessarily mean that it has a large population. Some regions cannot support more than a few people whilst others, with fertile soils and good communication, can support many. The world map below shows the average number of people who live in a square kilometre, or mile, in each country. This is known as population density.

*This chart shows the size of each continent or region, together with the percentage of the world's population who live there. Far more people live in Asia than anywhere else on Earth.*

Asia: 60.5%

Africa: 13.3%

North America: 6.8%

Australasia and Oceania: 0.5%

Europe: 12.1%

Antarctica: 0%

South America: 6.8%

**World map showing the population density of each country**

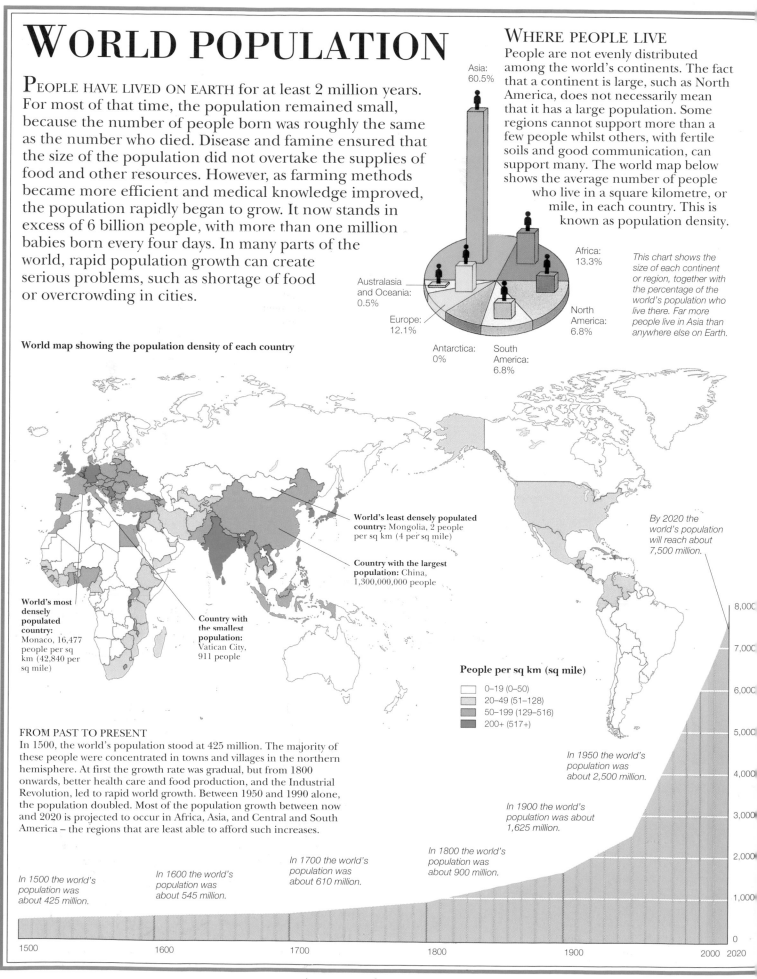

World's least densely populated country: Mongolia, 2 people per sq km (4 per sq mile)

Country with the largest population: China, 1,300,000,000 people

World's most densely populated country: Monaco, 16,477 people per sq km (42,840 per sq mile)

Country with the smallest population: Vatican City, 911 people

By 2020 the world's population will reach about 7,500 million.

**People per sq km (sq mile)**
- 0–19 (0–50)
- 20–49 (51–128)
- 50–199 (129–516)
- 200+ (517+)

## FROM PAST TO PRESENT

In 1500, the world's population stood at 425 million. The majority of these people were concentrated in towns and villages in the northern hemisphere. At first the growth rate was gradual, but from 1800 onwards, better health care and food production, and the Industrial Revolution, led to rapid world growth. Between 1950 and 1990 alone, the population doubled. Most of the population growth between now and 2020 is projected to occur in Africa, Asia, and Central and South America – the regions that are least able to afford such increases.

In 1950 the world's population was about 2,500 million.

In 1900 the world's population was about 1,625 million.

In 1800 the world's population was about 900 million.

In 1700 the world's population was about 610 million.

In 1600 the world's population was about 545 million.

In 1500 the world's population was about 425 million.

8,000

7,000

6,000

5,000

4,000

3,000

2,000

1,000

0

1500    1600    1700    1800    1900    2000  2020

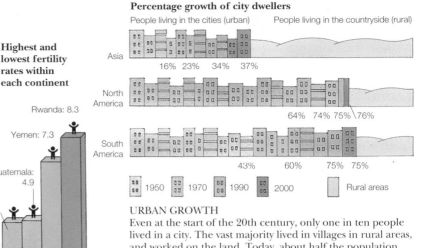

## Percentage growth of city dwellers

People living in the cities (urban) — People living in the countryside (rural)

Asia: 16% 23% 34% 37%

North America: 64% 74% 75% 76%

South America: 43% 60% 75% 75%

1950 | 1970 | 1990 | 2000 | Rural areas

**Highest and lowest fertility rates within each continent**

Rwanda: 8.3
Yemen: 7.3
Guatemala: 4.9
Papua New Guinea: 4.8
Mexico: 3.3
Albania: 2.9

San Marino: 1.5
Canada: 1.8
Uruguay: 2.5
Australia: 1.8
Hong Kong: 1.3
Tunisia: 3

## BIRTH AND DEATH

The number of babies a woman has varies from one country to another. In Sudan, above, the fertility rate is high with an average of 4.9 babies per mother. Better health care, even in the poorer countries of the world, means that less babies now die of hunger or disease, and fewer women die in childbirth. In wealthy countries, such as Canada, the birth rate is low because people can choose to have small families. Advances in medical knowledge also mean that people are living longer.

## URBAN GROWTH

Even at the start of the 20th century, only one in ten people lived in a city. The vast majority lived in villages in rural areas, and worked on the land. Today, about half the population are city dwellers. There are various reasons for this growth. In South America, for example, people have been pushed out of the countryside by poverty and loss of land. They are drawn to the cities in search of work. By 2020, if the growth continues, almost half of all people will live in a city.

| WORLD'S BIGGEST CITIES IN 1950 | |
|---|---|
| New York, USA | 12,300,000 |
| London, UK | 8,700,000 |
| Tokyo, Japan | 6,700,000 |
| Paris, France | 5,400,000 |
| Shanghai, China | 5,300,000 |

| WORLD'S BIGGEST CITIES IN 2005 | |
|---|---|
| Tokyo, Japan | 36,510,000 |
| New York, USA | 22,310,000 |
| Mexico City, Mexico | 22,090,000 |
| Seoul, South Korea | 21,740,000 |
| Mumbai, India | 19,470,000 |

## CITY SLUMS

One effect of the move of large numbers of people from the countryside to the cities is overcrowding. There are simply not enough houses and resources to go round. In many large cities, such as Mumbai (Bombay), India, this has led to the growth of shanty towns on the edges of cities. Conditions in these slums are often unhygienic. Families survive in crowded homes made of make-shift materials, often with no electricity or running water.

## SUPER CITIES

Before the 19th century, cities with more than a million people were rare. In the last 100 years, however, the number of large cities has grown dramatically. Today, several cities, such as Tokyo, already have populations of more than 20 million. This means that some cities have more people than the population of countries such as New Zealand or Sweden. Large cities often suffer from pollution caused by car exhausts, factory emissions, and domestic waste.

## LOOKING TO THE FUTURE

Although world population growth is slowing down, numbers are still rising quickly, especially in developing countries. To encourage people to have fewer children, programmes have now been set up to teach women about family planning and health care so that they have more choice about the size and health of their families. Today, almost half the married women in the developing world report that they or their partner use birth control, compared with less than a quarter in 1980.

*This doctor is writing out a prescription for contraceptives, now used by 43 per cent of the women in Zimbabwe.*

# THE POLITICAL WORLD

AS WELL AS BEING DIVIDED into physical land masses, the world is also split into countries. These countries are separated from one another by language, government, and culture, and this creates the political world. As recently as 1950, there were only 82 countries. Today there are more than twice that many – some vast, others tiny. New countries are created when people want freedom from their past colonial rulers or when separate peoples living within one country seek independence. The break-up of Yugoslavia in the 1990s, for example, created five new countries.

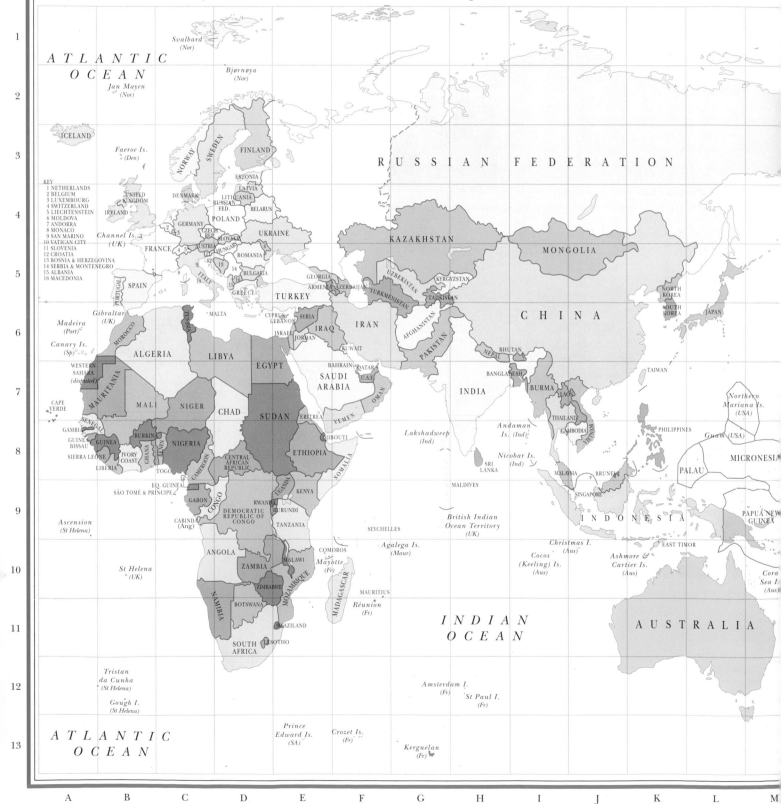

**KEY**
1 NETHERLANDS
2 BELGIUM
3 LUXEMBOURG
4 SWITZERLAND
5 LIECHTENSTEIN
6 MOLDOVA
7 ANDORRA
8 MONACO
9 SAN MARINO
10 VATICAN CITY
11 SLOVENIA
12 CROATIA
13 BOSNIA & HERZEGOVINA
14 SERBIA & MONTENEGRO
15 ALBANIA
16 MACEDONIA

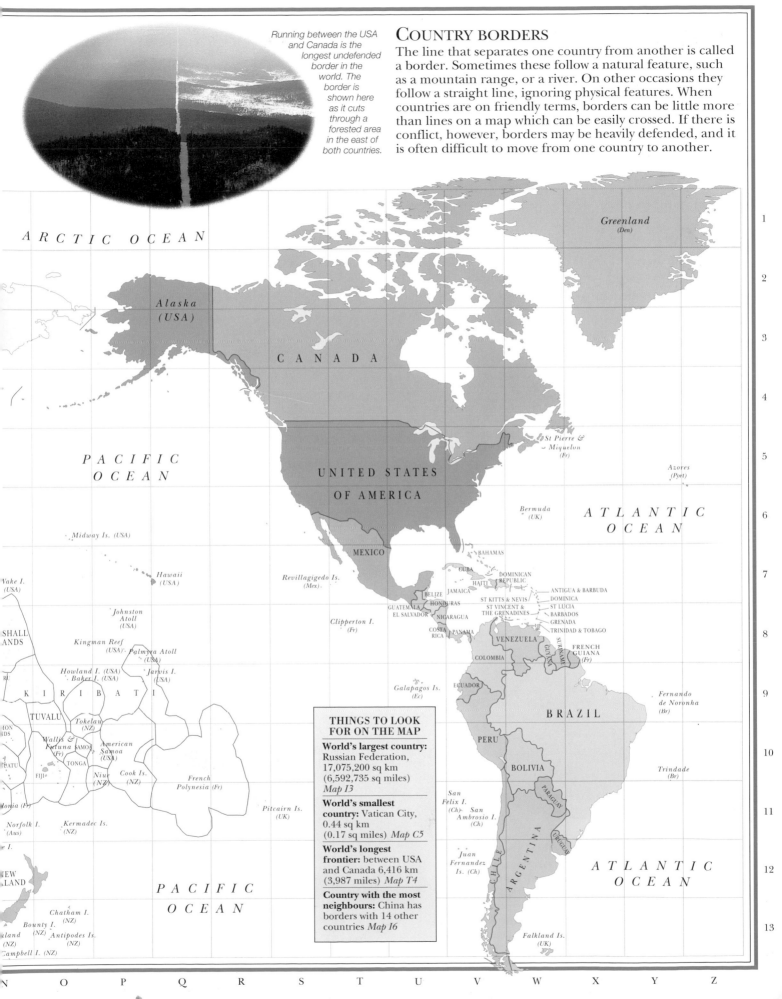

*Running between the USA and Canada is the longest undefended border in the world. The border is shown here as it cuts through a forested area in the east of both countries.*

# COUNTRY BORDERS

The line that separates one country from another is called a border. Sometimes these follow a natural feature, such as a mountain range, or a river. On other occasions they follow a straight line, ignoring physical features. When countries are on friendly terms, borders can be little more than lines on a map which can be easily crossed. If there is conflict, however, borders may be heavily defended, and it is often difficult to move from one country to another.

**THINGS TO LOOK FOR ON THE MAP**

**World's largest country:** Russian Federation, 17,075,200 sq km (6,592,735 sq miles) *Map I3*

**World's smallest country:** Vatican City, 0.44 sq km (0.17 sq miles) *Map C5*

**World's longest frontier:** between USA and Canada 6,416 km (3,987 miles) *Map T4*

**Country with the most neighbours:** China has borders with 14 other countries *Map I6*

# NORTH AMERICA

NORTH AMERICA INCLUDES THE COUNTRIES of Canada, the United States, and Mexico, as well as the world's largest island, Greenland. During the last Ice Age, a great sheet of ice flowed across the continent, scouring the landscape, deepening the depressions that now hold the Great Lakes, and dumping fertile soil onto the central plains. The Rocky Mountains form the backbone of the continent, running from Alaska to New Mexico. In the east are the Appalachian Mountains, flanked by coastal lowlands to the east and south. In eastern Canada lies the Canadian Shield, a huge basin of ancient eroded rocks now covered with thin soils. Deserts stretch from the southwestern United States down into northern Mexico.

**Section across the USA**

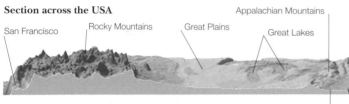

San Francisco · Rocky Mountains · Great Plains · Appalachian Mountains · Great Lakes · Washington, DC

## MOUNTAIN RANGES

The main mountain ranges of North America, the snow-capped Rockies, and the forested Appalachians, vary greatly in appearance (see above cross-section). The difference can be explained by their age. The Rockies, shown right, are relatively young mountains that have not yet been worn down. The Appalachians, however, are among the world's oldest mountains and have been gradually eroded by the scouring action of wind, water, and the movement of glaciers.

*This view shows the Rockies in Canada.*

## THE GRAND CANYON

The Grand Canyon was formed over millions of years as the waters of the Colorado River and its tributaries carved their way through the solid rock. At some points the canyon is 1.6 km (1 mile) deep, and cuts through rocks that are 2,000 million years old. Different types of fossils found in the canyon walls reveal the dates of its changing history.

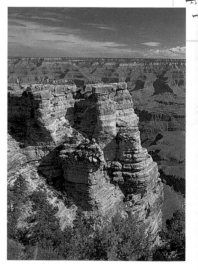

## THE GREAT PLAINS

Across the centre of Canada and the USA lie the Great Plains, also called the prairies. This huge area has hot summers and cold snowy winters. Trees are rare except along rivers and lakeshores, but the region was once covered with grasses and grazed by millions of buffalo. Today, little natural prairie survives, and in its place farmers cultivate vast fields of maize and wheat.

## THE GREAT LAKES

Estimated to contain one-fifth of the world's fresh water, the five Great Lakes straddle the border between Canada and the USA. Only Lake Michigan, shown left, lies entirely within the USA. The lakes are linked by waterways, and drained by the St Lawrence River, which empties into the Atlantic Ocean. The Niagara River, which joins lakes Erie and Ontario, passes over the famous Niagara Falls.

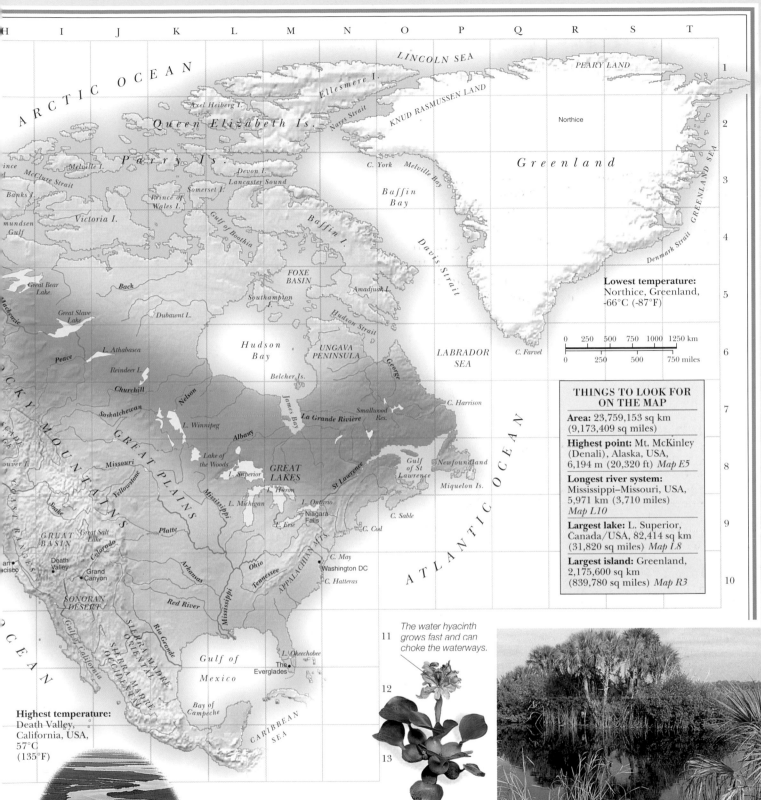

H I J K L M N O P Q R S T

ARCTIC OCEAN

LINCOLN SEA

PEARY LAND

Ellesmere I.

Axel Heiberg I.

Queen Elizabeth Is.

KNUD RASMUSSEN LAND

Northice

Melville I.

Prince

McClure Strait

Banks I.

Parry Is.

Devon I.

Lancaster Sound

Somerset I.

Prince of Wales I.

Gulf of Boothia

C. York

Melville Bay

Greenland

Baffin Bay

GREENLAND SEA

Victoria I.

mundsen
Gulf

Baffin I.

Davis Strait

Denmark Strait

Great Bear
Lake

Back

FOXE
BASIN

Southampton
I.

Amadjuak L.

Mackenzie

Great Slave
Lake

Dubawnt L.

Hudson Strait

UNGAVA
PENINSULA

LABRADOR
SEA

**Lowest temperature:**
Northice, Greenland,
-66°C (-87°F)

Peace

L. Athabasca

Reindeer L.

Hudson
Bay

George

C. Farvel

Churchill

Belcher Is.

0   250   500   750   1000   1250 km
0        250        500        750 miles

ROCKY

Nelson

Saskatchewan

James Bay

La Grande Rivière

Smallwood
Res.

C. Harrison

L. Winnipeg

Albany

ATLANTIC OCEAN

**THINGS TO LOOK FOR
ON THE MAP**

**Area:** 23,759,153 sq km
(9,173,409 sq miles)

**Highest point:** Mt. McKinley
(Denali), Alaska, USA,
6,194 m (20,320 ft) *Map E5*

**Longest river system:**
Mississippi–Missouri, USA,
5,971 km (3,710 miles)
*Map L10*

**Largest lake:** L. Superior,
Canada/USA, 82,414 sq km
(31,820 sq miles) *Map L8*

**Largest island:** Greenland,
2,175,600 sq km
(839,780 sq miles) *Map R3*

MOUNTAINS

GREAT PLAINS

Lake of
the Woods

L. Superior

GREAT
LAKES

St Lawrence

Gulf
of St
Lawrence

Newfoundland

Missouri

Yellowstone

Snake

L. Michigan

L. Huron

Mississippi

L. Ontario

Niagara
Falls

Miquelon Is.

COAST RANGES

couver I.

Platte

GREAT
BASIN

Great Salt
Lake

Colorado

L. Erie

Ohio

C. Sable

C. Cod

Death
Valley

Grand
Canyon

Arkansas

Tennessee

APPALACHIAN MTS.

C. May

Washington DC

C. Hatteras

SONORAN
DESERT

Red River

Mississippi

11

*The water hyacinth
grows fast and can
choke the waterways.*

SIERRA MADRE ORIENTAL

SIERRA MADRE OCCIDENTAL

Gulf of California

Rio Grande

L. Okeechobee

The
Everglades

12

Gulf of
Mexico

13

CARIBBEAN
SEA

Bay of
Campeche

OCEAN

**Highest temperature:**
Death Valley,
California, USA,
57°C
(135°F)

## THE MISSISSIPPI RIVER

The great Mississippi flows from
Minnesota to the Gulf of Mexico.
At the turn of the last century,
the destruction of forest and
the ploughing of prairies around
the river basin caused severe soil
erosion. Soil washed into the river,
raised the water level, and caused
floods. Replanting forests and building
dams has helped control the flow, but
exceptionally heavy rains still cause floods.

## THE EVERGLADES

Florida's Everglades is a protected wetland habitat, home
to many rare plants and animals. Originally covering a
much larger area, part of the Everglades has been drained
and used for the cultivation of sugarcane. The northern
part of the surviving wetland is now a sawgrass prairie,
covered by shallow water with islands of higher land.
In the south, fresh water mixes with water from the sea,
creating saltmarshes fringed by mangrove swamps.

# PEOPLES OF NORTH AMERICA

ONCE POPULATED BY GROUPS of native peoples who lived off the land, the vast majority of North America's population arrived as immigrants over the last 400 years. Today, in terms of both population and economic wealth, the continent is dominated by the USA, the richest country in the world. To the north, Canada covers a vast area, much of it cold and inhospitable, and so has a much smaller population. Both of these countries were once British colonies and are still mostly English speaking. In contrast, Mexico is Spanish speaking, reflecting its past as a Spanish colony. Mexico is a relatively poor country, despite its vast oil and gas reserves.

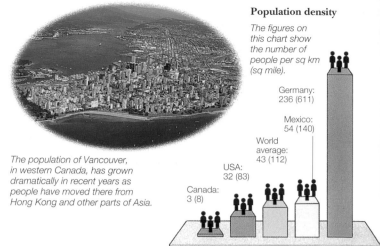

The population of Vancouver, in western Canada, has grown dramatically in recent years as people have moved there from Hong Kong and other parts of Asia.

**Population density**

The figures on this chart show the number of people per sq km (sq mile).

Germany: 236 (611)
Mexico: 54 (140)
World average: 43 (112)
USA: 32 (83)
Canada: 3 (8)

## POPULATION DISTRIBUTION

In general, North America is one of the most sparsely populated continents. Over two-thirds of the population live in the USA. Mexico has the next largest population, followed by Canada. Historically, the east of the USA was the most densely populated area, but in the past few decades, many people have moved to the warmer southern and western states. In Canada, people have also left the east coast for the Great Lakes and cities such as Toronto, or for west coast cities, such as Vancouver.

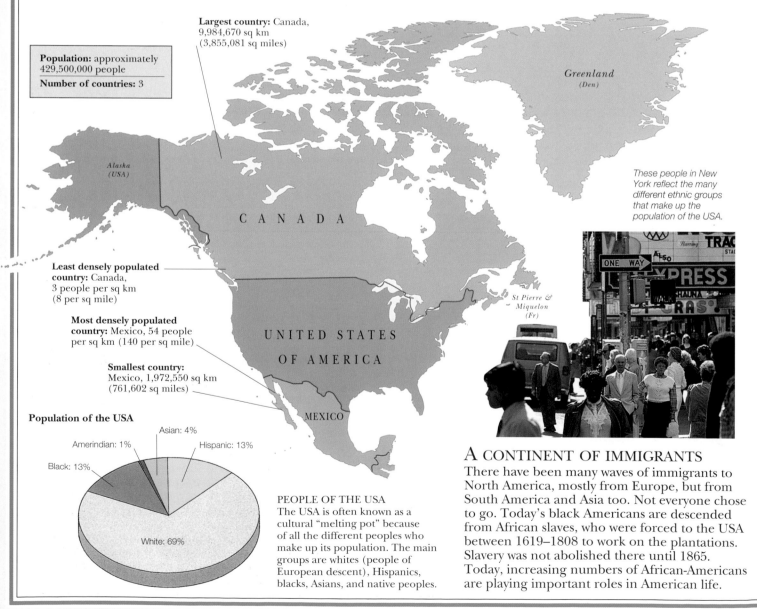

**Largest country:** Canada, 9,984,670 sq km (3,855,081 sq miles)

**Population:** approximately 429,500,000 people

**Number of countries:** 3

*Greenland (Den)*

*Alaska (USA)*

These people in New York reflect the many different ethnic groups that make up the population of the USA.

**Least densely populated country:** Canada, 3 people per sq km (8 per sq mile)

**Most densely populated country:** Mexico, 54 people per sq km (140 per sq mile)

**Smallest country:** Mexico, 1,972,550 sq km (761,602 sq miles)

CANADA

UNITED STATES OF AMERICA

*St Pierre & Miquelon (Fr)*

MEXICO

**Population of the USA**

Asian: 4%
Amerindian: 1%
Hispanic: 13%
Black: 13%
White: 69%

### PEOPLE OF THE USA

The USA is often known as a cultural "melting pot" because of all the different peoples who make up its population. The main groups are whites (people of European descent), Hispanics, blacks, Asians, and native peoples.

## A CONTINENT OF IMMIGRANTS

There have been many waves of immigrants to North America, mostly from Europe, but from South America and Asia too. Not everyone chose to go. Today's black Americans are descended from African slaves, who were forced to the USA between 1619–1808 to work on the plantations. Slavery was not abolished there until 1865. Today, increasing numbers of African-Americans are playing important roles in American life.

## CANADIAN CULTURE

Canadians often display their distinctive maple-leaf flag outside their homes. They are very proud of their country with its wide open spaces, lakes, mountains, and extensive national and provincial parks. But there is always the issue of US entertainment and culture flooding across the border and dominating the Canadian identity. To encourage Canada's own cultural development, the government gives grants to the arts, and the broadcasting, publishing, and film industries.

*This Canadian "patriotic workshop" is painted in the colours of the country's flag.*

*This Mayan family are cooking tortillas.*

## GOOD NEIGHBOURS

There has not been a war between the countries of North America for nearly 150 years. Recently, Canada, the USA, and Mexico agreed to abolish trade barriers and open their markets to each other's exports. The full effects of this agreement are yet to be discovered, but Mexican workers like these farmers have already lost out, as cheaper US food and goods have flooded into Mexico. By contrast, cheaper food can benefit the poor.

## NATIVE PEOPLES

Native Americans are the descendants of people who probably migrated from Asia via a land bridge across the Bering Strait about 20,000 years ago. Today, native peoples form only a small proportion of the population of the USA and Canada. In the USA, many native Americans were moved into special reservations in the 19th century as settlers took over their lands. In Mexico, native peoples, like these Maya, form about 30 per cent of the population and are spread throughout the country.

## EUROPEAN SETTLERS

Europeans have been settling in the USA and Canada since the 16th century, but in the 19th century, immigrants began to flood in. They were often driven from Europe by economic hardship, political unrest, and religious persecution. North America was seen as a land of opportunity, where there was plenty of cheap land and people were promised their freedom. The first immigrants settled on the east coast, but began to move northeast in the 1800s as industry began to grow.

*This building in the city of Sacramento is home to the government of the state of California, USA.*

*In the USA, local matters, such as the police, running hospitals, and maintaining the highways, are decided by individual states. Matters which affect all the states, such as foreign policy, defence, and issuing currency, are dealt with centrally.*

| State government | | Federal government | |
|---|---|---|---|
| 📖 | Education | 💼 | Foreign policy |
| 🚌 | Highways | $ | Currency |
| 🏠 | Housing | ✚ | Health care |
| 🚗 | State police | 🌲 | National parks |

## FEDERAL GOVERNMENTS

All three countries in North America have federal systems of government. This means that each country is divided into a number of states or provinces. These make their own local laws and also have representatives in the national government. Tension sometimes develops between the interests of the individual states or provinces and the interests of the country as a whole. In Canada, for example, a strong independence movement has grown up in the French-speaking province of Québec.

# CANADA

THE SECOND LARGEST COUNTRY in the world, Canada occupies two-fifths of the North American continent, stretches across five time zones, and is divided into 10 provinces and three territories. It was once inhabited only by native peoples including the Inuit. The French were the first Europeans to settle in Canada, but after years of fighting the British gained control in 1763. Gradually they took over the rest of the country, as pioneers and settlers moved west and north. Today, Canada is an important industrial nation and one of the world's richest countries. Most of its manufacturing is based on the natural resources of wood, metals, and mineral fuels.

## CANADA

**Capital city:** Ottawa

**Area:** 9,984,670 sq km (3,855,081 sq miles)

**Population:** 31,500,000

**Official languages:** English, French

**Major religions:** Roman Catholic 44%, Protestant 29%, other 27%

**Government:** Multi-party democracy

**Currency:** Canadian dollar

**Adult literacy rate:** 99%

**Life expectancy:** 79 years

**People per doctor:** 476

**Televisions:** 715 per 1,000 people

### OTTAWA
Ottawa, which is named after the native people who used to live in the area, was chosen as Canada's capital city in 1857 by Queen Victoria of Britain. Today, the city boasts many magnificent copper-roofed government buildings, museums, and art galleries, and a park-lined canal that turns into the world's longest skating rink once the winter freeze sets in.

**Canadian vegetation zones**

- Tundra and polar
- Mountain
- Taiga
- Grassland
- Temperate forest

## THE CHANGING LANDSCAPE
About one-third of Canada lies within the Arctic Circle and can remain frozen for up to nine months of the year. In these cold northern areas, known as the tundra, any vegetation is limited to lichens, grasses, and small shrubs and trees. Further south, large areas of land are covered by dense coniferous forests, known as taiga. Towards the border with the USA lie the mixed, temperate forests and the grasslands of the prairies.

Edmonton
Calgary
Winnipeg
Vancouver
Montreal
Ottawa
Toronto
Hamilton
Great Lakes

### WHERE PEOPLE LIVE
Canada is such a large country, much of it uninhabitable, that on average there are only three people living in each square kilometre (eight per square mile). About three-quarters of all Canadians live near the US border, in towns and cities around the shores of the Great Lakes, and along the St Lawrence River. The rest live in fishing villages along the coasts or on farms and villages inland.

### CALGARY STAMPEDE
Every year since 1923, thousands of people have flocked to Calgary for the famous Calgary Stampede. People dress up in cowboy style to celebrate the old Wild West and Alberta's origins as a cattle trading centre. Attractions include a rodeo, complete with bucking broncos.

## PEOPLE OF CANADA
Until quite recently, most Canadians were descendants of British or French settlers. Most of the French, like those at the winter carnival shown here, live in Québec province. Germans and Italians are also large ethnic groups but, recently, increased numbers of people have come from eastern Europe, South America, and Southeast Asia. Native peoples make up less than 3 per cent of the population.

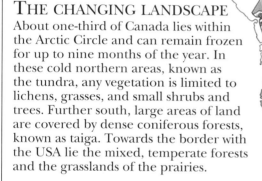

# THE FIRST CANADIANS

Native peoples, including the Inuit, are sometimes called Canada's "First Nations" because they lived in Canada long before European settlers arrived and took over their lands. Since 1970, the government has tried to draw these peoples into Canadian society, but many prefer their own culture and traditions. Across Canada colourful ceremonies and festivals demonstrate their proud spirit. Recently, First Nations have begun to win battles for their rights to ancestral lands. In 1999, the Nunavut area in the Northwest Territories became a self-governing Inuit territory, the first part of Canada to be governed by native Canadians in modern history.

*The Inuit live in such cold conditions that they depend on warm clothing for survival.*

*Caribou fur is used by the Inuit as it traps warm air between each of the hairs.*

*Traditional Inuit jacket, called a parka.*

*Insulated boots keep feet warm in freezing winter weather.*

## JAMES BAY

In 1971, construction began on a vast hydroelectric project to dam the rivers that flow into James Bay and Hudson Bay, and generate electricity for use in Canada and the USA. However, the project threatened thousands of Cree Indians who live in this region. Strong opposition from both the Cree Indians and environmental groups means that the project is unlikely to be finished.

## CANADIAN PACIFIC RAILWAY

The last spike of the transcontinental rail link of the Canadian Pacific Railway was pounded in at Eagle Pass, British Columbia, on November 7, 1885. It was the start of a new era for Canada, opening up the west for trade and settlement, and finally making the vast country seem like one nation. One of the railway's most amazing engineering feats is a spiral tunnel drilled into the Rocky Mountains. Curving steadily round, the tunnel rises for more than 914 m (3,000 ft). In spite of quicker alternatives, tourists often take the spectacular trip across Canada by train, although the railroad is mostly used for cargo.

## MINERAL WEALTH

Most of Canada's wealth comes from its abundance of natural resources, many of them mineral. It is the world's largest producer of uranium, zinc, and nickel, and also has reserves of aluminium, gold, copper, and silver.
Underground work has begun on what are thought to be some of the world's richest diamond deposits in an area near Yellowknife in the Northwest Territories.

*Zinc can be galvanized onto steel to prevent it from rusting.*

*Nickel can be mixed with other metals to to make jet engines.*

**Main cargo loads**

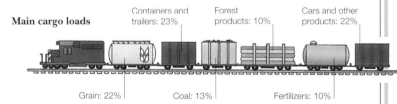

Containers and trailers: 23%
Forest products: 10%
Cars and other products: 22%
Grain: 22%
Coal: 13%
Fertilizers: 10%

## AGRICULTURE

Wheat and cattle farming dominate Canada's main farming area, the prairies. Elsewhere, a wide variety of fruit and vegetables is grown. Apples, shown growing here in British Columbia, are the country's most important fruit crop. Between Lakes Ontario and Erie lies the Niagara fruit belt. The lakes protect this area from the worst of Canada's weather, making it the ideal place for growing tender fruits such as pears, plums, peaches, and cherries.

## COPING WITH THE COLD

Winters are long and cold throughout Canada but when the first snow falls, snow ploughs and grit lorries are out making sure the roads are safe. Next to some parking places there are even electric outlets where motorists can plug in heaters to keep their car's engine warm. During winter people can play hockey on frozen lakes and ponds. Skiing and snowboarding are also popular winter sports.

*Snow ploughs clear the roads to make them safe.*

**Find out more**

DIAMONDS: *150, 226, 248*
EARLY SETTLERS: *23, 31*
INUIT: *266*
VEGETATION ZONES: *15*

# WESTERN CANADA

A WEALTH OF NATURAL RESOURCES first attracted European settlers to the wilds of western Canada. Fur trappers, gold prospectors, and loggers all hoped to make their fortune from the land. Today, natural resources are still the basis of the economy. The fertile soils of the prairie provinces of Alberta, Manitoba, and Saskatchewan make up four-fifths of Canada's farmland. Fishing is a major industry along the Pacific coast, where the main catch is salmon, most of which is canned for export. By contrast, the remote Yukon, Northwest, and Nunavut territories have important reserves of gold, zinc, and lead. These territories are also the only part of Canada where the native peoples form the majority of the population.

**VANCOUVER**
Situated between the mountains and the sea, Vancouver is an attractive city and an industrial centre, as well as a busy port. Its ice-free harbour provides Canada with year-round access for trade with Asian countries across the Pacific Ocean. Many Chinese families settled here rather than staying in Hong Kong when it reverted to China in 1997.

*The most used softwood trees are spruce, shown left, then pine and fir.*

*The most used hardwood trees are poplar, then birch, shown right, and maple.*

## TIMBER INDUSTRY
Moist winds from the Pacific Ocean deposit rain on the western slopes of the Rocky Mountains, making ideal conditions for trees to grow to enormous sizes. Canada is the world's largest exporter of forest products, and British Columbia produces almost half of Canada's timber. Some logs are floated to the sawmills, but today they are often transported by road or helicopter. Most of the timber is softwood, used for building materials as well as to make chopsticks for Japan. Hardwoods can be used for furniture.

*At the sawmill the timber is cut into planks or pulped for papermaking.*

*Logs may be floated downriver from the forests to the sawmills in the form of huge rafts.*

*Logs are sawn when they are still "green", or full of sap. The method shown here produces boards with a decorative grain.*

**TOTEM POLES**
For generations, native peoples of the northwest coast carved wooden totem poles to record their family trees. Part of the pole shows which of the main clans the family belongs to, such as the raven or the wolf clan. Totem poles often guarded doorways to village homes.

*The animals carved on the totem pole are symbols of the family's ancestors.*

**COAL, OIL, AND GAS WEALTH**
Once grain and beef processing centres for the prairies, Edmonton and Calgary grew rich during the 1970s from the coal, oil, and gas found in the prairies and nearby Rocky Mountains. Now Edmonton boasts a gigantic shopping mall with an ice-hockey rink, a swimming pool, a rollercoaster ride, and even a hotel where people can stay while they shop.

## LIVING IN THE WILD
Large parts of the extreme north of Canada are home to more animals than people. Although part of the area is forested most of it is icy wilderness known as tundra. Animals that live here are adapted to the very cold conditions, and waterproof fur helps them to survive the snow and ice. Caribou, or reindeer, live on the tundra but migrate to the forests further south in winter to escape the cold. Grizzly bears are found in the Rocky Mountains and can be dangerous.

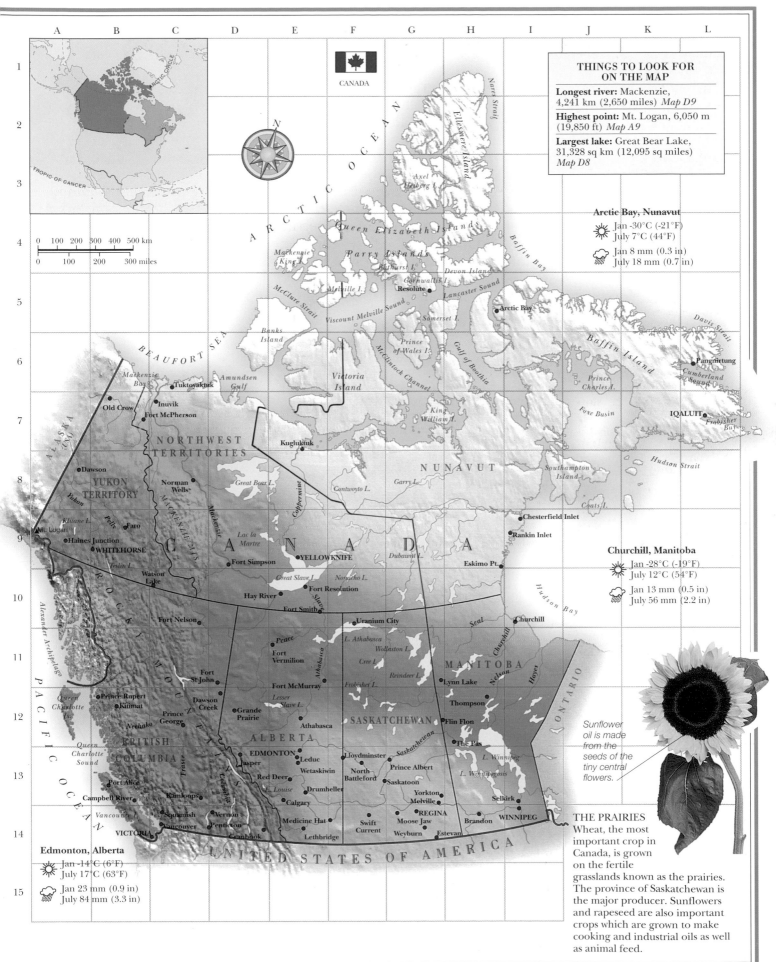

A B C D E F G H I J K L

1 2 3 4 5 6 7 8 9 10 11 12 13 14 15

CANADA

### THINGS TO LOOK FOR ON THE MAP

**Longest river:** Mackenzie, 4,241 km (2,650 miles) *Map D9*

**Highest point:** Mt. Logan, 6,050 m (19,850 ft) *Map A9*

**Largest lake:** Great Bear Lake, 31,328 sq km (12,095 sq miles) *Map D8*

**Arctic Bay, Nunavut**
☀ Jan -30°C (-21°F)
July 7°C (44°F)
🌧 Jan 8 mm (0.3 in)
July 18 mm (0.7 in)

**Churchill, Manitoba**
☀ Jan -28°C (-19°F)
July 12°C (54°F)
🌧 Jan 13 mm (0.5 in)
July 56 mm (2.2 in)

**Edmonton, Alberta**
☀ Jan -14°C (6°F)
July 17°C (63°F)
🌧 Jan 23 mm (0.9 in)
July 84 mm (3.3 in)

ARCTIC OCEAN

Ellesmere Island
Axel Heiberg I.
Queen Elizabeth Islands
Parry Islands
Mackenzie King I.
Bathurst I.
Melville I.
Cornwallis I.
Devon Island
Resolute
Banks Island
McClure Strait
Viscount Melville Sound
Victoria Island
Prince of Wales I.
Somerset I.
Lancaster Sound
Baffin Bay
Arctic Bay
Amundsen Gulf
McClintock Channel
Gulf of Boothia
Prince Charles I.
Davis Strait
Baffin Island
Cumberland Sound
Pangnirtung
King William I.
Foxe Basin
IQALUIT
Frobisher Bay
BEAUFORT SEA
Mackenzie Bay
Tuktoyaktuk
Inuvik
Fort McPherson
Old Crow
Kugluktuk
Southampton Island
Hudson Strait
Coats I.
NUNAVUT
Garry L.
Contwoyto L.
Chesterfield Inlet
Rankin Inlet
Dawson
NORTHWEST TERRITORIES
Norman Wells
Great Bear L.
Coppermine
YUKON TERRITORY
Yukon
Mt. Logan
Haines Junction
WHITEHORSE
Kluane L.
Pelly
Faro
Teslin L.
Watson Lake
Lac la Martre
Fort Simpson
YELLOWKNIFE
Dubawnt L.
Eskimo Pt.
Great Slave L.
Nonacho L.
Hudson Bay
Hay River
Fort Resolution
Fort Smith
Slave
Churchill
ALASKA (USA)
ROCKY MOUNTAINS
MACKENZIE MTS.
Mackenzie
CANADA
Churchill
Seal
Fort Nelson
Uranium City
L. Athabasca
Wollaston L.
Nelson
Peace
Athabasca
Cree L.
Reindeer L.
Frobisher L.
MANITOBA
Lynn Lake
Hayes
ONTARIO
Fort Vermilion
Fort St. John
Fort McMurray
Thompson
Alexander Archipelago
PACIFIC OCEAN
Prince Rupert
Kitimat
Dawson Creek
Grande Prairie
Lesser Slave L.
Flin Flon
The Pas
Nechako
Prince George
Athabasca
SASKATCHEWAN
Saskatchewan
L. Winnipeg
Queen Charlotte Is.
BRITISH COLUMBIA
Fraser
EDMONTON
Jasper
Leduc
Wetaskiwin
Lloydminster
North Battleford
Prince Albert
Saskatoon
L. Winnipegosis
Queen Charlotte Sound
Red Deer
Columbia
L. Louise
Drumheller
Yorkton
Melville
Selkirk
Vancouver I.
Port Alice
Campbell River
Kamloops
Squamish
Vancouver
Vernon
Penticton
Calgary
Medicine Hat
Cranbrook
Lethbridge
Swift Current
Moose Jaw
Weyburn
REGINA
Estevan
Brandon
WINNIPEG
VICTORIA
UNITED STATES OF AMERICA

*Sunflower oil is made from the seeds of the tiny central flowers.*

### THE PRAIRIES
Wheat, the most important crop in Canada, is grown on the fertile grasslands known as the prairies. The province of Saskatchewan is the major producer. Sunflowers and rapeseed are also important crops which are grown to make cooking and industrial oils as well as animal feed.

# EASTERN CANADA

SOME OF THE RICHEST AND POOREST areas of Canada are found within the eastern part of the country. The provinces of Ontario and Québec that lie around the Great Lakes and the St Lawrence River form Canada's wealthy industrial region, and contain most of the population. Canada's capital, Ottawa, and other major cities, including Toronto and Montréal, are in this region. At the end of Lake Erie, on the border with the United States, is Niagara Falls, one of the main tourist attractions in the region. The Atlantic, or maritime, provinces along the stormy east coast have few natural resources and are suffering from a decline in the fishing industry, but enjoy a distinctive culture, and a rugged coastline and landscape.

### HOCKEY
Canadians take advantage of long winters by playing hockey on frozen lakes and ponds, as well as community ice rinks. Hockey is the world's fastest team game, with the puck moving at speeds of up to 190 km (118 miles) per hour. It can get rather rough, and the action stops frequently, when players are sent to sit out penalties in the "sin bin".

### TORONTO
On the north shore of Lake Ontario lies Toronto, Canada's leading industrial city, financial capital, and fastest growing urban area. The city has a reputation for being safe, with the lowest crime rate of any major city in North America. It also boasts SkyDome, the world's first stadium with a moving roof, and the Canadian National (CN) Tower, the world's second tallest free-standing structure.

### ST LAWRENCE SEAWAY
Completed in 1959, the Great Lakes-St Lawrence Seaway system made it possible for ships to travel 3,769 km (2,342 miles) from the industrial centre of North America to the Atlantic Ocean. Ships carrying cargoes of grain, timber, iron ore, and coal descend 183 m (600 ft) from Lake Ontario to sea level through a system of locks. Tolls are charged for ships that use the system. The Seaway is closed because of ice for four months during the winter.

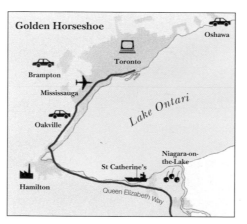

Golden Horseshoe

Oshawa

Toronto

Brampton

Mississauga

Oakville

*Lake Ontari*

Niagara-on-the-Lake

St Catherine's

Hamilton

Queen Elizabeth Way

### GOLDEN HORSESHOE
Canada's leading industrial region, known as the Golden Horseshoe, curves around the western end of Lake Ontario, from the car-industry centre of Oshawa, through Toronto and Hamilton and on to Niagara. Its location makes it easy to move products by water, by rail, and by road via a major highway called the Queen Elizabeth Way (QEW). Plentiful job opportunities attract people here and they earn some of the highest incomes in Canada.

Car assembly   Steelworks   Shipbuilding
Aircraft assembly   Finance   Fruit canning

### QUÉBEC
In 1608, Frenchman Samuel de Champlain set up a fur trading post on the St Lawrence River at a place the native peoples called Kébec. By 1763, the French settlements had been taken over by the British. Under British control, the province grew into a major commercial centre. Today, over 80 per cent of Canadians whose native language is French live in the province of Québec. Although laws guarantee the right of French Canadians to their own language, laws, and culture, some Québécois want to separate from the rest of Canada.

*Cranberries are used to make sauces and syrups.*

### CRANBERRIES
Along the coast of New Brunswick the land is marshy and ideal for growing cranberries. The plants are grown in bogs and the ripe berries are collected by hand or by special machines that scoop the fruit from the water. Berries are ready to pick in September or October.

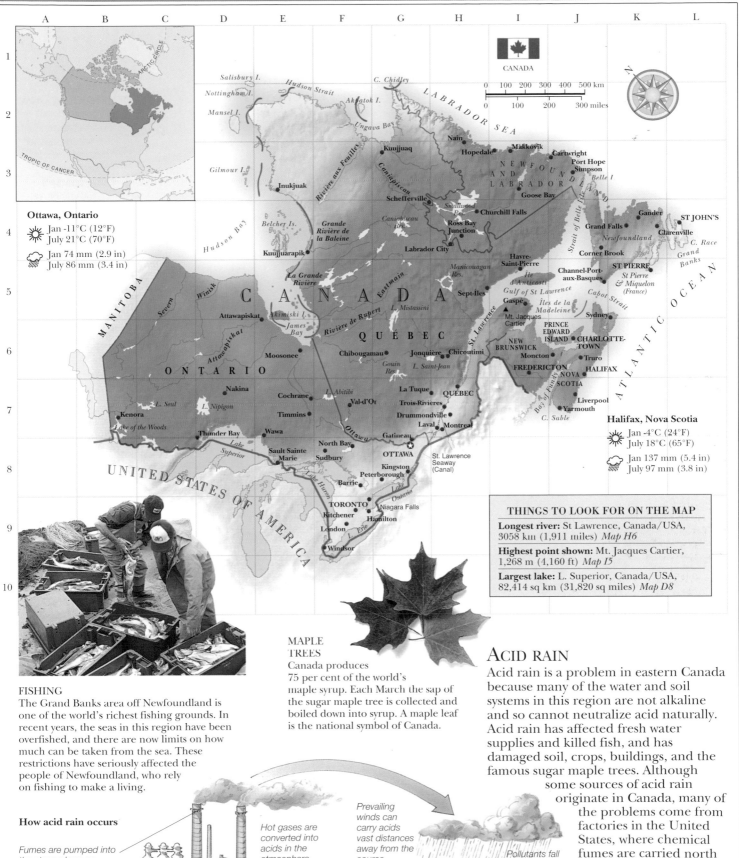

CANADA

0  100  200  300  400  500 km
0     100     200     300 miles

**Ottawa, Ontario**
Jan -11°C (12°F)
July 21°C (70°F)
Jan 74 mm (2.9 in)
July 86 mm (3.4 in)

**Halifax, Nova Scotia**
Jan -4°C (24°F)
July 18°C (65°F)
Jan 137 mm (5.4 in)
July 97 mm (3.8 in)

**THINGS TO LOOK FOR ON THE MAP**

**Longest river:** St Lawrence, Canada/USA, 3058 km (1,911 miles) *Map H6*

**Highest point shown:** Mt. Jacques Cartier, 1,268 m (4,160 ft) *Map I5*

**Largest lake:** L. Superior, Canada/USA, 82,414 sq km (31,820 sq miles) *Map D8*

### FISHING
The Grand Banks area off Newfoundland is one of the world's richest fishing grounds. In recent years, the seas in this region have been overfished, and there are now limits on how much can be taken from the sea. These restrictions have seriously affected the people of Newfoundland, who rely on fishing to make a living.

### MAPLE TREES
Canada produces 75 per cent of the world's maple syrup. Each March the sap of the sugar maple tree is collected and boiled down into syrup. A maple leaf is the national symbol of Canada.

## ACID RAIN
Acid rain is a problem in eastern Canada because many of the water and soil systems in this region are not alkaline and so cannot neutralize acid naturally. Acid rain has affected fresh water supplies and killed fish, and has damaged soil, crops, buildings, and the famous sugar maple trees. Although some sources of acid rain originate in Canada, many of the problems come from factories in the United States, where chemical fumes are carried north by the wind.

**How acid rain occurs**

*Fumes are pumped into the atmosphere as waste matter.*

*Power stations and factories produce sulphur dioxide. Also, exhaust from cars and trucks produces nitrogen oxide.*

*Hot gases are converted into acids in the atmosphere.*

*Prevailing winds can carry acids vast distances away from the source.*

*Pollutants fall as acid rain or snow.*

*Acid rain destroys trees and other plants. It kills fish and plant life in lakes and rivers.*

# UNITED STATES OF AMERICA

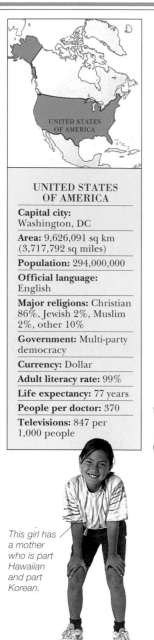

**UNITED STATES OF AMERICA**

**Capital city:** Washington, DC

**Area:** 9,626,091 sq km (3,717,792 sq miles)

**Population:** 294,000,000

**Official language:** English

**Major religions:** Christian 86%, Jewish 2%, Muslim 2%, other 10%

**Government:** Multi-party democracy

**Currency:** Dollar

**Adult literacy rate:** 99%

**Life expectancy:** 77 years

**People per doctor:** 370

**Televisions:** 847 per 1,000 people

IN LESS THAN 400 YEARS, the United States of America (USA) has grown from wild countryside inhabited by native peoples to the world's most powerful industrial nation. The country is made up of 50 states, including Alaska in the far north and Hawaii in the Pacific Ocean. There are two major mountain ranges, the Appalachians to the east and the Rockies in the west, while much of its centre is covered by the gently sloping Great Plains. Vast supplies of coal, oil, and minerals, together with mass immigration in the 19th and early 20th centuries, helped business and industry to grow fast. Today, American products and culture are recognized throughout the world.

**STARS AND STRIPES**
On the US flag, the stars stand for the 50 modern states, while the stripes represent the original 13 states on the East Coast. Until independence in 1776, these were governed by Britain. Today, each state has its own laws but is ruled by the national government in Washington, District of Columbia.

## PEOPLE OF AMERICA

People in the USA belong to a wide range of different ethnic groups. Most are descended from immigrants – people who moved there from other parts of the world, such as Europe and Asia. Many African-Americans are descendants of slaves forced to the USA in the 17th, 18th, and early 19th centuries. Today the population is increasingly Hispanic (Spanish speaking), Asian, and African-American. By 2050, these groups will make up almost half the population.

*This girl has a mother who is part Hawaiian and part Korean.*

*This child has Japanese parents who moved to the US during the 1970s.*

*African-Americans now make up 13 per cent of the population.*

**WORLD LEADER**
The USA is the world's richest country, and its leading products include iron and steel, timber and paper products, electronic equipment, cars, and aircraft, shown above. These industries create many jobs, and women now make up almost half of the country's total workforce.

## LIVING IN THE CITY

Almost 80 per cent of Americans live in cities or the surrounding suburbs. Most people who live in the suburbs own their own homes and travel to work by car. New York is the biggest city, with about 22 million inhabitants, followed by Los Angeles, and then Chicago. People from different backgrounds mingle in most cities. Often they have their own neighbourhoods, with names such as Little Italy or Chinatown. This view shows the island of Manhattan, New York.

*As cities became more crowded, and land more expensive, architects began to design taller and taller buildings where people could live and work.*

*Every day, half a million people use Grand Central Station to get to work.*

*Many US cities are laid out on a simple grid system where main roads, or avenues, run north to south and streets run east to west.*

*Americans live in a variety of homes – detached houses, townhouses, and high-rise apartment buildings.*

*Places of worship, like the Holy Family Church, can be found in every city.*

*Skyscrapers, such as the Empire State Building, now dominate the skyline of most cities in the US.*

## MOVING WEST

The people of the USA have always been quite mobile, often moving to a new state in search of work or a better lifestyle. Major events, such as the Great Depression in the 1930s, also forced people to move in the hope of finding work. The general pattern of movement since settlers first arrived is shown on this map. Over the past 30 years or so, more and more people have moved to the Sun Belt states of the South and West. These include California, Arizona, Texas, and Florida.

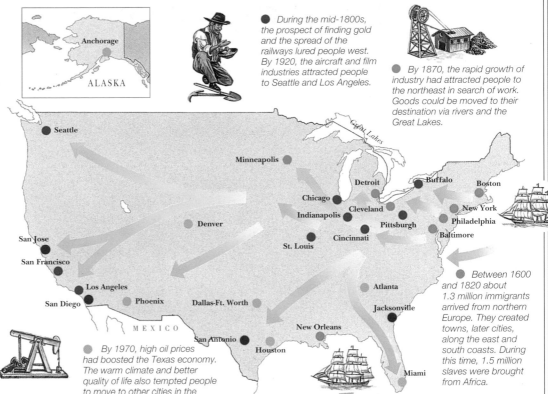

● During the mid-1800s, the prospect of finding gold and the spread of the railways lured people west. By 1920, the aircraft and film industries attracted people to Seattle and Los Angeles.

● By 1870, the rapid growth of industry had attracted people to the northeast in search of work. Goods could be moved to their destination via rivers and the Great Lakes.

● Between 1600 and 1820 about 1.3 million immigrants arrived from northern Europe. They created towns, later cities, along the east and south coasts. During this time, 1.5 million slaves were brought from Africa.

● By 1970, high oil prices had boosted the Texas economy. The warm climate and better quality of life also tempted people to move to other cities in the south and west. Cheap labour from Mexico was also important.

● Major cities that have grown up over the last 50 years

### NATIONAL PARKS

Large areas of America's most spectacular countryside are protected in more than 350 national parks. Yellowstone National Park, above, in Wyoming and Montana, was the first park to open, in 1872. Yellowstone provides a safe environment for animals including bison, elk, antelope, grizzly bear, moose, and deer.

## THE FIRST AMERICANS

Native Americans, the first inhabitants of the USA, make up less than 1 per cent of the population. Since Europeans arrived in the 1500s, the Native American tribes have had to fight long and hard to keep their homelands. Despite these struggles, they have held on to many tribal traditions and languages. Today, about one-fifth live on reservations – land returned to them by the American government.

| LARGEST TRIBES | |
| --- | --- |
| Cherokee | 308,000 |
| Navajo | 219,000 |
| Chippewa | 104,000 |
| Sioux | 103,000 |
| Choctaw | 82,000 |
| Pueblo | 53,000 |

This Zuni artist, a member of the Pueblo tribe, makes and sells silver and turquoise jewellery.

### BASEBALL

Baseball is the country's national sport. The first game played between two organized teams took place in New Jersey in 1846. The National League was formed in 1876 and today baseball is the most popular spectator sport. It is traditional for the president to pitch the first ball at the start of each new baseball season. The batter shown in action here played for the Minnesota Twins.

### AMERICAN CULTURE

The influence of US culture can be seen all over the world. Fast foods, such as hamburgers, hot dogs, and soft drinks, as well as characters from films and TV shows, are recognized in cities from Berlin to Beijing. This "selling of America" is a billion-dollar industry and plays a vital part in the US economy.

Strawberry milkshake

Double hamburger

*Find out more*

NATIVE PEOPLES: *22–23*
SETTLING THE CONTINENT: *23, 24–25*
US GOVERNMENT: *23, 270*

# USA: WESTERN STATES

FROM THE ICY LANDSCAPE OF ALASKA, through the deserts of Nevada and Arizona, to the semi-tropical islands of Hawaii, the western states cover a dramatic range of scenery. Down the Pacific Coast, large cities such as Seattle, Portland, and San Francisco ship timber, fish, and fruit all over the world. The West is also home to Hollywood, capital of the multi-million dollar film industry, and Silicon Valley, a stretch of northern California which lies at the heart of the high-tech computer business. Sun Valley in Idaho ranks as one of the country's leading ski and summer resorts.

**THE NORTHERN FORESTS**
Great forests of pine, cedar, and fir trees thrive in the wet climate near the coasts of Oregon and Washington. These states are the country's major suppliers of timber and wood pulp. The trees are cut into logs and transported by road to the coast. Environmental groups are now trying to protect the trees, many of which are more than 200 years old.

## EARTHQUAKE COUNTRY

People in California have to live with the constant threat of earthquakes. The area lies on the boundary, or fault line, between two plates of the Earth's crust. When these plates push and slide against each other, it causes earthquakes which can destroy roads and homes. It is difficult to predict an earthquake, so most people keep a survival kit in case they are trapped or left without supplies. Some of the items included in such a kit are displayed here.

**FAULT LINES**
The San Andreas Fault runs for 1,207 km (750 miles) across California, passing through the cities of San Francisco and Los Angeles. There are also hundreds of other smaller faults that constantly cause minor tremors.

— Major fault
— Minor faults

Lightweight bag of emergency items, including first-aid supplies (not shown)

Bar of dried food with vitamins

Heavy-duty torch

Packet of pure drinking water

Mini rolls of toilet tissue

Towelette

Disposable toothbrush with toothpaste

Light sticks work for 12 hours and do not need batteries.

Emergency blanket designed to reflect body heat

## FIELDS OF PLENTY

Fertile soil, plenty of sunshine, and water diverted from rivers that flow from the Sierra Nevada Mountains, make California the leading agricultural state. The land is used to grow more than 40 per cent of the fresh fruit and vegetables eaten in the USA, including peaches, oranges, strawberries, artichokes, and brussels sprouts. The Napa Valley, north of San Francisco, is an important grape-growing and wine-producing area. Mexicans often cross into California illegally to find work on the fruit farms.

**CAR CULTURE**
When Henry Ford introduced the first cheap car in 1910, it promised freedom on the open road. Today, there are more cars on the road in the USA than in any other country. Networks of 6-lane freeways weave across cities such as Los Angeles, shown above. Fumes from the cars contribute to the city's smog problem.

**SOUTH OF THE BORDER**
The majority of immigrants living in the western states come from nearby Mexico. They are called Hispanics because their ancestors came from Spain and they speak Spanish. Many still follow the religion and festivals of Mexico. Hispanics also arrive from Cuba, Puerto Rico, and El Salvador.

| CARS PER 100 PEOPLE | | |
|---|---|---|
| USA | | 77 |
| France | | 47 |
| Denmark | | 35 |
| Brazil | | 14 |
| India | | 0.7 |

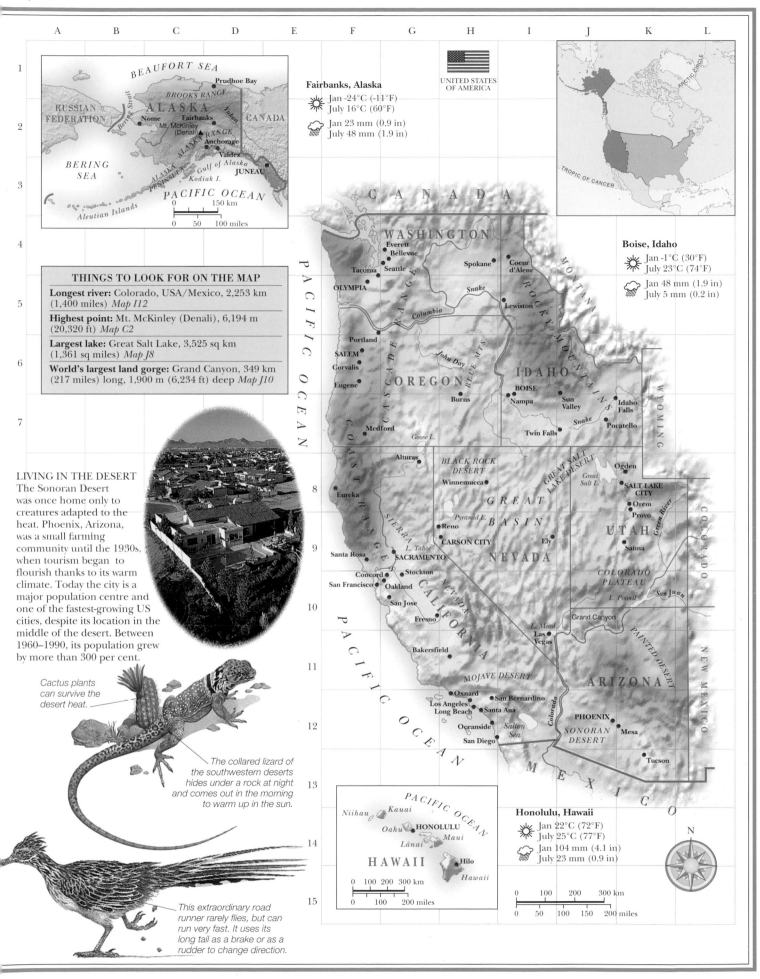

UNITED STATES
OF AMERICA

**Fairbanks, Alaska**
Jan -24°C (-11°F)
July 16°C (60°F)

Jan 23 mm (0.9 in)
July 48 mm (1.9 in)

**Boise, Idaho**
Jan -1°C (30°F)
July 23°C (74°F)

Jan 48 mm (1.9 in)
July 5 mm (0.2 in)

## THINGS TO LOOK FOR ON THE MAP

**Longest river:** Colorado, USA/Mexico, 2,253 km (1,400 miles) *Map I12*

**Highest point:** Mt. McKinley (Denali), 6,194 m (20,320 ft) *Map C2*

**Largest lake:** Great Salt Lake, 3,525 sq km (1,361 sq miles) *Map J8*

**World's largest land gorge:** Grand Canyon, 349 km (217 miles) long, 1,900 m (6,234 ft) deep *Map J10*

**LIVING IN THE DESERT**
The Sonoran Desert was once home only to creatures adapted to the heat. Phoenix, Arizona, was a small farming community until the 1930s, when tourism began to flourish thanks to its warm climate. Today the city is a major population centre and one of the fastest-growing US cities, despite its location in the middle of the desert. Between 1960–1990, its population grew by more than 300 per cent.

*Cactus plants can survive the desert heat.*

*The collared lizard of the southwestern deserts hides under a rock at night and comes out in the morning to warm up in the sun.*

*This extraordinary road runner rarely flies, but can run very fast. It uses its long tail as a brake or as a rudder to change direction.*

**Honolulu, Hawaii**
Jan 22°C (72°F)
July 25°C (77°F)

Jan 104 mm (4.1 in)
July 23 mm (0.9 in)

# USA: CENTRAL STATES

FAMOUS FOR COWBOYS AND CATTLE RANCHES, the central states of the USA are also the country's cereal bowl and oil refinery. This vast region includes high mountains, fertile plains, and the Mississippi River system. Texas and Oklahoma have major oil and gas fields, while coal is mined in Wyoming and Montana. The Rocky Mountains contain important national parks, such as Yellowstone and Glacier, and are rich in mineral resources. Hot summers and cold winters, as well as violent hailstorms and tornadoes, make the region's climate one of extremes.

*Ears of the type of wheat used for making bread.*

*Grains of wheat*

### THE GREAT PLAINS

Once home to millions of buffalo, the vast open plains between the Rocky Mountains and the Mississippi River are now planted with cereals. Farmers on the Great Plains produce more wheat and maize than anywhere else on Earth. Farming is highly mechanized, with huge machines to harvest the grain. In the drier parts, the land can be farmed only if it is irrigated using water taken from a natural underground reservoir, known as an aquifer.

### TORNADO ALLEY

Several hundred tornadoes a year strike "Tornado Alley", an area that runs through Kansas, Oklahoma, and Missouri. They occur when hot air from the Gulf of Mexico hits cold dry air from Canada. The violent storms, known as "twisters", cut through the towns and countryside, destroying everything in their path.

*A twisting column of rising air forms beneath a thunder cloud.*

*The air spirals up the column and sucks up dirt and objects in its way.*

*Tornadoes can travel at 180 km/h (112 mph).*

### RURAL AMERICA

Today, most Americans live in cities and towns, but at the start of the 20th century, two out of every five adults lived on farms. There are still many small towns with populations of less than 10,000 people. These towns are often in farming country, and are where people go for supplies, and attend school or church. This fair is taking place in a Montana town.

### COWBOY COUNTRY

Cattle are raised on the Great Plains and foothills of the Rocky Mountains. In summer, cowboys on horseback used to drive the cattle to fresh pastures; in winter, they herded them back to the ranch to be sold at auction for food. Hollywood films turned cowboys into heroes, but life in the saddle was not easy. Pay was poor and men often spent 15 hours a day on horseback in scorching heat or driving rain. Today, ranches are smaller and cowboys and horses may be ferried from ranch to pasture by truck and trailer.

*Hats keep off the sun and the rain, and were once used to carry water.*

*Leather cuffs*

*Chaps protect the rider from cattle horns.*

*Fringe helps to drain away any rainwater.*

*Spurs*

*A lasso is used to rope cattle.*

*Boots have heels to keep feet firmly in the stirrups.*

### CITIES OF THE DEAD

Cemeteries in New Orleans are built above ground to protect them when the Mississippi floods. The burial grounds are called Cities of the Dead.

*A wreath of flowers*

### MISSISSIPPI RIVER

From Minnesota in the north to its enormous delta in the Gulf of Mexico, the mighty Mississippi River flows through the central states. It is one of the world's busiest waterways, suitable for cargo boats for almost 2,900 km (1,802 miles). This view of the river shows it flowing through Iowa, where it forms a natural border with Illinois and Wisconsin. In the south, severe flooding often occurs after heavy rains.

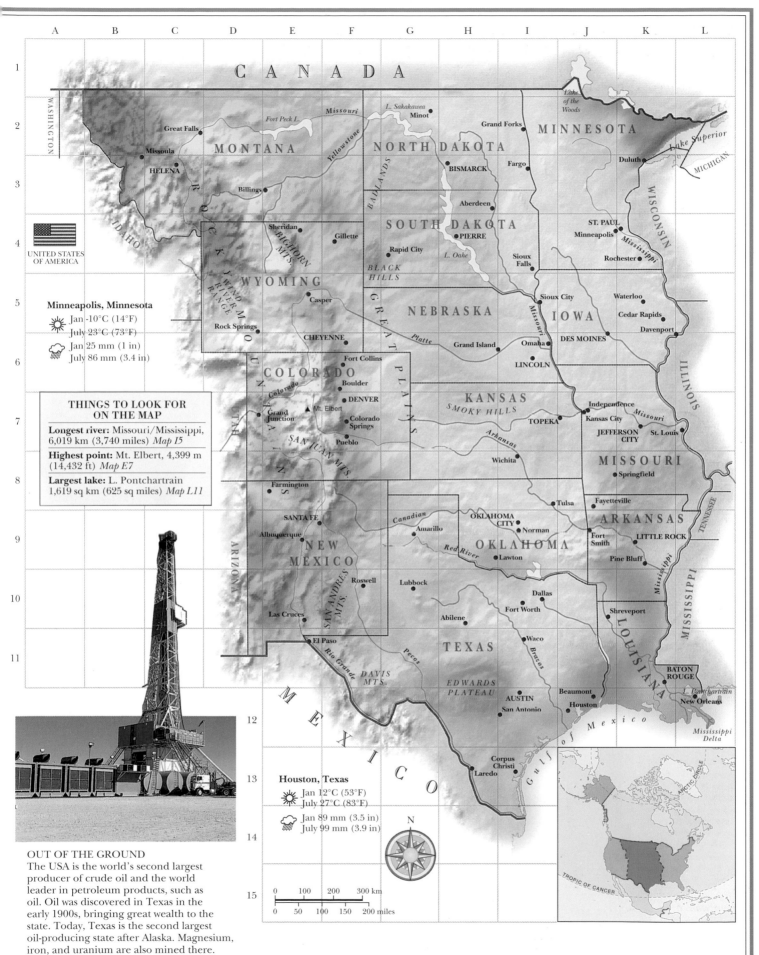

A B C D E F G H I J K L

1

C A N A D A

WASHINGTON

2

Great Falls
Missoula
HELENA
MONTANA
Fort Peck L.
Missouri
Yellowstone
L. Sakakawea
Minot
NORTH DAKOTA
BISMARCK
Grand Forks
Fargo
MINNESOTA
Duluth
Lake of the Woods
Lake Superior
MICHIGAN
WISCONSIN

3

Billings
BADLANDS

4

UNITED STATES
OF AMERICA

Sheridan
Gillette
BIGHORN MTS.
SOUTH DAKOTA
Aberdeen
Rapid City
PIERRE
BLACK HILLS
L. Oahe
Sioux Falls
ST. PAUL
Minneapolis
Rochester
Mississippi

**Minneapolis, Minnesota**
☀ Jan -10°C (14°F)
☀ July 23°C (73°F)
🌧 Jan 25 mm (1 in)
🌧 July 86 mm (3.4 in)

5

Casper
Rock Springs
WYOMING
WIND RIVER RANGE
ROCKY MOUNTAINS
IDAHO
GREAT PLAINS
NEBRASKA
Grand Island
Sioux City
Missouri
IOWA
Waterloo
Cedar Rapids
Davenport

6

CHEYENNE
Fort Collins
Boulder
COLORADO
Colorado
DENVER
Platte
Omaha
LINCOLN
DES MOINES
ILLINOIS

**THINGS TO LOOK FOR
ON THE MAP**

**Longest river:** Missouri/Mississippi,
6,019 km (3,740 miles) *Map I5*

**Highest point:** Mt. Elbert, 4,399 m
(14,432 ft) *Map E7*

**Largest lake:** L. Pontchartrain
1,619 sq km (625 sq miles) *Map L11*

7

Grand Junction
▲ Mt. Elbert
Colorado Springs
Pueblo
SAN JUAN MTS.
KANSAS
SMOKY HILLS
TOPEKA
Arkansas
Independence
Kansas City
Missouri
JEFFERSON CITY
St. Louis
MISSOURI

8

Farmington
UTAH
Wichita
Springfield
Fayetteville

9

SANTA FE
Albuquerque
NEW MEXICO
Canadian
Amarillo
OKLAHOMA CITY
Norman
OKLAHOMA
Red River
Lawton
Tulsa
Fort Smith
ARKANSAS
LITTLE ROCK
Pine Bluff
Mississippi
TENNESSEE

10

Roswell
Lubbock
SAN ANDRES MTS.
ARIZONA
Dallas
Fort Worth
Shreveport
Mississippi

11

Las Cruces
El Paso
Rio Grande
Pecos
Abilene
Waco
Brazos
TEXAS
LOUISIANA
BATON ROUGE

MEXICO

DAVIS MTS.
EDWARDS PLATEAU
AUSTIN
San Antonio
Beaumont
Houston
New Orleans
L. Pontchartrain
Mississippi Delta

12

13

**Houston, Texas**
☀ Jan 12°C (53°F)
☀ July 27°C (83°F)
🌧 Jan 89 mm (3.5 in)
🌧 July 99 mm (3.9 in)

Corpus Christi
Laredo
Gulf of Mexico

N

14

0  100  200  300 km

0  50  100  150  200 miles

ARCTIC CIRCLE

TROPIC OF CANCER

15

**OUT OF THE GROUND**
The USA is the world's second largest
producer of crude oil and the world
leader in petroleum products, such as
oil. Oil was discovered in Texas in the
early 1900s, bringing great wealth to the
state. Today, Texas is the second largest
oil-producing state after Alaska. Magnesium,
iron, and uranium are also mined there.

# USA: EASTERN STATES

EXCELLENT HARBOURS, FERTILE LANDS, and rich mineral resources have made this region one of the most densely populated in the country. It was along the East Coast that the first settlers from Europe arrived in the 16th century. Today the area includes some of the country's largest cities, such as New York and Washington DC, as well as the once-great industrial centres of Chicago, Detroit, and Cleveland on the Great Lakes. Further south, farmers use the land to cultivate cotton, tobacco, and vegetables grown for their oil. Each year, hurricanes are a threat to people living on the Gulf and Atlantic coasts.

*The White House has been the home of every US president since 1800.*

**RULING THE COUNTRY**
The USA has a written set of laws, known as a constitution, which sets out how the country should be governed. The centre of government is Washington, DC, where the President and his family live in The White House. The President is the head of state and is chosen in elections which are held once every four years.

**THE APPALACHIANS**
The Appalachian Mountains run through North Carolina, Virginia, and West Virginia. For many years, coal was mined here and used to power the steel mills. Today, many mines and factories have closed and taken away jobs. Despite a plan to open up the area to tourists, Appalachia remains one of the poorest parts of the USA.

## BIG BUSINESS IN NEW YORK

Originally a fur-trading post at the mouth of the Hudson River, New York is now the US's financial capital. Wall Street, so called because it marked the line of the old city wall, is the home of the New York Stock Exchange. Financial deals worth billions of dollars are made there every day. Nasdaq, short for National Association of Securities Dealers Automated Quotation System, based in New York, was the world's first electronic stock market. Because it is a purely computer-based system, shares can be traded around the globe, 24 hours a day.

*This huge machine picks the cotton bolls from the plant.*

*Flower buds form on the cotton plants.*

*Flowers turn pink and then fall off.*

*The sign on this blues club in Memphis, Tennessee, is shaped like a giant guitar.*

**THE BIRTH OF THE BLUES**
This part of the USA is the birthplace of some of the world's most popular music. Jazz and blues were based on the spirituals and work songs of the black population. Country music began as poor white people's music in Kentucky and Tennessee, and the soul label Motown grew up in Detroit, or Motor Town.

*Neon, used to light up so many buildings across America, was first invented in 1898.*

*After the flower falls off, a tiny seed ripens and grows into a pod, or boll.*

*The cotton boll opens into a fluffy fibre ready for harvesting.*

*Cotton is woven into fabric for shirts, trousers, and towels, which are sold at home and abroad.*

## COTTON – FROM FIELD TO FABRIC

In the mid-1800s, the southern states produced 80 per cent of the world's cotton and grew rich on the profits. Cotton was grown on huge plantations, then hand-picked by black slaves who had been brought by force from Africa. Slavery was finally abolished in the USA in 1865. Cotton is still an important crop, although modern machinery now does the hard work. Soya beans, used mainly for oil, is now the biggest crop in this region.

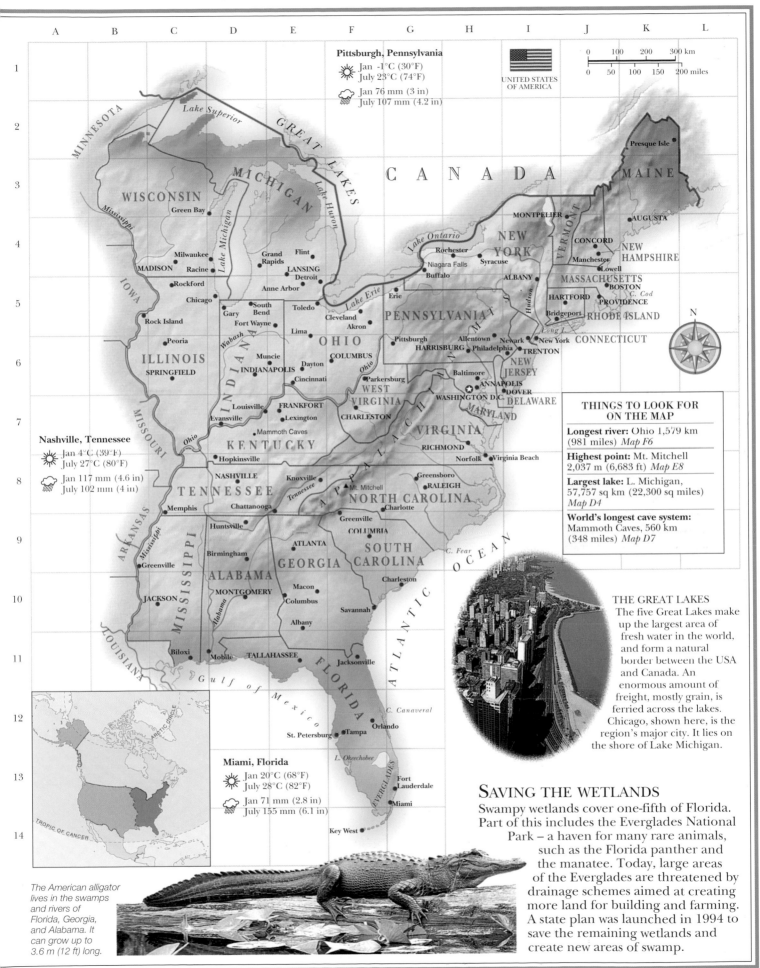

**Pittsburgh, Pennsylvania**
☀ Jan -1°C (30°F)
   July 23°C (74°F)
🌧 Jan 76 mm (3 in)
   July 107 mm (4.2 in)

UNITED STATES OF AMERICA

0  100  200  300 km
0  50  100  150  200 miles

MINNESOTA
Lake Superior
GREAT LAKES
MICHIGAN
CANADA
MAINE
Presque Isle
WISCONSIN
Green Bay
Lake Michigan
Lake Huron
NEW YORK
VERMONT
MONTPELIER
AUGUSTA
CONCORD
NEW HAMPSHIRE
Rochester
Niagara Falls
Syracuse
Manchester
Lowell
MASSACHUSETTS
Milwaukee
MADISON
Racine
Rockford
Grand Rapids
Flint
LANSING
Detroit
Anne Arbor
Buffalo
ALBANY
Lake Ontario
Hudson
BOSTON
C. Cod
HARTFORD
PROVIDENCE
IOWA
Chicago
South Bend
Gary
Fort Wayne
Toledo
Cleveland
Akron
Lake Erie
Erie
PENNSYLVANIA
Bridgeport
RHODE ISLAND
Long I.
New York
CONNECTICUT
Rock Island
Peoria
Lima
Muncie
Dayton
COLUMBUS
OHIO
Pittsburgh
Allentown
Newark
N
ILLINOIS
SPRINGFIELD
INDIANAPOLIS
Cincinnati
Ohio
Parkersburg
HARRISBURG
Philadelphia
TRENTON
NEW JERSEY
Wabash
Louisville
FRANKFORT
WEST VIRGINIA
Baltimore
ANNAPOLIS
DOVER
DELAWARE
MISSOURI
Evansville
Lexington
CHARLESTON
WASHINGTON D.C.
MARYLAND
Ohio
Mammoth Caves
KENTUCKY
VIRGINIA
Nashville, Tennessee
☀ Jan 4°C (39°F)
   July 27°C (80°F)
🌧 Jan 117 mm (4.6 in)
   July 102 mm (4 in)
Hopkinsville
NASHVILLE
Knoxville
RICHMOND
Norfolk
Virginia Beach
TENNESSEE
Tennessee
APPALACHIAN
Mt. Mitchell
Greensboro
RALEIGH
Memphis
Mississippi
Chattanooga
Huntsville
NORTH CAROLINA
Charlotte
Greenville
COLUMBIA
C. Fear
ARKANSAS
Birmingham
ATLANTA
SOUTH CAROLINA
Greenville
ALABAMA
GEORGIA
Charleston
ATLANTIC OCEAN
JACKSON
MONTGOMERY
Macon
Columbus
MISSISSIPPI
Alabama
Savannah
Albany
LOUISIANA
Biloxi
Mobile
TALLAHASSEE
Jacksonville
FLORIDA
Gulf of Mexico
C. Canaveral
Orlando
St. Petersburg
Tampa
Miami, Florida
☀ Jan 20°C (68°F)
   July 28°C (82°F)
🌧 Jan 71 mm (2.8 in)
   July 155 mm (6.1 in)
L. Okeechobee
EVERGLADES
Fort Lauderdale
Miami
Key West
ARCTIC CIRCLE
TROPIC OF CANCER

**THINGS TO LOOK FOR ON THE MAP**

**Longest river:** Ohio 1,579 km (981 miles) *Map F6*

**Highest point:** Mt. Mitchell 2,037 m (6,683 ft) *Map E8*

**Largest lake:** L. Michigan, 57,757 sq km (22,300 sq miles) *Map D4*

**World's longest cave system:** Mammoth Caves, 560 km (348 miles) *Map D7*

**THE GREAT LAKES**
The five Great Lakes make up the largest area of fresh water in the world, and form a natural border between the USA and Canada. An enormous amount of freight, mostly grain, is ferried across the lakes. Chicago, shown here, is the region's major city. It lies on the shore of Lake Michigan.

## SAVING THE WETLANDS
Swampy wetlands cover one-fifth of Florida. Part of this includes the Everglades National Park – a haven for many rare animals, such as the Florida panther and the manatee. Today, large areas of the Everglades are threatened by drainage schemes aimed at creating more land for building and farming. A state plan was launched in 1994 to save the remaining wetlands and create new areas of swamp.

*The American alligator lives in the swamps and rivers of Florida, Georgia, and Alabama. It can grow up to 3.6 m (12 ft) long.*

# MEXICO

MEXICO

| **MEXICO** |
|---|
| **Capital city:** Mexico City |
| **Area:** 1,972,550 sq km (761,602 sq miles) |
| **Population:** 104,000,000 |
| **Official language:** Spanish |
| **Major religions:** Christian 93%, other 7% |
| **Government:** Multi-party democracy |
| **Currency:** Mexican peso |
| **Adult literacy rate:** 91% |
| **Life expectancy:** 74 years |
| **People per doctor:** 667 |
| **Televisions:** 261 per 1,000 people |

THE COLOURFUL LAND OF MEXICO was once home to the golden civilizations of the Maya and Aztecs. These ancient empires were destroyed by the Spanish, who invaded in the 1500s and ruled the country until its independence in 1821. Descendants of the native peoples still live in Mexico, but most people are *mestizo*, of mixed Spanish and native Indian descent. Almost half of all Mexicans are under 20 years old, and the population is growing rapidly, leading to overcrowding in the cities. Mexico has limited farmland and cannot produce enough food for the growing population.

A LAND OF CONTRASTS
Mexico's landscape ranges from vast deserts in the north, through snow-capped mountains and a central plateau in the centre, to tropical rainforests in the south. The Sonoran Desert, shown here, stretches across the border into the USA. This desert is home to the giant saguaro cactus, and to poisonous animals such as rattlesnakes and scorpions.

SITE SEEING
Tourism is one of Mexico's biggest sources of income. Visitors from all over the world come to see Chichén Itzá, Tenochtitlán, Palenque, and other sites of the ancient Maya and Aztec civilizations. The warm sea and sandy beaches at coastal resorts, such as Acapulco and Cancun, also attract many tourists.

*Mexico City's most famous street is the wide Paseo de la Reforma, with its tall buildings, cafés, and theatres.*

*These buildings at Teotihuacán, near Mexico City, are the remains of an ancient religious centre.*

## MEXICO CITY

With a population of more than 22 million, Mexico City is one of the world's largest cities. But its size and location bring many problems. It lies at high altitude and is ringed by mountains, so pollution from cars and factories cannot escape and poisons the air. Children sometimes do not leave for school until after the rush hour to avoid car fumes. Mexico City is very overcrowded, and the area is also prone to earthquakes; the most recent one devastated the city centre in 1985.

*Most Mexicans are Roman Catholic and worship in churches often named after saints.*

*Women carry decorated baskets of flowers. They wear wrap-around skirts, called enrados, and white blouses.*

*Men parade with large cotton globes on which the name of their town is written.*

*A dip called guacamole is made with avocados.*

*Beer with a slice of lime*

*Avocado*

*Chillies*

*Tortillas are eaten like bread or made into a snack called a taco.*

## VILLAGE FESTIVALS

Festivals, or *fiestas*, are a common part of Mexican village life. Each village has its own patron saint and on the saint's day there is a colourful celebration. There are 115 separate saints' days in Mexico. Here the people of a small town near Oaxaca celebrate their *fiesta* with a street procession. Although most people in Mexico are Roman Catholic, native Indian beliefs are also important and many festivals are a mixture of Christian and Indian traditions.

MEXICAN FOOD
Mexicans eat a variety of spicy foods using chillies. Most of their food is based on home-grown produce, such as avocados, beans, tomatoes, and maize. Pancakes, called *tortillas*, are made from maize flour and filled with meat or vegetables, and cheese. Cooks also mix chillies and chocolate to make a spicy sauce called *mole* which is served on chicken.

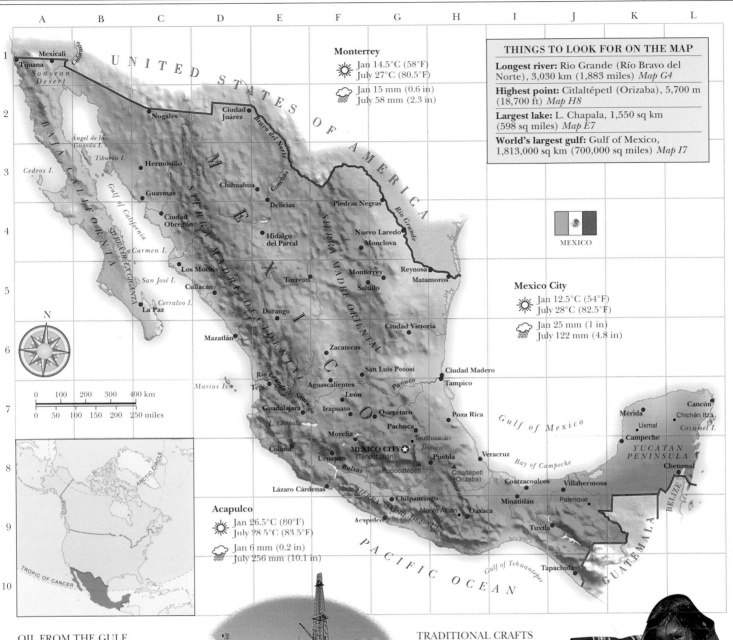

A B C D E F G H I J K L

1 2 3 4 5 6 7 8 9 10

UNITED STATES OF AMERICA

MEXICO

Mexicali
Tijuana
Sonoran Desert
Ángel de la Guarda I.
Tiburón I.
Cedros I.
Nogales
Hermosillo
Guaymas
Ciudad Obregón
Carmen I.
Los Mochis
San José I.
Culiacán
Cerralvo I.
La Paz
BAJA CALIFORNIA
Gulf of California
SIERRA DE LA GIGANTA
Ciudad Juárez
Bravo del Norte
Chihuahua
Conchos
Delicias
Hidalgo del Parral
Durango
Mazatlán
SIERRA MADRE OCCIDENTAL
Colorado
Piedras Negras
Rio Grande
Nuevo Laredo
Monclova
Torreón
Monterrey
Saltillo
Reynosa
Matamoros
Ciudad Victoria
Zacatecas
San Luis Potosí
Ciudad Madero
Tampico
SIERRA MADRE ORIENTAL
Marías Is.
Tepic
Rio Grande de Santiago
Aguascalientes
León
Guadalajara
L. Chapala
Irapuato
Querétaro
Pachuca
Panuco
Poza Rica
Gulf of Mexico
Mérida
Cancún
Chichén Itzá
Cozumel I.
Uxmal
Campeche
YUCATAN PENINSULA
Morelia
Teotihuacán
Colima
MEXICO CITY (Tenochtitlán)
L. Texcoco
Puebla
Veracruz
Bay of Campeche
Chetumal
Uruapan
Balsas
Popocatépetl
Citlaltépetl (Orizaba)
Coatzacoalcos
Villahermosa
Palenque
BELIZE
Lázaro Cárdenas
SIERRA MADRE DEL SUR
Chilpancingo
Monte Albán
Oaxaca
Minatitlán
Tuxtla
GUATEMALA
Acapulco
PACIFIC OCEAN
Gulf of Tehuantepec
Tapachula

N

0 100 200 300 400 km
0 50 100 150 200 250 miles

TROPIC OF CANCER
ARCTIC CIRCLE

**Monterrey**
☀ Jan 14.5°C (58°F)
July 27°C (80.5°F)
🌧 Jan 15 mm (0.6 in)
July 58 mm (2.3 in)

**Mexico City**
☀ Jan 12.5°C (54°F)
July 28°C (82.5°F)
🌧 Jan 25 mm (1 in)
July 122 mm (4.8 in)

**Acapulco**
☀ Jan 26.5°C (80°F)
July 28.5°C (83.5°F)
🌧 Jan 6 mm (0.2 in)
July 256 mm (10.1 in)

MEXICO

| THINGS TO LOOK FOR ON THE MAP |
|---|
| **Longest river:** Rio Grande (Río Bravo del Norte), 3,030 km (1,883 miles) *Map G4* |
| **Highest point:** Citlaltépetl (Orizaba), 5,700 m (18,700 ft) *Map H8* |
| **Largest lake:** L. Chapala, 1,550 sq km (598 sq miles) *Map E7* |
| **World's largest gulf:** Gulf of Mexico, 1,813,000 sq km (700,000 sq miles) *Map I7* |

## OIL FROM THE GULF

Huge reserves of oil were found along the Gulf of Mexico in 1976, and today Mexico is the world's fifth largest producer. There are about 3,000 oil platforms in the gulf, extracting oil from the sea bed. Mexico is also rich in other minerals, including iron, zinc, copper, and silver, of which it is the world's biggest producer.

## TRADITIONAL CRAFTS

Weaving and embroidery are among the traditional crafts of Mexico's native Indian peoples. Images of gods, birds, and flowers are often used in their designs. Just like their ancestors, women bring brightly decorated clothes into the towns to sell in the markets.

*Blue, red, and black are the main colours used in traditional Mexican designs.*

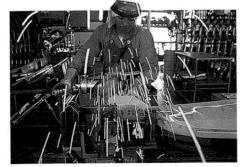

## MADE IN MEXICO

Clustered along Mexico's border with the USA are some 2,000 factories, called *maquiladoras*. Here, huge numbers of cars, computers, shoes, and other manufactured goods are assembled from parts, ready to be exported. Most of the factories are owned by foreign companies, who are attracted to Mexico by the cheap labour costs. The *maquiladoras* are an important source of income for Mexico, and help to prevent its economy from being too dependent on oil.

| *Find out more* |
|---|
| OIL: *137, 152, 281* |
| POPULATION GROWTH: *16–17* |
| ROMAN CATHOLICS: *274* |
| TRADE (*MAQUILADORAS*): *280* |

# CENTRAL AND SOUTH AMERICA

CENTRAL AMERICA IS A NARROW BRIDGE of land linking Mexico in the north to South America in the south. A string of mountains runs down its length, capped by volcanoes. The beautiful, palm-fringed islands of the Caribbean Sea lie off the east coast. South America, the fourth largest continent, contains a range of very different landscapes. About 60 per cent of the continent is covered in vast, grassy plains. The towering Andes Mountains stretch along the west coast, with the long, thin Atacama Desert sandwiched between the mountains and the sea. Tropical rainforests spread in a lush, green blanket across huge areas of the northeast.

*The Andean condor has a wingspan of 3 m (10 ft). Its huge wings help it to soar above the mountain peaks.*

## THE AMAZON RIVER

The world's largest rainforest grows in the vast basin of the mighty Amazon, the longest river in South America. The Amazon rises high in the snow-capped Andes in Peru, then flows 6,439 km (4,001 miles) across Peru and Brazil to its mouth in the Atlantic Ocean. The Amazon carries more water than any other river. At its mouth, the Amazon is so wide that you cannot see from one bank to the other. The river discharges so much water into the ocean that the water is still fresh 180 km (112 miles) out to sea.

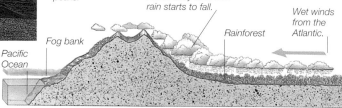

*As the winds reach the Andes they cool and rain starts to fall.*

*Wet winds from the Atlantic.*

*Rainforest*

*Fog bank*

*Pacific Ocean*

*Very little rain falls on the west side of the Andes, which is mostly desert.*

## THE ANDES

Stretching for 7,250 km (4,505 miles) along the entire length of South America, the Andes are the world's longest mountain range. Many peaks rise above 6,000 m (19,685 ft). The mountains were formed when two plates of the Earth's crust collided. The plates are still moving, causing numerous earthquakes and volcanoes along the range. An extinct volcano, Aconcagua, is the highest Andean peak and the highest mountain in South America at 6,960 m (22,835 ft). The world's highest navigable lake, Titicaca, lies in the Andes between Peru and Bolivia.

### THE ANDES AND CLIMATE

The Andes have a major effect on the weather of South America. Warm, wet winds from the Atlantic rise up the eastern slopes. As they rise, they cool and the water in them falls as rain. On the dry, western slopes, the weather conditions are completely different. Here the winds pass over the cold Humboldt Current as they blow in off the sea. This causes them to cool and form a bank of fog.

*Patagonia covers about 700,000 sq km (270,272 sq miles) of southern Argentina and Chile.*

### PATAGONIA

In the far southeast of South America lies a huge, dry, windswept plateau of land, called Patagonia. This region is sparsely populated, but some small groups of sheep farmers live near the Colorado and Negro rivers. They include a community of Welsh-speakers whose ancestors settled in the region during the 1860s. Northern Patagonia is semi-desert with some scrubby vegetation. The south is colder, drier, and bleaker with very little plant life.

### THE PAMPAS

Rolling grasslands cover the centre of Argentina and extend into neighbouring Paraguay. These are the pampas, vast open plains which stretch across an area of 650,000 sq km (250,967 sq miles). The western pampas are dry, semi-desert, but the eastern part has frequent rainfall. The pampas form the economic heartland of Argentina. Large herds of beef cattle are grazed on the plains. Other areas have been ploughed up to grow huge amounts of wheat, maize, beans, and other crops.

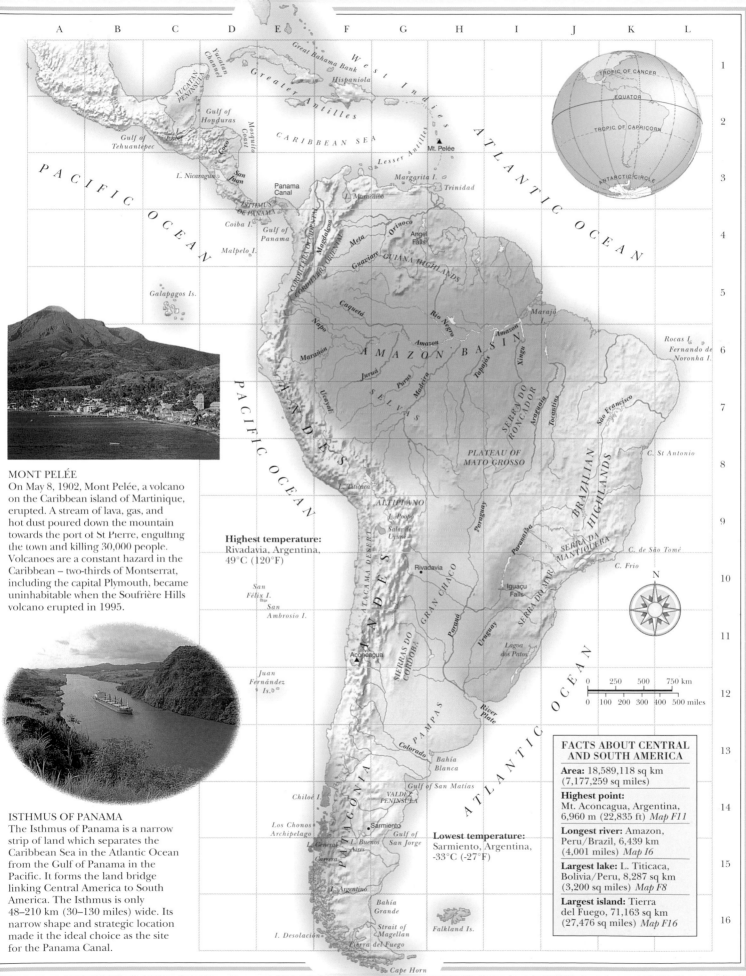

**MONT PELÉE**

On May 8, 1902, Mont Pelée, a volcano on the Caribbean island of Martinique, erupted. A stream of lava, gas, and hot dust poured down the mountain towards the port of St Pierre, engulfing the town and killing 30,000 people. Volcanoes are a constant hazard in the Caribbean – two-thirds of Montserrat, including the capital Plymouth, became uninhabitable when the Soufrière Hills volcano erupted in 1995.

**ISTHMUS OF PANAMA**

The Isthmus of Panama is a narrow strip of land which separates the Caribbean Sea in the Atlantic Ocean from the Gulf of Panama in the Pacific. It forms the land bridge linking Central America to South America. The Isthmus is only 48–210 km (30–130 miles) wide. Its narrow shape and strategic location made it the ideal choice as the site for the Panama Canal.

**Highest temperature:**
Rivadavia, Argentina,
49°C (120°F)

**Lowest temperature:**
Sarmiento, Argentina,
-33°C (-27°F)

---

### FACTS ABOUT CENTRAL AND SOUTH AMERICA

**Area:** 18,589,118 sq km
(7,177,259 sq miles)

**Highest point:**
Mt. Aconcagua, Argentina,
6,960 m (22,835 ft) *Map F11*

**Longest river:** Amazon,
Peru/Brazil, 6,439 km
(4,001 miles) *Map I6*

**Largest lake:** L. Titicaca,
Bolivia/Peru, 8,287 sq km
(3,200 sq miles) *Map F8*

**Largest island:** Tierra
del Fuego, 71,163 sq km
(27,476 sq miles) *Map F16*

# PEOPLES OF CENTRAL AND SOUTH AMERICA

**Population:** approximately 433,500,000 people
**Number of countries:** 32

THE LANGUAGE, HISTORY, and culture of Central and South America have been shaped by colonization. Until 1492, when Christopher Columbus first landed in the Bahamas, the continent had been inhabited by native peoples. After that time, European settlers arrived from Spain and Portugal, and huge numbers of Africans were imported as slaves, especially to the Caribbean and Brazil. The Caribbean also became home to English, French, and Dutch settlers. As a result, the population of the continent today is a combination of these different ethnic groups. Spanish is the main language spoken throughout most of the continent, together with Portuguese in Brazil. English and French are more common in the Caribbean, while Dutch can still be heard in Suriname.

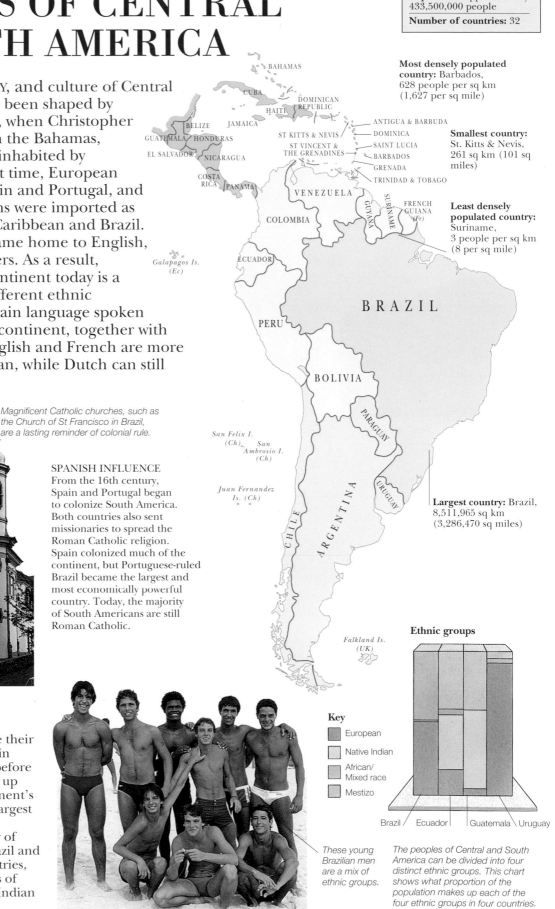

**Most densely populated country:** Barbados, 628 people per sq km (1,627 per sq mile)

**Smallest country:** St. Kitts & Nevis, 261 sq km (101 sq miles)

**Least densely populated country:** Suriname, 3 people per sq km (8 per sq mile)

**Largest country:** Brazil, 8,511,965 sq km (3,286,470 sq miles)

*Magnificent Catholic churches, such as the Church of St Francisco in Brazil, are a lasting reminder of colonial rule.*

### SPANISH INFLUENCE
From the 16th century, Spain and Portugal began to colonize South America. Both countries also sent missionaries to spread the Roman Catholic religion. Spain colonized much of the continent, but Portuguese-ruled Brazil became the largest and most economically powerful country. Today, the majority of South Americans are still Roman Catholic.

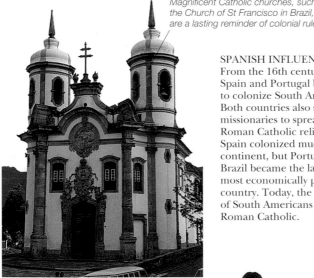

## ETHNIC GROUPS
Native Indians, who can trace their history back to people living in Central and South America before the Europeans arrived, make up just two per cent of the continent's population today. The next largest group are people of African descent, the greatest number of whom are today found in Brazil and the Caribbean. In most countries, the largest group of people is of mixed European and native Indian descent, known as *mestizos*.

**Ethnic groups**

**Key**
- European
- Native Indian
- African/Mixed race
- Mestizo

Brazil / Ecuador / Guatemala \ Uruguay

*These young Brazilian men are a mix of ethnic groups.*

*The peoples of Central and South America can be divided into four distinct ethnic groups. This chart shows what proportion of the population makes up each of the four ethnic groups in four countries.*

**Key**

- 50% and more
- 10–49%
- Less than 10%

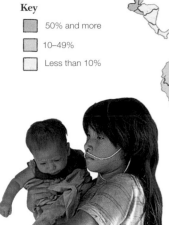

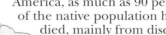

*This map is shaded to show the percentage of native Indians in each country across the continent. Some native Indians, such as this Yaminahva Indian woman and child, in Peru, now live in special reservations.*

# NATIVE PEOPLES

Within a hundred years of the Spanish arrival in South America, as much as 90 per cent of the native population had died, mainly from diseases brought by Europeans, such as smallpox or measles, against which the native peoples had no natural immunity. Today, native Indians make up a very small minority, except in Guatemala, where Mayan people still inhabit the highlands in large numbers, and in the Andean ranges of Bolivia where descendants of the Incas live.

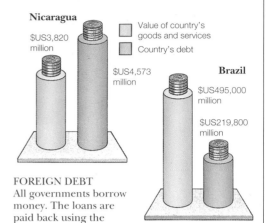

**Nicaragua**

$US3,820 million

$US4,573 million

Value of country's goods and services

Country's debt

**Brazil**

$US495,000 million

$US219,800 million

## FOREIGN DEBT

All governments borrow money. The loans are paid back using the money that the country earns by exporting its goods. However, many countries in Central and South America have huge debts. Brazil has a very large foreign debt, but it is still relatively small compared to Brazil's earnings. Nicaragua has a much smaller debt, but the country's earnings are even less.

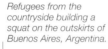

*Refugees from the countryside building a squat on the outskirts of Buenos Aires, Argentina.*

## CROWDED CITIES

Nearly three-quarters of the continent's population live in cities. In some countries, such as Chile and Uruguay, more than a third of the population live in the capital. Many people have been forced to migrate from rural areas to escape widespread poverty, or have been drawn to the cities by the chance of work, and now live in crowded shanty towns that have grown up on the city outskirts.

## SMALL-SCALE FARMS

Most of the continent's farmers have only enough land to support one or two people. People grow crops, like this Bolivia family does, and keep a few animals such as chickens or pigs to eat rather than to sell. Since the farm cannot provide enough food for all the family, some family members are forced to move elsewhere in search of work.

## LARGE-SCALE FARMS

Across the region, ranches for cattle and sheep and plantations growing export crops, such as bananas and sugar, often extend over a vast area and are operated as profit-making businesses. These huge farms may be owned by foreign companies or by a handful of rich and powerful families. Cuba is different, for the government controls these large estates.

**Average number of children**

Kenya: 4.5

Bolivia: 4.0

Peru: 3.1

Argentina: 2.5

Germany: 1.4

# POPULATION GROWTH

Since 1900, population growth across the continent has been rapid, particularly in Brazil and the northern countries. In most countries, birth rates are now beginning to fall. However, since so many of the population are young, and improvements in health allow more children to survive into adulthood, the population is still growing. By the end of 2005, another 80 million people were living there.

*This birth rate chart shows the average number of children per woman in five countries. Birth rates in Central and South America are lower than in Africa, but higher than birth rates in Europe where most families have 1 or 2 children.*

# CENTRAL AMERICA AND THE CARIBBEAN

THE SEVEN SMALL COUNTRIES OF CENTRAL AMERICA lie within a neck of land that joins North and South America. To the east, hundreds of Caribbean islands stretch from the USA almost to Venezuela. When Christopher Columbus and his Spanish crew dropped anchor in the Caribbean in 1492, they thought it was Asia, and the islands became known as the West Indies. From that time on, Europeans competed for control of the region, bringing slaves from Africa to work on the land. Central America's greatest influence is still Spanish, while the Caribbean retains its African culture. The entire area is affected by natural hazards with volcanoes, earthquakes, and hurricanes.

### FARMING THE LAND
Even before the arrival of Europeans, Central America was an agricultural region. The land divides into three main zones: the fertile Pacific plain, ideal for growing crops such as bananas; the central highlands, with coffee plantations (above) and cattle ranches; and the forested northeast, where the soil is less suitable for farming. Intensive farming has damaged much of the environment.

## HURRICANE STRENGTH
Powerful tropical storms, known as hurricanes, affect the Caribbean between May and October. A hurricane starts off as a normal storm over the ocean, but grows in force if the waters are particularly warm. Winds then blow the swirling mass of cloud, wind, and rain westwards, towards the islands, where it can cause massive destruction when it hits land. The word hurricane comes from Huracan, the local name for the god of storms.

Arrows indicate the movements of storms and show how they die out once they hit land and "spend" all their energy.

The red line across the map marks the southern limit of the area of hurricane activity.

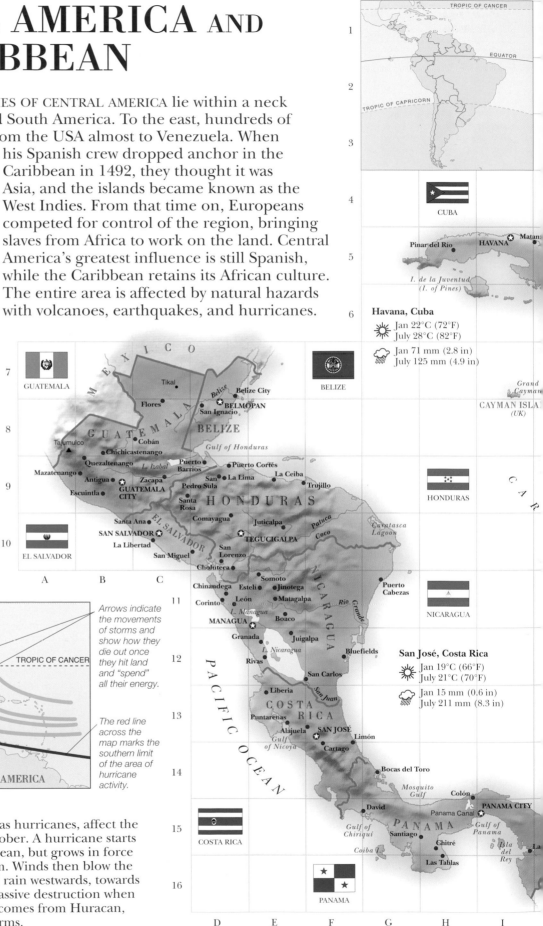

**Havana, Cuba**
Jan 22°C (72°F)
July 28°C (82°F)
Jan 71 mm (2.8 in)
July 125 mm (4.9 in)

**San José, Costa Rica**
Jan 19°C (66°F)
July 21°C (70°F)
Jan 15 mm (0.6 in)
July 211 mm (8.3 in)

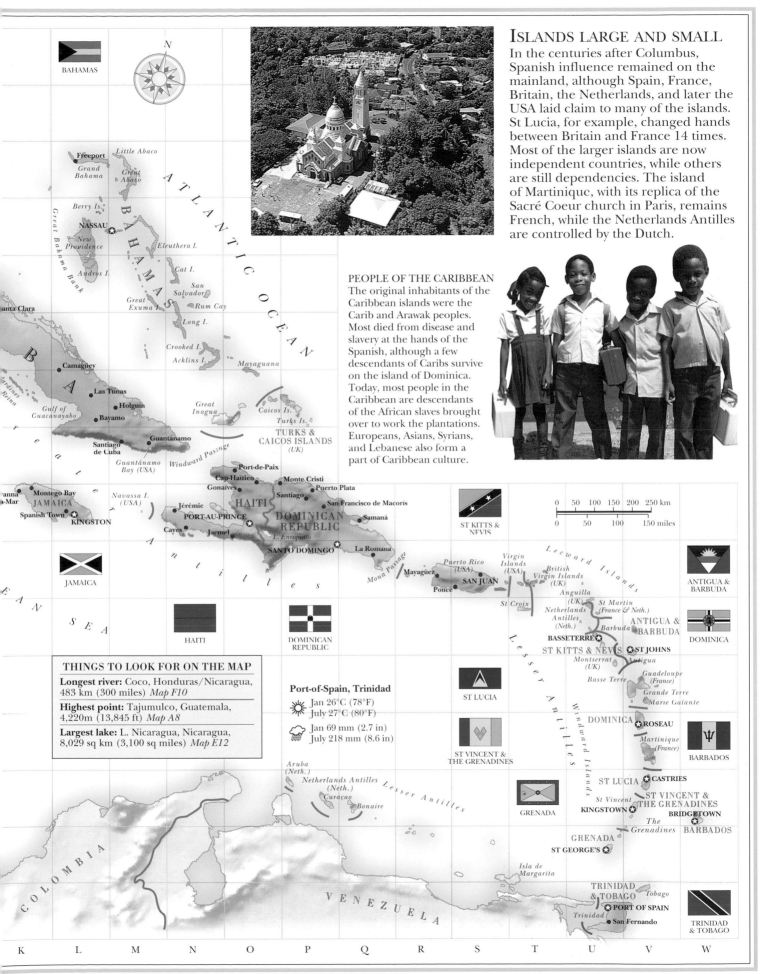

## ISLANDS LARGE AND SMALL

In the centuries after Columbus, Spanish influence remained on the mainland, although Spain, France, Britain, the Netherlands, and later the USA laid claim to many of the islands. St Lucia, for example, changed hands between Britain and France 14 times. Most of the larger islands are now independent countries, while others are still dependencies. The island of Martinique, with its replica of the Sacré Coeur church in Paris, remains French, while the Netherlands Antilles are controlled by the Dutch.

### PEOPLE OF THE CARIBBEAN

The original inhabitants of the Caribbean islands were the Carib and Arawak peoples. Most died from disease and slavery at the hands of the Spanish, although a few descendants of Caribs survive on the island of Dominica. Today, most people in the Caribbean are descendants of the African slaves brought over to work the plantations. Europeans, Asians, Syrians, and Lebanese also form a part of Caribbean culture.

### THINGS TO LOOK FOR ON THE MAP

**Longest river:** Coco, Honduras/Nicaragua, 483 km (300 miles) Map F10

**Highest point:** Tajumulco, Guatemala, 4,220m (13,845 ft) Map A8

**Largest lake:** L. Nicaragua, Nicaragua, 8,029 sq km (3,100 sq miles) Map E12

**Port-of-Spain, Trinidad**

☀ Jan 26°C (78°F)
July 27°C (80°F)

☂ Jan 69 mm (2.7 in)
July 218 mm (8.6 in)

45

# GUATEMALA

FROM THE RUINED CITIES of the ancient Maya civilization to the Catholic churches of the Spanish, Guatemala represents a blend of cultures. Today, more than half the people are direct descendants of the Maya Indians and live mainly in highland villages; the remainder of the population is part Indian and part Spanish. Many Maya work for rich landowners who grow the coffee, sugar, and bananas that are the country's main cash crops. Guatemala also exports fresh-cut flowers, mostly roses, which are grown in the valleys around Antigua.

*Villagers carry a statue of the Virgin Mary.*

**HOLY WEEK**
Most Guatemalans are Roman Catholic, the religion the Spanish brought with them in the 16th century. However, many people are now becoming Protestant. Guatemalans also practise their own form of worship based on traditional beliefs. This procession in Antigua forms part of their celebration of Holy Week.

| GUATEMALA | |
|---|---|
| **Capital city:** Guatemala City | |
| **Area:** 108,890 sq km (42,042 sq miles) | |
| **Population:** 12,300,000 | |
| **Official language:** Spanish | |
| **Major religions:** Christian 98%, other 2% | |
| **Government:** Multi-party democracy | |
| **Currency:** Quetzal | |
| **Adult literacy rate:** 70% | |
| **Life expectancy:** 65 years | |
| **People per doctor:** 1,111 | |
| **Televisions:** 126 per 1,000 people | |

| BELIZE | |
|---|---|
| **Capital city:** Belmopan | |
| **Area:** 22,966 sq km (8,867 sq miles) | |
| **Population:** 256,000 | |
| **Official language:** English | |
| **Major religion:** Christian 87%, other 13% | |
| **Government:** Multi-party democracy | |
| **Currency:** Belizean dollar | |
| **Adult literacy rate:** 77% | |
| **Life expectancy:** 74 years | |
| **People per doctor:** 2,000 | |
| **Televisions:** 183 per 1,000 people | |

## MARKET DAY
Markets such as this one in Chichicastenango, in the highlands near Lake Atitlán, are a feature of daily life. Many native Guatemalans farm small plots of land where they grow corn, beans, and squash, as well as fruit. They regularly walk long distances from outlying villages to sell crops, flowers, and handcrafted goods such as pottery and baskets.

*People worship Catholic saints and ancient gods at the Church of Santo Tomas.*

*Lilies and roses, as well as carnations and gladioli, are grown in the valleys. Many are sold to North America.*

*Goods are weighed in a simple, hand-held balance.*

*Village women wear brightly coloured ankle-length skirts. Patterns date back hundreds of years.*

*Maize and other cereals are the main foods.*

*Maya crafts, such as baskets and handwoven textiles, are popular with tourists.*

*A basket of fruit, called papayas (pawpaws).*

*Avocados have been cultivated in Central America for thousands of years.*

**WEAVING STYLES**
Weaving is a traditional craft. Cloth is made from coloured yarn, using patterns that have been handed down through the generations. There are more than 300 different styles, each with a special historical meaning.

*Weavers use a backstrap loom that can be moved from place to place.*

**CITIES OF THE MAYA**
Tourism is one of Guatemala's fastest growing industries. Each year almost one million tourists visit the country to see its ancient sites. Spectacular ruins mark the site of Tikal, one of the great Mayan cities. Tikal was mysteriously abandoned in about AD 900. Today its ruined temples lie in a huge area of tropical forest.

### REFUGEES

Life for the Maya is a constant struggle for survival, and many have suffered hardship and death in their attempts to avoid being forced into mainstream society. Persecution was particularly bad in the early 1980s when the then military government set out to destroy them. Some 60,000 Maya fled to safety in refugee camps in Mexico. Today, they are returning to Guatemala, but their safety is uncertain, and many of their lands have been seized.

### STREET CHILDREN

Guatemala City is home to growing numbers of so-called street children. Forced to leave home because of poverty and abuse, children live in small groups and survive through crime, begging, and selling whatever they can find. Recently, human rights groups such as Amnesty International have drawn attention to their plight.

# BELIZE

LYING ON THE CARIBBEAN COAST, Belize is both an old and a new country. Ancient ruins dot the landscape, reminders of its Maya history, but the country itself only achieved full independence in 1981. For many years, Belize was a British colony, the only one in Central America. English is the official language, but Belizeans are descended from several ethnic groups – Caribs, Africans, Mayas, Asians, and Europeans – and many people speak a Creole or African dialect. Caribbean foods and music are popular, and the country is famous for its wildlife.

### CORAL REEF

A chain of coral reefs, dotted with small sandy islands called cayes, runs 290 km (180 miles) along the coastline of Belize. It is the world's second largest barrier reef, after Australia's, and is home to turtles, sea anemones, and spiny lobsters, as well as a wonderful array of tropical fish. The clear, warm water attracts divers from around the world.

*Flooding and hurricanes can cause serious problems along the coast of Belize, so a new capital, Belmopan, has been built further inland than Belize City, the old capital.*

### DEEP IN THE FOREST

Dense tropical rainforest covers half of Belize's land area. Rosewood and other products from the forest such as chicle, used to make chewing gum, and kapok, a silky cotton from the giant Ceiba tree, are important to the economy. So, too, are the increasing number of citrus groves. But cultivation is limited. Much of the rainforest is protected and provides a rich habitat for plants and animals.

### BELMOPAN

In 1961, a massive hurricane and tidal wave devastated the coastal capital, Belize City. In 1970, a new capital, Belmopan, was built 80 km (50 miles) inland to protect it from tropical storms. Although people and businesses are gradually moving to the new capital, Belize City remains the country's most populated city.

### FOREST WILDLIFE

The forests are filled with an amazing variety of wildlife. Jaguars, tapirs, howler monkeys, and coatimundi are just a few of the world's endangered species still thriving in the forests of Belize. Butterflies and tropical birds fly through the trees. And there are 250 different types of orchids, including the black orchid, Belize's national flower.

*Toucans live in the treetops so they can fly around the open areas.*

*The howler monkey defends its part of the rainforest with a noisy howl.*

**Find out more**

CORAL REEFS: *255, 258*
HURRICANES: *44*
RAINFORESTS: *15, 69, 204*
RELIGION: *274–275*

# HONDURAS

HONDURAS
EL SALVADOR

### HONDURAS

**Capital city:** Tegucigalpa

**Area:** 112,090 sq km (43,278 sq miles)

**Population:** 6,900,000

**Official language:** Spanish

**Major religion:** Christian 100%

**Government:** Multi-party democracy

**Currency:** Lempira

**Adult literacy rate:** 80%

**Life expectancy:** 66 years

**People per doctor:** 1,250

**Televisions:** 90 per 1,000 people

### EL SALVADOR

**Capital city:** San Salvador

**Area:** 21,040 sq km (8,124 sq miles)

**Population:** 6,500,000

**Official language:** Spanish

**Major religion:** Christian 98%, other 2%

**Government:** Multi-party democracy

**Currency:** Salvadorean colón, US dollar

**Adult literacy rate:** 80%

**Life expectancy:** 70 years

**People per doctor:** 909

**Televisions:** 675 per 1,000 people

THE HOT, STEAMY CLIMATE of Honduras is ideal for growing fruit, and for many years the banana industry has dominated the life of the country. Today, Honduras has developed other exports such as coffee, sugar, and beef. About half of the Honduran population lives in the countryside, in small villages or isolated settlements. Many are poor farmers, growing maize, beans, or rice for their own use. Life is hard, and many people go hungry. Land is unevenly distributed – wealthy families and the fruit companies own 60 per cent of the land.

HONDURAN PEOPLE
Most Hondurans are *mestizos* – mixed descendants of native Indians and the Europeans who arrived in the 16th century. Some are descended from black Africans who were shipped to the Caribbean as slaves. Some are white (European) or Indian.

As the bananas grow, they begin to point upwards.

Bananas take between 9 and 13 weeks to ripen.

Workers cut down the bananas when they are still green.

Coloured tags identify which bunches are ready for picking.

The stalk has a flower on the end made of thick, purple petals.

Workers cover bananas with bags to protect them from insects and the spray from pesticides.

### BANANA PLANTATIONS

Banana exports are important to the economy of Honduras. Many are grown on huge plantations, particularly around La Lima in northeastern Honduras. Labourers work long hours and the pay is low. Cutters regularly have to carry loads of bananas weighing about 40 kg (88 lb). Once cut down, the bananas are washed, inspected, and weighed into boxes, ready to be shipped abroad.

# EL SALVADOR

THE SMALLEST COUNTRY in Central America, El Salvador has suffered a history of civil war and revolution. Historically, a handful of rich families have controlled the land and wealth while most Salvadoreans have lived in poverty. A line of volcanoes, many still active, dominates the landscape. Forests, once rich with cedar, mahogany, and oak, have been cut down for farmland.

THE FOOTBALL WAR
In 1969 long-standing border disputes erupted when El Salvador played Honduras to qualify for the World Cup. The incident led to the Salvadoran army invading Honduras. More than 3,000 people were killed during the Football War.

SAN SALVADOR
San Salvador was founded by Spanish colonists in 1525. Since then it has been damaged by earthquakes many times. Much of the original Spanish architecture has been replaced with modern buildings. Overcrowded slum areas have developed around the city as thousands of refugees have arrived in search of work.

PEACE ACCORD
Between 1979 and 1991, a bitter civil war raged between the US-backed government and left-wing guerilla forces. Some 75,000 Salvadoreans died. On 16 January 1992, the country celebrated a peace agreement signed by guerilla leader Chano Guevara (left).

*Find out more*
COFFEE: *50, 62, 66*
PEOPLES OF THE CONTINENT: *42*
SUGAR: *52*
VOLCANOES & EARTHQUAKES: *13*

# NICARAGUA

SOMETIMES CALLED "the land of lakes and volcanoes", Nicaragua is a beautiful country. It could also be one of the richest in Central America, except that its recent history has been as violent as its earthquakes, and the economy has been thrown into chaos by past political events. The economy is mainly based on agriculture with fishing along the coasts, but Nicaragua also has large deposits of minerals, including copper and gold, which are mined for export. The country has a young population with more than half the people under 15 years of age.

| NICARAGUA | |
|---|---|
| **Capital city:** Managua | |
| **Area:** 129,494 sq km (43,278 sq miles) | |
| **Population:** 5,500,000 | |
| **Official language:** Spanish | |
| **Major religions:** Christian 97%, other 3% | |
| **Government:** Multi-party democracy | |
| **Currency:** Gold córdoba | |
| **Adult literacy rate:** 77% | |
| **Life expectancy:** 69 years | |
| **People per doctor:** 1,429 | |
| **Televisions:** 190 per 1,111 people | |

## SANDINISTA REVOLUTION

For over 40 years, the Somoza family ruled Nicaragua as a dictatorship. But in 1979, rebels took control and formed the left-wing Sandinista government. They provided better health care, and set up a programme of taking land from the rich and giving it to peasants. However, they were opposed by the Contras, anti-Sandinista forces backed by the USA, and thousands lost their lives in fighting during the next decade. In 1990 the Sandinistas lost the elections, but have retained their popularity among the poor.

## FAMILY LIFE

Extended families are common in Nicaragua. Parents and children often live with their grandparents under one roof. Until 1979, more than half the population could not read or write. Under the Sandinistas, a literacy campaign was set up, and newly trained teachers, many of them women, were sent into rural areas to teach reading and writing. Within just a few months, literacy levels rose to 87 per cent. However, when the Sandinistas lost power, the campaign faded and reading levels dropped again.

*Overcrowding is a problem and large families are often crammed into very small living spaces.*

## LIVING DANGEROUSLY

Most of Nicaragua's population lives on the Pacific coast, where many of the major cities are located. There are active volcanoes here, but earthquakes are the most serious danger. In 1972, the country's capital, Managua, was nearly destroyed by an earthquake that killed more than 6,000 people and left 300,000 homeless. In 1998, powerful Hurricane Mitch devastated Nicaragua's east coast, killing at least 3,800 people and causing damage estimated at $US1 billion.

*The maize ear, or cob, needs plenty of sunshine to grow and ripen.*

*Maize kernels are ground into flour and used to make tortillas, a type of pancake.*

### FARMING THE LAND
The fertile volcanic soil near the Pacific coast forms the main farming region of Nicaragua. Maize (shown growing here), beans, and sorghum are the main food crops, and are harvested twice a year. Coffee, cotton, and bananas are also important export crops.

### LAKE NICARAGUA
The west of the country is dominated by Lake Nicaragua, the largest lake in Central America. It is also the only freshwater lake in the world to contain sea fish, including sharks and swordfish. Scientists now think that sharks find their way to the lake by swimming up the San Juan River from the Caribbean Sea.

*Lake Nicaragua is named after Nicarao, an ancient Indian chief whose people lived by the lake.*

### Find out more
LITERACY: *277*
POLITICAL SYSTEMS: *270–271*
POPULATION GROWTH: *43*
VOLCANOES & EARTHQUAKES: *13*

# COSTA RICA

BORDERED BY SEA on both sides, Costa Rica differs from its Central American neighbours in many ways. It is a peaceful country with a democratically elected government and, since 1948, no army. The country is also relatively wealthy. Schools are free and Costa Rica spends much of its budget on education. There is not much poverty and life expectancy is the highest in Central America. Exports include coffee, bananas, and sugar which grow on the country's fertile volcanic soils. The main port is Limón on the Caribbean coast.

| COSTA RICA |
| --- |
| **Capital city:** San José |
| **Area:** 51,060 sq km (19,714 sq miles) |
| **Population:** 4,200,000 |
| **Official language:** Spanish |
| **Major religions:** Christian 95%, other 5% |
| **Government:** Multi-party democracy |
| **Currency:** Costa Rican colón |
| **Adult literacy rate:** 96% |
| **Life expectancy:** 78 years |
| **People per doctor:** 1,111 |
| **Televisions:** 387 per 1,000 people |

**THE WAY TO SAN JOSÉ**
San José lies in the mountainous centre of the country directly on the Pan-American Highway. It is the processing centre for the crops which grow in the nearby valleys. The area developed as a tobacco growing centre under Spanish rule and became the capital in 1823.

*Pickers work by hand, harvesting about 25 kg (55 lb) of beans per day.*

## COFFEE BEANS

Costa Rica was the first country in Central America to grow coffee, and for more than 100 years this has been its leading export. From time to time this success is affected by falling international prices. Coffee is made from the fruit of the coffee tree, which grows best on well-drained soil. Trees need a warm, but not hot, climate, and are often grown in areas partly shaded with larger trees. They can produce good crops for 15 years.

*The sweet-smelling flowers last about 3 to 4 days.*

*The coffee fruit is called a cherry.*

*Coffee trees grow to about 3 m (9.8 ft) tall.*

*Berries turn from dark green to yellow to ripe red.*

*Coffee is made from the two beans inside the cherry.*

**TRAIN TO THE COAST**
The Atlantic Railway, completed in 1890, was built to take coffee from the plantations to the coast for export. The project was fraught with problems. Thousands of workers lost their lives due to terrible working conditions, and the cost plunged the government into debt.

## SAVING THE FORESTS

Costa Rica was once covered with forests that included mahogany and tropical cedar trees. But now its tree cover has been greatly reduced because forests have been cut down for timber and to make room for coffee plantations. However, the government is aware that loss of forest also means loss of valuable plant and animal life, and it is now working to conserve its forests. Today, much of the forest is protected in reserves and national parks.

*This tiny violet-ear hummingbird is just 12 cm (4.75 in) long. It hovers in the air and takes nectar from flowers through its long beak.*

*The hummingbird's wings can beat 55 times per second.*

*Nectar is a sweet liquid.*

| ***Find out more*** |
| --- |
| COFFEE: *62, 66* |
| DEMOCRACY: *270* |
| LOGGING: *69, 244* |
| TRADE (COMMODITIES): *281* |

# PANAMA

THE COUNTRY OF PANAMA forms a land link between the North and South American continents. The Panama Canal, which cuts through the country and joins the Atlantic and Pacific Oceans, is a vital link in international sea trade. Panama has a hot steamy climate with heavy rainfall, especially on its Caribbean coast. The interior is mountainous and the best farmland is in the lowlands of the Pacific coast where the main cash crops, bananas, coffee, and sugar, are grown. Shrimp, caught in the coastal waters, are also an important export.

## PANAMA

**Capital city:** Panama City

**Area:** 78,200 sq km (30,193 sq miles)

**Population:** 3,100,000

**Official language:** Spanish

**Major religions:** Christian 92%, Jewish and other 8%

**Government:** Multi-party democracy

**Currency:** Balboa

**Adult literacy rate:** 92%

**Life expectancy:** 75 years

**People per doctor:** 588

**Televisions:** 187 per 1,000 people

### FROM OCEAN TO OCEAN
There is a 26 m (85 ft) difference in height between Gatun Lake and the two oceans. From the Atlantic, ships are raised up through the Gatun locks (1, 2, and 3). Then they are lowered via the Pedro Miguel locks (4) and, finally, through the Miraflores locks (5 and 6) into the Pacific.

## PANAMA CANAL
Every year some 14,000 ships negotiate the locks of the Panama Canal. First opened in 1914, the canal is 82 km (51 miles) long, with a minimum depth of 12 m (39 ft). Forty thousand workers, mostly from the Caribbean, worked on the canal which took 10 years to build and cost US$380 million. It also cost thousands of lives. After sharing the canal with the USA for many years, Panama took complete control of the canal in December 1999.

*Nine months of tropical rain each year keeps Gatun Lake full. Water from the lake feeds the locks.*

**Cross-section of canal**

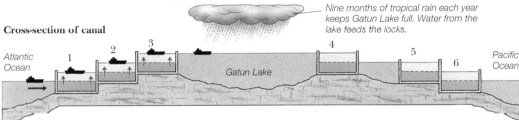

Atlantic Ocean    1    2    3    Gatun Lake    4    5    6    Pacific Ocean

### CANAL AT THE CROSSROADS
The canal puts Panama at the crossroads of international trade. Revenue from the canal, and from the Free Trade Zone at its mouth in Colón, is vital to the economy. Since 1970, Panama has been one of the world's main financial centres, and its tax-free banking attracts investors from around the world.

*Banks and business centres line the canal approach to Panama City.*

**Detail of lock chamber**

*A ship waits in a lock chamber while water is piped in to lift the ship to the next level.*

*Water is fed through huge pipes, called culverts, down the sides of the lock.*

*Trains, called mules, help pull the ship through the lock.*

*Ships travel in the opposite direction along this channel.*

*A series of smaller pipes feeds water into the lock from the culverts.*

## CUNA INDIANS
The original inhabitants of Panama were mostly Cuna, Guaymi, and Choco Indians, but their numbers were severely reduced after the arrival of European explorers in the 16th century. The Cuna once held considerable power in the area and traded, mainly by canoe, along the Caribbean coast. Important chiefs were carried by hammock. Today, the Cuna live in small villages and depend on agriculture for a living.

*Hammocks are made of woven fibre from plants that grow on the coast.*

*Embroidered clothing designs, known as molas, are a feature of the Cuna culture.*

### THE GOOD SOIL
Panama has many rivers. The soil that develops from clays, sand, and silt deposited from these rivers is called alluvial soil, and is good for growing crops such as the vegetables shown here. On poorer soils the land is used for a few years and then left until its natural fertility returns. This system of land use is called *roza*.

***Find out more***
BANANAS: *48*
COFFEE: *50, 62, 66*
PEOPLES OF THE CONTINENT: *42*

# CUBA

MORE THAN 200 RIVERS WIND their way across Cuba, watering the lush green scenery of the Caribbean's largest island. The land is made up of mountains, rolling hills, and flat plains, all covered in a fertile soil that is ideal for growing sugar, tobacco, and a variety of tropical fruits and vegetables. Most Cubans are descended from the early Spanish settlers, or from Africans brought over later to work as slaves on the plantations. Over recent decades, the socialist policies of the long-standing leader, Fidel Castro, have kept Cuba isolated from much of the world.

| CUBA | |
|---|---|
| **Capital city:** Havana | |
| **Area:** 110,860 sq km (42,803 sq miles) | |
| **Population:** 11,300,000 | |
| **Official language:** Spanish | |
| **Major religions:** Christian 41%, other 59% | |
| **Government:** One-party state | |
| **Currency:** Cuban peso | |
| **Adult literacy rate:** 97% | |
| **Life expectancy:** 77 years | |
| **People per doctor:** 189 | |
| **Televisions:** 239 per 1,000 people | |

## MUSIC AND DANCE
Cuba's lively music reflects its mix of Spanish and African influences. The Spanish brought their distinctive melodies, along with the guitar and violin, and the Africans brought a very different style, as well as various drums and short wooden sticks called claves. The music has gradually fused to create rhythms such as the mambo and salsa. A thriving Afro-Cuban jazz scene has also developed.

## CUBAN POLITICS
In 1959, Fidel Castro and a group of rebels overthrew the ruling dictator, Fulgencio Batista. Since then, Cuba has been a communist state, aided by the Soviet Union until its breakup in 1991. Many of Castro's social policies have been successful. Housing and health care have greatly improved, and most people can now read and write. However, the USA remains hostile to the communist government.

*Cigars are stored in boxes made from cedar wood to keep them fresh.*

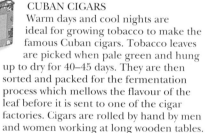

### CUBAN CIGARS
Warm days and cool nights are ideal for growing tobacco to make the famous Cuban cigars. Tobacco leaves are picked when pale green and hung up to dry for 40–45 days. They are then sorted and packed for the fermentation process which mellows the flavour of the leaf before it is sent to one of the cigar factories. Cigars are rolled by hand by men and women working at long wooden tables.

*A good cigar is made from at least five different types of tobacco.*

*Dark brown sugar has not been refined to remove all the syrup.*

*Light brown sugar has been part refined.*

*Sugarcane is a giant grass that needs plenty of rain as well as sunshine.*

*Rum is made from the distilled juice of sugarcane.*

*Sugar is stored inside the stalk, in a firm pulp.*

*A dark syrup, known as molasses, is a by-product of cane juice.*

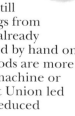

## HAVANA
The largest city in the Caribbean, Cuba's capital, Havana, has a population of more than 2 million. It was founded by the Spanish in 1515 and some areas of the city are extremely old, with cobbled streets and elegant colonial buildings. Today, parts of Havana have become rather run down and in need of improvement. However, housing policies mean there are no shanty towns around the city. Havana is a major port and exports most of Cuba's sugar, tobacco, and tropical fruit.

## SUGAR INDUSTRY
Sugar has long been important to Cuba and still makes up 75 per cent of the country's earnings from exports. By the 1800s, the sugar industry was already booming, fuelled by African slaves who worked by hand on the vast colonial plantations. Today the methods are more modern and the cane is usually cut down by machine or bulldozer. However, the collapse of the Soviet Union led to a steep decline in demand for sugar, and reduced supplies of imported oil. To overcome this crisis, many of the mills started to use *bagasse*, a by-product of sugarcane, to run their machinery.

| **Find out more** |
|---|
| BREAK-UP OF THE USSR: *136* |
| CITIES: *17, 14* |
| PEOPLES OF THE CONTINENT: *42* |
| POLITICAL SYSTEMS: *270–271* |

# JAMAICA

THE BEAUTIFUL ISLAND OF JAMAICA is a place of strong contrasts. On one hand, there is the relaxed attitude of people enjoying the national passions – cricket and reggae music. On the other hand, there is tension between the few powerful families and the poor in the violent slums of Kingston. This side of life is rarely seen by the tourists who flock here each year, attracted by the tropical climate. As well as tourism, a mineral ore called bauxite is a valuable source of income. Sadly the landscape is being damaged by the bauxite mines, which leave red mud lakes with an acid content that kills the vegetation.

| JAMAICA | |
|---|---|
| **Capital city:** Kingston | |
| **Area:** 10,990 sq km (4,243 sq miles) | |
| **Population:** 2,700,000 | |
| **Official language:** English | |
| **Major religions:** Christian 55%, other 45% | |
| **Government:** Multi-party democracy | |
| **Currency:** Jamaican dollar | |
| **Adult literacy rate:** 88% | |
| **Life expectancy:** 75 years | |
| **People per doctor:** 714 | |
| **Televisions:** 182 per 1,000 people | |

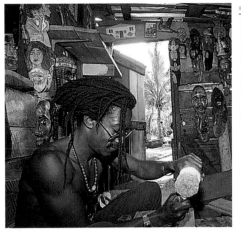

## RASTAFARIANISM

The Rastafarian religion began among the poor of Kingston, Jamaica, in the 1930s. Members believe that Haile Selassie, the former emperor of Ethiopia (Ras Tafari), was a god. They also believe that God (Jah) will lead black people back to Ethiopia, the promised land. Rastafarians do not usually eat pork, they are against violence, and wear their hair in long dreadlocks. Their clothes are often green, yellow, and red because these are the colours of the Ethiopian flag.

### REGGAE MUSIC

The driving rhythms of reggae music can be heard everywhere across the island. Its songs often tell of hardship and political struggle, and are linked to Rastafarianism. Reggae developed in Jamaica from ska, which was a blend of African, European, and South American styles. Jamaican singer Bob Marley (1945–81) made reggae music popular around the world.

## KINGSTON

Jamaica's capital city and chief port, Kingston, is one of the largest urban centres in the Caribbean. Founded by the British, the city first grew as a major port for shipping cane sugar to Europe. However, an earthquake in 1907 damaged the city. It has now been rebuilt with modern hotels, banks, and financial offices. Crowded shanty towns also exist on the western side of the city. Violence frequently breaks out here, connected either to political unrest or to the long-established trade in illegal drugs.

## ISLAND INDUSTRIES

A variety of industries brings money to Jamaica, from oil refining to producing clothes, such as the jeans being made here. Various minerals are mined, with bauxite being the most important. One rapidly growing industry is data processing, which involves typing data into computers and sending it to companies in the USA. Unlike many other Caribbean countries, however, Jamaica's data processing companies are mostly owned by Jamaicans, and not by large foreign organizations.

### FARMING THE LAND

Not everyone in Jamaica works in industry or tourism – agriculture is also important. Plantations growing sugar, bananas, coffee, and cocoa employ large numbers of people. Many Jamaicans also fish for a living or farm their own small plots of land, producing food for themselves, as shown here, with a little left over to sell at local markets.

Okra is used in soups and stews or eaten as a vegetable.

Dasheen is grown for its edible root and leaves.

The breadfruit tree produces fruit with a pulp that is eaten as a vegetable.

**Find out more**
ETHIOPIA: *218*
GROWTH OF CITIES: *17*
RELIGION: *274–275*
SUGAR: *52*

# THE BAHAMAS

THIS LONG LINE OF ABOUT 700 coral islands snakes its way across the warm Caribbean Sea. It was on the island of San Salvador that Christopher Columbus first set foot when he arrived in the "New World" of the Americas in 1492. The Spanish, who called the islands *Bajamar*, meaning "shallow seas", were followed by British settlers and the islands remained a British colony until 1973. Today, the islands are a paradise for holiday-makers of every nationality. They are also a major financial centre, because tax laws make it profitable for banks and foreign businesses to have offices here.

THE BAHAMAS

| | |
|---|---|
| **Capital city:** Nassau | |
| **Area:** 13,940 sq km (5,382 sq miles) | |
| **Population:** 314,000 | |
| **Official language:** English | |
| **Major religions:** Christian 83%, other 17% | |
| **Government:** Multi-party democracy | |
| **Currency:** Bahamian dollar | |
| **Adult literacy rate:** 96% | |
| **Life expectancy:** 70 years | |
| **People per doctor:** 667 | |
| **Televisions:** 230 per 1,000 people | |

PUERTO RICO*

| | |
|---|---|
| **Capital city:** San Juan | |
| **Area:** 8,875 sq km (3,427 sq miles) | |
| **Population:** 3,890,000 | |
| **Official language:** Spanish | |
| **Major religions:** Christian 85%, other 15% | |
| **Government:** Multi-party democracy | |
| **Currency:** US dollar | |

\* Puerto Rico is not an independent country. It is a self-governing commonwealth state of the USA.

**JUNKANOO FESTIVAL**
At the end of each year, the streets come alive with the dancing and music of the Junkanoo parades. This festival forms a link with the country's past. It is said that when an African chief, given the name John Canoe (Junkanoo), came here as a slave he was granted the right to celebrate in true African style.

**Main overseas tourists**

| USA | Canada | Europe | Others |
|---|---|---|---|
| 87% | 5% | 5% | 3% |

## TOURIST DESTINATION

More than five million tourists a year come to relax on the white sandy beaches and in the warm waters of the Bahamas. Tourism is vital to the economy and almost half the local people work in jobs linked to the tourist trade, such as in hotels, restaurants, and shops. The city of Freeport on Grand Bahama is the largest resort, with a deep-water harbour for cruise ships. However, passengers often eat and sleep on the ships, which does not help the local economy.

# PUERTO RICO

ALTHOUGH SPANISH IS THE MAIN language of Puerto Rico, it is strongly American in flavour. Colonized by Spain in the years after Columbus, the Spanish stayed in control until 1898, when the USA took over. The cultivation of tobacco, sugar, and tropical fruits remains important despite the increasing number of factories set up here by US companies. Most people have a good standard of living with excellent education and health care schemes.

PEOPLE OF PUERTO RICO
Puerto Ricans are mainly of Spanish and African descent. Most live in the cities, with one-third in the capital of San Juan. Overcrowding forces others into housing projects outside the main cities. Some people choose to move to the USA.

## OPERATION BOOTSTRAP

This plan, which began in 1948 with backing from the USA, was set up to tackle the island's economic problems. Attracted by low taxes and cheap labour, many US companies moved here and, over the years, the plan helped raise living standards on the island. The main industries include petrochemicals, textiles, and medicines.

*Find out more*

CORAL ISLANDS: *202*
EDUCATION: *277*
HEALTH: *276*
PEOPLES OF THE CONTINENT: *42*

# HAITI

THE POOREST COUNTRY IN the western world, Haiti shares the island of Hispaniola with the Dominican Republic. A revolution by African slaves in 1791, led by Toussaint Ouverture, broke French rule and Haiti became the first black republic. Recent politics have been turbulent. The long dictatorship of the Duvalier family ("Papa" and "Baby Doc"), gave way to a series of military coups. Political unrest continues and the country suffers from great poverty. Many Haitians practise the religious cult of voodoo which blends traditional African beliefs with Roman Catholicism. Followers believe in powerful spirits, and dancing to the beat of sacred drums is part of the voodoo ritual.

## ART AND CULTURE
Many Haitians try to make extra money by selling crafts, such as straw hats and woodcarvings, to visitors as well as acting as unofficial tourist guides. Since the 1930s, artists have been noted for producing simple, bold paintings, in a style derived from the decorations in voodoo temples.

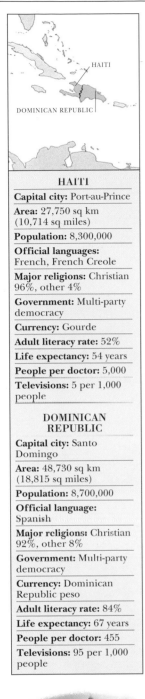

### HAITI
**Capital city:** Port-au-Prince

**Area:** 27,750 sq km (10,714 sq miles)

**Population:** 8,300,000

**Official languages:** French, French Creole

**Major religions:** Christian 96%, other 4%

**Government:** Multi-party democracy

**Currency:** Gourde

**Adult literacy rate:** 52%

**Life expectancy:** 54 years

**People per doctor:** 5,000

**Televisions:** 5 per 1,000 people

### DOMINICAN REPUBLIC
**Capital city:** Santo Domingo

**Area:** 48,730 sq km (18,815 sq miles)

**Population:** 8,700,000

**Official language:** Spanish

**Major religions:** Christian 92%, other 8%

**Government:** Multi-party democracy

**Currency:** Dominican Republic peso

**Adult literacy rate:** 84%

**Life expectancy:** 67 years

**People per doctor:** 455

**Televisions:** 95 per 1,000 people

## SOIL EROSION
Farming is the main occupation here and most Haitians live on small plots of land, growing food and keeping goats. They make very little money and pressure for more land to farm means that trees are constantly being cut down. Some wood is turned into charcoal, shown here, and used as fuel in rural areas. Goats overgraze on the remaining woodland. The exposed soil has now become so severely eroded that crop yields are poor. It has been estimated that one-third of the land in Haiti is no longer usable.

**Island of Hispaniola**

HAITI

DOMINICAN REPUBLIC

# DOMINICAN REPUBLIC

THE LANDSCAPE OF MOUNTAINS and forests in the Dominican Republic may be similar to that of its island neighbour, but other aspects of life are very different. Spain was the main colonial power here and US influences are also strong. The people and the culture are a mix of Spanish, African, and native peoples. The island is rich in natural resources, with deposits of silver, platinum, uranium, and nickel, and one of the largest gold mines in the world. However, tourism is by far the most important source of foreign earnings.

## SANTO DOMINGO
The capital city of Santo Domingo was founded by Columbus' brother Bartolomé in 1496. The city became the main base from which Spain launched its conquest of the region. The city has many recently restored colonial buildings which date back to the 16th century.

| | HAITI | DOMINICAN REP. |
|---|---|---|
| 🚗 | 12 cars per 1,000 people | 66 cars per 1,000 people |
| ☎ | 16 telephones per 1,000 people | 110 telephones per 1,000 people |
| 📖 | 6,288 university students | 176,995 university students |

## THE ECONOMY
People in the Dominican Republic have a better standard of living than those who live in Haiti, where most cannot even afford health care. The economy is stronger in the Republic because it is boosted by earnings from tourism and mining and by a government that encourages new industries, such as textiles. In recent years holiday resorts have sprung up across the country, creating jobs. Many Haitians come here in search of work.

***Find out more***

DICTATORSHIP: *271*
PEOPLES OF THE CONTINENT: *42*
RELIGION: *274–275*
SOIL EROSION: *55, 244*

# LESSER ANTILLES

THE ISLANDS OF the Lesser Antilles stretch in a gentle curve from the Greater Antilles island of Puerto Rico in the north down to the coast of South America. Once European colonies, most of the islands are now independent. However, the background of African, European, and Asian influences has resulted in a vibrant and distinctive culture, highlighted in the music and festivals. Bananas, which thrive in the heat and high rainfall, remain a major export, although some producers are at risk from hurricanes which can devastate the land.

### ST KITTS AND NEVIS
**Capital city:** Basseterre

**Area:** 261 sq km (101 sq miles)

**Population:** 38,763

### ANTIGUA AND BARBUDA
**Capital city:** St Johns

**Area:** 442 sq km (170 sq miles)

**Population:** 67,897

### DOMINICA
**Capital city:** Roseau

**Area:** 754 sq km (291 sq miles)

**Population:** 69,655

### ST LUCIA
**Capital city:** Castries

**Area:** 620 sq km (239 sq miles)

**Population:** 162,157

### ST VINCENT AND THE GRENADINES
**Capital city:** Kingstown

**Area:** 389 sq km (150 sq miles)

**Population:** 116,812

### BARBADOS
**Capital city:** Bridgetown

**Area:** 430 sq km (166 sq miles)

**Population:** 270,000

### GRENADA
**Capital city:** St George's

**Area:** 340 sq km (131 sq miles)

**Population:** 89,258

### TRINIDAD AND TOBAGO
**Capital city:** Port-of-Spain

**Area:** 5,130 sq km (1,981 sq miles)

**Population:** 1,300,000

## CRICKET
Cricket is the national game of the English-speaking islands. Children learn to play on sun-dried pitches which allow the ball to be bowled at high speeds. As adults they can play for the West Indies team, drawn from the best players on each island. The team has included many great bowlers and batsmen.

*Brian Lara from Trinidad has played for the West Indies cricket team since 1990.*

## TRANSPORT
In the past, people and goods were transported by boat between the islands. Today ships are still the most economic way to move cargo, and ports, such as Castries in St Lucia, handle the islands' exports. Most islands have no railways and main roads are often confined to the coasts, making the interior difficult to reach. Antigua, Barbados, Martinique, and other islands now have large airports capable of taking jumbo jets.

## TOURISM
The main industry in the Caribbean is tourism which provides work for local people in restaurants, hotels, shops, and beach stalls. However the work is mainly seasonal, as most visitors only come when it is cold at home. Also many hotels are owned by foreign companies and money does not always remain on the islands. Some local governments are trying to reduce their dependence on tourism.

## SCARLET IBIS
The Caribbean is a haven for colourful birdlife, notably the scarlet ibis of Trinidad and Tobago. The ibis lives in the islands' mangrove swamps, flying off during the day to feed on crabs and other small sea creatures that live in the coastal mudflats.

*Curved beak for digging in mud*

## FOOD FROM THE LAND
Because of the shortage of land, most island farms are small. Farmers grow food for themselves, and sell a wide range of crops in local markets, including yams, sweet potatoes, okra, and salad crops, as well as fruit such as mangoes, limes, coconuts, and bananas. They also grow cash crops for export. The main crop varies from island to island, with nutmeg grown in Grenada, coffee in Trinidad, arrowroot in St Vincent, and sugar and bananas almost everywhere.

# INDUSTRY

The most industrialized country in the area is Trinidad and Tobago, which has petrochemical, iron, and steel industries based on its reserves of oil and natural gas. Apart from Barbados, the other islands have few mineral resources and rely on bananas, sugar, cotton, and cocoa for export. In recent years, all the islands have tried to produce a wider range of exports. St Vincent now has a flour mill, and Martinique an oil refinery. Light industrial estates have been set up on a number of islands.

**PITCH LAKE**
La Brea, in the south of Trinidad, boasts one of the world's most unusual sights. Near to the town is a lake filled not with water but with natural pitch, a black, sticky tar that is mainly used for surfacing roads. The lake, which is 60 m (200 ft) deep, is the world's largest single supply of natural pitch. It is thought to be linked to the underground rocks that supply nearby South America with oil.

| LESSER ANTILLES INDUSTRIES | |
|---|---|
| **ANTIGUA AND BARBUDA** <br> Tourism, cotton, rum | |
| **ST KITTS AND NEVIS** <br> Sugar, cotton production, tourism | |
| **DOMINICA** <br> Bananas, citrus fruits, essential oils | |
| **ST LUCIA** <br> Bananas, tourism, electrical parts | |
| **ST VINCENT AND THE GRENADINES** <br> Tourism, bananas, food processing, cement works | |
| **BARBADOS** <br> Sugar, tourism, petroleum products | |
| **GRENADA** <br> Tourism, bananas, nutmeg | |
| **TRINIDAD AND TOBAGO** <br> Oil refining, chemicals, sugar | |

## ISLAND MUSIC

Almost every Caribbean island resounds to the beat of calypso music, which has its origins in the slave songs brought from west Africa. Calypso has a strong beat and lyrics that tell about social and political problems. In recent years soca, a mixture of soul and calypso, has started to become popular with younger people.

*Steel band music originated in Trinidad, using pans or drums made from large oil drums.*

*This steel band is playing music for tourists in Tobago.*

*The Jinnah Memorial Mosque in Trinidad serves the Muslim community. People are called to prayer from the minarets.*

*Minaret*

## ISLAND SPICES

The island of Grenada is the world's second largest producer of nutmeg, after Indonesia, and grows almost one-quarter of the world's total crop. Nutmeg, a spice used to flavour food, originated in the East Indies, and was introduced to Grenada by the Dutch in the 19th century. The trees flourished in the fertile volcanic soil, warm temperatures, and high annual rainfall. Ginger, cinnamon, pepper, and cloves are also grown on the island.

*The single brown nutmeg seed is protected within a green fruit.*

*Ginger comes from the thick underground stem of this flowering plant.*

*The oil from nutmeg can be added to perfume and soap.*

*Ground nutmeg used in cooking*

*Ginger root can be used fresh or dried.*

## PEOPLE OF THE CARIBBEAN

Most people who live on the islands are a mixture of descendants of African slaves, Europeans, and local Carib Indians. The exception are the people of Trinidad, where almost 40 per cent are originally from the Indian subcontinent. Shipped over to work in the plantations, the immigrants brought their religions with them, setting up Hindu temples and Muslim mosques and continuing to observe their own religious customs.

**Find out more**
BANANAS: *48*
HURRICANES: *44*
SPICES: *198, 264*
SUGAR: *52*

# NORTHERN SOUTH AMERICA

ARCHING AROUND THE RAINFORESTS of the great Amazon River, the countries in northern South America are dominated by the Andes Mountains. Running north to south from Venezuela to Ecuador, and then through Chile, the mountains were once home to the Inca Empire. In search of gold, the Spanish arrived in the 16th century and carved out a huge empire. British, French, and Dutch colonies were also established in the northeast. All but French Guiana are now independent, although not without problems. Extremes of wealth and poverty, overcrowded cities, and the illegal drugs trade are features of most of the countries in this region.

### ANIMALS OF THE ANDES

The llama is used to carry goods.

For centuries, the people of the Andes have relied on a group of versatile mammals for food and clothing. The wild guanaco and vicuña, as well as the domesticated llama and alpaca, are all treasured for their wool and meat. Vicuña wool is as fine as silk, while coarse llama wool is used to make blankets, ropes, and other goods.

### QUECHUA INDIANS

The Quechua have lived high in the Andes in Bolivia, Peru, and Ecuador for hundreds of years. The Quechua were once farmers who had a system where their work and their land was shared equally between men and women. Today many Quechua have moved to the cities in search of work. Those who remain farm tiny plots of land.

The Andes is the longest unbroken mountain chain over 3,000 m (9,850 ft) in the world.

Lake Titicaca straddles the border between Peru and Bolivia.

The Altiplano, or high plain, is used for growing potatoes and grazing animals.

La Paz

## CULTIVATING THE ANDES

Fertile land is in such short supply in the Andes that every available scrap of soil must be used. Farmers often cut terraces into the hillsides to get maximum use from their land. Crops are grown to suit the temperature, which is hot and humid on the lower slopes near the coast but gets cooler as the mountains rise upwards. On the high plains beyond the Andes only the potato will ripen successfully. To the right is a section of the Andes from Peru to Bolivia.

3,000 m (9,850 ft)

Potatoes, wheat, and barley grow in the cool highland areas of the Andes.

2,000 m (6,550 ft)

Potato plant

Sugarcane

Sugarcane, coffee, tobacco, and corn flourish in the temperate zone.

1,000 m (3,280 ft)

Bananas, cocoa, cotton, and rice all grow well in the warm climate of the lowlands.

Sea level

Bananas

### World drug routes

USA

To Mexico

To Eastern USA

To Europe

To North Africa

To Western USA and Canada

SOUTH AMERICA

Main growing areas

Main traffic routes

## THE DRUG TRADE

For many centuries, people in this region have chewed the leaves of the coca plant to reduce hunger. Today the leaves are processed to make cocaine, an illegal drug much in demand in North America and Europe. Coca bushes thrive on poor soil and need little attention, unlike food crops which need tending. Growing coca is also more profitable than growing food. As a result, large quantities of coca are grown in isolated areas of the Andes. Once refined into cocaine, the drug is smuggled out of the region.

### ANGEL FALLS

Angel Falls is the highest waterfall in the world. It was discovered in 1935 by Jimmy Angel, an American pilot who was flying across Venezuela in search of a river he had once prospected for gold. Instead he flew over a vast waterfall, that plunges 980 m (3,215 ft) into the River Churún.

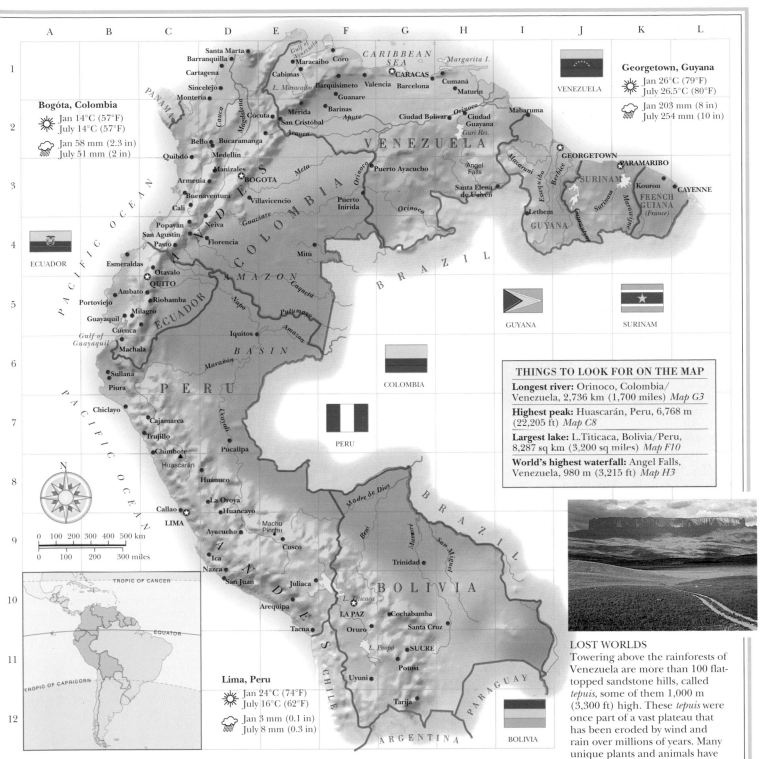

**Bogóta, Colombia**
☀ Jan 14°C (57°F)
July 14°C (57°F)
🌧 Jan 58 mm (2.3 in)
July 51 mm (2 in)

**Georgetown, Guyana**
☀ Jan 26°C (79°F)
July 26.5°C (80°F)
🌧 Jan 203 mm (8 in)
July 254 mm (10 in)

VENEZUELA

ECUADOR

GUYANA

SURINAM

COLOMBIA

PERU

**Lima, Peru**
☀ Jan 24°C (74°F)
July 16°C (62°F)
🌧 Jan 3 mm (0.1 in)
July 8 mm (0.3 in)

BOLIVIA

### THINGS TO LOOK FOR ON THE MAP

**Longest river:** Orinoco, Colombia/
Venezuela, 2,736 km (1,700 miles) *Map G3*

**Highest peak:** Huascarán, Peru, 6,768 m
(22,205 ft) *Map C8*

**Largest lake:** L.Titicaca, Bolivia/Peru,
8,287 sq km (3,200 sq miles) *Map F10*

**World's highest waterfall:** Angel Falls,
Venezuela, 980 m (3,215 ft) *Map H3*

### LOST WORLDS

Towering above the rainforests of
Venezuela are more than 100 flat-
topped sandstone hills, called
*tepuis*, some of them 1,000 m
(3,300 ft) high. These *tepuis* were
once part of a vast plateau that
has been eroded by wind and
rain over millions of years. Many
unique plants and animals have
evolved in these "lost worlds".

### THE CARIBBEAN COASTLINE

In most of South America,
the population is made up
of a mixture of European
immigrants and the native
Indian peoples. But the
Caribbean coast and islands
are home to a largely black
population, like these
Colombians. They are the
descendants of slaves brought
over from Africa to work on the
sugar plantations. Many have
remained among the poorest
members of society.

### BORDER DISPUTES

There is not a country in South
America that has not fought
with its neighbours about
its borders, and many
frontiers are still disputed
today. Wars between
Bolivia and Paraguay in
the 1930s, and Ecuador
and Peru in the 1940s,
resulted in thousands of
deaths. The checkpoint
shown here marks the border
between Bolivia and Chile.

# VENEZUELA

WHEN THE ITALIAN EXPLORER Amerigo Vespucci first visited the southern shores of the Caribbean Sea in 1499, he named the land Venezuela, or "Little Venice". The lake dwellings of the native Indians reminded him of the houses and canals of the Italian city of Venice. Part of the Spanish Empire for three centuries, Venezuela became independent in 1811. Today it is a country of huge contrasts: the oil industry produces immense wealth, yet many people live in shanty towns. Most people live in cities, yet the tribes of the interior are barely touched by modern life.

### VENEZUELA

| | |
|---|---|
| **Capital city:** Caracas | |
| **Area:** 912,050 sq km (352,143 sq miles) | |
| **Population:** 25,700,000 | |
| **Official language:** Spanish | |
| **Major religions:** Christian 99%, other 1% | |
| **Government:** Multi-party democracy | |
| **Currency:** Bolívar | |
| **Adult literacy rate:** 93% | |
| **Life expectancy:** 74 years | |
| **People per doctor:** 417 | |
| **Televisions:** 185 per 1,000 people | |

**HIGH-RISE CARACAS**
For most of its 400-year history, Caracas was a sleepy town 900 m (2,950 ft) up in the hills near the Caribbean coastline. With the discovery of oil, the population rapidly rose from a few thousand to more than 4 million. Today Caracas is a modern city, with steel and glass architecture, an extensive motorway, and a subway system.

**SLASH AND BURN AGRICULTURE**
In parts of the Amazon rainforest in Venezuela farmers practice a type of agriculture called slash and burn. This is where virgin rainforest is cut down and burned in order to provide farm land. The land cannot sustain being cultivated for long, so after a few years more forest must be destroyed for farmers to carry on growing crops.

**Where people live**

87% live in cities                              13% live in the country

## RAINFOREST TRIBES

The few native peoples who still survive in Venezuela live in the remote interior of the country near the border with Brazil. The main group is the Yanomami, who number about 10,000 people. The Yanomami are hunters and gatherers who live in enormous thatched huts, called *yanos*, built in clearings in the forest. Their way of life is threatened both by the timber companies and mineral prospectors anxious to exploit the wealth of the region, and by measles and other diseases against which they have no defence.

*Women tend the gardens as well as bringing up the children.*

*Yanos are made from beams covered with palm branches.*

*Circular yanos contain between 10 and 20 families, each living in their own section.*

*Yanomami men hunt wild animals for food. Boys are trained to hunt from an early age.*

## OIL WEALTH

The discovery of oil in Lake Maracaibo in 1917 transformed Venezuela from one of the poorest countries in South America to one of the richest. The reserves underneath Lake Maracaibo are the biggest outside the Middle East; oil-bearing beds of tar by the Orinoco River add to the country's wealth. Despite these reserves, many people remain poor. Public services and agriculture have been neglected, and the rise and fall in oil prices has affected the economy.

**CABLE CAR**
Far above the city of Mérida is the world's highest cable car system. It carries passengers from the city up to 4,765 m (15,600 ft) above sea level. The journey is in four stages and takes more than an hour.

**YOUNG VENEZUELA**
Out of a total population in Venezuela of 25 million, more than 7 million are under the age of 15. The majority of them live in the cities of the north. Many enjoy North American activities such as playing baseball (which was introduced by workers in the oil industry), as well as listening to rock music.

*Find out more*

NATIVE PEOPLES: 43
OIL: 137, 152, 281
POPULATION GROWTH: 43
RAINFORESTS: 15, 69, 204

# GUYANA

ONLY ABOUT 765,000 PEOPLE live in Guyana, most of them on the coastal plain in and around the capital city of Georgetown. Guyana takes its name from a native Indian word meaning "Land of Many Waters", for the country is crossed by numerous rivers draining north into the Atlantic Ocean. Guyana was once a British colony, but gained independence in 1966. Today the country exports sugar and bauxite, and also possesses vast natural resources, including timber and minerals.

### SUGAR PLANTATIONS
The Dutch were the first Europeans in Guyana, establishing a settlement on the Essequibo river in 1615. They planted sugar, cocoa, and other tropical crops, importing slaves from West Africa to help them run the plantations. The British took control of the country in 1814 and concentrated on growing sugar. Today sugar, rice, bauxite, and gold are the main exports.

### THE POPULATION
Most people in Guyana are descendants of workers or slaves brought into the country to labour on the sugar plantations. Black African slaves were shipped in between the 17th and 19th centuries. After slavery was abolished in the British Empire in 1833, people from the Indian Subcontinent arrived to take their place. The Caribs, the original Indian inhabitants, now number no more than 50,000 people.

| GUYANA | |
|---|---|
| **Capital city:** | Georgetown |
| **Area:** | 214,970 sq km (83,000 sq miles) |
| **Population:** | 765,000 |
| **Official language:** | English |
| **Major religions:** | Christian 57%, Hindu 33%, Muslim 9%, other 1% |
| **Government:** | Multi-party democracy |
| **Currency:** | Guyana dollar |
| **Adult literacy rate:** | 97% |
| **Life expectancy:** | 62 years |
| **People per doctor:** | 5,000 |
| **Televisions:** | 55 per 1,000 people |

| SURINAME | |
|---|---|
| **Capital city:** | Paramaribo |
| **Area:** | 163,270 sq km (63,039 sq miles) |
| **Population:** | 436,000 |
| **Official language:** | Dutch |
| **Major religions:** | Christian 48%, Hindu 27%, Muslim 20%, other 5% |
| **Government:** | Multi-party democracy |
| **Currency:** | Suriname dollar |
| **Adult literacy rate:** | 94% |
| **Life expectancy:** | 70 years |
| **People per doctor:** | 3,333 |
| **Televisions:** | 153 per 1,000 people |

| FRENCH GUIANA* | |
|---|---|
| **Capital city:** | Cayenne |
| **Area:** | 90,000 sq km (34,749 sq miles) |
| **Population:** | 186,917 |
| **Official language:** | French |
| **Major religions:** | Christian 75%, other 25% |
| **Government:** | Ruled from France as part of multi-party democracy |
| **Currency:** | Euro |

*French Guiana is not an independent country. It is a French overseas department.

# SURINAME

FORMERLY KNOWN AS DUTCH GUIANA, Suriname was originally owned by the British who exchanged it for the Dutch island of Nieuw Amsterdam, now called Manhattan, in 1667. Suriname became independent from the Netherlands in 1975. Because the country is so poor, about 200,000 Surinamese live in the Netherlands and send money back to support their families at home.

### PARAMARIBO
The capital city of Suriname lies just inland from the Atlantic coastline. The Dutch origins of the city can be seen in the Dutch-style architecture and in street names such as Konigstraat. Most of the city is built of wood, including the 19th-century cathedral of St Peter and St Paul with its tall spires. Half the population of Suriname lives in Paramaribo.

# FRENCH GUIANA

THE ONLY REMAINING colony in South America is French Guiana. For years the colony was famous for its offshore prison on Devil's Island, but today it is better known for its role in the European space programme. The colony is dependent on France for much of its income, with the result that it now has one of the highest standards of living in South America.

*The ocelot is an endangered animal.*

### FORESTS
Most people live on the coast and the interior is largely untouched tropical rainforest. Thousands of different species of flora and fauna, including ocelots, jaguars, and pumas, plus a variety of reptiles, inhabit the forests.

### KOUROU
More than 15,000 people live and work at Kourou, the launch site for the European Space Agency. *Ariane* rockets put satellites and probes into space on behalf of European nations.

---

### Find out more
DEPENDENT TERRITORIES: *271*
NATIVE PEOPLES: *43*
RAINFORESTS: *15, 69, 204*
SUGAR: *52*

# COLOMBIA

| COLOMBIA | |
| --- | --- |
| **Capital city:** Bogotá | |
| **Area:** 1,138,910 sq km (439,733 sq miles) | |
| **Population:** 44,200,000 | |
| **Official language:** Spanish | |
| **Major religions:** Christian 95%, other 5% | |
| **Government:** Multi-party democracy | |
| **Currency:** Colombian peso | |
| **Adult literacy rate:** 92% | |
| **Life expectancy:** 72 years | |
| **People per doctor:** 833 | |
| **Televisions:** 217 per 1,000 people | |

**CARTAGENA**
The bustling port of Cartagena was founded by the Spanish in the 1500s. Great Spanish galleons bound for home set off from here piled high with riches looted from the native peoples. The old city walls, enclosing beautiful mansions and churches, are still there today, along with the many fortifications built by the Spanish to ward off pirates and attacks from other countries.

WHEN SPANISH CONQUERORS reached Colombia in 1499 they discovered a civilization that was rich in gold. They spread tales of a mysterious lost city called *El Dorado,* filled with wealth, but it has never been found. Since 1819, when Colombia became an independent country, it has suffered decades of violent political battles and, more recently, bloody rivalry between gangs involved in the drugs trade. Today Colombia is the world's largest producer of cocaine. Large rivers, such as the Orinoco and Amazon, form an important means of transport for goods across the country.

## BURIED TREASURE
Mining has become very important to the Colombian economy since large deposits of oil were found northeast of Bogotá. Petrochemical plants, like this one at Barranquilla, convert oil into fuel for cars and planes. New sources of coal, the largest in Latin America, as well as deposits of nickel, are also helping to boost the economy. The USA and Venezuela are Colombia's main trading partners.

*The women's skirts look like those worn by Spanish flamenco dancers.*

**THE CUMBIA**
All Colombians know how to dance the *cumbia,* even young children. The dance is a blend of traditions from the black slaves who were brought to Colombia from Africa in the 1800s, together with Spanish and native Indian influences. The men wear white which was the colour of slaves' clothes. Women's clothes are more Spanish in origin.

*A small pouch, called a mochila, is traditionally worn to hold coca leaves or rum.*

*Men wear sombreros – hats which have wide brims to keep off the sun.*

*Skirts have weights in the hems to keep them from swirling too high.*

**EMERALDS**
Many people consider Colombian emeralds to be the finest in the world. The earliest civilizations to live in this region made beautiful objects from gold and emeralds. Today, Colombia produces more than half of the world's emeralds.

*Veins of natural emeralds are found in rocks such as calcite or pyrite.*

## AGRICULTURE
The variety of climate zones in Colombia means that a wide range of crops can be grown. For many years coffee was the country's main export and Colombia is still the world's third largest producer. Once picked, coffee beans are spread out in trays to dry naturally in the sun. Falling world coffee prices have forced Colombia's farmers to develop other products, such as sugar, bananas, cotton, and cut flowers, which are all grown for export.

**SAN AGUSTIN**
This small village near the southern mountains is famous for its ancient stone figures. The statues are at least 800 years old, but very little is known about the people who carved them. Some experts believe that the site was a ceremonial centre where the Agustinians buried their dead, placing statues near the tombs.

*About 500 statues have been found at San Agustin. Many are shaped like birds or animals.*

***Find out more***
COFFEE: *50, 66*
DRUG TRADE: *58*
GEMSTONES: *172, 191*
OIL: *137, 152, 281*

# ECUADOR

CUT THROUGH BY THE EQUATOR, after which it is named, Ecuador is a small country with a varied landscape. A journey of just 200 km (125 miles) takes you from humid coastal lowlands, up into the cold air of the Andes, and down into tropical rainforest. Ecuador also includes the Galápagos Islands, which lie about 1,000 km (620 miles) west in the Pacific Ocean. Ecuador has large reserves of oil and natural gas, and these products account for nearly half of the country's export earnings.

## ECUADOR

**Capital city:** Quito

**Area:** 283,560 sq km (109,483 sq miles)

**Population:** 13,000,000

**Official language:** Spanish

**Major religions:** Christian 95%, other 5%

**Government:** Multi-party democracy

**Currency:** US dollar

**Adult literacy rate:** 91%

**Life expectancy:** 70 years

**People per doctor:** 588

**Televisions:** 293 per 1,000 people

### COTOPAXI
Ecuador is home to the notorious "volcano boulevard" – four rows of volcanic mountains which form part of the Andes chain. At least 10 of them are still active. One of the most famous is Cotopaxi. A towering 5,897 m (19,348 ft) in height, this is one of the world's tallest active volcanoes. It last erupted in the early 1900s.

## MANGROVE SWAMPS
Along the coast are swamps filled with trees, called mangroves, that can grow in salt water. This watery habitat is very important: the trees provide firewood and timber, while the fish, crustaceans, and shellfish that live here are an important source of food. Shrimps in particular have become a major export. Large shrimp farms have created thousands of much-needed jobs, but they are gradually destroying the coastal environment on which they depend.

*The roots trap silt from the sea and help to prevent erosion of the land.*

*At high tide, the sea comes in and covers the roots.*

*Statice*

*Carnations*

### AGRICULTURE
Twenty years ago, Ecuador's economy was based on three crops – bananas, coffee, and cocoa. Today, agriculture is less dominant, but about a third of the workforce still makes a living from farming. Fishing is also important, with shrimps, sardines, and tuna among the main catches. A recently introduced crop is cut flowers, such as roses, carnations, and statice, which are exported to North America and Europe.

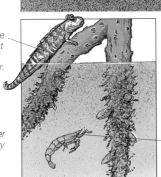

*Mudskippers are the only fish that can live on land and in the water.*

*Swamp water is usually very muddy.*

*Shrimps are washed in with the tide. They feed on plankton.*

*The mangroves' tangled roots spread far and wide, some even emerging above water to trap oxygen.*

*Panama hats are made from the leaves of the jipijapa plant.*

### PANAMA HAT
Panama hats have never been made in Panama. They come from Ecuador, where they were originally made for export to Panama – hence the name. A good-quality hat takes three months to make and can be rolled up without being spoiled.

## THE OTAVALO INDIANS
The town of Otavalo, high in the Andes, is home to one of the wealthiest groups of Indians in South America. The Otavalo make blankets, ponchos, rugs, and other woven goods, which they sell to tourists and export all over South America, the USA, and Europe. Demand for Otavalo goods is so great that many of them are now mass-produced, using artificial dyes and fibres and machines for weaving. The money raised allows the Otavalo to continue their traditional way of life.

*Otavalo market is so popular with tourists that it now occupies all five squares in the centre of town.*

*Otavalo rug, decorated with llamas.*

***Find out more***
ANDES: *40, 58*
GALÁPAGOS ISLANDS: *265*
NATIVE PEOPLES: *43*
VOLCANOES: *13*

# PERU

FOUR HUNDRED YEARS AGO, Peru was the centre of the great Inca Empire that stretched the length of South America. Descendants of the Incas still continue their traditional way of life in the Andes Mountains, and make up about half of Peru's population. In recent years, unemployment, poverty, and other social problems have led to much political violence in Peru. This has stopped foreign companies investing in Peru and kept it one of the poorest countries in South America.

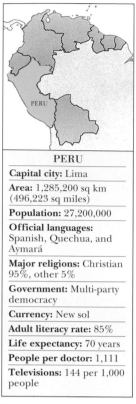

| PERU | |
|---|---|
| **Capital city:** Lima | |
| **Area:** 1,285,200 sq km (496,223 sq miles) | |
| **Population:** 27,200,000 | |
| **Official languages:** Spanish, Quechua, and Aymará | |
| **Major religions:** Christian 95%, other 5% | |
| **Government:** Multi-party democracy | |
| **Currency:** New sol | |
| **Adult literacy rate:** 85% | |
| **Life expectancy:** 70 years | |
| **People per doctor:** 1,111 | |
| **Televisions:** 144 per 1,000 people | |

## LIMA

Grey skies and damp mists hang over Lima for much of the year. But the population of Peru's capital city has grown rapidly to more than 6 million as people flock there in search of work. Although the rich live in new apartment buildings or suburban houses, the poor survive in *calampas*, huge, overcrowded shanty towns that have sprung up on the outskirts. Lima was founded in 1535 by the Spaniard, Francisco Pizarro.

### PACIFIC FISHING

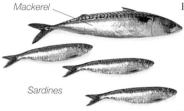

*Mackerel*

*Sardines*

Peru's cool coastal waters are teeming with plankton, which provide food for huge numbers of anchovies, sardines, pilchards, and mackerel. Anchovies, caught and processed into fishmeal, are a major export. Every nine or 10 years a warm water current, called *El Niño*, upsets the balance of plankton and the fish move to better feeding areas. It struck throughout the 1990s, devastating Peru's fishing industry.

*The islands are built from layers of reeds which rot away at the bottom and are replaced at the top.*

*New reeds are cut and stacked ready for use.*

*Villagers grow potatoes in fields by the lake.*

*The Urus build their homes and boats from the totora reeds that grow at the edge of the lake.*

*Remains of the city of Machu Picchu*

*Women untangling fishing nets.*

## LAKE TITICACA

Lying 3,810 m (12,500 ft) above sea level, Lake Titicaca is the world's highest navigable lake. It stretches across the border into Bolivia and, for thousands of years, native peoples have fished its waters. One group, the Urus, live by the lake in floating villages built on huge rafts made from reeds. They grow potatoes, one of the few crops that will ripen at such high altitudes, fish, and hunt birds that live by the lake.

### THE LOST CITY OF THE INCAS

Perched high in the Andes, Machu Picchu was an important Inca city in the 15th and 16th centuries. This fortress city escaped the notice of the Spanish conquerors who arrived in 1532, and remained a "lost city" until it was rediscovered by American archaeologist, Hiram Bingham, in 1911. The site includes the remains of ceremonial buildings, such as temples, and 143 homes.

*Women wear their hair in a single plait which they tuck into their hats.*

*The Urus build boats from tightly bundled reeds. A well-built boat can last a family up to six months.*

### SHINING PATH

During the 1980s a guerilla group called the Shining Path conducted a terrorist campaign in Peru. The group wanted to introduce a communist government and proceeded to terrorize the country. They were able to assassinate people and bomb targets in Peru's cities. Their leader, Abimael Guzmán, was captured in 1992 and later imprisoned.

# BOLIVIA

THE SMALL, MOUNTAINOUS country of Bolivia has no coastline. In 1883, its coastal region was lost to Chile in the Pacific Wars, and now its main means of export are by roads and railways running through Peru and Chile. Bolivia has many resources, such as silver and tin, but its isolated position and frequent changes of government have kept it poor. About 70 per cent of the population are Aymará or Quechua Indians who live on the high windswept plains, called the *altiplano*, growing barely enough food to feed themselves and their families.

**BOLIVIA**

**Capital city:** Sucre (official), La Paz (administrative)

**Area:** 1,098,580 sq km (424,162 sq miles)

**Population:** 8,800,000

**Official languages:** Spanish, Quechua, and Aymará

**Major religions:** Christian 93%, other 7%

**Government:** Multi-party democracy

**Currency:** Boliviano

**Adult literacy rate:** 87%

**Life expectancy:** 64 years

**People per doctor:** 769

**Televisions:** 116 per 1,000 people

**SIMÓN BOLÍVAR**
Bolivia is named after Simón Bolívar (1783–1830), the Venezuelan freedom fighter known as "The Liberator". From 1812, Bolívar devoted his life to freeing South America from Spanish control. He liberated New Granada (Colombia), Venezuela, Ecuador, Panama, and finally Bolivia, then known as Upper Peru. Bolívar dreamed of a united South America, but his dream has not come true.

It is cold living on the high plains of Bolivia. The soil is poor and villagers break up the ground to sow potatoes.

## MINING

Bolivia is rich in tin, silver, lead, zinc, and other minerals. Tin mining is an important industry and, even though production has fallen, Bolivia still ranks among the world's top five tin producers. Thousands of people work in the mines, but conditions are dangerous and wages are low. Many miners believe that a spirit, called *El Tio*, lives in the mines, and they leave cigarettes as offerings for him.

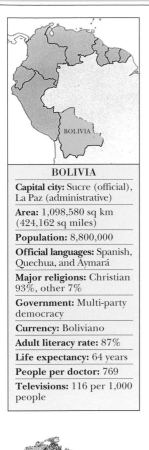
Tin

Silver

## LIFE ON THE HIGH PLAINS

Life is hard for the Aymará Indians who live in villages without electricity or plumbing. Most are poor farmers who grow potatoes as well as maize and barley stalks to feed their cows, sheep, and chickens. Sometimes they kill an animal for food. Llamas provide wool for warm clothing and llama droppings are used as fuel. Aymará women and girls wear dark green, black, or brown hats.

This lamb will later provide milk for the family.

Many Aymará wear plastic shoes, called ojotas.

### COCA GROWING
The leaf of the coca plant is used in the production of the illegal drug cocaine. Coca grows well in Bolivia's mountain valleys and provides a much-needed source of income for local people. The government has tried to stop coca production by offering farmers money to destroy their plantations and grow other crops, such as coffee, cocoa, or bananas, instead. However, this policy has not succeeded, and coca is still Bolivia's main crop.

Traditional pan-pipes are made from reeds.

**FESTIVAL IN THE SUN**
Although Bolivia is Roman Catholic, many traditional beliefs still survive. The Isla del Sol (Island of the Sun) in Lake Titicaca is thought to be the birthplace of the Sun and is the location for the celebration shown here. Music is important at Bolivian festivals, when pan-pipes, drums, and brass instruments are played.

Loose seeds inside the maracas make a noise when they are shaken.

Maracas are pairs of rattles made from dried gourds.

# BRAZIL

THE LARGEST COUNTRY in South America, Brazil covers almost half the continent. From the 16th–19th centuries it was ruled by the Portuguese who named it after the brazilwood tree. The country contains deserts in the northeast, rainforests in the north and west, and rolling grasslands in the south. Because the climate is so varied, it is possible to grow almost any crop. Brazil also has crowded modern cities and areas that have never been explored. In the south, the forces of the Paraná and Paraguay rivers have been harnessed to form one of the world's largest hydroelectric project, the Itaipú Dam.

## PEOPLE OF BRAZIL

The population of Brazil is a mixture of peoples. Some are descended from native Indians who have always lived in Brazil, others from the Portuguese who ruled there for 300 years. Many Brazilians have African ancestors who were brought over in the 17th century to work as slaves on the sugar plantations. At the beginning of the 20th century many Japanese sailed to Brazil to escape crop failures at home. Also during the 20th century, large numbers of European migrants settled in the south of the country.

*This Brazilian girl is of African descent.*

*This boy has both Portuguese and African ancestors.*

*The girl in the middle is a rainforest Indian from the Tembé tribe.*

**World's top coffee producers**
(Figures show percentage of world production)

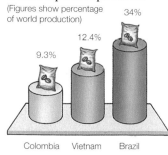

9.3% Colombia | 12.4% Vietnam | 34% Brazil

## AGRICULTURE

Brazil is the world's major producer and exporter of coffee which is grown on

huge plantations, mostly in the states of Paraná and São Paulo. However, coffee is only one of the country's main crops; soya beans, sugarcane, and cotton are also produced on a large scale. Brazil is also one of the world's main producers of oranges, bananas, and cocoa beans. About a quarter of all Brazilians work in agriculture, although the size of farms varies from tiny plots of land to vast estates. Many people work in the fields for little pay while a few rich landowners benefit from the huge profits.

## CITY LIFE

About 80 per cent of Brazilians live in cities, most of which have developed near the coast. Over the years many people have moved to the cities from the countryside in search of work and a better standard of living. For many years the cities grew rapidly, although this has now slowed down. More than 20 million people live in or around the city of São Paulo, more than the populations of London and Paris put together.

| TOP CITIES BY POPULATION | |
|---|---|
| São Paulo | 10,677,019 |
| Rio de Janeiro | 5,974,081 |
| Salvador | 2,556,429 |
| Belo Horizonte | 2,305,812 |
| Fortaleza | 2,256,233 |

*The homes in this shanty town in São Paulo are built from wood and corrugated metal.*

## SHANTY TOWNS

Housing shortages in Brazil mean that about 25 million people live in sprawling shanty towns, called *favelas*, that surround the cities. Most of the homes are built by the families themselves, sometimes from waste materials but more often from wood, bricks, and cement bought from builder's merchants. Services such as running water and sanitation are poor.

**Favela homes**

*No running water: 70%* | *No toilets or drains: 60%* | *No waste collection: 52%*

## FOOTBALL

Everyone in Brazil plays or watches football (soccer), and there is a stadium in every city. The huge Maracana stadium in Rio de Janeiro was built for the 1950 World Cup and holds 200,000 spectators. Brazil has won the World Cup more times than any other country, most recently in 2002. Many Brazilian stars play football abroad for teams in England, Spain, and Italy.

**Manaus**

☀ Jan 27°C (82°F)
   July 27°C (82°F)

🌧 Jan 249 mm (9.8 in)
   July 58 mm (2.3 in)

### THINGS TO LOOK FOR ON THE MAP

**Longest river:** Amazon, Brazil/Peru, 6,439 km (4,001 miles) *Map G3*

**Highest point:** Pico da Neblina, 3,014 m (9,888 ft) *Map C3*

**World's largest lagoon:** Lagoa dos Patos, 10,145 sq km (3,917 sq miles) *Map G12*

**Porto Alegre**

☀ Jan 25°C (77°F)
   July 14°C (57°F)

🌧 Jan 89 mm (3.5 in)
   July 114 mm (4.5 in)

## PIRANHA FISH

These vicious fish live in the rivers of the rainforest. They have razor-sharp teeth and when hundreds of them attack together, they can kill and strip a large animal in minutes.

## AMAZON

The Amazon River starts life in the Andes Mountains of Peru and flows for 6,439 km (4,001 miles) across South America until it gushes into the Atlantic Ocean. For more than half of its length, the Amazon flows through Brazil. It is the country's most important waterway, and large boats can travel inland as far as the modern city of Manaus, about 1,600 km (994 miles) from the sea. Every year the river floods and deposits fertile silt on the land.

*The Amazon, its tributaries, swamps, and lakes, form a vast network of fresh water.*

FUN IN THE SUN

Brazil's eastern coastline stretches for 7,400 km (4,598 miles) along the Atlantic Ocean. In Rio de Janeiro, local people and tourists flock to the wide, sandy beaches to meet friends and play volleyball. The most popular beach in Rio de Janeiro is Copacabana, which is overlooked by Sugarloaf Mountain. Only good swimmers brave the waves here because of the strong currents.

# BRAZIL

**BRAZIL**

**Capital city:** Brasília

**Area:** 8,511,965 sq km (3,286,470 sq miles)

**Population:** 179,000,000

**Official language:** Portuguese

**Major religions:** Christian 95%, other 5%

**Government:** Multi-party democracy

**Currency:** Réal

**Adult literacy rate:** 86%

**Life expectancy:** 69 years

**People per doctor:** 769

**Televisions:** 316 per 1,000 people

BOOM AND BUST BEST DESCRIBES the pattern of the economy in Brazil. In the 1960s and 1970s the country enjoyed a period of massive industrial growth. Then the boom ended, Brazil went bust, and the country became the world's greatest debtor. Paying back the loans is now the government's biggest problem. But Brazil has a great supply of natural resources, including gold and iron ore, and mining is one of the country's most important industries. Brazil has both extremes of wealth and poverty. Some landowners and business people are very rich while most of the rural population is very poor. Although there has been a democratic government since 1985, corruption is still a problem in Brazilian politics.

## CARNIVAL

For four days and nights before Lent each year (February or March), it is carnival time in Brazil. People come from all over the world to join the celebration in Rio de Janeiro where there are street parties, balls, and a contest for the best costume. Day and night the streets are crammed with people in wonderful costumes moving to the rhythm of the music. A parade of brightly coloured floats, organized by neighbourhood samba schools, is the highlight of the carnival.

### FOOD FROM BAHIA

The state of Bahia in northeast Brazil was the first to be colonized by Europeans. Later, black slave cooks created lots of tasty dishes using fish from the sea mixed with spices from their native Africa. Along the beaches of Bahia, women still sell these dishes as well as snacks of coconut sweets and delicious spicy fish patties.

*Electrical goods such as refrigerators, washing machines, and food mixers*

*Leather goods such as bags, shoes, jackets, tennis shoes, and footballs*

## ECONOMY

Brazil produces most of its own food and manufactured goods but needs money to pay off its enormous debts. The country's major exports, some of which are shown here, include coffee, minerals, and aeroplanes, as well as large numbers of Brazilian cars which are sold in Argentina. Most of Brazil's manufacturing takes place in a rough triangle formed by the industrial cities of Rio de Janeiro, São Paulo, and Belo Horizonte.

*Textiles of cotton and silk, and finished goods including towels and sports clothes*

*Agricultural produce including oranges, tangerines, lemons, and limes*

## RELIGION

Almost all Brazilians are Roman Catholic, the religion the Portuguese brought with them, and every town and village has its own patron saint to protect it. Millions of Brazilians also exercise their right to freedom of belief and worship gods and spirits from African religions. In December and January, for example, people leave gifts of flowers, soap, and fruit on the beaches in honour of *Iemanjá*, the Afro-Brazilian goddess of the sea, who they hope will grant their wishes for the new year. The goddess is linked with the Catholic Virgin Mary.

### GREEN FUEL

In the 1970s, the rising cost of oil forced Brazil to look for an alternative fuel. Researchers came up with ethanol, a fuel which is made from fermented sugarcane. Ethanol is cheaper than ordinary petrol and produces less carbon monoxide, which is much better for the environment. Today, about one-third of Brazil's cars run on this "green petrol".

# AMAZON RAINFOREST

Covering an area the size of Australia, the Amazon rainforest is the largest remaining tropical rainforest anywhere on Earth. It covers about one-third of South America, mostly growing around the Amazon River in Brazil. Many animals, birds, insects, and reptiles rely on the trees for food and shelter, as do the tribes of Amazonian Indians who have lived in the forest for thousands of years. But the rainforest is a fragile environment and both wildlife and people are under serious threat as vast areas of the forest are cut down.

*This village chief is from the Tembé tribe.*

**Native Indian homelands**

Brazilian rainforest

① Tikuna
② Yanomani
③ Guajajara
④ Xavante
⑤ Sateré Maué

## INDIAN TRIBES

At one time there were about 5 million native Indians living in the rainforest; today only about 220,000 remain. The largest of these tribes are located on the above map.
Most live as shifting cultivators, which means they settle for a while to hunt and grow basic food crops and then move on. This way the forest soil can recover its fertility. Since the arrival of people from outside the forest, the Indians are at risk from diseases, such as influenza and measles, to which they have no resistance.

### MINING
In the last 20 years large deposits of gold and other minerals have been discovered in the Amazon rainforest. At Carajas, a huge iron mountain was accidentally discovered when a geologist crash-landed his helicopter. The rock contains massive amounts of iron ore as well as manganese and copper. Mining is one of Brazil's major industries, despite the damage it does to the rainforest.

## PLANT POWER
The forests contain plants that provide the basis for many valuable products such as rubber, varnish, paint, cosmetics, and most importantly medicines. The bark of *chinchona*, for example, supplies the quinine used to treat malaria. Other plants have properties that help fight cancer.

*Quinine is obtained from the chinchona plant.*

*Brazil nuts contain vitamins.*

*Bark*

*Shelled nut*

## LOSS OF FOREST
Vital areas of forest are lost through logging, cattle ranching, and relocation (moving people). Building roads also opens up the interior to further destruction. If the present rate of deforestation continues, there will be no forest left by the end of the century.

### RELOCATION
The Brazilian government has cleared large areas of forest and encouraged landless people to buy small plots of land there for farming. But the soil is shallow and rapidly loses its fertility.

### CATTLE BREEDING
About 30 per cent of Brazil's rainforest has been cut down for cattle ranches. But the land can only support cattle for a few years before all its grazing is used up. Then the ranchers have to move on and clear another site.

### LOGGING
Thousands of ebony, teak, and mahogany trees are cut down each year for export. People are now encouraged to buy furniture made of softwoods, such as pine, which take less time to regrow.

**Plan of Brasília**

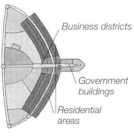

*Business districts*

*Government buildings*

*Residential areas*

## BRASÍLIA
The city of Brasília was built in the late 1950s as part of a government scheme to encourage people to move into the interior of the country. It became Brazil's capital in 1960, taking over from Rio de Janeiro. The city is laid out in the shape of an aeroplane with the business district in the centre, residential areas in the wings, and the government in the cockpit. Bold architecture, such as the glass cathedral shown here, is a feature of this modern city.

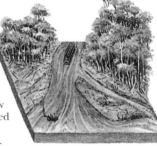

> *Find out more*
> CITIES: *17, 43*
> COFFEE: *50, 62*
> RAINFORESTS: *15, 204*
> ROMAN CATHOLICS: *274*

# SOUTHERN SOUTH AMERICA

FROM THE TROPICAL INTERIOR OF Paraguay, through the warm Mediterranean climate of central Chile, to the freezing conditions around the glaciers of Argentina, southern South America is a region of great contrasts. Four countries – Chile, Argentina, Paraguay, and Uruguay – make up this half of the continent, often called the "southern cone" because of its shape. An important land resource is the pampas, a vast fertile plain that stretches across Argentina and Uruguay, where huge quantities of wheat are grown. During the 1970s, all four countries were known for their brutal military dictatorships. These have since been overturned and the countries are now run as democracies.

### ATACAMA DESERT
This desert in northern Chile is the driest place on Earth, often with no rain for years on end. When rain does fall, devastating flash floods are often the result. The Atacama is a barren wilderness of sun-baked rock and shifting sand dunes, where the night-time temperature can fall dramatically in just one hour. The only paved road across this empty desert is the Pan-American Highway.

**Main migration routes from 1860–1926**

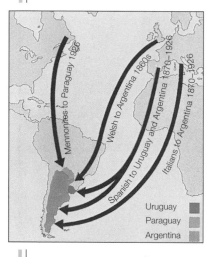

Uruguay
Paraguay
Argentina

### MIGRANT GROUPS
Many people from Europe have settled in South America. During the 19th and early 20th centuries, poverty in Italy drove labourers to Argentina for the wheat harvest; many never went home. Workers also left Spain for Argentina and Uruguay. A German religious group, the Mennonites, moved to Paraguay from Canada to find freedom of worship, and the Welsh set up a community in Argentina to escape English rule and preserve their language.

### INDIAN PEOPLES
Unlike northern South America, the countries in the south have only a few native Indian groups, with Paraguay home to the largest proportion. Uruguay has no Indian population at all. The main surviving groups include the Kolla of Argentina, shown here, the Mataco and Mapuche of central and southern Chile, and the Ache who live in Paraguay.

### WHERE PEOPLE LIVE
In the past 50 years, there has been a great shift as people have moved from the country to the cities in search of work. In Argentina and Uruguay, city populations were already swollen by large numbers of immigrants. In each country, the capital city has grown very quickly while the population in other cities has remained fairly small. Almost 40 per cent of Argentinians, for example, live in the vicinity of Buenos Aires, shown here. Since the 1970s, the move to the cities has begun to slow down.

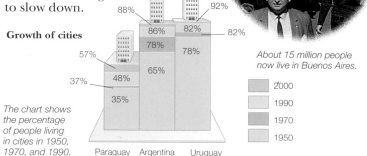

*About 15 million people now live in Buenos Aires.*

**Growth of cities**

88%
92%
86%
82%
82%
57%
78%
78%
37%
48%
65%
35%

*The chart shows the percentage of people living in cities in 1950, 1970, and 1990.*

2000
1990
1970
1950

Paraguay   Argentina   Uruguay

### CATTLE BREEDING
In Argentina and Uruguay, cattle breeding for beef exports is a major source of income. Vast herds of cattle graze the pampas, many feeding on alfalfa plants which produce a leaner meat. The main breeds are Aberdeen Angus and Hereford, brought over from Europe during the last century. Sheep are grazed in the cooler area of Patagonia, and both Argentina and Uruguay are among the world's top wool-producing nations.

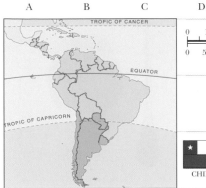

**Asunción, Paraguay**
☀ Jan 28°C (83°F)
July 17°C (63°F)

🌧 Jan 140 mm (5.5 in)
July 56 mm (2.2 in)

PARAGUAY

**Buenos Aires, Argentina**
☀ Jan 23°C (74°F)
July 10°C (50°F)

🌧 Jan 79 mm (3.1 in)
July 56 mm (2.2 in)

CHILE

### ITAIPÚ DAM
Huge amounts of earth were cleared to build the Itaipú Dam on the River Paraná in Paraguay. One of the world's largest hydroelectric projects, the dam was built jointly by Paraguay and Brazil, and can produce massive amounts of electricity. Unfortunately, the lake made by the dam drowned a set of waterfalls and created a breeding ground for malaria-carrying mosquitoes.

### MORENO GLACIER
At the southern tip of Argentina lies one of the region's most dramatic natural spectacles, the vast Moreno Glacier. Every few years, the glacier advances across Lake Argentino, creating a dam of bluish-white ice that can be up to 60 m (197 ft) high. Eventually, the dammed water in the lake bursts through the icy barrier. The ice collapses and cracks, while torrents of water gush over it.

### GIANT ANTEATER
The giant anteater is one of South America's most striking animals. It spends the day roaming the pampas in search of ants and termites. If it finds a nest, the anteater breaks it open with its powerful claws and then laps up the insects with its long, sticky tongue.

### THINGS TO LOOK FOR ON THE MAP

**Longest river:** Paraná, Argentina/Paraguay/Brazil, 2,940 km (1,827 miles) *Map J7*

**Highest point:** Mt. Aconcagua, Argentina, 6,960 m (22,835 ft) *Map F7*

**Largest lake:** L. Buenos Aires/L. General Carrera, Argentina/Chile, 2,240 sq km (865 sq miles) *Map G13*

**World's driest place:** Atacama Desert, Chile *Map F4*

# URUGUAY

URUGUAY HAS BEEN DESCRIBED as a giant city with a ranch attached. Half the population of 3 million plus live in the capital city of Montevideo, while the rest earn a living on the rich lowland pastures that spread out across the rest of the country. The rearing of livestock has brought great wealth to Uruguay, although in recent years tourism and banking have also contributed to the national income. Apart from a period of brutal military rule in the 1970s, the country enjoys a stable government that has built up an impressive welfare system to look after its people.

Silver straw, called a bombilla

Carved gourd for holding the maté tea

### MATÉ TEA
The national drink of Uruguay and other South American nations is a herbal tea called *maté*. The hot drink, which is rich in caffeine, can be mixed with sugar and aromatic herbs. *Maté* is sipped by straw from a dried gourd, a type of fruit with a hard rind.

| URUGUAY | |
| --- | --- |
| **Capital city:** Montevideo | |
| **Area:** 176,220 sq km (68,039 sq miles) | |
| **Population:** 3,400,000 | |
| **Official language:** Spanish | |
| **Major religions:** Christian 68%, Jewish 2%, other 30% | |
| **Government:** Multi-party democracy | |
| **Currency:** Uruguayan peso | |
| **Adult literacy rate:** 98% | |
| **Life expectancy:** 75 years | |
| **People per doctor:** 270 | |
| **Televisions:** 241 per 1,000 people | |

| PARAGUAY | |
| --- | --- |
| **Capital city:** Asunción | |
| **Area:** 406,750 sq km (157,046 sq miles) | |
| **Population:** 5,900,000 | |
| **Official languages:** Spanish, Guaraní | |
| **Major religions:** Christian 100% | |
| **Government:** Multi-party democracy | |
| **Currency:** Spanish, Guaraní | |
| **Adult literacy rate:** 92% | |
| **Life expectancy:** 71 years | |
| **People per doctor:** 909 | |
| **Televisions:** 101 per 1,000 people | |

### CATTLE AND SHEEP
Twelve million cattle and ten million sheep live on the grassy plains of Uruguay, easily outnumbering the population. In the 1860s the country's first meat-processing factory was set up in Fray Bentos, a name forever linked with corned beef. The town became the centre of the national meat industry when a huge refrigeration plant opened in 1901. Today, Uruguay exports animal products all over the world, and is one of the world's largest exporters of wool.

# PARAGUAY

TUCKED INLAND, LARGELY EMPTY with few natural resources, Paraguay is one of the world's forgotten countries. Once part of the Spanish Empire, it gained its independence in 1811. For most of its history, it has been ruled by military dictators. The most famous of these was General Alfredo Stroessner, who governed for 35 years until he was overthrown in a sudden coup in 1989. Today, Paraguay is struggling to modernize itself. The vast Itaipú Dam generates sufficient electricity to export supplies to neighbouring Brazil. Efforts are also being made to widen the economy so it does not depend on agricultural products.

### JESUIT MISSIONS
Almost a century after the occupation of Paraguay by Spain in 1536, Jesuit missionaries began to convert the local people to Christianity. The Jesuits, a Roman Catholic order of priests, set up missions and built huge stone churches, protecting the local Guaraní Indians from attack by their enemies. When the Jesuits were expelled in 1767, many of their buildings fell into disrepair, but are now being restored.

### ASUNCIÓN
The capital, and almost only, city of Paraguay is Asunción, home to about 1.2 million people. Situated on the eastern bank of the Paraguay River, the city is laid out in a rectangular grid, with wide, tree-lined avenues and beautiful parks. Asunción still retains the atmosphere of the Spanish colonial town it once was.

### PEOPLE OF THE CHACO
The north of Paraguay is dominated by the Gran Chaco, a vast stretch of grassland and forest. The only people who live there are the Guaraní and Macá Indians. The Macá sell woven bags to tourists.

*Find out more*

CATTLE FARMING: 75
NATIVE PEOPLES: 43
POLITICAL SYSTEMS: 270–271
ROMAN CATHOLICS: 274

# CHILE

CHILE

| | |
|---|---|
| **Capital city:** Santiago | |
| **Area:** 756,950 sq km (292,258 sq miles) | |
| **Population:** 15,800,000 | |
| **Official language:** Spanish | |
| **Major religions:** Christian 80%, other 20% | |
| **Government:** Multi-party democracy | |
| **Currency:** Chilean peso | |
| **Adult literacy rate:** 96% | |
| **Life expectancy:** 76 years | |
| **People per doctor:** 909 | |
| **Televisions:** 232 per 1,000 people | |

A NATIVE OF CHILE ONCE SAID that his country had a mad geography, because it is the longest, thinnest country in the world. Protected by the Andes, it was the last country in the Americas to be occupied by the Spanish, but gained its independence in 1818. Since the end of a cruel military dictatorship, which lasted from 1973–1990, the country has enjoyed a more stable political life. Most people live in central Chile around the capital, Santiago, and the main port of Valparaiso. Fruit, cereals, and grapes are cultivated in the valleys which are well-watered by rivers from the Andes. Fishing off the long Pacific coast is also important.

## CHILEAN WINE
Vines were first brought to Chile by the Spanish, to grow for their communion wine. Today, the valleys that surround Santiago contain some of the best vineyards on the American continent. Chilean red and white wines are so good that they are exported around the world.

## CHANGING SCENERY
From the dry, barren lands of the Atacama Desert in the north to the icy rocks of Cape Horn in the south, Chile includes almost every type of climate and landscape in the world. The northern desert is one of the driest places on Earth, while the central agricultural valley has a Mediterranean climate similar to California or southern Europe. In the cold and stormy south, 55 volcanoes are currently active, and huge glaciers block the valleys. More than 80 per cent of the country is mountainous, and much of the rest is forested. Not much land is available for growing crops.

## COPPER MINING
Chile is the world's largest exporter of copper, and also mines significant quantities of iron ore, coal, gold, silver, and other minerals. High up in the Atacama Desert, in the north of Chile, lies one of the world's largest deposits of copper. The mine at Chuquicamata is 4,115 m (13,500 ft) long and 670 m (2,200 ft) deep. Every week millions of tonnes of rock are blasted out of the ground and taken away to be turned into copper.

## MAPUCHE INDIANS
For centuries, the Mapuche Indians have fought for their independence, first against the Incas of Peru, then against invading Spaniards, and most recently against the Chilean government. Today, most of the 600,000 Mapuche live on reservations in the south. One of Chile's main football teams, Colo-Colo, is named after an old Mapuche chief.

## PUNTA ARENAS
The city of Punta Arenas lies on the Straits of Magellan, the route used by ships to avoid stormy Cape Horn. The port is filled with fishing and Antarctic research vessels, and is a base for oil exploration. It lies under the hole in the ozone layer above Antarctica, and people are easily burned by the Sun's rays.

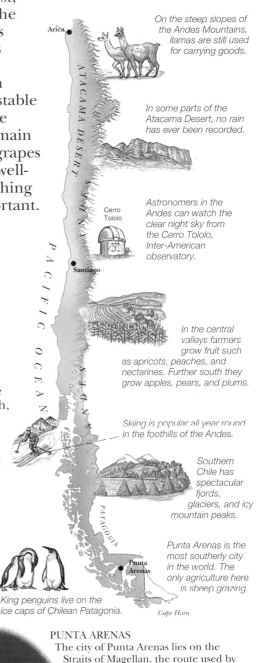

**From north to south**
Chile is 4,200 km (2,610 miles) long from north to south, the same as the distance from Norway to Nigeria. At no point is the country more than 180 km (112 miles) wide.

Arica

On the steep slopes of the Andes Mountains, llamas are still used for carrying goods.

In some parts of the Atacama Desert, no rain has ever been recorded.

Cerro Tololo

Astronomers in the Andes can watch the clear night sky from the Cerro Tololo, Inter-American observatory.

Santiago

In the central valleys farmers grow fruit such as apricots, peaches, and nectarines. Further south they grow apples, pears, and plums.

Skiing is popular all year round in the foothills of the Andes.

Southern Chile has spectacular fjords, glaciers, and icy mountain peaks.

Punta Arenas is the most southerly city in the world. The only agriculture here is sheep grazing.

Punta Arenas

King penguins live on the ice caps of Chilean Patagonia.

Cape Horn

### Find out more
ANDES: *40, 58*
COPPER MINING: *237, 245*
NATIVE PEOPLES: *43*
VEGETATION ZONES: *15*

# ARGENTINA

STRETCHING FROM THE SUBTROPICAL forests of the north down across the vast central plains of the Pampas to the snow-capped mountains of Patagonia in the south, Argentina occupies most of southern South America. The country is bounded by the Andes Mountains in the west, and slopes gently downhill to the Atlantic Ocean in the east. Today's population is a mixture of native Indians, Spanish settlers, and immigrants from southern Europe who arrived during the past 100 years. The country is relatively wealthy, but has suffered from years of political instability, with periods of army rule alternating with elected governments.

## ARGENTINA

**Capital city:** Buenos Aires

**Area:** 2,766,890 sq km (1,068,296 sq miles)

**Population:** 38,400,000

**Official language:** Spanish

**Major religions:** Christian 92%, Jewish 2%, other 6%

**Government:** Multi-party democracy

**Currency:** Argentine peso

**Adult literacy rate:** 97%

**Life expectancy:** 74 years

**People per doctor:** 370

**Televisions:** 289 per 1,000 people

### DANCING THE TANGO
Tango, the national music of Argentina, began in the slums of Buenos Aires. The music, and the dramatic dance style that goes with it, reflects the hopes of working people and is sometimes happy, but often sad. Tango music is played on a *bandoneon*, a type of concertina, with a piano and violin accompaniment.

## BUENOS AIRES
Almost 40 per cent of Argentinians live in or near the capital city of Buenos Aires, making it one of the major cities in the southern half of the world. The city was founded by the Spanish in 1536 as a port on the Río de la Plata, and inhabitants are still called *porteños*, meaning "people of the port". Modern Buenos Aires is highly sophisticated, with grand avenues, a subway system, and expensive shops. It is the trading centre of the country, and most of Argentina's exports are shipped through its docks.

## MEDIA AND NEWSPAPERS
Argentinians can choose from a range of about 180 daily newspapers, among them *El Cronista, La Nación*, and *Clarín*, which has the biggest circulation of any newspaper in South America. Most are published in Spanish, but German, English, and French language papers circulate widely. The constitution of Argentina guarantees freedom of the press, but during the military dictatorship newspapers and television were both heavily censored.

*Simple potato pasta is traditionally eaten at the end of the month, just before payday.*

### ITALIAN IMMIGRANTS
In the years leading up to World War I in 1914, about 2 million people fled the poverty of southern Europe to start a new life in Argentina. More than half came from Italy, finding work on the land or in the expanding cities of Buenos Aires and Rosario. Italian food, such as the potato pasta *ñoquis*, is still served in restaurants throughout Argentina.

### FALKLAND ISLANDS
Some 480 km (300 miles) east of Argentina lie the disputed Islas Malvinas. Occupied by Spain in 1767, the islands were invaded by Britain in 1833 and renamed the Falkland Islands. Britain and Argentina have contested ownership ever since. In 1982 an Argentinian invasion was repelled by Britain, which now has a military garrison there.

### TIERRA DEL FUEGO
When Ferdinand Magellan and his Spanish crew first saw the rocky islands at the tip of Argentina in 1520, they named them Tierra del Fuego, or Land of Fire, because they saw fires lit by the Fuegian Indians to keep warm. The islands, shared between Argentina and Chile, are wet and windswept, with glaciers carving out huge valleys in the mountains.

## THE ECONOMY

With its rich farmland and mineral resources, Argentina is one of South America's most important economies. It is also self-sufficient in energy supplies and has large reserves of oil and gas. Despite its resources, Argentina has been badly run and has substantial overseas debts. A huge economic crisis in 2001 led to a collapse of confidence in the banking system. Many people withdrew their money from the banks.

*Buenos Aires residents were among thousands of Argentinians who queued for hours to withdraw their savings during the crisis of 2001.*

### STEAM TRAINS

In 1857 a steam train made its way slowly south from Buenos Aires to the inland town of Las Flores, opening the first railway line in Argentina. Within 40 years, the country was linked by more than 34,000 km (21,000 miles) of track. Largely built by British engineers and using rolling stock constructed in British factories, this vast railway system still runs carriages and freight wagons, although diesel locomotives are now taking over.

*The car industry is important to Argentina, and many of the leading manufacturers have factories there. Cars are made in the industrial centres of Buenos Aires, Córdoba, and Rosario.*

### GOING TO SCHOOL

The literacy level of Argentina is one of the highest in South America. Primary education is compulsory up to the age of 12, although attendance is often low in country areas. In most state primary schools children wear white coats called *guarda polvo*, meaning "dust guard". The coats protect their clothes from chalk dust. About one-third of the students go on to attend one of the free state universities.

## GAUCHOS OF THE PAMPAS

As famous as his northern cousin, the American cowboy, the Argentine gaucho has roamed the rolling plains of the pampas for about 300 years. The name gaucho comes from a Quechua word for outcast, as gauchos have always chosen to live beyond the law of the cities. The men work on the vast *estancias*, or ranches, fixing fences and corrals (pens for animals), tending the horses, and looking after the large herds of cattle. Tough, self-reliant, and free, the gauchos have become legendary heroes and a national symbol of Argentina.

*Gauchos ride criollos, a breed of wild horse that originally came from Mexico.*

*Beef cattle feed on pasture, or alfafa mixed with grains of sorghum grass to produce a leaner meat.*

*Gauchos regularly have to "throw a steer" to check for ticks and fleas.*

*To throw a steer, one man holds the animal by the horns, while another two men hold on to the tail.*

*The gaucho wears a hat with a broad brim to protect him from the hot sun.*

*A cotton or woollen cape, called a poncho, provides warmth at night.*

*The gaucho's broad leather belt has a silver buckle and is decorated with silver coins.*

*Bombachas, or baggy trousers, are worn tucked into boots.*

*Boleadoras were whirled around and flung at the legs of a running animal to trip it up. Today, a gaucho would use a lasso.*

*The round stones of a boleadora are covered with horsehide.*

*Horse bridle of plaited raw horsehide.*

*Boots are made of tough leather to withstand wear and tear in the stirrups.*

### Find out more

DEBT: 280
EDUCATION: 277
POLITICAL SYSTEMS: 270–271
VEGETATION ZONES: 15

# THE ATLANTIC OCEAN

| ICELAND | |
|---|---|
| **Capital city:** Reykjavik | |
| **Area:** 103,000 sq km (39,768 sq miles) | |
| **Population:** 290,000 | |
| **Official language:** Icelandic | |
| **Major religions:** Christian 94%, other 6% | |
| **Government:** Multi-party democracy | |
| **Currency:** Icelandic krónur | |
| **Adult literacy rate:** 99% | |
| **Life expectancy:** 80 years | |
| **People per doctor:** 286 | |
| **Televisions:** 358 per 1,000 people | |

| CAPE VERDE | |
|---|---|
| **Capital city:** Praia | |
| **Area:** 4,030 sq km (1,556 sq miles) | |
| **Population:** 463,000 | |
| **Official language:** Portuguese | |
| **Major religions:** Christian 99%, other 1% | |
| **Government:** Multi-party democracy | |
| **Currency:** Cape Verde escudo | |
| **Adult literacy rate:** 76% | |
| **Life expectancy:** 69 years | |
| **People per doctor:** 5,000 | |
| **Televisions:** 4 per 1,000 people | |

**Key to currents**

Warm currents

Cold currents

BORDERED BY THE AMERICAS to the west, and Africa and Europe to the east, the Atlantic covers about 82 million sq km (31.7 million sq miles), one-fifth of the Earth's surface. Down the ocean's entire length runs the Mid-Atlantic Ridge, a great underwater mountain chain formed by lava which oozes up from the seabed, cools, and then hardens. Some peaks break the surface to form volcanic islands. The Atlantic contains some of the world's richest fishing grounds, but is also the most polluted ocean because of the industry around its shores.

## ICELAND

The volcanic island of Iceland is part of the Mid-Atlantic Ridge. Intense heat generated deep underground creates bubbling hot springs and mud pools. Iceland has the most *solfataras* (volcanic vents) and hot springs in the world, and many of its towns are heated by underground hot water. Cape Verde, off the west coast of Africa, is also volcanic.

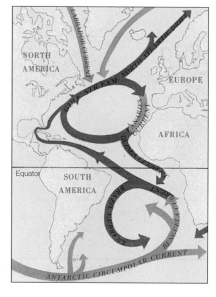

## OCEAN CURRENTS

Water in the oceans is never still but moves in huge belts of water known as currents. In the open ocean, surface winds drive these currents in vast, roughly circular patterns. The currents can be as warm as 30°C (86°F) or as cold as -2°C (30°F) and affect the world's weather. Warm water from the Equator moves towards the cooler poles helping to spread the warmth across the globe.

FISHING
About 90 per cent of the world's fish live in the shallow waters of the continental shelves that surround the land, feeding on the plankton that live there. Over the past 20 years, stocks of cod, herring, and other fish in the Atlantic have run low as the number and size of fishing fleets has increased.

## ICEBERGS

Icebergs, which are made of frozen fresh water, occur when warmer weather causes icesheets and glaciers on icy coastlines to break up, or calve. At sea, icebergs are moved by the wind and ocean currents and can be a danger to ships. Icebergs vary in size from small Arctic growlers, which are about as big as a grand piano, to much larger Antarctic icebergs, which can be 8 km (5 miles) long.

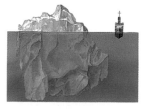

*Only about one-seventh of an iceberg shows above the surface of the ocean. The rest of the ice remains hidden below the waterline.*

GULF STREAM
The Gulf Stream is a warm current, only about 100 km (60 miles) wide, that moves across the North Atlantic. It raises the temperature of northern Europe and helps keep its ports ice-free in winter. It also allows tropical plants to grow in normally cool places, such as the west coast of Scotland.

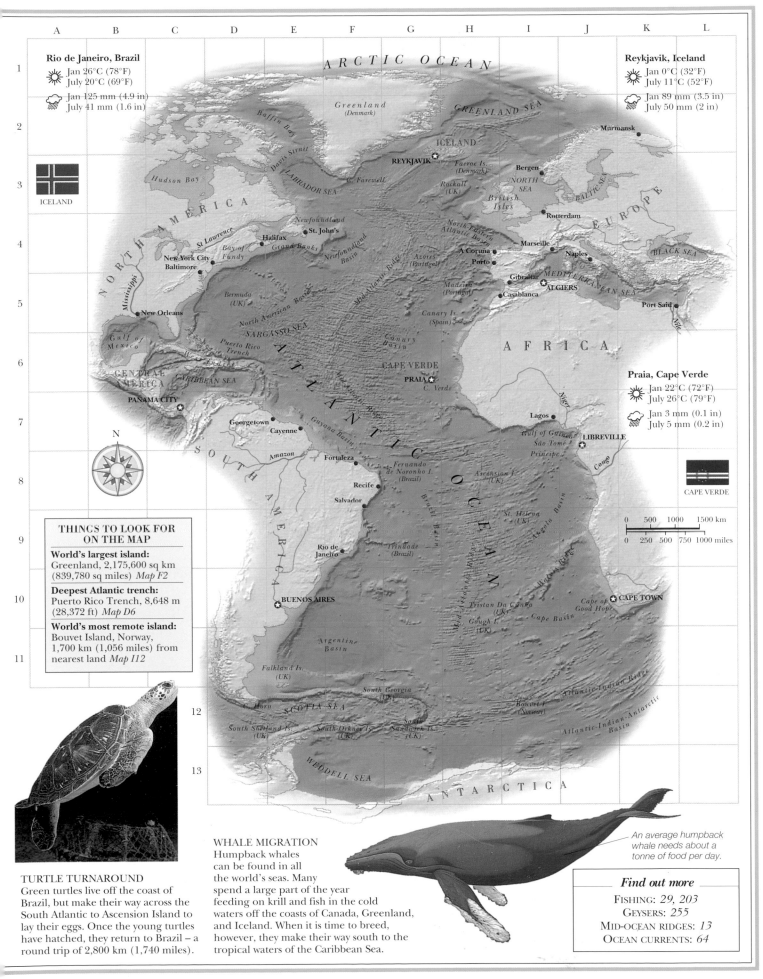

**Rio de Janeiro, Brazil**
☀ Jan 26°C (78°F)
July 20°C (69°F)
🌧 Jan 125 mm (4.9 in)
July 41 mm (1.6 in)

ICELAND

**Reykjavik, Iceland**
☀ Jan 0°C (32°F)
July 11°C (52°F)
🌧 Jan 89 mm (3.5 in)
July 50 mm (2 in)

**Praia, Cape Verde**
☀ Jan 22°C (72°F)
July 26°C (79°F)
🌧 Jan 3 mm (0.1 in)
July 5 mm (0.2 in)

CAPE VERDE

0   500   1000   1500 km
0   250   500   750   1000 miles

### THINGS TO LOOK FOR ON THE MAP

**World's largest island:**
Greenland, 2,175,600 sq km (839,780 sq miles) *Map F2*

**Deepest Atlantic trench:**
Puerto Rico Trench, 8,648 m (28,372 ft) *Map D6*

**World's most remote island:**
Bouvet Island, Norway, 1,700 km (1,056 miles) from nearest land *Map I12*

### TURTLE TURNAROUND
Green turtles live off the coast of Brazil, but make their way across the South Atlantic to Ascension Island to lay their eggs. Once the young turtles have hatched, they return to Brazil – a round trip of 2,800 km (1,740 miles).

### WHALE MIGRATION
Humpback whales can be found in all the world's seas. Many spend a large part of the year feeding on krill and fish in the cold waters off the coasts of Canada, Greenland, and Iceland. When it is time to breed, however, they make their way south to the tropical waters of the Caribbean Sea.

*An average humpback whale needs about a tonne of food per day.*

### Find out more
FISHING: *29, 203*
GEYSERS: *255*
MID-OCEAN RIDGES: *13*
OCEAN CURRENTS: *64*

# EUROPE

A GREAT CURVE OF mountain ranges, that includes the Pyrenees and the Alps, roughly divides the cooler north of Europe from the warmer south. In the far north, treeless tundra merges into the cool coniferous forests that extend across Scandinavia and into Russia. South of this lies the fertile North European Plain, which supports most of the continent's agriculture and mixed woodland. By contrast, the Mediterranean region to the south is hot and almost desert-like in places. Volcanic activity is confined to Iceland and southern Italy, where Mount Etna is constantly active. The Ural and Caucasus Mountains form Europe's eastern borders.

Bird's Eye primrose

THE ALPS
The mountains that form the Alps run from southeastern France, through Switzerland and Italy, into Austria. In the last 2 million years, ice has moulded the scenery, carving pyramid-shaped peaks, like the Matterhorn (above), knife-edged ridges, dramatic waterfalls, and armchair-shaped basins filled with lakes. Alpine plants, such as the Bird's Eye primrose, have adapted to growing at high altitudes.

**Highest temperature:**
Seville, Spain, 50°C (122°F)

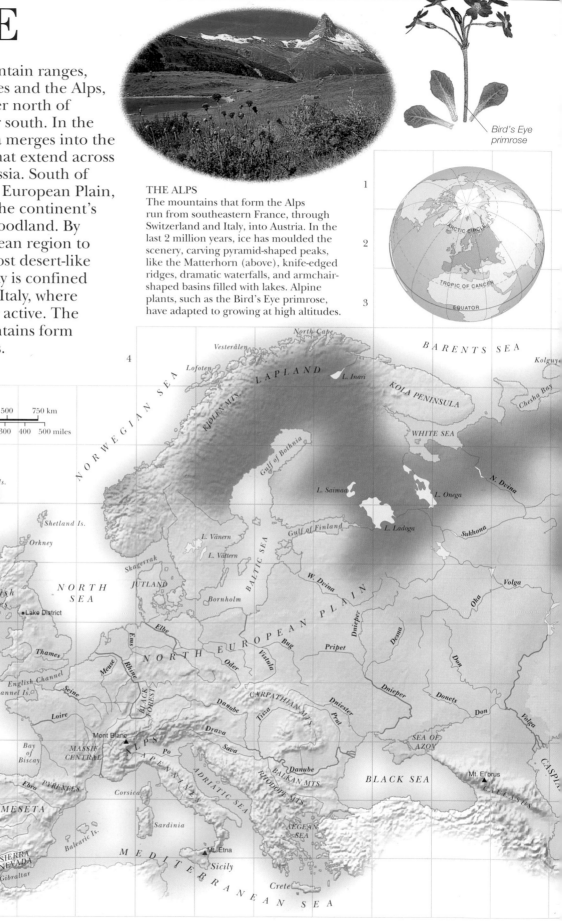

*This is a river valley before the arrival of a glacier. Glaciers are huge masses of ice that grind the shape of the land as they move slowly forwards.*

# THE LAKE DISTRICT

The 15 lakes of the Lake District in northwestern England lie in U-shaped valleys extending outwards like the spokes of a wheel from an uplifted dome of low mountains. Long ago, the valleys contained rivers, but during the Ice Age these were deepened by the movement of glaciers and most were dammed by eroded rock left behind when the glaciers melted. The erosion of the main valleys has cut off tributary valleys and left them "hanging" above the main valleys, often with waterfalls cascading from them.

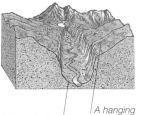

*When glaciers retreat, at the end of an Ice Age for example, they leave behind U-shaped valleys.*

*A hanging valley on the side of the main valley.*

*Ullswater is a lake that lies in a U-shaped valley.*

KARA SEA

N

**Lowest temperature:** Ust'Shchugor, Russian Federation, -55°C (-67°F)

# NORTHERN PLAINS

The North European Plain stretches from southern England across France and Germany as far as Russia, ending at the Ural Mountains. Most of the plain is low-lying, and in the Netherlands it even lies partly below sea level. Some of the world's most fertile farmland is found here, as well as important deposits of coal, oil, and natural gas. This is Europe's most densely populated area and contains many major cities.

## NORTHERN FORESTS

A thick band of dense coniferous forest, known as taiga, covers northern Europe. Conifers (trees that have cones), such as spruce and pine, keep their leaves all year round and can withstand heavy snow. They also provide winter food and shelter for many animals.

*Wheat, sugarbeet, and apples are grown on the plains of northern France.*

*Foxes are often found in the fields and woodlands of Europe, although many now live in towns. They eat almost anything from rabbits to apples or worms.*

## THINGS TO LOOK FOR ON THE MAP

**Area:** 10,400,000 sq km (4,000,000, sq miles)

**Highest point:** Mt. El'brus, Russian Federation, 5,642 m (18,510 ft) *Map K11*

**Longest river:** Volga, Russian Federation, 3,530 km (2,194 miles) *Map L8*

**Largest lake:** L. Ladoga, Russian Federation, 18,389 sq km (7,100 sq miles) *Map J7*

**Largest island:** Great Britain, 229,850 sq km (88,745 sq miles) *Map D9*

N   O   P

## THE MEDITERRANEAN

The region around the Mediterranean Sea has a distinctive climate of hot, dry summers and mild, rainy winters. These conditions are perfect for growing crops such as citrus fruits, grapes, and olives, shown here in southern Spain. Many trees, such as cork oaks, develop thick bark as a protection against the heat.

## THE DANUBE

The Danube, western Europe's longest river, flows eastwards from its source in Germany to its mouth on the Black Sea. It serves as a trade route between the nine countries that lie along its course. The Danube delta, where the river divides into numerous channels, is an important wetland area. About 300 different bird species have been recorded in the delta as well as boars, deer, and wild cats.

# PEOPLES OF EUROPE

EUROPE IS A CROWDED CONTINENT. It is the second smallest of the continents by area, yet it has the third highest population. As a result, population densities are very high, and most Europeans live in cities. Europe is also crowded with countries – more than 40 different nations jostle for position on the continent. Conflicts between these countries have often erupted into war. Two world wars have started on European soil in the last 100 years. Yet, despite these problems, Europe is by and large a rich continent, and many European countries are among the wealthiest in the world. Some pockets of poverty exist, but in general the population enjoys a high standard of living compared to most other parts of the world. Much of this wealth has come as a result of industrial growth, and because of the large colonial empires established by many European countries in Africa, Asia, and the Americas.

**EUROPEAN CITIES**
A large proportion of Europeans live in cities. The most densely populated part of Europe lies in the west and forms a belt that stretches more or less continuously from southeast Britain, through northern France, Belgium, the Netherlands, and into Germany. In these densely populated areas, individual cities can merge into one another, forming what are known as conurbations. The largest of these is in the German industrial region known as the Ruhr. By contrast, in eastern Europe a greater proportion of the population live in country areas.

**Population:** approximately 774,000,000 people

**Number of countries:** 43

**Largest country:** Russian Federation straddles northern Europe and Asia (see page 138) and its European part covers 3,955,818 sq km (1,527,341 sq miles)

**Least densely populated country:** Iceland, 3 people per sq km (8 per sq mile)

**KEY**
1 NETHERLANDS
2 BELGIUM
3 LUXEMBOURG
4 SWITZERLAND
5 LIECHTENSTEIN
6 MOLDOVA
7 ANDORRA
8 MONACO
9 SAN MARINO
10 VATICAN CITY
11 SLOVENIA
12 CROATIA
13 BOSNIA AND HERZEGOVINA
14 SERBIA AND MONTENEGRO
15 ALBANIA
16 MACEDONIA

**Most densely populated country:** Monaco, 16,477 people per sq km (42,840 per sq mile)

**Smallest country:** Vatican City, 0.44 sq km (0.17 sq miles)

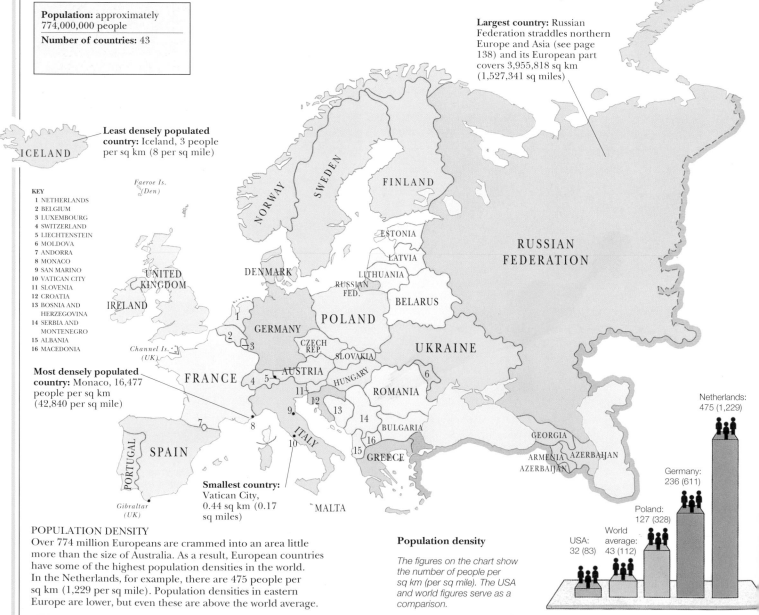

**POPULATION DENSITY**
Over 774 million Europeans are crammed into an area little more than the size of Australia. As a result, European countries have some of the highest population densities in the world. In the Netherlands, for example, there are 475 people per sq km (1,229 per sq mile). Population densities in eastern Europe are lower, but even these are above the world average.

**Population density**

*The figures on the chart show the number of people per sq km (per sq mile). The USA and world figures serve as a comparison.*

USA: 32 (83)
World average: 43 (112)
Poland: 127 (328)
Germany: 236 (611)
Netherlands: 475 (1,229)

## THE CHANGING POPULATION

Compared to Asia and Africa, the populations of most European countries are stable – they are not increasing or decreasing to any great extent. Birth rates are low, and average life expectancy is very high – about 75 years in most countries, compared to less than 50 years in Afghanistan and most of Africa. As a result of these two factors, Europe's population is relatively elderly, with a large number of people aged 60 years and over.

### THE TWO EUROPES

Economically, Europe can be divided into two main sets of countries. Western Europe contains some very rich countries, such as Germany, Switzerland, and France, which have strong economies. By contrast, eastern Europe contains former communist countries such as Poland, Hungary, and Romania, which are much poorer. They are still struggling to adjust their economies in order to compete in world markets.

*A market in the Russian Federation. Under communism all commerce was controlled by the state.*

### Age of population

| | | | |
|---|---|---|---|
| Germany (Europe) | 21.6% | 57% | 21.4% |
| Kenya (Africa) | 59.1% | 36.2% | 4.7% |
| India (Asia) | 45.7% | 47.5% | 6.8% |

Ages 0–19
Ages 20–59
Ages 60+

## CULTURAL MELTING POT

Europe's wealth and relative political stability have attracted large numbers of migrants to its shores, many from former colonies. As a result, most countries, particularly in western Europe, contain large numbers of people from ethnic minorities. In France, for example, north Africans from Algeria and other former colonies have settled in cities such as Marseilles and Paris.

*The UK's population contains migrants from many countries, including the Caribbean, India, Pakistan, and Bangladesh.*

**New European countries**

*Former Czechoslovakia split apart peacefully in 1993, when the Czech Republic and Slovakia voted to separate.*

CZECH REPUBLIC
SLOVAKIA
CZECHOSLOVAKIA

*Former Yugoslavia was shattered by war in the 1990s, as various regions declared themselves independent countries.*

SLOVENIA
CROATIA
BOSNIA & HERZEGOVINA
YUGOSLAVIA
SERBIA & MONTENEGRO
MACEDONIA

*The European Parliament, elected by the people of the EU, meets in this building in Strasbourg, France.*

*New European countries have also been formed from the former USSR – see page 136.*

New European countries have also been formed from the former USSR – see page 136.

### SPLITTING APART

Europe is a fragmented continent made up of more than 40 independent countries. Even within individual countries there are sometimes separate groups, such as the Basques in Spain, who claim some form of independence from the national government. New countries are still being formed. The former USSR, Yugoslavia, and Czechoslovakia are among the European countries that have split apart in recent years, sometimes violently.

*The stars on the flag of the European Union represent solidarity, perfection, and unity.*

## THE EUROPEAN UNION

In 1957, six European countries agreed to form the European Economic Community (EEC). They believed that economic co-operation would reduce the likelihood of wars between the member countries, and would bring prosperity to the peoples of Europe. Since that time, more countries have joined, and the EEC has been renamed the European Union (EU). Today it consists of 25 member states and as well as closer economic co-operation, there are moves to encourage greater political union.

# SCANDINAVIA AND FINLAND

THE NORTHERN EUROPEAN countries of Norway, Sweden, and Denmark are together known as Scandinavia. Along with neighbouring Finland, all four countries have small populations and enjoy a high standard of living with extensive social welfare systems that distribute wealth evenly among the people. Much of Norway, Sweden, and Finland is covered by forests of pine, spruce, and birch trees and contains many lakes gouged out by glaciers during the last Ice Age. Norway and Sweden are mountainous, while Finland and fertile Denmark are low-lying.

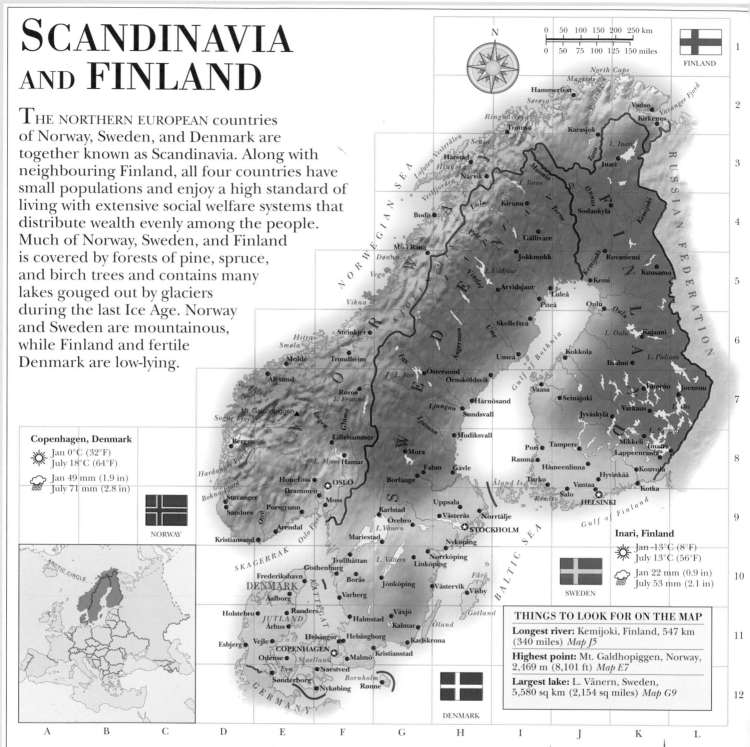

FINLAND

**Copenhagen, Denmark**
- Jan 0°C (32°F)
- July 18°C (64°F)
- Jan 49 mm (1.9 in)
- July 71 mm (2.8 in)

NORWAY

**Inari, Finland**
- Jan -13°C (8°F)
- July 13°C (56°F)
- Jan 22 mm (0.9 in)
- July 53 mm (2.1 in)

SWEDEN

## THINGS TO LOOK FOR ON THE MAP

**Longest river:** Kemijoki, Finland, 547 km (340 miles) *Map J5*

**Highest point:** Mt. Galdhøpiggen, Norway, 2,469 m (8,101 ft) *Map E7*

**Largest lake:** L. Vänern, Sweden, 5,580 sq km (2,154 sq miles) *Map G9*

DENMARK

## THE MIDNIGHT SUN

Much of northern Norway, Sweden, and Finland lie in the Arctic Circle. Here the Sun never sets at the height of summer – giving 24 hours of light – and never rises in the middle of winter – giving 24 hours of darkness. The periods of light or dark lengthen the further north you go. In the far north the winter darkness lasts for almost two months.

*Midnight Sun in Senja, Norway.*

## COASTLINE CITIES

Most people in the region live in towns and cities around the coast or on lakesides. These stretches of water provide the best form of transport in an area where fast-flowing rivers are unsuitable for transport and where much of the interior is rugged. The capitals of all four countries are on the coast, including Stockholm, the Swedish capital, which lies on the edge of the Baltic Sea.

# NORWAY

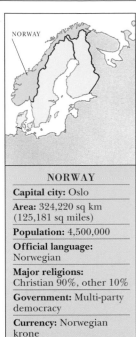

NORWAY LIES ALONG the western coast of Scandinavia. It is a long country, narrow in its northern half and only 80 km (50 miles) wide at one point. Despite its northerly location, Norway's lengthy coastline is kept free of ice by the warm Gulf Stream. Most of the country is mountainous, the spectacular landscape containing thousands of lakes and offshore islands. Many people work in industry, including offshore oil and gas production, shipbuilding, and mining. Fishing, forestry, and agriculture employ only about 5 per cent of the total workforce.

| NORWAY | |
| --- | --- |
| **Capital city:** Oslo | |
| **Area:** 324,220 sq km (125,181 sq miles) | |
| **Population:** 4,500,000 | |
| **Official language:** Norwegian | |
| **Major religions:** Christian 90%, other 10% | |
| **Government:** Multi-party democracy | |
| **Currency:** Norwegian krone | |
| **Adult literacy rate:** 99% | |
| **Life expectancy:** 79 years | |
| **People per doctor:** 333 | |
| **Televisions:** 579 per 1,000 people | |

## OIL INDUSTRY

The discovery of oil and gas under the North Sea in 1969 transformed the Norwegian economy, turning the country into Europe's largest oil producer. Thousands of people work in the industry, constructing tankers and oil rigs and refining the crude oil. Today Norway is self-sufficient in energy, and exports most of its oil and natural gas to the rest of Europe.

## FJORDS

Only 3 per cent of Norway is suitable for farming, as most of the country consists of rugged mountain ranges and deep lakes. Most farmland is situated at the head of fjords, the long inlets of sea which cut into Norway's coast. Fjords were created by glaciers gouging out valleys as they descended to the sea. The fjords are natural harbours, sheltering small communities of fishermen and farmers. Tourists visit the spectacular scenery in cruise ships.

*Low-lying meadows are suitable for livestock.*

*Deep water allows cruise and other ships to sail far inland.*

*Rough upland grazing for herds of sheep and goats.*

*Once-thriving coastal fishing communities are declining as fish stocks diminish, but fish farming is increasing.*

*Traditional stave church in Sogne Fjord.*

*South facing slopes are warm enough to support crops of soft fruit in the summer months.*

## WOODEN CHURCHES

Ancient stave churches are found throughout Norway. Unlike log cabins, which are made of horizontal logs, stave churches are built with vertical, curved strips of wood, called staves. Not a single nail is used in the construction, which is powerful enough to withstand heavy winter snowfalls.

## SHIPPING

Norway has one of the largest shipping fleets in the world. Many thousands of people are employed in shipyards and repair docks, and on board the many merchant ships and ferries that supply the ports and islands of the west coast. The most important port is the capital city, Oslo. Over half a million people live in this bustling, lively city, which is the cultural, intellectual, and industrial centre of the country.

## SKIING

Norway is the home of skiing. The earliest remains of skis were found in a glacier here, and the word "ski" is of Norwegian origin. During the snowy winter months, the most efficient way for many Norwegians to travel is on skis. The ski jump is a feature of most towns in Norway. Annual ski festivals are popular events, as is the sport of cross-country skiing.

| ***Find out more*** |
| --- |
| GAS: *163, 198, 211* |
| GLACIERS: *79* |
| GULF STREAM: *76* |
| OIL: *152, 281* |

# DENMARK

THE LONG, NARROW Jutland Peninsula that makes up mainland Denmark extends away north of Germany towards Norway and Sweden. To the east of the peninsula, more than a hundred islands make up the rest of the country. Denmark is the most southerly country in Scandinavia and is one of the flattest lands in the world. Like its neighbours, it enjoys political stability and a high standard of living. Industry has developed rapidly, and today a third of the people work in small factories.

| DENMARK | |
|---|---|
| **Capital city:** | Copenhagen |
| **Area:** | 43,094 sq km (16,639 sq miles) |
| **Population:** | 5,400,000 |
| **Official language:** | Danish |
| **Major religions:** | Christian 90%, other 10% |
| **Government:** | Multi-party democracy |
| **Currency:** | Danish kroner |
| **Adult literacy rate:** | 99% |
| **Life expectancy:** | 77 years |
| **People per doctor:** | 294 |
| **Televisions:** | 585 per 1,000 people |

## ARCHITECTURE

Like the rest of the region, Denmark is famous for its architecture. Danish architects combine local materials such as cement, brick, and timber to create beautiful buildings that harmonize with the environment. Many housing developments have been built where each house runs on a designed system of solar panels and insulation designed to keep energy wastage to a minimum. Design is very important in Denmark, especially for furniture, glassware, kitchenware, and porcelain.

*Solar panels use the Sun's rays to heat the water.*

*The ventilation system ensures that fresh air is taken in and stale air is drawn out.*

*Sun rooms made almost entirely from glass attract the warmth of the Sun's rays.*

*Air trapped between the inner and outer walls of the house acts as insulation and keeps out the cold.*

## COPENHAGEN

Denmark's capital is situated on the island of Sjaelland. It is the biggest city in Scandinavia and the largest trading centre in Denmark. Visitors wandering down old alleyways and pedestrianized streets will soon find historic churches, colourful market places, and a network of canals. This is also a city of bicycles, with bike paths leading out towards areas where many city-dwellers have summer homes.

PIG AND DAIRY FARMING
Denmark is well known for its co-operative organizations. To keep up with modern agricultural development, the farmers have had to work together closely. Part of their strategy has been to establish co-operatively owned dairies and bacon factories and to concentrate their energies on promoting these foods abroad.

LEGOLAND
"Lego" – the colourful interlocking building blocks designed for children – was first produced by a carpenter in Jutland in the 1930s. Now Jutland is home to a massive Legoland theme park, where all the buildings are made of Lego. The name "Lego" comes from the two Danish words, *leg* and *godt*, meaning "play well".

## ROYAL DANISH BALLET

The Royal Danish Ballet was established at the opening of the Royal Theatre in Copenhagen in 1748, and is one of the oldest and most renowned ballet companies in the world. Much of its fame is due to August Bournonville (1805–79), who directed the company from 1828 until his death and choreographed more than 50 ballets.

HANS CHRISTIAN ANDERSEN
The Danish writer Hans Christian Andersen (1805–75) was one of the first authors to write new fairy tales. His first collection, *Fairy Tales*, was published in 1835. He wrote more than 160 stories, including *The Snow Queen* and *The Ugly Duckling*.

***Find out more***
CYCLING: *92, 192*
EUROPEAN FAMILIES: *81*
INSULATED HOUSES: *143*
WORKING WOMEN: *137, 141*

# SWEDEN

LYING BETWEEN NORWAY and Finland, Sweden stretches from the Arctic north to the fertile south, where most of its small population lives. Sweden's long industrial traditions and a highly skilled workforce have made it one of the world's most advanced manufacturing countries. Like its neighbours, Sweden is a prosperous place, where equal rights for all groups in society is a very important issue.

### SWEDEN
**Capital city:** Stockholm
**Area:** 449,964 sq km (173,371 sq miles)
**Population:** 8,900,000
**Official language:** Swedish
**Major religions:** Christian 85%, other 15%
**Government:** Multi-party democracy
**Currency:** Swedish krona
**Adult literacy rate:** 99%
**Life expectancy:** 80 years
**People per doctor:** 333
**Televisions:** 530 per 1,000 people

## SOCIAL WELFARE

Sweden has led the way in social welfare, and a small population means that it is easier for the government to take care of everyone. Childcare and facilities for the sick and the elderly are excellent. Unemployment figures have been relatively low (see chart below). However, to pay for these benefits the government must impose high taxes. Economic problems could threaten some of the benefits system.

**Recycling system**

*Customers return their empty aluminium cans to shops with machines that flatten the cans, allowing many more to be collected.*

## CONSERVATION

Swedes are very concerned about conserving their environment. This includes their historic buildings as well as the countryside. There are many nature reserves in Sweden and some of Europe's largest national parks in the mountainous north. Many people are worried about water pollution and Sweden is a leading campaigner in the movement to clean up the Baltic Sea. It has also restricted industrial development in some coastal areas. Conserving resources is part of everyday life and Sweden runs a highly successful recycling system (right).

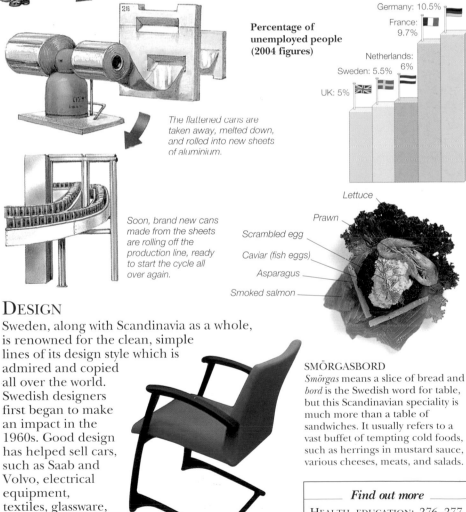

*The flattened cans are taken away, melted down, and rolled into new sheets of aluminium.*

*Soon, brand new cans made from the sheets are rolling off the production line, ready to start the cycle all over again.*

**Percentage of unemployed people (2004 figures)**

Germany: 10.5%
France: 9.7%
Netherlands: 6%
Sweden: 5.5%
UK: 5%

Lettuce
Prawn
Scrambled egg
Caviar (fish eggs)
Asparagus
Smoked salmon

## DESIGN

Sweden, along with Scandinavia as a whole, is renowned for the clean, simple lines of its design style which is admired and copied all over the world. Swedish designers first began to make an impact in the 1960s. Good design has helped sell cars, such as Saab and Volvo, electrical equipment, textiles, glassware, and furniture by internationally known companies such as Ikea.

*This office chair is practical and hardwearing.*

## SMÖRGASBORD

*Smörgas* means a slice of bread and *bord* is the Swedish word for table, but this Scandinavian speciality is much more than a table of sandwiches. It usually refers to a vast buffet of tempting cold foods, such as herrings in mustard sauce, various cheeses, meats, and salads.

### SUMMER HOMES
Holiday homes are common in this wealthy country. Pretty wooden houses, often painted red, are found along the coast, lakeshores, and river valleys. They provide the perfect escape for city-dwellers at the weekend or during holidays. When they are not there themselves, families often rent out these retreats to friends or to the growing number of tourists that visit Sweden.

***Find out more***
HEALTH, EDUCATION: *276–277*
RECYCLING: *94*
RICH AND POOR: *278–279*
STOCKHOLM: *82*

# FINLAND

KNOWN AS "SUOMI" to its people, Finland is one of the most northerly countries in the world. An aerial view of this land would show a spectacular pattern of forests, swampy peatland, massive lakes, and islands – scattered in the lakes and along the coastline. Most of it is covered with pine, spruce, and birch trees, and for up to half of the year it is carpeted with snow. After centuries of Swedish rule, Finland became part of Russia before independence in 1917. Finland has a distinctive language and culture that marks it apart from Scandinavia.

### FINLAND

**Capital city:** Helsinki

**Area:** 337,030 sq km (130,127 sq miles)

**Population:** 5,200,000

**Official languages:** Finnish, Swedish

**Major religions:** Christian 91%, other 9%

**Government:** Multi-party democracy

**Currency:** Euro

**Adult literacy rate:** 99%

**Life expectancy:** 78 years

**People per doctor:** 323

**Televisions:** 640 per 1,000 people

## LAPLAND

The icy north of Norway, Sweden, and Finland is called Lapland. The people who live in the scattered villages of this region, the Sami, or Lapps, have their own language and customs and some herd reindeer for their meat and milk. However, their traditional way of life is slowly changing. Lapland is also known as the home of Father Christmas, and thousands of children send letters to him there each year.

### HELSINKI

Surrounded on three sides by water, Finland's capital, Helsinki, has an open, spacious feel. Its magnificent harbour boasts a colourful street market selling fish, fruit, vegetables, and flowers. The city is filled with exciting modern buildings that are designed to blend with the old and create a distinctive national style.

## LOGGING INDUSTRY

Timber is a major industry in this forested country – Finland and Sweden are Europe's top producers of the softwoods pine and spruce. The timber is transported by truck to processing plants where the wood is boiled down to a pulp. The liquid produced, wood alcohol, is used in various chemicals, while the pulp is made into plywood, board, and paper. Sawdust, bark, and waste are burned to produce electricity.

**What the land is used for**

Forest: 76%

Other: 15%
Crops: 8%
Grassland: 1%

**LAND OF LAKES**
Well over 50,000 lakes take up about 10 per cent of the country's area and are a major tourist attraction. Lake Saimaa is the largest lake and contains hundreds of islands. Ferries provide a vital link between the coastal islands. During the long, cold winters, lakes may freeze up and icebreakers keep coastal waters open for merchant shipping.

*People beat themselves with birch twigs to stimulate their blood circulation and so refresh their bodies.*

*After a session in the sauna, it is time to cool off under a cold shower – or in the nearby lake!*

*Saunas are fuelled by wooden logs in the country and by electricity in towns and cities.*

## SAUNAS

Finland is the home of the sauna. The Finns have used the steam bath for centuries, and today most houses in Finland have one. A sauna is a small, very warm room which people sit in to relax and cleanse their bodies. From time to time they throw water over hot stones and, as the water crackles and spits, the air fills with clouds of steam. Most families enjoy a shared sauna every week.

*Find out more*

ARCTIC PEOPLES: 25, 266
LOGGING: 26, 69, 244
NORTHERN FORESTS: 15, 132

# THE BRITISH ISLES

TUCKED AWAY IN THE NORTHWEST corner of Europe, the British Isles consist of the United Kingdom (UK) and Ireland. The UK includes Scotland, England, Wales, and Northern Ireland. The rest of Ireland is an independent country. Once, the whole of Ireland was dominated by England, a Protestant nation. This caused resentment among the Catholic Irish and in 1922 the south broke away. Despite differences between the two countries – Ireland is mainly rural, while the UK is heavily urbanized – both share a strong sense of identity that comes from being isolated from the rest of Europe by sea.

**UNITED KINGDOM**

**Oban, UK**
Jan 4°C (39°F)
July 14°C (57°F)
Jan 146 mm (5.8 in)
July 120 mm (4.7 in)

## THINGS TO LOOK FOR ON THE MAP

**Longest river:** Shannon, Ireland, 386 km (240 miles) *Map F8*

**Highest point:** Ben Nevis, UK, 1,343 m (4,406 ft) *Map H5*

**Largest lake:** Lough Neagh, UK, 396 sq km (153 sq miles) *Map G7*

**Deepest reservoir in Europe:** Loch Morar, UK, 310 m (1,017 ft) *Map H4*

**Cork, Ireland**
Jan 6°C (42°F)
July 16°C (61°F)
Jan 119 mm (4.7 in)
July 70 mm (2.8 in)

**IRELAND**

N

0   50   100   150 km
0   25   50   75   100 miles

**London, UK**
Jan 4°C (39°F)
July 18°C (64°F)
Jan 54 mm (2.1 in)
July 57 mm (2.2 in)

A   B   C   D   E   F   G   H   I   J   K   L

### THE EMERALD ISLE
Ireland gets its nickname, "The Emerald Isle", from the lush green grass that thrives in the island's mild and wet climate. This pasture makes excellent grazing land for cattle, and so dairy produce and beef are major products in a land where agriculture has always been the main industry. The beauty of the landscape, particularly its dramatic west coast, has also made Ireland a major tourist destination.

*North Yorkshire coastline, England.*

### LANDSCAPE
The landscape of the British Isles varies greatly within a small area. High, craggy mountains in northern England, Scotland, Wales, and Ireland contrast with the flat Fens (marshlands) of East Anglia and the rolling green fields of southern England. Three-quarters of the land is used for farming, and the crops grown vary from region to region, depending on the climate and soil.

# UNITED KINGDOM

FOR A SMALL COUNTRY, the United Kingdom (UK) has had a huge influence on world affairs. At one time it controlled a vast empire, which is why English is now spoken across the globe. The Industrial Revolution of the late 1700s, which brought large-scale factory production, began here before spreading worldwide. Today many of the UK's traditional industries have declined. This highly urban society is now more reliant on service industries, such as banking and insurance, while huge reserves of oil in the North Sea meet much of its energy needs.

UNITED KINGDOM

## UNITED KINGDOM

**Capital city:** London

**Area:** 244,820 sq km (94,525 sq miles)

**Population:** 59,300,000

**Official language:** English

**Major religions:** Christian 60%, Muslim 3%, Hindu 1%, other 36%

**Government:** Multi-party democracy

**Currency:** Pound sterling

**Adult literacy rate:** 99%

**Life expectancy:** 77 years

**People per doctor:** 500

**Televisions:** 645 per 1,000 people

### A MULTICULTURAL SOCIETY

Since the 1950s, the UK has become an increasingly multicultural society. Large numbers of people from the UK's former colonies in Africa, the West Indies, and the Indian Subcontinent have made their home here, establishing their own distinctive communities and enriching British life with their culture and traditions.

EDINBURGH

The beautiful city of Edinburgh lies on the chilly east coast of Scotland. Perched on a hill, Edinburgh Castle looks out over a city of winding medieval streets and splendid Georgian townhouses. The city is home to a major international arts festival held every summer.

*Street performers at the Edinburgh Festival.*

**Visitor numbers to 7 of the top UK tourist sites**

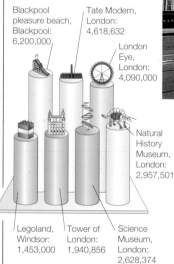

Blackpool pleasure beach, Blackpool: 6,200,000

Tate Modern, London: 4,618,632

London Eye, London: 4,090,000

Natural History Museum, London: 2,957,501

Legoland, Windsor: 1,453,000

Tower of London: 1,940,856

Science Museum, London: 2,628,374

*Red London buses rush past the Houses of Parliament, home of the United Kingdom's government.*

## LONDON

Founded by the Romans in AD 43, London is now a city of 7 million people, and is one of the largest cities in Europe. It is one of the world's leading centres of culture, finance, and tourism. Each year millions of people visit London to sample its theatres, museums, and historic buildings. Tourism is now a major industry throughout the whole of the UK. Places such as the west coast of Scotland and the historic cities of Bath and York attract thousands of tourists.

## HOMES

Many people in the UK live in suburbs on the outskirts of towns and cities. Suburbs offer a cleaner environment, more space, and transport links, making commuting to jobs in city centres possible. British life is closely centred on the home, which most people aim to buy. Houses tend to be more popular than flats, and gardening or home improvements are popular leisure activities.

**Where people live**

90% live in the city.

10% in the country.

**Typical styles of housing in the UK**

*1960s apartment block, or flats, with communal garden at the front.*

*Victorian terraced house, 1880s.*

*Semi-detached house, 1930s.*

*Detached house, 1980s.*

## WELSH MINING

Wales was until recently a major supplier of coal, and many towns and villages depended on the mines for their existence. But the coal industry has now been dismantled and large amounts of coal are imported, so that mines all over the UK have closed down. Wales especially was badly affected, leading to high unemployment in former mining areas. Some towns, however, have succeeded in attracting new industries and the beautiful mountainous scenery brings increasing numbers of tourists.

### SPORT

Sport is close to the hearts of many British people. Football (soccer) and rugby are generally played in the winter, and cricket and golf are popular in the summer months. Rugby, cricket, and golf – now played all over the world – originated in the UK, and the rules of football developed from games played in English boys' schools.

*Hat made from Welsh wool.*

*Scottish tartan scarf*

*Waistcoat made from Irish linen.*

### NATIONAL IDENTITIES

The UK's government is based at Westminster in London, England, but a separate Scottish Parliament and Welsh Assembly – both with certain "devolved" powers – were approved by referendum and were first elected in May 1999. Strong national identities are also deeply rooted through cultural and historic ties as well as by traditional arts, crafts and customs.

## INDUSTRY

Heavy industry once supplied many jobs in the UK, but this pattern has changed. Now light engineering products, machinery, cars, and weapons are the major exports, and large numbers of people are employed in financial and service industries. These have helped an economy that was flagging, partly because the UK has to import so much of its food and raw materials. Many powerful multinational companies, with offices throughout the world, are also based here.

*Call centres let firms make savings by taking away the need to staff a network of branches.*

### FINANCE

Each day more currency changes hands in London than in any other city in the world. The City of London, or the "square mile" as it is also known, contains more than 500 banks, attracted to the capital because of its leading role in world finance. This situation partly stems from the former importance of the British Empire, but today it is more to do with the city's convenient location – midway between Tokyo and New York, the other main world financial centres – and the expertise in banking and financial services built up over many years.

*The Lloyd's Insurance Building in the heart of the City of London.*

## NORTHERN IRELAND

Since the 1960s Northern Ireland and its capital, Belfast (above), have suffered violent conflict. The Protestant community, descended from British settlers, wants to stay in the UK, while Irish Catholics, who have been discriminated against in jobs and housing, wish to join the Republic of Ireland. Both sides have kept up terrorist campaigns, and the Catholic Irish Republican Army have bombed the British mainland. A peace agreement was signed on Good Friday in April 1998, but getting the two communities to share political power has proved difficult.

*Find out more*
COAL MINING: *96, 114, 162*
ETHNIC MIX: *81*
EUROPEAN CITIES: *80*
SERVICE INDUSTRIES: *281*

# IRELAND

THE GREEN PASTURES of Ireland are kept fertile by the country's mild, wet climate. Ireland was once ruled by Britain. In 1922, southern Ireland – which makes up about two-thirds of the island – became an independent nation, while Northern Ireland remained part of the United Kingdom. Natural resources are few and traditionally much of the population was employed in agriculture. However a dramatic growth in tourism and light industry has radically altered Irish working habits and has turned the country into one of Europe's recent economic success stories.

| IRELAND | |
|---|---|
| **Capital city:** Dublin | |
| **Area:** 70,280 sq km (27,135 sq miles) | |
| **Population:** 4,000,000 | |
| **Official languages:** Irish, English | |
| **Major religions:** Christian 91%, other 9% | |
| **Government:** Multi-party democracy | |
| **Currency:** Euro | |
| **Adult literacy rate:** 99% | |
| **Life expectancy:** 77 years | |
| **People per doctor:** 500 | |
| **Televisions:** 417 per 1,000 people | |

## RELIGIOUS LIFE

The Irish are a devout people and the Catholic Church plays an important role in daily life. Religious processions are held regularly, and shrines, many dedicated to the Virgin Mary (Jesus's mother), are dotted around the country. As well as running schools and hospitals, the Church has an influence on the social life of the country and opposes abortion and birth control. Divorce was illegal in Ireland until 1995.

### IRISH PUBS
Much social life in Ireland centres on the pub, or bar, where people meet to drink, chat, and exchange news. Stories from Irish history are told through songs, and bars are often alive with the sound of folk music. Irish stout – a strong, dark beer with a creamy, pale head – is the favourite drink. One of Europe's largest breweries is in Dublin and was opened by the Guinness family 200 years ago.

Bustling O'Connell Street is Dublin's major roadway.

## DUBLIN

The capital of Ireland, Dublin, is steeped in the country's history. This compact city was the focus for the revolt against British rule and it was here, in 1922, that the Irish state was born. In recent years, Dublin has attracted manufacturing and service industries, as well as many people from other parts of the country that have come here in search of work.

### RACEHORSES
The lush pastures of Ireland provide excellent grazing land for racehorses. These fine Irish thoroughbreds are world famous and frequently win major international races. The animals, bred on stud farms, are valuable sources of income for the Irish economy. Buying and selling horses is also popular, and country horse fairs are a familiar sight.

*Many Irish peat bogs are a distinctive domed shape.*

*Over thousands of years, mud and plants compress to form peat.*

*The peat is cut out in blocks and then stacked and left to dry.*

*Peat is still gathered by hand in many parts of Ireland.*

## PEAT

Ireland has few natural resources, such as coal or oil, that produce energy. What it does have are huge peat bogs. Peat consists of dead, rotted plants that have been compressed and can be burned as fuel. Some villages have their own peat supplies, and there are also vast government-owned areas that are dug out by mechanical cutters. These provide fuel for large power stations that generate electricity.

*Find out more*
BEER-BREWING: *117*
COAL AND OIL: *96, 152, 162*
NORTHERN IRELAND: *89*
RELIGIONS: *274–275*

# THE LOW COUNTRIES

THE THREE COUNTRIES IN THIS REGION – Belgium, the Netherlands, and Luxembourg – are known as the Low Countries because much of their land is flat and low-lying. The Low Countries are also called "Benelux" after the customs union they formed in 1948. The Benelux union allows the free flow of goods between the three countries, although each keeps its own tax system. These are the most densely populated countries in Europe, yet their people generally enjoy a high standard of living. Although the region's traditional heavy industries, such as coal mining, are declining, they are being replaced by modern, manufacturing industries and service activities, such as banking and administration.

**THINGS TO LOOK FOR ON THE MAP**

**Longest river:** Meuse, France/Belgium/Netherlands, 901 km (560 miles) *Map J8*

**Highest point:** Botrange, Belgium, 694 m (2,277 ft) *Map J10*

**Largest lake:** Ijsselmeer, Netherlands, 1,210 sq km (467 sq miles) *Map I5*

NETHERLANDS

**De Bilt, Netherlands**
☀ Jan 2°C (36°F)
☀ July 18°C (64°F)
🌧 Jan 68 mm (3 in)
🌧 July 77 mm (3 in)

BELGIUM

**Luxembourg, Luxembourg**
☀ Jan 1°C (33°F)
☀ July 18°C (64°F)
🌧 Jan 61 mm (2 in)
🌧 July 60 mm (2 in)

LUXEMBOURG

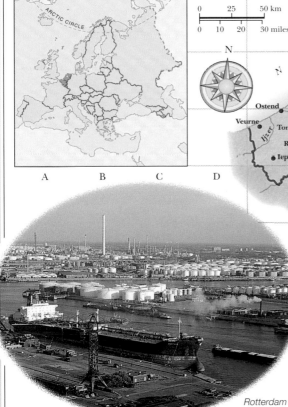

*Rotterdam is one of the world's busiest ports.*

## RIVERS

Some of Europe's most important rivers flow through these countries, linking the interior of the region with the coast. The most useful rivers for transport and trade are the Rhine, Mosel, and Meuse. At the mouth of the River Rhine stands the port of Rotterdam. Stretching for 20 km (12 miles) along the river, the port can handle 300 cargo ships at a time. Canals are also important for linking the ports with the rivers and inland areas.

## FARMLAND

The region's flat plains are used for grazing dairy cattle and for growing flowers and vegetables. Much of the farmland has been reclaimed from the sea by enclosing an area with earth barriers, called dykes, and draining the water from it. The only areas of high land are the forested Ardennes Mountains which run across the south of Belgium and into Luxembourg.

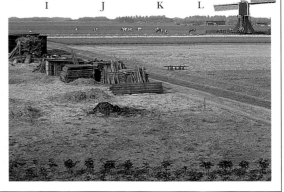

NETHERLANDS

# NETHERLANDS

THIS SMALL, DENSELY POPULATED country is also referred to as Holland, the name of two of its provinces. In the 16th and 17th centuries, Dutch merchants and sailors travelled far and wide, trading in gold and spices. The empire they established stretched from southeast Asia to the Caribbean. Trade is still of great importance to the Netherlands today, since several large international companies are Dutch, and exports make up about half the country's income. The Dutch are known for their tolerance and for their liberal social attitudes.

**NETHERLANDS**

**Capital cities:** Amsterdam, The Hague

**Area:** 41,526 sq km (16,033 sq miles)

**Population:** 16,100,000

**Official language:** Dutch

**Major religions:** Christian 63%, Muslim 3%, other 34%

**Government:** Multi-party democracy

**Currency:** Euro

**Adult literacy rate:** 97%

**Life expectancy:** 78 years

**People per doctor:** 303

**Televisions:** 543 per 1,000 people

## AMSTERDAM
This historic city is the capital of the Netherlands and is much visited by tourists. In the 17th century, Amsterdam was a centre of world trade. Merchants built the network of canals which crisscross the city and the tall, narrow houses which line the canals. Today, Amsterdam is a world centre for diamond cutting and polishing.

### CYCLING
The extreme flatness of the Dutch countryside makes cycling one of the easiest and most popular ways of getting about. Country areas have long-distance cycle routes, clearly signposted and shown on maps. Town centres are planned for bicycles rather than for motor cars. The lack of traffic means that more people can live in town centres, and so small, family-run shops are still thriving businesses.

More than half a million people in Amsterdam use a bicycle to travel to school or work.

Tulips were first brought to the Netherlands from Turkey in the 1630s, as much for their edible bulbs as for their flowers.

Asian lily bulb

Gladioli bulbs

### AGRICULTURE
The Dutch have developed intensive farming methods to get the most from their limited but fertile land. Among the main crops grown are potatoes, barley, and salad vegetables, such as lettuce and tomatoes. Bulbs and flowers are probably the Netherlands' most famous export, particularly tulips. Other major exports are meat and dairy products, including cheeses, such as Gouda and Edam.

**Making a polder**

Earth dykes are built around a shallow area of water.

A mat of woven twigs is laid across the land surface.

A plane sows the seeds of reeds which grow up through the twigs.

The reeds are burned down. Their ashes are dug into the soil.

Years 1–2
The water is gradually drained off the land and pumped away.

Years 3–6

### ETHNIC MIX
Many people from the former Dutch colonies in southeast Asia settled in the Netherlands in the 1940s and 1950s. They were followed in the 1960s by a flow of foreign workers from southern Europe, Turkey, and Morocco. Immigrants now make up more than a fifth of the population of the Netherland's major cities. Most have full Dutch citizenship. The Dutch pride themselves on their policy of welcoming immigrants and refugees.

## LAND RECLAMATION
Year 7

About a third of the Netherlands is land which has been reclaimed from the sea. These areas of land are called polders. Most of the reclaimed land is used for crop production and dairy farming, although about 25 per cent is set aside for housing, roads, and open spaces. Since so much of the land lies at or below sea-level, flooding is a serious problem. Huge barrier dams are built to keep the sea at bay, and water levels are monitored.

Year 8

Only eight years since it was beneath the sea, the land is now ready to be used for farming and for building houses and roads.

*Find out more*
CYCLING: *192*
ETHNIC MIX: *81*
POPULATION DENSITY: *80*
TRADE: *280–281*

# BELGIUM

BELGIUM IS A FAIRLY NEW country that became independent from its Dutch rulers in 1830. Its current borders were only settled in 1919. The country is split in two by the valley of the River Meuse. To the north lie flat, fertile plains stretching to the coast. A thriving textile industry grew up here in the 16th century around cities such as Bruges, which is still known for its lace-making. To the south lie the Ardennes Mountains, a region of poor soil and scattered farms.

| BELGIUM | |
|---|---|
| **Capital city:** Brussels | |
| **Area:** 30,510 sq km (11,780 sq miles) | |
| **Population:** 10,300,000 | |
| **Official languages:** Dutch, French, and German | |
| **Major religions:** Christian 88%, Muslim 2%, other 10% | |
| **Government:** Multi-party democracy | |
| **Currency:** Euro | |
| **Adult literacy rate:** 99% | |
| **Life expectancy:** 79 years | |
| **People per doctor:** 256 | |
| **Televisions:** 510 per 1,000 people | |

| LUXEMBOURG | |
|---|---|
| **Capital city:** Luxembourg | |
| **Area:** 2,585 sq km (998 sq miles) | |
| **Population:** 453,000 | |
| **Official language:** Letzeburgish | |
| **Major religions:** Christian 99%, other 1% | |
| **Government:** Multi-party democracy | |
| **Currency:** Euro | |
| **Adult literacy rate:** 99% | |
| **Life expectancy:** 78 years | |
| **People per doctor:** 400 | |
| **Televisions:** 391 per 1,000 people | |

## LANGUAGES

Three languages are spoken in Belgium. People in the southern part of the country, close to the border with France, speak French. North of Brussels, most people speak Flemish, a dialect of Dutch. In the far east, the official language is German. In Brussels, most people speak French, but Dutch is also widely spoken.

**Main languages**

BELGIUM

☐ Dutch
☐ French
☐ German

*The three languages Dutch, French, and German are spoken in Belgium.*

*The medieval Grand Place is at the heart of Brussels.*

## BRUSSELS

Brussels is the capital of Belgium and the centre of government and trade. It is also an important international city. As a centre of the Benelux union, Brussels has a long history of administering international relations. The city is now home to the administrative centre of the European Union.

Chips

Mussels

## FOOD AND DRINK

Belgian food is a mixture of French and Flemish influences. Soup is very popular and many regions have their own local recipes. A speciality is mussels and chips, which can be eaten in an expensive restaurant or bought from a street stall.

*A Brussels newsstand sells papers in three languages.*

## INDUSTRY

Belgium's traditonal heavy industries, such as coal mining and steel-making are now in decline. They are being replaced by newer industries such as the manufacture of chemicals and electrical equipment (shown here), and service industries, such as banking and administration. Two out of three Belgians now work in service industries.

# LUXEMBOURG

SQUEEZED BETWEEN Germany, France, and Belgium, the Grand Duchy of Luxembourg is a tiny state. Living standards are among the highest in Europe and it is famous as a centre of international banking and finance. Despite its small size, Luxembourg plays a vital part in the European Union. Home to headquarters of major EU institutions, it hosts the European Court of Justice and the secretariat of the European parliament.

*This tiny country has been at the crossroads of Europe for centuries. Walled towns and castles, built to offer protection from passing armies, are still dotted across the landscape.*

## TOURISM

As part of the Ardennes Mountain region, much of Luxembourg's countryside is hilly and forested. Tourism is a growing industry as visitors come to discover the unspoilt scenery with its picturesque castles and ancient walled towns.

***Find out more***
EUROPEAN PLAIN: *79*
EUROPEAN UNION: *81, 273*
RICH AND POOR: *278–279*
SERVICE INDUSTRIES: *281*

# GERMANY

LYING AT THE HEART OF EUROPE, Germany is one of the world's wealthiest nations. In its present form, Germany is also one of the newest countries in Europe. After World War II, it was divided into two separate countries – West Germany, a western-style democracy, and East Germany, a communist state. In 1990, the two parts of Germany were reunited as one country. The eastern part is now struggling to overcome the legacy of economic decay and pollution left by its communist past.

| GERMANY | |
|---|---|
| **Capital city:** Berlin | |
| **Area:** 357,021 sq km (137,846 sq miles) | |
| **Population:** 82,500,000 | |
| **Official language:** German | |
| **Major religions:** Christian 67%, Muslim 3%, other 30% | |
| **Government:** Multi-party democracy | |
| **Currency:** Euro | |
| **Adult literacy rate:** 99% | |
| **Life expectancy:** 78 years | |
| **People per doctor:** 303 | |
| **Televisions:** 580 per 1,000 people | |

### EDUCATION
Young German children go to nursery school, then to primary school. At the age of 10, they move to either a *Gymnasium* (grammar school), a *Hauptschule* (secondary school) or a *Realschule* (middle school). These last two types of schools specialize in training students in technical skills.

## RECENT HISTORY
The reunification of Germany took place on October 3, 1990. Growing protests in East Germany, and the collapse of communism in the USSR, finally led the government to make changes. The Berlin Wall, symbol of Germany's division, was demolished, and East Germans started to flood into West Berlin. The unified city has now regained its status as the country's capital and the seat of parliament.

## FEDERAL STATES
Germany has only been a single country since 1871. Before that, it was divided into many independent states. Today, Germany is still made up of 16 states, or *Länder* (shown left), with a federal system of government, similar to the USA. Each *Land* has its own state government and controls local issues such as education. Many Germans still have a strong sense of regional identity, thinking of themselves as Bavarians, for example, first, and Germans second.

HAMBURG
SCHLESWIG-HOLSTEIN
BREMEN
BERLIN
MECKLENBURG-WEST POMMERANIA
LOWER SAXONY
BRANDENBURG
NORTH RHINE-WESTPHALIA
SAXONY-ANHALT
SAXONY
THURINGIA
HESSE
RHINELAND-PALATINATE
SAARLAND
BAVARIA
BADEN-WURTTEMBERG

*Many provincial cities in Germany were formerly the capitals of independent states. Dresden, shown here, is now the capital of Saxony, a region that was once part of the former East Germany.*

### THE ENVIRONMENT
Thanks to the success of the Green Party, Germans are well aware of the need to protect the environment. There are very strict controls on pollution – Germany has led the way in fitting catalytic converters to cars and in using lead-free petrol. Most houses have three separate dustbins for different types of waste, so that household rubbish can be recycled.

*Paper waste is collected separately from people's houses and taken to a refuse site like this one for recycling.*

### FOOD AND DRINK
The annual Munich *Oktoberfest* is the biggest of the many beer festivals held all over Germany. It lasts for two weeks and attracts millions of beer-drinkers. Beer is Germany's national drink, with wine a close second. Popular types of food include bread, pastries, pretzels, cold meats, and cheese. *Wurst* (sausage) is another German speciality. Many regions make their own local sausages.

*Wine from the Rhine Valley*

*Pretzels*

*Smoked cheese*

*Blue-veined cheese*

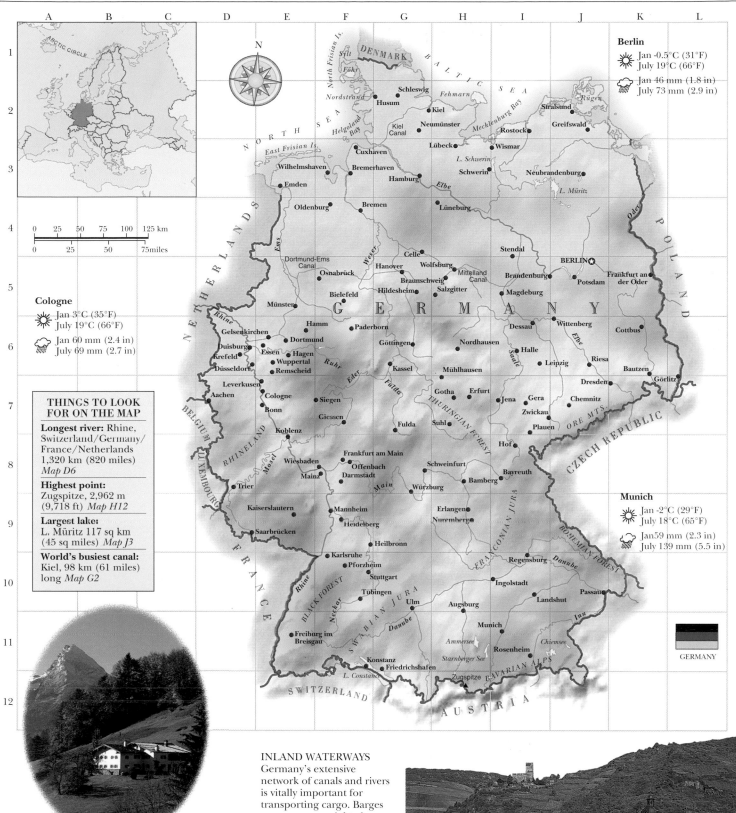

A B C D E F G H I J K L

**Berlin**
☀ Jan -0.5°C (31°F)
July 19°C (66°F)
☂ Jan 46 mm (1.8 in)
July 73 mm (2.9 in)

ARCTIC CIRCLE

**Cologne**
☀ Jan 3°C (35°F)
July 19°C (66°F)
☂ Jan 60 mm (2.4 in)
July 69 mm (2.7 in)

DENMARK

BALTIC SEA

North Frisian Is.
Sylt
Föhr
Nordstrand
Husum
Schleswig
Fehmarn
Rügen
Stralsund
Kiel
Greifswald
Neumünster
Kiel Canal
Rostock
Wismar
Lübeck
Neubrandenburg
Cuxhaven
Bremerhaven
Schwerin
L. Schwerin
L. Müritz
Wilhelmshaven
Hamburg
Emden
Elbe
Oldenburg
Bremen
Lüneburg
Celle
Stendal
BERLIN ✪
Frankfurt an der Oder
Hanover
Wolfsburg
Brandenburg
Potsdam
Osnabrück
Braunschweig
Mittelland Canal
Magdeburg
Bielefeld
Hildesheim
Salzgitter
Münster
Wittenberg
Cottbus
Hamm
Paderborn
Dessau
Gelsenkirchen
Göttingen
Nordhausen
Halle
Riesa
Dortmund
Leipzig
Bautzen
Duisburg
Essen
Hagen
Kassel
Mühlhausen
Dresden
Görlitz
Krefeld
Wuppertal
Remscheid
Gotha
Erfurt
Düsseldorf
Leverkusen
Siegen
Jena
Gera
Chemnitz
Aachen
Cologne
Zwickau
Bonn
Giessen
Suhl
Plauen
ORE MTS.
Fulda
Hof
THURINGIAN FOREST
CZECH REPUBLIC
Frankfurt am Main
Schweinfurt
Koblenz
Offenbach
Bayreuth
Wiesbaden
Darmstadt
**Munich**
☀ Jan -2°C (29°F)
July 18°C (65°F)
☂ Jan 59 mm (2.3 in)
July 139 mm (5.5 in)
Mainz
Würzburg
Bamberg
Trier
Erlangen
Nuremberg
Kaiserslautern
Mannheim
Heidelberg
FRANCONIAN JURA
BOHEMIAN FOREST
Saarbrücken
Heilbronn
Regensburg
Danube
Karlsruhe
Pforzheim
Stuttgart
Ingolstadt
Passau
Landshut
Tübingen
Ulm
Augsburg
Inn
Freiburg im Breisgau
SWABIAN JURA
Danube
Munich
GERMANY
Konstanz
Ammersee
Rosenheim
Chiemsee
Friedrichshafen
Starnberger See
L. Constance
Zugspitze
BAVARIAN ALPS
SWITZERLAND
AUSTRIA

NETHERLANDS
Rhine
Ems
Dortmund-Ems Canal
Weser
BELGIUM
LUXEMBOURG
RHINELAND
Mosel
Ruhr
Eder
Fulda
Main
Neckar
BLACK FOREST
FRANCE

POLAND
Oder
Elbe
Saale

**THINGS TO LOOK FOR ON THE MAP**
**Longest river:** Rhine, Switzerland/Germany/France/Netherlands 1,320 km (820 miles) *Map D6*
**Highest point:** Zugspitze, 2,962 m (9,718 ft) *Map H12*
**Largest lake:** L. Müritz 117 sq km (45 sq miles) *Map J3*
**World's busiest canal:** Kiel, 98 km (61 miles) long *Map G2*

0 25 50 75 100 125 km
0 25 50 75 miles

**THE LANDSCAPE**
From the flat, fertile plains of the north, to the snow-capped peaks of the Bavarian Alps, shown here, the German landscape is extremely varied. One of the country's most famous and most picturesque regions is the Black Forest in the southwest, which gets its name from its dark coniferous trees.

**INLAND WATERWAYS**
Germany's extensive network of canals and rivers is vitally important for transporting cargo. Barges are a common sight along rivers, such as the Rhine, carrying goods around Germany and into other parts of Europe. In eastern Germany, the River Oder is an important waterway for taking goods into Poland. On land, Germany has excellent motorways and a fast, efficient railway system.

## RELIGION
In the 16th century, a German monk, Martin Luther, attacked the teachings of the Roman Catholic Church in Germany and preached his own brand of Christianity. The movement he started was called the Reformation, and his followers, Protestants. His movement gained most support in northern Germany which is still largely Protestant. Most people in southern Germany are Catholic.

*This Gutenberg Bible was printed in Germany.*

## SPORT
Many of the world's top sports stars have come from Germany, including Boris Becker in tennis, brothers Michael (shown right) and Ralf Schumacher (shown left) in motor racing, and Katja Seizinger in skiing. Football is Germany's most popular spectator sport. The West German team was outstandingly successful, winning the World Cup several times. A single, unified German squad first entered competition for the 1992 European Cup.

## NEW GERMANS
As the German economy grew, so did the need for labour. In the 1960s, thousands of people came from Turkey and former Yugoslavia to work in Germany. Life has not been easy for them. They have suffered discrimination and been refused citizenship, despite their contribution to German life. Since 1990, more than a million German-speaking immigrants have arrived from eastern Europe.

*Foreign workers often took unskilled jobs that Germans were unwilling to do.*

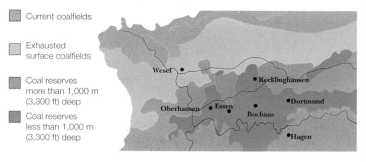

*Around a third of German workers are employed in industry.*

## THE ECONOMY
Germany's industries were completely rebuilt and modernized after World War II. Today, Germany is one of the world's leading industrial nations. This success is largely due to its very strong manufacturing industry. Germany is one of the world's top producers of trucks, ships, electrical goods, and cars, with such famous makes as Volkswagen, Mercedes, and BMW. These are exported for sale all over the world.

**Cross-section through a deep coal mine**

Coal deposits, or seams, are removed from the Earth by mining.

Surface works of coal mine

Upper layers of rock are younger and do not contain coal.

Vertical shaft leads down to the coal seams.

Seam of coal

Horizontal shafts lead to the seams where the coal is mined.

### Coalfields in the Ruhr Valley

- Current coalfields
- Exhausted surface coalfields
- Coal reserves more than 1,000 m (3,300 ft) deep
- Coal reserves less than 1,000 m (3,300 ft) deep

Wesel
Recklinghausen
Oberhausen · Essen
Dortmund
Bochum
Hagen

## THE RUHR VALLEY
The Ruhr Valley is the most heavily industrialized region in Germany, and also the most densely populated area, with many large towns and cities. In the 19th century, huge deposits of coal were discovered there. This led to the region's development as the centre of iron and steel production, vital for Germany's car industry. At first, coal was mined in the south of the coalfield where it lay near the surface. These seams are now exhausted. Today, mining is concentrated in deeper mines in the north.

### COAL MINING
The Ruhr coalfield is one of the largest in the world, producing both black coal and brown coal (lignite). Brown coal is found on the surface, but black coal has to be extracted from deep mines, like the one shown here. Today, the Ruhr region faces serious problems. Coal supplies are running out, and other sources of fuel are being found, leaving many people without jobs.

*Find out more*
BREAK-UP OF USSR: *136*
COAL MINING: *114, 162*
EUROPEAN IMMIGRANTS: *81*
PROTESTANTS: *274*

# FRANCE

THE LARGEST COUNTRY IN western Europe, France includes the island of Corsica in the Mediterranean Sea. Two major mountain chains, the Pyrenees to the south and the Alps to the east, provide dramatic natural borders to neighbouring countries. Several rivers, including the Loire, the Rhône, and the Seine, are important for transport and irrigation of farmland. The tiny countries of Monaco and Andorra lie tucked in the south.

**LANDSCAPE**
The landscape and climate of France varies from north to south. Northern France has gently rolling farmland with cool, wet weather, while the middle of the country is dominated by the rugged hills of the Central Massif. The south, with its Mediterranean climate, is dry and warm with lavender fields a typical scene in the region of Provence.

FRANCE

**THINGS TO LOOK FOR ON THE MAP**

**Longest river:** Loire, 1,020 km (634 miles) *Map D5*

**Highest point:** Mont Blanc, 4,807 m (15,772 ft) *Map J6*

**Largest lake:** L. Geneva, 580 sq km (224 sq miles) *Map I6*

**Paris**
- Jan 6°C (43°F)
- July 23°C (73°F)
- Jan 43 mm (1.7 in)
- July 11 mm (0.4 in)

**Lyon**
- Jan 2°C (36°F)
- July 21°C (70°F)
- Jan 52 mm (2.1 in)
- July 56 mm (2.2 in)

**Marseille**
- Jan 5°C (42°F)
- July 23°C (73°F)
- Jan 43 mm (1.7 in)
- July 11 mm (0.4 in)

MONACO

ANDORRA

## FRENCH HISTORY

For hundreds of years, France was ruled by kings and queens. They built magnificent palaces and castles, such as Chenonceau, along the River Loire. All this was swept away in the revolution of 1789. The monarchy was overthrown and King Louis XVI and his queen, Marie Antoinette, were publicly beheaded. In 1792, France became a republic. Despite some efforts to restore the monarchy, France remains a republic.

# FRANCE

THE INFLUENCE OF French culture, fashion, and food can be seen all over the world. As a leading industrialized nation, and founder member of the European Union, France also plays a key role in world affairs. Since the end of the Second World War, the country has become Europe's major agricultural producer and exporter with main crops of wheat, sugar beet, sunflower seeds, apples, and grapes used for wine. France boasts the world's fastest train, the TGV, which can travel at speeds up to 515 km/h (320 mph).

The Eiffel Tower is 300 m (984 ft) high and was built for the Paris World Exposition of 1889. The observation gallery can hold 800 people.

The second level is reached by lift or by climbing a further 700 steps.

Visitors reach the first level by lift or by climbing up 360 steps.

## CITY OF CULTURE
Situated on the banks of the River Seine, Paris is the capital of France and its cultural and political centre. One of the world's most visited cities, its famous landmarks include the Eiffel Tower, the Louvre, and the cathedral of Notre Dame. There are also many museums, shops, and restaurants. Each spring, the world's leading fashion designers arrive in Paris to present their latest collections.

## VILLAGE LIFE
Although many French people have moved from the countryside to live in the cities, village life is still important. Throughout France villages have kept a strong identity, with local festivals, fairs, and weekly food markets. Life centres around the village square where people often gather to play *boules*, the national game of France.

## INDUSTRY
One of the world's leading industrial nations, France has large manufacturing, steel, and chemical industries, and competes at the forefront of engineering and technology. The country is a major producer of cars and aircraft, such as this Airbus in its Toulouse factory. France has a large nuclear industry which generates over 75 per cent of the country's electrical power. With millions of visitors a year, tourism is also important to the economy.

## FOOD OF FRANCE
Famous for its excellent food and fine wines, France has such a range of climates and landscapes that it can produce many different types of food. Each region has its own speciality dish. Central France, for example, is famous for *boeuf bourguignon* (beef in red wine), while Marseille on the Mediterranean coast specializes in *bouillabaisse* (fish soup with garlic). France is also known for its breads and pastries, such as *croissants*, and different types of cheeses.

Crottins de Chavignol cheese

Croissant

Garlic

French people relax with friends in a café or restaurant.

## A FINE FRAGRANCE
Some of the world's finest perfumes, or scents, come from France. Most perfume is made in Grasse in southern France where fields of lavender, roses, and jasmine are grown. Their essential oils are extracted and blended to make a variety of scents. As many as 300 oils may be used in one perfume.

Oil from the lavender flower is an important ingredient in many perfumes, as well as in soaps and bath oils.

| FRANCE | |
| --- | --- |
| Capital city: | Paris |
| Area: | 547,030 sq km (211,208 sq miles) |
| Population: | 60,100,000 |
| Official language: | French |
| Major religions: | Christian 90%, Muslim 8%, Buddhist 1%, Jewish 1% |
| Government: | Multi-party democracy |
| Currency: | Euro |
| Adult literacy rate: | 99% |
| Life expectancy: | 79 years |
| People per doctor: | 303 |
| Televisions: | 601 per 1,000 people |

| MONACO | |
| --- | --- |
| Capital city: | Monaco |
| Area: | 1.95 sq km (0.75 sq miles) |
| Population: | 32,130 |
| Official language: | French |
| Major religions: | Christian 95%, other 5% |
| Government: | Multi-party democracy |
| Currency: | Euro |
| Adult literacy rate: | 99% |
| Life expectancy: | 79 years |
| People per doctor: | 152 |
| Televisions: | 768 per 1,000 people |

| ANDORRA | |
| --- | --- |
| Capital city: | Andorra la Vella |
| Area: | 468 sq km (181 sq miles) |
| Population: | 69,150 |
| Official language: | Catalan |
| Major religions: | Christian 94%, other 6% |
| Government: | Multi-party democracy |
| Currency: | Euro |
| Adult literacy rate: | 99% |
| Life expectancy: | 83 years |
| People per doctor: | 385 |
| Televisions: | 391 per 1,000 people |

FRANCE

## WINE-MAKING

France produces about a fifth of the world's wine, and vineyards are a feature of the French landscape. Wine is made from the juice of black or white grapes (which are actually red or pale green in colour). Although juice was once extracted by people trampling on the picked grapes, today's methods are generally more modern. There are several processes in the production of wine, including fermentation, which mixes a natural yeast on the grape skin with the sugar in the grape. Pressing grapes using a modern press is shown here.

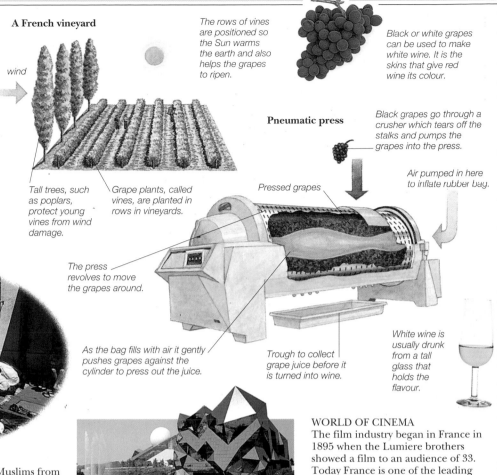

**A French vineyard**

The rows of vines are positioned so the Sun warms the earth and also helps the grapes to ripen.

Black or white grapes can be used to make white wine. It is the skins that give red wine its colour.

wind

Tall trees, such as poplars, protect young vines from wind damage.

Grape plants, called vines, are planted in rows in vineyards.

**Pneumatic press**

Black grapes go through a crusher which tears off the stalks and pumps the grapes into the press.

Air pumped in here to inflate rubber bag.

Pressed grapes

The press revolves to move the grapes around.

As the bag fills with air it gently pushes grapes against the cylinder to press out the juice.

Trough to collect grape juice before it is turned into wine.

White wine is usually drunk from a tall glass that holds the flavour.

### IMMIGRATION

France has about 6 million immigrants, mainly Muslims from Morocco, Tunisia, and Algeria – France's former colonies in North Africa. People also arrive from Italy, Spain, and Poland in the hope of finding work. Immigrants often face problems such as discrimination, unemployment, and poor housing.

### WORLD OF CINEMA

The film industry began in France in 1895 when the Lumiere brothers showed a film to an audience of 33. Today France is one of the leading makers of internationally acclaimed films. The crystal-shaped Kinemax in Poitiers has 10 different cinemas and one of the biggest screens in Europe.

# MONACO

A TINY COUNTRY ON THE Mediterranean coast, Monaco lies close to the Italian border. The heart of the country is the sophisticated city of Monte-Carlo, famous for its gambling casinos and motor racing Grand Prix. Monaco is an independent principality, ruled for more than 700 years by the Grimaldi family. Only a small part of the country's population is originally from Monaco; more than half the people are citizens of France.

### TOURISM

Monaco's warm climate and glamorous image attracts thousands of tourists. Many rich people, with yachts moored in the old harbour, also choose to live there because it has a low rate of tax. Monaco is also a major international business centre.

# ANDORRA

HIGH IN THE PYRENEES MOUNTAINS, on the border between France and Spain, nestles the country of Andorra. The country is nominally ruled by the president of France and the bishop of Urgel in northeastern Spain. Catalan is the official language, although many people also speak French and Spanish. The country's only large town is the capital city of Andorra la Vella.

### THE PYRENEES

The main source of income in Andorra is tourism. Many people come to ski in the Pyrenees, although the only road between France and Spain is often blocked by heavy snow in winter.

*Find out more*

ETHNIC GROUPS: *81*
EUROPEAN CITIES: *80*
EUROPEAN UNION: *81, 273*
FORMER COLONIES: *208–212*

# SPAIN AND PORTUGAL

SPAIN AND PORTUGAL OCCUPY a peninsula of land in southwest Europe called Iberia. For hundreds of years the area was ruled by the Moors, North African Muslims, who introduced orange trees to the region. Iberia is separated from the rest of Europe by the Pyrenees Mountains in the north, and from Africa by the Strait of Gibraltar to the south. Both countries share a warm Mediterranean climate and have economies based on tourism. Fishing off the Atlantic coast is also important.

## LANDSCAPE

The landscape of Iberia is dominated by a vast, almost treeless, central plain called the *Meseta*. In summer, it is so hot here that nearly all the streams dry up. In winter, the temperature often falls below freezing and blizzards are common. Rain is in such short supply that farmers have to rely on irrigation to water their crops.

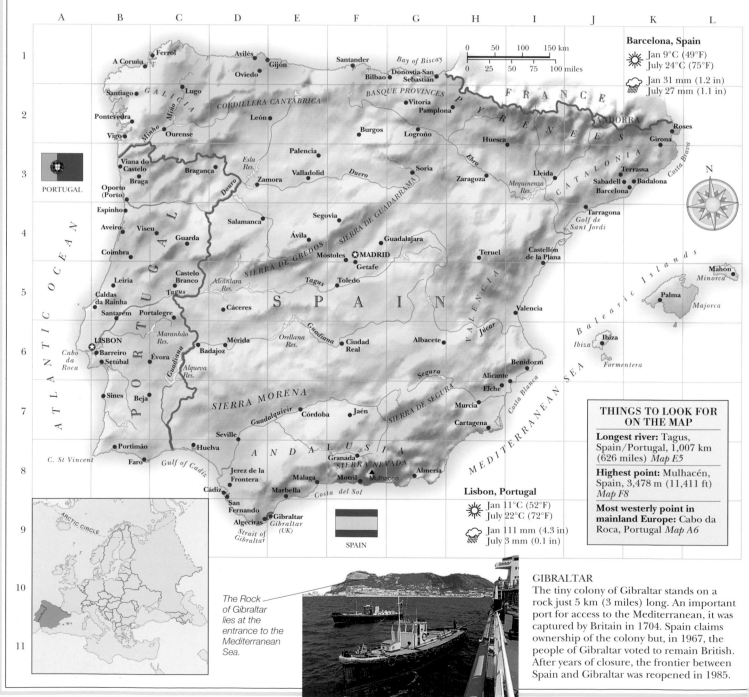

**Barcelona, Spain**
- Jan 9°C (49°F)
- July 24°C (75°F)
- Jan 31 mm (1.2 in)
- July 27 mm (1.1 in)

**Lisbon, Portugal**
- Jan 11°C (52°F)
- July 22°C (72°F)
- Jan 111 mm (4.3 in)
- July 3 mm (0.1 in)

PORTUGAL

SPAIN

### THINGS TO LOOK FOR ON THE MAP

**Longest river:** Tagus, Spain/Portugal, 1,007 km (626 miles) *Map E5*

**Highest point:** Mulhacén, Spain, 3,478 m (11,411 ft) *Map F8*

**Most westerly point in mainland Europe:** Cabo da Roca, Portugal *Map A6*

The Rock of Gibraltar lies at the entrance to the Mediterranean Sea.

## GIBRALTAR

The tiny colony of Gibraltar stands on a rock just 5 km (3 miles) long. An important port for access to the Mediterranean, it was captured by Britain in 1704. Spain claims ownership of the colony but, in 1967, the people of Gibraltar voted to remain British. After years of closure, the frontier between Spain and Gibraltar was reopened in 1985.

# SPAIN

FIESTAS AND FLAMENCO provide much of the flavour of Spain. Most Spaniards are Roman Catholic and fiestas, often to celebrate a local saint's day, include processions of people in traditional costume, music, and dancing. After a bitter civil war in 1936–39, Spain was ruled by a dictator, Francisco Franco, until 1975. His successor, King Juan Carlos I, has restored democracy. Today, Spain is a major industrial nation, with a large agricultural sector, and a booming tourist trade. These activities are mainly based near the coasts while central regions are less developed.

**CITIES OF SPAIN**
Madrid, shown here, became Spain's capital in 1561 because King Philip II liked its climate and central location. Today, the city has a population of over 4 million people, and is Spain's centre of finance and government. Barcelona is Spain's vibrant second city and the capital of Catalonia. It lies at the heart of a large industrial area in the north and was the site of the 1992 Olympic Games.

| SPAIN | |
| --- | --- |
| **Capital city:** Madrid | |
| **Area:** 504,782 sq km (194,896 sq miles) | |
| **Population:** 41,100,000 | |
| **Official language:** Spanish, Galician, Basque, Catalan | |
| **Major religions:** Christian 96%, other 4% | |
| **Government:** Multi-party democracy | |
| **Currency:** Euro | |
| **Adult literacy rate:** 98% | |
| **Life expectancy:** 78 years | |
| **People per doctor:** 303 | |
| **Televisions:** 506 per 1,000 people | |

*Fan held by flamenco dancer.*

*Wooden castanets played by dancers.*

**FLAMENCO**
Flamenco is the name given to the music and dance style developed by the gypsies of Andalusia in the 15th century. Dancers in traditional costumes, men in black and women in frilled dresses, stamp their heels and click castanets while flamenco music is played on a guitar

*The guitar originated in Spain in the 16th century. This model is a 19th century court guitar.*

## PEOPLE OF SPAIN

The Spanish are divided into regional groups, some with their own language and culture. Local languages include Catalan, Galician, and Euskera from the Basque region which stretches from northern Spain into France. The official language of Spain is Castilian, which is taught in all schools, along with either English or French. Children in Spain tend to stay up late. They have a snack called *merienda* after school, then play outside before eating a late family dinner at around 9 p.m.

## INDUSTRY

Farming and fishing used to be the basis of the Spanish economy. The country has now developed a large steel industry, centred around Barcelona, and is also an important centre for making cars. In the 1980s, many new electronics and high-tech industries were set up, often supported by money from foreign investment. Major agricultural products include cereals, olives, grapes for wine, and citrus fruits, especially oranges from around Seville.

**Top six exports**

*Figures show percentage of country's total exports*

Cars and other vehicles: 23.7%

Heavy machinery: 9.8%

Electrical goods: 7%

Chemicals: 6.5%

Textiles: 4.6%

Fruit: 3.5%

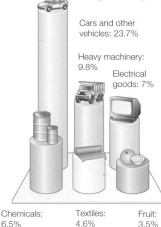

**SPANISH RESORTS**
About 50 million tourists flock to Spain each year to enjoy the Mediterranean Sea and sunshine, and to admire the churches and palaces of cities such as Barcelona and Seville. The number-one summer destination for many European tourists remains the beaches on Spain's Costa del Sol and the Balearic Islands of Majorca, Minorca and Ibiza.

*Find out more*
OLIVE GROWING: *130*
POLITICAL SYSTEMS: *270–271*
ROMAN CATHOLICS: *274*
SPANISH EMPIRE: *42*

# PORTUGAL

A NATION OF GREAT SEAFARERS, Portuguese explorers sailed the world in the 15th and 16th centuries. They claimed territories as far apart as Africa and Asia, and they also colonized Brazil. From 1932–1968 Portugal was ruled by the dictator, António Salazar, but after a military coup in 1974 the armed forces finally withdrew from politics. In 1986 Portugal joined the European Community, but it remains one of the poorest countries in western Europe. Tourism, particularly in the Algarve, is important to the economy.

| PORTUGAL | |
|---|---|
| **Capital city:** Lisbon | |
| **Area:** 92,391 sq km (35,672 sq miles) | |
| **Population:** 10,100,000 | |
| **Official language:** Portuguese | |
| **Major religions:** Christian 98%, other 2% | |
| **Government:** Multi-party democracy | |
| **Currency:** Euro | |
| **Adult literacy rate:** 93% | |
| **Life expectancy:** 76 years | |
| **People per doctor:** 312 | |
| **Televisions:** 452 per 1,000 people | |

## LISBON

The capital of Portugal, Lisbon lies at the mouth of the River Tagus. In the 15th century, Lisbon was a major port and world centre for the spice and gold trade. The Tower of Belem, shown here, sits on the site where the explorer Vasco da Gama set sail. Today, many old palaces and mansions have been converted into elegant restaurants and bars, shops, and art galleries.

## RURAL LIFE

Traditional farming methods, unchanged for centuries, are still used in many parts of Portugal. In some villages, oxen wearing carved wooden yokes still pull the ploughs. One of the country's main crops is maize, which was brought back from the Americas by Christopher Columbus in the 15th century. Other crops include olives and figs. Wine, cork, and tomatoes are exported abroad and fishing remains important along the Atlantic coast.

## CRAFTS

Traditional Portuguese handicrafts include ceramic tiles, called *azulejos* which are often used to decorate buildings. Street markets also display other local specialities, such as brightly coloured pottery, painted furniture, glassware, and porcelain. Delicate silver filigree jewellery and richly embroidered cloth from the island of Madeira are exported all over the world.

**The cork process**

*The cork oak tree grows to about 20 m (65 ft).*

*Bark has been removed from tree but will grow back over the years.*

*Workers strip cork away from the tree.*

## THE CORK INDUSTRY

Almost 10 per cent of Portugal is covered with cork oak trees, the bark of which is used to make cork products. The thick, spongy bark is expertly stripped off and left to dry. It is then steamed or boiled to soften it and pressed into sheets ready for use. Portugal is the world's leading exporter of cork for products such as stoppers, tiles, and the insides of shuttlecocks. By law, the bark is only removed every nine years so the trees can recover. Trees can provide cork for more than 100 years.

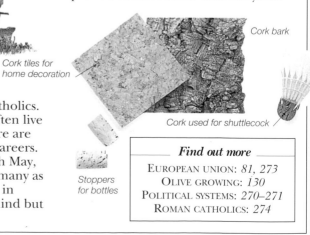

*Cork bark*

*Cork tiles for home decoration*

*Cork used for shuttlecock*

*Students celebrate the end of university.*

## THE PORTUGUESE

Most Portuguese people are Roman Catholics. Family life is very important and girls often live at home until they marry, although more are now going to university and taking up careers. The *Queima das Fitas*, a festival held each May, celebrates the end of university life. As many as 3 million Portuguese have gone abroad in search of work. Some leave families behind but send money home to support them.

*Stoppers for bottles*

*Find out more*

EUROPEAN UNION: *81, 273*
OLIVE GROWING: *130*
POLITICAL SYSTEMS: *270–271*
ROMAN CATHOLICS: *274*

# ITALY

FOR MUCH OF ITS HISTORY, Italy has been a divided land. It was first united under the ancient Romans, whose great empire spread right across Europe. However, during the Middle Ages, Italy split into many separate states and did not reunite until 1861. This boot-shaped country stretches from the glaciers and lakes of the mountainous north to the rocky Mediterranean coastline of the hot south. The two nearby Mediterranean islands of Sicily and Sardinia both belong to Italy. Just south of Sicily lies a group of islands that make up the separate country of Malta. The mainland of Italy also includes the two tiny independent states of San Marino and Vatican City.

**Milan, Italy**
Jan 2.5°C (36°F)
July 25°C (76°F)
Jan 44 mm (1.6 in)
July 64 mm (2.5 in)

**Brindisi, Italy**
Jan 9°C (48.5°F)
July 25°C (77°F)
Jan 77 mm (3 in)
July 14 mm (0.6 in)

**Valletta, Malta**
Jan 12°C (54°F)
July 25°C (78°F)
Jan 90 mm (3.5 in)
July 0 mm (0 in)

SAN MARINO

VATICAN CITY

ITALY

MALTA

### THINGS TO LOOK FOR ON THE MAP

**Longest river:** Po, 652 km (405 miles) *Map B4*

**Highest active volcano in Europe:** Mt. Etna, 3,263 m (10,705 ft) *Map H13*

**Largest lake:** L. Garda, 370 sq km (143 sq miles) *Map D3*

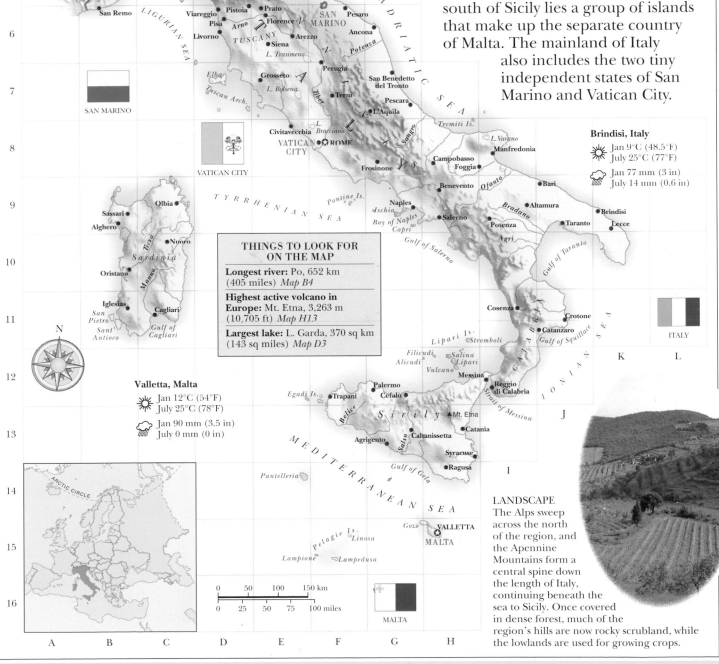

LANDSCAPE
The Alps sweep across the north of the region, and the Apennine Mountains form a central spine down the length of Italy, continuing beneath the sea to Sicily. Once covered in dense forest, much of the region's hills are now rocky scrubland, while the lowlands are used for growing crops.

0  50  100  150 km
0  25  50  75  100 miles

# ITALY

ANCIENT TRADITIONS and historic wealth have left Italy a rich legacy of art and architecture. Although Italy is today one of the world's leading industrial powers, there is a great divide between the wealthy, industrial north and the poorer, agricultural south. This economic division affects many aspects of Italian life and is one of the reasons behind the country's rapid turnover of governments. Most people throughout Italy follow the Roman Catholic religion.

## ITALY

**Capital city:** Rome
**Area:** 301,230 sq km (116,305 sq miles)
**Population:** 57,400,000
**Official language:** Italian
**Major religion:** Christian 85%, Muslim 2%, other 13%
**Government:** Multi-party democracy
**Currency:** Euro
**Adult literacy rate:** 99%
**Life expectancy:** 78 years
**People per doctor:** 233
**Televisions:** 420 per 1,000 people

## TOURISM
Some of the world's most stunning sights can be found in Italy's cities. Tourists flock to the ancient ruins of Rome, and to the palaces and churches of Florence, where the great revolution in art known as the Renaissance was born in the 15th century. The northern ski resorts and lakes are also much visited. Tourism is vital to Italy's economy.

## OPERA
The three great national passions are fast cars, football (soccer) – and opera. Opera was virtually invented in Italy and performers such as Luciano Pavarotti are household names worldwide. Italian opera is unique in being a part of everyday life, and not a pastime for the wealthy few, as it tends to be elsewhere.

*An opera performance in Verona's Roman arena.*

*Tall vines scramble up rows of posts and any available fruit trees.*

*A cereal crop such as maize is grown in a block between a row of vines and land left for grazing cattle.*

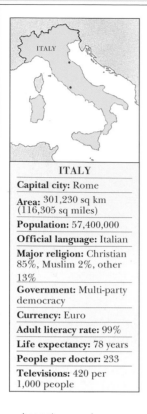

*On many small farms, a variety of different crops are grown mixed up together in what is known as polyculture. Vines, fruit, vegetables, and cereals are main crops.*

*Crops such as potatoes are grown in the soil beneath vines.*

*Vine roots reach down to a deep layer of soil.*

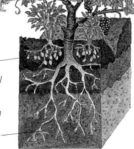

## AGRICULTURE
Small, family-run farms cover the Italian countryside, and many farmers are part-time. In the fertile northern plain surrounding the River Po, small-scale farmers get the most from their land by growing a variety of different crops close together. Cereals, fruit trees, vines, and vegetables are widely grown, and there are olive groves in the south. Italy is a leading producer of fruit, wine, and olive oil.

## INDUSTRY
Once a mainly agricultural nation, Italy is now a leading industrial country. Since it does not have many natural resources, Italy imports raw materials and uses its highly skilled workforce to turn them into manufactured goods, like the scooter shown here. Italy is a major player in industrial and product design, and fashion.

*The hard, strong-tasting Parmesan cheese is made from cow's milk in the north of Italy.*

*A popular meal is pasta with tomatoes, and often Parmesan cheese.*

*Tomatoes grow well in the warm sun around Naples.*

*Pasta comes in many shapes.*

## FAMILY MEALTIMES
To Italians, life revolves around the family, which means a large, extended network of different generations, usually living nearby. Mealtimes are important family gatherings, where the food differs from region to region. In the north, the popular pasta is often replaced by rice or polenta, made from maize flour. Olive oil and fresh vegetables are also important in Italian cooking.

*A family enjoying a lunch together of pasta and fresh vegetables on the southern Italian island of Lipari.*

*Find out more*
EUROPEAN CITIES: *80*
OLIVE GROWING: *131*
ROMAN CATHOLICS: *274*
WINE MAKING: *99*

# MALTA

DUE TO ITS STRATEGIC POSITION on Mediterranean shipping routes, Malta has been ruled by many powers over the centuries. It finally became an independent country in 1964. Perhaps because of this history, the Maltese people cling to a strong sense of national identity, mostly following Roman Catholicism and speaking their own language. The country consists of two main islands, Malta and Gozo, and the smaller island of Comino.

### MALTA

| | |
|---|---|
| **Capital city:** | Valletta |
| **Area:** | 316 sq km (122 sq miles) |
| **Population:** | 394,000 |
| **Official languages:** | Maltese and English |
| **Major religion:** | Christian 98% Other 2% |
| **Government:** | Multi-party democracy |
| **Currency:** | Maltese lira |
| **Adult literacy rate:** | 93% |
| **Life expectancy:** | 78 years |
| **People per doctor:** | 345 |
| **Televisions:** | 735 per 1,000 people |

### VATICAN CITY

| | |
|---|---|
| **Capital city:** | Vatican City |
| **Area:** | 0.44 sq km (0.17 sq miles) |
| **Population:** | 911 |
| **Official languages:** | Italian and Latin |
| **Major religion:** | Christian 100% |
| **Government:** | Ruled by the Pope |
| **Currency:** | Euro |
| **Adult literacy rate:** | 80% |
| **Life expectancy:** | 66 years |

### SAN MARINO

| | |
|---|---|
| **Capital city:** | San Marino |
| **Area:** | 61 sq km (24 sq miles) |
| **Population:** | 28,119 |
| **Official language:** | Italian |
| **Major religions:** | Christian 93%, other 7% |
| **Government:** | Multi-party democracy |
| **Currency:** | Euro |
| **Adult literacy rate:** | 99% |
| **Life expectancy:** | 81 years |

## SHIPPING

The busy Grand Harbour of Malta's capital, Valletta, is a sign of how vital shipping is to the Maltese economy. This has been true for centuries, due to Malta's position on the trade route between Europe and Africa. Many ships still come here to use the port and facilities for ship refitting.

## TOURISM

A major source of Malta's income is provided by tourism. Visitors are drawn by its sheltered beaches and coves, and its pleasant climate. Another attraction is the country's imposing architecture, a legacy of its history as part of the Roman and Byzantine empires, and later as a British colony. As for other industries, the poor soil means that farming produces little income and is now overshadowed by light industry, such as clothes manufacture.

# VATICAN CITY

THE WORLD'S SMALLEST independent state, Vatican City lies at the heart of Rome. This tiny state is the centre of the Roman Catholic Church and the home of the Pope. States ruled by the Pope once stretched right across Italy, and the Vatican is the last survivor. Many visitors are drawn by its religious significance and also its rich cultural legacy. The Vatican has its own flag, national anthem, and stamps, as well as a newspaper and radio station.

*This spectacular view is from St Peter's basilica. The Pope delivers his messages and blessings to packed crowds in this grand piazza.*

# SAN MARINO

SITUATED IN ITALY'S MOUNTAINOUS NORTH, San Marino is Europe's smallest republic. It is also one of the oldest, possibly founded around AD900. During the Middle Ages, Italy was divided into powerful "city-states", such as Venice and Florence. These states gradually became absorbed into other, larger territories, but San Marino held on to its independence. The country consists of the capital, also called San Marino, and eight villages. The landscape is dominated by the three peaks of Mount Titano.

## TOURISM

The fairytale fortress of Rocca Tower, perched high on a rocky outcrop, overlooks San Marino. With few resources, the republic relies heavily on a thriving tourist trade.

**Find out more**

POLITICAL SYSTEMS: *270–271*
ROMAN CATHOLICS: *274*
SMALL EUROPEAN STATES: *80–81*

# SWITZERLAND AND AUSTRIA

HOME TO EUROPE'S TALLEST MOUNTAINS, the Alps, this region includes Switzerland, Austria, and the tiny state of Liechtenstein. The mountains have shaped the way Switzerland and Austria are organized politically, since communication has been difficult. Each is split up into individual districts which have great control over their own affairs. With no direct access to the sea and few natural resources, both countries have had to maintain good relations with their neighbours and develop specialized industries.

## MOUNTAINS AND LAKES
Idyllic scenes of towns and villages next to peaceful lakes are just one of the sights that inspire so many tourists to visit this part of the world. Europe's largest lakes and its highest mountains are found in these two countries.

**Innsbruck, Austria**
☀ Jan -3°C (27°F)
☀ July 19°C (66°F)
🌧 Jan 54 mm (2.1 in)
🌧 July 134 mm (5.3 in)

AUSTRIA

**Zurich, Switzerland**
☀ Jan 1°C (31°F)
☀ July 20°C (66°F)
🌧 Jan 74 mm (2.9 in)
🌧 July 136 mm (5.4 in)

LIECHTENSTEIN

SWITZERLAND

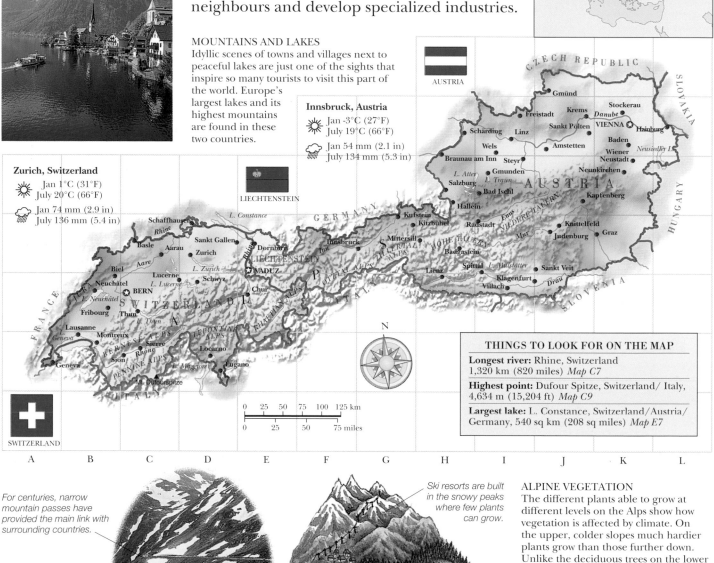

### THINGS TO LOOK FOR ON THE MAP
**Longest river:** Rhine, Switzerland 1,320 km (820 miles) *Map C7*

**Highest point:** Dufour Spitze, Switzerland/ Italy, 4,634 m (15,204 ft) *Map C9*

**Largest lake:** L. Constance, Switzerland/Austria/ Germany, 540 sq km (208 sq miles) *Map E7*

*For centuries, narrow mountain passes have provided the main link with surrounding countries.*

## COMMUNICATIONS
The towering Alps cut through these two countries and form a massive wall that separates northern Europe from the Mediterranean countries further south. In the past, people had to cross the mountains via steep passes that were often blocked by snow. Today, tunnels and high bridges provide year-round access for road and rail transport, and Swiss engineering firms have become world experts in tunnel construction.

*Ski resorts are built in the snowy peaks where few plants can grow.*

*On the higher slopes, patches of conifer trees are cleared for small farms.*

*The lower slopes are used as meadowland where cows can graze.*

## ALPINE VEGETATION
The different plants able to grow at different levels on the Alps show how vegetation is affected by climate. On the upper, colder slopes much hardier plants grow than those further down. Unlike the deciduous trees on the lower slopes, conifer trees have downward sloping branches so they can shed heavy snow. Above the tree line, there is scrubland where only small, flowering plants and shrubs can thrive.

*Crops such as fruit and vines are grown in the fertile valley bottom.*

# SWITZERLAND

SWITZERLAND HAS BEEN a neutral country since 1815, and has stayed out of all the wars that have affected Europe since that time. It is a country of isolated mountain communities, whose people speak several different languages. Despite this, Switzerland is remarkably unified in many ways, and has pooled its few resources to create a flourishing economy. Its neutrality and political stability have helped make it a major financial centre.

| SWITZERLAND | |
|---|---|
| **Capital city:** Bern | |
| **Area:** 41,290 sq km (15,942 sq miles) | |
| **Population:** 7,200,000 | |
| **Official languages:** German, French, Italian, and Romansch | |
| **Major religions:** Christian 86%, Muslim 2%, other 12% | |
| **Government:** Multi-party democracy | |
| **Currency:** Swiss franc | |
| **Adult literacy rate:** 99% | |
| **Life expectancy:** 79 years | |
| **People per doctor:** 286 | |
| **Televisions:** 525 per 1,000 people | |

| LIECHTENSTEIN | |
|---|---|
| **Capital city:** Vaduz | |
| **Area:** 160 sq km (62 sq miles) | |
| **Population:** 33,145 | |
| **Official language:** German | |
| **Major religions:** Christian 88%, other 12% | |
| **Government:** Multi-party democracy | |
| **Currency:** Swiss franc | |
| **Adult literacy rate:** 99% | |
| **Life expectancy:** 79 years | |
| **People per doctor:** 763 | |

### MANUFACTURING
Even though it has virtually no raw materials, Switzerland has made itself a major industrial power. The Swiss have a skilled workforce specializing in producing high-value, lightweight products. Since Switzerland is a small country, Swiss companies have had to export goods in order to find large markets and many businesses now have branches worldwide.

*Making medicines and drugs is an important industry.*

*Switzerland is famous for making clocks and watches.*

### GENEVA
Many of Switzerland's banks and businesses are based in the beautiful lakeside city of Geneva. This city is also home to many international organizations, who have been attracted here by Switzerland's political stability and its neutral status. These include the Red Cross, the World Health Organization, and the European headquarters of the United Nations.

### AGRICULTURE
Farming is not easy in such mountainous terrain, but the fertile valley bottoms are used extensively, and fruit and vines are grown on warmer, south-facing slopes. Dairy farming is a traditional way of life here. Cattle, sheep and goats graze the rich pasture of the upland slopes in the warmer months, and are brought down to the valleys for the winter. Their milk is used to produce a variety of cheeses, such as Emmental.

# LIECHTENSTEIN

NESTLING IN THE RHINE VALLEY between Switzerland and Austria, this tiny, German-speaking principality is one of very few small European states to hold on to its independence. It is not totally independent, though, as Liechtenstein's Swiss neighbour provides its currency, as well as its postal and telephone services, and also directs the country's foreign policy.

*French-speaking Swiss people at a street market in Lausanne.*

### SWISS LANGUAGES
Four different languages are spoken in Switzerland, Europe's most multi lingual country. German, French, and Italian are the official languages, but a fourth, Romansch, spoken in remote Alpine villages, has been given the status of a national language.

*Liechtenstein produces highly decorative postage stamps that are much sought after by collectors. This one celebrates the anniversary of the prince and princess.*

*Stamp sales are an important source of income for Liechtenstein.*

### THE ECONOMY
Financial services are vital to the economy, and investors are drawn here by liberal banking laws and political stability. Intensive agriculture, a thriving small-scale manufacturing industry, and tourism bring in large amounts of revenue. Its varied economy makes this is an extremely wealthy state.

*Find out more*

INTERNATIONAL ORGANIZATIONS: *273*

RICH AND POOR: *278–279*

SERVICE INDUSTRIES: *281*

# AUSTRIA

THE SMALL, MOUNTAINOUS republic of Austria was once the centre of the vast Austro-Hungarian empire. It first became an independent country in 1918. The Alps cover much of western Austria and fertile lowlands stretch across the east. Dairy herds graze on the mountain slopes and crops such as cereals and fruit grow well in the north. Modern-day Austria is an industrialized nation, with cities such as Linz producing iron, steel, heavy engineering, and chemicals. Austria joined the European Union in 1995.

| AUSTRIA | |
|---|---|
| **Capital city:** Vienna | |
| **Area:** 83,858 sq km (32,378 sq miles) | |
| **Population:** 8,100,000 | |
| **Official language:** German | |
| **Major religions:** Christian 83%, Muslim 2%, other 1% | |
| **Government:** Multi-party democracy | |
| **Currency:** Euro | |
| **Adult literacy rate:** 99% | |
| **Life expectancy:** 79 years | |
| **People per doctor:** 312 | |
| **Televisions:** 516 per 1,000 people | |

## VIENNA

Austria's capital city was once the glittering centre of the Austro-Hungarian empire, and the Imperial Palace (above), was the residence of its emperors. In the late 1700s and 1800s, Vienna was one of the most sophisticated cities in Europe, and the architecture still attracts visitors. Others come to soak up musical history – the city was a magnet for composers, such as Beethoven and Mozart, who hoped to win commissions from the aristocracy.

## HYDROELECTRIC POWER

Austria has little coal and no oil of its own, and so other ways of producing power have been developed. Plentiful rivers and steep Alpine valleys provide the opportunity of harnessing the power of moving water to generate electricity. This is known as hydroelectric power. In the mountains, as water is released from an upper to a lower reservoir, it powers generators that produce electricity.

*Water is collected in a reservoir high up in the mountains.*

*The movement of the turbine drives an electricity generator.*

*Steep roofs are built to shed heavy winter snowfalls.*

*The water falls down to a motor called a turbine.*

*The energy of the falling water drives the turbine.*

**Tourism in the Austrian Alps**

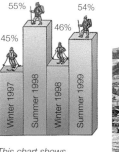

55%  54%

45% 46%

Winter 1997 | Summer 1998 | Winter 1998 | Summer 1999

*This chart shows the percentage of tourists visiting Austria in the winter or summer. Winter visitors go skiing; summer visitors go hill-walking.*

## TOURISM

Tourism accounts for nearly 20 per cent of the country's income. As well as exploring Austria's historic cities, visitors come to go skiing and hill-walking. Some of the world's best ski resorts are found here, and favourite summer haunts include the huge lakes nestling in the Alps. Conservation measures are being introduced to protect the land from damage by large numbers of visitors.

## MOUNTAIN HOUSES

In the past, Austrians farming in the Alps built their steep-roofed houses from wood because trees were plentiful. Animals, hay, and humans were often housed in the same building. Hay was kept under the roof; cattle were kept in the basement; and the farmer's family lived in between. This kind of housing can still be seen in some farming villages, although tourism is changing the face of rural areas.

## VARIED TASTES

Viennese coffee houses are famous worldwide for their vast choice of coffee, cakes, and pastries. Austrian food blends a range of influences – the result of all the different countries that once fell within the empire. For example, the famous *Wiener Schnitzel* (Viennese cutlet) – a breaded and fried piece of veal or pork – may have come originally from Italy.

*Austrians drink their coffee with milk, whipped cream, or strong and black.*

### Find out more

ALPINE LANDSCAPE: *106*
EUROPEAN UNION: *81, 273*
HYDROELECTRIC POWER: *262*
RIVER DANUBE: *78*

# SLOVENIA AND CROATIA

THE COUNTRIES of Slovenia and Croatia stretch from the snow-clad Alps in the north to the sunny Adriatic coast in the south. The area is crossed by the River Sava, which flows past the capital cities of Ljubljana and Zagreb, across a fertile plain, eventually joining the River Danube. In the west, the Karst region of Slovenia has given its name to a type of scenery associated with limestone rock formations and deep caves. Some caves, such as those at Postojna, are as large as cathedrals. Ruled by Austria and Hungary for centuries, both countries retain strong cultural ties with the rest of Europe. At the end of World War I, Slovenia and Croatia were incorporated into the newly formed Yugoslavia but declared themselves independent in 1991.

## WALLED CITY OF DUBROVNIK
This ancient Croatian port, with its narrow streets and massive walls, was founded by the Romans in the 7th century. Protected by its fortifications, Dubrovnik grew into a thriving city with trade links throughout the region. The wealth brought by trade encouraged a strong artistic tradition which persists today. Most of the damage from the war in the 1990s has now been repaired.

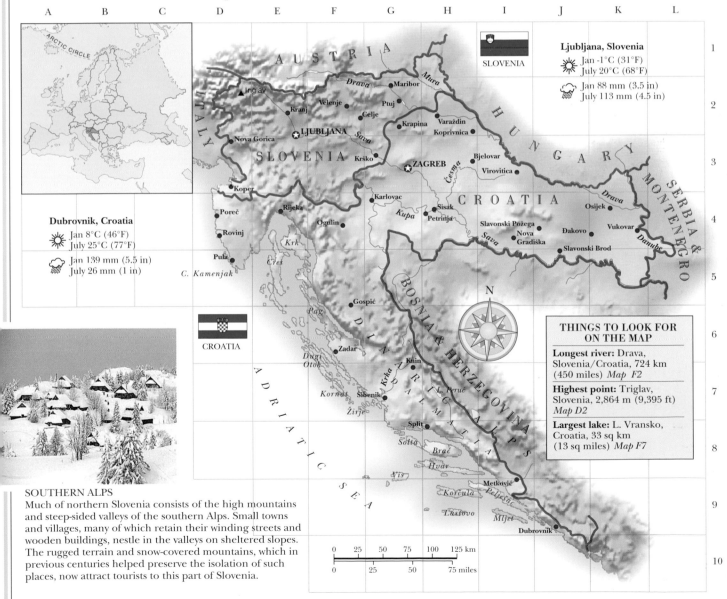

**Ljubljana, Slovenia**
Jan -1°C (31°F) July 20°C (68°F)
Jan 88 mm (3.5 in) July 113 mm (4.5 in)

**Dubrovnik, Croatia**
Jan 8°C (46°F) July 25°C (77°F)
Jan 139 mm (5.5 in) July 26 mm (1 in)

### THINGS TO LOOK FOR ON THE MAP
**Longest river:** Drava, Slovenia/Croatia, 724 km (450 miles) *Map F2*
**Highest point:** Triglav, Slovenia, 2,864 m (9,395 ft) *Map D2*
**Largest lake:** L. Vransko, Croatia, 33 sq km (13 sq miles) *Map F7*

## SOUTHERN ALPS
Much of northern Slovenia consists of the high mountains and steep-sided valleys of the southern Alps. Small towns and villages, many of which retain their winding streets and wooden buildings, nestle in the valleys on sheltered slopes. The rugged terrain and snow-covered mountains, which in previous centuries helped preserve the isolation of such places, now attract tourists to this part of Slovenia.

# SLOVENIA

THE SMALL, alpine country of Slovenia lies at the northeastern end of the Adriatic Sea. Formerly ruled by Austria, and later part of Yugoslavia, Slovenia regained its independence in 1991 without getting involved in the ensuing war. It maintains a strategic position in this corner of Europe, and its ports provide Austria with its main maritime outlets. Slovenia joined the EU in 2004.

## RIDING SCHOOLS
As long ago as 1580, a stud farm was set up in what is now Slovenia to supply horses to the Spanish Riding School in Vienna. The farm eventually bred the famous snow-white Lippizaner horse. Today they are considered the finest riding horses in the world.

| SLOVENIA |
| --- |
| **Capital city:** Ljubljana |
| **Area:** 20,250 sq km (7,820 sq miles) |
| **Population:** 2,000,000 |
| **Official language:** Slovene |
| **Major religions:** Christian 96%, Muslim 1%, other 2% |
| **Government:** Multi-party democracy |
| **Currency:** Tolar |
| **Adult literacy rate:** 99% |
| **Life expectancy:** 76 years |

| CROATIA |
| --- |
| **Capital city:** Zagreb |
| **Area:** 56,542 sq km (21,831 sq miles) |
| **Population:** 4,400,000 |
| **Official language:** Croatian |
| **Major religions:** Christian 92%, Muslim 1%, other 7% |
| **Government:** Multi-party democracy |
| **Currency:** Kuna |
| **Adult literacy rate:** 98% |
| **Life expectancy:** 74 years |

## ECONOMY
Widespread forests provide wood for sawmills, furniture, and paper-making industries in Slovenia. In recent years, licence agreements with companies in western Europe have allowed local factories to produce a range of cars, trucks, motorcycles, and refrigerators.

## SLOVENE PEOPLE
Despite being ruled for almost a thousand years by German-speaking Austrians, the Slovenes have kept their Slav language and folk culture. Colourful embroidery and distinctive headwear, as worn by women at this wedding, are part of that culture. Most people live in small towns or in one of the numerous villages scattered across the country. Only 300,000 people live in Ljubljana, making it one of Europe's smallest capitals.

*Slovene women attend a village wedding.*

*The islands along the Adriatic coast are popular with tourists.*

# CROATIA

THE CRESCENT-SHAPED COUNTRY of Croatia was part of Hungary until it was joined to Yugoslavia in 1918. Along with Slovenia, it was the first province to declare independence in 1991. War erupted almost immediately with Serbia. Until then the economy had prospered. Mineral wealth provided the basis for industry while vast areas of fertile land were used for crops. Although the war devastated much of the country, the economy was quick to recover.

## TOURISM
A long, rugged coastline with hundreds of islands, bays, and secluded beaches, backed by the dramatic Dinaric Alps, has drawn tourists to Croatia for many years. The historic cities of Zagreb, Dubrovnik and Split have repaired much of the damage they received from the war, and tourist levels are returning to what they were before the conflict, with over 50 per cent coming from Germany, Italy and the UK.

*The flax plant is harvested when the lower stalk starts to turn yellow.*

*Linen fibre is obtained by crushing the stalks of the flax plant.*

## CROATIAN CROPS
The fertile river valleys in the north have a warm climate that is ideal for growing fruits such as plums, apricots, and grapes. Flax is also grown, both for its fibre, which is made into linen clothing and canvas, and for its seeds, which are used for linseed oil.

---

### *Find out more*
BREAK-UP OF YUGOSLAVIA: *81, 124*
OIL AND COAL: *96, 152, 162*
TIMBER INDUSTRY: *26*

# BELARUS AND THE BALTIC STATES

TUCKED AWAY in the northwestern corner of the vast landmass that was once the USSR, these four states are now independent countries. Three of the states – Estonia, Latvia, and Lithuania – border the chilly Baltic Sea. The fourth, Belarus, lies inland. The countries are low-lying, with hills, lakes, and marshes and a cool, moist climate. There are few natural resources in this thinly populated area. The peoples represent many different cultural groups and have suffered centuries of hardship from invasions and uprisings.

**Tallinn, Estonia**
- Jan -7°C (20°F)
- July 16°C (61°F)
- Jan 39 mm (1.5 in)
- July 68 mm (2.7 in)

**THINGS TO LOOK FOR ON THE MAP**

**Longest river:**
Western Dvina, Russian Federation/Belarus/Ukraine, 1,018 km (633 miles) *Map J8*

**Highest point:**
Gaizin Kalns, Latvia, 312 m (1,024 ft) *Map H6*

**Largest lake:** L. Peipus, Estonia/Russian Federation, 3,626 sq km (1,400 sq miles) *Map I4*

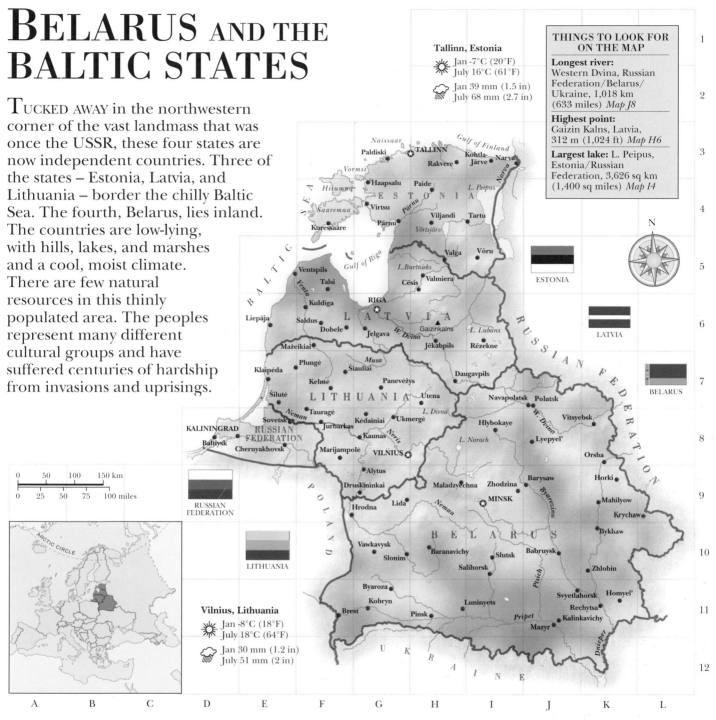

**Vilnius, Lithuania**
- Jan -8°C (18°F)
- July 18°C (64°F)
- Jan 30 mm (1.2 in)
- July 51 mm (2 in)

## FARMING AND FISHING
Lack of good farmland, together with the cold, damp climate, limits the range of crops that can be grown in this region. The main crops are cereals, potatoes, and sugar beet. Cattle graze on the wet pastures. Fishing is an important industry in the Baltic States.

*Tawny owls find shelter in the region's dense forests. At night they fly over farmland hunting for prey.*

## INDEPENDENCE
The three Baltic States' struggle for independence during the 1980s played a large part in the USSR's break-up into many separate republics in 1991. At one point, the people of these states formed a massive human chain across their lands, as a form of protest. These Baltic peoples are now trying to forge closer links with neighbouring countries, and all three states have joined the EU.

# BELARUS

THIS POOR, RURAL republic is sparsely populated and has few natural resources. However, living conditions have improved greatly since the 1960s when a drive began to develop industry and to provide better housing. In 1986, an explosion at the Chernobyl nuclear power station in the Ukraine seriously affected people's health across the country. Two hundred years of Russian rule ended in 1991 with the break-up of the former USSR, and Belarus became an independent republic.

## BELARUS

**Capital city:** Minsk

**Area:** 207,600 sq km (80,154 sq miles)

**Population:** 9,900,000

**Official language:** Belorussian, Russian

**Major religions:** Christian 68%, other 32%

**Government:** Multi-party democracy

**Currency:** Belorussian rouble

**Adult literacy rate:** 99%

**Life expectancy:** 68 years

**People per doctor:** 222

**Televisions:** 314 per 1,000 people

### PRIPET MARSHES
Huge areas of southern Belarus are covered in misty, marshy land. The Pripet Marshes form the largest expanse of marshland in Europe. Much of this area is forested with pine, alder, aspen, and oak trees which supply a growing timber industry. Animals such as elk, lynx, wild boar, and grouse have made the marshes and forests their home.

### LOCAL FOODS
Mushrooms and potatoes are staple foods. Potatoes cooked in different ways are eaten for breakfast, lunch, and dinner. Mushrooms and sour cream are served with meat dishes, such as baked rabbit or pork. As well as being enjoyed fresh, mushrooms may be dried or salted and pickled.

**Glass-making**
Glass is actually cooled liquid sand. It is made from sand, limestone, soda, and waste glass. These four ingredients are fed into a furnace where they are heated to produce molten glass.

*Dried chanterelle mushrooms*

*Mushrooms flourish in the country's thick, damp forests, and mushroom-picking is so popular it has been called the national sport.*

*Boletus or cèpe mushrooms*

## INDUSTRY
Heavy industries such as oil refining and the manufacture of machinery are important to Belarus. Under the former USSR, large factories were located here to process raw materials from Russia and the Ukraine. Reserves of useful minerals, such as oil, rock salt, and types of sand have been discovered. The sands are used to make high-quality glassware.

*The furnace is heated up to 1400°C (2550°F) to melt the raw ingredients.*

*As glass cools, it can be carefully shaped. To make sheets of glass, the liquid glass is floated on a river of molten tin. To make bottles, the glass is poured into bottle-shaped moulds.*

*A lump of molten glass called a gob is dropped into a mould.*

*The liquid glass sinks to the far end.*

*Air is blown in to make the glass fill the mould.*

*The glass bottle is left to cool and set before being taken out of the mould.*

## MINSK
The centrally placed capital city has a history of changing fortunes. Although it was devastated by bombing in World War II, in peaceful times Minsk has blossomed as a centre of government, education, culture, and communications. Recently, industrial growth has brought rapid expansion to the city. It is also the headquarters of the Commonwealth of Independent States (CIS), an organization that brings together former Soviet states.

### EDUCATION
During the rule of the USSR, almost everyone in Belarus was taught to read and write and education was free between the ages of 7 and 17. This firm educational foundation has led to the development of a strong literary and musical heritage within the republic.

### Find out more
EDUCATION: *277*
EUROPEAN CITIES: *80*
FORMER USSR: *134*
OIL: *135, 152, 281*

# ESTONIA

A LAND OF FORESTS, low hills, and lakes, Estonia is the smallest of the Baltic States. Once a farming nation, the Soviets transformed Estonia into an urban, industrialized region. Today its industries include timber, shipbuilding, and food processing. Since becoming independent from the former USSR in 1991, tensions have sprung up between the native Estonians and the third of the population that is Russian.

**TALLINN**
Roughly one-third of the people of Estonia live in or around the capital city of Tallinn. Many of the state's regular flow of tourists come to wander around the narrow, medieval streets of the city's old quarter.

# LATVIA

SANDWICHED BETWEEN the other Baltic States, Latvia's central position, with easy access to the coast and three major ports, has done much to help trade. The cool, damp climate is well suited to dairy farming and meat production. Since becoming independent from the USSR in 1991, Latvia has concentrated on developing its farming, fishing, and timber industries, which had been overshadowed by large-scale factory production under the Soviets.

**RIGA**
The capital has been an important trading port since the Middle Ages. This is perhaps the most lively capital in the Baltic States and it is a vital cultural centre. Latvia has strong historic links with Germany, and this can be seen at every turn in Riga — in the buildings, the fashions, and the many German visitors.

# LITHUANIA

IN MANY WAYS, LITHUANIA is the odd one out among the Baltic States. First, most of its people are native Lithuanians, whereas Estonia and Latvia have large Russian populations. Second, life here tends to be concentrated in the interior of the country, and away from the coast. The third major difference lies in the fertile soil, which makes farming vital to the economy.

**FOLK TRADITIONS**
The songs, dances, music, and crafts of their folk history have great value for the people of the Baltic States. Keeping their folk traditions alive became especially important as a way of maintaining a sense of identity under Russian rule. Now, each country has annual folk festivals and parades.

Amber can be cut or polished to make jewellery.

A fly is attracted to the tree's sticky resin and then caught as it hardens into amber.

**AMBER**
Up to 90 per cent of the world's amber comes from the shores of Lithuania, buried in sands dating back 50 million years. Amber is a fossilized tree resin, found in chunks of different shapes and sizes. Some is opaque and brown, but the most sought-after amber is yellow or gold. One small piece may contain the remains of insects or plants, trapped forever in the golden resin.

| ESTONIA | |
|---|---|
| **Capital city:** Tallinn | |
| **Area:** 45,226 sq km (17,462 sq miles) | |
| **Population:** 1,300,000 | |
| **Official language:** Estonian | |
| **Major religion:** Christian 81%, other 19% | |
| **Government:** Multi-party democracy | |
| **Currency:** Kroon | |
| **Adult literacy rate:** 99% | |
| **Life expectancy:** 71 years | |
| **People per doctor:** 323 | |
| **Televisions:** 480 per 1,000 population | |

| LATVIA | |
|---|---|
| **Capital city:** Riga | |
| **Area:** 64,589 sq km (24,938 sq miles) | |
| **Population:** 2,300,000 | |
| **Official language:** Latvian | |
| **Major religion:** Christian 100% | |
| **Government:** Multi-party democracy | |
| **Currency:** Lats | |
| **Adult literacy rate:** 99% | |
| **Life expectancy:** 70 years | |
| **People per doctor:** 333 | |
| **Televisions:** 492 per 1,000 population | |

| LITHUANIA | |
|---|---|
| **Capital city:** Vilnius | |
| **Area:** 65,200 sq km (25,174 sq miles) | |
| **Population:** 3,400,000 | |
| **Official language:** Lithuanian | |
| **Major religion:** Christian 88%, other 12% | |
| **Government:** Multi-party democracy | |
| **Currency:** Litas | |
| **Adult literacy rate:** 99% | |
| **Life expectancy:** 73 years | |
| **People per doctor:** 250 | |
| **Televisions:** 459 per 1,000 population | |

*Find out more*
EUROPEAN CITIES: *80*
FOLK TRADITIONS: *116, 118*
FORMER USSR: *134*
SHIPBUILDING: *183*

# CENTRAL EUROPE

THE HEART OF EUROPE consists of a block of four countries: Poland, the Czech Republic, Slovakia, and Hungary. This region lies on the north European plain and is largely flat, broken only by low mountains in the south. The country borders within Central Europe have been redrawn many times over the centuries. This is because the flat landscape provides an easy target for invaders, and because the region was surrounded by four mighty empires: Russia, Austro-Hungary, Prussia, and the Ottoman Turks. After World War II, Central Europe came under the control of the former Soviet Union. Now independent, all four countries joined the European Union in 2004.

### ROMAN CATHOLICISM
The celebration of saints' days and religious festivals is a regular feature of life in Central Europe, where Roman Catholicism is the main religion. This region was first converted to Christianity about 1,000 years ago. Repeated invasions have led its people to cling to their sense of national identity, and Roman Catholicism is an important part of this.

*Each year, thousands of people visit the Black Madonna at Czestochowa, Poland's holiest shrine.*

*A Hungarian musician in traditional costume.*

### FOLK MUSIC
Weddings, harvest festivals, Christmas, and other kinds of family and religious occasions are marked by music, song, and dance. Local styles vary widely, but traditions are particularly strong in rural areas. In Poland, for example, most musicians are amateurs, only picking up their instruments after a hard day's work. Slovakian folk music traditions survive mainly in the mountain villages and are associated with brightly coloured folk dress.

## THE RIVER DANUBE

This major waterway links Slovakia and Hungary to Germany and the River Rhine in the west, and to the Black Sea in the southeast. In the past, the Danube has been a vital trading route for Central Europe, although river traffic has declined recently as trade with the former Soviet Union has fallen off sharply. However, the waters have been dammed to produce an important source of hydroelectric power – a dam at Gabcikovo now provides 15 per cent of Slovakia's electricity.

**How coal and lignite are formed**

*In swamps millions of years ago, plants died and were covered in mud.*

*The dead plant material was gradually compressed into peat.*

*Over centuries, layers of peat and rock sediment are laid down.*

*Underlying bedrock*

*The weight of all the layers pushes downwards.*

*The pressure turns the peat into lignite.*

*A chunk of lignite, also known as brown coal.*

*Over time, lignite may eventually become harder, black coal.*

*Cabbage is very popular and is often eaten stuffed, or pickled as sauerkraut.*

*Potatoes are served with most main courses.*

*Root vegetables such as beetroot are used to make thick soups.*

*Meat, such as this Polish salt pork called oczek, is a central part of most meals.*

## HEARTY FOOD
The more northerly areas of Central Europe tend to have warm summers but very cold winters. Plummeting temperatures have made heavy, warming foods popular here. Influences are strongly German, Austrian, and Russian, and potatoes, dumplings, soups, and meat stews are favourite dishes. To the south, Hungary has a more exotic tradition, featuring highly spiced foods such as goulash – its famous beef stew.

## LIGNITE
Brown coal, or lignite, is traditionally the main fuel in Central Europe. It is burned in power stations to produce much of the region's electricity. However, lignite is very rich in sulphur and, when it is burned, its fumes join with moisture droplets in the air to produce a mild form of sulphuric acid, or "acid rain". This can eat into stone buildings and destroy plant life. Air pollution in this region is made even worse by vehicle exhaust fumes. Although car ownership is relatively low, the cars on the road are frequently old models running on inefficient engines.

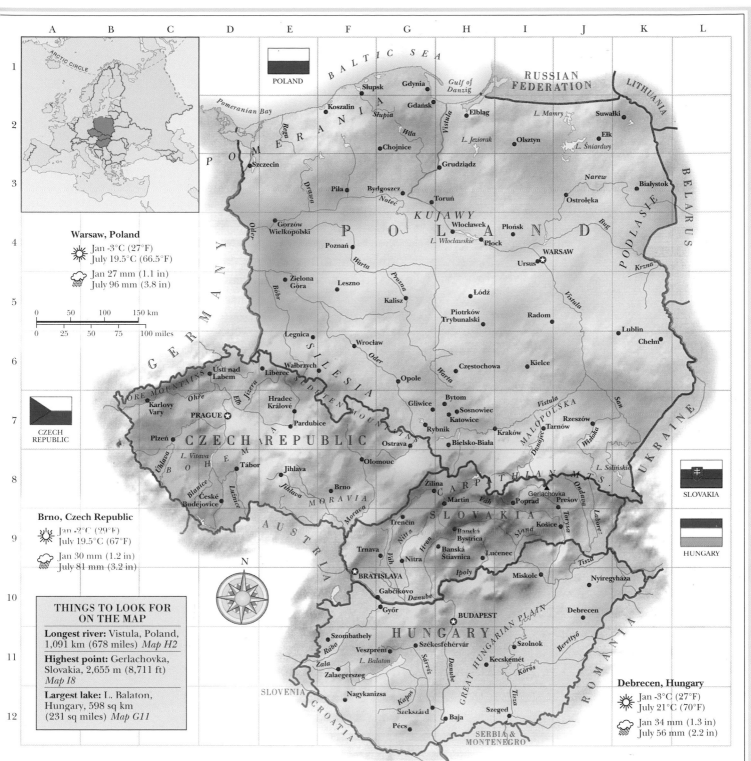

A B C D E F G H I J K L

**Warsaw, Poland**
☀ Jan -3°C (27°F)
☀ July 19.5°C (66.5°F)
☁ Jan 27 mm (1.1 in)
☁ July 96 mm (3.8 in)

POLAND

CZECH REPUBLIC

**Brno, Czech Republic**
☀ Jan -2°C (29°F)
☀ July 19.5°C (67°F)
☁ Jan 30 mm (1.2 in)
☁ July 81 mm (3.2 in)

SLOVAKIA

HUNGARY

**Debrecen, Hungary**
☀ Jan -3°C (27°F)
☀ July 21°C (70°F)
☁ Jan 34 mm (1.3 in)
☁ July 56 mm (2.2 in)

### THINGS TO LOOK FOR ON THE MAP

**Longest river:** Vistula, Poland, 1,091 km (678 miles) *Map H2*

**Highest point:** Gerlachovka, Slovakia, 2,655 m (8,711 ft) *Map I8*

**Largest lake:** L. Balaton, Hungary, 598 sq km (231 sq miles) *Map G11*

## WILD FOREST ANIMALS

The Bialowieza National Park in Poland is northern Europe's largest area of woodland. Wild animals native to the forest include elk, deer, wolves, and bears, and conservation campaigns have done much to protect them. Special animal breeding programmes have been set up here, and it is now the only natural breeding place for wild bison in Europe.

*A bison cow feeding her calf in Bialowieza National Park, Poland.*

## FOREST AREAS

Woodland covers a quarter of Central Europe. In some places, the forest dates back many thousands of years – there are centuries-old oaks near Poznan, in Poland. Acid rain has harmed trees across the region, but especially in Poland, where almost half the trees have been affected.

*Ancient forest in Bialowieza National Park, Poland.*

# POLAND

POLAND IS A MIX OF SCATTERED farming villages and magnificent medieval towns. This mainly flat country is larger than the other three countries of Central Europe put together. Once a land of many different peoples, warfare, migration, and border changes in 1945 have meant that the majority of the people are now Polish-speaking Roman Catholics. During the 1980s, Poland broke free from Soviet communist control and began the difficult journey towards a more democratic political system.

| POLAND | |
|---|---|
| **Capital city:** Warsaw | |
| **Area:** 312,685 sq km (120,728 sq miles) | |
| **Population:** 38,600,000 | |
| **Official language:** Polish | |
| **Major religions:** Christian 95%, other 5% | |
| **Government:** Multi-party democracy | |
| **Currency:** Zloty | |
| **Adult literacy rate:** 99% | |
| **Life expectancy:** 74 years | |
| **People per doctor:** 455 | |
| **Televisions:** 413 per 1,000 people | |

## DEVELOPING INDUSTRIES

Poland is making the transition from a planned, communist-style economy to a free market. It no longer relies on heavy industry such as ship building and coal mining, but is starting to develop industries such as tourism (above) and electronics. A "shock therapy" programme during the early 1990s helped the country transform its economy into one of the strongest in Central Europe. Poland joined the NATO alliance in 1999 and the European Union in 2004.

Market in Warsaw

Machinery: 30%   Manufacturing: 26%   Other: 21%

Textiles: 3%   Fuels: 5%   Chemicals: 6%   Food: 9%

**Polish exports**

*Major exports include vehicles, machinery for industry and farming, and crops such as potatoes and other vegetables. Poland is also a major world exporter of coal and metals.*

## HEAVY INDUSTRY

Under the former Soviet Union, Poland was part of a vast centralized economy. For example, iron would be shipped into Poland, where it was then made into goods such as tractors for export to other parts of the Soviet Union. However, with the arrival of democracy, the country has attempted to find new markets for its goods in the West, and Germany is now its biggest trading partner.

Painted wooden eggs are exchanged at Easter.

Wooden box carved with a traditional pattern.

## A TRADITIONAL WAY OF LIFE

This nation of small-scale farmers clung fiercely to its local traditions throughout the years of Soviet control. As a result, unlike other countries under Soviet rule, the many small farms were not merged into larger state-run farms. Today, traditions such as horse-drawn ploughing are still common in parts of Poland. Local folk arts and crafts flourish too. Embroidery and woodcarving are often used to decorate household objects, and wooden furniture may be colourfully painted.

## MEDIEVAL KRAKOW

The superb medieval buildings found along the city streets of Krakow are a reminder that Poland was a major power during the 15th and 16th centuries, before it was divided up among other countries. Poland has some of the finest old churches, palaces, and public buildings in Europe. Many were destroyed or damaged during World War II, but Krakow's buildings escaped relatively unscathed. Unfortunately, this is also one of the most air-polluted cities in Europe, due mainly to the nearby Nowa Huta steelworks.

The main market square in Krakow

## AGRICULTURE

About a quarter of the nation's workforce is employed in agriculture. The most important products are potatoes, sugar beet, cereals, and livestock. Some farms specialize in commercial crops, but most grow some crops for selling and some for feeding the family. This is partly because most farms are still small and privately owned, often operated part-time, frequently by elderly or retired owners.

*Find out more*

AIR POLLUTION: *114*
POLITICAL SYSTEMS: *270–271*
ROMAN CATHOLICS: *274*
SOVIET UNION: *136*

# CZECH REPUBLIC

**CZECH REPUBLIC**

| | |
|---|---|
| **Capital city:** Prague | |
| **Area:** 78,866 sq km (30,450 sq miles) | |
| **Population:** 10,200,000 | |
| **Official language:** Czech | |
| **Major religions:** Christian 44%, other 56% | |
| **Government:** Multi-party democracy | |
| **Currency:** Czech koruna | |
| **Adult literacy rate:** 99% | |
| **Life expectancy:** 75 years | |
| **People per doctor:** 294 | |
| **Televisions:** 447 per 1,000 people | |

As CENTRAL EUROPE'S most industrialized country, the Czech Republic has a modern economy and a good standard of living. From 1918 until 1993, the Republic was part of the union forming Czechoslovakia. By the 1950s, Czechoslovakia was under Soviet control, but democratic elections in 1990 led to its peaceful split into two countries – the Czech Republic and Slovakia. Much of the Republic lies on a high, mountain-ringed plateau, and its people have a strong national identity.

*Bridges over the Vltava River in Prague.*

PRAGUE
Not far from the historic core of this ancient city, one of the most beautiful capitals in Europe, a booming commercial centre has sprung up. The capital is now host to ever-increasing numbers of visitors, coming for both pleasure and business. However, as elsewhere in Central Europe, air pollution is a major problem. It is caused mainly by factories in the commercial quarter, and in the extensive industrial suburbs beyond.

*The main grain crops are wheat, maize and rye.*

## AGRICULTURE

In contrast to Poland, most of the agricultural land in the Czech Republic is given over to large farms owned by the state or by co-operatives. But, as in Poland, the changeover from a communist to a capitalist economy has proved difficult for farmers as they fight to compete in an open "market economy". Czech farms are very productive, with the highest grain yields in Central Europe. But, as in neighbouring countries, a large proportion of this grain is fed to livestock, since the Republic concentrates on meat and milk production.

THEATRE
It is extremely appropriate that the Czech Republic's first president, Vaclav Havel, was also a playwright, since this region has a powerful theatrical tradition that stretches back to the 13th century. It has also made contributions to other areas of the arts, particularly music, literature, and film.

*The Smetana Concert Hall, in Prague, was named after a Czech composer.*

*Intricate, highly decorated glassware.*

BOHEMIAN GLASS
For centuries, the fine sands found in this region, once known as Bohemia, have been used for glass-making. Medieval craftsmen were praised for their breathtaking stained-glass windows. Bohemian glass is renowned for its high quality and delicacy and is still made today.

**The brewing process in the Czech Republic**

*Malted barley grains and water are fed into the mash tun.*

*When heated, the starch in the barley is converted into sugar.*

*Dried hops are added for flavour.*

*Yeast is added. It converts the sugar into alcohol.*

*The mixture is boiled with hops for 1–2 hours.*

*The beer stays in the fermenting tank for about a week.*

*The beer is bottled or stored in casks.*

## INDUSTRY

Beer is one of the best-known products to come out of this highly industrialized country. Its centuries-old brewing traditions have created such famous brands as Pilsner, made in Plzen since 1925, and Budweiser Budvar. As long ago as the 1200s, mountains were excavated for their rich mineral deposits. One of Europe's leading industrial and technological regions since the late 19th century. its industries produce vehicles, explosives, plastics, and textiles.

*Budweiser Budvar is a well-known export.*

*Find out more*
AIR POLLUTION: *114*
GLASS-MAKING: *112*
NEW EUROPEAN COUNTRIES: *81*
POLITICAL SYSTEMS: *270–271*

# SLOVAKIA

ONCE THE EASTERN PART of Czechoslovakia, this small, beautiful country is much more rural than its highly industrialized neighbour, the Czech Republic. When Czechoslovakia broke free of Soviet control in 1990, the Slovaks felt they were being dominated by the wealthier Czechs and campaigned for independence, which came in 1993. The Slovakian economy was hit hard by the split, as it relied on Czech money and resources. In this mountainous land, the Slovak population is divided between different valleys, and the country lacks a geographical focus. Most people speak Slovak, but various dialects are still spoken in the more isolated areas.

### SLOVAKIA

**Capital city:** Bratislava

**Area:** 48,845 sq km (18,859 sq miles)

**Population:** 5,400,000

**Official language:** Slovak

**Major religions:** Christian 72%, other 28%

**Government:** Multi-party democracy

**Currency:** Slovak koruna

**Adult literacy rate:** 99%

**Life expectancy:** 73 years

**People per doctor:** 278

**Televisions:** 402 per 1,000 people

**Distribution of timber and mining**

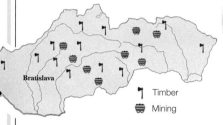

Bratislava

🌲 Timber

⚒ Mining

## BRATISLAVA

This city is one of the youngest capitals in the world – it became the new capital of a new country in 1993. This former residence of an archbishop has been made into the Presidential Palace. Bratislava is the only large city in Slovakia and historically has good links with Austria and Hungary. However, the city's good communications and modern industry have helped attract interest from foreign investors.

### BANSKA STIAVNICA

As early as 1156, the term 'terra banensium' (land of miners) was used to describe the region. Around 1237 Banská Štiavnica acheived legal status as a town, making it the oldest mining town in Slovakia. Then, in 1735, the first mining university in Europe was founded here. Ironically, economic stagnation in the 19th century, which halted the town's development, has led to a valuable tourist revenue in the 21st century, as the scheme and architecture of the town have remained intact.

*The castle used to control the mine revenues.*

## INDUSTRY

Today, one-third of the workforce have jobs in industry, as Slovakia fights for a place in the industrialized world. But the large state-owned companies set up by the former communist rulers have proved difficult to break up. The major Slovak industries are metallurgy and metalwork (which count for 33% of all their industry), chemicals, and the alimentary industry, which is industrial production of food. Much of east Slovakia is still forested, so timber and paper-making are also important.

*Spis Castle is a national monument and is one of the largest castles in Central Europe.*

## VILLAGE LIFE

This is a country of mountain villages and small towns. Slovakian farms are either tiny, family-run affairs, or they are large businesses run by the state or a group of people called a co-operative. As in the Czech Republic, the main crops are potatoes, sugar beet, and cereals, as well as livestock. Although Slovakia is traditionally rural, only a small proportion of the population are now employed in agriculture. There has been a great drive to develop industry, and many people are moving from the country to the towns.

*Traditional wooden houses in Cicmany, Slovakia.*

### UNSPOILED LANDSCAPE

The natural beauty of Slovakia's countryside gives it huge potential as a tourist destination, as long as it remains unspoiled. There are stunning mountain landscapes, castles perched on rocky outcrops, ancient walled towns, and mineral-rich spas. Great efforts are being made to develop the tourist trade, since there are as yet few facilities for visitors.

*Find out more*

CEREALS: *34, 122, 162*

NEW EUROPEAN COUNTRIES: *81*

POTATOES: *112*

SOVIET UNION: *136*

# HUNGARY

A BROAD, FERTILE PLAIN sweeps across much of this country, while gentle hills and low mountains are found in northern and western parts. The most southern country in Central Europe, Hungary has been home to many different peoples, including Germans, Slovaks, Serbs, Croats, Romanians, and Roma (Gypsies). Most Hungarians, however, are descended from the Magyars, who were fierce nomadic horsemen. After World War II, the communists established a harsh rule here, putting down a rebellion in 1956. A democratic government is now in place.

| HUNGARY | |
|---|---|
| **Capital city:** Budapest | |
| **Area:** 93,030 sq km (35,919 sq miles) | |
| **Population:** 9,900,000 | |
| **Official language:** Hungarian (Magyar) | |
| **Major religions:** Christian 71%, other 29% | |
| **Government:** Multi-party democracy | |
| **Currency:** Forint | |
| **Adult literacy rate:** 99% | |
| **Life expectancy:** 72 years | |
| **People per doctor:** 345 | |
| **Televisions:** 437 per 1,000 people | |

*Flowers being gathered at a vast flower farm run by a co-operative.*

*Paprika*

*Paprika is used in many recipes, and Hungary produces a large proportion of the world's total.*

*Goulash was originally a basic dish eaten by shepherds.*

### AGRICULTURE
Since this fertile land is warmed by hot summers and short, mild winters, a wide variety of crops are found here. Cereals flourish, as in other parts of Central Europe, but Hungary also produces sunflowers, fruit, and vegetables, as well as olives, figs, and grapes – there is a thriving wine trade. However, the changeover from a communist to a capitalist economy has caused problems.

*The parliament buildings on the River Danube in Budapest.*

### THERMAL SPRINGS AND SPAS
The grand architecture of Budapest's old Turkish baths is a distant echo of the country's past as part of the Ottoman Empire. There are baths and spas right across Hungary, centred on the hundreds of warm springs that gush naturally from the ground. Since earliest times, people have flocked to bathe in these mineral-rich waters, often seeking to cure their ailments.

### CUISINE
The varied crops produced in Hungary mean that it has developed some distinctive dishes. Hungary's national dish is a famous beef and vegetable mix called goulash, served as a stew or a thick soup. A hot red pepper called paprika is added to give goulash its spicy flavour. Other examples of the rich and heavy cuisine include carp in paprika sauce, pastry filled with liver pâté, and a mixed grill served with stuffed peppers.

*A sauce of tomatoes, paprika, onions, and sour cream is served with fish, as well as with meat dishes such as goulash.*

## BUDAPEST
If you were to take a cruise ship through Budapest along the great River Danube, you would discover that the capital is actually two cities. Buda, on one bank of the river, is the old royal capital, filled with ancient buildings. Across the water lies Pest, the heart of modern business and political life, where the government buildings are found. Budapest attracts a greater proportion of foreign visitors than any other Central European capital, and almost two-thirds of foreign money invested in Hungary is centred on the city.

*The wine industry is modernizing with great speed and is continuing to expand its export markets.*

## INDUSTRY
Hungary's wide range of industries produces metals, chemicals, and vehicles as well as textiles and electrical goods. Since a democratic government gained control in 1990, the country has had to compete in a worldwide market. Many firms have been privatized, and some industry has declined. However, Hungary's population has highly developed skills, especially in science and engineering, and has attracted tens of millions of dollars in foreign investment.

***Find out more***
CEREALS: *34, 122, 162*
EUROPEAN PLAINS: *79*
POLITICAL SYSTEMS: *270–271*
WINE MAKING: *99*

# UKRAINE, MOLDOVA, AND THE CAUCASIAN REPUBLICS

THE GRASSY STEPPE LOWLANDS of Ukraine and Moldova lie in the east of Europe. Further east, the three mountainous Caucasian Republics of Georgia, Armenia, and Azerbaijan lie between the Black Sea and the Caspian Sea, cradled by the Caucasus Mountains. From the 17th century, the Russian Empire dominated this region, and in the 20th century it became part of the USSR, regaining independence only in the 1990s. Fertile farmland and a wealth of natural resources have made this area one of the richest parts of the former USSR. The region's mountains give it protection from the extreme cold of the Russian winters, and this may help encourage a future tourist industry, particularly along the Black Sea coast.

Kiev, Ukraine
Jan -7°C (19°F)
July 20°C (68°F)
Jan 58 mm (2.3 in)
July 91 mm (3.6 in)

MOLDOVA

Simferopol, Ukraine
Jan -1°C (31°F)
July 22°C (71°F)
Jan 46 mm (1.8 in)
July 64 mm (2.5 in)

*These children at a wedding in Azerbaijan are from different ethnic groups.*

## PEOPLES
The people of Ukraine and Moldova are mostly European, while over 50 different ethnic groups exist in the Caucasian Republics. The USSR tried to wipe out differences between the peoples of its empire by forcing them to use the Russian language and by suppressing local culture. However, many of the people of this region have a proud and ancient history and have struggled to hold on to their own languages and culture.

## NATURAL RESOURCES
Large deposits of coal, gas, and oil have made this region among the world's leading producers of energy. In 1990, a quarter of all the energy used in the USSR came from this area. In addition to coal from the Donbass Basin in Ukraine, and oil and natural gas from the Caspian Sea off Azerbaijan, nuclear reactors, hydroelectric schemes, and wind-power plants have been built in the region. Metal ores such as iron, manganese, lead, zinc, copper, and uranium are also mined here.

**Key**
🔴 Coal mine
🔹 Gas field
Power station
⚓ Oil field

*Azerbaijan's oil fields have only recently begun to be exploited.*

120

## THINGS TO LOOK FOR ON THE MAP

**Longest river:** Dnieper, Russian Federation/Belarus/Ukraine, 2,285 km (1,420 miles) *Map G5*

**Highest point:** Shkhara, Georgia, 5,203 m (17,071 ft) *Map O12*

**Largest lake:** L. Sevan, Armenia, 1,414 sq km (546 sq miles) *Map Q14*

## FARMING

The Caucasus Mountains protect the three republics from cold northerly winds and allow farmers to cultivate many exotic crops that cannot be grown elsewhere in the region. Crops such as tea, grapes, nuts, tobacco, and cotton are sold to countries of the former USSR. Cattle and sheep are grazed on the high mountain pastures.

*Figs*

*Tea*

*A variety of crops are grown in Armenia on the broad plain beneath Mount Ararat.*

*Almonds and raisins*

*Soldiers prepare for battle in Georgia.*

## CONFLICTS IN THE REGION

Since these countries gained their independence from the USSR, several conflicts have sprung up. Different ethnic groups are trying to stake their claim to territory, particularly in the Caucasian Republics. Tension exists in Ukraine and Moldova between the local ethnic groups and the large numbers of Russians who were brought into the area under Soviet rule.

UKRAINE

**Tbilisi, Georgia**
Jan 3°C (37°F)
July 25°C (77°F)
Jan 17 mm (0.7 in)
July 46 mm (1.8 in)

GEORGIA

AZERBAIJAN

ARMENIA

**Yerevan, Armenia**
Jan -6°C (22°F)
July 26°C (78°F)
Jan 23 mm (0.9 in)
July 15 mm (0.6 in)

## FERTILE PLAINS

Vast fields of cereal crops such as wheat, barley, oats, and maize cover the gently rolling, treeless steppes of Ukraine and Moldova. There is less rain here than in the Caucasian Republics, but broad, slow-flowing rivers, such as the Dnieper and the Dniester, provide plentiful water to irrigate the fertile, dark soil.

# UKRAINE

WITH ITS VAST, FERTILE PLAINS and huge coal resources, Ukraine could be one of the most powerful countries of the former USSR. Following independence in 1991, relations with the Russian Federation were poor, as the two countries argued over ownership of weapons and ships belonging to the former USSR. Ethnic tension is a problem too, as one in five of the population is Russian. In 1986, the world's worst nuclear accident, at the Chernobyl nuclear power plant, contaminated a huge area, affecting people, animals, and even the soil.

| UKRAINE | |
|---|---|
| **Capital city:** Kiev | |
| **Area:** 603,700 sq km (223,090 sq miles) | |
| **Population:** 47,700,000 | |
| **Official language:** Ukrainian | |
| **Major religions:** Christian 95%, Jewish 1%, other 4% | |
| **Government:** Multi-party democracy | |
| **Currency:** Hryvna | |
| **Adult literacy rate:** 77% | |
| **Life expectancy:** 75 years | |
| **People per doctor:** 556 | |
| **Televisions:** 490 per 1,000 people | |

| MOLDOVA | |
|---|---|
| **Capital city:** Chisinau | |
| **Area:** 33,843 sq km (13,067 sq miles) | |
| **Population:** 4,300,000 | |
| **Official language:** Moldovan | |
| **Major religions:** Christian 99%, Jewish 1% | |
| **Government:** Multi-party democracy | |
| **Currency:** Moldovan leu | |
| **Adult literacy rate:** 99 % | |
| **Life expectancy:** 67 years | |
| **People per doctor:** 370 | |
| **Televisions:** 297 per 1,000 people | |

*Kiev is situated on the Dnieper River, Ukraine's main waterway.*

**KIEV**
Ukraine's capital city has been overrun repeatedly by powerful invaders. In the 9th century, it was the centre of a trading empire founded by the Vikings. It was invaded by the Mongols, and then by the Polish–Lithuanian Empire in the 14th century. In the 17th century, Kiev fell to the Russian Empire, later to become part of the USSR. Heavily bombed in World War II, Kiev was rebuilt in the 1950s–1960s and is now a centre for communications, culture, and education.

**HEAVY INDUSTRY**
The Donbass Basin in eastern Ukraine is Europe's largest coalfield. It is also a major industrial area, with local coal and hydroelectricity powering one of the world's largest iron and steel industry. Factories process metals into finished products, including ships and machinery. However, many mines and factories are inefficient and new investment is needed.

## CEREAL CROPS
Almost three-quarters of Ukraine is covered by fertile plains known as the steppes. Much of this land is used to grow cereals. The huge quantities of wheat, maize, barley, oats, buckwheat, and rye that Ukraine produced earned it the title "bread-basket of the Soviet Union". However Ukrainian farmers are not realizing the potential of their land due to a lack of investment in new technology.

*Oats*

*Rye*

*Wheat germ*

*Grains of cereal grow on the ears of each plant. This grain can be eaten whole or ground into flour.*

*Wholemeal bread*

*Caraway roll*

*Rye bread*

*Bread is the main food and is eaten with every meal. Ukrainians bake a great variety of bread in all shapes, sizes, and textures.*

*Granary loaf*

# MOLDOVA

THIS SMALL, RURAL country was part of Romania, before being taken over by the USSR in 1940. Although it is the most densely populated republic of the former USSR, native Moldovans make up fewer than two-thirds of the population. After independence ethnic unrest broke out with the minority populations of Russians and Ukrainians calling for their own states. Although there is now peace, tensions still remain.

*Most of the population live in country areas and make their living from small-scale farming.*

**AGRICULTURE**
Moldova's fertile soil and mild climate allow a variety of crops to be grown, such as maize, sunflower seeds, tobacco, and vines. Much of the produce is exported to countries of the former USSR to raise cash for vital imports such as oil, as Moldova has few mineral resources of its own. Industries related to farming, such as food processing, are important too.

*Find out more*
BREAK-UP OF USSR: *136*
CEREALS: *34, 162*
COAL MINING: *96, 114, 162*
ROMANIA: *128*

# GEORGIA

GEORGIA IS A LAND OF MOUNTAINS. The Caucasus range forms a barrier with Russia in the north, while snowy peaks overlook the Black Sea in the west. The country's sheltered fertile soil is suited to growing grapes, and Georgia is said to be the birthplace of wine. Its position between the Caspian and Black Seas, gives Georgia control over the movement of oil and other goods between countries in the region.

**A LONG LIFE**
Georgia holds a remarkable world record. More people living here live to be over 100 years old than anywhere else in the world. Many centenarians continue to lead active lives, some up to the age of 120. Scientists cannot explain this, but they think the combination of good climate, a healthy, balanced diet, the rural environment, and outdoor work are all part of the secret.

**GEORGIA**

| | |
|---|---|
| **Capital city:** Tbilisi | |
| **Area:** 69,700 sq km (26,911 sq miles) | |
| **Population:** 5,100,000 | |
| **Official language:** Georgian, Abkhazian | |
| **Major religions:** Christian 83%, Muslim 11%, other 6% | |
| **Government:** Multi-party democracy | |
| **Currency:** Lari | |
| **Adult literacy rate:** 99% | |
| **Life expectancy:** 73 years | |
| **People per doctor:** 256 | |
| **Televisions:** 473 per 1,000 people | |

**TBILISI**
The buildings of Georgia's capital rise steeply from the banks of the Kura River. Tbilisi is a uniquely multicultural city, with a synagogue, mosque, Georgian basilica, Armenian church, and a Zoroastrian fire-worshipper's temple within a few minutes walk of each other.

# AZERBAIJAN

THIS HOT, DRY COUNTRY lies along the coast of the Caspian Sea. In the 8th century, the Persians named the area Azerbaijan, "the land of flames", when they saw burning natural gas seeping from the ground. The Azerbaijani people are Muslims who conquered the region in the 11th century. Tensions exist over the Nagorno Karabakh region, which is populated mainly by Armenians.

**OIL PRODUCTION**
Before oil was discovered in the Gulf states, Azerbaijan supplied half the world's oil output from oil fields near its capital, Baku. Today, villages on floating platforms house workers who drill for oil under the Caspian Sea. A new pipeline opened in 2005 taking oil from Baku via Tbilisi in Georgia to Ceyhan in Turkey on the Mediterranean Sea, promising great wealth for Azerbaijan.

**AZERBAIJAN**

| | |
|---|---|
| **Capital city:** Baku | |
| **Area:** 86,600 sq km (33,436 sq miles) | |
| **Population:** 8,400,000 | |
| **Official language:** Azerbaijani | |
| **Major religions:** Muslim 87%, Christian 12%, other 1% | |
| **Government:** Multi-party democracy | |
| **Currency:** Manat | |
| **Adult literacy rate:** 97% | |
| **Life expectancy:** 65 years | |
| **People per doctor:** 278 | |
| **Televisions:** 254 per 1,000 people | |

**ARMENIA**

| | |
|---|---|
| **Capital city:** Yerevan | |
| **Area:** 29,800 sq km (11,506 sq miles) | |
| **Population:** 3,100,000 | |
| **Official language:** Armenian | |
| **Major religions:** Christian 94%, other 6% | |
| **Government:** Multi-party democracy | |
| **Currency:** Dram | |
| **Adult literacy rate:** 99% | |
| **Life expectancy:** 75 years | |
| **People per doctor:** 328 | |
| **Televisions:** 218 per 1,000 people | |

# ARMENIA

THIS TINY, MOUNTAINOUS state is the smallest of all the former republics of the USSR. Armenia was the first state in the world to adopt Christianity and is today bordered by three Islamic countries. Having no access to the sea, Armenia relies on its neighbours for road and rail links with the outside world, but conflict with Azerbaijan has affected much-needed supplies of raw materials and fuel.

**FARMING**
Farming is the main source of employment in Armenia. Sheep and cattle graze on the high mountain slopes, while fruit trees and cereals are grown lower down.

*Find out more*

BREAK-UP OF USSR: *136*
GAS: *163, 198, 211*
OIL: *135, 152, 281*
RELIGIONS: *274–275*

# SOUTHEAST EUROPE

MUCH OF SOUTHEAST EUROPE consists of rugged mountains separated by deep river valleys. The area was called the Balkans, meaning "mountains" by the Turks, who ruled this area for 500 years until the early part of the 20th century. From 1918 until 1991 all these states, together with Croatia and Slovenia, were part of the newly created Yugoslavia; only Albania remained independent. Under communist leader, General Marshal Tito, friction between the different cultures was kept under control. His death, and the fall of communism in Europe, allowed age-old rivalries to emerge. This led to the collapse of Yugoslavia and a vicious war that lasted from 1991–95.

## CROSSROADS OF CULTURE
History has placed this area at the crossroads of many different empires and each has left its influence on the language, customs, and religions of the people. Here, in the Bosnian city of Mostar, church spires belonging to Orthodox Christian and Roman Catholic churches mingle with the mosque minarets of Islam, the religion introduced by the Turks in the 15th century. Today, new cultural landscapes are being created as groups try to re-establish their national identity.

**Belgrade, Serbia and Montenegro**
☀ Jan 0°C (32°F)
July 23°C (73°F)
☁ Jan 47 mm (1.9 in)
July 61 mm (2.4 in)

BOSNIA AND HERZEGOVINA

SERBIA & MONTENEGRO

**Sarajevo, Bosnia**
☀ Jan -1°C (31°F)
July 20°C (68°F)
☁ Jan 66 mm (2.6 in)
July 71 mm (2.8 in)

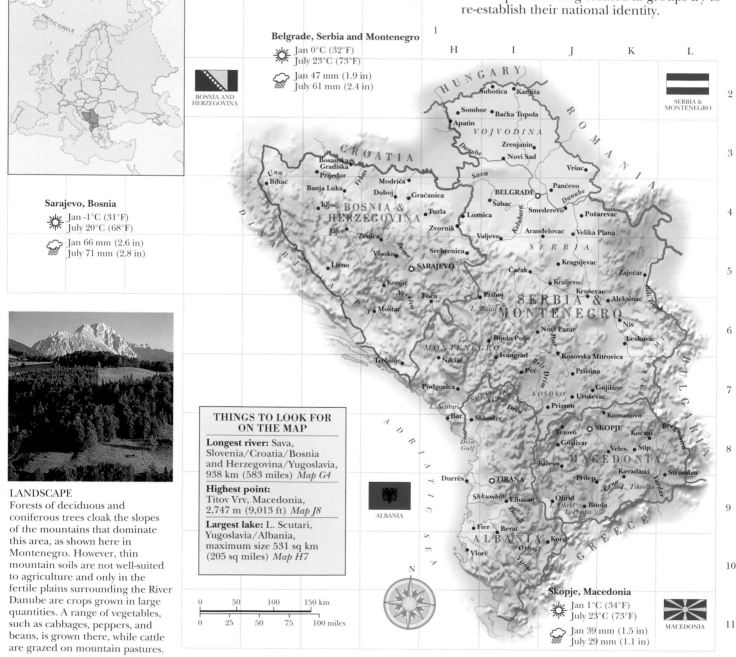

### THINGS TO LOOK FOR ON THE MAP
**Longest river:** Sava, Slovenia/Croatia/Bosnia and Herzegovina/Yugoslavia, 938 km (583 miles) *Map G4*

**Highest point:** Titov Vrv, Macedonia, 2,747 m (9,013 ft) *Map J8*

**Largest lake:** L. Scutari, Yugoslavia/Albania, maximum size 531 sq km (205 sq miles) *Map H7*

ALBANIA

## LANDSCAPE
Forests of deciduous and coniferous trees cloak the slopes of the mountains that dominate this area, as shown here in Montenegro. However, thin mountain soils are not well-suited to agriculture and only in the fertile plains surrounding the River Danube are crops grown in large quantities. A range of vegetables, such as cabbages, peppers, and beans, is grown there, while cattle are grazed on mountain pastures.

0 50 100 150 km
0 25 50 75 100 miles

N

**Skopje, Macedonia**
☀ Jan 1°C (34°F)
July 23°C (73°F)
☁ Jan 39 mm (1.5 in)
July 29 mm (1.1 in)

MACEDONIA

SERBIA AND MONTENEGRO

| SERBIA AND MONTENEGRO | |
|---|---|
| **Capital city:** Belgrade | |
| **Area:** 102,350 sq km (39,517 sq miles) | |
| **Population:** 10,500,000 | |
| **Official language:** Serbo-Croat | |
| **Major religions:** Christian 70%, Muslim 19%, other 11% | |
| **Government:** Multi-party democracy | |
| **Currency:** Dinar (Serbia), Euro (Montenegro) | |
| **Adult literacy rate:** 98% | |
| **Life expectancy:** 73 years | |
| **People per doctor:** 476 | |

| BOSNIA AND HERZEGOVINA | |
|---|---|
| **Capital city:** Sarajevo | |
| **Area:** 51,130 sq km (19,741 sq miles) | |
| **Population:** 4,200,000 | |
| **Official language:** Serbo-Croat | |
| **Major religions:** Christian 50%, Muslim 40%, other 10% | |
| **Government:** Multi-party democracy | |

# SERBIA AND MONTENEGRO

WHEN THE FORMER YUGOSLAVIA broke up in 1991, Serbia and Montenegro emerged from the wreckage as a joint republic, dominated by Serbia. Serbia then supported local Serbs in the Bosnian War of 1992–5 and in Kosovo in 1998–9, leading to international intervention to bring a fragile peace to the region. The country is now trying to repair the economic and structural damage caused by the conflicts; Montenegro is keen to pursue its dream of independence.

**Industry in former Yugoslavia**

- 🜹 Chemical
- △ Metallurgy
- ❋ Light engineering
- ✿ Heavy engineering
- ⌑ Electronics
- ❋ Textiles
- ▯ Food processing
- ✦ Pharmaceuticals

Novi Sad
Belgrade
Pancevo
Kragujevac
Paracin
Krusevac
Nis

INDUSTRY
Serbia was once the industrial heartland of the former Yugoslavia, with extensive engineering, food, and textile industries. Reserves of coal, as well as hydroelectricity from the Danube and Drina rivers, provided power, while oil deposits in the north supplied one-third of oil needs. However, sanctions applied in the late 1990s severely damaged Serbian industry.

PEOPLE
More than 60 per cent of people are Serbs, with Hungarians in Vojvodina, and Albanians in and around Kosovo. They speak a variety of languages. Serbs and Montenegrins speak a similar language and write in the Cyrillic script as used in Russian. Hungarians and Albanians use the Latin alphabet, as used in English, and speak separate, unrelated languages. Voting papers, being handed in here, are printed in all languages.

*Green and red peppers*

*Raznjici is made with skewers of grilled lamb.*

*Skewer*

DISHES OF SERBIA
A wide variety of tasty dishes are eaten in Serbia. *Raznjici*, grilled lamb with sweet peppers, shown here, is usually served with a bowl of yogurt. Meatballs served with onions and cream, called *cevapcici*, and vegetables such as cabbage stuffed with meat, onions, herbs, and garlic, are all popular dishes.

# BOSNIA AND HERZEGOVINA

BOSNIA AND HERZEGOVINA was the last of the former republics of Yugoslavia to declare independence, in 1992. For centuries, the area contained a mixture of Muslim Bosnians, Catholic Croats, and Orthodox Serbs. After independence, civil war broke out and many thousands of people were killed on all sides. The war ended in 1995 and the country was split into two separate halves – a Serb republic and a Muslim-Croat federation.

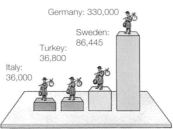

CITY OF SARAJEVO
By 1990, the ancient town of Sarajevo had grown into a large, modern city. But war exposed the city to Serb gunfire from the surrounding hills, and many citizens were killed. Those that remained led a primitive existence, often with no food, heat, or proper housing.

ETHNIC CLEANSING
Serbs fighting in Bosnia undertook a policy of ethnic cleansing. This involved removing, or "cleansing", Muslims and Croats from areas they inhabited alongside Serbs. Thousands of non-Serbs were murdered. Others were frightened into leaving their homes and seeking safety in more welcoming countries. Many Muslims sought refuge in Germany and Turkey.

**Bosnian refugees in Europe**

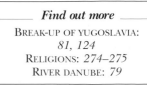

Germany: 330,000
Sweden: 86,445
Turkey: 36,800
Italy: 36,000

*Muslim girls and women traditionally wear a headscarf to cover their hair.*

**Find out more**
BREAK-UP OF YUGOSLAVIA: *81, 124*
RELIGIONS: *274–275*
RIVER DANUBE: *79*

# MACEDONIA

LANDLOCKED MACEDONIA has been controlled by its larger neighbours for many centuries. Historically linked to Greece, it has more recently been a part of Bulgaria and Yugoslavia. Since the country's independence, however, the greatest threat has come from ethnic tensions between Macedonan Slavs and ethnic Albanians. In this part of Southeast Europe, the warm climate allows the cultivation of early fruit crops and industrial crops such as rice, cotton, and tobacco. However, its location also means that fuel, machinery, and manufactured goods have to be imported.

Freshwater carp

| MACEDONIA | |
|---|---|
| **Capital city:** Skopje | |
| **Area:** 25,333 sq km (9,781 sq miles) | |
| **Population:** 2,020,000 | |
| **Official language:** Macedonian, Albanian | |
| **Major religions:** Christian 64%, Muslim 26%, other 10% | |
| **Government:** Multi-party democracy | |
| **Currency:** Denar | |
| **Adult literacy rate:** 94% | |
| **Life expectancy:** 73 years | |

| ALBANIA | |
|---|---|
| **Capital city:** Tirana | |
| **Area:** 28,748 sq km (11,100 sq miles) | |
| **Population:** 3,200,000 | |
| **Official language:** Albanian | |
| **Major religions:** Muslim 70%, Christian 30% | |
| **Government:** Multi-party democracy | |
| **Currency:** Lek | |
| **Adult literacy rate:** 99% | |

## EARTHQUAKES

The capital city of Skopje is located where several geological fault lines meet, making it a likely place for earthquakes. In fact, earth tremors in Skopje are frequent, and the city has been destroyed four times in its history. In 1963 an earthquake registering 6.8 on the Richter scale destroyed much of the city. Fortunately, the Turkish area, parts of which date from 1392, survived the destruction.

## LAKELAND AREAS

The mountainous area of southwest Macedonia contains two of Europe's most beautiful freshwater lakes. When the country had more tourists, visitors flocked to Lake Ohrid, and to the smaller Lake Prespa, to enjoy the scenery, and visit the ancient towns along the shores. Both lakes are teeming with fish, particularly carp, trout, and eels, that are used for local fish dishes. Colonies of pelicans and cormorants also feed on fish from Lake Prespa.

# ALBANIA

ONE OF THE POOREST countries in Europe, Albania is mostly rugged mountains. For much of its history, the country was ruled by the Ottoman Turks, who withdrew in 1913 leaving no roads, railways, or industries. In the last century, Albania has been ruled by a fascist king and a communist dictator. Democracy has been hindered by corruption and economic hardships. Violence erupted in 1997 after the collapse of an insurance scheme in which many Albanians had invested.

### Employment

*Jobs are scarce in Albania, and rates of pay are low. Over half of those with jobs work in agriculture, while the rest work in industry or services, such as education. Recently, thousands of people have moved to Greece or Italy to look for work.*

Services: 21%  Industry: 25%  Agriculture: 54%

## FAMILY LIFE

The family is an important part of Albanian life and, until recently, men were encouraged by the state to father large families. From an early age, Albanians are taught the importance of the promised word, known as *besa*. To break one's word, in a business deal for example, is considered a disgrace.

## COMMUNISM

From 1944–1985, Albania was led by the communist leader Enver Hoxha. Under his rule, Albania was cut off from the rest of Europe. The borders with Yugoslavia and Greece were sealed, and no contact with Italy was permitted. All trade after 1960, through ports in Durres and Vlore, was with China. The communists developed heavy industry at the expense of agriculture, leaving the country poor and undeveloped. This mural at Tirana Museum represents the people's struggle.

### Find out more

EARTHQUAKES: *13*
HYDROELECTRIC POWER: *108*
MEDITERRANEAN CLIMATE: *15*
POLITICAL SYSTEMS: *270–271*

# ROMANIA AND BULGARIA

DIVIDED BY THE MIGHTY River Danube, which flows eastwards along most of the shared border to the Black Sea, Romania and Bulgaria have much in common. The most fertile land in the region is found in the valley of the Danube, while forests of oak, pine, and fir grow on the sides of the Carpathian and the Balkan Mountains. For hundreds of years, Black Sea ports, around areas such as Constanta and Burgas, provided access to trade routes and remain important for international shipping.

### TOURIST ATTRACTIONS
Picturesque landscapes and colourful folk traditions make Romania popular with tourists. The legend of Count Dracula, from the forested region of Transylvania, shown here, attracts tourists who come to visit his castle. Black Sea beaches as well as mountain ski resorts cater for both summer and winter visitors.

### THINGS TO LOOK FOR ON THE MAP

**Longest river:** Danube, Germany/Austria/Hungary Yugoslavia/Romania/ Bulgaria, 2,850 km (1,771 miles) *Map F10*

**Highest point:** Musala, Bulgaria, 2,925 m (9,597 ft) *Map F12*

**Largest lake:** L. Razim, Romania, 390 sq km (151 sq miles) *Map L8*

**Bucharest, Romania**
Jan -3°C (27°F)
July 23°C (73°F)

Jan 46 mm (1.8 in)
July 53 mm (2.1 in)

ROMANIA

**Sofia, Bulgaria**
Jan -1°C (30°F)
July 22°C (71°F)

Jan 36 mm (1.4 in)
July 68 mm (2.7 in)

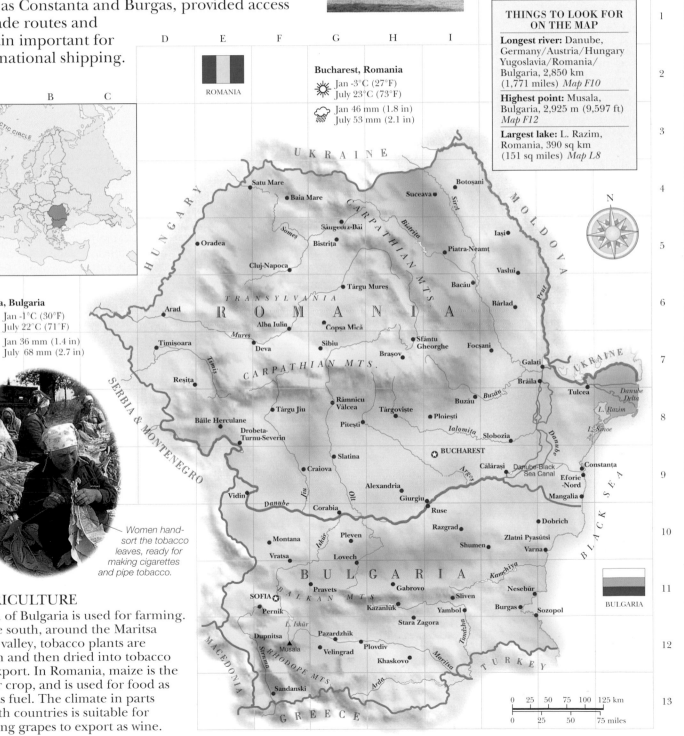

*Women hand-sort the tobacco leaves, ready for making cigarettes and pipe tobacco.*

BULGARIA

### AGRICULTURE
Much of Bulgaria is used for farming. In the south, around the Maritsa River valley, tobacco plants are grown and then dried into tobacco for export. In Romania, maize is the major crop, and is used for food as well as fuel. The climate in parts of both countries is suitable for growing grapes to export as wine.

0  25  50  75  100  125 km
0  25  50  75 miles

127

# ROMANIA

ONCE THE FRONTIER OF THE ROMAN EMPIRE, Romania is one of the largest countries in Europe. The Carpathian Mountains form an arc across the country, curving around the region of Transylvania. Elsewhere the land is rich and fertile. Romania became independent from Turkey in 1878, but its borders have been redrawn several times as a result of war. A revolution in 1989 overthrew the harsh communist government and today Romania is struggling to improve the life of its people. Although Romanians can now travel and worship in freedom, there is also high unemployment and food has become more expensive.

| ROMANIA |
| --- |
| **Capital city:** Bucharest |
| **Area:** 237,500 sq km (91,699 sq miles) |
| **Population:** 22,300,000 |
| **Official language:** Romanian |
| **Major religions:** Christian 98%, other 2% |
| **Government:** Multi-party democracy |
| **Currency:** Leu |
| **Adult literacy rate:** 97% |
| **Life expectancy:** 70 years |
| **People per doctor:** 526 |
| **Televisions:** 223 per 1,000 people |

**POLITICS**
From 1965 until his overthrow and execution in 1989, communist leader Nicolae Ceaucescu ruled Romania. During his brutal dictatorship, he tried to boost the population by encouraging women to have large families. Many people could not afford to keep their babies. The plight of the Romanian orphans attracted international attention and many were adopted abroad.

## WOODEN BUILDINGS

The vast forests of Romania provide an ideal material for building, and wooden houses and churches are found throughout the country. Many are surrounded by wooden fences and elaborately carved gateways. The walls are constructed using horizontal planks of wood, unlike the rest of Europe where they are placed vertically. House styles vary from one region to another. The steep-roofed home shown here is from a snowy area in the Carpathian Mountains; homes in wine-growing areas would have large cellars to store wine and fruit from the orchards.

*Homes in the mountains have steep roofs so that snow will slide off.*

*Wood from pine, beech, or spruce trees is used to build houses.*

*Columns may be hand-carved in a local design.*

*Houses are built on foundations of local stone to prevent the wood from rotting.*

*Rooms are decorated with carved wooden furniture and brightly painted plates.*

*Bedspreads are embroidered with traditional designs.*

**FOREIGN ORDERS**
In order to modernize old industries and create new jobs, foreign companies are being encouraged to set up business in Romania. France, Spain, Italy, the USA, and South Korea all now have manufacturing plants in or near Bucharest.

## PEOPLE OF ROMANIA

Romania is home to many peoples, with Hungarians and Germans sharing the land with native Romanians. Ukrainians and Turks settled areas near the Black Sea coast, now popular as a holiday resort. In the past, people lived and worked on the land, but with the growth of industry the majority now live in Bucharest, the capital, and other towns and cities.

**ROMA POPULATIONS**
Despite their name, the 500,000 Roma who live in Romania belong to a different ethnic group to the rest of the population. Although they used to live as travellers, they are now mostly settled on the outskirts of towns.

*Find out more*
CITIES: *80*
COUNTRIES OF EASTERN EUROPE: 81
POLITICAL SYSTEMS: *270–271*

# BULGARIA

FOR MUCH OF ITS HISTORY, the area that is now Bulgaria has lived in the shadow of stronger neighbours. The Greeks, Romans, and Turks have all ruled here, and from 1944–1989 Bulgaria was part of the Soviet communist bloc. Most of today's population are Bulgars, with sizcablc minorities of Macedonians and Turks. Since the move to democracy, state-run farms have been reorganized, and western tourists are encouraged to visit the old towns and villages as well as lakes and resorts on the Black Sea.

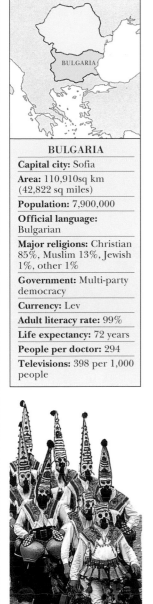

| BULGARIA | |
|---|---|
| **Capital city:** Sofia | |
| **Area:** 110,910sq km (42,822 sq miles) | |
| **Population:** 7,900,000 | |
| **Official language:** Bulgarian | |
| **Major religions:** Christian 85%, Muslim 13%, Jewish 1%, other 1% | |
| **Government:** Multi-party democracy | |
| **Currency:** Lev | |
| **Adult literacy rate:** 99% | |
| **Life expectancy:** 72 years | |
| **People per doctor:** 294 | |
| **Televisions:** 398 per 1,000 people | |

*Women wear traditional costumes during the Festival of the Roses.*

*Roses are picked before fully open to avoid exposure to the sun.*

*Damask rose*

## ROSE GROWING

Situated in the foothills of the Balkan Mountains, near the town of Kazanluk, lies the Valley of the Roses. Fields of roses are grown here for their csscntial oil, callcd attar, which is uscd to make perfume. At dawn each day in May and June, before the sun has time to dry out their oil, blossoms of the damask rose are picked, and the petals packed into sacks. These are taken by donkey cart to a distillery where they are made into attar. Every June there is a festival to celebrate the rose harvest.

### CITY OF SOFIA
The capital city of Sofia is home to more than a million people. Set in an area of mountains and lowland dairy farming, the city is a thriving industrial centre. It is also a showcase for many fine Roman buildings, as well as the Alexander Nevsky cathedral, shown here, that was built to honour Russian soldiers who liberated Sofia from Turkish rule in 1878. Bulgaria has a good transport system. Many people in Sofia travel by trolleybuses that get their power from overhead electric cables.

### FESTIVAL MASKS
Folk customs play an important part in keeping Bulgarian traditions alive. Many towns have their own festival, featuring music and parades. People often make and paint their own masks, and decorate them with beads and ribbons.

## ECONOMY
Bulgaria lacks the high-grade coal and iron necessary to support heavy industry. In the past, its factories relied on cheap supplies of coal and oil from the former USSR, but now have to buy these on the open market. Bulgaria has been forced to arrange large loans from the West to finance development of new industries, such as computer technology. Textile mills and food processing are important.

**Bulgarian industries**

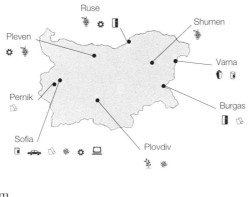

Ruse
Shumen
Pleven
Varna
Pernik
Burgas
Sofia
Plovdiv

| | |
|---|---|
| 🚗 Vehicle assembly | ▢ Steel |
| ⚙ Engineering | 🌿 Textiles |
| 🌱 Tobacco | 🚢 Shipbuilding |
| ▤ Oil refining | 🖳 Food processing |
| 🌾 Wine | 💻 Computers |

### NUCLEAR POWER
Bulgaria does not have enough coal or power from its hydroelectric plants to provide itself with energy. Forty per cent of its electricity now comes from the Kozloduy nuclear power station. Because the station was built by the Soviet Union, and lies in an earthquake zone, there has been great concern about its safety. Since 1990, the European Union has helped to make the plant safer.

*Find out more*
BREAK-UP OF USSR: *136*
COUNTRIES OF EASTERN EUROPE: *80*
POLITICAL SYSTEMS: *270–271*

# GREECE

GREECE HAS A RICH HISTORY stretching back thousands of years. Yet the modern nation state only won its independence from the Turks in 1829, and it took control of some islands as recently as 1947. With its mountainous terrain, more than 2,000 scattered islands, and lack of natural resources, Greece was one of the poorest members of the European Union. However, its large shipping fleet and earnings from tourism have helped the economy: Greece adopted the Euro in 2002 and hosted the Olympic Games in Athens in 2004.

| GREECE | |
|---|---|
| **Capital city:** Athens | |
| **Area:** 131,940 sq km (50,942 sq miles) | |
| **Population:** 11,000,000 | |
| **Official language:** Greek | |
| **Major religions:** Christian 98%, Muslim 1%, other 1% | |
| **Government:** Multi-party democracy | |
| **Currency:** Euro | |
| **Adult literacy rate:** 97% | |
| **Life expectancy:** 78 years | |
| **People per doctor:** 227 | |
| **Televisions:** 477 per 1,000 people | |

**Main tourist nationalities**

*The majority of tourists visiting Greece are European, although large numbers of people also travel to Greece from North America and Australasia.*

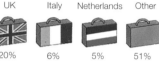

| Germany | UK | Italy | Netherlands | Other |
|---|---|---|---|---|
| 18% | 20% | 6% | 5% | 51% |

## TOURISM

More than 14 million tourists a year come to Greece to enjoy the beautiful island scenery, the historic monuments, and the summer sun. Hotels, shops, and restaurants employ thousands of people to cater for the visitors, whose spending boosts the national economy enormously. The Greek government encourages tourism by giving grants for hotel building, and the many Aegean islands are linked together by a comprehensive network of ferries. However, some islands are being developed too rapidly and suffer from problems such as water shortages.

*Holidaymakers enjoying the beach on the island of Samos.*

### SHIPPING

The cheapest and easiest way to travel round Greece is still by boat. Fleets of merchant ships connect the many islands with the mainland, moving supplies and industrial products, while ferries carry vehicles, local people, and tourists. Ship-owners have built up huge fleets of ships, with the result that Greece now has the largest merchant fleet in the world.

*Icons being blessed at an Easter ceremony.*

### GREEK ORTHODOX CHURCH

The state religion of Greece is Greek Orthodox, making it the only officially Orthodox Christian country in the world. Almost every Greek is a member of the church. Priests play an important part in national events, and are recognized as leaders of their local communities. The churches are not allowed statues, but many contain holy pictures of saints known as icons.

*Olives are treated, pickled, and fermented before being eaten whole.*

*To make olive oil, the olives are ground to a thick paste before being pressed.*

*Olives can be eaten when green or black, but must ripen to black when used for oil.*

### FARMING

Only a third of the mountainous terrain of Greece can be farmed, and much of the soil is poor. Many people are needed to work this land – nearly one-fifth of the Greek workforce is employed in agriculture, which is more than anywhere else in European Union. The most important crop is olives, grown on hillsides across the country. Greece is the third biggest producer of olive oil after Italy and Spain, as well as a major producer of grapes and wine, citrus and other fruits, figs, cotton, tomatoes, and tobacco.

*Olive trees are usually quite small but they can live for hundreds of years.*

*Olives are harvested in autumn. The trees are shaken by hand or by machine, and the olives are gathered up in large nets and sorted.*

### ATHENS

The ancient capital of Greece is dominated by the Acropolis and the dramatic ruins of the Parthenon temple. Much of the city, however, consists of modern buildings, for many people have left the countryside to seek employment in the city. As a result, Athens is one of Europe's most polluted cities; cars are banned from entering the city on certain days of the week in order to reduce the level of smog.

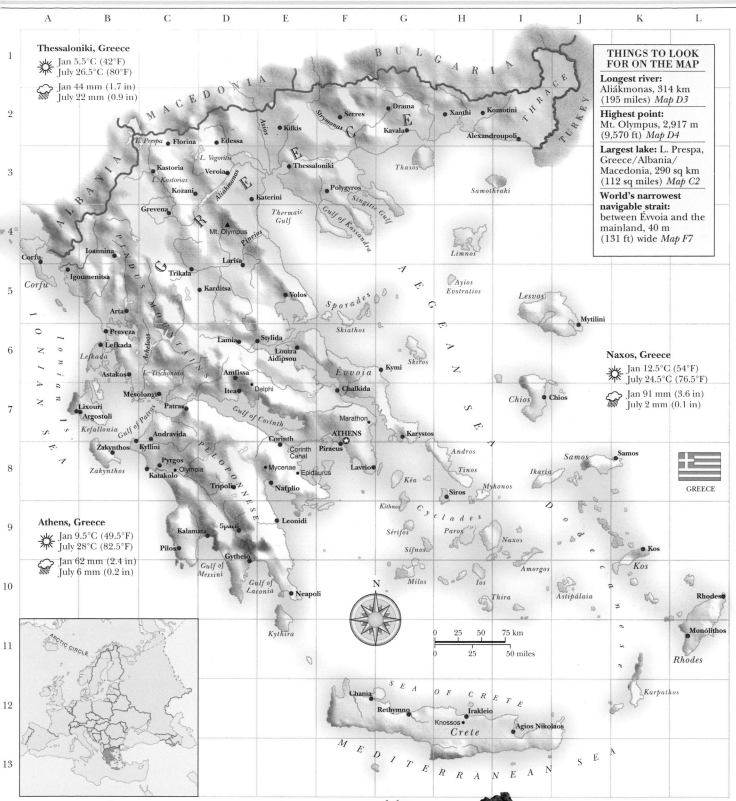

A B C D E F G H I J K L

**Thessaloniki, Greece**
☀ Jan 5.5°C (42°F)
July 26.5°C (80°F)
🌧 Jan 44 mm (1.7 in)
July 22 mm (0.9 in)

1

BULGARIA

MACEDONIA

2

THRACE

Drama
Serres
Strymonas
Kilkis
Xanthi
Komotini
Axios
Kavala
TURKEY
Alexandroupoli

L. Prespa
Florina
Edessa
L. Vegoritis
Kastoria
Veroia
L. Kastorias
Kozani
Katerini
Polygyros
Thasos
Samothraki
Grevena
Thermaic Gulf
Singitic Gulf
Gulf of Kassandra

ALBANIA

GREECE

Mt. Olympus
Pineios

3

Thessaloniki

Larisa

4

Corfu
Ioannina
Igoumenitsa
Trikala
Karditsa

PINDUS MOUNTAINS

Limnos
AEGEAN SEA

Ayios Evstratios
Lesvos
Mytilini

5

Corfu
IONIAN Is.
Arta
Preveza
Lefkada
Lefkada
Astakos
L. Trichonida
Acheloos
Volos
Sporades
Skiathos

Lamia
Stylida
Loutra Aidipsou
Évvoia
Kymi
Skiros
Chios
Chios

6

Mesolongi
Amfissa
Itea
Delphi
Chalkida
Lixouri
Argostoli
Patras
Gulf of Patras
Gulf of Corinth
Marathon
Karystos
Andros

7

Kefallonia

ATHENS
Piraeus
Corinth
Corinth Canal
Samos
Samos

Zakynthos
Kyllini
Andravida
PELOPONNESE
Mycenae
Epidauros
Lavrio
Kêa
Tinos
Ikaria

8

Pyrgos
Olympia
Katakolo
Tripoli
Nafplio
Siros
Mykonos
Zakynthos

**Athens, Greece**
☀ Jan 9.5°C (49.5°F)
July 28°C (82.5°F)
🌧 Jan 62 mm (2.4 in)
July 6 mm (0.2 in)

9

Kalamata
Sparti
Leonidi
Kithnos
CYCLADES
Sérifos
Paros
Nuxos
Kos

Pilos
Gytheio
Sífnos
Milos
Ios
Amorgos

10

Neapoli
Gulf of Messini
Gulf of Laconia
Thira
Astipálaia
DODECANESE
Rhodes
Monólithos

N

Kythira

11

Rhodes

0 25 50 75 km
0 25 50 miles

Karpathos

12

SEA OF CRETE
Chania
Rethymno
Irakleio
Knossos
Agios Nikolaos
Crete

13

MEDITERRANEAN SEA

**THINGS TO LOOK FOR ON THE MAP**
**Longest river:**
Aliákmonas, 314 km (195 miles) *Map D3*
**Highest point:**
Mt. Olympus, 2,917 m (9,570 ft) *Map D4*
**Largest lake:** L. Prespa, Greece/Albania/Macedonia, 290 sq km (112 sq miles) *Map C2*
**World's narrowest navigable strait:** between Évvoia and the mainland, 40 m (131 ft) wide *Map F7*

**Naxos, Greece**
☀ Jan 12.5°C (54°F)
July 24.5°C (76.5°F)
🌧 Jan 91 mm (3.6 in)
July 2 mm (0.1 in)

GREECE

ARCTIC CIRCLE

## ANCIENT GREEK HISTORY
The remains of temples and other buildings from Greece's long and complex history can still be seen today. From about 2000BC, advanced civilizations existed on Crete and on the mainland at Mycenae. By the 5th century BC, powerful city states emerged, including Athens and Sparta. Philosophers, mathematicians, architects, and dramatists contributed to a rich culture that spread around the Mediterranean.

*Signs of Greece's rich classical past are revealed in its many ancient ruins, such as this temple of Apollo at Delphi.*

*Find out more*
EUROPEAN UNION: *81, 273*
MEDITERRANEAN LANDSCAPE: *79*
ORTHODOX CHURCH: *274*
WINE MAKING: *99*

# ASIA

STRETCHING FROM THE frozen Arctic to the hot Equator, Asia is by far the world's largest and most mountainous continent. Much of the land is barren, with vast, empty deserts in southwest and central Asia, and the remote, windswept plateau of Tibet to the north of the Himalayan Mountains. Asia also has some of the world's most fertile plains and valleys beside rivers that include the Mekong, Indus, and Euphrates. In southeast Asia, the land is mainly mountainous or covered in tropical rainforests that are teeming with wildlife.

Away from the mainland, scattered either side of the Equator, lie thousands of islands, many of them volcanic.

## SIBERIA
Most of Siberia, the Asian part of Russia, is bitterly cold in winter. In the north lies the tundra, where part of the soil has been frozen since the end of the last Ice Age. Beneath its surface there are vast supplies of minerals. To the south lies the world's largest coniferous forest. This cold forest makes way for a dry grassland area, known as steppe, which forms Russia's main farming region.

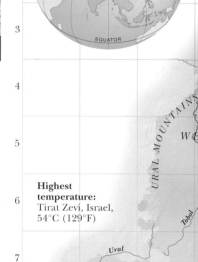

**Highest temperature:** Tirat Zevi, Israel, 54°C (129°F)

### THE YANGTZE RIVER
From its source in the Tanggula Mountains on the plateau of Tibet, the Yangtze River flows through mountainous land for most of its course. On its final stages, it follows the southern edge of the Great Plain of China until it reaches the East China Sea. In the flatter areas, the Yangtze supplies water for irrigation. In the past, flooding has caused thousands of deaths.

## CENTRAL DESERTS
Unlike most deserts, the Takla Makan and Gobi in central Asia have hot summers but extremely cold winters. Much of their landscape is made up of bare rock with huge expanses of shifting sand. Vegetation is sparse, except in river valleys, as shown here in the Takla Makan. Some animals, including wild camels, can survive cold winters in the Gobi.

*A Bactrian camels has two humps.*

## THE HIMALAYAS
The Himalayas, right, form a massive land barrier between the Indian Subcontinent and Tibet. The range is permanently snow-capped, and contains the world's highest peak, Mount Everest. The mountains began to form about 50 million years ago when a moving plate, carrying the subcontinent, began to push against the Eurasian plate. When the plates collided, the edge of the Indian plate was forced under the Eurasian plate, and the sea-bed in between was folded up to form the Himalayas.

HIMALAYAS

EURASIAN PLATE

INDIAN PLATE

Map labels: URAL MOUNTAINS, WE, Tobol, Ural, KHIRGHIZ STEPPE, USTYURT PLATEAU, CASPIAN SEA, ARAL SEA, Syr D, TURAN LOWLAND, KARA KUM, Amu Darya, BLACK SEA, CAUCASUS, ELBURZ MTS, Cyprus, Euphrates, Tigris, IRANIAN PLATEAU, Tirat Zevi, SYRIAN DESERT, ZAGROS MTS., DEAD SEA, Persian Gulf, Gulf of Oman, RED SEA, AR RUB' AL KHALI, ARABIA SEA, Gulf of Aden, Socotra, Lakshad

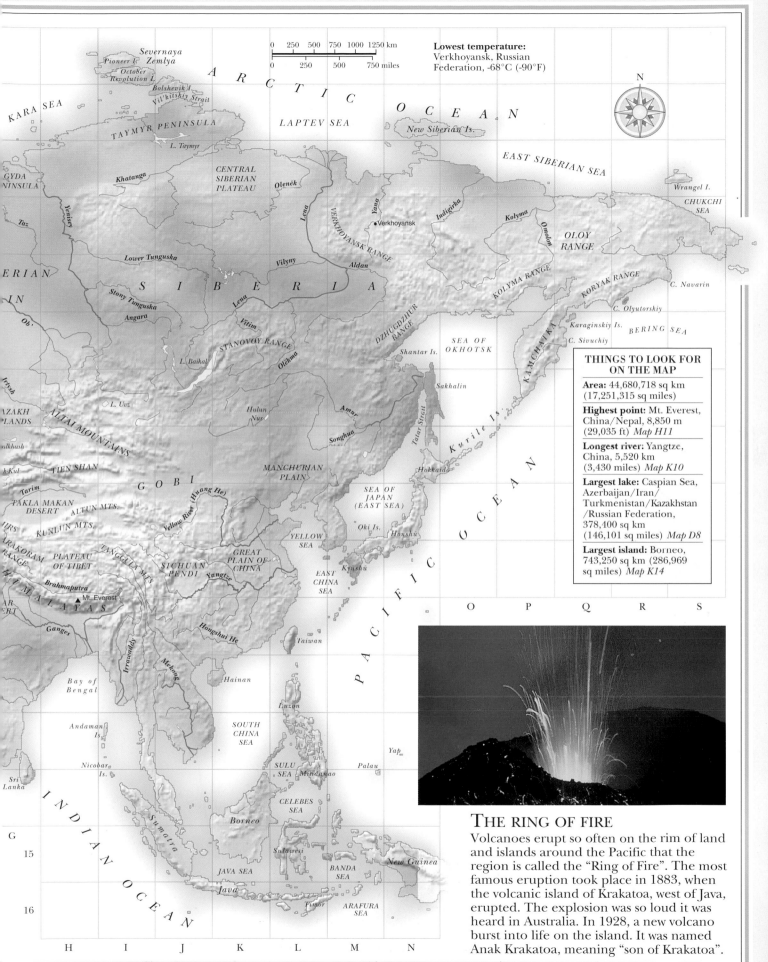

A R C T I C   O C E A N

KARA SEA

*Severnaya*
Pioneer I. *Zemlya*
October
Revolution I.
Bolshevik I.
Vil'kitskiy Strait

TAYMYR PENINSULA

LAPTEV SEA

New Siberian Is.

EAST SIBERIAN SEA

Wrangel I.

CHUKCHI
SEA

**Lowest temperature:**
Verkhoyansk, Russian
Federation, -68°C (-90°F)

N

GYDA
NINSULA

L. Taymyr

CENTRAL
SIBERIAN
PLATEAU

Khatanga

Olenëk

Lena

Yana

Indigirka

Kolyma

Omolon

OLOY
RANGE

C. Navarin

Taz

Yenisey

Lower Tunguska

S  I  B  E  R  I  A

Verkhoyansk

VERKHOYANSK RANGE

Aldan

KOLYMA RANGE

KORYAK RANGE

C. Olyutorskiy

Karaginskiy Is.

BERING SEA

ERIAN
IN

Ob'

Stony Tunguska

Angara

Vilyny

Vitim

Lena

DZHUGDZHUR
RANGE

C. Sivuchiy

Irtysh

STANOVOY RANGE

Olëkma

L. Baikal

Amur

Shantar Is.

SEA OF
OKHOTSK

KAMCHATKA

AZAKH
LANDS

ALTAI MOUNTAINS

L. Uvz

Hulun
Nur

Sakhalin

Kurile Is.

Ikul

TIEN SHAN

G O B I

MANCHURIAN
PLAIN

Songhua

Tatar Strait

Hokkaido

P A C I F I C   O C E A N

Tarim

TAKLA MAKAN
DESERT

ALTUN MTS.

Yellow River (Huang He)

SEA OF
JAPAN
(EAST SEA)

Oki Is.

Honshū

IRS

KUNLUN MTS.

Oki Is,

ARAKORAM
RANGE

PLATEAU
OF TIBET

TANGGULA MTS.

SICHUAN
PENDI

YELLOW
SEA

GREAT
PLAIN OF
CHINA

Yangtze

Kyūshū

Brahmaputra

Mt. Everest

H I M A L A Y A S

EAST
CHINA
SEA

Ganges

Hongshui He

Taiwan

Bay of
Bengal

Irrawaddy

Mekong

Hainan

Andaman
Is.

Luzon

SOUTH
CHINA
SEA

Yap

Sri
Lanka

Nicobar
Is.

SULU
SEA

Mindanao

Palau

I N D I A N   O C E A N

CELEBES
SEA

Sumatra

Borneo

Sulawesi

JAVA SEA

BANDA
SEA

New Guinea

Java

Timor

ARAFURA
SEA

O   P   Q   R   S

G

15

16

H   I   J   K   L   M   N

---

**THINGS TO LOOK FOR
ON THE MAP**

**Area:** 44,680,718 sq km
(17,251,315 sq miles)

**Highest point:** Mt. Everest,
China/Nepal, 8,850 m
(29,035 ft) *Map H11*

**Longest river:** Yangtze,
China, 5,520 km
(3,430 miles) *Map K10*

**Largest lake:** Caspian Sea,
Azerbaijan/Iran/
Turkmenistan/Kazakhstan
/Russian Federation,
378,400 sq km
(146,101 sq miles) *Map D8*

**Largest island:** Borneo,
743,250 sq km (286,969
sq miles) *Map K14*

---

## THE RING OF FIRE

Volcanoes erupt so often on the rim of land
and islands around the Pacific that the
region is called the "Ring of Fire". The most
famous eruption took place in 1883, when
the volcanic island of Krakatoa, west of Java,
erupted. The explosion was so loud it was
heard in Australia. In 1928, a new volcano
burst into life on the island. It was named
Anak Krakatoa, meaning "son of Krakatoa".

# PEOPLES OF ASIA I

OF ALL THE CONTINENTS, Asia has the largest population with the greatest variety of cultures. The history of civilization here stretches back for many thousands of years. Cities and writing, the development of which are closely connected, first appeared in Asia. More than 5,000 years ago the earliest cities, such as Babylon, emerged in the valley of the Tigris and Euphrates rivers, an area known as Mesopotamia (modern-day Iraq). Today, Asia contains over 60 percent of the world's population, much of which is concentrated in the southern and eastern regions of the continent. Although most of the population are farmers, city populations are growing very rapidly.

*Stone reliefs in Persepolis, capital of the ancient Persian Empire.*

EARLY CIVILIZATIONS
The world's earliest civilizations grew up around river valleys in Asia, in an area known as the fertile crescent which stretches in an arc from the Persian Gulf to the Mediterranean Sea. Many cities here can trace their history back for several thousand years.

| **Population:** approximately 3,823,390,000 people |
| --- |
| **Number of countries:** 48 |

**Largest country:** Russian Federation – the Asian part covers 13,444,468 sq km (5,190,909 sq miles)

**Smallest country:** Maldives 300 sq km (116 sq miles)

**Least densely populated country:** Mongolia, 2 people per sq km (4 per sq mile)

**Most densely populated country:** Singapore, 7,049 people per sq km (18,220 per sq mile)

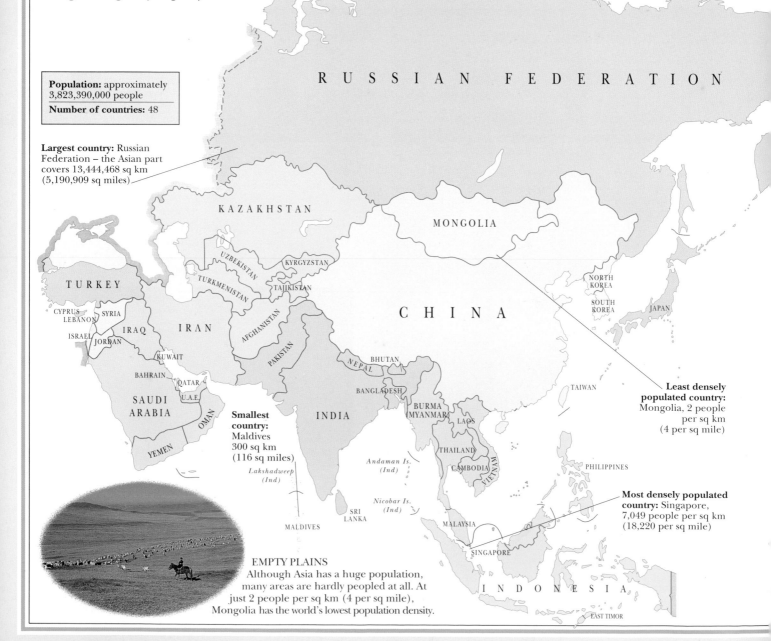

EMPTY PLAINS
Although Asia has a huge population, many areas are hardly peopled at all. At just 2 people per sq km (4 per sq mile), Mongolia has the world's lowest population density.

Map labels: RUSSIAN FEDERATION, KAZAKHSTAN, MONGOLIA, UZBEKISTAN, KYRGYZSTAN, TURKMENISTAN, TAJIKISTAN, NORTH KOREA, SOUTH KOREA, JAPAN, TURKEY, CYPRUS, LEBANON, SYRIA, IRAQ, IRAN, AFGHANISTAN, CHINA, ISRAEL, JORDAN, KUWAIT, PAKISTAN, NEPAL, BHUTAN, TAIWAN, BAHRAIN, QATAR, U.A.E., BANGLADESH, BURMA MYANMAR, LAOS, SAUDI ARABIA, OMAN, INDIA, THAILAND, CAMBODIA, VIETNAM, PHILIPPINES, YEMEN, *Andaman Is. (Ind)*, *Lakshadweep (Ind)*, *Nicobar Is. (Ind)*, SRI LANKA, MALDIVES, MALAYSIA, SINGAPORE, INDONESIA, EAST TIMOR

# GROWING CITIES

A large proportion of Asia's population still live in the countryside as farmers, but the number living in cities is rising steeply. The largest cities in Asia now have populations of over 10 million people. These super-cities, along with many other cities in the continent, are destined to grow even faster as people move from the countryside to towns.

*This crowded street scene is in India's capital, New Delhi. India is one of the world's most densely populated countries.*

| LARGEST CITIES IN ASIA | |
| --- | --- |
| Tokyo, Japan | 35,510,000 |
| Seoul, South Korea | 21,740,000 |
| Mumbai, India | 19,470,000 |
| Jakarta, Indonesia | 17,590,000 |
| Osaka, Japan | 17,510,000 |

**Population density**

The figures on the chart show the number of people per sq km (per sq mile). Countries outside Asia are included as a comparison.

Bangladesh: 1,096 (2,837)

China: 140 (362)

World: 43 (112)

Oman: 14 (35)

USA: 32 (83)

## POPULATION DENSITY

Large areas of the Middle East and central Asia are empty wilderness, unsettled by people because of their extreme dryness or cold temperatures. Most of the continent's population is concentrated in the fertile river valleys and coastal lowlands of south and east Asia. Apart from the island city-state of Singapore, Bangladesh is the most densely populated country in Asia with 1,096 people per sq km (2,837 per sq mile).

*A Bedouin man in Jordan may have more than one wife and many children.*

# POPULATION GROWTH

Three out of every five people in the world live in Asia. Seven of the world's 10 most populated countries are located here, with China and India heading the list. Between them these two countries account for about 40 per cent of the world's population. In mainland China a strictly enforced government policy to restrict family size to just one child has slowed the rate of population growth, but elsewhere in the continent it is still very high. By 2000, India's population had risen to over 1,000 million and Indonesia's had passed 210 million inhabitants.

*In China, a family with just one child receives free education and a housing allowance.*

## RIVER VALLEYS

The first peoples settled in fertile river valleys where they could grow crops. They built irrigation systems to channel water from the river to the crops. Today, rivers are still of great importance to the people of southern and eastern Asia. As well as irrigation, rivers are used for fishing and for drinking. They are dammed to produce hydroelectric power. Rivers often provide a country's main means of transport, and some are the focus around which countries have grown up.

**World's top rice-growing countries (2003)**

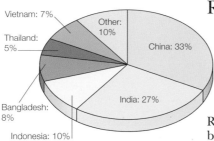

Vietnam: 7%

Thailand: 5%

Other: 10%

China: 33%

India: 27%

Bangladesh: 8%

Indonesia: 10%

# RICE

Half the world's population depend on rice as their principal source of food, so a rice shortage can cause terrible famine. This plant, which is native to southeast Asia, has been cultivated in the region for at least 7,000 years. In recent decades, new varieties of rice have been developed to help feed Asia's growing population. These new strains of rice are part of the "Green Revolution", which applies scientific knowledge to plant breeding and uses technology to increase productivity.

# PEOPLES OF ASIA II

ALTHOUGH SOME ASIAN COUNTRIES, such as Japan and China, have been independent for a long time, others have only recently emerged from being colonies. At the start of the 20th century, much of the Middle East, the whole Indian Subcontinent, and large areas of southeast Asia were controlled by European powers. Nationalist movements grew up across Asia and the countries regained their independence. Many countries here have had very fast economic growth which, together with the recent pressures for change, means that societies across the region are now changing very rapidly.

**INDEPENDENCE**
Each year, many countries in the region celebrate their freedom from colonial rule in independence day celebrations, like those in Pakistan shown above. Some countries, like India, gained independence through largely peaceful protest, while fierce fighting occurred in others, such as Indonesia. These countries are now struggling to forge a sense of national unity.

**The former USSR**
This map shows the former USSR and the 15 republics that it divided up into.

**USSR**
*(Much of this area is now the Russian Federation.)*

## BREAK-UP

The Soviet Union, or USSR, was the world's largest nation. However, in 1991, it split up into 15 republics which set up their own governments. Nine of the republics are in Europe and five in Asia, while Russia straddles both. Now they are no longer part of a large, centralized economy, the republics are struggling to compete in a world market. The USSR's collapse also freed some eastern European countries from Soviet control.

*Chechnya's capital Grozny was heavily bombed by the Russian Federation in 1994–95 and again in 1999–2000.*

*Most young men in Thailand live in a monastery as monks for a few months.*

**WORLD RELIGIONS**
Asia was the birthplace of all the main world religions, including Hinduism, Buddhism, Judaism, Christianity, and Islam. Religious beliefs still have a strong influence on the people of the region today. Religions often emphasise modesty in wealth and the importance of donating to charity for spiritual reward rather than any personal gain.

*This temple is in Thailand, where Buddhism is the main religion.*

## ETHNIC GROUPS

Fighting between ethnic groups is still continuing in several parts of the former USSR. The Russian Federation, for example, includes some regions where the Russian population is in the minority and greater numbers of people belong to native ethnic groups. In Chechnya, only about a third of the population is Russian. Since the break-up of the USSR, the Chechens have been fighting for independence. However, the Russian Federation is not prepared to grant independence to any of these territories since this could lead to the break-up of Russia itself.

# PRESSURES FOR CHANGE

In Asian societies today, the traditional rural ways of life and religious beliefs conflict with an increasingly money-oriented way of life, influenced by the West. As Asian societies become more open to western influences, so the pressures on traditional ways of life will intensify. Societies react to pressures for change in different ways. In Afghanistan, for example, religious leaders violently opposed Western ideas, leading to the setting up of a hardline republic based on a strict interpretation of Islamic law.

*In Afghanistan, the hardline Islamic Taliban government banned videos and ordered them all to be destroyed.*

## OIL AND THE MIDDLE EAST

Before oil was discovered, many desert countries in the Middle East were very poor. Oil has transformed their fortunes. More than two-thirds of the world's known reserves of crude oil and a third of all natural gas occur here and the countries have become wealthy through the export of oil and natural gas throughout the world. New cities have sprung up such as Dubai (shown above) and foreign workers have arrived in great numbers.

*The influence of the USA and capitalism can be seen on the streets of Tokyo, in Japan.*

## WESTERN INFLUENCE

In some societies, change happens gradually and without violent demonstrations. In Japan, for example, economic development was seen by its rulers as a way of avoiding becoming dependent on European nations. Japan has therefore accepted western capitalism while still managing to preserve traditional Japanese values. Even China, so long closed to western ideas, is now enthusiastically embracing capitalism.

*Shaded areas on the map show southeast Asia's newly industrializing countries.*

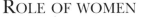

**Asia's "Little Tiger" economies**

SOUTH KOREA
HONG KONG
TAIWAN
PHILIPPINES
THAILAND
MALAYSIA
SINGAPORE

## LITTLE TIGERS

Following in the footsteps of Japan, a number of Southeast Asian countries looked to make the most of their cheap and plentiful supply of workers to rapidly boost their economies. These "Little Tigers" achieved great success in the final decades of the 20th century. However, they are now having to deal with the side effects of rapid industrialization – pollution, unemployment, poverty in rural areas, and new cheaper competition that has begun to emerge from elsewhere.

*Kazakh people in northern China outside a tent, known as a yurt.*

## NOMADIC EXISTENCE

The collapse of the USSR has led to a revival of traditional ways of life among the nomads of central Asia. Goods that were made in factories, such as felt which is used to line the inside of nomads' tents, ceased to be available and now have to be made by hand using traditional methods. The same is true when it comes to moving home. In recent years, many nomads have moved their belongings around in motor vehicles, but petrol is now in very short supply and nomads have returned to using camels and horses.

# ROLE OF WOMEN

Women's lives differ hugely over such a large continent, influenced by each nation's culture, religion, and politics. In some areas, such as India and the Islamic countries of the Middle East, the vast majority of the workforce is male. Yet Islamic women in southeast Asian countries such as Indonesia often work outside the home. In other areas, such as communist China and North Korea, and the former communist republics of the USSR, women make up a large proportion of the workforce and carry out most household chores.

*This chart shows the percentage of men and women in the workforce in five countries.*

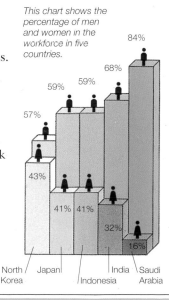

84%
68%
59%   59%
57%
43%
41%   41%
32%
16%

North Korea | Japan | Indonesia | India | Saudi Arabia

# RUSSIAN FEDERATION

STRETCHING ACROSS two continents –
Europe and Asia – and extending halfway
around the globe, the Russian Federation
is by far the largest country in the world.
Because of the bitterly cold climate and
harsh living conditions, this vast land is
sparsely populated. However, Russia has
areas of fertile land, rich mineral deposits,
and abundant natural resources. The
country was once the head of a powerful
communist state, the Union of
Soviet Socialist Republics (USSR).
During the collapse of communism
in 1991, many parts of the old Soviet
Union declared independence.
The government of the newly
formed Russian Federation is now
struggling to establish a Western-
style democracy and economy.

*Surrounded by high
red-brick walls, the
Kremlin (fortress)
contains four gilt-
domed cathedrals
and the grand
palace of the
tsars.*

**RUSSIAN FEDERATION**

**St Petersburg**
☀ Jan -10°C (14°F)
July 17°C (63°F)
☔ Jan 35 mm (1.4 in)
July 72 mm (2.8 in)

**Perm**
☀ Jan -17°C (2°F)
July 19°C (65°F)
☔ Jan 40 mm (1.6 i
July 89 mm (3.5

---

**THINGS TO LOOK FOR
ON THE MAP**

**Longest river:** Lena, 4,261 km
(2,648 miles) *Map N6*

**Highest point:** Klyuchevsk, 4,750 m
(15,585 ft) *Map T5*

**Largest lake:** Baikal, 31,468 sq km
(12,150 sq miles) *Map M10*

**World's largest straits:** Tatar Strait,
800 km (497 miles) long *Map S9*

## POLITICAL CHANGE

The Moscow Kremlin reflects the
changing political face of Russia. Once
the home of the tsars (emperors), who
ruled Russia for many centuries, it later
became the headquarters of the world's
first communist government in 1917.
The government created the USSR,
which became an industrial and military
superpower, but at great cost to its people.
The communist state collapsed in 1991,
and the Kremlin is now the symbolic home
of the new rulers of the Russian Federation.

## VOLGA RIVER

The mighty Volga River rises
northwest of Moscow and
flows 3,530 km (2,193 miles)
southwards to the Caspian
Sea. The Volga is the
most important inland
waterway in Russia.
Hundreds of ships use
it every day to transport
goods to vast industrial
sites that lie alongside the
river. Huge dams have created
a string of reservoirs providing
water and electricity for the people
who live on or near its banks.

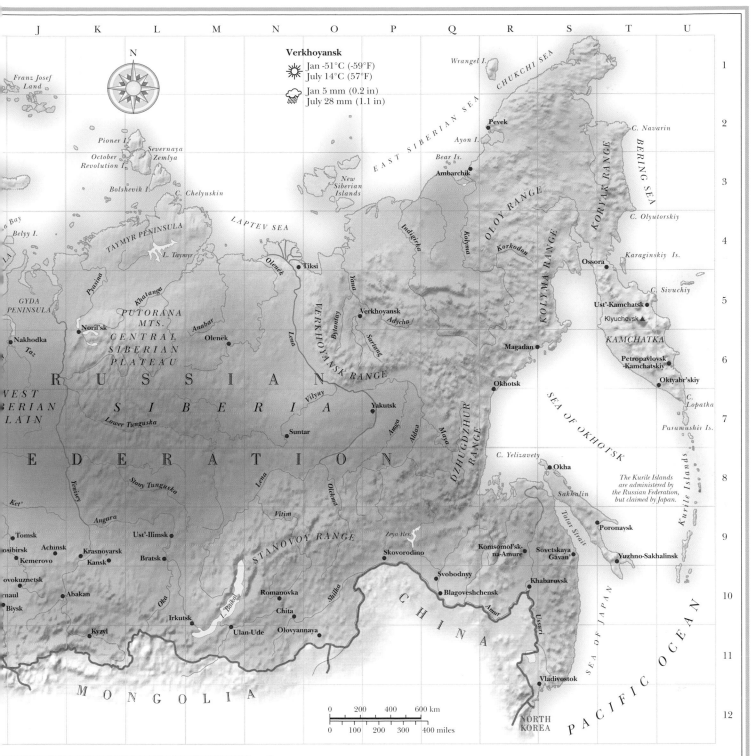

**Verkhoyansk**
- Jan -51°C (-59°F)
  July 14°C (57°F)
- Jan 5 mm (0.2 in)
  July 28 mm (1.1 in)

*Wrangel I.*

CHUKCHI SEA

*Franz Josef Land*

N

*Pioner I.*

*October Revolution I.*

*Severnaya Zemlya*

*Bolshevik I.*

*C. Chelyuskin*

EAST SIBERIAN SEA

*New Siberian Islands*

LAPTEV SEA

*C. Navarin*

BERING SEA

Pevek

*Ayon I.*

*Bear Is.*

Ambarchik

OLOY RANGE

KORYAK RANGE

*C. Olyutorskiy*

*Belyy I.*

a Bay

TAYMYR PENINSULA

*L. Taymyr*

*Pyasina*

*Khatanga*

*Oleněk*

Tiksi

*Yana*

*Indigirka*

*Kolyma*

*Korkodon*

Ossora

*Karaginskiy Is.*

GYDA PENINSULA

PUTORANA MTS.

CENTRAL SIBERIAN PLATEAU

*Anabar*

VERKHOYANSK RANGE

*Bytantay*

Verkhoyansk

*Adycha*

*Suntang*

KOLYMA RANGE

*C. Sivuchiy*

Ust'-Kamchatsk

Klyuchevsk ▲

Noril'sk

*Nakhodka*

*Taz*

Oleněk

*Lena*

Magadan

KAMCHATKA

Petropavlovsk-Kamchatskiy

R U S S I A N   S I B E R I A

WEST SIBERIAN PLAIN

*Lower Tunguska*

*Vilyuy*

Yakutsk

Okhotsk

Oktyabr'skiy

*C. Lopatka*

F E D E R A T I O N

*Yenisey*

*Stony Tunguska*

*Ket'*

*Suntar*

*Lena*

*Amga*

*Aldan*

*Maya*

DZHUGDZHUR RANGE

*C. Yelizavety*

SEA OF OKHOTSK

*Paramushir Is.*

Okha

*Sakhalin*

The Kurile Islands are administered by the Russian Federation, but claimed by Japan.

*Olëkma*

*Angara*

*Vitim*

Tomsk

Achinsk

osibirsk

Krasnoyarsk

Ust'-Ilimsk

Kansk

Bratsk

STANOVOY RANGE

*Zeya Res.*

Skovorodino

Komsomol'sk-na-Amure

Sovetskaya Gavan'

Poronaysk

*Tatar Strait*

*Kurile Islands*

Yuzhno-Sakhalinsk

ovokuznetsk

Abakan

*Oka*

*L. Baikal*

Romanovka

Svobodnyy

Khabarovsk

Biysk

*Stilka*

Chita

Irkutsk

Kyzyl

Ulan-Ude

Olovyannaya

C H I N A

Blagoveshchensk

*Amur*

*Ussuri*

SEA OF JAPAN

M O N G O L I A

Vladivostok

PACIFIC OCEAN

NORTH KOREA

0  200  400  600 km

0  100  200  300  400 miles

---

## SIBERIA

To the east of the Ural Mountains lies Siberia, a vast tract of largely uninhabited land that stretches across to the Pacific Ocean. Most of Siberia is covered with coniferous forest known as the taiga, which contains about a quarter of the world's wood reserves. In the north, the forest thins out as the climate gets colder and the land becomes a barren waste, called tundra. Here, the ground remains frozen throughout the year.

SIBERIAN WILDLIFE
The forests of Siberia provide a vital source of food for animals, such as reindeer, bears, and squirrels, especially during the long winter months. The region is also home to the largest tiger in the world, the Siberian tiger, which has thick fur to withstand the bitter winters.

*Arctic ground squirrel*

# RUSSIAN FEDERATION

THE URAL MOUNTAINS form the boundary between European and Asian Russia. European Russia lies to the west of the mountains. This vast stretch of land is home to more than 100 million people, two-thirds of the entire Russian population. Most people live in the big cities of Moscow – the capital of the country – and St Petersburg, or along the Volga river valley. The land is rich in minerals. It is also intensively farmed, with wheat and other grains in the north giving way to tobacco, citrus fruit, and a variety of crops in the warmer south.

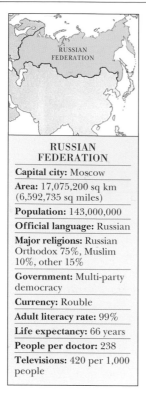

**RUSSIAN FEDERATION**

**Capital city:** Moscow

**Area:** 17,075,200 sq km (6,592,735 sq miles)

**Population:** 143,000,000

**Official language:** Russian

**Major religions:** Russian Orthodox 75%, Muslim 10%, other 15%

**Government:** Multi-party democracy

**Currency:** Rouble

**Adult literacy rate:** 99%

**Life expectancy:** 66 years

**People per doctor:** 238

**Televisions:** 420 per 1,000 people

## ST PETERSBURG
With its network of canals and rivers, the elegant city of St Petersburg is known as the "Venice of the North". It is a centre for arts and culture, and has many fine 18th century buildings. It was the capital of Russia between 1713 and 1917. Under communist rule the city was renamed Leningrad to honour Lenin, the leader of the 1917 Russian revolution. With the collapse of communism in 1991, it reverted to its old name.

## AGRICULTURE
Because of the harsh climate, only 10 percent of Russian land is used for growing crops, mostly in an area known as the "fertile triangle" (see map right). The country is the world's leading producer of oats and rye, and the world's second biggest producer of barley and potatoes. During the 1950s a vast area of barren land in south-central Russia was cultivated, the largest expansion of agriculture in the last 100 years. The new wheat fields freed up more fertile areas in the West to grow fodder for animals.

*Potatoes are grown on a huge scale in Russia. The large, open fields are ploughed into furrows and then the potatoes are planted in neat rows by machine.*

*At harvest time, the potatoes are dug out of the ground.*

*The potatoes are sorted and graded according to size and condition.*

**The fertile triangle**

*Most of Russia's crops are grown in "the fertile triangle" which stretches from St Petersburg and Ukraine in the west to southern Siberia in the east.*

**RUSSIAN BALLET**
Ballet arrived in Russia from France in the 19th century, thanks to close cultural and diplomatic ties between Paris and St Petersburg, the old Russian capital. By the early 20th century, Russia had transformed traditional ballet, making it more creative and exciting. Today, the Bolshoi Ballet of Moscow and the Kirov Ballet of St Petersburg are known throughout the world.

## RELIGIOUS REVIVAL
The Russian Orthodox Church was suppressed for many years by the former Soviet government, but became legal once more with the ending of communism. Today churches and monasteries are reopening across the country, and many people regularly attend religious services. As Russian society continues to change rapidly, the unchanging traditions of the Orthodox Church are a great comfort to many people.

*The head of the Russian Orthodox Church is known as the "Patriarch of Moscow and All Russia".*

## FOOD AND DRINK

The basic Russian diet, consisting of grain, potatoes, oil, and sugar, tends to be fattening. Fresh fruit, vegetables, and meat are regarded as a luxury. In the last few years, however, increased food production and a better system of supply has led to a wider range of foods on sale in the big cities.

*Sour cream*

*Borscht, a soup made from beetroot.*

*Vodka, a strong alcohol made from grain or potatoes, is the national drink. Alcoholism is a problem throughout Russia.*

*Black bread made from hard wheat.*

## THE TATARS

The ancient town of Kazan, on the Volga, is the capital of Tatarstan, home to around two million Tatars. These Islamic peoples are descendants of the Mongols, who overran Russia in the 13th century. Under the Soviet Union, the Tatars were suppressed and their Islamic mosques closed. Today the Tatars – along with other non-Russian peoples – are asserting their independence within the Russian Federation. The Tatars are reviving their traditional customs, and are taking steps to gain control of the local economy.

## INDUSTRY

The former Soviet Union invested heavily in its industry. Vast industrial complexes were built in the iron-rich Ural Mountains and in the Kuzbass coalfield of southern Siberia. The production of coal, iron, and other minerals soared, and heavy industries, such as engineering, steel, iron, and chemical production, dominated the economy. However, Russia is now paying a price for this big advance. Many factories are old and inefficient, polluting the environment with harmful emissions.

**Russian exports**

Basic goods: 25%

Metals: 22%

Minerals: 19%

Petroleum: 18%

Other: 4%

Chemicals: 5%

Machinery: 7%

## THE MOSCOW METRO

During the 1930s, the Soviet government built a huge underground railway system beneath the streets of Moscow. The system is fast and efficient and is used daily by more than 7 million people. The stations were built deep down in the ground so that they could be used as air-raid shelters during wartime. Many are beautifully decorated with paintings, sculptures, and mosaics.

*Well-known Western brands were sold quickly on the newly opened Russian market.*

### MARKET ECONOMY

When the USSR collapsed in 1991, the state-run, planned economy went with it. Switching abruptly to a liberal Western-style economy caused many problems for ordinary Russians, widening the gap between rich and poor. A severe crisis in 1998 has been largely overcome, but Russia is still struggling to achieve Western-style prosperity.

## WOMEN WORKERS

Many more Russian men than women died during World War II and in the labour camps set up by the Soviet leader Stalin. As a result, there are far more women than men in Russia, and women make up around 50 per cent of the workforce. Good child care and medical services enable women with children to go out to work. Many work on the railways or drive buses and trams. Most factories have large female workforces and many professions, such as medicine, dentistry, and teaching, are dominated by women.

*This woman worker is helping to clear heavy snow in Moscow.*

# RUSSIAN FEDERATION

To the east of the Ural Mountains lies Asian Russia. This vast expanse of land, known as Siberia, is bigger than the combined size of the USA and western Europe. Yet, because of the harsh climate, only 40 million people live here. Parts of Siberia are colder in winter than the North Pole. To the north are frozen plains, or tundra, while further south it is just warm enough to grow some hardy crops. For centuries, Siberia remained undeveloped, home only to peoples who trapped animals for their meat and fur and caught fish in the local rivers. But the discovery of minerals, such as gold and diamonds, has opened the region up to economic and industrial development.

## KAMCHATKA

Hanging off the eastern end of Siberia, the Kamchatka Peninsula is one of the most isolated parts of Russia. Under the Soviet Union, Kamchatka bristled with military bases because of its closeness to both Japan and the USA. Today the military presence is reduced and people are returning to more traditional ways of making a living. Once more, people are fishing in the many rivers, herding reindeer, or hunting seals, sea otters, and bears for their skins.

**Major mineral deposits**

Moscow

URAL MTS

Omsk

Trans-Siberian railway

Vladivostock

## RAW MATERIALS

Siberia is rich in natural resources, with huge reserves of oil, gas, coal, metals, diamonds, and gold. The Trans-Siberian railway transports vast amounts of minerals from Siberia to European Russia. Western Siberia contains one-third of the world's natural gas reserves, as well as a huge oilfield producing 8.4 million barrels of oil a day, more than two-thirds of the entire Russian output. Development of these resources, however, is difficult, for the climate is harsh and laying pipelines to carry fuel over such long distances is expensive.

Coal
Gas
Oil
Copper
Diamonds
Gold
Iron

*The elegant dining car of the Trans-Siberian Express.*

### THE TRANS-SIBERIAN RAILWAY

The Trans-Siberian railway is the world's longest continuous rail line. It begins at Moscow's Yaroslavl station in the west and stretches 9,440 km (5,866 miles) across to Vladivostok in the east. Trains cross eight time zones and take eight days to complete the journey. In recent years the line has become increasingly congested. New lines, including the Baikal-Amur Mainline, have been built alongside to relieve this problem.

### CLOSED AND SECRET CITIES

Under Soviet Union rule, two types of city were out of bounds for security reasons to all but an authorized few. Closed cities, including Vladivostok (shown left), were sites of military or industrial importance. Secret cities were places of research in chemical and nuclear warfare. They did not appear on a map and were located in remote areas surrounded by no-go zones and patrolled by armed guards. Today, most of the closed cities are open to visitors, but the secret cities remain out of bounds.

*The boxes are often decorated with scenes from fairy tales.*

### ARTS AND CRAFTS

The rise in Russian nationalism has been accompanied by a return to traditional crafts, folk tales, and music and dance. Skilled craftworkers make boxes and other items from wood or *papier mâché*. The lacquered boxes are decorated with miniature paintings.

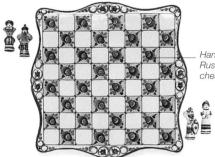

*Hand-painted Russian chess set.*

## CHESS

The ancient game of chess became popular in Russia as a way of spending long, dark winter evenings by the fireside. Today, chess is still widely played here. Russian Grand Masters such as Karpov and Spassky have dominated world chess tournaments. During a big match, giant chessboards are displayed in big city squares for the public to follow the competitors' moves.

# FORESTRY

The taïga forest of northern Russia and Siberia provides work in logging, paper production, chemicals, and furniture making. In the past, most forestry jobs were in the more accessible parts of northern Russia. But many of these forests have been cleared, and new seedlings take up to 80 years to produce mature wood. As a result, the centre of the forestry industry has moved south and east into Siberia. Today, most timber production is located in southern Siberia near Lake Baikal or on the Amur River near the Pacific coast.

# LIVING IN A COLD CLIMATE

The Yakut people of eastern Siberia are used to living in a cold climate, as winter temperatures drop to –43°C (–45°F). Engines are kept running 24 hours a day to prevent them freezing up. Drinking water is delivered as chunks of ice sawn out of the local river. Even during the brief summer, most ground remains frozen hard. Houses are often built on raised concrete platforms or wooden stilts to protect them from frost damage.

*The Yakut survive the winter by wearing many layers of warm clothing made from animal skins and fur. People wear felt or reindeer-fur boots, as leather freezes and cracks quickly.*

*Window frames are often attractively decorated.*

*Food is stored in bags outside the windows and defrosted when needed.*

*Milk is sold in frozen brick form with wooden handles inserted so that it can be carried home easily.*

*A sled pulled by dogs or reindeer is a traditional way of travelling through the snow.*

*The Yakut people make their living by herding reindeer in the north of the region and rearing cattle in the centre.*

*Windows are triple-glazed to keep out the cold. The air between the three layers of glass acts as insulation.*

*Fur hats with ear-flaps protect their wearers from Russian winters.*

## FUR FARMS

For centuries, hunters and trappers have worked the Siberian forests to catch ermine, mink, sable, lynx, and fox. In order to protect some species from over-hunting, the Soviet government introduced fur farms, where breeders raise rare animals for their furs. Furs from Siberian animals are turned into hats, coats, and linings for boots and gloves.

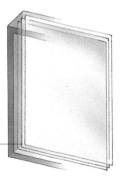

*Lake Baikal is home to the world's only freshwater seal, the nerpa or Baikal seal. A wide variety of flora and fauna, unique to the area, are found in and around the lake.*

# LAKE BAIKAL

Known as the "blue eye of Siberia", Lake Baikal in southeastern Siberia covers 31,468 sq km (12,150 sq miles) and is up to 1,940 m (6,367 ft) deep. It is the deepest lake in the world and the largest freshwater lake, containing more than 20 per cent of the world's entire supply of fresh water. In recent years, logging and chemical industries have polluted the water, prompting a major campaign to protect this unique environment.

*Find out more*

BREAK-UP OF USSR: *136*
FORESTRY: *69, 86, 244*
ORTHODOX CHURCH: *274*
POLITICAL SYSTEMS: *270–271*

# TURKEY

TURKEY LIES PARTLY IN EUROPE and partly in Asia, and is divided by a narrow waterway. For more than 600 years, Turkey was part of the powerful Ottoman Empire. Today, Turkey is a republic and the country is a mix of Islamic and Western traditions. Most people are Turkish-speaking Muslims, although there is no official state religion. Turkey has a varied landscape and climate, and is a popular tourist destination. Many types of crop are grown, and the country is self-sufficient in food.

| TURKEY | |
|---|---|
| **Capital city:** Ankara | |
| **Area:** 780,580 sq km (301,382 sq miles) | |
| **Population:** 71,300,000 | |
| **Official language:** Turkish | |
| **Major religions:** Muslim 99%, other 1% | |
| **Government:** Multi-party democracy | |
| **Currency:** Turkish lira | |
| **Adult literacy rate:** 87% | |
| **Life expectancy:** 70 years | |
| **People per doctor:** 769 | |
| **Televisions:** 286 per 1,000 people | |

| CYPRUS | |
|---|---|
| **Capital city:** Nicosia | |
| **Area:** 9,250 sq km (3,571 sq miles) | |
| **Population:** 802,000 | |
| **Official languages:** Greek and Turkish | |
| **Major religions:** Greek Orthodox 85%, Muslim 12%, other 3% | |
| **Government:** Multi-party democracy | |
| **Currency:** Cyprus pound and Turkish lira | |
| **Adult literacy rate:** 97% | |
| **Life expectancy:** 78 years | |
| **People per doctor:** 381 | |

## KEMAL ATATURK
Kemal Ataturk was the founder and first president of the modern state of Turkey after the collapse of the Ottoman Empire in the early 20th century. He brought about many reforms in Turkish society, including greater freedom for women and better education for all.

*This depiction of Kemal Ataturk towers over Antalya, in southern Turkey.*

*Kurdish children living in Harran in Turkey.*

## THE KURDS
The Kurds, numbering about 25 million, are one of the largest groups of people in the world who have no homeland. They live in a mountainous area split between four countries: Turkey, Iran, Iraq, and Syria. The Kurds have sought to form their own state – Kurdistan.

## AGRICULTURE
About half of the Turkish workforce is employed in agriculture – growing crops such as wheat, cotton, tobacco, sugar beet, and fruit. Tea is grown along the Black Sea coast and is a popular drink. Much of the work in the fields is done by women. With plenty of fertile farmland, Turkey can produce enough food not only for its own needs, but for export too.

## EPHESUS
Each year, millions of tourists visit Turkey for its sunny weather, sandy beaches, and ancient sites. These include the ruined city of Ephesus on the Aegean coast, famous for its huge, open-air theatre, carved out of the hillside in the first century AD, with seating for 24,000 people. Tourism is one of Turkey's major industries.

## MARKETS
Bustling street markets, or bazaars, are a common sight in many Turkish towns and cities. Turkey is famous for its arts and crafts, particularly for its fine carpets, pottery, beaten copperware, and leatherwork. Carpets are woven from silk, wool, and cotton and decorated with beautiful geometric and floral designs, often symbolizing the maker's family or area of origin.

*This carpet stall is in the Grand Bazaar in Kusadasi in western Turkey.*

## STREET CAFES
Street cafés are popular meeting places, especially with men. They visit them to drink tea or Turkish coffee, smoke pipes, and chat. Games, such as cards or backgammon, are often played.

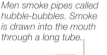

*Men smoke pipes called hubble-bubbles. Smoke is drawn into the mouth through a long tube.*

*Rich, dark Turkish coffee is a popular drink.*

*Men often play cards in street cafés.*

TURKEY

**Istanbul, Turkey**
Jan 5.5°C (41.5°F)
July 23°C (73.5°F)
Jan 109 mm (4 in)
July 34 mm (1.3 in)

**Kars, Turkey**
Jan -12°C (10°F)
July 17°C (63°F)
Jan 28 mm (1.1 in)
July 53 mm (2.1 in)

**Nicosia, Cyprus**
Jan 10°C (50.5°F)
July 29°C (84°F)
Jan 76 mm (3.0 in)
July 1 mm (0 in)

CYPRUS

## ISTANBUL

Istanbul is the only city in the world to lie in two continents. It is split between Europe and Asia by a narrow channel of water called the Bosphorus. Bridges link the two parts of the city. Istanbul is a mixture of old and new, eastern and western, with elegant mosques side-by-side with sprawling slums. It is Turkey's largest city and main port. Until the move to Ankara in 1923, it was also Turkey's capital.

# CYPRUS

CYPRUS IS A LARGE, picturesque island in the eastern Mediterranean, popular as a tourist destination. It was under Turkish, then British control until its independence in 1960. The majority of the islanders are Greeks; about a fifth are Turkish. Conflict between the two groups led to the division of the island in 1974, into the Greek south and Turkish north.

*This house stands on Hermes Street in Nicosia, the capital of Cyprus. The street marks the division between the Greek south and Turkish north. Turkey is the only country to officially recognize Turkish Northern Cyprus.*

*Find out more*

CARPET MAKING: *155, 165, 210*
ISLAM: *275*
TEA: *172, 238*

# THE NEAR EAST

BETWEEN EUROPE AND THE MIDDLE EAST, at the eastern edge of the Mediterranean Sea, lies the region known as the Near East. The area includes the countries of Israel, Lebanon, Jordan, and Syria. It is the birthplace of some of the world's oldest civilizations and has close ties with three major religions – Judaism, Christianity, and Islam. The land is mostly dry and barren, particularly to the east, but is lusher and more fertile along the Mediterranean coast. After centuries of invasion by Arabs, Christian Crusaders, and Turks, the present-day countries took shape in the last 100 years. Since then, they have been plagued by civil wars and conflicts.

### A LAND OF CONTRASTS

A range of mountains stretches from Lebanon in the north to Israel in the south, which contrasts with the deserts to the east and the coast to the west. In Lebanon, the mountains drop away to rich, fertile plains where cereal crops are grown. The mountain tops are covered in snow for most of the year and are popular with skiers.

*Noisy or smelly market stalls, such as those belonging to metalsmiths (above) or leatherworkers, are placed at a distance from the main mosque.*

### A CITY IN THE NEAR EAST

Many traditional Muslim cities follow a distinctive pattern. At the heart of the city is the main mosque, which is usually the largest building. This is surrounded by other important buildings and market stalls. The narrow, irregular streets which radiate out towards the city walls provide shade and keep down wind and dust. Privacy is important – doors opening on to narrow streets must not face each other.

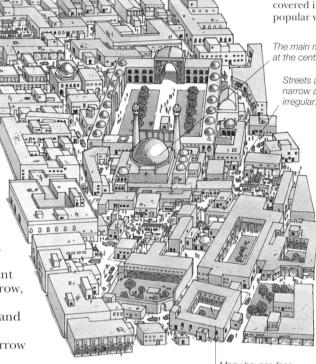

*The main mosque stands at the centre of the city.*

*Streets are narrow and irregular.*

*Many houses face on to courtyards.*

*The market stalls selling religious goods, such as candles, incense, and books (above), are placed closest to the main mosque in the centre of the city.*

### PALESTINE

In 1948, the Jewish state of Israel was created from the country of Palestine, the ancient land of the Jews and the home of the Palestinian Arabs. Thousands of Palestinians were driven from their homes and land. Many went to live in the West Bank and the Gaza Strip. In 1967, Israel captured and occupied these areas. After agreeing to peace accords in 1993, the Palestinians were given control over parts of these areas, and Israel intends to leave Gaza by 2006. However, violence between the two communities continues.

*Yasser Arafat (1929–2004) was leader of the Palestine Liberation Organization (PLO), which represented the interests of Palestinian Arabs.*

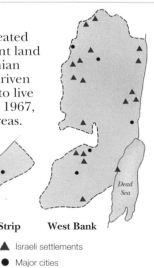

**Gaza Strip**   **West Bank**

Dead Sea

▲ Israeli settlements
● Major cities

### THE DEAD SEA

On the border between Israel and Jordan lies a large lake known as the Dead Sea. It is the lowest place on Earth – some 400 m (1,312 ft) below sea level. Salt deposits rise up like pillars out of the water. No fish can live there, which is how the lake got its name. Mud from the shores of the Dead Sea is said to have healing properties.

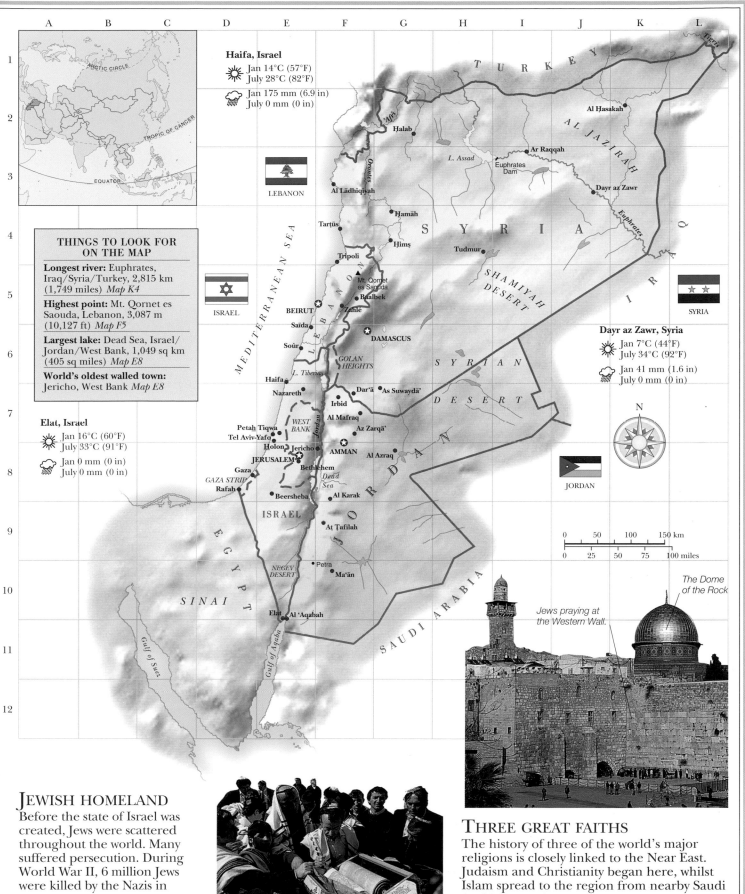

**Haifa, Israel**
☀ Jan 14°C (57°F)
July 28°C (82°F)
🌧 Jan 175 mm (6.9 in)
July 0 mm (0 in)

LEBANON

ISRAEL

SYRIA

**THINGS TO LOOK FOR ON THE MAP**

**Longest river:** Euphrates, Iraq/Syria/Turkey, 2,815 km (1,749 miles) *Map K4*

**Highest point:** Mt. Qornet es Saouda, Lebanon, 3,087 m (10,127 ft) *Map F5*

**Largest lake:** Dead Sea, Israel/ Jordan/West Bank, 1,049 sq km (405 sq miles) *Map E8*

**World's oldest walled town:** Jericho, West Bank *Map E8*

**Elat, Israel**
☀ Jan 16°C (60°F)
July 33°C (91°F)
🌧 Jan 0 mm (0 in)
July 0 mm (0 in)

**Dayr az Zawr, Syria**
☀ Jan 7°C (44°F)
July 34°C (92°F)
🌧 Jan 41 mm (1.6 in)
July 0 mm (0 in)

JORDAN

0   50   100   150 km
0   25   50   75   100 miles

*The Dome of the Rock*

*Jews praying at the Western Wall.*

*Map labels:* TURKEY, Al Ḥasakah, AL JAZIRAH, Afri, Ḥalab, L. Assad, Ar Raqqah, Euphrates Dam, Dayr az Zawr, Al Lādhiqīyah, Orontes, Ḥamāh, SYRIA, Euphrates, Tartūs, Ḥimṣ, Tudmur, Tripoli, Mt. Qornet es Saouda, SHAMIYAH DESERT, IRAQ, Baalbek, LEBANON, BEIRUT, Zahlé, Saïda, DAMASCUS, Soûr, MEDITERRANEAN SEA, GOLAN HEIGHTS, SYRIAN DESERT, L. Tiberias, Haifa, Dar'ā, As Suwaydā', Nazareth, Irbid, Al Mafraq, Petah Tiqwa, WEST BANK, Az Zarqā', Tel Aviv-Yafo, Holon, Jericho, AMMAN, Al Azraq, JERUSALEM, Bethlehem, Jordan, Gaza, Dead Sea, GAZA STRIP, Rafah, Beersheba, Al Karak, ISRAEL, JORDAN, EGYPT, Aṭ Ṭafīlah, NEGEV DESERT, Petra, Maʿān, SINAI, SAUDI ARABIA, Elat, Al ʿAqabah, Gulf of Suez, Gulf of Aqaba, Tigris

# JEWISH HOMELAND

Before the state of Israel was created, Jews were scattered throughout the world. Many suffered persecution. During World War II, 6 million Jews were killed by the Nazis in Europe. After the war, thousands of Jews from all over the world emigrated to Israel, the home of their ancestors.

# THREE GREAT FAITHS

The history of three of the world's major religions is closely linked to the Near East. Judaism and Christianity began here, whilst Islam spread to the region from nearby Saudi Arabia. Jerusalem in Israel is a holy city for all three faiths. The Dome of the Rock, sacred to Muslims, and the Western Wall, sacred to Jews, stand on the same site.

# SYRIA

SYRIA IS AN ANCIENT LAND. Its capital, Damascus, is one of the world's oldest cities. Because of its important position on major trade routes, Syria has been invaded and occupied many times – by the Romans, Arabs, Greeks, and Turks. After World War I, it came under French control, becoming independent in 1941. Since then Syria has been involved in several wars with Israel. Most Syrians are Muslim and speak Arabic. More than half of Syria is desert, but the river floodplains provide fertile land.

### SYRIA

**Capital city:** Damascus

**Area:** 185,180 sq km (71,498 sq miles)

**Population:** 17,800,000

**Official language:** Arabic

**Major religions:** Muslim 90%, Christian 10%

**Government:** One party dictatorship

**Currency:** Syrian pound

**Adult literacy rate:** 83%

**Life expectancy:** 70 years

**People per doctor:** 769

**Televisions:** 70 per 1,000 people

## PALMYRA

The rich and varied history of Syria is reflected in the many ancient ruins from past civilizations found scattered throughout the country. In the 3rd century AD, Palmyra, with its palaces, temples, and theatres, was a flourishing city, but it was destroyed by the Romans for refusing to give up its independence. It lies in an oasis on the edge of the desert, and is one of the best preserved ancient cities in the world.

## MARKET LIFE

Markets, or *souks*, are held in villages and towns throughout Syria. The *souks* are lively, bustling places, with market stalls set out on winding alleyways, selling anything from spices and vegetables, to carpets, jewellery, basketwork, and coffee pots. People come here to buy and sell, meet their friends, and haggle (bargain) over prices. *Souks* are more than just trading centres, they are a central feature of the Arab way of life.

*Craftsmen and women are often seen working at their stalls in the souk: beating and engraving copper, carving wood, and weaving baskets.*

*The stalls selling fresh bread, fruit, and vegetables jostle for space with the craft stalls.*

### MUSLIM GROUPS

The majority of Syrians belong to the traditionally powerful Sunni Muslim group. But there are other Muslim sects, such as the Shi'as, Ismailis, and Alawis. The Alawis believe not only in Islam, but in some aspects of Christianity. For example, they celebrate Christmas and Easter. The Alawis were persecuted in the past, but many have now become rich and powerful. President Assad of Syria was himself an Alawi Muslim.

*A minaret (tower) on a Muslim mosque, from which the faithful are called to prayer five times a day.*

## THE EUPHRATES DAM

The Euphrates River flows through the northeast of Syria, on its journey from Turkey to Iraq. A gigantic dam has been built across the river to harness the power of the water and produce hydro-electricity. Sharing the waters of the Euphrates is a big issue for Turkey, Syria and Iraq. A huge lake, Lake Assad, was also created by the dam. Water from the lake is used to grow crops.

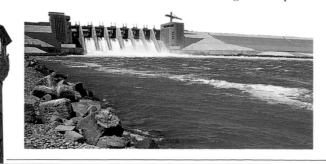

### THE GOLAN HEIGHTS

The mountainous area known as the Golan Heights was seized from Syria by Israel in 1967. It is important to the Israelis because it overlooks the Hula Valley in Israel, offering a good strategic position. It has been a major issue in past peace talks between the two countries, but the renewed Israeli-Palestinian conflict since 2001 has left the issue unresolved.

### *Find out more*

HYDRO-ELECTRICITY: *108, 262*
ISLAM: *275*
ISRAELI TERRITORY: *146*
OASES: *213*

# LEBANON

LEBANON IS A SMALL COUNTRY at the eastern end of the Mediterranean, bordered by Syria and Israel. The people of Lebanon are mostly Arabs, belonging to a great variety of religious groups. Lebanon was once the cultural and business centre of the Near East. But in 1975, tensions between Muslim and Christian groups led to the outbreak of a violent civil war which almost destroyed the country. Peace terms were agreed in 1989 and some stability was restored.

| LEBANON | |
|---|---|
| **Capital city:** Beirut | |
| **Area:** 10,400 sq km (4,015 sq miles) | |
| **Population:** 3,700,000 | |
| **Official language:** Arabic | |
| **Major religions:** Muslim 70%, Christian 30% | |
| **Government:** Multi-party democracy | |
| **Currency:** Lebanese pound | |
| **Adult literacy rate:** 87% | |
| **Life expectancy:** 71 years | |
| **People per doctor:** 476 | |
| **Televisions:** 352 per 1,000 people | |

## RELIGIOUS GROUPS

The Lebanese population is a jigsaw of religious groups, including different Christian and Muslim sects. The largest Christian group is the Maronites, who practise a form of Catholicism. Other Christian groups include the Greek Orthodox and Greek Catholics. The Muslims are divided into the Sunnis and the Shi'as.

*Although Beirut is no longer formally divided into Muslim West and Christian East, both groups have remained in their own area.*

Beirut

- Greek Orthodox
- Maronites
- Sunni Muslim
- Shi'a Muslim
- Druze

### DRUZES

The Druze faith is an offshoot of Islam that is now considered a religion in its own right. There are about 200,000 Druzes in Lebanon, mainly living in the southern mountains. They have many customs designed to protect their community. It is impossible to become a Druze unless you are born one, and you cannot give up your faith. Marriage is only allowed within the community to ensure that the Druze faith continues.

## REBUILDING BEIRUT

Before its destruction in the civil war, Beirut was a cultured and lively city. It was known as the "Paris of the East" and was one of the region's most important ports and business centres. For many years the city lay in ruins, but a government project to rebuild Beirut has managed to restore its financial centre and has succeeded in attracting visitors back to the capital.

**Where people live**

90% live in cities          10% live in the country

### CEDAR TREES

The cedars of Lebanon are the country's symbol and appear on the national flag. In biblical times, great forests of cedar trees covered the slopes of the Lebanese mountains. Today, they survive only in a few protected groves. Some of these trees are more than 1,500 years old.

## LEBANESE FOOD

The national dish of Lebanon is *kibbe*, made of lamb, burghul (cracked wheat), and onions, pounded together. The mixture is shaped into balls or patties and baked or fried. Sweet pastries, stuffed with nuts and dates and covered in honey, are also popular.

*Baklava*

*Kibbe is the Lebanese national dish.*

*Vegetables, such as swede, and spicy foods, such as chillies, are often eaten with the main meal.*

*Swede*          *Chillies*

### TYRE AND SIDON

The civil war ruined Lebanon's thriving tourist industry. Attempts are now being made to attract visitors back to the country's fine beaches and historical sites, such as the two cities of Tyre and Sidon. These were built by the Phoenicians some 3,000 years ago and were famous in Roman times for their glassware and purple dyes.

*Find out more*
LEBANESE FLAG: *147*
LEBANESE LANDSCAPE: *146*
RELIGION: *274–275*
WARS IN THE REGION: *146*

# ISRAEL

ISRAEL IS A LONG, THIN STRIP of land running along the eastern coast of the Mediterranean Sea. Its landscape is varied, with fertile valleys, dry deserts, mountains, lakes, and rivers. It has a wide range of industries and a modern agricultural system. The state of Israel was created in 1948 as a homeland for Jews from all over the world. The country was previously called Palestine. Much of the Palestinian Arab population was forced to leave Israel and live as refugees in Jordan and Lebanon. This has created conflict between Israel, the Palestinians, and neighbouring Arab states ever since.

| ISRAEL* |
|---|
| **Capital city:** Jerusalem |
| **Area:** 20,770 sq km (8,109 sq miles) |
| **Population:** 6,400,000 |
| **Official languages:** Hebrew and Arabic |
| **Major religions:** Jewish 80%, Muslim 16%, Christian 2%, other 2% |
| **Government:** Multi-party democracy |
| **Currency:** Shekel |
| **Adult literacy rate:** 95% |
| **Life expectancy:** 79 years |
| **People per doctor:** 270 |
| **Televisions:** 318 per 1,000 people |
| * Figures include the West Bank and Gaza Strip. |

## JERUSALEM
The city of Jerusalem is a holy place for Jews, Muslims, and Christians. Within the walls of the Old City is the Jewish Western Wall, the only remaining part of Herod's Temple, and the Temple Mount from where the Muslim prophet Mohammad rose up to heaven. The major Christian shrine is the Church of the Holy Sepulchre, the traditional site of Christ's burial and resurrection.

## KIBBUTZ
Almost half of Israel's food is grown on large communal farms, called *kibbutzim*, on which many families live and work together. People share everyday tasks such as cleaning and cooking, as well as work on the farm. Use of computerized irrigation to water the land has made large areas of barren desert fertile.

*Families live and work together on a kibbutz.*

*Some crops, such as tomatoes, are grown inside plastic greenhouses.*

*People from other countries, attracted by the way of life, come to stay and work on kibbutzim during busy periods.*

*Citrus fruits, such as oranges, lemons, and grapefruit, are grown.*

*Water is pumped through pipes to irrigate the land.*

*Efficient irrigation is essential for farming in a hot, dry climate.*

## AT PRAYER
Judaism is one of the world's oldest religions. Jews believe in one God and follow the teachings of the *Torah*, the first five books of the Bible. At prayer, many Jewish men wear blue-edged prayer shawls and small boxes called phylacteries, or *tephilin*, which contain verses from the *Torah*. Saturday is the Jewish holy day, or Sabbath.

**ISRAELI SOLDIERS**
Because of the conflict between Israel and the Palestinians, and repeated wars with neighbouring countries, the army plays a crucial part in Israeli life. From the age of 18, Israeli men and women must serve in the army for a number of years. Women receive the same training as men, but do not take part in direct combat.

*Tephilin are worn on the head and left arm, near the heart, to show that God's teachings control a person's thoughts and feelings.*

*Knotted tassels serve to remind Jews of God's commandments.*

*Prayer shawl*

**DIAMOND CUTTING**
About 25 per cent of Israel's export earnings come from its diamond industry. The rough diamonds are imported, and then skilfully cut and polished for use in jewellery settings.

| *Find out more* |
|---|
| DIAMONDS: *226, 248* |
| IRRIGATION: *155, 156, 217* |
| JUDAISM: *275* |
| PALESTINE: *146* |

# JORDAN

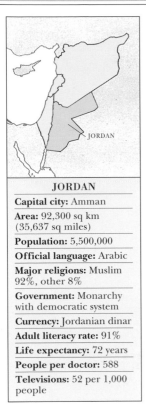

JORDAN LIES TO THE NORTHWEST of the Arabian Peninsula. Apart from a short coastline along the Gulf of Aqaba, it is completely landlocked, or cut off from the sea. Much of eastern Jordan is desert, with mountains in the north and south. Most of its people are Muslim and speak Arabic. Jordan is a relatively new country (it became fully independent in 1946), but some of the world's oldest sites are found here. In recent years, the government has played a part in peace talks between the Israelis and their Arab neighbours.

**JORDAN**

**Capital city:** Amman

**Area:** 92,300 sq km (35,637 sq miles)

**Population:** 5,500,000

**Official language:** Arabic

**Major religions:** Muslim 92%, other 8%

**Government:** Monarchy with democratic system

**Currency:** Jordanian dinar

**Adult literacy rate:** 91%

**Life expectancy:** 72 years

**People per doctor:** 588

**Televisions:** 52 per 1,000 people

*Ed-Deir (The Monastery) is the largest monument in Petra.*

### PETRA
The spectacular rose-red city of Petra was carved out of desert rock by the Nabateans in the 4th century BC. It is Jordan's most famous historic site. Among the amazing rock-cut buildings are the Khazneh (Treasury) and the Royal Tombs, reached on horseback through a narrow, winding gully.

### REFUGEE CAMPS
When Israel was formed in 1948, tens of thousands of Palestinians were forced to flee their homes and become refugees in Jordan and other Arab countries. More than 40 years later, they are still there. In Jordan alone, there are 1.6 million Palestinian refugees. Many have been born and brought up in refugee camps. This Palestinian refugee camp is near Amman.

*Houses being built in Amman.*

### POPULATION GROWTH
The population of Jordan, roughly equally divided between Jordanians and Palestinians, is growing rapidly. Providing housing, jobs, schools, and healthcare for the growing number of people is one of the Jordanian government's most urgent problems.

### GULF OF AQABA
The Gulf of Aqaba is the narrow, northeastern arm of the Red Sea between Saudi Arabia and the Sinai Peninsula. It is 160 km (99 miles) long and up to 27 km (17 miles) wide. At its head lies Jordan's one seaport, Aqaba. This short stretch of coastline is Jordan's only outlet to the sea. It is also popular with holidaymakers.

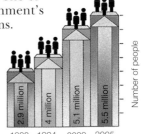

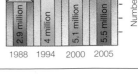

**Population growth in Jordan**

| 2.9 million | 4 million | 5.1 million | 5.5 million |
|---|---|---|---|
| 1988 | 1994 | 2000 | 2005 |

Number of people

### RIVER JORDAN
Water is in short supply throughout the Near East. Control of the River Jordan, which forms the border between Jordan and Israel, has become an important issue in peace talks between the two countries. Jordan, a relatively poor country, has a particular need for a greater share of the water to irrigate its land and produce more crops.

*Find out more*

ANCIENT SITES: *134*
ISLAM: *275*
NEAR EAST HISTORY: *146–147*
POPULATION GROWTH: *16–17*

# THE MIDDLE EAST

THE MIDDLE EAST IS IN SOUTHWEST ASIA. Much of the area is covered by dry, barren desert or rugged mountains. Earlier this century, large deposits of oil were discovered around the Persian Gulf. Today, oil is the main source of income for many Middle Eastern countries. Historically, the Middle East was the site of the world's first cities and the birthplace of one of the world's great religions – Islam. The majority of the population today is Muslim and the most widely spoken language is Arabic. In recent years, the region has suffered a series of wars and conflicts between neighbouring countries.

**ROCKY DESERT**
Part of the Middle East is rocky desert, where the bare rock floor has been stripped clean by intense heat, drying winds, and occasional but heavy rainstorms.

*Sand dunes are created by a build-up of sand carried along by strong winds.*

*Sand storms arise when strong winds blow sand and dust across the desert, causing the sky to darken.*

*Settlements may grow up around oases – these are often created by water coming to the surface through a fault (split) in the rock.*

## DESERT

Apart from fertile patches of land along the Tigris and Euphrates rivers, by the coast, and near isolated oases, much of the Middle East is covered by hot, dry deserts, both rocky and sandy. These include the Rub'Al Khali, the Empty Quarter, a vast sandy desert in Saudi Arabia. Large areas of desert are uninhabited because of the lack of water for drinking and farming.

*When the wind blows in one direction, it causes a ripple effect in the sand.*

*Some hardy plants can survive all year in the desert because their long roots collect water over a wide area.*

*Bedouin nomads face a constant fight for survival as they move from place to place with their animals in search of food and water.*

## OIL PRODUCTION

More than 65 per cent of the world's oil is found in the Middle East, and the region supplies almost a third of the world's daily oil production. The discovery of oil has brought great wealth to the Middle East, leading to rapid industrial and social change in a formerly underdeveloped region. It has also greatly increased the region's international importance and influence on world affairs.

**Drilling for oil**

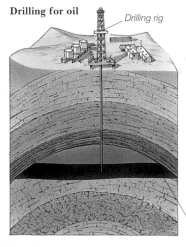

*Drilling rig*

*Oil wells are drilled deep down into the ground to extract the oil trapped between layers of rock.*

**Distribution of oil production in the Middle East**

Yemen and Bahrain: 2.1%
Qatar: 3.7%
Oman: 4.9%
Iraq: 8.3%
Kuwait: 10.3%
United Arab Emirates: 11.3%
Iran: 16.8
Saudi Arabia: 42.6%

## WARFARE

In recent years, the Middle East has been frequently troubled by wars, in which thousands of people have lost their lives. In 1980, the long-standing rivalry and border disputes between Iran and Iraq erupted into a war which lasted until 1988. In 1991 and again in 2003, an international force led by the US attacked Iraq, overthrowing its dictator, Saddam Hussein.

*A sign marks part of the border between Iran and Iraq.*

*Rusting tanks in Iraq serve as a reminder of recent warfare.*

**DISPUTED BORDERS**
Many Middle Eastern countries are relatively new, created earlier this century when the region was divided up by its Western rulers. These artificial divisions, sometimes poorly defined, have led to many border disputes, especially between Iraq and its six neighbouring countries.

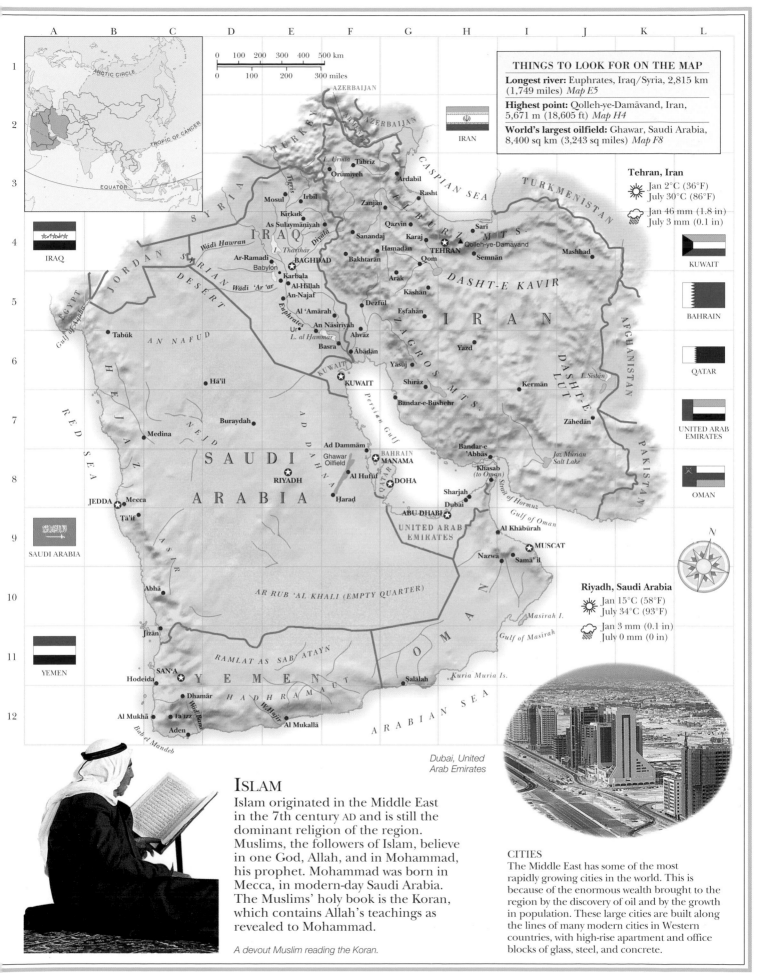

ARCTIC CIRCLE

TROPIC OF CANCER

EQUATOR

0 100 200 300 400 500 km

0 100 200 300 miles

**THINGS TO LOOK FOR ON THE MAP**

**Longest river:** Euphrates, Iraq/Syria, 2,815 km
(1,749 miles) *Map E5*

**Highest point:** Qolleh-ye-Damāvand, Iran,
5,671 m (18,605 ft) *Map H4*

**World's largest oilfield:** Ghawar, Saudi Arabia,
8,400 sq km (3,243 sq miles) *Map F8*

IRAN

**Tehran, Iran**
☀ Jan 2°C (36°F)
☀ July 30°C (86°F)
🌧 Jan 46 mm (1.8 in)
🌧 July 3 mm (0.1 in)

IRAQ

KUWAIT

BAHRAIN

QATAR

UNITED ARAB
EMIRATES

OMAN

SAUDI ARABIA

**Riyadh, Saudi Arabia**
☀ Jan 15°C (58°F)
☀ July 34°C (93°F)
🌧 Jan 3 mm (0.1 in)
🌧 July 0 mm (0 in)

YEMEN

N

AZERBAIJAN

TURKEY

SYRIA

JORDAN

EGYPT

Gulf of Aqaba

RED SEA

HEJAZ

NEJD

ASIR

AN NAFUD

AD DAHNA

AR RUB 'AL KHALI (EMPTY QUARTER)

RAMLAT AS SAB'ATAYN

HADHRAMAUT

ARMENIA

AZERBAIJAN

CASPIAN SEA

ELBURZ MTS.

TURKMENISTAN

DASHT-E KAVIR

IRAN

ZAGROS MTS.

DASHT-E LUT

AFGHANISTAN

PAKISTAN

L. Sīstān

Jaz Mūrīān Salt Lake

Strait of Hormuz

Gulf of Oman

OMAN

Masīrah I.

Gulf of Masīrah

Kuria Muria Is.

ARABIAN SEA

Bab el Mandeb

*L. Urmia* Tabrīz
Orūmīyeh
Ardabīl
Rasht
Mosul
Kirkūk
Irbīl
Zanjān
Qazvīn
Sarī
As Sulaymānīyah
Diyālā
Sanandaj
Hamadān
Karaj
TEHRAN Qolleh-ye-Damāvand
Semnān
Mashhad
Tigris
*L. Tharthār*
Ar-Ramādī
BAGHDAD
Bakhtarān
Qom
Babylon
Karbala
Arāk
Al-Hillah
Kāshān
An-Najaf
Dezful
Eşfahān
Al 'Amārah
An Nāsirīyah
Ur
Ahvāz
*L. al Hammar*
Ābādān
Yazd
Basra
Yāsūj
Tabūk
Kermān
Hā'il
Shīrāz
Bandar-e-Būshehr
KUWAIT
Zāhedān
KUWAIT
Buraydah
Medina
Ad Dammām
BAHRAIN
Bandar-e 'Abbās
Ghawar Oilfield
MANAMA
Khasab (to Oman)
Al Hufūf
DOHA
Sharjah
RIYADH
Dubai
Harad
Al Khābūrah
JEDDA Mecca
ABU DHABI
MUSCAT
Tā'if
UNITED ARAB EMIRATES
Nazwā
Samā'il
Abhā
Jīzān
SALĀLAH
SAN'A
Hodeida
Dhamār
Ta'izz
Al Mukhā
Al Mukalla
Aden
*Wadi Hawran*
*Wadi 'Ar 'ar*
Euphrates
Persian Gulf
SYRIAN DESERT

*Dubai, United Arab Emirates*

## ISLAM
Islam originated in the Middle East
in the 7th century AD and is still the
dominant religion of the region.
Muslims, the followers of Islam, believe
in one God, Allah, and in Mohammad,
his prophet. Mohammad was born in
Mecca, in modern-day Saudi Arabia.
The Muslims' holy book is the Koran,
which contains Allah's teachings as
revealed to Mohammad.

*A devout Muslim reading the Koran.*

## CITIES
The Middle East has some of the most
rapidly growing cities in the world. This is
because of the enormous wealth brought to the
region by the discovery of oil and by the growth
in population. These large cities are built along
the lines of many modern cities in Western
countries, with high-rise apartment and office
blocks of glass, steel, and concrete.

153

# IRAQ

IRAQ IS ONE OF THE LARGEST and most powerful countries in the Middle East. Most of its people are Muslim and Arabic speaking. There are also some 4 million Kurds living in the north. Apart from the fertile plains of the Tigris and Euphrates rivers, most of Iraq is mountainous or covered in desert. Only about a sixth of the country is suitable for farming and much of Iraq's food is imported. Since Iraq became a republic in 1958, it has experienced great political unrest. In 2003, a US-led international force invaded Iraq and removed its dictatorial leader, Saddam Hussein. The country is now moving towards democracy.

| IRAQ | |
|---|---|
| **Capital city:** Baghdad | |
| **Area:** 437,072 sq km (168,753 sq miles) | |
| **Population:** 25,200,000 | |
| **Official language:** Arabic, Kurdish | |
| **Major religions:** Muslim 95%, other 5% | |
| **Government:** Multi-party democracy | |
| **Currency:** New Iraqi dinar | |
| **Adult literacy rate:** 40% | |
| **Life expectancy:** 63 years | |
| **People per doctor:** 1,667 | |

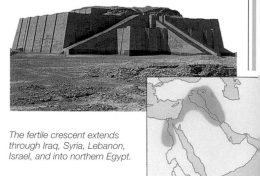

This ziggurat is in Ur, once a thriving city in Mesopotamia.

The fertile crescent extends through Iraq, Syria, Lebanon, Israel, and into northern Egypt.

## MESOPOTAMIA
Many ancient peoples settled in Mesopotamia (part of which is now Iraq) because it lay in the fertile crescent of land formed by the Tigris and Euphrates rivers. The area has many ancient ruins, including stepped, pyramid-like structures, called ziggurats, found at Babylon and Ur. The steps led to a temple at the top.

### BAGHDAD
Baghdad, the capital of Iraq, lies on the banks of the River Tigris. It is the largest city in Iraq and the country's centre of business and government. A city of contrasts, it is a mixture of ancient mosques, modern high-rise buildings, and packed bazaars. Baghdad has been a centre of Islamic culture for more than a thousand years.

### SADDAM HUSSEIN
In 1979, Saddam Hussein became leader of Iraq. Under his dictatorship, many Iraqis, especially Kurds, were killed or imprisoned as opposition to his rule was savagely crushed. During the invasion of Iraq in 2003, statues of the dictator were pulled down by his victorious opponents.

### PIPING OIL
Iraq's most important natural resources are oil and natural gas. Oil production began on a large scale in 1945 and now dominates the economy. Because Iraq has only a short stretch of coastline along the Persian Gulf, it relies on pipelines through Turkey, Syria, and Saudi Arabia to export its oil.

## MARSH ARABS
The Marsh Arabs have hunted and fished in the marshes of southern Iraq for more than 5,000 years. In recent years they were under threat because of their opposition to Saddam Hussein, whose government drained the marshes to water crops elsewhere. This endangered both the Marsh Arabs and the region's unique wildlife.

The huts, or mudhifs, are made of reeds bound tightly together.

The Marsh Arabs wend their way through the narrow reed-lined waterways in small wooden canoes, or mashhufs.

The white pelican is one species of bird that makes its home in the marsh lands in winter.

The reed huts are built on platforms made of mud.

*Find out more*
ANCIENT SITES: *134*
DICTATORSHIP: *271*
KURDS: *144*
OIL: *137, 152, 281*

# IRAN

IRAN IS THE LARGEST NON-ARAB country in the Middle East; its people are Persian in origin. In ancient times, Iran was called Persia, and it was at the centre of a great empire. The Persian language has survived from that time and is spoken by most Iranians. The country consists of a huge, central plateau, ringed by the Zagros and Elburz mountains. In 1979, the last shah, or king, of Iran was overthrown by an Islamic revolution and the country was declared a republic. Today, oil is Iran's biggest export.

Minaret

| IRAN | |
|---|---|
| **Capital city:** Tehran | |
| **Area:** 1,648,000 sq km (636,293 sq miles) | |
| **Population:** 68,900,000 | |
| **Official language:** Farsi | |
| **Major religions:** Muslim 99%, other 1% | |
| **Government:** Islamic republic | |
| **Currency:** Iranian rial | |
| **Adult literacy rate:** 77% | |
| **Life expectancy:** 69 years | |
| **People per doctor:** 2,625 | |
| **Televisions:** 157 per 1,000 people | |

## MOSQUE

Mosques are Muslim places of worship. All mosques have at least one tall tower, or minaret, from which the faithful are called to prayer. Many mosques are beautifully decorated with abstract patterns and verses from the Koran, the holy book of Islam. Artists avoid representing living things, as Muslims believe nothing should be worshipped except for God, and that God is the only creator of life.

## QANAT IRRIGATION

Less than half of the Iranian countryside is suitable for farming, and then only if it is well irrigated, or watered. Traditional irrigation methods include dams, wells, and qanats. A qanat is an underground channel that transports water from a source to an area that can be farmed. Some qanats are more than 40 km (25 miles) long.

Shepherds leading their flock of sheep through the Elburz Mountains.

### AGRICULTURE

In recent years, Iran has tried to become less dependent on food imports, and has returned to growing more crops, such as cereals, tea, and cotton. Herds of cattle, sheep, and goats continue to be kept by many farming families.

The wells are used as ventilation and repair shafts, as well as to draw water.

Rainwater runs down and seeps into the ground.

The water flows along an underground channel that slopes gently downwards.

A series of wells are used to dig the channel and then to draw water from it.

A settlement often grows up near the mouth of the qanat.

A class of girls in traditional dress. In Iran girls and boys are educated separately.

## THE AYATOLLAH

Ayatollah Khomeini was a key figure in the Iranian revolution and remained Iran's political and religious leader until his death in 1989. The shah had tried to introduce Western ideas to Iran, but Khomeini wanted the country to be governed by traditional Islamic laws and values. His ideas still dominate Iran.

### PERSIAN CARPETS

Iran is famous for its hand-woven Persian carpets. Each consists of thousands of pieces of wool knotted into elaborate patterns. The weavers always make a deliberate mistake in their work because, as Muslims, they believe that nothing is perfect except God. Carpets are Iran's second largest export, after oil.

This woman is weaving a carpet on a vertical loom.

Graceful patterns of flowers and leaves combined with abstract shapes are a feature of Persian carpets.

*Find out more*

CARPET MAKING: *144, 165, 210*
IRRIGATION: *156, 217*
ISLAM: *275*
POLITICAL SYSTEMS: *270*

# SAUDI ARABIA

SAUDI ARABIA IS BY FAR the largest country in the Arabian Peninsula. Some 90 per cent of this Muslim nation is covered by the hot, dry, sandy Arabian Desert, including the vast Rub'Al Khali, or Empty Quarter, in the south. There are no permanent rivers, and years may pass without any rainfall. The discovery of huge oil reserves has made Saudi Arabia extremely rich and powerful, and enabled it to develop and improve its industry, agriculture, and standard of living.

| SAUDI ARABIA | |
| --- | --- |
| **Capital city:** Riyadh | |
| **Area:** 1,960,582 sq km (756,981 sq miles) | |
| **Population:** 24,200,000 | |
| **Official language:** Arabic | |
| **Major religion:** Muslim 100% | |
| **Government:** Absolute monarchy | |
| **Currency:** Saudi riyal | |
| **Adult literacy rate:** 78% | |
| **Life expectancy:** 73 years | |
| **People per doctor:** 588 | |
| **Televisions:** 262 per 1,000 people | |

*Many Islamic women wear a veil, or burqa.*

*The Ka'ba stands on the remains of an ancient shrine, which, according to the Koran (the Muslim holy book), was built by Abraham.*

OPEC
Saudi Arabia has the largest oil reserves in the world. Oil accounts for over 90 per cent of the country's exports. Saudi Arabia is a key member of OPEC (Organization of Petroleum Exporting Countries). OPEC sets guidelines for the production and export of oil, and protects the interests of its member countries.

## MECCA

Mecca, the birthplace of the prophet Mohammad and the holiest city of Islam, is in the west of Saudi Arabia. Each year, more than a million pilgrims from all over the world flock to Mecca to visit the sacred Ka'ba shrine in the Great Mosque. Muslims are expected to undertake the *hajj*, or pilgrimage to Mecca, at least once in their lives.

## WOMEN'S ROLE

Women in Saudi Arabia and some other Muslim countries live restricted lives by Western standards. Many women wear traditional Muslim dress, with long robes and veils covering their heads and faces. In Saudi Arabia, women are not allowed to work with men or to drive cars, although every girl has the right to a good education.

WATERING THE LAND
Much of Saudi Arabia's land is scrubby, barren, and unsuitable for growing food. Farmers rely on irrigation to water their fields. Recent projects have been so successful that farmers can now grow melons, tomatoes, wheat, and barley in the desert.

*Disc-shaped fields are created by sprinklers that rotate to water the land.*

## THE BEDOUIN

For centuries, Bedouin nomads have roamed the deserts of Saudi Arabia in search of food and water for their animals. Some Bedouin are camel herders; others keep sheep and goats. The Bedouin traditionally live in tents that are light and easy to transport. Today, their way of life is under threat as the government encourages people to settle in towns and cities.

*Camels are ideally suited to desert life and are highly valued by the Bedouin.*

*A Bedouin tent is made from long strips of tightly woven goat's hair.*

*The tent is divided into male and female quarters.*

*Modern Bedouin use cars and trucks for transport as well as camels and horses.*

*Bedouin women weave tent cloth, drapes, and cushion covers, and saddle bags for their camels and horses.*

*Long, loose-fitting robes protect the skin from the sun, and keep the body cool during the day.*

*Find out more*
DESERT NOMADS: *181, 209*
DESERTS: *15, 132, 152*
ISLAM: *275*
OIL: *137, 152, 281*

# KUWAIT

KUWAIT LIES AT THE NORTHERN end of the Persian Gulf. It is a small country, largely covered by sandy desert. Huge oil reserves have made Kuwait rich, and oil-refining has become its chief industry. In 1990, at the start of the Gulf War, Kuwait was occupied by Iraq. It was liberated in 1991 by an international force.

## KUWAIT'S WEALTH

Until the discovery of oil in the 1940s, Kuwait was a poor, underdeveloped country. The wealth gained by selling oil has transformed it into one of the most prosperous nations in the world. Its people enjoy a high standard of living, with free education, free health care and social services, and no income tax.

POLLUTION
Kuwait suffered badly during its invasion by Iraq. Many of its oil wells were set on fire, causing enormous damage to the economy and the environment. A huge slick of oil spilled into the Gulf, poisoning the water and killing wildlife. Abandoned ammunition and unexploded mines litter the desert and the clearing up process continues today.

*Kuwait's wealth is reflected in its impressive buildings, such as these water towers which dominate Kuwait's skyline.*

## KUWAIT
**Capital city:** Kuwait
**Area:** 17,820 sq km (6,880 sq miles)
**Population:** 2,500,000
**Official language:** Arabic
**Major religions:** Muslim 85%, other 15%
**Government:** Absolute monarchy with parliament
**Currency:** Kuwaiti dinar
**Adult literacy rate:** 83%
**Life expectancy:** 77 years
**People per doctor:** 526
**Televisions:** 491 per 1,000 people

## BAHRAIN
**Capital city:** Manama
**Area:** 655 sq km (253 sq miles)
**Population:** 724,000
**Official language:** Arabic
**Major religions:** Muslim 99%, other 1%
**Government:** Absolute monarchy
**Currency:** Bahrain dinar
**Adult literacy rate:** 89%
**Life expectancy:** 73 years
**People per doctor:** 1,000
**Televisions:** 472 per 1,000 people

## QATAR
**Capital city:** Doha
**Area:** 11,437 sq km (4,416 sq miles)
**Population:** 610,000
**Official language:** Arabic
**Major religions:** Muslim 95%, other 5%
**Government:** Absolute monarchy
**Currency:** Qatar riyal
**Adult literacy rate:** 82%
**Life expectancy:** 75 years
**People per doctor:** 769
**Televisions:** 404 per 1,000 people

# BAHRAIN

BAHRAIN IS MADE UP OF A SMALL GROUP of islands in the Persian Gulf. Little rain falls, so farming is only possible on irrigated, or watered, land. Bahrain was one of the first Arab states to discover oil in the 1930s. Its oil reserves are now running out.

PEARLING
As Bahrain's oil runs low, traditional industries such as pearling are once again growing in importance. The pearl season lasts from June to September. Divers descend on weighted ropes, equipped only with nose-clips, knives, and collecting bags. The most valuable pearls are bright white, tinged with pink.

*A pearl taken from an oyster shell.*

## LINKED ISLANDS

The main island of Bahrain is linked by a series of road causeways to the neighbouring islands of Al Muharraq and Sitrah, and to the Saudi Arabian mainland, with which Bahrain has close relations. Bahrain island is only 48 km (30 miles) long, and the other islands are even smaller.

# QATAR

*An Indian construction worker.*

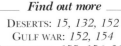

QATAR IS A LONG PENINSULA of land jutting out into the Persian Gulf. It is mainly desert with a hot, dry climate. Oil production and refining form the basis of its economy. The government is trying to encourage the growth of fishing and agriculture to reduce the country's dependence on oil.

WORKERS FROM ABROAD
In the 1940s, the smaller oil states such as Qatar and Kuwait encouraged workers from other parts of the Middle East, India, and Pakistan to work in their rapidly growing oil industries. Their own labour forces were simply too small to cope. Today, these migrant workers outnumber the local Qatari people.

*Find out more*
DESERTS: *15, 132, 152*
GULF WAR: *152, 154*
IRRIGATION: *155, 156, 217*
OIL: *137, 152, 281*

# UNITED ARAB EMIRATES

THE UNITED ARAB EMIRATES (UAE) lies on the southern coast of the Persian Gulf. Three-quarters of this Islamic country is sandy desert, with a hot, dry climate all year round. Only a tiny proportion of the land is suitable for farming and most food has to be imported. Oil was discovered in 1958 and has turned the UAE into one of the world's most prosperous countries, with a high standard of living for most people. There are many huge oil refineries along the coast.

*Abu Dhabi*

| UNITED ARAB EMIRATES | |
|---|---|
| **Capital city:** Abu Dhabi | |
| **Area:** 82,880 sq km (32,000 sq miles) | |
| **Population:** 3,000,000 | |
| **Official language:** Arabic | |
| **Major religions:** Muslim 96%, other 4% | |
| **Government:** Federation of monarchies | |
| **Currency:** UAE dirham | |
| **Adult literacy rate:** 77% | |
| **Life expectancy:** 75 years | |
| **People per doctor:** 556 | |
| **Televisions:** 294 per 1,000 people | |

| OMAN | |
|---|---|
| **Capital city:** Muscat | |
| **Area:** 212,460 sq km (82,030 sq miles) | |
| **Population:** 2,900,000 | |
| **Official language:** Arabic | |
| **Major religion:** Muslim 90%, other 10% | |
| **Government:** Absolute monarchy | |
| **Currency:** Omani rial | |
| **Adult literacy rate:** 74% | |
| **Life expectancy:** 74 years | |
| **People per doctor:** 769 | |
| **Televisions:** 595 per 1,000 people | |

## TOURISM
The UAE has a growing tourist industry. Some 2.5 million people arrive each year, mainly from Europe and Japan. Most visit in winter when it is warm but not too hot. Attractions include luxury hotels and duty-free shops, traditional markets, fine beaches, and trips into the desert.

*Al Mamza Beach Park, Dubai.*

## SEVEN STATES
The United Arab Emirates is a federation of seven small states, or emirates, each ruled by an emir, or sheik. The emirs have absolute power over their own states, but they also meet regularly to make decisions affecting the whole federation. Abu Dhabi is the largest of the emirates and its capital is also that of the UAE.

## ISLAMIC FESTIVALS
The two most important festivals of the Islamic year are *Id al-Fitr* and *Id al-Adha*. *Id al-Fitr* literally means "the breaking of the fast". It celebrates the end of the holy month of Ramadan, during which Muslims must fast from dawn to dusk. *Id al-Adha* is the festival of sacrifice. Prayers are followed by the sacrifice of a sheep, cow, or camel.

*A Muslim family celebrating Id al-Fitr (left). The feast consists of typical Middle Eastern foods, such as those shown on the right.*

*Dates*

*Apricots and dates are often eaten as appetizers.*

*Dried apricots*

*Lentils are used to make soups.*

*Courgettes (zucchinis) often accompany a meat dish.*

# OMAN

THE SULTANATE (KINGDOM) OF OMAN lies on the southeast coast of the Arabian Peninsula. Much of the land is desert, dotted with oases, but parts of the coastline are more fertile. Here farmers grow dates, pomegranates, limes, tobacco, and wheat. People also raise goats, sheep, and cattle. Oil is Oman's main export.

*Omani fishermen*

## FISHING
The Oman coastline is 1,700 km (1,056 miles) long, and fishing is a valuable source of income and food. Omani fishermen catch large amounts of sardines, tuna, anchovies, cod, and cuttlefish. They use traditional dug-out canoes, fitted with outboard motors for greater speed.

### LOST CITY OF THE SANDS
According to Arabian legend, a magnificent city called Ubar lies buried under the desolate sands of southern Oman. Archaeologists have excavated a watering hole and the remains of a city dating from about 3000 BC near the Yemen border. Some experts believe that this is the lost city of Ubar.

**Find out more**
DESERTS: *15, 132, 152*
ISLAM:. *275*
OIL: *137, 152, 281*
OIL WEALTH: *137, 278*

# YEMEN

THE COUNTRY OF YEMEN was formed in 1990 when North and South Yemen were reunited. Yemen lies at the southern tip of the Arabian Peninsula. It is more fertile than other Middle Eastern countries, with good farmland in the western highlands where there is regular rainfall. The coast and mountains of the east are hot, dry, and barren. Yemen is a poorer, less developed country than its neighbours. It is hoped that oil reserves, discovered in the 1980s, may help increase its prosperity in the future.

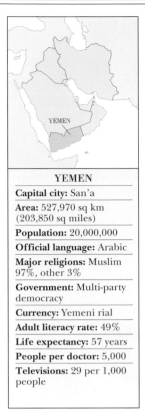

| YEMEN | |
|---|---|
| **Capital city:** San'a | |
| **Area:** 527,970 sq km (203,850 sq miles) | |
| **Population:** 20,000,000 | |
| **Official language:** Arabic | |
| **Major religions:** Muslim 97%, other 3% | |
| **Government:** Multi-party democracy | |
| **Currency:** Yemeni rial | |
| **Adult literacy rate:** 49% | |
| **Life expectancy:** 57 years | |
| **People per doctor:** 5,000 | |
| **Televisions:** 29 per 1,000 people | |

**THE PORT OF ADEN**
Aden is one of the biggest cities in Yemen and the country's main port. Because of its location on the Gulf of Aden, it has been the region's chief trading city since ancient times. Today, it is an important industrial centre, with a huge oil refinery, factories, and an international airport.

## YEMENI TERRACES

In many places, the mountain slopes of Yemen are terraced to provide extra space for crops. Some terraces are more than 1,300 years old. About half of all Yemeni workers are farmers. They grow cereal crops, such as wheat and sorghum, along with citrus fruits and dates, and raise sheep, goats, and cattle. Coffee and cotton are grown mainly for export.

*Traditional Yemeni tower houses are scattered throughout the terraced hills.*

*The remaining floors are used as living quarters.*

*The terraces are built up into the mountains.*

*The first floor is often used for storage.*

*Animals, such as goats and sheep, are kept on the ground floor of the house.*

*A variety of crops, such as coffee and cotton, are grown on the Yemeni terraces.*

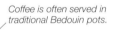

*Coffee is often served in traditional Bedouin pots.*

**COFFEE AND QAT**
Coffee is thought to have originated as a drink in Yemen, and the country produces some of the world's finest quality beans. Yemen is also famous for a plant called qat. Its leaves contain a mild drug and are often chewed. Qat parties are an important part of Yemeni social life.

*Tribal men often wear a ceremonial dagger, or jambiya, strapped to the waist.*

## TRIBAL SOCIETY

Most Yemeni people are Muslim Arabs belonging to various tribal groups. Each tribe elects a sheik as its leader and has its own customs, costumes, and folklore. Within each tribe, people live in large, closely knit, extended families. Several generations of the same family usually share the same house. The tribal tradition is particularly strong in north Yemen.

## SAN'A

San'a, the capital of Yemen, is an ancient city, famous for its traditional Yemeni-style architecture. In the old city you can still see clusters of 400-year-old multi-storeyed, mud and brick tower houses, their outer walls often decorated with friezes. An international conservation effort has been launched to protect this unique city and preserve it for the future.

# CENTRAL ASIA

CENTRAL ASIA LIES FAR FROM the world's oceans. The winds are dry and there is little rainfall, so the area is generally arid. With cold, dry winters, and hot, dry summers, lack of water is a problem for farmers. The north consists of a flat, grass-covered plain, or steppe. In the centre of the region are two vast deserts, the Kyzyl Kum ("Red Sands") and the Kara Kum ("Black Sands"). In the south are long chains of snow-capped mountain ranges that join the neighbouring Himalayas. The entire region, apart from Afghanistan, used to be part of the Soviet Union. Industrialization and collective farms brought huge changes to a region once occupied mainly by nomads.

## INDEPENDENCE

In 1991, the communist state of the Soviet Union fell apart and the central Asian countries became independent. While the countries were under Soviet rule, many Russian people settled there and Russian replaced the local languages. Today, the peoples of central Asia have re-established their own languages and national identities.

Nomadic herders in the hills of Afghanistan.

Child's hat from Afghanistan.

*This girl's hat from Uzbekistan is embroidered with gold thread.*

## A LAND OF MANY PEOPLES

There is a great variety of peoples living in central Asia. The original inhabitants include the Kazakhs, Turkmens, and Uzbeks, related to the Turks, and the Tajiks and Afghans, related to the Iranians. Each group has its own distinctive style of hat, often woven in silk with brightly coloured geometric patterns.

*Silver ornaments adorn this Turkmen girl's hat.*

## NOMADIC LIFESTYLE

Many people living in central Asia are nomads, moving from place to place with their animals in search of new pastures. Nomads live in tents and have few belongings, making travelling easier and quicker. They live by herding animals such as camels, goats, and sheep, which give them milk, meat, and wool, some of which they sell, but most of which they use themselves. Nomads mostly stay in the open country, but they visit the towns and cities occasionally to sell their products.

**The Aral Sea in 1960**

*Fishing village on the coast.*

*Fishing village stranded inland.*

**The Aral Sea in 1995**

*The lake is about half its original size. By 2010, it may have almost disappeared.*

### DRILLING FOR OIL

The northern states of central Asia are sitting on huge reserves of oil and gas. Kazakhstan is slowly exploiting one of the world's biggest oil fields under the Caspian Sea, while Turkmenistan is beginning to make use of a vast reservoir of natural gas trapped beneath its land. Exploitation of these riches is hampered by lack of investment and a poorly skilled workforce.

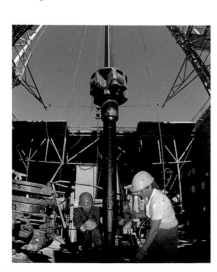

*Miners drilling for oil in the Tengiz oil field in Kazakhstan.*

## SHRINKING SEA

The Aral Sea, once the fourth largest freshwater lake in the world, is shrinking. Fishing villages that once stood on the sea coast are now stranded inland, depriving villagers of their livelihood. This environmental disaster has been caused by water from the Amu Darya River, which flows into the Aral Sea, being drained for irrigation projects. Huge areas of useless land have been laid bare. Wind storms are common, sweeping up polluted dust and dumping it on the surrounding countryside.

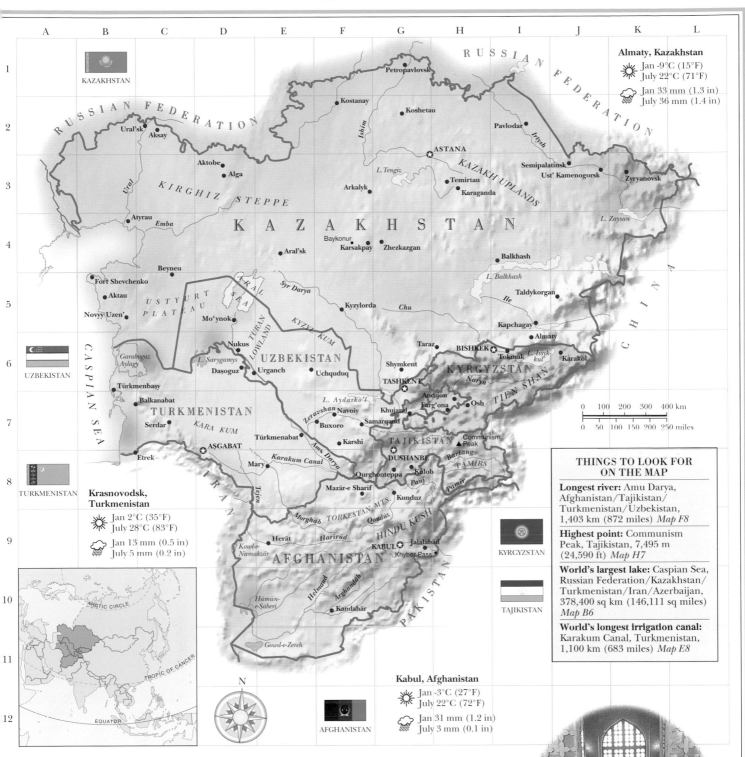

**Almaty, Kazakhstan**
Jan -9°C (15°F)
July 22°C (71°F)

Jan 33 mm (1.3 in)
July 36 mm (1.4 in)

RUSSIAN FEDERATION

Petropavlovsk

Kostanay

Koshetau

KAZAKHSTAN

Ural'sk
Aksay

Aktobe
Alga

Pavlodar

ASTANA

Semipalatinsk
Ust' Kamenogorsk
Zyryanovsk

KIRGHIZ STEPPE

Arkalyk
Temirtau
Karaganda

L. Tengiz

KAZAKH UPLANDS

Atyrau
Emba

L. Zaysan

Beyneu

Baykonur
Karsakpay  Zhezkazgan

Aral'sk

Balkhash

L. Balkhash

Fort Shevchenko

USTYURT PLATEAU

Aktau

ARAL SEA

Syr Darya

Kyzylorda

Chu

Taldykorgan

Ile

Novyy Uzen'

Mo'ynok

TURAN LOWLAND

KYZYL KUM

Kapchagay
Almaty

CASPIAN SEA

Garabogaz Aylagy

Nukus
L. Sarygamys
Dașoguz  Urganch

UZBEKISTAN

Uchquduq

Taraz

Shymkent

BISHKEK
Tokmak  Karakol

KYRGYZSTAN

L. Issyk-kul'

Türkmenbașy

TASHKENT

Naryn

TIEN SHAN

CHINA

Balkanabat

L. Aydarko'l

Andijon
Farg'ona  Osh

TURKMENISTAN

Serdar

KARA KUM

Zeravshan  Navoiy
Samarqand

Khujand

Communism
Peak

AȘGABAT

Türkmenabat

Buxoro

Karshi

TAJIKISTAN

Barlang
PAMIRS

Etrek

Mary

Karakum Canal

Amu Darya

DUSHANBE

Kulob
Panj

Pomir

Qurghonteppa

Tejen

Mazār-e Sharif

Kunduz

Qonduz

0  100  200  300  400 km
0  50  100 150 200 250 miles

Morghāb

TORKESTAN MTS.

HINDU KUSH

Herāt

Harīrūd

KABUL  Jalālābād

Kōwl-e-Namakzār

AFGHANISTAN

Khyber Pass

KYRGYZSTAN

Helmand

Arghandāb

PAKISTAN

TAJIKISTAN

Hāmūn-e-Sāberi

Kandahār

Gowd-e-Zereh

**Krasnovodsk, Turkmenistan**
Jan 2°C (35°F)
July 28°C (83°F)

Jan 13 mm (0.5 in)
July 5 mm (0.2 in)

**Kabul, Afghanistan**
Jan -3°C (27°F)
July 22°C (72°F)

Jan 31 mm (1.2 in)
July 3 mm (0.1 in)

AFGHANISTAN

N

### THINGS TO LOOK FOR ON THE MAP

**Longest river:** Amu Darya, Afghanistan/Tajikistan/ Turkmenistan/Uzbekistan, 1,403 km (872 miles) *Map F8*

**Highest point:** Communism Peak, Tajikistan, 7,495 m (24,590 ft) *Map H7*

**World's largest lake:** Caspian Sea, Russian Federation/Kazakhstan/ Turkmenistan/Iran/Azerbaijan, 378,400 sq km (146,111 sq miles) *Map B6*

**World's longest irrigation canal:** Karakum Canal, Turkmenistan, 1,100 km (683 miles) *Map E8*

## CAVIAR

The largest inland lake in the world, the Caspian Sea covers 378,400 sq km (146,111 sq miles) and borders five countries. The lake is home to a variety of fish, such as sturgeon, from which caviar (fish eggs) is made. However, pollution of the waters by industrial waste has led to a drop in the numbers of fish.

*Caviar served on toast.*

## Islam

Throughout central Asia, Islam is the main religion. It arrived in the region in the early 8th century. While central Asia was part of the Soviet Union, Islam was suppressed. Traditional Muslim wedding ceremonies were forbidden. Throughout this time, however, people continued to worship in secret. With the end of communism, Islam has gained strength in every country.

# KAZAKHSTAN

STRETCHING FROM THE Caspian Sea to China, Kazakhstan is a vast country, almost the size of western Europe. It is also one of the most underpopulated countries in the world. With vast mineral reserves, fertile soil, and a stable government, Kazakhstan has the potential to be a wealthy country. However, industrial and agricultural pollution, particularly the use of pesticides and the way in which crops like cotton are grown, have caused considerable environmental problems.

### KAZAKHSTAN

**Capital city:** Astana

**Area:** 2,717,300 sq km (1,049,150 sq miles)

**Population:** 15,400,000

**Official language:** Kazakh

**Major religions:** Muslim 47%, Christian 44%, other 9%

**Government:** Democracy

**Currency:** Tenge

**Adult literacy rate:** 99%

**Life expectancy:** 62 years

**People per doctor:** 278

**Televisions:** 231 per 1,000 people

## THE VIRGIN LANDS

In the 1950s the Russian government increased grain production by cultivating the vast grassland steppes, or plains, of Kazakhstan. Huge farms were set up to grow corn and wheat on land that had been barren. Millions of Russians migrated or were forced to move to this empty region, known as the "Virgin Lands". The programme met with mixed success. It left Kazakhstan self-sufficient in grain and other crops, but it led to enormous environmental damage.

## RICH IN MINERALS

Mining is the most important industry in Kazakhstan. The country has huge coal and iron-ore reserves, the world's largest chrome mine, and one of its biggest gold fields, as well as plentiful supplies of copper, zinc, lead, uranium, and other minerals. Most coal in Kazakhstan comes from open-cast mines, rather than from deep mine shafts.

*At the processing plant, the coal is cleaned and dried and sorted into different sizes.*

*In the filter bed, any remaining pieces of rock and clay are removed.*

*Trucks transport the extracted coal along a haul road.*

*Steps are cut into the sides of the pit so that the coal can be reached safely.*

*Surface rock is loosened by explosives so that the digging machines can remove the rock and reach the coal.*

*Machines dig the coal out of the pit.*

## THE KAZAKHS

Native Kazakhs make up only about 50 per cent of the total population of their country and live mainly in the west and south. Many are farmers and have worked hard to preserve the natural beauty of the land, setting up reserves to protect wildlife and the environment. The rest of the population consists mainly of Russians, Germans, and Ukranians.

*A government building in Almaty, the former capital of Kazakhstan.*

### THE CITY OF APPLES

Almaty means "father of apple trees", and the former capital is known for its apple orchards. The city nestles at the foot of the Tien Shan mountains in the far south of the country. It has many parks and fountains, and narrow canals called *aryks* run along the sides of streets to cool the city during the hot summers. In 1994 the capital was moved to Astana in the north.

### SPACE RACE

History was made in Kazakhstan in 1957 when the world's first artificial satellite, *Sputnik I*, was launched from the Baykonur Cosmodrome, or space station, in the centre of the country. The first person in space, Yuri Gagarin, was sent into orbit around the Earth from Baykonur in 1961. The site is still used today by the Russian government for its space programme.

### Find out more

# UZBEKISTAN

UZBEKISTAN IS ONE OF the wealthiest and one of the more populated countries in central Asia. It also has a varied landscape. While two-thirds of the land is made up of desert and arid steppe land, there are also fertile areas, fast-flowing rivers, and snowy mountain tops. The ancient cities of the Silk Road are beginning to attract large numbers of tourists, and foreign investors are helping to develop the country's huge mineral and energy resources. Uzbekistan is also the world's fifth largest producer of cotton, known locally as "white gold".

## ISLAMIC CITIES

The Silk Road is an old trading route that linked China with central Asia, the Middle East, and Europe. Ancient Islamic cities, once major trading centres, are found along its route. These include Samarkand, which contains many fine examples of Islamic architecture, Bukhara, an important place of pilgrimage for Muslims, and Tashkent, the capital of Uzbekistan and known as the "city of fountains".

NATURAL GAS
Uzbekistan is rich in natural resources. It has plentiful supplies of oil, natural gas, coal, gold, and uranium. A huge pipeline used for exporting natural gas stretches from Bukhara to the Urals in Russia. Much of the local industry, producing machinery, chemicals, and aircraft, is based on energy from gas.

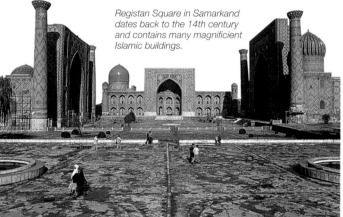

*Registan Square in Samarkand dates back to the 14th century and contains many magnificent Islamic buildings.*

| UZBEKISTAN | |
|---|---|
| **Capital city:** Tashkent | |
| **Area:** 447,400 sq km (172,741 sq miles) | |
| **Population:** 26,100,000 | |
| **Official language:** Uzbek | |
| **Major religions:** Muslim 88%, Christian 9%, other 3% | |
| **Government:** Presidential dictatorship | |
| **Currency:** Som | |
| **Adult literacy rate:** 99% | |
| **Life expectancy:** 67 years | |
| **People per doctor:** 345 | |

| TAJIKISTAN | |
|---|---|
| **Capital city:** Dushanbe | |
| **Area:** 143,100 sq km (55,251 sq miles) | |
| **Population:** 6,200,000 | |
| **Official language:** Tajik | |
| **Major religions:** Muslim 85%, other 15% | |
| **Government:** Democracy | |
| **Currency:** Somoni | |
| **Adult literacy rate:** 99% | |
| **Life expectancy:** 67 years | |
| **People per doctor:** 476 | |

# TAJIKISTAN

THE POOREST OF THE FORMER SOVIET UNION states, Tajikistan is a mountainous country with only about six per cent of its land available for farming. Most people work on the land, growing fruit, cotton, and tobacco and herding animals, or work in small factories producing textiles, silk, and carpets. From independence in 1991 until 1997, Tajikistan was split by armed conflict between the government and rebel groups.

*In the Pamir mountain region, a different tribal group is found in almost every valley.*

Peaches

Melon

Pistachios

FERTILE VALLEYS
In spring, melted snow from the Tien Shan and Pamir mountains flows down into the Fergana and other river valleys of Tajikistan, bringing with it rich, fertile mud. Irrigation channels direct this water into the surrounding fields, enabling farmers to grow a variety of crops, such as those above.

## PAMIR VALLEY PEOPLES
Less than 100,000 people live in the Pamir mountain region, growing grain and fruit in the deep valleys, or herding sheep and yaks on the bleak high plains in the east. Because of the remoteness of the area and the isolation of the valleys from each other, there is a bewildering variety of peoples, languages, and dialects.

*Find out more*
COTTON: *36, 215, 216*
GAS: *198, 211*
ISLAM: *275*
ISLAMIC ARCHITECTURE: *155*

# TURKMENISTAN

ALMOST 90 PER CENT of Turkmenistan consists of the vast Kara Kum ("Black Sands") Desert, where temperatures reach more than 50°C (122°F). A fertile strip of land stretches around the southern borders of the desert; here people grow cotton and other crops for export. Since Turkmenistan became independent in 1991, Turkmen has replaced Russian as the state language and Islam is once again the major religion. The country is poor and isolated from the rest of the world, but possesses huge reserves of natural gas.

**ASHGABAT**
In 1948, the bustling market town of Ashgabat was totally destroyed by a huge earthquake. The town was completely replanned and rebuilt and is now the capital city of Turkmenistan. Ashgabat is the centre for food processing and silk, lace, and carpet manufacturing.

| TURKMENISTAN | |
|---|---|
| **Capital city:** Ashgabat | |
| **Area:** 488,100 sq km (188,455 sq miles) | |
| **Population:** 4,900,000 | |
| **Official language:** Turkmen | |
| **Major religions:** Muslim 87%, Christian 11%, other 2% | |
| **Government:** Presidential dictatorship | |
| **Currency:** Manat | |
| **Adult literacy rate:** 98% | |
| **Life expectancy:** 65 years | |
| **People per doctor:** 382 | |

| KYRGYZSTAN | |
|---|---|
| **Capital city:** Bishkek | |
| **Area:** 198,500 sq km (76,640 sq miles) | |
| **Population:** 5,100,000 | |
| **Official language:** Kyrgyz, Russian | |
| **Major religions:** Muslim 72%, Christian and other 28% | |
| **Government:** Democracy | |
| **Currency:** Som | |
| **Adult literacy rate:** 97% | |
| **Life expectancy:** 65 years | |
| **People per doctor:** 385 | |

## THE TURKMENS

The Turkmen people live in various parts of central Asia and many follow a nomadic lifestyle. In Turkmenistan, however, many Turkmens have settled as farmers and expert horse breeders. They visit local horse fairs and buy and sell horses for export to neighbouring countries. The Turkmens are known for producing highly prized racehorses, such as the Akhal-Teke, a breed able to move quickly in desert conditions.

Main towns
Cotton

**KARAKUM CANAL**
The world's longest irrigation canal stretches from the Amu Darya River in the east to beyond Ashgabat in the west, a distance of 1,100 km (683 miles). Known as the "River of Life", the Karakum Canal provides water for a large area of arid land, so that cotton and other crops can be grown.

# KYRGYZSTAN

KNOWN AS THE SWITZERLAND of central Asia because of its mountainous landscape, over half of Kyrgyzstan is 2,500 m (8,200 ft) or more above sea level. The snow-capped Tien Shan mountains dominate the countryside, but the river valleys are fertile and green. Most people are farmers. Animal breeding is particularly important because there is so little land to farm.

*The Kyrgyz people follow Islam. They speak a Turkic language and live a nomadic life in the countryside.*

## THE KYRGYZ PEOPLE

Over half the population are native Kyrgyz – nomadic people known for their skilled horsemanship. The largest minority group are Russians, who live in the towns and, until independence in 1991, ran the economy. As a result of rising nationalist feeling among the Kyrgyz, many Russian people have now returned to Russia.

*Gold nugget*

**MOUNTAIN RICHES**
The mountains of Kyrgyzstan are rich in minerals. Gold and mercury are mined for export, while coal, oil, and gas are exploited for domestic use. The fast-flowing rivers are ideal for generating electricity and new hydro-electric power stations have been built.

*Find out more*
DESERTS: *15, 132, 152*
GAS: *163, 198, 211*
NOMADS: *160*
USSR BREAK-UP: *136, 160*

# AFGHANISTAN

AFGHANISTAN OCCUPIES AN IMPORTANT position between central Asia and the Indian Subcontinent. As a result, the country has been fought over for centuries. It has few paved roads and no railways, and three-quarters of the land is inaccessible. In 1979, Russian troops occupied the country to support its communist government but by 1989 they had been driven out by Islamic mujahideen. The Taliban took power in 1996; however, their links with Islamic extremists, including Osama Bin Laden, suspected of masterminding the destruction of New York's World Trade Centre, led to their overthrow by opposition forces supported by the USA and its allies in 2001.

**CULTURAL DESTRUCTION**
In 2001 the Taliban destroyed two of the world's largest statues of Buddha at Bamiyan. Built in 5 AD, the tallest of the statues was over 53 m (174 ft) high. The Taliban justified this act by saying Islam forbids the depiction of the human form in art, but many Islamic nations disagreed with what they had done.

| AFGHANISTAN | |
| --- | --- |
| **Capital city:** Kabul | |
| **Area:** 647,500 sq km (250,000 sq miles) | |
| **Population:** 23,900,000 | |
| **Official languages:** Dari (Persian), Pashtu | |
| **Major religions:** Muslim 99%, other 1% | |
| **Government:** Islamic republic | |
| **Currency:** New Afghani | |
| **Adult literacy rate:** 36% | |
| **Life expectancy:** 43 years | |
| **People per doctor:** 10,000 | |
| **Televisions:** 13 per 1,000 people | |

*Some mujahideen groups are based in the hills of Afghanistan. "Mujahideen" comes from the Arabic word for "fighter".*

*The Turkmen nomads in the north of the country live in reddish-brown, dome-shaped tents.*

*The Pushtoon nomads of the south live in black tents spread low over the ground.*

## THE TALIBAN

In Pashtu, an Afghani language, Taliban means "religious student", and it was from religious schools in Pakistan and southern Afghanistan that the Taliban developed their extreme ideology. The Taliban governed according to a strict interpretation of the Koran, the Muslim holy book, compelling all men to wear beards, outlawing TV and radio, and forbidding music, dance, and even chess.

**TENTS**
Some Afghans are nomads, or *kochis*, as they are known locally. The different groups can be distinguished by the unique designs of the felt or animal-skin tents they live in, each design having been passed down through countless generations.

## OPPRESSION OF WOMEN

Under the Taliban, girls were banned from school and women from work. They were not even allowed to leave the home without a male member of their family as an escort. When they did venture outside, they had to wear a burqa – a traditional Afghan robe that covered them from head to toe. Since the fall of the Taliban, women have begun to rejoin society and have started education and work.

**CARPET WEAVING**
The Turkmens of northern Afghanistan are skilled carpet makers, hand-knotting and weaving fine wool from the karakul sheep into geometric red, brown, and maroon patterns. The carpets are usually made by women and are used as saddle-cloths, tent hangings, and prayer mats.

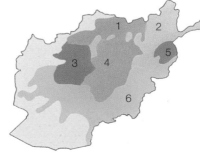

**Major peoples in Afghanistan**
1. Uzbek
2. Tajik
3. Aimaq
4. Hazara
5. Nuristani
6. Pushtoon

*Find out more*
CARPET MAKING: *144, 155, 210*
ISLAM: *275*
NOMADS: *160*
TENTS: *156, 181*

# THE INDIAN SUBCONTINENT

FRINGED BY THE INDIAN OCEAN, the Arabian Sea, and the Bay of Bengal, and bordered to the north by the mighty Himalayas, the Indian Subcontinent covers a vast area. More than a fifth of the world's people live here. Dominated by India, the area also includes Pakistan, Bangladesh, Nepal, the island of Sri Lanka, and the tiny state of Bhutan. The Subcontinent has a long and turbulent history and has been invaded many times. In the 19th and early 20th centuries, most of the area, apart from Nepal and Bhutan, was ruled by Britain. The landscape and climate of the Subcontinent vary greatly, with snow-capped mountains in the north, dry, sandy desert in the northwest, and hot, tropical rainforest in the south.

### INDEPENDENCE
India became independent in 1947. The country was divided into Hindu India and the new Muslim country of Pakistan, split into West and East. In 1971, East Pakistan became the independent country of Bangladesh.

*Mahatma Gandhi, a central figure in India's struggle for independence, believed in using peaceful methods to achieve his country's aims.*

*Most villagers are farmers, but others follow a trade such as weaving or pottery-making.*

*Most village people live in small houses with two or three rooms.*

## VILLAGE LIFE
Most people in the Subcontinent live in closely knit villages and make their living from farming. In India alone, more than 70 per cent of the population live in some 500,000 villages scattered across the country. Some consist of small clusters of houses, others have thousands of inhabitants. Most families have lived in the same village for many years, passing on their knowledge and skills from one generation to the next.

*The houses of many villages are clustered round a village square. Here the village council (Panchayat) will meet to make decisions.*

*The well is one of the focal points of village life. Women collect water every day and meet to exchange news.*

## MONSOON
The climate of much of the Subcontinent is dominated by the monsoon winds which bring rain to the area each summer. Farmers rely on this rainfall to water their crops. If the rains fail, they face ruin. Sometimes the rainfall is very heavy and causes terrible floods. Whole villages and fields of crops may be swept away.

### SEASONAL WINDS
These winds blow from the southwest in summer and from the northeast in winter. As the summer winds sweep across the Indian Ocean, they pick up moisture which turns into rain on reaching the hot, dry land.

*Because Bangladesh is flat and low-lying, it is particularly prone to flooding.*

→ Southwest winds (June to October)

⇉ Northeast winds (November to February)

### TREKKING IN THE HIMALAYAS
Each year, thousands of tourists travel to Nepal to trek in the mountains. The Nepalese Himalayas include eight peaks more than 8,000 m (26,247 ft) high. The world's tallest mountain, Everest, stands on the border between Nepal and China. Many expeditions are accompanied by Sherpas. These Nepalese people are skilled climbers.

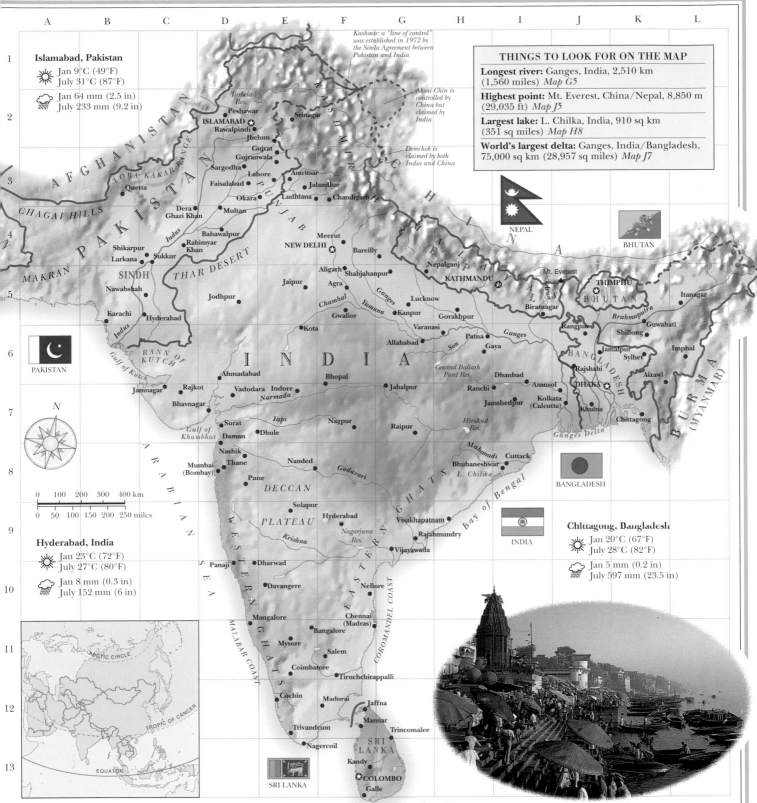

A B C D E F G H I J K L

**Islamabad, Pakistan**
☀ Jan 9°C (49°F)
☀ July 31°C (87°F)
🌧 Jan 64 mm (2.5 in)
🌧 July 233 mm (9.2 in)

Kashmir: a "line of control"
was established in 1972 by
the Simla Agreement between
Pakistan and India

Aksai Chin is
controlled by
China but
claimed by
India

Demchok is
claimed by both
India and China

**THINGS TO LOOK FOR ON THE MAP**

**Longest river:** Ganges, India, 2,510 km
(1,560 miles) *Map G5*

**Highest point:** Mt. Everest, China/Nepal, 8,850 m
(29,035 ft) *Map J5*

**Largest lake:** L. Chilka, India, 910 sq km
(351 sq miles) *Map H8*

**World's largest delta:** Ganges, India/Bangladesh,
75,000 sq km (28,957 sq miles) *Map J7*

NEPAL

BHUTAN

AFGHANISTAN

TOBA KAKAR RANGE

CHAGAI HILLS

MAKRAN

Tarbela Res.
Peshawar
ISLAMABAD
Rawalpindi
Jhelum
Gujrat
Gujranwala
Sargodha
Lahore
Faisalabad
Okara
Multan
Dera
Ghazi Khan
Bahawalpur
Rahimyar
Khan
Shikarpur
Larkana
Sukkur
Nawabshah
Karachi
Hyderabad

PAKISTAN

PUNJAB

SINDH

THAR DESERT

Indus

Srinagar

Amritsar
Jalandhar
Ludhiana
Chandigarh

KASHMIR

HIMALAYA

Meerut
NEW DELHI
Bareilly
Aligarh
Shahjahanpur
Jaipur
Agra
Jodhpur
Gwalior
Kota

Chambal
Yamuna

Lucknow
Kanpur
Varanasi
Allahabad
Gorakhpur

Ganges

Son

NEPAL
Nepalganj
KATHMANDU
Mt. Everest

Biratnagar

Patna
Gaya

Ganges

BHUTAN
THIMPHU

Itanagar

Rangpur
Jamalpur
Shillong
Guwahati
Sylhet
Imphal
Aizawl

Brahmaputra

Indus

CHINA

Dhanbad
Asansol
Ranchi
Jamshedpur
Kolkata
(Calcutta)
Khulna

BANGLADESH
DHAKA

Chittagong

BURMA
(MYANMAR)

Govind Ballash
Pant Res.

RANN OF
KUTCH

Gulf of Kutch

ARABIAN SEA

PAKISTAN

Jamnagar
Rajkot
Bhavnagar

Ahmadabad
Vadodara
Indore
Narmada

Bhopal

Jabalpur

Tapi
Surat
Daman
Dhule
Nashik
Mumbai
(Bombay)
Thane
Pune

Nanded

Nagpur

Raipur

Godavari

INDIA

Hirakud
Res.

Mahanadi

Bhubaneshwar
L. Chilika

Cuttack

Ganges Delta

Bay of Bengal

BANGLADESH

100 200 300 400 km
50 100 150 200 250 miles

N

DECCAN
PLATEAU

Krishna

Solapur
Hyderabad

Nagarjuna
Res.

Visakhapatnam
Rajahmundry
Vijayawada

INDIA

**Chittagong, Bangladesh**
☀ Jan 20°C (67°F)
☀ July 28°C (82°F)
🌧 Jan 5 mm (0.2 in)
🌧 July 597 mm (23.5 in)

**Hyderabad, India**
☀ Jan 23°C (72°F)
☀ July 27°C (80°F)
🌧 Jan 8 mm (0.3 in)
🌧 July 152 mm (6 in)

Panaji
Dharwad
Davangere

Mangalore
Bangalore
Mysore
Salem
Coimbatore
Tiruchchirappalli
Cochin
Madurai
Trivandrum
Nagercoil

WESTERN GHATS

EASTERN GHATS

MALABAR COAST

COROMANDEL COAST

Nellore
Chennai
(Madras)

Jaffna
Mannar
Trincomalee

SRI
LANKA

Kandy
COLOMBO
Galle

SRI LANKA

ARCTIC CIRCLE
TROPIC OF CANCER
EQUATOR

**SACRED RIVER**
Followers of five of the world's major religions
live in the Indian Subcontinent – Hindus,
Muslims, Buddhists, Sikhs, and Christians. The
majority of people are Hindu and their holiest
city is Varanasi, in northern India. The city
stands on the banks of the Ganges, the sacred
river of the Hindus. Millions of pilgrims come to
Varanasi each year to bathe in the river. This is
believed to wash away their sins.

**ENDANGERED WILDLIFE**
The Subcontinent is rich in wildlife,
from elephants and rhinoceroses to
monkeys and mongooses. Loss of
habitat and poaching are serious
threats to India's most famous
animals, including tigers. Despite the
establishment of protected reserves,
illegal tiger-hunting continues. Only
around 3,000 tigers are left in the wild.

# PAKISTAN

PAKISTAN WAS CREATED IN 1947 as a home for Muslims in India. The country was originally divided into East and West, but in 1971 East Pakistan broke away to become Bangladesh and West Pakistan became Pakistan. Today most people make their living from farming, but industry – especially cotton and textiles – is growing steadily. Handicrafts, such as carpet-making and metal work, are also important. Since Pakistan became independent, it has been in dispute with India over the largely Muslim state of Kashmir, which forms part of India, but is claimed by Pakistan.

## PAKISTAN

| | |
|---|---|
| **Capital city:** Islamabad | |
| **Area:** 803,940 sq km (310,401 sq miles) | |
| **Population:** 154,000,000 | |
| **Official language:** Urdu | |
| **Major religions:** Muslim 97%, other 3% | |
| **Government:** Multi-party democracy | |
| **Currency:** Pakistani rupee | |
| **Adult literacy rate:** 44% | |
| **Life expectancy:** 64 years | |
| **People per doctor:** 1,436 | |
| **Televisions:** 88 per 1,000 people | |

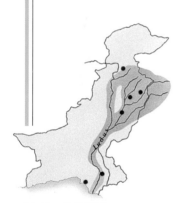

● major cities
▦ irrigated land

### WHERE PEOPLE LIVE
The population of Pakistan is unevenly distributed across the country. More than 80 per cent live in the provinces of Punjab and Sind, on the fertile floodplains of the rivers.

### ISLAMABAD
About a third of Pakistani people live in cities. The capital is Islamabad (right), a brand new city built in the early 1960s. The name Islamabad means the "place of Islam." The city is well planned, with lots of open spaces and wide, tree-lined avenues. Karachi is the major port and largest city, with around 10 million people living there.

### WATERING THE LAND

The flat, fertile plains of the Punjab form the farming heartland of Pakistan. The rich soil is watered by the River Indus, which also provides water for drinking and for electricity. The river has five tributaries, the Jhelum, Chenab, Ravi, Sutlej, and Beas, which give the region its name, as Punjab means "five waters". In other parts of the country, huge irrigation (watering) schemes have converted scrubland and semi-desert into fertile farmland.

### PEOPLES OF PAKISTAN
There are many different groups of people living in Pakistan, all of whom have their own distinctive language and culture. The Pathan tribes of the Northwest Frontier are known for their fierce loyalty to family and tribe. The Sindhis (above) are a farming community living in the south of the country with a rich tradition in literature and music. The Punjabis live in the fertile plains of the Punjab.

**BRIGHT BUSES**
Many people in Pakistan travel on the brightly coloured buses that run between the towns and cities. The buses often have flowers and patterns painted on them and are decorated with tinsel and fairy lights. Trucks used to transport all kinds of goods are also often highly decorated.

### WOMEN'S LIFE
Islamic law is very important in Pakistan. It determines how people worship and behave. It is Islamic custom for women to live in *purdah* (behind the veil). This means that when women appear in public, they cover themselves with a *burqa* (hooded gown) or a *chaddar* (veil) to ensure that men cannot see their faces. Traditional households are often divided into a men's section at the front and a women's section at the back.

Chaddar, or veil

Kamiz, or tunic

> **Find out more**
> COTTON: *36, 215, 216*
> IRRIGATION: *155, 156, 217*
> ISLAM: *275*
> RIVER VALLEYS: *135*

# BANGLADESH

In 1971, EAST PAKISTAN broke away from West Pakistan to become the independent country of Bangladesh. Like Pakistan, it remains a largely Muslim country. The official language is Bengali. Bangladesh is one of the poorest and most crowded countries in the world, suffering from frequent cyclones and floods which cause devastation, especially along the coast. Efforts are being made to control the floods, to slow down the rate of population growth, and to modernize industry and farming.

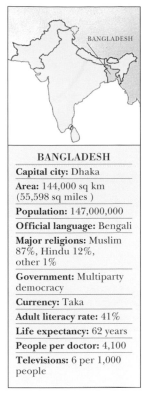

### BANGLADESH

**Capital city:** Dhaka

**Area:** 144,000 sq km (55,598 sq miles )

**Population:** 147,000,000

**Official language:** Bengali

**Major religions:** Muslim 87%, Hindu 12%, other 1%

**Government:** Multiparty democracy

**Currency:** Taka

**Adult literacy rate:** 41%

**Life expectancy:** 62 years

**People per doctor:** 4,100

**Televisions:** 6 per 1,000 people

## GROWING JUTE

Known to Bangladeshis as "the golden fibre," jute is a tough, fibrous plant which has proved a valuable source of income for farmers. Jute is used to make sacking, rope, and carpet backing. It has traditionally been Bangladesh's most important export, but now faces competition from artificial fibres. Rice is a major food crop in Bangladesh, with tea and sugarcane grown for export.

*Most Bangladeshi people make their living from fishing and farming. The annual floods provide plenty of fish and keep the land very fertile.*

**The flooded delta**
*The map shows the varying depths of water during the annual flood.*

## FLOODED LAND

Much of Bangladesh is made up of the delta (mouth) of three major rivers – the Ganges, Brahmaputra, and Meghna. During the monsoon season (June to October) the rivers flood, and huge amounts of rich silt are left behind, making the soil extremely fertile for farming. But the flooding can also cause devastation, killing many people and animals, and sweeping away homes and crops. Despite the risks, most Bangladeshis live in tiny villages scattered across the floodplains.

**Depth of water**
- up to 1 m (3 ft)
- 1–2 m (3–6 ft)
- more than 2 m (6 ft )

*Houses are often raised up on stilts or embankments to protect them from the floods.*

*Boats are a vital means of transport. People travel in all types of boats, which are often very crowded. Huge rafts are used to carry jute, bamboo, and other goods.*

## HEALTH CARE

Despite government health-care programmes, the death rate in Bangladesh is very high, especially among children in remote, rural areas. This is largely due to poor diet and to unclean water, which helps spread diseases such as cholera. Medical teams travel around the country immunizing people from disease and teaching them about diet and birth control.

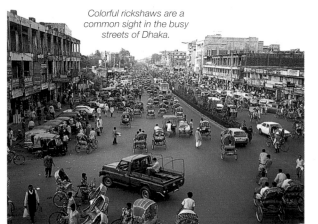

*Colorful rickshaws are a common sight in the busy streets of Dhaka.*

## LIFE IN THE CITY

Only about a third of Bangladeshis live in cities, mainly in Dhaka, the capital, or the two ports of Chittagong and Khulna. City dwellers can enjoy a higher standard of living than people in the villages, with better homes and facilities such as piped water and electricity supplies. As the cities become more crowded with people looking for work, however, many new arrivals are being forced to live in slums and shanty towns.

*Find out more*

HEALTH: *276*
ISLAM: *275*
MONSOON: *166*
RIVER VALLEYS: *135*

# INDIA

THE WORLD'S SEVENTH LARGEST and second most populated country, India is a vast, colourful land, full of variety in religion, language, and culture. Three of the world's major faiths, Hinduism, Buddhism, and Sikhism, originated here. More than 200 languages are spoken, though 40 per cent of the population speak Hindi. Despite much poverty, India is one of the world's top industrialized nations. Both agriculture and industry have expanded during the past 20 years and have attracted investment from international companies. India is also the world's largest democracy. Some 600 million people are eligible to vote.

**INDIA**

| | |
|---|---|
| **Capital city:** | New Delhi |
| **Area:** | 3,287,590 sq km (1,269,338 sq miles) |
| **Population:** | 1,070,000,000 |
| **Official languages:** | Hindi, English |
| **Major religions:** | Hindu 83%, Muslim 11%, Christian 2%, Sikh 2%, other 2% |
| **Government:** | Multi-party democracy |
| **Currency:** | Rupee |
| **Adult literacy rate:** | 61% |
| **Life expectancy:** | 63 years |
| **People per doctor:** | 1,885 |
| **Televisions:** | 69 per 1,000 people |

## BOLLYWOOD

More films are produced in India than anywhere else in the world, including the USA. About 800 full-length feature films are shot each year, mainly in Mumbai (Bombay), nicknamed "Bollywood". Indian films are often packed with songs, dancing, romance, glamorous stars, and non-stop action. Going to the cinema is a favourite pastime in India, and many films last for four or five hours.

*These farm workers are winnowing, or sifting, grain after the harvest. Huge amounts of grain are kept in reserve in case the harvest fails.*

## GREEN REVOLUTION

One of India's most pressing problems has been to produce enough food for its ever-growing population. Today, it is self-sufficient in food, production of rice and wheat having risen more than 200 per cent since independence. This improvement is partly due to the "Green Revolution" of the 1960s, when farming methods were modernized and higher yielding varieties of rice and wheat were planted.

### FOOD PRODUCTION
India is the world's biggest producer of the crops shown below. Percentages indicate India's share in world production.

- sugar 11%
- bananas 13%
- tea 28%
- sesame seeds 33%
- jute 44%
- mangoes 60%

*Cinnamon is used in both sweet and savoury dishes.*

*Garlic is added to many spice mixtures.*

*Coriander is an essential ingredient in many Indian dishes.*

*Turmeric is used as a spice and a dye.*

## INDIAN FOOD

Many Indian people are vegetarians. They do not believe in killing animals to eat. Most Hindus never eat beef because they consider cows to be sacred, and Muslims do not eat pork. Food varies from place to place, but a typical meal might consist of several spicy vegetable dishes, *dhal* (lentils), *dahi* (yoghurt), rice or *chappatis* (flat bread), and *poppadums*. The food is flavoured with many spices, including turmeric, chilli, coriander, cumin, and cardamom.

*Rice*

*Vegetables in a spicy sauce.*

## INDUSTRY

Since independence, industry has expanded in India. Factories produce and process goods such as cars, chemicals, food and drink, and computers. Jet aeroplanes and space rockets are now being made. Textiles and leather goods are major exports. Traditionally much of India's industrial output has come from small, family-run industries producing traditional handicrafts such as brasswork, mirror work, and tie-dye.

## MODERNIZATION

India's cities are bustling, chaotic places where modern, high-rise office blocks stand next to ancient temples, mosques, and monuments. New Delhi is the capital, but Mumbai (Bombay, left) is the biggest. Bangalore is carving out a reputation as the high-tech capital of India and is home to a growing electronics and telecommunications industry. However much of India is still underdeveloped and many people live below the poverty line.

### MEMORY IN MARBLE

The Taj Mahal in Agra was built in the 17th century by Shah Jahan, one of the Mughal emperors who ruled India from the 16th to the 19th centuries. Built in white marble as a tomb for his beloved wife, it is a fine example of Islamic architecture and attracts many visitors. Tourism is an increasingly important industry in India, bringing millions of people every year.

## HINDU WEDDING

Hindu weddings are elaborate affairs, with ceremonies and feasting lasting for several days. Most marriages take place among members of the same *caste*, or social group, and are arranged by the couple's parents. After the wedding, the bride lives with her husband's family. Family life is very important to Hindus. They often live as part of an extended family, with several generations sharing the same house.

*The bride and groom wear garlands round their necks.*

*After the sheet has been lifted, the bride and groom take seven steps around the sacred fire. Each step represents an aspect of their future life together, such as happiness, children, and lifelong friendship.*

*At the beginning of the wedding ceremony, the bride and groom sit facing each other, holding hands through a silk sheet held as a screen between them.*

*Traditionally, a Hindu bride wears a red silk sari, embroidered with gold thread, together with special jewellery and make-up. Her hands and feet are decorated with mehndi (henna).*

*The henna lasts for weeks, reflecting the woman's new status as a wife.*

*A silk sari*

### SARI

The traditional dress for Indian women is the sari, a length of brightly coloured silk or cotton, some 20 m (66 ft) long, which is wrapped around the body and draped over one shoulder. One end of the sari is left hanging or used to cover the head. Traditional dress for men is a *dhoti*, a length of cotton cloth usually wrapped around the waist and between the legs.

### OTHER FAITHS

Most people in India are Hindu, but many other faiths are followed, such as Sikhism and Jainism. Sikhs believe in one god. Their holiest shrine is the Golden Temple, in Amritsar. Male Sikhs wear turbans (left), a symbol of purity. Jainism is similar to Hinduism. Jains have respect for all life, and monks wear masks to prevent insects from entering their mouths.

*Find out more*

DEMOCRACY: *270*
GROWING CITIES: *17, 135*
RELIGION: *274–275*
SPICES: *57, 198, 264*

# SRI LANKA

SRI LANKA IS A TEARDROP-SHAPED island that lies off the southeast coast of India. It is known for its tropical, palm-fringed beaches, rugged mountains, and varied wildlife which attracts thousands of tourists. In recent years, Sri Lanka and its tourist trade have been badly hit by fighting between the Sinhalese people and the minority Tamil group, who want an independent state. Agriculture is important to Sri Lanka. Tea, rubber, and coconuts are grown on large plantations and are the island's main export crops. Rice is the main food crop.

### SRI LANKA
**Capital city:** Colombo

**Area:** 65,610 sq km (25,332 sq miles)

**Population:** 19,100,000

**Official language:** Sinhala, Tamil

**Major religions:** Buddhist 69%, Hindu 15%, Christian 8%, Muslim 8%

**Government:** Multi-party democracy

**Currency:** Sri Lanka rupee

**Adult literacy rate:** 92%

**Life expectancy:** 74 years

**People per doctor:** 2,319

**Televisions:** 92 per 1,000 people

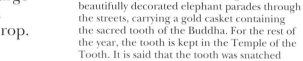

*Sapphire stone*

*Sapphire earrings*

## SAPPHIRE BLUE
Sri Lanka is known for its gemstones, particularly those from Ratnapura, the "City of Gems". Sapphires, rubies, topazes, amethysts, and garnets are all found in the rocks nearby. Many are made into superb jewellery or exported abroad.

## THE SACRED TOOTH
The most important Buddhist festival in Sri Lanka takes place in Kandy in August. A beautifully decorated elephant parades through the streets, carrying a gold casket containing the sacred tooth of the Buddha. For the rest of the year, the tooth is kept in the Temple of the Tooth. It is said that the tooth was snatched from the Buddha's funeral pyre (fire) in 543 BC.

## THE TAMILS
Tensions between the Sinhalese government and the Tamils erupted into civil war between 1983 and 2002. The Tamils object to the domination of the island by the Sinhalese and are demanding their own independent state in the north. Tamils, who are mostly Hindu, make up about 20 per cent of the population. The mainly Buddhist Sinhalese form the majority, accounting for about 75 per cent.

*Many Tamil women are employed as tea pickers*

## BEAUTIFUL BEACHES
Tourism has become one of Sri Lanka's most important industries. The country is well known for its beautiful sandy beaches, especially on the south and southwest coasts, its Buddhist temples and monuments further inland, particularly the ancient city of Kandy. However, the effects of the civil war and the Indian Ocean tsunami in 2004 have recently kept tourists away.

*Tea seeds are first sown in a nursery bed and then the young plants are transplanted to a field.*

*The women hang the baskets from their heads, so that both hands are free for picking.*

## TEA GROWING
Tea is grown mainly on large plantations in the central highlands. The cooler climate allows the tea to grow slowly, adding to its flavour. Only the youngest, most tender leaves are harvested, and then processed quickly to retain quality. Tea makes up about a third of the island's exports. Recently, the tea industry has suffered fierce competition from countries producing cheaper, lower quality tea.

*The tea plants are plucked once a week. Picking is still done by hand as machines would bruise the leaves and spoil their flavour.*

*When the tea picker's basket is full, it is taken for weighing. The picker is paid by the basket.*

*The leaves are then fermented and dried to produce the final product.*

*Find out more*
BUDDHISM: *275*
GEMSTONES: *62, 191*
TEA GROWING: *238*
TSUNAMI: *197, 273*

# NEPAL

THE SMALL, ISOLATED country of Nepal lies in the Himalayan mountains and is landlocked (cut off from the sea). Although it is a Hindu state, many people practise both Hinduism and Buddhism. Until 1991, the king was the absolute ruler. In that year, democratic elections were held for the first time, but in 1996 revolutionary communists launched a military campaign to overthrow the government. In 2002 and 2005, the king suspended constitutional government and introduced monarchial rule once again.

KATHMANDU
Kathmandu is the capital and largest city in Nepal. In the old part of the city there are many narrow streets and squares lined with ancient temples and monuments. In one temple lives the Kumari Devi, or living goddess. She is a young girl chosen to represent the Hindu goddess, Parvati, until she reaches puberty.

| NEPAL | |
|---|---|
| Capital city: Kathmandu | |
| Area: 140,800 sq km (54,363 sq miles) | |
| Population: 25,200,000 | |
| Official language: Nepali | |
| Major religions: Hindu 90%, Buddhist 5%, Muslim 3%, other 2% | |
| Government: Absolute monarchy | |
| Currency: Nepalese rupee | |
| Adult literacy rate: 46% | |
| Life expectancy: 60 years | |
| People per doctor: 12,500 | |
| Televisions: 6 per 1,000 people | |

| BHUTAN | |
|---|---|
| Capital city: Thimpu | |
| Area: 47,000 sq km (18,147 sq miles) | |
| Population: 2,300,000 | |
| Official language: Dzongkha | |
| Major religions: Buddhist 70%, Hindu 24%, other 6% | |
| Government: Absolute monarchy | |
| Currency: Ngultrum | |
| Adult literacy rate: 47% | |
| Life expectancy: 63 years | |
| People per doctor: 6,384 | |
| Televisions: 6 per 1,000 people | |

MOUNTAIN TERRACES
About 90 per cent of Nepalese people work on the land. Crops such as rice are grown on immaculately kept terraces cut into the mountainside. This allows farmers to grow crops on land that would otherwise be inaccessible. Farmers depend on the monsoon rains for a good harvest.

These Sherpa women are carrying heavy loads as they trek through the mountains.

## NEPALESE PEOPLES

There are many different groups of people living in Nepal. The Sherpas of the eastern mountains are known for their climbing skill. The Gurkha people are famous for their courage and military skills. Their reputation has spread all over the world. The Newars of Kathmandu Valley are known for their magnificent wood carvings which decorate many Nepali temples and houses. More than half of the people are Nepalese, of Indian descent.

# BHUTAN

THE HIMALAYAN KINGDOM of Bhutan is a mysterious, isolated place because of its location in the mountains and its restrictions on tourism. With limited natural resources, Bhutan has been trying to exploit the fast-flowing mountain rivers to produce hydroelectricity. Bhutan is a Buddhist country, ruled by an absolute monarch, the Dragon King.

Drupkas speak Dzonghkha, the national language of Bhutan, which is closely related to Tibetan.

Bhutanese people eat yak meat, use their milk to make butter and cheese, and use their dung as fuel.

Yak hair is used for tents and clothes and yak tails are used as fans or dusters.

USEFUL YAKS
For many people living in the mountains of Bhutan, life revolves around their herds of yaks. These tough, hardy animals can carry heavy loads and survive freezing temperatures.

## DRUPKAS

About 70 per cent of the Bhutanese are Drupkas of Tibetan origin. Clashes between the Drupkas and the Nepali-speaking Lhotsampa people of the south led to violent demonstrations against the government in 1990. Further immigration into Bhutan is banned.

*Find out more*

HIMALAYAS: *132, 166*
HINDUISM & BUDDHISM: *275*
POLITICAL SYSTEMS: *270–271*
TERRACE FARMING: *159, 201*

# EAST ASIA

EAST ASIA IS DOMINATED by the vast country of China, but it also includes the windswept plains of Mongolia, North and South Korea, and the fertile island of Taiwan. China itself is full of contrasts. In the west, high ranges of mountains tower over rocky valleys and semi-desert plains. Tibet, a previously independent country occupied by China since 1950, is known as the "roof of the world" because it is so high above sea level. In the north of the country is the harsh and empty Gobi Desert. In eastern China and North and South Korea, river valleys and flood plains are farmed intensively, providing food for the millions of people who live in the cities on or near the coast.

### THE YELLOW RIVER

The Yellow River, or Huang He, is one of the world's most destructive rivers. It has flooded the surrounding land many times, causing enormous loss of life. For this reason, the river is known as "China's Sorrow". As it slowly glides eastwards through central China, it erodes huge amounts of fertile loess (fine soil) from the land which stains the river yellow, hence its name.

**Urumqi, China**
Jan -17°C (3°F)
July 21°C (70°F)

Jan 15 mm (0.6 in)
July 18 mm (0.7 in)

### THE GREAT WALL

Snaking across northern China, from the Yellow Sea in the east to the deserts of central Asia in the west, is one of the technological wonders of the ancient world. Much of the Great Wall was built in the 1400s to protect Chinese farmers from invasion by nomads from Mongolia. At almost 6,400 km (4,000 miles) long, it is the world's longest structure, and is a popular tourist destination.

## ANCESTOR WORSHIP

One of the main ideas of Confucianism, the ancient religion of China, is the importance of family loyalties and the honouring of ancestors. Because of this, traditional funerals in East Asia follow a set ritual to ensure that the soul of the dead person is well provided for. At the graveside, mourners make food offerings and burn paper money and paper models of cars, bikes, and other goods to accompany the soul to heaven.

*People throw paper money to pacify spirits that are thought to haunt the road.*

*Mourners often wear over-garments made of sackcloth, and white headdresses.*

*Buddhist priests often lead the funeral procession. They chant prayers and play musical instruments.*

*Effigies (models) of Confucius, the founder of Confucianism, are carried along the way.*

*The richer the family, the more ornate the coffin.*

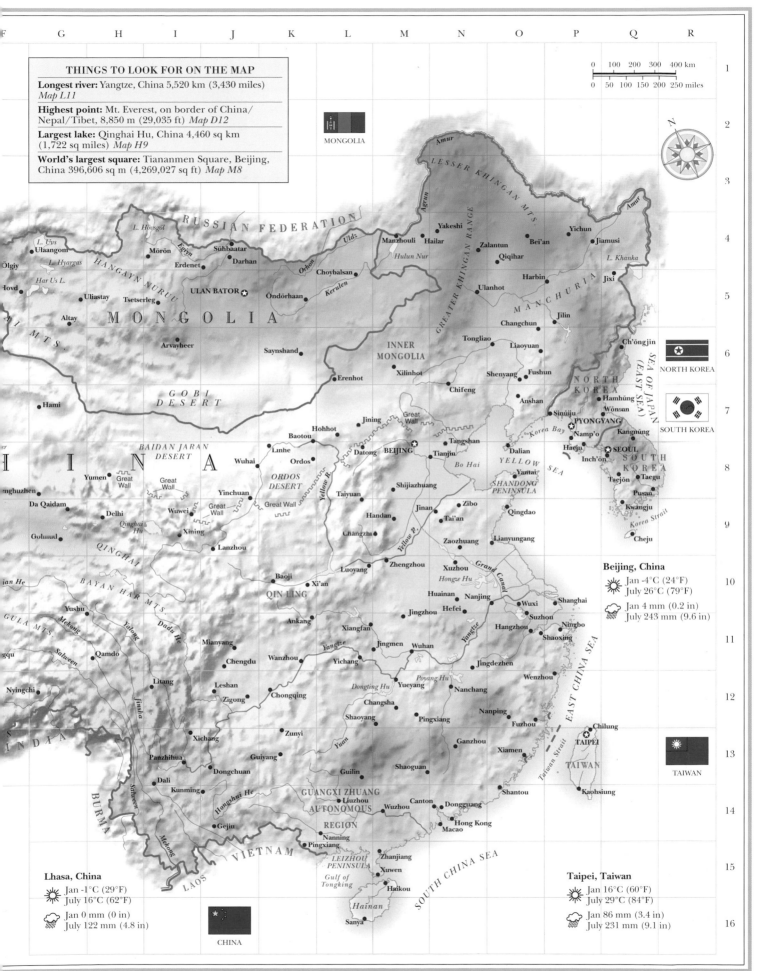

F G H I J K L M N O P Q R

1 2 3 4 5 6 7 8 9 10 11 12 13 14 15 16

### THINGS TO LOOK FOR ON THE MAP

**Longest river:** Yangtze, China 5,520 km (3,430 miles) *Map L11*

**Highest point:** Mt. Everest, on border of China/ Nepal/Tibet, 8,850 m (29,035 ft) *Map D12*

**Largest lake:** Qinghai Hu, China 4,460 sq km (1,722 sq miles) *Map H9*

**World's largest square:** Tiananmen Square, Beijing, China 396,606 sq m (4,269,027 sq ft) *Map M8*

0 100 200 300 400 km
0 50 100 150 200 250 miles

MONGOLIA

NORTH KOREA

SOUTH KOREA

TAIWAN

CHINA

RUSSIAN FEDERATION

**Beijing, China**
Jan -4°C (24°F)
July 26°C (79°F)
Jan 4 mm (0.2 in)
July 243 mm (9.6 in)

**Lhasa, China**
Jan -1°C (29°F)
July 16°C (62°F)
Jan 0 mm (0 in)
July 122 mm (4.8 in)

**Taipei, Taiwan**
Jan 16°C (60°F)
July 29°C (84°F)
Jan 86 mm (3.4 in)
July 231 mm (9.1 in)

L. Uvs
Ulaangom
Ölgiy
L. Hyargas
Hovd
Har Us L.
MTS.
ALTAI
Hami
Yumen
enghuzhen
Da Qaidam
Golmud
Yushu
GULA MTS.
gqu
Nyingchi
INDIA
BURMA
LAOS
VIETNAM

L. Hövsgöl
Mörön
Egiyn
Erdenet
Darhan
Sühbaatar
ULAN BATOR
Tsetserleg
Uliastay
Altay
HANGAYN NURUU
MONGOLIA
Arvayheer
GOBI DESERT
BAIDAN JARAN DESERT
Wuhai
Yumen
Great Wall
Great Wall
Great Wall
Delhi
Wuwei
Xining
Lanzhou
QINGHAI
Qinghai Hu
BAYAN HAR MTS.
Mekong
Yalong
Dadu He
Litang
Qamdo
Mianyang
Chengdu
Leshan
Zigong
Xichang
Panzhihua
Dali
Kunming
Dongchuan
Gejiu

RUSSIAN FEDERATION
Choybalsan
Öndörhaan
Orhon
Uldz
Kerulen
Saynshand
Erenhot
INNER MONGOLIA
Xilinhot
Hohhot
Baotou
Linhe
Ordos
ORDOS DESERT
Great Wall
Yinchuan
Wuwei
Yellow R.
Taiyuan
Baoji
Xi'an
QIN LING
Ankang
Wanzhou
Yichang
Yangtze
Chongqing
Zunyi
Guiyang
Guilin
Nanning
Pingxiang
GUANGXI ZHUANG AUTONOMOUS REGION
Hongshui He
Liuzhou
Wuzhou

Amur
LESSER KHINGAN MTS.
Argun
GREATER KHINGAN RANGE
Manzhouli
Hailar
Hulun Nur
Yakeshi
Zalantun
Qiqihar
Ulanhot
MANCHURIA
Tongliao
Chifeng
Great Wall
Jining
Datong
BEIJING
Tangshan
Tianjin
Shijiazhuang
Handan
Changzhi
Luoyang
Zhengzhou
Jingzhou
Xiangfan
Jingmen
Wuhan
Dongting Hu
Yueyang
Changsha
Shaoyang
Pingxiang
Shaoguan
Canton
Dongguang
Hong Kong
Macao
Zhanjiang
LEIZHOU PENINSULA
Xuwen
Haikou
Gulf of Tongking
Hainan
Sanya

Bei'an
Yichun
Jiamusi
L. Khanka
Harbin
Jixi
Changchun
Jilin
Liaoyuan
Shenyang
Fushun
Anshan
NORTH KOREA
Ch'ŏngjin
SEA OF JAPAN (EAST SEA)
Sinŭiju
Hamhŭng
Wŏnsan
PYONGYANG
Namp'o
Kangnŭng
Haeju
SEOUL
Inch'ŏn
SOUTH KOREA
Taejŏn
Taegu
Pusan
Kwangju
Cheju
Korea Strait
Dalian
Yantai
YELLOW SEA
Qingdao
SHANDONG PENINSULA
Korea Bay
Bo Hai
Jinan
Zibo
Tai'an
Zaozhuang
Lianyungang
Xuzhou
Grand Canal
Hongze Hu
Huainan
Nanjing
Hefei
Wuxi
Shanghai
Suzhou
Hangzhou
Ningbo
Shaoxing
Jingdezhen
Wenzhou
Nanchang
Poyang Hu
Nanping
Fuzhou
Ganzhou
Xiamen
Shantou
EAST CHINA SEA
Taiwan Strait
Chilung
TAIPEI
TAIWAN
Kaohsiung
SOUTH CHINA SEA

# CHINA

ONE IN FIVE PEOPLE in the world today lives in just one country – China. This vast country is almost the same size as the whole of Europe, and is the third largest country in the world after Russia and Canada. It also has one of the world's oldest civilizations, with a history stretching back more than 7,000 years. Ruled by a succession of emperors, China became a republic in 1911 and a communist state in 1949. Under the communists, every aspect of life is controlled by the state and China has become a major industrial and military power. In recent years it has begun to move towards a more competitive economy which encourages investment from other countries.

| CHINA | |
|---|---|
| **Capital city:** Beijing | |
| **Area:** 9,596,960 sq km (3,705,386 sq miles) | |
| **Population:** 1,300,000,000 | |
| **Official language:** Mandarin | |
| **Major religions:** Traditional religions 20%, Buddhist 6%, Muslim 2%, other 72% | |
| **Government:** One-party state | |
| **Currency:** Yuan | |
| **Adult literacy rate:** 91% | |
| **Life expectancy:** 71 years | |
| **People per doctor:** 714 | |
| **Televisions:** 272 per 1,000 people | |

THE FORBIDDEN CITY
When the emperor Zhu Di rebuilt China's capital, Beijing, in the 15th century, he created a vast imperial palace in the centre of the new city. The palace became known as the Forbidden City as only the emperor's family and closest advisers could enter it. Encircled by walls, it contains nearly 1,000 buildings, including temples, stables, and a library.

*The art of handwriting, or calligraphy, is highly prized in China because great care is required to draw each character correctly.*

## CHINESE WRITING
Unlike English or French, which use an alphabet of 26 letters, Chinese writing uses more than 50,000 characters or symbols. Each character depicts a different word or idea. Simple words, such as "sky", or "rain", use one character. Complex words use two or more – "telephone" uses the characters for "electric" and for "talk".

## CHINESE COMMUNISM
The Communist Party took control of China in 1949. Led by Mao Zedong, the party believed in a society in which everyone was equal and property was owned by the whole community. Land was taken from wealthy landowners and given to groups of peasant farmers who worked together on large, collective farms. Industry was put under state control. These attempts to transform China met with mixed success. Since Mao's death in 1976, private ownership has again been allowed to develop.

*Portraits of Mao Zedong still hang in Tiananmen Square in Beijing, the largest public square in the world.*

## RICE GROWING
Two-thirds of China's large population live and work on the land. The most fertile areas are found in the south. The main crop is rice, though tea, cotton, fruit, and vegetables are also grown. The rice is planted in flooded paddy fields (shown below). Two crops of rice and one of vegetables or cereals are harvested in a good year. In the north and west of the country, which is drier and hillier, farmers grow a single crop of cereals and tend sheep and cattle.

**Ploughing**
*Water buffaloes are used to plough, rake, and flatten the muddy paddy fields ready for planting.*

*Low earth barriers known as bunds separate the paddy fields.*

**Planting**
*Women do the back-breaking work of planting the rice shoots.*

**Sowing**

*While the paddy fields are being prepared, rice seeds are sown in a separate flooded field, or seed-bed.*

*After a month, the tightly packed rice shoots are ready for transplanting into the paddy fields.*

*Some farms in China have tractors, but most use water buffaloes or oxen.*

*Water in the paddy fields keeps down the weeds.*

# CHINESE FOOD

Chinese people take great pleasure in their food, which varies from region to region. Western cuisine from Sichuan province uses spices, while northern cuisine from Beijing is famous for its tasty roast duck. Cantonese food from the south is renowned across the world for its fish dishes and delicate flavours. Meals are cooked by steaming or stir-frying in a large pan called a wok. Rice is served in the south of the country, wheat buns or noodles in the north. The food is held in small bowls and chopsticks are used for eating.

*Bean sprouts*

*Green mung beans are eaten as a savoury or sweet.*

*Native to China, star anise is a spice that has a similar flavour to aniseed.*

*Root ginger adds a fresh, spicy taste to many dishes in western China.*

*Chilli peppers are added to make hot, spicy dishes.*

*Rice, whether boiled, steamed, or fried, forms the basis of many Chinese dishes.*

*China bowl*

*Tea is served in handleless china cups.*

*Tea, made without milk and sugar, is the most popular drink in China.*

*Chopsticks are used for eating.*

*Knives are not needed because food is sliced before cooking.*

*Jasmine tea is a light, refreshing drink made from green leaves. Black and Oolong are other types of Chinese tea.*

### Harvesting

*Farmers cut the stalks with sickles and tie them into bundles.*

*The rice stalks are beaten to shake off the grain.*

*Piles of rice grains are left in the sun to dry.*

*When the rice is dry, the outer shells, or husks, are removed, and the rice is sifted.*

## FOOD PRODUCTION

Every patch of fertile soil in China is used for agriculture. Crops are planted alongside roads and railway lines, and one type of crop is often planted between rows of another. China is the world's biggest producer of the crops shown below. Percentages indicate China's share in world production.

| carrots | rice | pears | cucumbers | water-melons | sweet potatoes |
|---------|------|-------|-----------|--------------|----------------|
| 26% | 32% | 52% | 56% | 61% | 86% |

# CITY LIFE

About 500 million Chinese people live in towns and cities, many of which are overcrowded. Accommodation is scarce and families usually live in one or two rooms rented from the company they work for. The city streets are full of bicycles, and public transport, while cheap and frequent, is always packed. The main industrial and commercial city is Shanghai, home to 17 million people and one of the biggest cities in the world.

# ONE-CHILD FAMILIES

The Chinese population is growing by about 9 million people a year, which is around the total population of Sweden. In order to reduce this rapid growth, the government introduced a policy in 1979 to limit each family to one child only. The single children are known as "Little Emperors" because they are often spoiled. The one-child policy has succeeded in the towns, but not in the country, where large families are needed to provide labour in the fields.

## NEW YEAR CELEBRATIONS

Every year, in late January or early February, Chinese people prepare to celebrate the New Year. They spring-clean their houses, put up red decorations to bring them luck, and give new clothes and toys to their children. The festival itself lasts for several days. Every shop and office is closed, and people take to the streets, letting off firecrackers and joining in the displays of lion and dragon dances.

## THE BUDDHISTS OF TIBET

Tibet, once an independent country, has been part of China since 1950. Tibetans are devout Buddhists and their religion has been suppressed by the Communist Party, which discourages any religious practice. However, the Buddhist faith remains strong in Tibet. Buddhists devote their lives to prayer. They hang up flags with prayers printed on them to bring fortune and good luck.

Tibetan Buddhists hang prayer flags from their houses, across bridges, or on mountainsides.

## THE GRAND CANAL

The world's longest waterway, the Grand Canal, stretches for 1,790 km (1,110 miles) across China. It was begun in the 5th century BC to connect the cities of the north with the rice growing valleys of the south. Near its southern end, the canal passes through Suzhou, a picturesque city known as the "Venice of the East" because it is crisscrossed by rivers and canals.

## LIFE IN THE PARK

Because most city people live in flats with no gardens, parks play an important part in everyone's life. Exercise is encouraged in China, and people go regularly to the park to keep fit. Early in the morning, many people practise *tai chi* or the more vigorous *kung-fu*. Children fly kites on windy days, and adults play table tennis, cards, or chess, or just sit and chat with their friends.

Table tennis is very popular in China; tables are set up in parks for people to enjoy a game out in the open air.

Kites are made by pasting brightly coloured paper on to simple bamboo frames, often in the shape of animals or birds.

People often play Chinese chess and cards.

Cycling is popular, as a means of transport and as a way of keeping fit.

Tai chi is a form of gentle exercise with slow movements, which resembles shadow boxing.

Chinese parks are beautifully kept and contain rockeries and trees that blossom in the spring.

## INDUSTRY

Over the last 20 years China has transformed itself from one of the world's poorest nations to a rapidly expanding economy. It is a leading producer of textiles, clothing and electronics. Western-style market reforms have led to a surge in growth and the rise of cities such as Shanghai with its new, futuristic economic quarter, Pudong (pictured). However, in spite of this, much of the population remains very poor.

## CHINESE MEDICINE

The Chinese believe that a person falls ill because the opposing forces of *yin* and *yang* in the body become unbalanced. Doctors rebalance the body with herbal remedies and acupuncture, which involves sticking thin needles into various parts of the body to relieve pain. Many people are treated by "barefoot doctors", or locally trained healers.

Bugbane rhizome (sheng ma) is used to treat headaches, colds, and measles.

Wolfberry (guo qi zi) is used for diabetes and is said to improve eyesight.

Chain fern bark (gou ji) helps ease back pain.

Senn leaf (fan xie ye) is a herb used to cleanse the system.

HONG KONG SHANGHAI BANK
In the central business district of Hong Kong stands the impressive Hong Kong Shanghai Bank. This masterpiece of technological engineering was completed in 1985. At every stage of its construction, experts in *feng shui*, the ancient Chinese belief in the natural forces of wind and water, were consulted to ensure that the building would bring health, prosperity, and good fortune to its many occupants.

# HONG KONG

Tucked into a corner of southeast China, Hong Kong occupies only a small area, yet almost 6 million people live squashed on its rocky islands and mountainous mainland. It is one of the world's most important finance centres and has one of its most prosperous economies. In 1898, the New Territories of Hong Kong were leased by China to Britain for 99 years. On 1st July 1997, Britain returned the whole of Hong Kong to China.

HAPPY VALLEY
Surrounded by the towering skyscrapers of Hong Kong, the Happy Valley racecourse is one of Hong Kong's most famous landmarks. Betting money on horse races is hugely popular and is the only legal form of gambling allowed. A season's takings at the race course can amount to over US$11 billion

TEXTILES
For over one hundred years Hong Kong has had a flourishing textiles industry, exporting its products all over the world. Across Hong Kong, thousands of people are still employed in workshops making T-shirts, suits, and shirts though there is now fierce competition from countries such as India.

## FLOATING HOMES

Many people in Hong Kong live not on the land but on boats. Families are squashed on to wooden junks and sampans, mostly making their living by fishing. Floating schools, shops, and restaurants serve their needs, while doctors, dentists, and hairdressers do their rounds by boat. Thousands of people still live in these floating villages, but, increasingly, deep-sea trawlers are replacing the traditional boats and forcing the fisherfolk to look for work on land.

TECHNOLOGY
As traditional industries have declined, Hong Kong's economy has diversified into producing high-tech products such as computers, digital cameras, watches and mobile phones.

*digital camera*

# MACAO

Overshadowed by Hong Kong, its richer and bigger neighbour, Macao consists of a mainland and two islands linked by a bridge and causeway. Macao was returned to China in 1999. When its Portuguese rulers gave up power – after almost 450 years – it was the end of the longest surviving European colony in Asia.

INDUSTRY
Macao produces a variety of goods for export, ranging from textiles and electronic goods to fireworks (shown above) and toys. Every day, low-paid workers from mainland China come to work in the many factories of Macao.

## TOURISM

Macao's skyline is dominated by casinos and hotels. The casinos are a big tourist attraction because gambling is very popular with the Chinese and casinos are outlawed in Hong Kong and China. Gambling is a major industry in Macao, and provides about one-third of the territory's income.

### Find out more

BUDDHISM: *275*
POLITICAL SYSTEMS: *270–271*
POPULATION GROWTH: *16–17*
RICE GROWING: *135, 185, 197*

# TAIWAN

WHEN PORTUGUESE SAILORS first visited this island in 1590, they named it *Ilha Formosa* – "Beautiful Island" – because of its lush, mountainous scenery. In 1949, at the end of civil war in China, the defeated Nationalist government fled here and established itself as a rival to the Communists on the mainland. Taiwan still officially calls itself the Republic of China. Since then, both Taiwan and China have tried to seek international recognition as the official Chinese government. However, few nations recognize Taiwan and it does not have a seat at the United Nations. Despite this, Taiwan has a thriving economy based on mass production and high-tech industries.

**TAIWAN**

| | |
|---|---|
| **Capital city:** Taipei | |
| **Area:** 35,980 sq km (13,892 sq miles) | |
| **Population:** 22,600,000 | |
| **Official language:** Mandarin | |
| **Major religions:** Buddhist, Confucian, and Taoist 93%, Christian 5%, other 2% | |
| **Government:** Multi-party democracy | |
| **Currency:** Taiwan dollar | |
| **Adult literacy rate:** 96% | |
| **Life expectancy:** 77 years | |
| **People per doctor:** 714 | |
| **Televisions:** 237 per 1,000 people | |

## INDUSTRY

Once a poor agricultural island, Taiwan has succeeded in developing one of the world's most successful industrial economies. It is a world exporter of electronic and electrical goods, machinery, textiles, shoes, sports equipment, TV sets, and watches. This huge export trade pays for the oil and other raw materials the economy needs, for Taiwan has few natural resources of its own.

## TAIPEI

For most of its history, Taipei has been a city of low-rise buildings. But during the last few decades the city has been transformed into the modern high-tech capital of the island, with many new tower blocks, public buildings, and landscaped gardens. Almost 3 million people live in Taipei, and the capital has problems with congestion and pollution. Most people travel to work on motorcycles, contributing to the smog that covers the city for most of the year.

### OPERA

Traditional Chinese opera is popular in Taiwan. The basic stories are simple – concerning good against evil, or boy meets girl – and there are few props on stage. Instead, the actor's movements, elaborate costumes, and facial make-up all convey character and plot.

*The largest surviving tribe is the Ami, who are expert potters and farmers. The Ami live in large villages, with women holding power in the family home.*

### TRIBAL GROUPS

Long before the Chinese first came to Taiwan, the island was home to a variety of peoples. Each tribe had its own distinct language, but all had many customs and skills in common. In the 1600s, the Chinese came to the island and fought the tribes for control. Today the surviving tribes make up only 2 per cent of the total population.

## TAOISM

The major religions practised in Taiwan are Buddhism, Taoism, and Confucianism. These faiths are closely linked and many people follow aspects of all three. Taoism, which began in China around 300 BC, teaches how people can follow the *tao* (path) to a life of simplicity and freedom from desire. Taoists aim to live in harmony with nature, balancing the calm, feminine side of the body (*yin*) with the active, male side (*yang*).

*Temples are used as social centres and playgrounds as well as places of worship.*

**Major tribes in Taiwan**

- Tsou
- Paiwan
- Ami
- Atayal
- Bunun

*Find out more*

GROWTH OF CITIES: *17*
PACIFIC RIM ECONOMIES: *137*
RELIGION: *274–275*
TRADE: *280–281*

# MONGOLIA

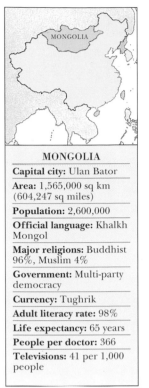

MONGOLIA

| MONGOLIA | |
|---|---|
| **Capital city:** Ulan Bator | |
| **Area:** 1,565,000 sq km (604,247 sq miles) | |
| **Population:** 2,600,000 | |
| **Official language:** Khalkh Mongol | |
| **Major religions:** Buddhist 96%, Muslim 4% | |
| **Government:** Multi-party democracy | |
| **Currency:** Tughrik | |
| **Adult literacy rate:** 98% | |
| **Life expectancy:** 65 years | |
| **People per doctor:** 366 | |
| **Televisions:** 41 per 1,000 people | |

THE REMOTE, SPARSELY POPULATED country of Mongolia was once the centre of a vast empire. However, for most of the 20th century Mongolia was a communist country linked to Soviet Russia, until democratic rule was introduced in 1990. Many people live on the grassy plains in the centre of the country, tending their flocks as they move in search of new pasture. The climate is harsh: summers are short, winters are long and cold. Mountain ranges ring the country to the north and west, while the south is bordered by the Gobi Desert. The country is rich in natural resources, with huge deposits of coal and oil, but it is only recently that these have been developed.

**GENGHIS KHAN**
During the 13th century, the Mongol leader Genghis Khan carved out a huge empire that stretched across much of central Asia and China. By the time of his death, it was said that it took almost a year to ride from one side of his empire to the other. His grandson, Kublai Khan, became emperor of China, but the Mongol empire fell apart during the 1300s.

*The framework of a yurt consists of a circular latticework frame with a central ring to support the roof. The frame is covered with felt lashed together with rope.*

*Smoke from the iron stove escapes through a chimney in the roof of the yurt.*

## NOMADIC LIFE

The nomadic farmers of Mongolia move with their yaks, sheep, goats, camels, and cattle from the summertime pastures high in the mountains down to the grassy lowland steppes during the winter months. Yaks are ideally suited to the harsh Mongolian climate, and provide milk, butter, meat, and wool. As the nomads move with their flocks, they take their portable dome-shaped yurts with them.

*A yurt may have as many as eight layers of felt to keep out the winter cold.*

*Flaps may be drawn over the single wooden or felt door.*

*The scroll is carved in the shape of a horse's head.*

## ULAN BATOR

The capital city of Mongolia lies at the centre of road and rail networks in the country. Until the 1920s Ulan Bator was a small country town, but development by its communist rulers has turned it into a major city. The influence of Soviet Russia is reflected in the style of many of the city's major buildings.

*Traditional wooden Mongolian fiddle*

*Bow*

**MAKING MUSIC**
Mongol nomads like to entertain themselves in the evening with music. Stringed instruments, such as the Mongolian fiddle, are popular.

**HORSE RIDERS**
Many Mongols are accomplished horse riders. From a very early age, Mongolian children learn to ride horses, becoming jockeys as early as three years old. Every July 11 they get the chance to show off their skills at the Nadam Festival, a nationwide sporting event which includes horse racing, archery, and wrestling competitions.

*Find out more*
NOMADS: *156, 160, 209*
POLITICAL SYSTEMS: *270–271*
STEPPE (GRASSLANDS): *15*
YAKS: *173*

# NORTH KOREA

WITH ITS RUGGED, HILLY INTERIOR and limited fertile land, North Korea is a harsh country. Winds from central Asia produce extreme winter temperatures, and snow covers the ground for many months. Politically, North Korea is equally harsh. The communist government maintains a tight grip on its people. It limits contact with the outside world and forbids all foreign newspapers. Its health and education services have been badly affected by a lack of money and many people face starvation every year. Recently there have been attempts to break the country's long isolation.

### NORTH KOREA

**Capital city:** Pyongyang

**Area:** 120,540 sq km (46,540 sq miles)

**Population:** 22,700,000

**Official language:** Korean

**Major religion:** No figures available

**Government:** One-party state

**Currency:** North Korean won

**Adult literacy rate:** 99%

**Life expectancy:** 62 years

**People per doctor:** 333

**Televisions:** 53 per 1,000 people

## A DIVIDED LAND

At the end of World War II, Korea was occupied by Russian and American armies. In 1948, the country was divided in two. A communist government ruled the North and an American-backed, democratic government ruled the South. Today, the two sides face each other along one of the most heavily armed borders in the world.

*Most farm houses are built of brick with tile or slate roofs.*

*Both men and women work on the land, growing rice, vegetables, grain, and fruit.*

## COLLECTIVE FARMING

Under the communist government, thousands of small, family-owned farms were abolished and replaced by 3,800 enormous state-controlled farms. These collective farms are run by people who work together to produce enough food to supply the country's needs. Because North Korea is so mountainous, every piece of available land is farmed intensively, with irrigation (watering) systems, advanced machinery, and fertilizers used to improve the annual harvest.

*Health services are free for everyone, with doctors and nurses employed on each collective farm.*

*Every farm has its own day-care centre and nursery school where babies and young children stay while their parents work on the land.*

### KOREAN FOOD

In North and South Korea, the whole meal is served at the same time, rather than in separate courses. Rice is always the main dish, often combined with barley and red beans and eaten with a range of spicy vegetables, herbs, and meats. Steamed rice cakes are prepared for important celebrations.

*Ginseng is exported around the world.*

*Kimchi, made from pickled cabbage and radishes mixed with garlic, salt, red pepper, and other spices, is a popular dish.*

### GINSENG

The root of the ginseng plant is grown in both North and South Korea. It is believed to promote good health and energy. After being washed, steamed, and dried it can be ground into pills or made into lotions.

*In jeolme, a type of rice-cake powdered with soya flour, is served as a sweet.*

### KIM IL SUNG

Kim Il Sung dominated North Korea from 1948 until his death in 1994. He established an image as the father of working people. His portrait was hung in every office and huge statues were erected to him in public places. Under his rule, North Korea became increasingly isolated politically and economically from the rest of the world. He was succeeded by his son, Kim Jong Il, but is still referred to as "the eternal president".

### *Find out more*

FARM "SHARING": *115, 140, 150*
HEALTH, EDUCATION: *276, 277*
IRRIGATION: *155, 156, 217*
POLITICAL SYSTEMS: *270–271*

# SOUTH KOREA

LIKE NORTH KOREA, much of South Korea is mountainous and forested. Compared with its northern neighbour, however, it has a strong economy that trades with many other countries, such as Japan and the USA. After becoming independent in 1948, South Korea was invaded by North Korea. By the end of the Korean War (1950–53), the cities and factories of South Korea were devastated and thousands of refugees had arrived in the country from the North. Within 20 years, a remarkable turnaround had taken place. New factories began to produce world-class products, and new cities sprang up. Today South Korea has a well-educated workforce producing high-technology goods for export.

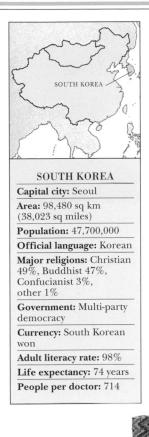

| SOUTH KOREA | |
|---|---|
| **Capital city:** Seoul | |
| **Area:** 98,480 sq km (38,023 sq miles) | |
| **Population:** 47,700,000 | |
| **Official language:** Korean | |
| **Major religions:** Christian 49%, Buddhist 47%, Confucianist 3%, other 1% | |
| **Government:** Multi-party democracy | |
| **Currency:** South Korean won | |
| **Adult literacy rate:** 98% | |
| **Life expectancy:** 74 years | |
| **People per doctor:** 714 | |

## SEOUL
More than 21 million people live in and around the capital Seoul. Most of this city has been built in the decades since the end of the Korean War. As more people have moved here from the countryside, the city has become more crowded. To cope with this, Seoul has an excellent public transport system, linking buses, trains, boats, and planes into one collective schedule.

*Shipbuilding has expanded rapidly in South Korea, which is now the biggest and most successful shipbuilder in the world.*

*A Korean shaman is usually a woman, called a mundang.*

*People bring offerings of money and food to the mundang.*

## SHAMANISM
People in South Korea belong to a number of religions. About half are Buddhists, the rest are Christian or Confucianist. Many people in rural areas still believe in shamanism – that an invisible spirit world lives alongside the visible human world. When the spirits interfere in the lives of humans, a shaman (priest) acts as a link between the two worlds.

*Burnt offerings are made to pacify the spirits.*

*Apart from obtaining blessings from spirits, a mundang will try to cure people's diseases and help with personal problems.*

## INDUSTRY
After the devastation of the Korean War, South Korea had to rebuild its industry from scratch. It concentrated on producing and exporting manufactured goods, setting up huge industrial companies, known as *chaebol*, to make shoes, clothes, ships, cars, and more recently computers and video sets. Large iron and steel works were built to supply the factories with raw materials. South Korea now has one of the most successful economies in the world.

*Figures show South Korea's share in world production.*

25%

12%

4%

**Ship production in South Korea**

1980 1990 2000

*The traditional Korean fan dance is performed by women only. As the women dance, they move faster and faster around each other while making patterns with their fans.*

## FARMING
Unlike North Korea, most farms in South Korea are small and family-owned. Rice is the main crop, but barley, wheat, fruit, vegetables, and spices are also grown. As much of the land is mountainous, farms can be found clustered along the river valleys and lowlands near the coast.

*Women wear long, brilliantly coloured, high-waisted dresses.*

## KOREAN DANCE
Korean dancing is popular in both the South and North. Dancers dress up in traditional clothes called *hanbok*. The aim of Korean dancing is to create a mood rather than to tell a story.

*Find out more*

PACIFIC RIM ECONOMIES: *137*
POLITICAL SYSTEMS: *270–271*
RELIGION: *274–275*
TRADE: *280–281*

# JAPAN

JAPAN IS A CHAIN OF SOME 4,000 ISLANDS stretching for more than 2,500 km (1,553 miles) off the east coast of mainland Asia. Most people live on the four largest islands – Honshu, Hokkaido, Shikoku, and Kyushu. Flat land is in short supply. More than three-quarters of the country is hilly, leaving less than a quarter suitable for building and farming. To create more level ground, hillsides are being cut back and land is being reclaimed from the sea. Japan's climate is a varied one. The islands in the south are warm all year round, while in the north it is cooler, with snowfall on the mountains in winter. The Japanese call their country *Nippon*, "the land of the rising Sun", as the Sun can be seen rising above the Pacific Ocean.

## ISLAND LINKS

Travel between the islands is made easier by a network of bridges and tunnels linking them together. The Seto Ohashi Bridge (above) connects several smaller islands. The Akashi Kaikyo Road Bridge, linking Honshu and Shikoku, opened in 1998 – it is the world's longest suspension bridge, with an overall span of 1,990 m (6,529 ft).

## THE EMPEROR

Japan has the oldest hereditary monarchy in the world, dating back to before the 6th century. In the past, the emperor was very powerful and many Japanese people believed he was a god. But the emperor's status changed after Japan's defeat in World War II, and his role was reduced to a symbolic one.

*The present emperor, Akihito, is the 125th in the imperial line. He is highly respected by Japanese people, but he has no political power.*

*Mount Fuji is a huge, cone-shaped volcano. It last erupted in 1707.*

## SACRED MOUNTAIN

At 3,776 m (12,388 ft), Mount Fuji on Honshu is Japan's highest mountain. For the followers of Shinto, one of Japan's major religions, Mount Fuji is a sacred mountain. Each year, thousands of pilgrims make the long climb to visit the Shinto shrine on the summit. Many Japanese consider Mount Fuji to be a symbol of their country and keep a photograph or painting of the mountain on display in their homes.

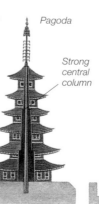

*Children are taught to duck under desks to protect themselves from falling objects.*

## UNSTABLE LAND

Japan suffers from hundreds of earthquakes a year. Slight shakes are recorded almost every day, while larger tremors causing minor damage can be felt several times a year. Strong earthquakes occur more rarely, causing damage, injury, and death. Buildings and bridges topple, roads, and railways are destroyed, and devastating fires break out. In 1995, a massive earthquake struck the port of Kobe and killed more than 5,000 people. Regular earthquake drills are held in schools, homes, and workplaces.

*Modern skyscraper*

*Pagoda*

*Strong central column*

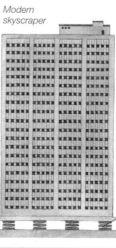

## BUILT TO LAST

Both new and old buildings in Japan have been designed with earthquakes in mind. A pagoda has a strong central column sunk into the ground to give it added stability. A modern skyscraper has a regular shape and thick walls reinforced by steel columns, which help make the building more secure.

*Skyscrapers are often built on pads made of steel and rubber that absorb earthquake tremors.*

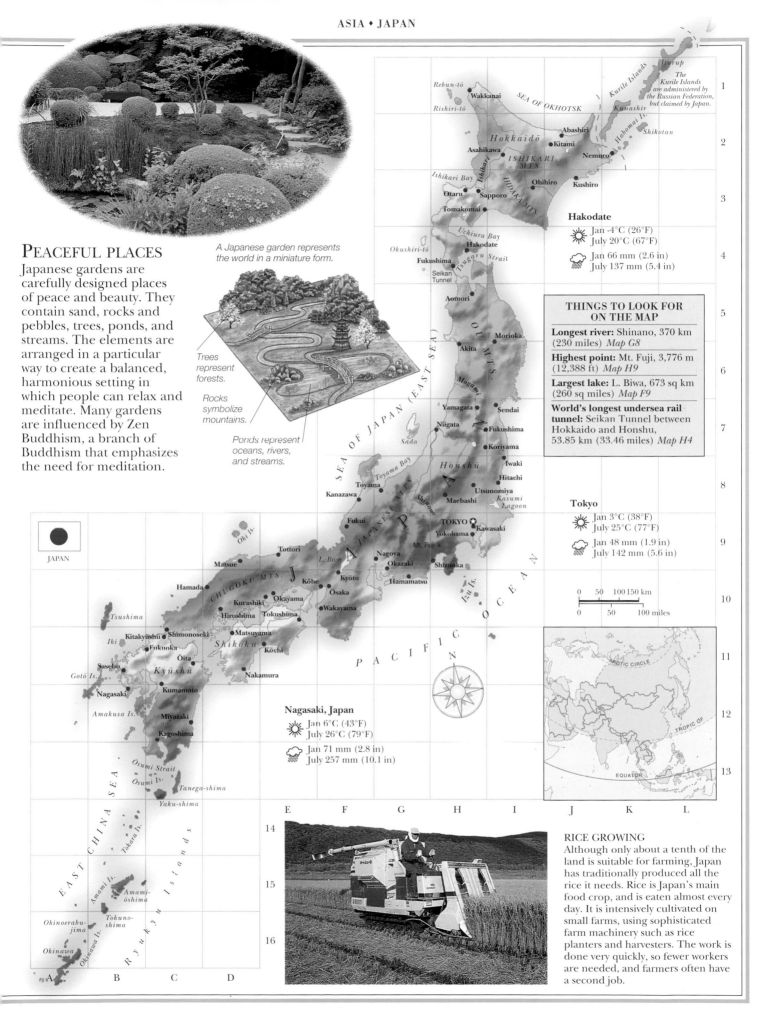

## PEACEFUL PLACES

Japanese gardens are carefully designed places of peace and beauty. They contain sand, rocks and pebbles, trees, ponds, and streams. The elements are arranged in a particular way to create a balanced, harmonious setting in which people can relax and meditate. Many gardens are influenced by Zen Buddhism, a branch of Buddhism that emphasizes the need for meditation.

*A Japanese garden represents the world in a miniature form.*

Trees represent forests.

Rocks symbolize mountains.

Ponds represent oceans, rivers, and streams.

The Kurile Islands are administered by the Russian Federation, but claimed by Japan.

### Hakodate
☀ Jan -4°C (26°F)
July 20°C (67°F)
🌧 Jan 66 mm (2.6 in)
July 137 mm (5.4 in)

### THINGS TO LOOK FOR ON THE MAP

**Longest river:** Shinano, 370 km (230 miles) *Map G8*

**Highest point:** Mt. Fuji, 3,776 m (12,388 ft) *Map H9*

**Largest lake:** L. Biwa, 673 sq km (260 sq miles) *Map F9*

**World's longest undersea rail tunnel:** Seikan Tunnel between Hokkaido and Honshu, 53.85 km (33.46 miles) *Map H4*

### Tokyo
☀ Jan 3°C (38°F)
July 25°C (77°F)
🌧 Jan 48 mm (1.9 in)
July 142 mm (5.6 in)

JAPAN

### Nagasaki, Japan
☀ Jan 6°C (43°F)
July 26°C (79°F)
🌧 Jan 71 mm (2.8 in)
July 257 mm (10.1 in)

0   50   100 150 km
0      50    100 miles

### RICE GROWING

Although only about a tenth of the land is suitable for farming, Japan has traditionally produced all the rice it needs. Rice is Japan's main food crop, and is eaten almost every day. It is intensively cultivated on small farms, using sophisticated farm machinery such as rice planters and harvesters. The work is done very quickly, so fewer workers are needed, and farmers often have a second job.

# JAPAN

FOR MANY CENTURIES, Japan was closed to foreigners and wary of the outside world. Today, it is a leading industrial and technological power and one of the world's richest countries. This transformation is even more remarkable given Japan's mountainous landscape and lack of natural resources. Most raw materials have to be imported from abroad. Japanese people are hard-working and enjoy a high standard of living, with good health and education systems. Average life expectancy is among the highest in the world. Western influence is strong, although people remain proud of their culture and traditions.

### JAPAN
**Capital city:** Tokyo

**Area:** 377,835 sq km (145,882 sq miles)

**Population:** 128,000,000

**Official language:** Japanese

**Major religions:** Shinto and Buddhist 92%, other 8%

**Government:** Multi-party democracy

**Currency:** Yen

**Adult literacy rate:** 99%

**Life expectancy:** 82 years

**People per doctor:** 496

**Televisions:** 707 per 1,000 people

## MAKING MONEY
Japan has huge economic power. It invests in land and property around the world, and many of the world's largest commercial banks are Japanese. Japan's economic and industrial heartland is in the capital, Tokyo. The world's second largest stock exchange and the headquarters of many major banks and corporations are found in Tokyo's Central Business District. It is said that if an earthquake hit this area, the world would suffer economic chaos.

**Electronic goods produced in Japan**

Electronic components: 34%

Computers: 24%

Other 5%

Consumer goods: 18%

Industrial equipment: 19%

*The Japanese excel at making electronic goods, such as televisions, cameras, digital watches, and computers, that are sold worldwide. Many Japanese companies are world leaders in research and development of new technology.*

*The Rainbow Bridge connects the port with the city.*

## ECONOMIC STRENGTH
Japan has a highly developed infrastructure and industrial base. One of the main reasons why the country's industries have grown so quickly is that the Japanese are very hard-working. Many of the larger companies are like families, providing housing and health care for their employees. However, society is slowly changing. Young people are starting to question this working culture, especially as the economy began to slow down in the 1990s and unemployment rose.

*Traditional folding fans made of bamboo covered with paper are carried by both men and women.*

## TRADITIONAL DRESS
People in Japan wear kimonos for religious festivals and other special occasions. A kimono (which means "clothing") is a long-sleeved, wrap-around robe, tied with a broad sash. It may be made of silk, cotton, or wool. Many formal silk kimonos are richly coloured and beautifully embroidered.

Black silk kimono

### CHERRY BLOSSOM
Japanese people share a love of nature and pay close attention to the changing seasons. The blossoming of the cherry trees is a reminder that spring has arrived. The first blossoms appear in southern Kyushu, and their progress is plotted on maps shown on the television news. The blossoms last for a few days, and people celebrate by picnicking under the cherry trees.

*Wooden clogs, or geta*

## RELIGION

Shinto and Buddhism, the two major religions of Japan, have always existed side by side and even merge together to a certain extent. Most Japanese people consider themselves Buddhist, Shintoist or Shinto-Buddhist. There is also a significant Christian community, making it the third most popular religion in Japan.

*A Japanese woman praying to a statue of Buddha.*

## OVERCROWDING

With a large population and a lack of flat land for settlement, Japan is a crowded country. Land is expensive, especially in the cities, and many people commute long distances to work. During rush hour, subway trains are so crowded that guards have to push commuters on board. The uncomfortable journeys that people endure inspired Japanese technicians to invent personal stereos so people could listen to music while travelling.

## FESTIVALS

There are plenty of festivals in Japan, each with their own emphasis and tradition. The parade shown here is from the Hakata Dontaku Festival in Kyushu, which is steeped in over 820 years of history. In the festival, Fukujin, Ebisu and Daikoku, the three gods of good fortune, make the rounds of the city.

## CHILDREN'S LIVES

Children are well looked after in Japan. There is even a national holiday, Children's Day, dedicated to them. In another festival, "seven-five-three day", children are dressed in traditional clothing and taken to religious shrines. Japanese children are expected to study hard at school. In addition to the long school day, many pupils attend extra classes on Saturdays and in the evenings.

## SPORTING LIFE

Whether watching or taking part, Japanese people love sport. The national team sport is baseball, which came to Japan from the USA. An ancient sport unique to Japan is sumo wrestling. Success in the ring depends on weight and strength, so wrestlers follow high-protein diets.

*Golf is very popular in Japan. Practice-ranges are often built on several levels to save space.*

## FISHING FOR FOOD

As a nation of islands, Japan depends heavily on the surrounding seas for food. The Japanese catch and eat more fish than any other country, and have the largest fishing fleet in the world. There are hundreds of villages dotted along the coast from which small fishing boats venture out, while deep-sea fish are caught by larger trawlers. Some trawlers are floating fish factories that process the catch on board. Millions of fish are also bred each year on fish farms.

*Deep-sea trawlers may stay at sea for months at a time.*

*Fish are cleaned and filleted on board.*

*Many types of fish and seafood are eaten raw, as sushi, and artistically presented on lacquered dishes or trays.*

*After filleting, the fish are frozen or canned.*

*Fish are stored in the hold.*

### Find out more

EARTHQUAKES: *13*
GROWING CITIES: *17, 136*
LIFE EXPECTANCY: *276*
PACIFIC RIM ECONOMIES: *137*

# MAINLAND SOUTHEAST ASIA

STRETCHING FROM THE FOOTHILLS of the Himalayas in the north almost to the Equator in the south, the seven countries of mainland Southeast Asia are largely mountainous. About half the region is covered with forest. Most people live in the river valleys that cut through the fertile countryside. Burma is isolated, poor, and underdeveloped. In comparison, Thailand, Malaysia, and, above all the island of Singapore are rich countries with modern industrial economies. Vietnam, Cambodia, and Laos have had to recover from years of war. The region has a monsoon climate, with a dry season from November to March and a wet season from May to October.

THE COMING OF THE RAIN
As the wet season starts in May, the people of Laos and northeast Thailand celebrate *bun bang fai*, the skyrocket festival. They build huge rockets up to 4 m (13 ft) long from steel or plastic pipes and pack them with up to 500 kg (1,100 lb) of gunpowder. The rockets are launched into the sky to prompt the rain god, Vassakarn, to send the annual rains.

*In the uplands, the river picks up silt which it carries down to the valleys.*

*During the monsoon season, the river bursts its banks and floods the surrounding fields.*

THE MEKONG DELTA
The delta of the Mekong River in Vietnam is one of the world's great rice-growing areas, producing much of the surplus that has made Vietnam the world's second largest rice exporter. Farmers in the delta also grow fruit and catch the many breeds of fish that thrive in the muddy river waters.

## RIVER VALLEYS

From ancient times, people have settled in the valleys of the great rivers, such as the Irrawaddy, Mekong, and Salween, because the land there is suitable for growing rice. All the major cities in the region are situated on a river. In the valleys, farmers cultivate every corner of the land, often constructing terraces on the hillsides to grow rice and other crops. They use the river waters to irrigate (water) their crops.

*Silt from the uplands helps to fertilize the paddy fields.*

*This Akha village on the border of Thailand and Burma is surrounded by land that is cleared for slash-and-burn farming.*

*Rice is grown near the river, where the paddy fields can be easily watered.*

*1 and 2: in January an area of forest is cut down and left to dry. During the dry season in April, the area is burnt.*

## SLASH-AND-BURN FARMING

In the uplands, where there is lots of land but few people to work it, farmers use a technique called slash-and-burn. An area of forest is cleared and cultivated for a few years, then the farmer moves on to another patch, leaving the original land to recover. In this way, the land is never exhausted, and the forest is not destroyed to create permanent fields.

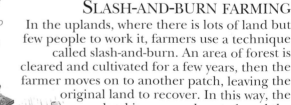

*3 and 4: crops are planted during the monsoon rains in May and harvested in October.*

*Stages 3 and 4 are repeated for 2–4 years, until the soil becomes less fertile.*

### THE UPLANDS
In contrast to the crowded river valleys, the uplands are sparsely populated and largely covered by forests. Here the hill peoples live in villages, farming small plots of land and gathering fruit and other food from the forests. This traditional way of life is now threatened by the region's growing population, which has brought more people to the uplands, and by logging companies cutting down the forests.

*5 and 6: the area is left fallow for 15–25 years and the forest grows back.*

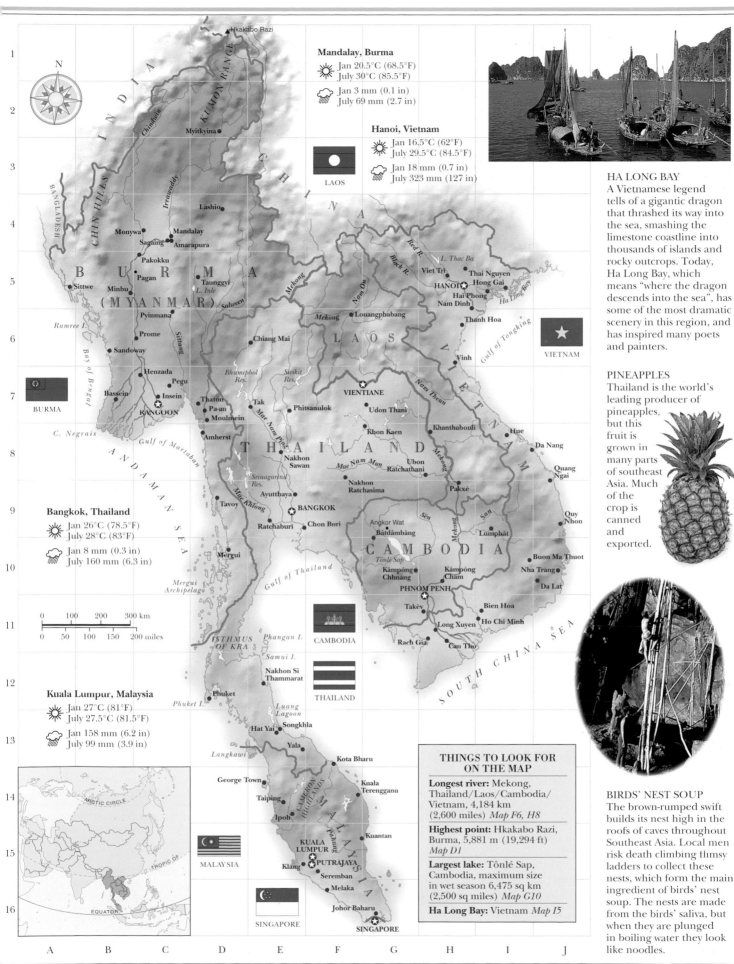

**Mandalay, Burma**
☀ Jan 20.5°C (68.5°F)
☀ July 30°C (85.5°F)
🌧 Jan 3 mm (0.1 in)
🌧 July 69 mm (2.7 in)

LAOS

**Hanoi, Vietnam**
☀ Jan 16.5°C (62°F)
☀ July 29.5°C (84.5°F)
🌧 Jan 18 mm (0.7 in)
🌧 July 323 mm (127 in)

VIETNAM

BURMA

**Bangkok, Thailand**
☀ Jan 26°C (78.5°F)
☀ July 28°C (83°F)
🌧 Jan 8 mm (0.3 in)
🌧 July 160 mm (6.3 in)

CAMBODIA

THAILAND

**Kuala Lumpur, Malaysia**
☀ Jan 27°C (81°F)
☀ July 27.5°C (81.5°F)
🌧 Jan 158 mm (6.2 in)
🌧 July 99 mm (3.9 in)

MALAYSIA

SINGAPORE

### THINGS TO LOOK FOR ON THE MAP

**Longest river:** Mekong, Thailand/Laos/Cambodia/Vietnam, 4,184 km (2,600 miles) *Map F6, H8*

**Highest point:** Hkakabo Razi, Burma, 5,881 m (19,294 ft) *Map D1*

**Largest lake:** Tônlé Sap, Cambodia, maximum size in wet season 6,475 sq km (2,500 sq miles) *Map G10*

**Ha Long Bay:** Vietnam *Map I5*

### HA LONG BAY
A Vietnamese legend tells of a gigantic dragon that thrashed its way into the sea, smashing the limestone coastline into thousands of islands and rocky outcrops. Today, Ha Long Bay, which means "where the dragon descends into the sea", has some of the most dramatic scenery in this region, and has inspired many poets and painters.

### PINEAPPLES
Thailand is the world's leading producer of pineapples, but this fruit is grown in many parts of southeast Asia. Much of the crop is canned and exported.

### BIRDS' NEST SOUP
The brown-rumped swift builds its nest high in the roofs of caves throughout Southeast Asia. Local men risk death climbing flimsy ladders to collect these nests, which form the main ingredient of birds' nest soup. The nests are made from the birds' saliva, but when they are plunged in boiling water they look like noodles.

# THAILAND

THE KINGDOM OF THAILAND was established in the 13th century, and the country has remained independent for most of its history. It was the only country in mainland Southeast Asia not to be colonized by Britain or France. Modern Thailand is an economically successful nation, with rapid economic growth and a huge tourist industry. The north, west, and south are mountainous and fairly empty. About a third of the people live in the fertile and densely populated centre of the country. Thailand was once covered in forest, but so much of it has been cut down for timber that logging is now banned.

| THAILAND |
| --- |
| **Capital city:** Bangkok |
| **Area:** 514,000 sq km (198,455 sq miles) |
| **Population:** 62,800,000 |
| **Official language:** Thai |
| **Major religions:** Buddhist 95%, Muslim 4%, other 1% |
| **Government:** Multi-party democracy |
| **Currency:** Baht |
| **Adult literacy rate:** 93% |
| **Life expectancy:** 69 years |
| **People per doctor:** 3,427 |
| **Televisions:** 236 per 1,000 people |

*These young men wear orange robes and have shaved their heads to show that they are monks.*

### THE KING OF THAILAND
King Bhumibol Adulyadej has ruled Thailand since 1946, making him the longest-serving head of state in the world. The king is a powerful unifying force in the country and has often intervened in politics to restore order. He is highly respected by Thais and any criticism of him or his family is frowned upon.

## BANGKOK
Officially 6 million people live in Bangkok, but the true figure is probably closer to 10 million. Originally built on a network of canals, the city still has relatively few major roads and a limited public transport system. As a result, Bangkok has some of the worst traffic jams in the world. In July 1992, after a monsoon storm, it took 11 hours for one jam to clear. Some commuters have converted their cars into mobile offices, even installing chemical toilets, so they can work while they are driven in.

## A MODERN ECONOMY
Thailand is the world's biggest producer of pineapples, and also exports large quantities of rubber and rice. However, in recent years manufacturing has overtaken agriculture in economic importance. American and Japanese companies have set up factories in Thailand, which is now a leading producer of electronic goods, such as integrated circuits for computers. Many of the workers in these new factories are women.

*Women are often employed in the electronics industry because they earn lower wages than men and their smaller hands can cope with the fiddly assembly work.*

## BUDDHISM
Monks from Sri Lanka introduced Theravada Buddhism to this region in the 12th century and it soon became Thailand's main religion. Theravada Buddhism – the "Way of the Elders" – encourages its followers to obey the Law of Karma and do all they can to reduce suffering in the world. Traditionally young men were expected to became monks for a period of their lives, and many still follow this custom today.

*The Emerald Temple in Bangkok is named after the green jade statue of the Buddha that it contains.*

## TOURISM
The thousands of ornate Buddhist temples and monasteries in Thailand have always drawn tourists from around the world to admire their beautiful architecture. Despite the Indian Ocean tsunami in 2004, visitors still come to lie on the unspoiled beaches, trek in the hills of the north, or play on one of the new golf courses that are designed to attract businessmen from Japan.

*Find out more*
BUDDHISM: *275*
GROWING CITIES: *17, 135*
PACIFIC RIM ECONOMIES: *137*
TSUNAMI: *197, 273*

# BURMA (MYANMAR)

OVERSHADOWED BY THE POWERFUL neighbouring countries of India, China, and Thailand, Burma (also known as Myanmar) is little known to the outside world. When the country became independent in 1948, it adopted a policy of political and economic isolation that reduced this once-rich nation to one of the poorest on Earth. Revolts by the hill peoples and, in recent years, political repression by a military government have kept nearly all foreign influences away. Yet Burma is rich in natural resources, is well watered by the great Irrawaddy River, and is fertile enough to support intensive farming.

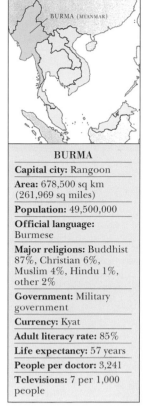

### BURMA
**Capital city:** Rangoon

**Area:** 678,500 sq km (261,969 sq miles)

**Population:** 49,500,000

**Official language:** Burmese

**Major religions:** Buddhist 87%, Christian 6%, Muslim 4%, Hindu 1%, other 2%

**Government:** Military government

**Currency:** Kyat

**Adult literacy rate:** 85%

**Life expectancy:** 57 years

**People per doctor:** 3,241

**Televisions:** 7 per 1,000 people

The Akha people value silver highly. This chief and his family wear silver neck-rings, bracelets, and ornaments on their clothes to show their wealth and status.

## THE HILL PEOPLES
In the upland areas of the east, north, and west of Burma live the hill peoples. They include the Shan, Akha, Karen, and Kachin tribes, and make up more than a quarter of the total Burmese population. Most hill peoples live in small villages and make their living from slash-and-burn farming on the land around their villages. They are fiercely independent and resent interference from outside. As a result, more than 200,000 Karen and others have lost their lives fighting the Burmese government for independence.

## TEAK
Hard, easily carved, and containing an oil that resists water and stops iron rusting, teak is a highly desirable wood for furniture, flooring, and other building uses. About 70 per cent of the world's teak trees grow on the hills of Burma, but intensive felling means that soon few trees will be left standing unless action is taken to replant the forests.

### NATURAL WEALTH
Rubies and sapphires are among the many gemstones produced in northern Burma. Many people consider these rubies to be the finest in the world because of their deep red colour. Burma is also rich in silver, copper, jade, lead, zinc, and tin, and has extensive reserves of oil and natural gas.

◆ Rubies

▨ Poppy-growing area

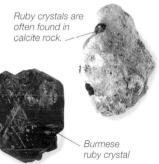

Ruby crystals are often found in calcite rock.

Burmese ruby crystal

### THE GOLDEN TRIANGLE
The area where Burma, Thailand, and Laos meet is known as the Golden Triangle. Here the hill peoples grow opium poppies as one of their few sources of income. Opium is a useful painkiller, but it can also be used to make narcotics. Two-thirds of the world's heroin comes from this region. In order to combat this lethal trade, the government is encouraging the local people to plant other crops for export, such as tobacco or flowers.

The opium poppy has white, pink, or purple flowers and can grow to a height of 1.2 m (4 ft).

Seed head

Opium is made from the sap that oozes out of cuts scored in the seed head.

## RANGOON
Situated in the delta of the great Irrawaddy River, the capital city of Burma was established in 1852 by the British, who laid out the streets in a grid pattern. Since then, Rangoon has grown to be the country's major port and industrial centre. Dominating the city is a Buddhist temple called the Shwe Dagon Pagoda. Situated on a hill just north of the city centre, the gold-covered pagoda towers 99 m (325 ft) above the city streets.

# VIETNAM

| VIETNAM | |
|---|---|
| **Capital city:** Hanoi | |
| **Area:** 329,560 sq km (127,243 sq miles) | |
| **Population:** 81,400,000 | |
| **Official language:** Vietnamese | |
| **Major religions:** Buddhist 55%, Christian 7%, other 38% | |
| **Government:** One-party state | |
| **Currency:** Dong | |
| **Adult literacy rate:** 93% | |
| **Life expectancy:** 70 years | |
| **People per doctor:** 1,919 | |
| **Televisions:** 47 per 1,000 people | |

EVERY DAY FOR 13 YEARS, Vietnam appeared on television sets and in newspapers around the world as the communist-led north of the country fought the American-backed south in a vicious war. When the war ended in 1975, with victory for the north, Vietnam had been devastated by the years of fighting and many of its people wanted to leave. Although the communist government struggled for years to recover, its policy of allowing foreign firms to invest in new industries slowly strengthened the economy. Today, tourists are beginning to visit this beautiful country in ever greater numbers. However, despite this success, most people in Vietnam remain very poor.

RUSH HOUR ON A BICYCLE
Cars dominate most large cities in the world, but in Vietnam the bicycle rules the road. Everyone has a bicycle which they use to get to work, or for shopping, because few people are rich enough to afford a car. In the morning and evening rush hours, streets like this one in Ho Chi Minh City are packed with cyclists, ringing their bells and shouting out loud to warn pedestrians and other cyclists to get out of the way.

## THE BIRTH OF A CHILD
In the past, many Vietnamese babies did not live for long, so families didn't celebrate the birth of a child, but its survival for a month. This ritual continues today. Later, when the child is a year old, the family celebrates *Thoi Noi*. The child is shown a tray with objects on it. Whichever one the child chooses shows which career he or she will follow – for example, a pen for a teacher, scissors for a tailor.

*Most villages have an electricity supply, and some families own a television set.*

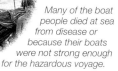

*Many of the boat people died at sea from disease or because their boats were not strong enough for the hazardous voyage.*

## THE BOAT PEOPLE
After the end of the war, many Vietnamese people tried to leave in search of jobs abroad or out of fear of persecution. They took to the sea in boats, hoping to reach the West via Hong Kong, Malaysia, or Singapore. By 1980 about half a million people had set sail. The flood of refugees stopped when neighbouring countries began to send them home.

## RICE GROWING
Two-thirds of the farmland in Vietnam is under water for part of the year, but deliberately so, because the fields are flooded to grow rice. During the rainy season, the fields slowly fill with rainwater, which is kept in place by low earth dykes. Soon a series of shallow, muddy paddy fields appear. Women plant the rice by hand. It takes two to three months to grow to full strength and is then harvested.

*House made of concrete.*  *Outdoor shower*  *Plot for growing vegetables and maize.*

## VILLAGE LIFE
Four out of every five people in Vietnam live in the countryside. Because cars are rare, and there are few railway lines, not many people will ever visit the great cities of Hanoi or Ho Chi Minh. The vast majority live in small villages and earn their living as farmers or labourers. Here they live in simple houses made of concrete, brick or, more traditionally, wood, straw, and palm leaves. A typical house has two rooms – one for eating and living, the other for sleeping – but no running water, which comes from a well outside.

*Families live on the fruits and vegetables they grow on their farms. They eat meat only on special occasions.*

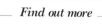

---

*Find out more*

# CAMBODIA

**F**EW COUNTRIES HAVE SUFFERED as much as Cambodia. In 1970 it was drawn into the fighting in neighbouring Vietnam. Then, from 1975–79, the country was ruled by Pol Pot and the Khmer Rouge, a revolutionary group who killed more than a million Cambodians. In 1979 the Vietnamese invaded to overthrow Pol Pot, and the country fell into civil war, which lasted until 1991. Today, Cambodia is slowly rebuilding its shattered society.

*Angkor Wat consists of a central temple building, surrounded by smaller temples and palaces, and huge moats and reservoirs.*

## CAMBODIA

**Capital city:** Phnom Penh

**Area:** 181,040 sq km (69,900 sq miles)

**Population:** 14,100,000

**Official language:** Khmer

**Major religions:** Buddhist 93%, Muslim 6%, Christian 1%

**Government:** Multi-party democracy

**Currency:** Riel

**Adult literacy rate:** 69%

**Life expectancy:** 54 years

**People per doctor:** 3,333

**Televisions:** 15 per 1,000 people

## LAOS

**Capital city:** Vientiane

**Area:** 236,800 sq km (91,428 sq miles)

**Population:** 5,700,000

**Official language:** Lao

**Major religions:** Buddhist 85%, other 15%

**Government:** One-party state

**Currency:** New kip

**Adult literacy rate:** 66%

**Life expectancy:** 56 years

**People per doctor:** 5,000

**Televisions:** 4 per 1,000 people

## ANGKOR WAT

For centuries, the vast temple complex of Angkor Wat lay hidden in the jungles of north Cambodia. It was built in the 12th century by the Khmer King, Suryavarman II, in honour of the Hindu god Vishnu, and was once the centre of a huge empire. When the Khmers fell from power, Angkor Wat was abandoned and the jungle gradually grew over the buildings. The site has been uncovered only in the last 100 years.

### CLASSICAL DANCE

In the temple of Angkor Wat, royal dancers performed religious dances based on the Indian epic tales of the Ramayana and the Mahabharata. This type of classical dance is highly stylized, with graceful movements requiring years of training to perfect. The dancers wear richly embroidered costumes so tight that they have to be sewn into them before each performance.

## THE WORLD'S BIGGEST MINEFIELD

The lengthy wars in Cambodia have left the country in a desperate state. The road and rail systems have collapsed, and industry barely exists. Up to 3 million mines are thought to lie buried in the ground. Despite the efforts of mine clearers, like the man in this picture, many mines are discovered only when someone steps on one. As a result, some 20,000 people have been disabled.

# LAOS

*Hmong men often have more than one wife. Each wife is responsible for bringing up her own children, and looks after her own poultry and vegetable garden.*

**L**AOS IS A COMMUNIST STATE, and one of the poorest and most isolated countries in the world. Three-quarters of its people are farmers; many of them grow only enough food to feed their families. Apart from the fertile Mekong Valley, the land is rugged and unsuitable for farming. Yet Laos is rich in gold and other minerals, and also produces timber and coffee.

## THE HILL PEOPLES

Peoples such as these Hmong have lived in the isolated hill areas of Laos for many years. They grow maize and rice to eat, and opium poppies to sell. But this traditional way of life has been badly affected by the wars in this region and many Hmong have left the country and settled in Thailand or the USA.

THE FRIENDSHIP BRIDGE
Spanning the Mekong River near the capital city of Vientiane is the Friendship Bridge, which opened in 1994. Laos is landlocked (it has no coastline), and the bridge provides the only direct route to Thailand and its sea ports.

*Find out more*

HILL PEOPLES: *188, 191*
HINDUISM: *275*
OPIUM: *191*
POLITICAL SYSTEMS: *270–271*

# MALAYSIA

SPREAD ACROSS THE SOUTH CHINA SEA is the divided land of Malaysia. Part of the country lies on the Malay Peninsula, which hangs off the corner of mainland Southeast Asia, but the states of Sarawak and Sabah are on the island of Borneo to the east. More than 24 million people live in the country, most of them in the rapidly growing cities on the peninsula. Every five years Malaysia gets a new head of state: nine sultans, who each rule one of the states that make up the country, take it in turns to be king.

THE PEOPLE OF MALAYSIA
Almost half the population of Malaysia are Malays, like this family. About one-third are Chinese; the rest are either descendants of settlers from the Indian Subcontinent or local tribespeople. This mix of peoples has led to racial conflict in the past.

**MALAYSIA**

**Capital city:** Kuala Lumpur

**Area:** 329,750 sq km (127,316 sq miles)

**Population:** 24,400,000

**Official language:** Malay

**Major religions:** Muslim 53%, Buddhist 19%, Chinese faiths 12%, Christian 7%, traditional beliefs 2%, other 7%

**Government:** Multi-party democracy

**Currency:** Ringgit

**Adult literacy rate:** 89%

**Life expectancy:** 73 years

**People per doctor:** 1,474

**Televisions:** 166 per 1,000 people

**SINGAPORE**

**Capital city:** Singapore

**Area:** 693 sq km (267 sq miles)

**Population:** 4,300,000

**Official languages:** Malay, Chinese, Tamil, and English

**Major religions:** Buddhist 55%, Taoist 22%, Muslim 16%, other 7%

**Government:** Multi-party democracy

**Currency:** Singapore dollar

**Adult literacy rate:** 93%

**Life expectancy:** 78 years

**People per doctor:** 698

**Televisions:** 348 per 1,000 people

## NATURAL RESOURCES

Malaysia is rich in natural resources, with large oil and gas reserves off the coast of Sarawak. The country is the world's top producer of palm oil, used to make soap and for cooking, and the third biggest producer of natural rubber. The rainforests of Sarawak are rich in hardwood trees, but experts are worried that the timber industry is cutting down trees faster than the forest can renew itself.

*Peas, beans, and other vegetables are often grown between the rows of trees.*

*Strips of bark are cut away to let the latex run down the trunk and into a collecting cup.*

RUBBER
Hidden inside the bark of the rubber tree is a white liquid, called latex, that is used to make natural rubber. Rubber trees grow in hot, wet climates and flourish on the lower slopes of the mountains that run down the length of the Malay Peninsula. Collected latex is sent to a local factory. There it is mixed with water and acid in a large pan to make a sheet of rubber that is then smoked or hung on a line to dry.

*Rubber tappers go out before dawn to collect the latex before the high daytime temperatures stop its flow.*

*Half of all cars sold in Malaysia are Protons.*

## MODERN INDUSTRY

The first car to be manufactured in Malaysia – the Proton – rolled off the production line outside Kuala Lumpur in 1985. Today, more than 90,000 Protons are produced every year, many for export to Indonesia, Singapore, and the UK. The Proton has been so successful that it has been followed by a second car project, the Perodua. Malaysia is also an international centre for the electronics industry and is the world's biggest producer of disk drives for computers.

THE CHANGING ECONOMY
**1970s:** in 1970 Malaysia had few factories, and most of its raw materials, such as rubber and tin, were exported to be manufactured into finished goods abroad.

**2000s:** today, Malaysia's economy is one of the most successful in the world. Malaysia continues to produce large amounts of raw materials, and its manufacturing sector has grown dramatically. Three-quarters of all exports are now finished goods, such as cars, electronics, textiles, and foods.

**Exports in 1970**
42.5%
15%
25%
12.5%
5%

**Exports in 1998**
Manufactured goods: 76%
Other: 16.5%
Oil and gas: 6.2%
Rubber: 1.1%
Tin: 0.2%

## ISLAM

In 1414, the people of Malacca (modern-day Melaka) converted to Islam when their ruler married a Muslim princess from Sumatra. The new faith spread rapidly throughout the country. Today, more than half the population of Malaysia is Muslim. Islamic law is widely obeyed and many women wear a head-dress in the street.

*Modern-day Kuala Lumpur is a mixture of skyscrapers and old colonial buildings.*

## KUALA LUMPUR

In 1857, a group of miners in search of tin set up a camp where the Kelang and Gombak rivers join. They called their settlement Kuala Lumpur, which is Malay for "muddy meeting place". The camp soon grew in size and importance as a centre of the tin mining and rubber industries. Today it is Malaysia's biggest city and home to more than 1.5 million people.

## LIFE ON STILTS

Faced with the problem of building on the banks of rivers or next to the sea, villagers developed an ingenious solution – they built their houses on stilts. Villages of these houses, called *kampungs*, are found throughout Southeast Asia. The wooden houses stand high enough above the water to protect them from flooding, while the raised floors and many windows help to keep the houses well ventilated.

*A high, steep roof protects the inhabitants from the heavy monsoon rains.*

*Animals are often kept under the raised floor.*

*Many kampung villagers make their living from fishing.*

*Fish are laid out to dry in the sun so that they can be stored for future use.*

# SINGAPORE

OFF THE TIP OF MALAYSIA lies the tiny island state of Singapore, one of the most densely populated countries on Earth. Singapore was originally a trading settlement on the shipping route between India and China. It was founded in 1819 by Sir Stamford Raffles, an official of the British East India Company. Today, rapid economic growth has turned the island into one of the world's most successful economies.

*Singapore's banks and stock exchange, based in this part of the city, generate about a quarter of the country's income.*

## THE PORT OF SINGAPORE

Every three minutes a ship enters or leaves the bustling harbour of Singapore, making it the busiest port in the world. Tankers from the Persian Gulf bring crude oil to be refined into petrol and other products, which are then shipped out to ports throughout eastern Asia. Cargo ships on the way to and from China and Japan stop to use the harbour's facilities, and most of Malaysia's large export trade goes out through this port.

*Singapore's skyline is dominated by modern high-rise buildings, built because land is in such short supply.*

## SINGAPORE SOCIETY

Three-quarters of the people of Singapore are Chinese; the rest are Malays and descendants of people from the Indian Subcontinent. Because Singapore is so wealthy, most people lead comfortable lives. The government keeps tight control over the country: it regulates the press, owns the television and radio services, and limits car ownership to prevent congestion on the roads. It is illegal to drop litter in the street, eat in the underground, or chew gum in public.

---

*Find out more*

ISLAM: *275*
OIL: *137, 152, 281*
PACIFIC RIM ECONOMIES: *137*
RUBBER: *226*

# MARITIME SOUTHEAST ASIA

MARITIME MEANS "CONNECTED WITH THE SEA" and maritime Southeast Asia is a belt of thousands of islands strung out across a vast expanse of ocean. Here, sandwiched between mainland Southeast Asia and Australia, are four countries: the eastern part of Malaysia, Brunei, Indonesia, and the Philippines. This is one of the world's most volcanic regions, and the monsoon climate makes some areas among the wettest places on Earth. A huge variety of animals and plants live here, because the environment is slightly different on each island. There are many different peoples, too. More than 250 languages are spoken on the islands of Indonesia alone.

**WATER TRANSPORT**
In this island region, boats have traditionally provided the main method of getting from place to place. Small boats, such as this outrigger canoe, are ideal for navigating the waterways between clusters of islands.

## TYPHOON CLIMATE

Each year, about 20 tropical storms called typhoons batter the islands of the Philippines. They bring flooding and winds travelling at over 100 km/h (62 mph). Many people are killed in storms, and thousands of homes are destroyed. Low-lying coastal areas are most at risk, but people are forced to live there because land is in short supply, and these areas are cheap.

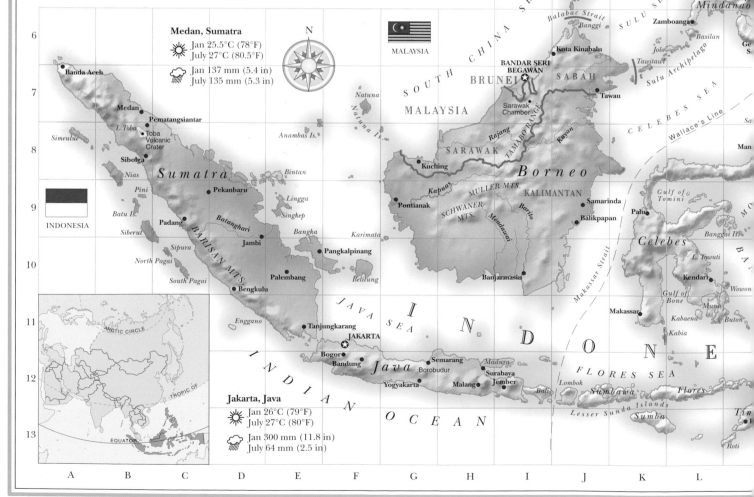

**PHILIPPINES**

**Manila, Philippines**
- Jan 25.5°C (77.5°F)
  July 27.5°C (81.5°F)
- Jan 23 mm (0.9 in)
  July 432 mm (17 in)

**BRUNEI**

**MALAYSIA**

**Medan, Sumatra**
- Jan 25.5°C (78°F)
  July 27°C (80.5°F)
- Jan 137 mm (5.4 in)
  July 135 mm (5.3 in)

N

**INDONESIA**

**Jakarta, Java**
- Jan 26°C (79°F)
  July 27°C (80°F)
- Jan 300 mm (11.8 in)
  July 64 mm (2.5 in)

Aparri
Tuguegarao
Baguio
Dagupan
*Luzon*
Cabanatuan
Mt. Pinatubo
MANILA
Lucena
Batangas
Naga
*Mindoro*
Legaspi
*Mindoro Strait*
Masbate
*Panay*
Iloilo
Cadiz
Bacolod
*Negros*
Cebu
Boho
*Palawan*
Puerto Princesa
PHILIPPINES
Iligan
*Mindanao*
*Balabac Strait*
Banggi
Zamboanga
Basilan
*SULU SEA*
Jolo
*Sulu Archipelago*
Tawitawi
Kota Kinabalu
SABAH
Tawau
*CELEBES SEA*
*Wallace's Line*
BANDAR SERI BEGAWAN
BRUNEI
Sarawak Chamber
*TAMABO RANGE*
*SOUTH CHINA SEA*
*Natuna*
Natuna Is.
*Anambas Is.*
MALAYSIA
SARAWAK
Kuching
Rajang
*Borneo*
Kayan
KALIMANTAN
Samarinda
Palu
*Gulf of Tomini*
Banda Aceh
Medan
Pematangsiantar
L. Toba
Toba Volcanic Crater
Sibolga
Simeulue
Nias
*Sumatra*
Bintan
Pekanbaru
Lingga
Singkep
Pontianak
MULLER MTS.
Balikpapan
*Celebes*
Banggai Is.
Pini
Batu Is.
Padang
Batanghari
Bangka
Kapuas
SCHWANER MTS.
Barito
Mandawai
Siberut
*BARISAN MTS.*
Jambi
Karimata
Kendari
Sipura
North Pagai
Pangkalpinang
Belitung
Banjarmasin
*Makassar Strait*
Wowon
South Pagai
Palembang
Makassar
Muna
Bengkulu
*Gulf of Bone*
Buton
Enggano
*JAVA SEA*
Kabaena
Kabia
Tanjungkarang
JAKARTA
*INDONE*
Bogor
Bandung
*Java*
Semarang
Borobudur
Madura
Surabaya
*FLORES SEA*
Yogyakarta
Malang
Jember
Bali
Lombok
Sumbawa
Flores
*Lesser Sunda Islands*
*INDIAN OCEAN*
Sumba
Roti
*ARCTIC CIRCLE*
*TROPIC OF*
EQUATOR

## VOLCANOES

Volcanic eruptions and earthquakes are a frequent part of life in this region. They are caused by the movement of huge pieces of the Earth's crust, called tectonic plates. Much of maritime Southeast Asia lies over a massive arc-shaped join between two of these plates. Despite the terrible destruction that eruptions cause, the islanders risk growing crops on the slopes of active volcanoes because their ash makes the soil fertile.

## NATURAL VARIETY

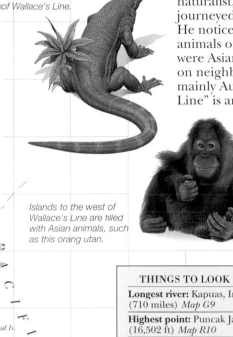

*This Australasian Komodo dragon lives on an island to the east of Wallace's Line.*

During the 1850s the British naturalist, Alfred Russel Wallace, journeyed through these islands. He noticed that most of the animals on the island of Bali were Asian in origin, but those on neighbouring Lombok were mainly Australasian. "Wallace's Line" is an imaginary line drawn across the region to divide the islands with Asian animals from those with Australasian animals.

*Islands to the west of Wallace's Line are filled with Asian animals, such as this orang utan.*

## TSUNAMI 2004

On December 26, 2004, a massive underwater earthquake off the northwest coast of Sumatra set off a giant wave, known as a tsunami, that quickly rippled out across the Indian Ocean. The tsunami was so powerful that it killed at least 225,000 people in 11 nations, including 170,000 in Indonesia. Coastal towns, such as the port of Banda Aceh (shown above) on the northern tip of Sumatra, were decimated, while people were killed as far away as Somalia on the east coast of Africa.

*Scientists studying the rainforests in this region have discovered that they contain one-sixth of all the world's bird species.*

### THINGS TO LOOK FOR ON THE MAP

**Longest river:** Kapuas, Indonesia, 1,142 km (710 miles) *Map G9*

**Highest point:** Puncak Jaya, Indonesia, 5,030 m (16,502 ft) *Map R10*

**World's largest volcano crater:** Toba, Indonesia, 1,775 sq km (685 sq miles) *Map B8*

**World's largest cave:** Sarawak Chamber, Malaysia, 700 m (2,296 ft) long *Map I7*

## THE TROPICAL RAINFORESTS

Individual islands provide different natural habitats, so the animals and plants that have evolved on one island may be very different to those on the next. This means that the region's dense rainforests contain the greatest variety of species in the world. This is why it is so vital that these forests should be protected and not cut down or cleared.

*PACIFIC OCEAN*

Morotai

Halmahera

Gulf of Weda

Waigeo

Biak

Sorong

Yapen

Jayapura

Misool

Gulf of Berau

Mamberamo

oluccas

CERAM SEA

Ceram

PAPUA IRIAN JAYA

Ambon

Banda Is.

MAOKE MTS

Puncak Jaya

Kai Is.

ARAFURA SEA

Aru Is.

Digul

PAPUA NEW GUINEA

Dolak

Leti Is.

Babar

Yamdena

Komoran

TIMOR

EAST TIMOR

**Ambon, Moluccas**

☀ Jan 27.5°C (82°F)
☀ July 25°C (77.5°F)

☁ Jan 127 mm (5 in)
☁ July 602 mm (23.7 in)

SEA

0   100   200   300   400   500 km
0   100   200   300 miles

O     P     Q     R     S     T

### THE RAFFLESIA FLOWER

This rare plant, found deep in the rainforests, is named after Sir Stamford Raffles, a British governor in this region during the 19th century. It has the world's largest flowers, measuring up to 91 cm (3 ft) across. *Rafflesia* is famous for its foul smell, which attracts insects.

# INDONESIA

EVERYTHING ABOUT INDONESIA IS BIG. It is the world's largest archipelago, made up of 18,108 islands, of which only about 1,500 are inhabited. It stretches for 5,100 km (3,169 miles), and is spread across 8 million sq km (3 million sq miles) of sea and three time zones. The population contains 362 different peoples, speaking over 250 languages and dialects. More than 190 million Indonesians are Muslim, making it the world's biggest Muslim country. It is also a land of contrasts: along with its modern cities and industries, Indonesia contains peoples whose lifestyles have not altered for centuries.

## INDONESIA

**Capital city:** Jakarta

**Area:** 1,919,440 sq km (741,096 sq miles)

**Population:** 220,000,000

**Official language:** Bahasa Indonesia

**Major religions:** Muslim 87%, Christian 9%, other 4%

**Government:** Multi-party democracy

**Currency:** Rupiah

**Adult literacy rate:** 88%

**Life expectancy:** 67 years

**People per doctor:** 6,564

**Televisions:** 136 per 1,000 people

## BRUNEI

**Capital city:** Bandar Seri Begawan

**Area:** 5,770 sq km (2,228 sq miles)

**Population:** 358,000

**Official language:** Malay

**Major religions:** Muslim 66%, Buddhist 14%, Christian 10%, other 10%

**Government:** Absolute monarchy

**Currency:** Brunei dollar

**Adult literacy rate:** 94%

**Life expectancy:** 77 years

**People per doctor:** 929

**Televisions:** 241 per 1,000 people

## EAST TIMOR

**Capital city:** Dili

**Area:** 15,007 sq km (5,794 sq miles)

**Population:** 778,000

**Official languages:** Tetum, Portuguese

**Major religions:** Roman Catholic 95%, other 5%

**Government:** Multi-party democracy

**Currency:** US Dollar

**Adult literacy rate:** 59%

**Life expectancy:** 65 years

**People per doctor:** 40,000

**Televisions:** 56 per 1,000 people

### THE SPICE ISLANDS

For centuries, the Moluccas islands in eastern Indonesia were Europe's main source of cloves, nutmeg, cinnamon, and other spices. While Indonesia was a Dutch colony, the merchants of the Dutch East India Company had total control of this trade and grew fabulously rich. Indonesia became an independent country in 1949.

Pepper    Nutmeg

Cloves    Cinnamon

*The temple of Borobudur is the world's largest Buddhist monument.*

### BOROBUDUR

Situated in the heart of Java is one of the architectural wonders of the world. The vast Buddhist temple of Borobudur – which means "monastery on the hill" in Javanese – was built between AD 778–856. The temple consists of a series of platforms, each one representing a different stage in the Buddhist's spiritual journey from ignorance, through enlightenment, to nirvana, or heavenly bliss.

## JAKARTA

Indonesia's capital is home to more than 17 million people, making it the largest city in southeast Asia. It was originally a small trading port at the mouth of the Ciliwung River, shipping spices throughout eastern Asia. In 1618 the Dutch made Jayakarta, as it was then called, the capital of their East Indies empire. They renamed the town Batavia and rebuilt it around canals to look like Amsterdam.

## OIL AND GAS

Oil has dominated the Indonesian economy since the first oil well was drilled in Sumatra in 1871. By 1981, oil and gas products made up over 80 per cent of exports, but this figure is now dropping as oil reserves run out. To reduce its dependence on oil, Indonesia is exploiting its huge reserves of natural gas. The gas is usually exported in a liquid form, called liquefied natural gas.

### THE ISLAND OF BALI

With lush plants and trees and sandy beaches stretching along the coast, Bali is one of the most beautiful places in the world. It is a favourite destination for tourists, who come to enjoy the scenery and to watch local groups of actors and musicians perform ancient dances. Most Balinese are Hindu, and processions, like these women taking offerings to the temple, are part of everyday life.

## PEOPLES OF INDONESIA

More than 220 million people live in Indonesia, 60 per cent of them on the island of Java. Yet this island forms just 7 per cent of the country's area. Many other islands are barely occupied despite their size. In 1950 the government began to resettle people from Java on other islands. More than 6 million have been relocated, despite protests from local people who are sometimes moved to make way for the new settlers.

### THE DANI

The people who live in Indonesia's easternmost province of Irian Jaya are related to the dark-skinned peoples of the Pacific Ocean rather than the lighter-skinned inhabitants of the rest of southeast Asia. Among the many tribes who live in this isolated area are the Dani, whose agricultural way of life has changed little in thousands of years.

*Field of crops*

*The Dani barter for goods, such as pigs.*

*Dani houses are made of wood and thatch.*

*A longhouse is usually constructed of timber and bamboo.*

*Covered gallery*

*Loft storage area, where rice is kept in large baskets.*

*Women separating rice grains from the chaff.*

*Sulawesi*

### THE DAYAKS

The native inhabitants of Borneo, the Dayaks, are expert builders who construct longhouses on stilts. Several families live in a longhouse, each with their own cooking and sleeping quarters. Meetings are held in a covered gallery which runs along the length of the building.

### THE BUGIS

The Bugis people of south Sulawesi are famous for their seafaring skills and, in previous centuries, for their ferocity in battle. They built elegant wooden ships in which they terrorized the inhabitants of neighbouring islands. It is thought that our English words "bogeyman" and "bugbear" come from Bugis.

*The Bugis still build their wooden ships, although they now have diesel engines.*

# BRUNEI

Squashed between the Malaysian state of Sarawak and the South China Sea lies the tiny kingdom of Brunei. Once a forgotten outpost of the British Empire and a haven for pirates, the country was transformed by the discovery of oil in 1929. Today it is one of the world's wealthiest nations. Brunei is so rich that the people pay no income tax, and receive free education, health care, and pensions.

### BRUNEI'S WEALTHY RULER

Brunei is governed by one of the wealthiest men on Earth. Thanks to the country's oil and gas reserves, Sultan Hassanal Bolkiah is worth about US$25 billion, although he denies this figure. He lives in the world's largest private royal residence in Brunei's capital city, Bandar Seri Begawan, and has his own fleet of aircraft, three hundred cars and two hundred polo ponies. In recent years the Sultan has spent more than US$450 million building one of the world's largest mosques.

*Brunei women dressed in the Muslim veil (hijab) greet the sultan.*

# EAST TIMOR

Being a portuguese colony for 400 years, gave East Timor a very different identity to its neighbours. Most people are Roman Catholic and the country is full of Portuguese architecture. It became independent in 1975 but was taken over by its giant neighbour, Indonesia, the same year. After 26 years of war and famine, which saw the death of 200,000 East Timorese, the tiny nation finally gained independence in 2002.

### STRUGGLE FOR INDEPENDENCE

East Timor's fight to rule itself followed a long guerrilla war with Indonesia in which over 200,000 East Timorese were killed. The Revolutionary Front for an Independent East Timor (known in Portuguese as Fretilin) consists of many of these former fighters and now runs the government of the world's newest nation.

FRETILIN

*Find out more*

ISLAM & BUDDHISM: *275*
OIL & GAS: *137, 152, 163, 211*
POPULATION DENSITY: *16, 135*
SPICES: *57, 264*

# THE PHILIPPINES

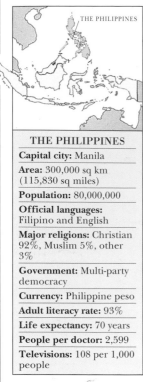

LOCATED ON THE "RING OF FIRE" – the arc of volcanoes running through maritime southeast Asia – and in the path of violent tropical storms, the Philippines suffers from earthquakes and volcanic eruptions. The country consists of 7,107 islands, of which only about 1,000 are inhabited. Most of the people live on the northern island of Luzon, which contains the capital, Manila. For almost 400 years the Philippines was governed by Spain; in fact the country is named after the Spanish king, Philip II. In 1898 control passed to the USA, then in 1946 the Philippines became an independent nation. Most Filipinos are of Malay origin, but there are some Chinese immigrants and mixed-blood *mestizos*.

## MANILA

Much of the Philippines' capital city lies below sea level, and it suffers from floods during the rainy summer season. The Spanish captured Manila in 1571, fortifying its walls and making it the centre of their Asian empire. Over the centuries Manila has been an important trading port, with merchants arriving from as far afield as Arabia, India, and Japan. Today, it is a bustling modern city with more than 10 million inhabitants.

*2 April 1991: the growth of a lava dome shows that Mt Pinatubo is about to erupt.*

*14 June 1991: the mountain begins to spew deadly clouds of gas and ash.*

*15 June 1991: a huge blast blows out the mountainside, and molten lava floods down the slopes.*

## MOUNT PINATUBO

In June 1991, Mount Pinatubo, a volcano north of Manila on the island of Luzon, burst into life. For 10 days, it spewed out volcanic ash and rocks in one of the biggest volcanic eruptions ever recorded. The landscape was soon covered with a layer of debris some 7 m (23 ft) deep. Heavy rainfall turned much of this to sludge, blocking rivers and filling up valleys. The local Aeta tribespeople lost their land and houses overnight.

### SMOKY MOUNTAIN

On the edge of Manila lies a vast mountain. Unlike other mountains, this one is not made of rock, but of rubbish. Every day the dust carts of Manila arrive there to dump their loads of household waste. Many people, some of them children as young as four, live on the mountain, searching the refuse daily for bottles, cans, plastics, and cardboard that they can sell for recycling.

**Filipinos working abroad 2000**

Europe: 3.8%

Asia: 47.8%

Middle East: 44.3%

The Americas: 2.1%

Africa: 1.2%

Australasia: 0.8%

*About 2% of the workforce are working abroad at any one time, sending money home to support their families. Each year, more than US$1 billion flows into the country's economy in this way.*

## THE ECONOMY

Once one of the richer nations in Asia, in the last few decades the Philippines has fallen behind its economically powerful neighbours. Half the population live in poverty, and many Filipinos can only support their families by working abroad. The Philippines is rich in natural resources, with reserves of gold, copper, and chrome. The main export crops are tobacco, sugar, and a wide range of tropical fruits.

### AMAZING JEEPS

At the end of World War II, the US Army left thousands of unwanted jeeps in the Philippines. Local people soon converted these for their own use, decorating them in amazing colours and patterns. The jeep can cope with the rugged conditions and poor roads of the countryside, and is now one of the main forms of transport in the Philippines.

# POLITICS

The presidential system of government in the Philippines has caused problems over the last few decades. In 1965 Ferdinand Marcos became president, but governed the country harshly, cheated in elections and used his position to make a personal fortune. He was finally forced to leave when thousands of people took to the streets in protests known as "People Power", organized by the Catholic Church. In 2001 another corrupt president, Joseph Estrada, a former film star, was also forced to step down after more mass protests from Filipinos.

# RELIGION

Roman Catholicism was introduced to the Philippines by the explorer, Magellan, who visited the island of Cebu in 1521 during his voyage round the world. Under Spanish rule, many Filipinos converted to Catholicism. It became the major religion in all but the southern, Muslim, island of Mindanao. Today, the Philippines is one of only two Christian countries in Asia, and the Catholic Church continues to exert a powerful influence on everyday life.

## ANCIENT TERRACES, MODERN METHODS

The Ifugao people have farmed the mountainous landscape in the north of Luzon island for thousands of years, laboriously constructing terraces on the steep hillsides to grow rice. These ancient terraces are now a major tourist attraction. But not all rice-growers in the Philippines use such traditional methods. The country is also home to the International Rice Research Institute, where scientists have bred new species of rice that yield more grains per plant, and are also developing rice-planting and harvesting machines.

*Farmers here sow rice in the ground like any other cereal crop, rather than in a flooded paddy field.*

*The terraces are held in place by stone walls, built entirely by hand.*

# COCONUTS

*Reaching a height of up to 30 m (100 ft), the coconut is one of the most beautiful palm trees in the world. Long leaves form on top of the slender trunk, and cream flowers grow on long spikes.*

The coconut palm flourishes in the warm, damp climate of the Philippines, producing nuts for up to 70 years. The nuts ripen in bunches of 15–20, and are harvested by farmers who knock them out of the trees with long bamboo poles. The Philippines is the world's second largest producer of coconuts after Indonesia, and the world's biggest producer of copra, the fleshy meat inside the nut, exporting its many products around the world.

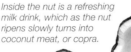

Copra
Coconut milk

Coconut

Outer husk

*Inside the nut is a refreshing milk drink, which as the nut ripens slowly turns into coconut meat, or copra.*

Copra

*Basket woven from palm leaves.*

## 101 USES OF THE COCONUT

Every part of the coconut tree has its use. The roots are turned into dyes and medicines, the trunk into timber and charcoal, and the leaves into thatch for roofs and woven material for mats and bags. The nut is used for matting, food, and cosmetics.

*Copra is used to make soap, cosmetics, and detergents.*

*Mat made from the outer husk of the coconut.*

## HUNTER-GATHERERS

On some of the more remote islands of the Philippines live groups of hunter-gatherers, who roam the countryside fishing, hunting animals, and gathering vegetables, fruit, and berries. These people are among the last in the world to continue this ancient way of life, but their lifestyle is under attack as the forests in which they live are felled for timber.

# THE INDIAN OCEAN

THE THIRD LARGEST of the world's oceans, the Indian Ocean, covers 73 million sq km (28 million sq miles) and contains some 5,000 islands, many of them surrounded by coral reefs. This ocean is unique because, unlike the Atlantic and Pacific, it has no outlet to the north. It has the saltiest sea (the Red Sea), and the warmest sea (the Persian Gulf) on Earth. The Indian Ocean is also at risk from pollution, especially from oil tankers leaving the Persian Gulf. Heavy monsoon rain and tropical storms can bring disastrous flooding to the northern coasts.

**ISLAND PARADISE**
The islands of the Indian Ocean include coral atolls, like the Maldives and Seychelles, which attract thousands of tourists every year. Although this brings money to the islands, it also threatens to damage the environment. Gradual erosion of the coral reefs also leaves the islands exposed to ocean tides and flooding. This Maldive island has a barrier to protect it from sea damage.

## CORAL ISLANDS

Coral is formed in warm waters by tiny creatures known as polyps. These marine creatures build limestone skeletons around themselves. Over many thousands of years, these skeletons gradually grow up towards the surface of the ocean to form a coral island. An atoll, shown right, is a form of circular coral reef that grows around an underwater volcano. As the volcano sinks, the coral forms an atoll. The water in the centre is called a lagoon.

*1. Corals grow in shallow waters around volcanic island.*

*2. Coral reef builds up as movements in the Earth's surface make the island sink.*

*3. Island finally disappears, leaving a coral atoll.*

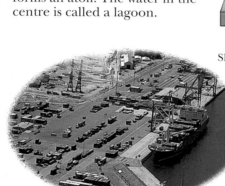

*This port in Fremantle, Australia handles freight from across the world.*

**SHIPPING ROUTES**
More than 200 large ships a day sail round the Cape of Good Hope at the southern tip of Africa as they enter or leave the Indian Ocean. Many are vast tankers laden with oil from the Persian Gulf. Smaller ships are able to pass through the Suez Canal. On the other side of the Indian Ocean, ships pass through the Strait of Malacca carrying cargo to ports in eastern Asia.

## MADAGASCAR

Madagascar lies off the east coast of Africa and, because of its isolation, is home to many unique plants and animals. Most people in Madagascar scratch a living by farming, clearing a new patch of land each year to plant their crops. One of the islands main crops is vanilla, grown for use as flavouring in food and drink. Women traditionally have elaborate hairstyles that indicate which village they are from.

**THE SALTY SEA**
Oceans are salty because minerals dissolved from rocks by rivers are washed into the seas. Around the shores of the Indian Ocean, people extract the salt by channelling water into shallow pans. The Sun's heat evaporates the water, leaving the salt behind, as shown here in Mauritius.

*The dried salt is stored in baskets. Workers then carry the heavy baskets on their heads to a waiting truck.*

---

### MALDIVES
**Capital city:** Male
**Area:** 300 sq km (116 sq miles)
**Population:** 318,000
**Official language:** Dhivehi
**Major religion:** Muslim 100%
**Government:** Non-party democracy
**Currency:** Rufiyaa

### COMOROS
**Capital city:** Moroni
**Area:** 2,170 sq km (838 sq miles)
**Population:** 768,000
**Official languages:** Arabic, French, Comoran
**Major religions:** Muslim 98%, other 2%
**Government:** Multi-party democracy
**Currency:** Comoros franc

### MAURITIUS
**Capital city:** Port Louis
**Area:** 2,400 sq km (788 sq miles)
**Population:** 1,200,000
**Official language:** English
**Major religions:** Hindu 52%, Christian 28%, Muslim 17%, other 3%
**Government:** Multi-party democracy
**Currency:** Mauritian rupee

### MADAGASCAR
**Capital city:** Antananarivo
**Area:** 587,040 sq km (226,656 sq miles)
**Population:** 17,400,000
**Official languages:** Malagasy and French
**Major religions:** Christian 41%, traditional beliefs 52%, Muslim 7%
**Government:** Multi-party democracy
**Currency:** Ariary

### SEYCHELLES
**Capital city:** Victoria
**Area:** 455 sq km (176 sq miles)
**Population:** 80,469
**Official language:** French Creole, English, French
**Major religions:** Christian 98%, other 2%
**Government:** Multi-party democracy
**Currency:** Seychelles rupee

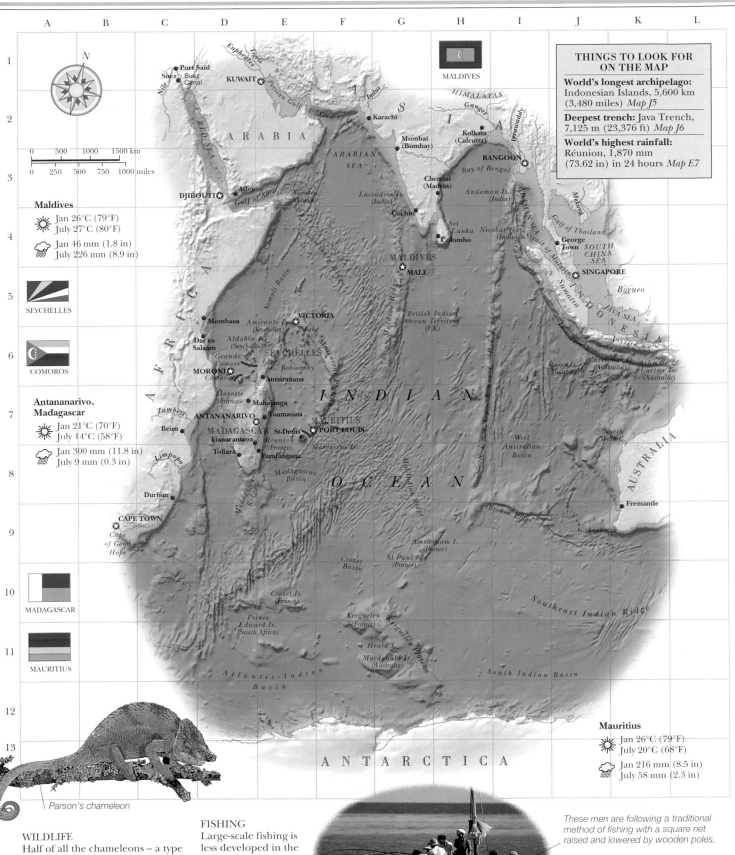

N

A B C D E F G H I J K L
1 2 3 4 5 6 7 8 9 10 11 12 13

0 500 1000 1500 km
0 250 500 750 1000 miles

**Maldives**
☀ Jan 26°C (79°F)
   July 27°C (80°F)
🌧 Jan 46 mm (1.8 in)
   July 226 mm (8.9 in)

SEYCHELLES

COMOROS

**Antananarivo, Madagascar**
☀ Jan 21°C (70°F)
   July 14°C (58°F)
🌧 Jan 300 mm (11.8 in)
   July 9 mm (0.3 in)

MADAGASCAR

MAURITIUS

**Mauritius**
☀ Jan 26°C (79°F)
   July 20°C (68°F)
🌧 Jan 216 mm (8.5 in)
   July 58 mm (2.3 in)

### THINGS TO LOOK FOR ON THE MAP

**World's longest archipelago:** Indonesian Islands, 5,600 km (3,480 miles) *Map J5*

**Deepest trench:** Java Trench, 7,125 m (23,376 ft) *Map J6*

**World's highest rainfall:** Réunion, 1,870 mm (73.62 in) in 24 hours *Map E7*

MALDIVES

Map labels: Port Said, Suez, Suez Canal, KUWAIT, Euphrates, Tigris, Nile, Persian Gulf, Karachi, Indus, Gulf of Oman, RED SEA, ARABIA, Aden, Gulf of Aden, Socotra (Yemen), DJIBOUTI, ARABIAN SEA, Mumbai (Bombay), Kolkata (Calcutta), Ganges, HIMALAYAS, ASIA, Irrawaddy, RANGOON, Chennai (Madras), Laccadive Is. (India), Cochin, Andaman Is. (India), Bay of Bengal, Sri Lanka, Colombo, Nicobar Is. (India), Mekong, Gulf of Thailand, George Town, SOUTH CHINA SEA, Strait of Malacca, SINGAPORE, MALDIVES, MALE, Maldive Ridge, British Indian Ocean Territory (UK), Sumatra, Borneo, JAVA SEA, INDONESIA, Java, AFRICA, Mombasa, Amirante Is. (Seychelles), Mahé, VICTORIA, Aldabra Is. (Seychelles), Dar es Salaam, Grande Comore, MORONI, Comoros, L. Bobaomby, Antsiranana, SEYCHELLES, Somali Basin, Carlsberg Ridge, Mascarene Basin, Mayotte (France), Mahajanga, Zambesi, ANTANANARIVO, Toamasina, MAURITIUS, PORT LOUIS, Beira, MADAGASCAR, St-Denis, Réunion (France), Fianarantsoa, Mascarene Is., Toliara, Farafangana, Madagascar Basin, Limpopo, Madagascar Ridge, Durban, INDIAN OCEAN, Mid-Indian Ridge, Cocos Is. (Australia), Christmas Is. (Australia), Ashmore & Cartier Is. (Australia), West Australian Basin, North West C., AUSTRALIA, CAPE TOWN, Cape of Good Hope, Fremantle, Broken Ridge, Amsterdam I. (France), St Paul I. (France), Crozet Basin, Southeast Indian Ridge, Crozet Is. (France), Prince Edward Is. (South Africa), Kerguelen (France), Kerguelen Plateau, Heard I., Macdonald Is. (Australia), Atlantic-Indian Basin, South Indian Basin, ANTARCTICA

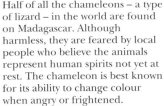

*Parson's chameleon*

### WILDLIFE
Half of all the chameleons – a type of lizard – in the world are found on Madagascar. Although harmless, they are feared by local people who believe the animals represent human spirits not yet at rest. The chameleon is best known for its ability to change colour when angry or frightened.

### FISHING
Large-scale fishing is less developed in the Indian Ocean than in the Atlantic or Pacific because there are not as many areas of shallow sea. Most of the fish are caught by shore-based fishermen for family use or to sell in a local market.

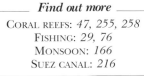

*Fishermen bring in the catch in the Maldives.*

These men are following a traditional method of fishing with a square net raised and lowered by wooden poles.

### Find out more
CORAL REEFS: *47, 255, 258*
FISHING: *29, 76*
MONSOON: *166*
SUEZ CANAL: *216*

# AFRICA

THE SECOND LARGEST CONTINENT, Africa is a land of contrasts. To the north lies the great Sahara, the largest desert in the world. The central parts, which the Equator runs through, are covered in dense tropical rainforests, while further south a series of grassy plateaux (areas of flat highland) give way to narrow coastal plains. Major mountain ranges include the Atlas in the north and the Ruwenzori range on the Uganda-Democratic Republic of Congo border. Africa's highest mountain is Kilimanjaro, a dormant volcano in Tanzania. To the east is the Great Rift Valley, which contains several huge lakes. Some of the world's longest rivers drain the continent, including the Nile, Niger, Congo, and the Zambezi.

## DESERTS

Africa has three huge deserts. The vast Sahara is the world's largest desert, and dominates the northern third of the continent. Thousands of years ago, the Sahara had a moist climate. Today, the path of wet winds blowing in from the sea is blocked by other winds blowing outwards from the desert. The Namib and Kalahari deserts cover large areas of southwest Africa. Although it lies along the coast, the Namib Desert (shown here), is particularly barren and dry.

## GREAT RIFT VALLEY

The Great Rift Valley stretches from Mozambique in the south, through east Africa and the Red Sea, into Syria. In most places the valley is 30–100 km (19–62 miles) wide, with steep sides rising up to 2,000 m (6,562 ft). The valley was formed as blocks of land sank between faults in the Earth's crust. In east Africa, the valley has two main branches. The Rift Valley is marked by volcanoes, hot springs, and a long chain of lakes.

**Formation of a rift valley**

*Movements deep within the Earth's crust cause stretching, and cracks appear on the surface.*

*Surface cracks*

*Block mountains*

*Lake*  *Volcano*

*The cracking creates long faults. Some blocks of land slip down between parallel faults to create a rift valley.*

### RAINFORESTS

The world's second largest rainforest, after the Amazon, lies in central Africa. It teems with plant and animal life, including rare creatures such as okapis. It was also the home of several groups of pygmies, but many now live in settled villages, as vast areas of forest have been destroyed for logging and farming. One group, the Bambuti, still live in the northeast forests of Democratic Republic of Congo.

*Millions of flamingos flock to Lake Turkana and other Rift Valley lakes to nest and feed on tiny water plants.*

## LAKE VICTORIA

Lake Victoria is Africa's largest lake and the second largest freshwater lake in the world. Lying on the Equator, between Kenya, Tanzania, and Uganda, it covers about 69,484 sq km (26,828 sq miles) and reaches 82 m (269 ft) at its deepest point. The River Nile flows out of the northern end of the lake. Lake Victoria is rich in fish, which provide an important source of income for the large numbers of people living along the lake shores.

### DRAKENSBERG MOUNTAINS

The highest mountains in southern Africa are the Drakensberg. They form part of the rim of a saucer-shaped plateau of high land, called the Great Escarpment. In the local Zulu language, the mountains are known as *Quathlamba*, which means the "barrier of pointed spears". The highest peak, Thabana Ntlenyana, rises 3,482 m (11,424 ft) above sea level, and is capped with snow in winter.

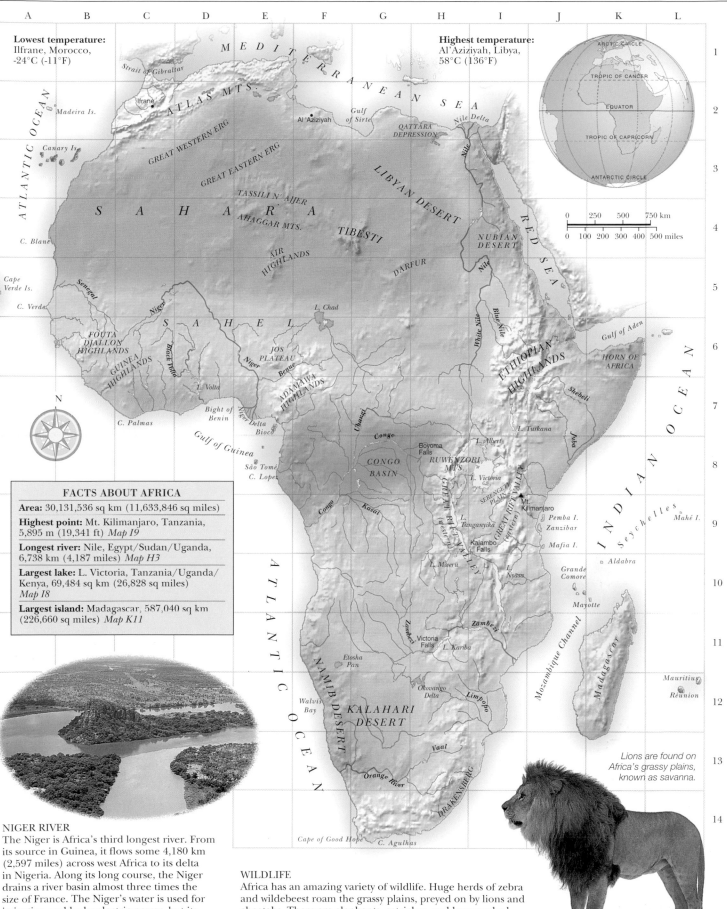

Lowest temperature:
Ilfrane, Morocco,
-24°C (-11°F)

Highest temperature:
Al'Aziziyah, Libya,
58°C (136°F)

## FACTS ABOUT AFRICA

**Area:** 30,131,536 sq km (11,633,846 sq miles)

**Highest point:** Mt. Kilimanjaro, Tanzania, 5,895 m (19,341 ft) *Map I9*

**Longest river:** Nile, Egypt/Sudan/Uganda, 6,738 km (4,187 miles) *Map H3*

**Largest lake:** L. Victoria, Tanzania/Uganda/Kenya, 69,484 sq km (26,828 sq miles) *Map I8*

**Largest island:** Madagascar, 587,040 sq km (226,660 sq miles) *Map K11*

*Lions are found on Africa's grassy plains, known as savanna.*

## NIGER RIVER

The Niger is Africa's third longest river. From its source in Guinea, it flows some 4,180 km (2,597 miles) across west Africa to its delta in Nigeria. Along its long course, the Niger drains a river basin almost three times the size of France. The Niger's water is used for irrigation and hydroelectric power, but its usefulness for transport is limited by its many waterfalls and rapids.

## WILDLIFE

Africa has an amazing variety of wildlife. Huge herds of zebra and wildebeest roam the grassy plains, preyed on by lions and cheetahs. There are elephants, ostriches, and long-necked giraffes. Hippos wallow in rivers and swamps. In the rainforests live chimpanzees and gorillas, among the rarest animals on Earth.

# PEOPLES OF AFRICA

Population: approximately
849,000,000 people
Number of countries: 53

AFRICA IS HOME TO about 849 million people – more than one in eight of the world's population. The most densely populated areas are along the northern and western coasts, especially in the fertile valleys of the Nile, Niger, Congo, and Senegal rivers. The population of Africa is growing rapidly, as birth rates in many African countries are extremely high. Families are often large, and about half the population is young, aged below 15 years. Although most Africans live in the countryside, a growing number are now found in towns and cities. Many people have moved there because of poverty and lack of work in country areas; others have gone to escape civil wars, droughts, and famines.

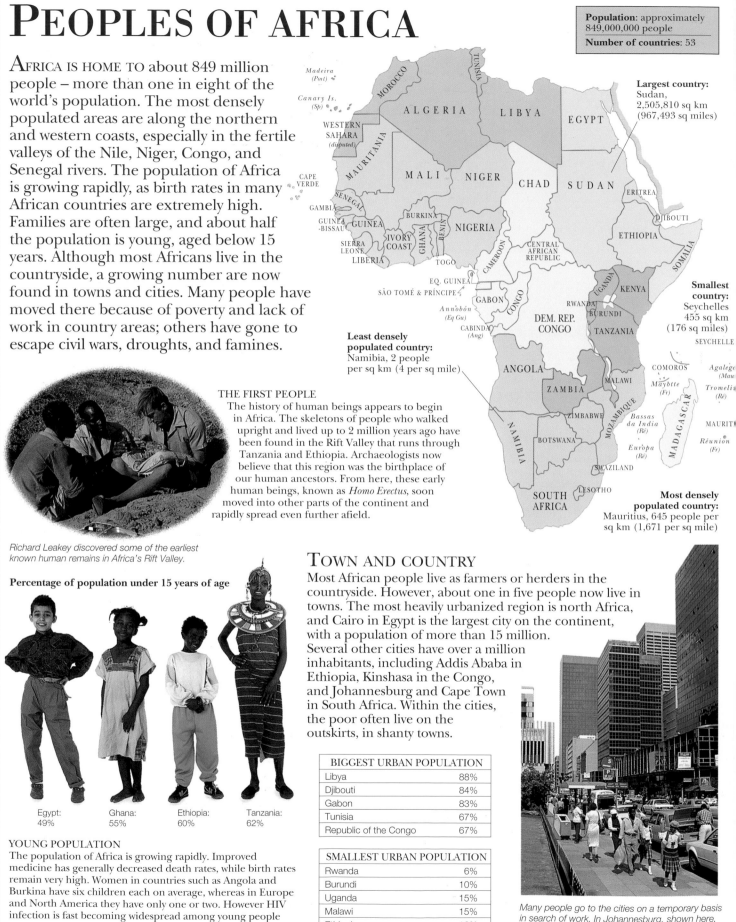

Largest country:
Sudan,
2,505,810 sq km
(967,493 sq miles)

Smallest country:
Seychelles
455 sq km
(176 sq miles)

Least densely populated country:
Namibia, 2 people per sq km (4 per sq mile)

Most densely populated country:
Mauritius, 645 people per sq km (1,671 per sq mile)

### THE FIRST PEOPLE

The history of human beings appears to begin in Africa. The skeletons of people who walked upright and lived up to 2 million years ago have been found in the Rift Valley that runs through Tanzania and Ethiopia. Archaeologists now believe that this region was the birthplace of our human ancestors. From here, these early human beings, known as *Homo Erectus*, soon moved into other parts of the continent and rapidly spread even further afield.

*Richard Leakey discovered some of the earliest known human remains in Africa's Rift Valley.*

**Percentage of population under 15 years of age**

Egypt:
49%

Ghana:
55%

Ethiopia:
60%

Tanzania:
62%

### YOUNG POPULATION

The population of Africa is growing rapidly. Improved medicine has generally decreased death rates, while birth rates remain very high. Women in countries such as Angola and Burkina have six children each on average, whereas in Europe and North America they have only one or two. However HIV infection is fast becoming widespread among young people and is likely to kill many in the near future.

## TOWN AND COUNTRY

Most African people live as farmers or herders in the countryside. However, about one in five people now live in towns. The most heavily urbanized region is north Africa, and Cairo in Egypt is the largest city on the continent, with a population of more than 15 million. Several other cities have over a million inhabitants, including Addis Ababa in Ethiopia, Kinshasa in the Congo, and Johannesburg and Cape Town in South Africa. Within the cities, the poor often live on the outskirts, in shanty towns.

| BIGGEST URBAN POPULATION | |
|---|---|
| Libya | 88% |
| Djibouti | 84% |
| Gabon | 83% |
| Tunisia | 67% |
| Republic of the Congo | 67% |

| SMALLEST URBAN POPULATION | |
|---|---|
| Rwanda | 6% |
| Burundi | 10% |
| Uganda | 15% |
| Malawi | 15% |
| Ethiopia | 16% |

*Many people go to the cities on a temporary basis in search of work. In Johannesburg, shown here, migrants seek work in the gold and diamond mines.*

## THE PEOPLE

The vast Sahara separates the peoples of northern Africa, who are mostly Berbers and Arabs, like these Tunisian men, from those to the south, who are mostly Negroid. Northern Africa is predominantly Islamic, but south of the Sahara people follow a variety of religions, including Christianity and traditional animist beliefs. Two other groups are also important: there are about 8 million people of European descent, who live mainly in southern Africa, as well as a large number of Indians who live along the eastern coast and in South Africa.

## ART

Africa has produced a great variety of art from prehistoric times to the present. Often, art was related to ritual or tribal ceremonies, as well as being used for decoration. In many tribes the artist was given high status and art was often regarded as an essential part of religion. It is possible to isolate different areas and different practices of African art. From around 7000 BC rock drawings include representations of animals and hunters. Tribal art has become a way of distinguishing one tribe from another and can take many forms, including body painting and sculptural masks.

*Bronze head of the Queen Mother of Benin, made using the lost wax process.*

# PEOPLES AND COUNTRIES

There are more than 600 ethnic or tribal groups in Africa, and only 53 countries. Many of today's national boundaries were created in the late 19th century by the colonial rulers. Borders sometimes follow natural features, such as rivers, but often they just follow straight lines on the map. As a result, tribes are often split between different countries. The Ewe people, for example, are divided between Ghana and Togo. After independence, it has often proved difficult to create unity among the different peoples in one country.

*Groups of nomadic Fulani people are found throughout the area shaded brown on this map of west Africa. They roam across many countries.*

WEST AFRICA

*Groundnuts (peanuts) are one of the main export crops in west Africa.*

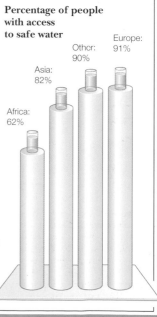

*These refugees at a camp in Rwanda are Hutu people from neighbouring Burundi. War between the Hutu and Tutsi peoples has forced thousands of people in this region to leave their homes.*

# ECONOMIC PROBLEMS

Most African countries rely on exporting raw materials, such as coffee, cocoa, or oil. In recent years, the prices of these products have been falling. In contrast, the cost of importing machinery and other manufactured goods has risen. So the amount that African countries can earn from their exports is often less than what they have to spend on imports. These factors, along with the growing population and the effects of drought and war, mean that the economies of many African countries are in difficulty.

# FRESH WATER

Only around 62 per cent of Africans have access to safe water. Often people must make long journeys to collect water and millions are forced to drink water that is contaminated by dangerous bacteria. The situation is worst across central Africa where the hot climate and lack of investment makes clean water scarce. Aid agencies have made access to clean water a key issue and have used funding to build safe water wells and educate people about the importance of hygiene.

**Percentage of people with access to safe water**

Africa: 62%
Asia: 82%
Other: 90%
Europe: 91%

# NORTHWEST AFRICA

THE FOUR COUNTRIES of Morocco, Algeria, Tunisia, and Libya make up the northwest corner of Africa. This region has a long and varied history, due to its situation between the rest of Africa, Western Europe, and the Middle East. Most of its people are Arabic-speaking Muslims whose ancestors came to northwest Africa from the Middle East. From the 1530s to the 1830s, the region was part of the Turkish Ottoman Empire. It was then ruled by the colonial powers of France, Italy, and Spain, until the various countries gained independence in the mid-1900s. The countries of northwest Africa are relatively wealthy, thanks largely to their rich supplies of oil and gas.

### ALONG THE COAST
The vast majority of northwest Africa's 75 million people live along the narrow coastal plain that borders the Mediterranean Sea and the Atlantic Ocean. Here, the climate is warm and wet in winter, and hot and dry in summer, making it more suitable for farming than the arid desert further inland. Citrus fruits, dates, olives, tomatoes, and flowers are grown. The major towns and cities are located here too.

## A GROWING POPULATION
One of the most serious problems facing northwest Africa is the rapid growth of its population. In Algeria alone, the population increased from 12 million to 31 million between 1966–2000. Millions of people have moved from the countryside to the cities in search of work. This has led to severe housing shortages in the city centres and to the rise of overcrowded shanty towns on the outskirts.

*This mosque with its rounded dome and towering minarets reveals the Arabic influence on religion and architecture.*

### ARAB INFLUENCE
The Arab invasions of the 7th and 8th centuries have had a long-lasting effect on northwest Africa. The Arabs soon outnumbered the local Berber people who rebelled against their rule. They quickly established their own language, Arabic, and their own religion, Islam, throughout the region. Despite the later arrival of European colonists, northwest Africa today, in its language, culture, religion, and architecture, remains firmly part of the Arab world.

MOROCCO

Tangier
Tétou
Kénitra
RABAT
Casablanca
Meknès
Safi
Khouribga
Essaouira
Beni Mellal
Er Ra
Marrakesh
Djebel Toubkal
Boumalne
-Dades
Agadir
Tiznit
ATL
Tan-Tan
MOROC

A T L A N T I C   O C E A N

LAYOUNE

Smara
Tindouf

W E S T E R N   S A H A R A

M A U R I T A N I A

Ad Dakhla

*Morocco occupied the whole of Western Sahara in 1979.*

Lagouira

**Marrakesh, Morocco**
Jan 11°C (53°F)
July 29°C (84°F)
Jan 25 mm (1 in)
July 3 mm (0.1 in)

| 0 | 100 | 200 | 300 | 400 km |
| 0 | 50 | 100 | 150 | 200 | 250 miles |

N

**In Salah, Algeria**
Jan 14°C (56°F)
July 37°C (98°F)
Jan 3 mm (0.1 in)
July 0 mm (0 in)

TROPIC OF CANCER
EQUATOR
TROPIC OF CAPRICORN

A     B     C     D     E     F     G

*The Tuareg ride on camel back, although motorbikes and four-wheeled drive trucks are increasingly used.*

# SAHARA DESERT

Much of northwest Africa is covered by the scorching sand and rocks of the Sahara Desert. The world's largest desert, the Sahara is expanding at an alarming rate as the land at its edges is overgrazed and gradually turned to dust. Despite daytime temperatures of up to 50°C (122°F), freezing nights, and years on end without rain, the desert is home to some amazing animals which have adapted to survive the conditions.

*The fennec fox's huge ears let heat escape from its body, cooling it down.*

## DESERT PEOPLES

Few people can survive in the harsh environment of the Sahara Desert. The hardy Tuareg are desert nomads who may travel vast distances a day, carrying salt to trade in markets. Traditionally, the Tuareg use camels for transport, and also to provide milk, meat, and hides. However, many Tuareg are now abandoning their centuries-old nomadic lifestyle and settling in the cities.

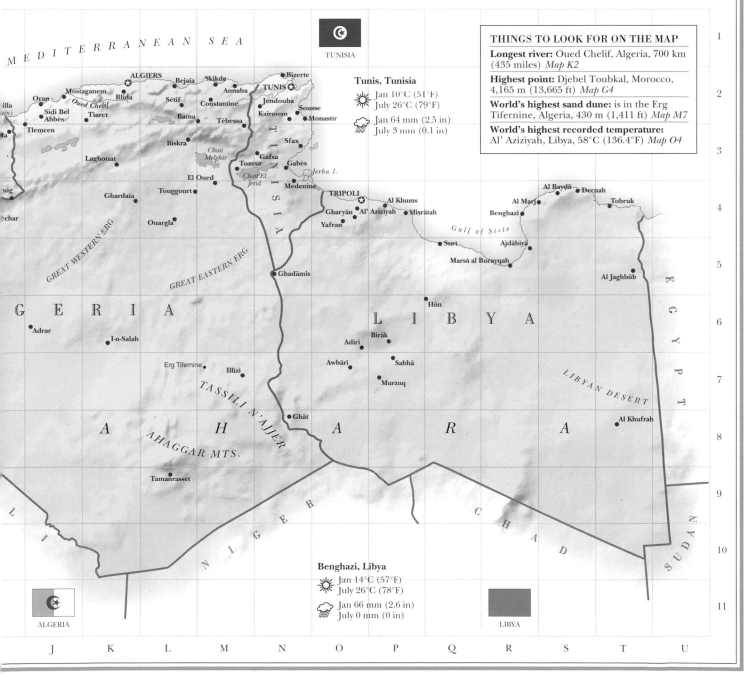

TUNISIA

**Tunis, Tunisia**
Jan 10°C (51°F)
July 26°C (79°F)
Jan 64 mm (2.5 in)
July 3 mm (0.1 in)

### THINGS TO LOOK FOR ON THE MAP

**Longest river:** Oued Chelif, Algeria, 700 km (435 miles) *Map K2*

**Highest point:** Djebel Toubkal, Morocco, 4,165 m (13,665 ft) *Map G4*

**World's highest sand dune:** is in the Erg Tifernine, Algeria, 430 m (1,411 ft) *Map M7*

**World's highest recorded temperature:** Al' Aziziyah, Libya, 58°C (136.4°F) *Map O4*

**Benghazi, Libya**
Jan 14°C (57°F)
July 26°C (78°F)
Jan 66 mm (2.6 in)
July 0 mm (0 in)

ALGERIA

LIBYA

# MOROCCO

MOROCCO'S WARM CLIMATE, sandy beaches, and stunning mountain scenery make it a popular winter destination for holiday makers. Tourism, along with agriculture and phosphate production, is vital to the country's economy. In 1956, Morocco gained its independence from the French who had governed it since 1912. It is one of the few Arab countries to be ruled by a king, Mohammed VI. Since coming to the throne in 1999, King Mohammed has won international recognition for his moderate leadership. The main issues facing Morocco today are Islamic fundamentalism and the undecided fate of the Western Sahara region in the south.

Berber wedding ceremony

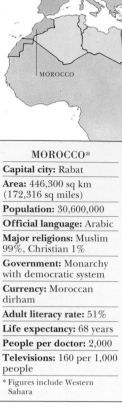

| MOROCCO* |
| --- |
| **Capital city:** Rabat |
| **Area:** 446,300 sq km (172,316 sq miles) |
| **Population:** 30,600,000 |
| **Official language:** Arabic |
| **Major religions:** Muslim 99%, Christian 1% |
| **Government:** Monarchy with democratic system |
| **Currency:** Moroccan dirham |
| **Adult literacy rate:** 51% |
| **Life expectancy:** 68 years |
| **People per doctor:** 2,000 |
| **Televisions:** 160 per 1,000 people |
| * Figures include Western Sahara |

## BERBERS

Since the Arab invasions of the 8th century, the local Berber people have lived in villages high up in the Atlas Mountains. Most Berbers converted to Islam but kept their own culture and way of life. They call themselves *Imazighen*, or "people of the land". Today, about a third of Moroccans are Berber-speaking, although most also speak Arabic and French.

*Carpets with symbolic patterns and ornate metalwork lanterns are made by local people.*

## AN ISLAMIC CITY

The ancient Moroccan city of Fez is a good example of a traditional Islamic town. Each part has been designed with a purpose, as set out in the Koran, the Muslim holy book. The streets are narrow to provide shade, but wide enough to let a pair of fully laden camels pass through. Houses have small, high-up windows on to the street, to guard their owners' privacy. In the city centre stands the largest mosque, surrounded by the *souks*, or markets.

*The numerous, carefully planned streets in the old city of Fez look chaotic from a distance.*

## ARTS AND CRAFTS

Millions of tourists visit Morocco each year to relax on the beaches along the Atlantic coast or to explore the historical cities of Fez and Marrakesh. The cities' colourful *souks*, or markets, are a treasure chest of traditional goods and handicrafts, such as Moroccan leather, silver jewellery, and hand-woven carpets.

*A supporter of the Polisario in the Western Sahara.*

### WESTERN SAHARA

This is a desert region south of Morocco with a population of some 200,000 people. It was formerly ruled by Spain. Since 1975, Morocco has been fighting a war for control of the region and its valuable mineral resources. Opposing the Moroccans are the Polisario, a guerilla force of desert tribesmen who are aiming for complete independence for the Western Sahara.

*A phosphate-processing factory in the south of Morocco.*

## ECONOMY

Morocco's economy depends on three major industries – tourism, agriculture, and phosphates. Farm products make up about a third of exports. The main crops are cereals, vegetables, citrus fruits, and dates. Irrigation systems pipe water to many dry areas for farming. Morocco is the world's third largest producer of phosphates, which are used to make chemicals and fertilizers. Large factories process the phosphates for export.

*Find out more*

CARPET MAKING: *144, 155, 165*
IRRIGATION: *155, 156, 217*
ISLAM: *275*
MONARCHY: *270–271*

# ALGERIA

STRETCHING FROM THE MEDITERRANEAN coast deep into the heart of the Sahara, Algeria is the second largest country in Africa. It won independence from France in 1962, after a bitter, eight-year struggle that claimed one million lives. During French rule, tens of thousands of Europeans arrived, many of them later leaving after independence. Since then, Algeria has played an important part in world affairs as a member of the United Nations and the Arab League. The main challenge facing the democratic government today comes from the Islamic fundamentalists who support the setting up of an Islamic government.

## ALGERIA

**Capital city:** Algiers

**Area:** 2,381,740 sq km (919,590 sq miles)

**Population:** 31,800,000

**Official language:** Arabic

**Major religions:** Muslim 99%, other 1%

**Government:** Democratic government

**Currency:** Algerian dinar

**Adult literacy rate:** 69%

**Life expectancy:** 71 years

**People per doctor:** 1,000

**Televisions:** 105 per 1,000 people

### ALGIERS
Algiers, the capital of Algeria, is the country's largest city and most important port. The city was founded in the 10th century by Muslims from Arabia. It was seized by the Turks in 1518 and by the French in 1830. The French influence can still be seen in these buildings in the modern part of the city along the Bay of Algiers. The old city, with its narrow streets, mosques, and markets, stands on the slopes of the Sahel Hills.

*The leaves of date palms are used for thatching.*

*Arabs selling local produce at a market in Ghardaia, Algeria.*

*Dates can be eaten in many ways.*

*Wood is used for timber*

*Date palms are grown at desert oases, where water comes up to the surface.*

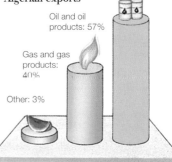

### Algerian exports
Oil and oil products: 57%

Gas and gas products: 40%

Other: 3%

### ETHNIC MIX
Almost 32 million people live in Algeria. Although the vast majority of Algerians are Arabs, about a quarter of the population are descendants of the earlier Berber settlers. Arabic is the official language and Islam the main religion. Of the million or so Europeans who settled in Algeria before independence, only a few thousand still live here. These include people of French, Spanish, and Italian descent.

### ECONOMY
Algeria's economy is dependent on its oil and gas reserves. These come from large deposits in the Sahara. Oil production began in 1958 and, by 1979, had reached 1.2 million barrels a day. Although falling world oil prices in the 1980s and 1990s caused a drop in oil production, the exploitation of natural gas has since increased. Algeria supplies both France and Italy with gas.

## FARMING
Algeria cannot grow enough crops to feed its rapidly increasing population and has to import about three-quarters of the food it needs. However, about a quarter of the workforce is employed in farming. Major crops include cereals, citrus fruits, grapes, olives, and tobacco. Figs and dates are important too. Algeria is one of the world's leading producers of dates and of cork, which is made from cork oak bark. Dates are eaten fresh, dried or ground into flour. Roasted and ground date stones are made into date coffee.

### TERRORIST ATTACKS
Islamic fundamentalists, like these members of the Islamic Salvation Front (FIS), are in open revolt against Algeria's government. Thousands of Algerians have died in recent years as a result of terrorist violence. Westerners have also been attacked and bombs have been planted in Paris and other French cities.

| *Find out more* |
| --- |
| COLONIAL PERIOD: *207* |
| ISLAM: *275* |
| OIL & GAS: *137, 152, 163, 211* |
| SAHARA: *204, 209* |

# TUNISIA

NORTHWEST AFRICA'S SMALLEST country, Tunisia lies between Libya to the south and Algeria to the west. Throughout its history, Tunisia has had close links with Europe. It was at the heart of the ancient empire of Carthage in the 4th century BC, and later became part of the mighty Roman empire. In the 7th century AD, Tunisia was colonized by Muslim Arabs, and, in the early 1880s, by French forces. It became independent in 1956. The government has since been restructured and a multi-party system introduced.

| TUNISIA | |
|---|---|
| **Capital city:** Tunis | |
| **Area:** 163,610 sq km (63,169 sq miles) | |
| **Population:** 9,800,000 | |
| **Official language:** Arabic | |
| **Major religions:** Muslim 98%, Christian 1%, Jewish 1% | |
| **Government:** Multi-party democracy | |
| **Currency:** Tunisian dinar | |
| **Adult literacy rate:** 73% | |
| **Life expectancy:** 73 years | |
| **People per doctor:** 1,429 | |
| **Televisions:** 334 per 1,000 people | |

*A heap of steamed couscous served with roast chicken and sausages.*

*Brightly dyed wool will soon be woven into carpets.*

## TUNISIAN FOOD

Traditional food is influenced by Arabic, Turkish, and French cooking. The national dish is *couscous*, a mix of semolina, meat, and vegetables. Spicy stews cooked in clay pots, called *tajines*, are also popular. For dessert, people eat fruit, dates stuffed with almond paste, or *baklava*, a sweet nut and honey pastry. To drink, there is strong black coffee or mint tea. Many Tunisian men go to cafés in the evening to meet friends and drink coffee.

*A glass of strong, sweet mint tea.*

## INDUSTRY

Until the collapse of world oil prices in the 1980s, Tunisia's major exports were oil and gas. Today, textiles and agricultural products have become much more important. Tunisia is also one of the world's leading producers of calcium phosphates, used to make chemicals and fertilizers. Most of the country's industries are located in and around the capital city, Tunis.

## TOURISM

Tunisia's warm winter climate and historic sites attract numerous tourists each year. Until 1976, tourism was Tunisia's highest earner of foreign currency. Numbers fell in the early 1980s but have now risen again to over 5 million per year. The government has encouraged the building of new hotels and the development of resorts to meet the growing demand. Hundreds of thousands of Tunisians are employed in the tourist industry.

Libya: 25%
Germany: 12%
France: 17%
Algeria: 14%
Other: 32%

*Most tourists come from neighbouring Algeria and Libya, and from Europe. Cheaper air travel and the search for an exotic holiday location have made Tunisia a favourite destination for Europeans.*

### ARTS AND CRAFTS

One of the liveliest parts of a Tunisian city is the *souk*, or market. The souk is a maze of narrow, winding streets, each crowded with traders and craftsmen selling their wares. Here, you can buy a wide range of traditional arts and crafts, including copper pots and pans, carpets, leather goods, jewellery, and embroidered cloth. Other stalls sell fish, meat, fruit, and vegetables.

*Grapes grow well in Tunisia's light soil and strong sunshine.*

*Oranges and limes come from groves along the fertile coast.*

*Dates are grown in the desert oases in the dry south.*

### AGRICULTURE

About two-thirds of Tunisia is suitable for farming. Many areas suffer from a lack of rainfall and rely on irrigation to water crops. The main crops include cereals, such as wheat and barley, citrus fruits, grapes, figs, dates, and olives. Tunisia is the world's fourth largest producer of olive oil. Despite efforts to improve output, however, Tunisia still has to import many basic foods.

*Find out more*

OIL & GAS: *137, 152, 163, 211*
OLIVES: *130*
POLITICAL SYSTEMS: *270–271*

# LIBYA

SITUATED ON THE MEDITERRANEAN COAST between Egypt and Algeria, Libya is the fourth largest country in Africa. It has been part of the Roman, Byzantine, Arab, and Ottoman empires, and from 1911 to 1943 was an Italian colony. The Sahara covers about 90 per cent of the country, so farming is only possible along the coastal strip, where many people work as sheep or goat herders. The discovery of oil in 1959 very quickly transformed Libya from a poor to a wealthy country. Many foreigners have since arrived to work in the oil industry.

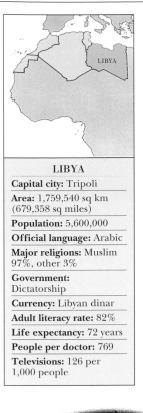

### LIBYA

**Capital city:** Tripoli

**Area:** 1,759,540 sq km (679,358 sq miles)

**Population:** 5,600,000

**Official language:** Arabic

**Major religions:** Muslim 97%, other 3%

**Government:** Dictatorship

**Currency:** Libyan dinar

**Adult literacy rate:** 82%

**Life expectancy:** 72 years

**People per doctor:** 769

**Televisions:** 126 per 1,000 people

## OIL AND GAS

The production of oil and gas dominates the Libyan economy, with oil making up 98 per cent of the country's exports. Before oil was discovered, Libya's major exports were rushes and scrap metal. Most of the oil is produced in western Libya but there are also some offshore oil reserves. As the oil industry has grown so have Libya's cities, providing more houses, jobs, and services. Some 88 per cent of the population are now city dwellers. Before this, many people lived in the countryside as farmers or nomads.

**Where people live**

88% live in cities          12% live in the country

## FAMILY GROUPS
Most Libyans are Arabs, with some Berbers and Tuaregs in the south. Almost all are Muslim. They belong to large, extended family groups, called tribes or clans. The clan is an important part of society and also has an influence on politics. Many of Colonel Gaddafi's government ministers are members of his clan. People's names often reveal which clan they belong to.

## COLONEL GADDAFI
Since 1969, Libya has been ruled by Colonel Muammar Gaddafi, who overthrew the king to become president. Gaddafi rules through military committees. His politics are a very personal mix of socialism, Islam, and Arab nationalism. Since all political parties were banned in 1971, any opposition to Gaddafi's rule has to come from outside Libya. In the past Colonel Gaddafi's support for terrorist organizations has brought him into conflict with Western governments.

## OASIS TOWN
In the vast, arid desert, small towns and villages have grown up around oases. Here, underground water rises to create rare patches of fertile land where crops are grown. The communities that live around oases rely on farming, receiving money from relations working in the cities, and dealing with passing traders. In the past, oasis towns were important stopping places for camel caravans transporting goods across the desert. Today, many of these journeys are made by truck instead.

*People grow crops such as date palms, grapes, figs, and peaches.*

*Rain falls in the mountains and sinks into the porous rock.*

*A small village grows up at the edge of the oasis.*

*Impermeable rock stops the water sinking further.*

*Rainfall is stored in porous rock called an aquifer.*

*Water seeps up through a split in the rock layers.*

## ROMAN RUINS
Signs of Libya's rich classical past can still be seen in its many historical ruins. It has some of the finest Roman ruins in North Africa, such as the impressive site of Leptis Magna which has a forum, aqueduct, and amphitheatre (shown left). This port was founded by the Phoenicians in about 800 BC and became a major centre for trade with Africa. It was then part of the Roman empire, before the Arab invasions of the 7th century AD led to the city's downfall.

*Find out more*

ISLAM: *275*
OIL: *137, 152, 281*
OIL WEALTH: *137, 278*
SAHARA: *204, 209*

# NORTHEAST AFRICA

NORTHEAST AFRICA CONTAINS EGYPT and Sudan, two desert lands watered by the River Nile, and the region known as the Horn of Africa, so-called because it is shaped like an animal horn. The region consists of Somalia, Djibouti, Ethiopia, and Eritrea, which are among the poorest countries in the world. The boundaries that divide them date from the last 100 years and follow the borders drawn up by the old colonial rulers of the area. Many people that live here are nomadic herders and take little notice of the borders as they travel over vast areas in search of pasture for their animals.

**BASIC TOOLS**
Farming methods in the area are often inefficient and simple tools, such as hoes, digging sticks, and sickles, are widely used. The ox-drawn scratch plough (above) is light and can be carried to scattered fields. But it only turns over the surface layer of the soil and does not allow nutrients to spread deeper, so after a few years the soil is no longer fertile.

## TROUBLED LANDS

In recent years, the countries of Somalia, Sudan, Ethiopia, and Eritrea have been devastated by war. In 1993, Eritrea gained independence from Ethiopia, after a civil war that lasted 20 years. Somalia has been torn apart by civil war between its rival groups, or clans. Conflict between the Arabic-speaking Muslims in the north and the African, non-Muslim peoples in the south of Sudan ravaged the country for years.

*Thousands of Eritrean women fought alongside men in the war against Ethiopia, and many held positions of command.*

**INTERNATIONAL AID**
Many parts of northeast Africa have suffered from drought and famine in recent years. In 1984–85, a terrible famine swept through Ethiopia. It was caused by a combination of drought, warfare, and population growth. The famine drew the world's attention to the region and a huge international aid effort was launched, helped by the pop charity, Band Aid.

*The White Nile meanders slowly through the Sudd, a vast region of dense reed swamps in Sudan.*

*The White Nile and the Blue Nile meet at Khartoum in Sudan to form the Nile River.*

*As the Nile reaches the border of Sudan and Egypt, it flows into Lake Nasser, one of the world's largest artificial lakes. The lake was created by the building of the Aswan High Dam.*

*Many birds, including storks, herons, and pelicans, make their home in the Sudd.*

*The Blue Nile begins at Lake Tana. It flows through the mountains of Ethiopia, collecting rainfall along the way.*

*Fertile farmland*

## THE RIVER NILE

The world's longest river, the River Nile, flows northwards from Lake Victoria in Kenya through the Sahara Desert to the Mediterranean Sea. It passes through Ethiopia, Sudan, and Egypt, providing precious water for drinking, farming, and fishing. The river is also a major tourist attraction. People travel along the Nile on cruise liners and traditional sailing boats, called *feluccas*, to see the ancient sites of Egypt.

*North of the Aswan Dam, the Nile is surrounded by desert, but rich, fertile land lies along the banks of the river.*

*Feluccas are now mainly used by tourists.*

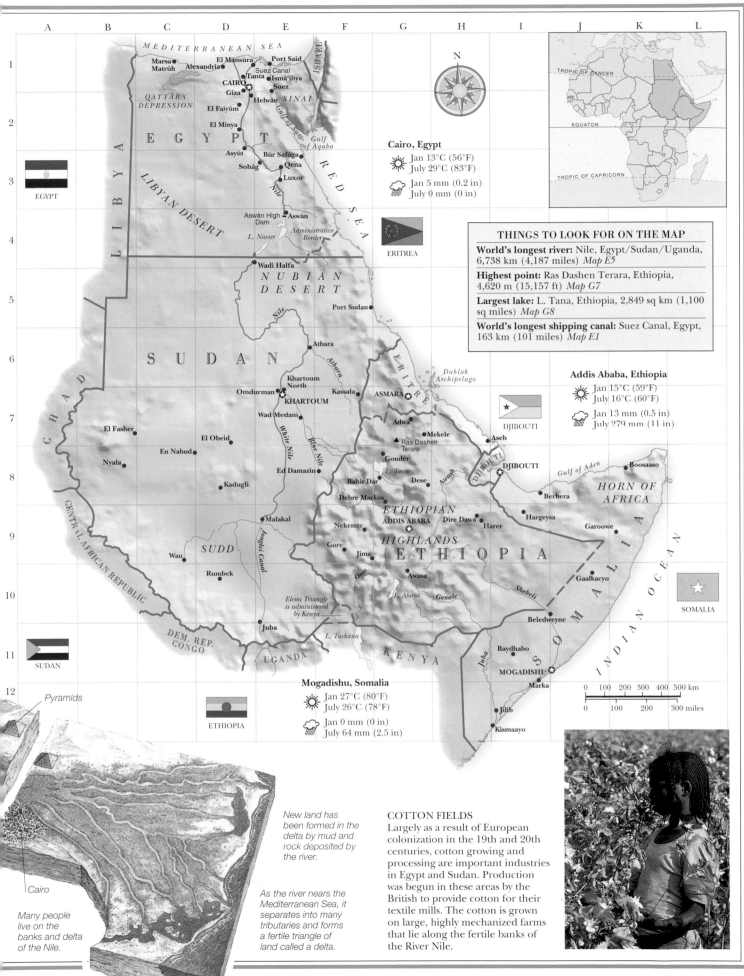

A B C D E F G H I J K L

1 2 3 4 5 6 7 8 9 10 11 12

**MEDITERRANEAN SEA**

Marsa
Matrûh
Alexandria
El Mansûra
Port Said
Suez Canal
Tanta Ismâ'iliya
CAIRO
Giza Suez
Helwan
EL Faiyûm
El Minya

**EGYPT**

SINAI

ISRAEL

Gulf of Suez

Gulf of Aqaba

QATTÂRA
DEPRESSION

Asyût Bûr Safâga
Sohâg Qena
Luxor

Nile

**RED SEA**

Aswân High Dam — Aswân
L. Nasser
Administrative Border

**LIBYAN DESERT**

LIBYA

Wadi Halfa

**NUBIAN DESERT**

Port Sudan

**SUDAN**

Nile

Atbara
Atbara

Khartoum North
Omdurman
KHARTOUM
Kassala
Wad Medani

White Nile
Blue Nile

**ERITREA**

ASMARA

Adwa
Mekele
Aseb

Adigrat

Ras Dashen Terara
Gonder
L. Tana

**DJIBOUTI**

DJIBOUTI

Gulf of Aden

Boosaaso

**HORN OF AFRICA**

Berbera

Hargeysa

Garoowe

El Fasher
En Nahud
El Obeid

Nyala
Kadugli

Ed Damazin

Bahir Dar
Debre Markos
Dese

Atbara

**ETHIOPIAN HIGHLANDS**

Nekemte
ADDIS ABABA
Dire Dawa
Harer

Gore
Jima

**ETHIOPIA**

Awasa

Malakal

Jonglei Canal

**SUDD**

Wau

Rumbek

Omo

L. Abaya
Genale

Shebeli

Gaalkacyo

**SOMALIA**

**INDIAN OCEAN**

Elemi Triangle is administered by Kenya

Juba

**UGANDA**

L. Turkana

**KENYA**

Beledweyne

Baydhabo

Juba

MOGADISHU

Marka

Jilib

Kismaayo

**CHAD**

**CENTRAL AFRICAN REPUBLIC**

**DEM. REP. CONGO**

N

**Cairo, Egypt**
☀ Jan 13°C (56°F)
July 29°C (83°F)
🌧 Jan 5 mm (0.2 in)
July 0 mm (0 in)

TROPIC OF CANCER
EQUATOR
TROPIC OF CAPRICORN

### THINGS TO LOOK FOR ON THE MAP

**World's longest river:** Nile, Egypt/Sudan/Uganda, 6,738 km (4,187 miles) *Map E5*

**Highest point:** Ras Dashen Terara, Ethiopia, 4,620 m (15,157 ft) *Map G7*

**Largest lake:** L. Tana, Ethiopia, 2,849 sq km (1,100 sq miles) *Map G8*

**World's longest shipping canal:** Suez Canal, Egypt, 163 km (101 miles) *Map E1*

**Addis Ababa, Ethiopia**
☀ Jan 15°C (59°F)
July 16°C (60°F)
🌧 Jan 13 mm (0.5 in)
July 279 mm (11 in)

Dahlak Archipelago

**Mogadishu, Somalia**
☀ Jan 27°C (80°F)
July 26°C (78°F)
🌧 Jan 0 mm (0 in)
July 64 mm (2.5 in)

EGYPT

ERITREA

DJIBOUTI

SOMALIA

SUDAN

ETHIOPIA

0 100 200 300 400 500 km
0 100 200 300 miles

Pyramids

New land has been formed in the delta by mud and rock deposited by the river.

Cairo

Many people live on the banks and delta of the Nile.

As the river nears the Mediterranean Sea, it separates into many tributaries and forms a fertile triangle of land called a delta.

### COTTON FIELDS

Largely as a result of European colonization in the 19th and 20th centuries, cotton growing and processing are important industries in Egypt and Sudan. Production was begun in these areas by the British to provide cotton for their textile mills. The cotton is grown on large, highly mechanized farms that lie along the fertile banks of the River Nile.

# EGYPT

IT IS SAID THAT EGYPT is the gift of the River Nile. The site of one of the world's first great civilizations, Egypt grew up under the rule of the pharaohs along the banks of the Nile more than 5,000 years ago. Most of the country is dry, sandy desert with a narrow, fertile strip which follows the river valley and widens into the delta. This is where the vast majority of Egypt's population lives. Most of the people are Arab and follow the Muslim faith. The economy is dominated by farming, oil, tourism, income from ships passing through the Suez Canal, and money earned by Egyptians working abroad.

### EGYPT

**Capital city:** Cairo

**Area:** 1,001,450 sq km (386,660 sq miles)

**Population:** 71,900,000

**Official language:** Arabic

**Major religions:** Muslim 94%, other 6%

**Government:** Multi-party democracy

**Currency:** Egyptian pound

**Adult literacy rate:** 56%

**Life expectancy:** 69 years

**People per doctor:** 625

**Televisions:** 122 per 1,000 people

## CAIRO

With a population of more than 15 million, Cairo is the largest city in Africa and one of the fastest growing. The city faces terrible housing problems. New arrivals often have to live in dirty, overcrowded slums. Some live among the graves of the City of the Dead, a huge cemetery on the outskirts of the city. People also live on the roofs of the many high-rise buildings in Cairo.

*The Suez Canal is used by more than 20,000 ships every year.*

## SUEZ CANAL

The Suez Canal runs from the Red Sea to the Mediterranean Sea. It is the one of the world's largest and most important artificial waterways, providing a short cut from Europe to India and East Asia. The canal was built with French and British help and was completed in 1869. It has since been made deeper and wider to allow for the increasing size of ships and tankers. In 1956 the canal came under Egyptian control. Today, the tolls taken from the ships that use the canal are an important source of income for the Egyptian government.

→ Route before Suez Canal
→ Route after Suez was built

*The Suez Canal offered a short cut from Europe to India and East Asia. Earlier, ships from Europe had sailed around Africa.*

**FUL MEDAMES**
This Egyptian dish is made by boiling brown beans with onions, vegetables, and spices. This may be eaten with an egg for breakfast. A similar mixture is used to stuff *aysh* (flat bread), to make sandwiches.

**THE RIVER NILE**
Some 99 per cent of Egyptians live in the valley or delta of the River Nile. The river is Egypt's lifeline, providing water for farming, industry, and home use. When the Aswan High Dam was built on the Nile, it created the world's largest reservoir, Lake Nasser.

*The Sphinx, built of soft sandstone, has the body of a lion and the head of a man.*

## FARMING IN EGYPT

Many Egyptian farmers, or *felahin*, use traditional farming methods to grow cotton, wheat, rice, sugar, fruit, and vegetables. Egypt is the world's second largest producer of dates. Another important crop is *berseem*, a type of clover that is grown for animal feed. Egypt is also one of the world's biggest cotton growers. Many people are employed in the textile industry, spinning, weaving, and dyeing the fine quality cotton to make clothes and other goods.

**ANCIENT SITES**
Egypt is littered with ancient monuments. Every years, millions of tourists flock to Egypt to see the pyramids and other sites, or to take a boat trip on the River Nile. The pyramids, built more than 4,000 years ago as tombs for the pharaohs, are one of the seven wonders of the ancient world, and the only one to survive.

*Cool and comfortable cotton tunics, called jellabas, are often worn by Egyptian men.*

# SUDAN

SUDAN, THE LARGEST COUNTRY in Africa, is one of the poorest and least developed countries in the world. The River Nile flows from south to north, and most people live along its fertile banks. The landscape ranges from rocky desert in the north, to swampland in the south. Sudan is also divided culturally. The people of the north are mainly Arabic-speaking Muslims, while in the centre and south, African languages and religions, together with Christianity, dominate. Clashes between the two sides have led to decades of civil war.

| SUDAN | |
| --- | --- |
| **Capital city:** Khartoum | |
| **Area:** 2,505,810 sq km (967,493 sq miles) | |
| **Population:** 33,600,000 | |
| **Official language:** Arabic | |
| **Major religions:** Muslim 70%, traditional beliefs 20%, Christian 9%, other 1% | |
| **Government:** Military government | |
| **Currency:** Sudanese dinar | |
| **Adult literacy rate:** 60% | |
| **Life expectancy:** 58 years | |
| **People per doctor:** 10,000 | |
| **Televisions:** 87 per 1,000 people | |

### WATERING THE LAND
Much of Sudan is too dry to live or farm in, and large areas of suitable farmland have been destroyed by war. The majority of people live by the River Nile and use its water to irrigate their fields. Two-thirds of workers make their living from the land, growing crops such as cotton, peanuts, gum arabic, millet, and dates. A large-scale irrigation scheme set up by the government has helped farmers to grow more crops for export.

### NOMADIC LIFE
Many of Sudan's tribal people live by herding cattle, moving from place to place in search of fresh pasture. The more cattle a person owns, the greater his importance in the tribe. The civil war has disrupted the lives of many herders, destroying their pastures and their herding routes.

*The Dinka tribe are nomadic cattle herders who live on the plains east of the Nile.*

### TRIBES
The people of Sudan are divided into more than 500 different tribes and groups speaking more than 100 languages and dialects. Each tribe shares a common ancestor. Many, such as the Dinka and Juhaynah tribes, are nomadic. Others have settled in particular areas, such as the Shilluk tribe, who are farmers living on the west bank of the Nile. The people shown left are from the Beni Amer tribe, a Muslim group.

### KHARTOUM
Since Sudan became independent in 1956, the Muslim government in the capital, Khartoum, has tried to impose Islam on the rest of the population, leading to civil war and famine. Millions of refugees have poured into Khartoum from the south and west to escape the fighting and to find food and work. Many now live in shanty towns on the outskirts of the city.

*Flat-roofed houses built of mud brick are common in northern Sudan.*

*Conical-roofed huts are common in central and southern Sudan. Each hut has its own purpose.*

*Storeroom*

*Living quarters*

### HOUSING
Life in the Arab north of Sudan is very different from that of the African south. There are differences in language, religion, customs, and style of housing. The Nubian people of the north (an African people who adopted Islam as their religion) build rectangular, flat-roofed houses of sun-dried bricks. The Nubans of central Sudan (a tribe of hill farmers) build round huts with conical roofs made of grass, wooden poles, and millet stalks.

*A small "keyhole" doorway helps keep the hut warm and dry inside.*

*Wrestling is a popular sport among the Nuban people.*

***Find out more***
IRRIGATION: *155, 156*
PEOPLES OF AFRICA: *206–207*
REFUGEES: *207*
RELIGION: *274–275*

# ETHIOPIA

A LAND RICH in its own unique traditions, Ethiopia has in recent years suffered from drought, famine, and warfare. In 1984–85, a terrible famine, caused by a combination of civil war, drought, overpopulation, and overfarming, struck the northern highlands. During this time, Ethiopia was involved in a long, bitter war with the Eritreans, which ended in 2000. Four out of five Ethiopians live off the land, growing crops such as *teff* (a type of grass) or herding cattle. Coffee is Ethiopia's major export crop. It is mostly grown in the mountains of Kaffa province, from which it gets its name.

## ADDIS ABABA

The capital, Addis Ababa, is the biggest city in Ethiopia with some 4 million inhabitants. It is a rapidly growing city, home to many refugees from the north and Eritrea. Housing is in short supply and there are about 20,000 children living on the streets. Many people live in crowded slums without toilets or running water. It is not unknown for a family of eight to ten people to share one room.

### ETHIOPIA

**Capital city:** Addis Ababa

**Area:** 1,127,127 sq km (435,184 sq miles)

**Population:** 70,700,000

**Official language:** Amharic

**Major religions:** Muslim 40%, Christian 40%, indigenous beliefs 15%, other 5%

**Government:** Multi-party democracy

**Currency:** Ethiopian birr

**Adult literacy rate:** 42%

**Life expectancy:** 42 years

**People per doctor:** 33,333

**Televisions:** 5 per 1,000 people

## MUSIC AND DANCE

There are many groups of Ethiopians, each with their own language and traditions in storytelling, music, and dance. Traditional dances tell stories from everyday life. The music and songs that accompany them are an important means of passing on information about local cultures and customs.

*Traditional instruments include the kra (a type of lyre).*

*Traditional Ethiopian dancers shake their shoulders as they dance.*

*Coffee-making ceremonies are elaborate. The coffee is brewed with added spices, incense is burned, and grass spread over the floor.*

*Traditional dress consists of an embroidered white dress and shawl for women, and white shirts and trousers for men.*

### FIREWOOD

Women are responsible for cutting, carrying, and selling firewood, a major source of fuel and income. Much of Ethiopia's forests have now been destroyed, however. This has led to the soil, no longer protected by trees, being blown or washed away and to the loss of valuable farmland.

*Ethiopian Orthodox priests at a religious festival in Addis Ababa.*

*A typical vegetable dish made from cabbage, carrots, garlic, and red lentils.*

*Wot, made from red onions, chillies, garlic, ginger, and other herbs and spices, is added to meat and vegetable dishes.*

*Hard-boiled eggs are often eaten with the meal.*

*Chicken stew, made from chicken, egg, and red peppers.*

*Enjera*

*Beef stew, made from beef, cinnamon, peppers, red chilli, and tomatoes.*

## ETHIOPIAN CHURCH

The Ethiopian Orthodox Church can be traced back to the 4th century AD. Its most impressive monuments are the 12th century churches in the village of Lalibela, which are carved out of solid rock. The Ethiopian Church has similarities with other Eastern churches and some Jewish customs have been retained, but its colourful ceremonies and festivals have their own distinctive flavour.

### FOOD

The national dish of Ethiopia is *enjera*, a type of soft, flat bread made from *teff*, eaten with a mixture of meat and vegetables. These are cooked in a hot, spicy sauce, called *wot*. Traditionally, the sauce is served on top of the *enjera*. Raw beef, served with hot spices and melted butter, is eaten at festival times.

# SOMALIA

SOMALIA GAINED INDEPENDENCE from Italy and Britain in 1960. However, this diverse country with a rich history did not achieve peace. Since 1991, Somalia has been torn apart by civil war, resulting in widespread famine. Many Somalis are nomadic herders, wandering through the dry, barren countryside with their camels, sheep, and goats in search of food and water.

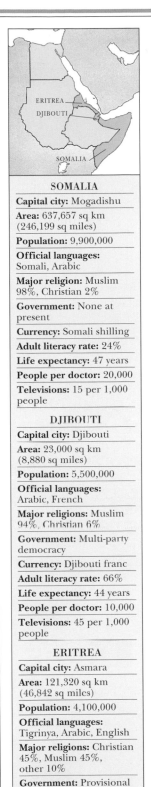

| SOMALIA | |
| --- | --- |
| **Capital city:** Mogadishu | |
| **Area:** 637,657 sq km (246,199 sq miles) | |
| **Population:** 9,900,000 | |
| **Official languages:** Somali, Arabic | |
| **Major religion:** Muslim 98%, Christian 2% | |
| **Government:** None at present | |
| **Currency:** Somali shilling | |
| **Adult literacy rate:** 24% | |
| **Life expectancy:** 47 years | |
| **People per doctor:** 20,000 | |
| **Televisions:** 15 per 1,000 people | |

| DJIBOUTI | |
| --- | --- |
| **Capital city:** Djibouti | |
| **Area:** 23,000 sq km (8,880 sq miles) | |
| **Population:** 5,500,000 | |
| **Official languages:** Arabic, French | |
| **Major religions:** Muslim 94%, Christian 6% | |
| **Government:** Multi-party democracy | |
| **Currency:** Djibouti franc | |
| **Adult literacy rate:** 66% | |
| **Life expectancy:** 44 years | |
| **People per doctor:** 10,000 | |
| **Televisions:** 45 per 1,000 people | |

| ERITREA | |
| --- | --- |
| **Capital city:** Asmara | |
| **Area:** 121,320 sq km (46,842 sq miles) | |
| **Population:** 4,100,000 | |
| **Official languages:** Tigrinya, Arabic, English | |
| **Major religions:** Christian 45%, Muslim 45%, other 10% | |
| **Government:** Provisional government | |
| **Currency:** Nakfa | |
| **Adult literacy rate:** 57% | |
| **Life expectancy:** 51 years | |
| **People per doctor:** 20,000 | |
| **Televisions:** 14 per 1,000 people | |

## RELIEF CAMPS

Since war broke out, many thousands of Somalis have moved into relief camps for food, safety, and shelter. The troubles, however, have made it difficult for international aid to be distributed. Up to one million Somalis sought refuge in neighbouring countries, although many began to return as the fighting decreased in 2000 and 2001.

### MOGADISHU
Mogadishu is the capital of Somalia and its major port and commercial centre. The various styles of the buildings reflect the history of the country. Arabs settled there in the 9th century, and it became a European colony in the 19th century.

### WOMEN'S DRESS
Many Somali women wear a cotton, sari-like garment called a *guntimo*, and a shawl, called a *garbasaar*. Unlike many Muslims in other countries, Somali women do not wear veils that cover the face.

# DJIBOUTI

THE SMALL, MAINLY DESERT country of Djibouti became independent in 1977. Many of its people are nomads. Djibouti is of great importance to this part of Africa because of its port and capital city, also called Djibouti. The country's economy relies almost entirely on income from the port.

*Fishing is a developing industry in Djibouti. Fishermen set out from the port of Djibouti on the Gulf of Aden.*

# ERITREA

AFTER 20 YEARS OF WAR, the mountainous land of Eritrea effectively became independent of Ethiopia in 1991. However, relations remained tense and a new war broke out in 1998. Ethopian troops finally left the country in 2001, leaving the Eritrean people to rebuild their shattered economy.

*This theatre in Asmara, the capital of Eritrea, is an example of the fine Italian-style architecture found in parts of the city. Eritrea was once an Italian colony.*

***Find out more***
COLONIAL PERIOD: *207*
DESERTS: *15, 204, 209*
ISLAM: *275*
REFUGEES: *207*

# WEST AFRICA

MANY CENTURIES AGO, great civilizations such as the Asanti and Mali were thriving in the region now known as West Africa. Word of rich gold deposits brought Europeans flocking here, and by the 1880s they had colonized nearly all of this vast region. West Africa did not win back its independence until the 1960s. Although this region is rich in oil, gold, timber, and other natural resources, most of the 15 countries in West Africa are very poor. There are large numbers of ethnic groups here – over 200 different peoples live in Nigeria alone. The combination of poverty and clashes between different peoples has made political turmoil another all-too-familiar feature of the region.

### RELIGION
West Africa divides roughly into northern and southern regions where the landscape and climate are concerned, and this also applies to its religions. Islam is dominant in the north, while there are more Christians in the south. Throughout the region, many people follow ancient traditional religions such as voodoo, which is especially strong in Benin.

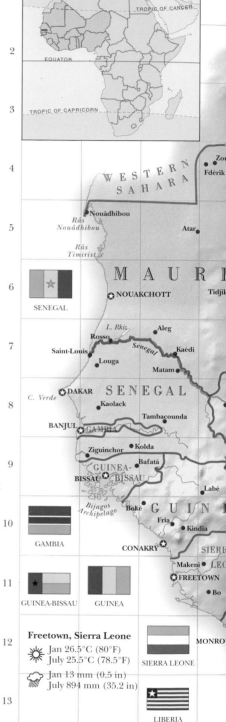

**Climate zones in West Africa**

Desert
Sahel
Savanna
Tropical forest

**Desert**
*The burning Sahara forms the northern "lid" of West Africa. Very little grows here. The border of the desert advances or retreats, depending on how dry it becomes in neighbouring areas.*

**Sahel**
*The arid northern grasslands that border the desert are called sahel – the word means "shore" of the desert in Arabic. Few trees can survive in this region.*

**Savanna**
*Moving south, a little more rain falls in the vast expanses of savanna – grassland scattered with acacias, baobabs, and other trees. Much of West Africa consists of savanna.*

**Tropical forest**
*Moist forests flourish under the heavy rains of the far south. Many animals and plants live here, although there are not as many different species as in the rainforests of central Africa.*

## THE CLIMATE
If you were to set out on a journey from north to south across this huge region, you would pass through a fascinating variety of hot, tropical landscapes. The vegetation of each zone has developed because of the amount of rain that falls there. Plenty of rain falls in the far south, whereas the arid northerly region is prone to serious drought. In some parts, there is a distinct wet season that lasts about 4–6 months and no rain at all falls for much of the rest of the year.

SENEGAL

GAMBIA

GUINEA-BISSAU

GUINEA

**Freetown, Sierra Leone**
☀ Jan 26.5°C (80°F)
July 25.5°C (78.5°F)
🌧 Jan 13 mm (0.5 in)
July 894 mm (35.2 in)

SIERRA LEONE

LIBERIA

MONRO

*There are many nomadic cattle herders in Burkina, which lies in the dry sahel region.*

### WEST AFRICAN FARMERS
This region is home to two very different types of farmer – settled and nomadic. Settled farmers live near small plots of land where they grow enough to feed their families and perhaps some cash crops such as cocoa or oil palms. Nomadic cattle herders, such as the Fulani, roam constantly across the region in search of good grazing land. They are more common towards the drier north, where the land is not as good for growing crops.

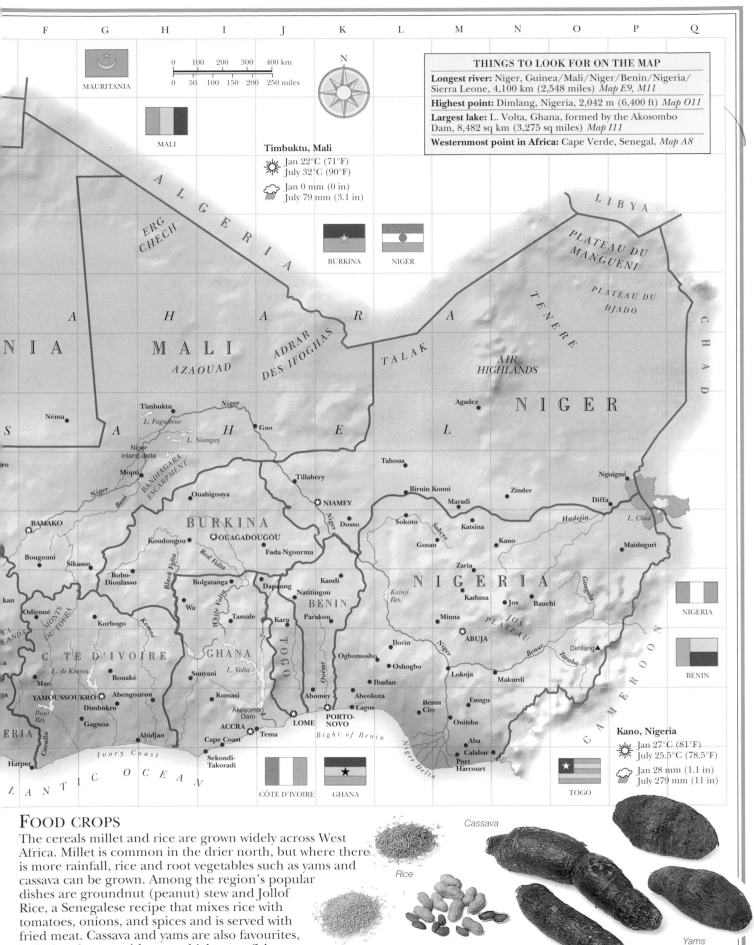

F G H I J K L M N O P Q

MAURITANIA

0 100 200 300 400 km
0 50 100 150 200 250 miles

N

MALI

**Timbuktu, Mali**
☀ Jan 22°C (71°F)
☀ July 32°C (90°F)
☂ Jan 0 mm (0 in)
☂ July 79 mm (3.1 in)

**THINGS TO LOOK FOR ON THE MAP**

**Longest river:** Niger, Guinea/Mali/Niger/Benin/Nigeria/Sierra Leone, 4,100 km (2,548 miles) *Map E9, M11*

**Highest point:** Dimlang, Nigeria, 2,042 m (6,400 ft) *Map O11*

**Largest lake:** L. Volta, Ghana, formed by the Akosombo Dam, 8,482 sq km (3,275 sq miles) *Map I11*

**Westernmost point in Africa:** Cape Verde, Senegal, *Map A8*

BURKINA    NIGER

ALGERIA

LIBYA

ERG CHECH

PLATEAU DU MANGUENI

PLATEAU DU DJADO

S A H A R A

MALI

AZAOUAD

ADRAR DES IFOGHAS

TALAK

TENERE

AÏR HIGHLANDS

NIGER

C H A D

Néma

Timbuktu    Niger
L. Faguibine

Gao

Agadez

L. Niangay

Niger inland delta

Mopti    BANDIAGARA ESCARPMENT

Tahoua

Nguigmi

L. Chad

Niger    Bani

Ouahigouya

Tillabéry

NIAMEY

Birnin Konni

Maradi

Zinder

Diffa

Hadejia

BAMAKO

BURKINA

Dosso

Sokoto

Sokoto

Katsina

Kano

Maiduguri

Bougouni

Koudougou    OUAGADOUGOU

Gusau

Sikasso

Zaria

Bobo-Dioulasso

Fada-Ngourma

Kaduna

Gongola

NIGERIA

Odienné

Bolgatanga

Kandi

Kainji Res.

Jos

Bauchi

MONTS DU TOURA

Wa

Natitingou

NIGERIA

Korhogo

Tamale

BENIN

Minna

JOS PLATEAU

CÔTE D'IVOIRE

GHANA

Dapaong

Parakou

ABUJA

Benue

BENIN

L. de Kossou

Sunyani

L. Volta

Kara

Ilorin

Niger

Taraba

Dimlang ▲

Man

Bouaké

Kumasi

Ogbomosho

Oshogbo

Lokoja

Makurdi

Buyo Res.

YAMOUSSOUKRO

Abengourou

Dimbokro

Abomey

Ibadan

Abeokuta

Benin City

Enugu

C A M E R O O N

Gagnoa

Akosombo Dam

ACCRA    Tema

LOME    PORTO-NOVO

Lagos

Onitsha

Abidjan

Cape Coast

Bight of Benin

Aba

**Kano, Nigeria**
☀ Jan 27°C (81°F)
☀ July 25.5°C (78.5°F)
☂ Jan 28 mm (1.1 in)
☂ July 279 mm (11 in)

Harper

Sekondi-Takoradi

Niger Delta

Port Harcourt

Calabar

ATLANTIC OCEAN

Ivory Coast

CÔTE D'IVOIRE    GHANA

TOGO

# FOOD CROPS

The cereals millet and rice are grown widely across West Africa. Millet is common in the drier north, but where there is more rainfall, rice and root vegetables such as yams and cassava can be grown. Among the region's popular dishes are groundnut (peanut) stew and Jollof Rice, a Senegalese recipe that mixes rice with tomatoes, onions, and spices and is served with fried meat. Cassava and yams are also favourites, boiled and eaten with goat, chicken, or fish.

*Cassava*

*Rice*

*Millet grains*    *Groundnuts (peanuts)*

*Yams*

# MAURITANIA

COVERING AN AREA TWICE THE SIZE of Spain, but with a population smaller than Madrid's, Mauritania is one of the emptiest countries in the world. In recent years, many of the people have left the countryside to live and work in the towns, and Nouakchott, the capital, has grown from 20,000 people in 1960 to more than 900,000 today. The country is dominated by the Arab Maures (Moors) from the north, but their political control is resented by the black peoples from the south. Mining is an important industry, as Mauritania is rich in phosphates, copper, gold, and other minerals. Drought is a major problem in this region.

**FISHING**
Fleets from all over the world come to fish off the coast of Mauritania, where some of the richest fish stocks in West Africa are found. By law, all fish caught here must be landed and processed in Mauritania before they are exported to overseas markets. However, overfishing of the seas by fleets of trawlers has led to concern about the future of the industry.

| MAURITANIA |
| --- |
| **Capital city:** Nouakchott |
| **Area:** 1,030,700 sq km (397,953 sq miles) |
| **Population:** 2,900,000 |
| **Official language:** Arabic |
| **Major religion:** Muslim 100% |
| **Government:** Multi-party democracy |
| **Currency:** Ouguiya |
| **Adult literacy rate:** 41% |
| **Life expectancy:** 51 years |
| **People per doctor:** 10,000 |
| **Televisions:** 91 per 1,000 people |

| NIGER |
| --- |
| **Capital city:** Niamey |
| **Area:** 1,267,000 sq km (489,188 sq miles) |
| **Population:** 12,000,000 |
| **Official language:** French |
| **Major religions:** Muslim 85%, traditional beliefs 14%, other 1% |
| **Government:** Multi-party democracy |
| **Currency:** CFA franc |
| **Adult literacy rate:** 17% |
| **Life expectancy:** 46 years |
| **People per doctor:** 25,000 |
| **Televisions:** 27 per 1,000 people |

*Projects like this one for planting trees and grass to hold the soil in place are helping to stop erosion.*

## THE SAHEL
Two-thirds of Mauritania is covered by the Sahara, and only the land along the Senegal River is suitable for farming. The semi-desert land in between, known as the sahel, is the grazing land for nomadic farmers. This area suffers from frequent droughts and from soil erosion, made worse by people cutting down the few trees for firewood and overgrazing cattle. For these reasons – both natural and human – the sahel is gradually becoming more desert-like.

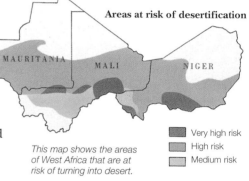

**Areas at risk of desertification**

*This map shows the areas of West Africa that are at risk of turning into desert.*

- Very high risk
- High risk
- Medium risk

# NIGER

THE VAST STATE OF NIGER is completely surrounded by other countries. Its main link to the sea is the River Niger, the only major river in the country. Most of Niger's 12 million people live in the semi-desert sahel region, which stretches in a narrow ribbon across the south of the country. North of the sahel lies the vast and inhospitable Sahara, home to the nomadic Tuareg peoples. Niger has few natural resources apart from uranium, which brought in considerable wealth during the 1980s. Most of the people, however, remain poor, earning their living herding flocks or growing crops in the few fertile parts of the country.

**FARMING**
Every year, the River Niger floods. As the floodwaters retreat, local farmers quickly plant their crops of cereals, rice, vegetables, groundnuts, and cotton in the fertile soils left behind. The banks of the Niger also provide pasture for cattle and other livestock reared for meat and milk.

**THE TUAREG**
As a result of frequent droughts in northern Niger, many Tuareg lost all their animals and were forced to give up their nomadic lifestyle. Many moved south to the towns in search of food and work. In reaction to this enforced move, some Tuareg have campaigned for a country of their own.

*Find out more*

RIVER NIGER: *205*
SAHEL: *220*
SOIL EROSION: *55, 244*
TUAREG: *209*

# MALI

THE LANDSCAPE OF MALI ranges from the vast desert plains of the Sahara in the north, through the semi-desert sahel region in the centre, to wetter savanna in the south. A thin belt of fertile land stretches on each side of the Niger and Senegal rivers. The country gets its name from the great Muslim empire of the Malinke people, which flourished in this region in the 13th and 14th centuries. Today, Mali is a poor country where most people make their living from farming or herding cattle.

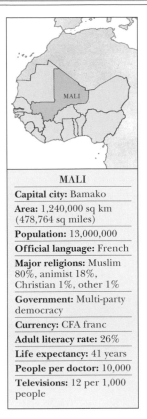

| MALI | |
|---|---|
| **Capital city:** Bamako | |
| **Area:** 1,240,000 sq km (478,764 sq miles) | |
| **Population:** 13,000,000 | |
| **Official language:** French | |
| **Major religions:** Muslim 80%, animist 18%, Christian 1%, other 1% | |
| **Government:** Multi-party democracy | |
| **Currency:** CFA franc | |
| **Adult literacy rate:** 26% | |
| **Life expectancy:** 41 years | |
| **People per doctor:** 10,000 | |
| **Televisions:** 12 per 1,000 people | |

## MOSQUES

Islam arrived in Mali with merchants travelling across the Sahara from the Arab north. By the 13th century, Mali was entirely Muslim, with mosques built in most towns. Mosques like this one at Mopti are constructed of clay around a wooden framework that sticks out in turrets above the roof. The wooden beams jutting out through the walls allow villagers to climb all over the building to carry out its annual repairs.

*The River Niger at Bamako, in southern Mali.*

### TIMBUKTU
Founded by Tuareg nomads in 1100, Timbuktu became one of the most famous cities in Africa. Because of its position on the trade route across the Sahara, it soon developed into a major town. Arab traders from the north brought salt, cloth, and horses to exchange for gold and slaves from the south. By 1400, Timbuktu had become a major centre of Islamic learning.

## THE NIGER

The River Niger is the lifeline of Mali, flowing through the country from west to east before turning south to pour into the Atlantic Ocean. Most people in the country live along its banks, using the river as a source of water and food and the main means of transport. The capital of Mali, Bamako, on the upper reaches of the river, is a major port, shipping cement and petrol down river and receiving rice and groundnuts (peanuts) for export in exchange.

*Granaries are built of thick clay to keep the grain cool and free of rats.*

*Dogon houses are made of clay, often with terraces above the main living area.*

*The flat rooftops are used to dry onions and to store pots and baskets.*

Compound

*Outer wall*  Entrance

*The Dogon live in walled compounds built on steep hillsides for protection against attack from their enemies.*

### RICE GROWING
In the centre of Mali, the River Niger splits into several branches. This area is called the river's inland delta, and is one of the most fertile regions of the country. Here, as the river begins to flood, farmers plant a special "floating" rice that grows up to 30 cm (12 in) a day to keep pace with the rising waters. When the crop is ready, the farmers harvest it from boats.

### THE DOGON
South of Timbuktu, the flat river plain gives way to sandstone cliffs surrounding the Bandiagara plateau. Living in the cliffs are the Dogon people, who first settled in the area in the 1500s. The Dogon worship their own gods, and have many legends about the creation of the world. Because of the harsh conditions in which they live, the Dogon are expert farmers, using every available strip of land to grow crops of rice, millet, and maize.

### Find out more
ISLAM: *275*
MALINKE PEOPLE: *225*
RICE GROWING: *135, 176, 197*
RIVER NIGER: *205*

# SENEGAL

THE MIGHTY SENEGAL RIVER dominates large areas of this country. Every year the river floods, and seasonal crops are grown on the fertile land that the flood waters leave behind. Senegal is relatively wealthy compared to other countries in this region, as it was once the capital of French West Africa and still has close links with France. Among the mix of ethnic groups, such as the Wolof and Mandinke, there are still many French inhabitants. There is a similar mix of religions – Islam exists side-by-side with traditional beliefs. Senegal's beautiful, palm-fringed coastline makes tourism an important feature of life here.

| SENEGAL | |
|---|---|
| **Capital city:** Dakar | |
| **Area:** 196,190 sq km (75,749 sq miles) | |
| **Population:** 10,100,000 | |
| **Official language:** French | |
| **Major religions:** Muslim 90%, traditional beliefs 5%, Christian 5% | |
| **Government:** Multi-party democracy | |
| **Currency:** CFA franc | |
| **Adult literacy rate:** 39% | |
| **Life expectancy:** 52 years | |
| **People per doctor:** 10,000 | |
| **Televisions:** 41 per 1,000 people | |

| GAMBIA | |
|---|---|
| **Capital city:** Banjul | |
| **Area:** 11,300 sq km (4,363 sq miles) | |
| **Population:** 1,400,000 | |
| **Official language:** English | |
| **Major religions:** Muslim 90%, Christian 9%, traditional beliefs 1% | |
| **Government:** Multi-party democracy | |
| **Currency:** Dalasi | |
| **Adult literacy rate:** 38% | |
| **Life expectancy:** 53 years | |
| **People per doctor:** 25,000 | |
| **Televisions:** 3 per 1,000 people | |

DAKAR
The lively city of Dakar, Senegal's capital, perches on a rocky peninsula that forms the westernmost point of Africa. This major port was once the capital of French West Africa, as can be seen from its grand colonial buildings. Today great poverty is found on the streets of Dakar, alongside the expensive restaurants and modern hotels.

## MUSICAL STORYTELLING

History is a living thing in West Africa. For centuries, history and other information has been passed on by word of mouth, and from one generation to the next, through stories, poems, and songs. In Senegal, the people who take these from village to village are called *griots*. They play a variety of traditional instruments, such as the *kora*.

The kora has 21 strings.

Front view of kora

The soundbox is made from a hollowed-out gourd.

## FARMING AND FISHING

Agriculture employs three-quarters of Senegal's workers. In the north, cereals such as millet and sorghum are the main food crops and groundnuts (peanuts) are a vital cash crop. Rice is common in the wetter southern areas. Groundnuts were once grown on nearly half the farmland, but fish is now taking over as the country's main export. A common sight is local fishermen setting out in dug-out canoes called *pirogues*, made from local trees.

# GAMBIA

THE TINY COUNTRY OF GAMBIA is a long, thin sliver of land carved out of Senegal, which surrounds it on three sides. At its widest point, Gambia measures no more than 80 km (50 miles) from north to south. Like Senegal, Gambia has a wide ethnic mix and Islam is very important. Most of the people work in farming, relying heavily on the groundnut crop. Women play a major role in agricultural life. Rice growing is their main occupation, but near the coast large areas of swampy rice land have been ruined by the build-up of salt in the soil. Many women now grow vegetables to sell in local markets.

*Most tourists come for the beaches, but many take trips inland to see the crocodiles, monkeys, and many species of bird that live along the Gambia River.*

TOURISM
The tourist trade is the fastest growing part of the Gambian economy. More and more North Europeans are coming here to escape their cold winters, attracted by the magnificent beaches. Gambia is particularly popular with visitors from the UK, because English is widely spoken in this former British colony. But fears are already mounting that the easy-going local lifestyle will soon be ruined by advancing tourism.

*Find out more*
AFRICAN CITIES: *206*
COLONIAL PERIOD: *207*
RELIGION: *274–275*
RICE GROWING: *135, 176, 197*

# GUINEA

ONCE A FRENCH COLONY, this fertile, hilly country is rich in minerals, and has perfect weather conditions for growing many crops, including bananas, citrus fruits, and rice. These factors should have made Guinea a rich country. Instead, it is one of the poorest in the world, with a life expectancy of just 46 years and very basic medical and education facilities. This is largely the result of the French leaving Guinea without financial support, poor management of the economy, and years of harsh political rule under Sekou Touré, who was president from 1958–84.

THE GUINEA HIGHLANDS
Thick forest covers the mountainous Guinea Highlands in the south of the country. As well as providing timber products, conditions in this highly fertile area are ideal for growing various crops, including coffee. Three of the region's major rivers – the Niger, the Gambia, and the Senegal – have their sources here. Rich iron deposits are also to be found, and the whole area is nourished by abundant rainfall.

| GUINEA |
| --- |
| **Capital city:** Conakry |
| **Area:** 245,860 sq km (94,926 sq miles) |
| **Population:** 8,500,000 |
| **Official language:** French |
| **Major religions:** Muslim 65%, traditional beliefs 33%, Christian 2% |
| **Government:** Multi-party democracy |
| **Currency:** Guinea franc |
| **Adult literacy rate:** 41% |
| **Life expectancy:** 46 years |
| **People per doctor:** 10,000 |
| **Televisions:** 41 per 1,000 people |

| GUINEA BISSAU |
| --- |
| **Capital city:** Bissau |
| **Area:** 36,120 sq km (13,946 sq miles) |
| **Population:** 1,500,000 |
| **Official language:** Portuguese |
| **Major religions:** Traditional beliefs 52%, Muslim 40%, Christian 8% |
| **Government:** Multi-party democracy |
| **Currency:** CFA franc |
| **Adult literacy rate:** 40% |
| **Life expectancy:** 45 years |
| **People per doctor:** 5,000 |
| **Televisions:** No figures available |

*About two-thirds of Guinea's population live in small villages like this one.*

## PEOPLE OF GUINEA

A varied mix of peoples, including the Malinke, Fulani, and Soussou, live in Guinea. Most of them are Muslim. The Malinke make up about a third of the population, and are named after a mountainous area on the Mali border. This was once part of the great Mali empire, which dominated West Africa in medieval times. Today, the Malinke are famous for their centuries-old storytelling and musical skills.

MINING
The mountainous areas of Guinea are rich in a mineral ore called bauxite. Ores are substances from which metals can be obtained, and bauxite is used to make aluminium. Guinea is the world's second largest producer of bauxite, after Australia, and it accounts for around 60 percent of the country's earnings from exports. Guinea's mountain regions yield other valuable minerals, including iron, gold, and diamonds.

# GUINEA BISSAU

SANDWICHED BETWEEN SENEGAL and Guinea, this low-lying, swampy country is a particularly unspoilt place. Once ruled by Portugal, Guinea Bissau was the first Portuguese colony to gain independence, in 1974. Today it is very poor and heavily dependent on financial aid from other countries. The people are a mix of ethnic groups, the largest of which are the Balante, from the south. Most people scrape a living by growing coconuts, cotton, groundnuts (peanuts), or cashew nuts. Timber and fishing are also important.

*Groundnuts (peanuts)*

GROUNDNUTS
As the name suggests, the actual nuts of the groundnut, or peanut, plant grow underground. The nut pods are pulled out of the ground and left to dry before being shelled and skinned. Some of the nuts are sold in local markets, but most are used to extract groundnut oil, used in food production, or crushed to make peanut butter.

ALONG THE COAST
Like its neighbours, Guinea Bissau has spectacular beaches. Its coastline is edged with mangrove swamps, mud flats, and estuaries leading to a maze of inland waterways. A huge variety of fish are found off the coast, and many people in this coastal region make their living from fishing.

*Cashew nuts*

*Find out more*

COLONIAL PERIOD: *207*
ISLAM: *275*
LIFE EXPECTANCY: *276*
POOR COUNTRIES: *298–299*

# SIERRA LEONE

IN 1787, THE BRITISH colonized this region and created a settlement for freed African slaves. This is how Sierra Leone's capital, Freetown, got its name. Today, there are still a few descendants of the freed slaves, known as Creoles, living here. The main peoples, however, are the Mende in the south and the Temne in the north. In recent years, conflicts between the various ethnic groups have led to civil war. Sierra Leone is one of the poorest countries in the world, and two-thirds of the workforce make their living from small-scale farming.

| SIERRA LEONE |
|---|
| **Capital city:** Freetown |
| **Area:** 71,740 sq km (27,698 sq miles) |
| **Population:** 5,000,000 |
| **Official language:** English |
| **Major religions:** Traditional beliefs 30%, Muslim 30%, other 30%, Christian 10% |
| **Government:** Multi-party democracy |
| **Currency:** Leone |
| **Adult literacy rate:** 36% |
| **Life expectancy:** 37 years |
| **People per doctor:** 10,000 |
| **Televisions:** 13 per 1,000 people |

| LIBERIA |
|---|
| **Capital city:** Monrovia |
| **Area:** 111,370 sq km (43,000 sq miles) |
| **Population:** 3,400,000 |
| **Official language:** English |
| **Major religions:** Christian 68%, traditional beliefs 18%, Muslim 14% |
| **Government:** Transitional government |
| **Currency:** Liberian dollar |
| **Adult literacy rate:** 56% |
| **Life expectancy:** 47 years |
| **People per doctor:** 20,000 |
| **Televisions:** 29 per 1,000 people |

Diamonds

Diamonds found among the gravel in rivers are called alluvial diamonds.

Cut diamond

**MINING**
Sierra Leone's rich mineral deposits have made mining a vital industry, with diamonds among the main products. Diamond mining methods vary from using fully mechanized diggers, to chipping gemstones out of the rock by hand, or panning for them in rivers. Other mineral exports include gold, iron ore, bauxite (from which aluminium is made), and rutile (from which titanium is made).

Rice grains

## FARMING
Sierra Leone's main cash crops are cocoa, coffee, nuts, and palm kernels (seeds from which oil is extracted). The main food crop is rice, which is grown in the river valleys. "Dry" rice is grown in the soil on the valley sides, and "wet" rice is grown in flooded fields on the valley floor. Attempts have been made to raise production – for example, clearing mangrove swamps to make way for extra rice-fields.

# LIBERIA

LIBERIA BECAME AN INDEPENDENT country in 1847 and has never been colonized, making it the oldest independent republic in Africa. In the 19th century, the American Colonization Society helped thousands of freed African slaves to return from the USA and settle here. They gave Liberia its name, which means "freed land". Links between the USA and Liberia still exist today. From 1990 to 2003, Liberia suffered from civil war, and the economy virtually collapsed.

THE RUBBER TRADE
One of Liberia's strongest links with the USA are the extensive, American-owned rubber plantations. Over the years, these have employed huge numbers of people and have accounted for a very large slice of the country's income from exports. The American Firestone company, which makes world-famous tyres, has been at the forefront of this rubber production. Rubber is made from a sticky substance called latex, which can be "tapped" from rubber trees by cutting slits in the bark.

Children as young as eight have been forced to fight in the war.

CIVIL WAR
In recent years there have been clashes between Liberia's different ethnic groups, which include the Kpelle, Bassa, and Kru peoples. These problems erupted into civil war in the early 1990s, which did a great deal of damage to an already weakened economy. The war has forced about half the population to leave their homes, and many people have starved because of food shortages.

| *Find out more* |
|---|
| DIAMONDS: *150, 248* |
| REFUGEES: *207* |
| RICE GROWING: *135, 176, 197* |
| RUBBER: *194* |

# IVORY COAST

BEING RULED BY ONE MAN, Félix Houphouët-Boigny for 33 years until his death in 1993, gave Ivory Coast a reputation as one of the most politically and economically stable countries in Africa. Many different ethnic groups lived largely in peace. However, some tensions between the Muslim north and the Christian south led to violence in 2000. The economy is based in a wide range of products and coffee and cocoa are the main cash crops. Other products include cotton, fruit, tobacco, and timber. Ivory Coast was a French colony until 1960, and is often know as Côte d'Ivoire.

These hardwoods all come from Ivory Coast.

Mahogany

Iroko

Idigbo

### TIMBER INDUSTRY
Ivory Coast once had vast areas of forest, containing ebony, mahogany, and other hardwood trees. Today hardly any is left. For years the country's economy was heavily dependent on the timber industry. Timber exports were seen as vital for paying off foreign debts, and large areas of forest were cleared to make way for coffee and cocoa plantations. A programme was recently started to help save the forests and plant new ones.

| IVORY COAST | |
|---|---|
| **Capital city:** Yamoussoukro | |
| **Area:** 322,460 sq km (124,502 sq miles) | |
| **Population:** 16,600,000 | |
| **Official language:** French | |
| **Major religions:** Muslim 38%, Christian 31%, traditional beliefs 25%, other 6% | |
| **Government:** Multi-party democracy | |
| **Currency:** CFA franc | |
| **Adult literacy rate:** 50% | |
| **Life expectancy:** 45 years | |
| **People per doctor:** 10,000 | |
| **Televisions:** 70 per 1,000 people | |

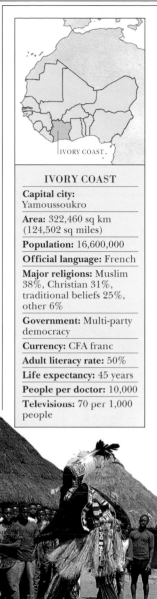

IVORY COAST.

### ETHNIC GROUPS
More than 60 ethnic groups live side-by-side in Ivory Coast, with relatively few clashes. The Dan people, for example, live deep in the heart of the western forests and are famous for their carving skills. They make wooden masks that are worn by the members of special secret societies to keep their identities hidden. Only members of these societies are allowed to take part in the Dan stilt dances.

### YAMOUSSOUKRO
The dome of the world's largest church rises up above the rooftops of Yamoussoukro, a small town in the centre of the country which became Ivory Coast's capital city in 1983. Personally overseen by former president Boigny, the cathedral was completed in 1989 at huge cost. It seats 7,000 people and has an open-air area for another 350,000 – more than double the city's population. There has been much controversy about undertaking such an extravagant project in a country where there is still widespread poverty.

Pineapple

Coffee beans

Bananas

### THE ECONOMY
Compared to much of West Africa, Ivory Coast is a fairly prosperous country. This is partly the result of the policy of growing a variety of crops. Ivory Coast is the world's leading cocoa grower – in some years, it produces about a third of the world's cocoa exports – but competition from elsewhere may change this. It is also Africa's biggest coffee producer and grows vast numbers of pineapples and bananas.

**World's top five cocoa producers**

Figures show the share of total world cocoa production.

Brazil: 7%
Nigeria: 7%
Indonesia: 11%
Ghana: 12.5%
Ivory Coast: 41%

Many of Abidjan's banks and businesses are based in the skyscrapers of the Plateau district.

### ABIDJAN
This modern port, with its glittering glass skyscrapers, is the country's largest city. Abidjan is filled with smart shops and restaurants that show a powerful French influence, reminding visitors of Ivory Coast's historical ties with France. It was also the country's capital until 1983, when Yamoussoukro took over that role.

*Find out more*
CHRISTIANITY: 274
COCOA: 228, 234
COFFEE: 50, 62, 66
LOGGING: 69, 244

# GHANA

GHANA SHOULD BE A RELATIVELY wealthy country. Its many riches include fertile farmland, reserves of gold, bauxite, and oil, and a young population that is among the best educated in Africa. However, years of unstable government, low earnings from exports, and bad management of the economy have hindered Ghana's development. More than 50 different ethnic groups live in Ghana, each with its own language and traditions. Among the largest groups are the Akan peoples, who include the Asante in the south of the country, the Dagomba in the north, and the Ewe in the southeast.

### SLAVERY
Between 1500 and 1800 over 10 million Africans were sold into slavery. Many were shipped from Ghana to work on plantations in America and the Caribbean. Elmina Castle (above) was built by the Portuguese to hold slaves before they crossed the Atlantic. Once on board the slaves were kept in terrible conditions and many died before they reached land.

| GHANA | |
|---|---|
| **Capital city:** Accra | |
| **Area:** 239,460 sq km (92,455 sq miles) | |
| **Population:** 20,900,000 | |
| **Official language:** English | |
| **Major religions:** Christian 69%, Muslim 16%, traditional beliefs 9%, other 6% | |
| **Government:** Multi-party democracy | |
| **Currency:** Cedi | |
| **Adult literacy rate:** 74% | |
| **Life expectancy:** 55 years | |
| **People per doctor:** 10,000 | |
| **Televisions:** 99 per 1,000 people | |

### THE AKOSOMBO DAM
One of the world's largest artificial lakes, Lake Volta, is formed by the Akosombo Dam on the Volta River. When the dam was built in the 1960s, about 85,000 people had to be moved from areas flooded by the lake. The dam's power station generates electricity for factories in the city of Tema and for domestic use. Some power is exported to Togo and Benin.

*Asante gold head showing a defeated enemy general.*

### MARKETS
Every Ghanaian town has a bustling market, drawing people in from the surrounding area. Here they can buy and sell a wide range of goods, from food and animals to household supplies and even false teeth. Many of the market traders are women. Some of them make a lot of money from it. Others are involved in marketing because it is part-time and leaves the rest of the day free for other work.

*Women traders at the market in Accra.*

## THE ASANTE
When Europeans first visited Ghana in the 15th century, they named it the Gold Coast because of the gold offered to them in trade by local people. The main gold workers were the Asante, whose kings and priests wore gold ornaments to show their high status. The symbol of Asante unity was a golden stool, which they believed had come down from the sky. Gold from the Asante mines is still an important export for Ghana.

*A mature cocoa tree produces 20–30 fruit pods a year.*

*Cocoa pods grow directly from the trunk. They are harvested once they have ripened to a yellow colour.*

## COCOA
Cocoa trees need plenty of shade when they are young and water when they are mature. This is why they grow so well in the humid forests of southern Ghana. Here young cocoa plants are grown between rows of other food crops, which provide the necessary shade. The trees only begin to produce fruit after about seven years. Cocoa production is a major industry, accounting for up to 34 per cent of the country's exports, but Ghana now faces stiff competition from neighbouring Ivory Coast and from southeast Asia.

*Each pod contains up to 40 pale pink beans covered in a pink pulp.*

*Roasted cocoa beans*

*Cocoa pod*

*Cocoa beans are fermented, roasted, and ground to produce a chocolate liquid. This is used to make cocoa butter for cosmetics, or is reheated and moulded to make blocks of chocolate.*

***Find out more***
COCOA: *227, 234*
COLONIAL PERIOD: *207*
GOLD MINING: *253*
TRADE DEPENDENCY: *281*

# BURKINA

LANDLOCKED BURKINA (formerly known as Upper Volta) is one of the world's poorest countries. Like the other countries in the sahel region, Burkina is at constant risk from drought, and in recent years large amounts of grazing land have turned to desert as the Sahara has expanded southwards. Burkina has few cities, and most of the people live in villages, making their living from farming and herding. Burkina's economy has suffered badly from political unrest. Because the country is so poor, millions of people from Burkina have to go abroad to find jobs.

## FOREIGN AID

Burkina is very dependent on foreign aid. Each year around US$400 million of aid comes into the country, much of it from Burkina's former colonial ruler, France, and from the European Union. The money is used for both large-scale projects, such as dams to generate hydroelectric power, and smaller schemes, like this well that provides clean water for a village.

| BURKINA | |
|---|---|
| **Capital city:** Ouagadougou | |
| **Area:** 274,200 sq km (105,869 sq miles) | |
| **Population:** 13,000,000 | |
| **Official language:** French | |
| **Major religions:** Muslim 55%, traditional beliefs 35%, Christian 10% | |
| **Government:** Multi-party democracy | |
| **Currency:** CFA franc | |
| **Adult literacy rate:** 25% | |
| **Life expectancy:** 43 years | |
| **People per doctor:** 33,333 | |
| **Televisions:** 9 per 1,000 people | |

| TOGO | |
|---|---|
| **Capital city:** Lomé | |
| **Area:** 56,785 sq km (21,924 sq miles) | |
| **Population:** 4,900,000 | |
| **Official languages:** French | |
| **Major religions:** Traditional beliefs 50%, Christian 35%, Muslim 15% | |
| **Government:** Multi-party democracy | |
| **Currency:** CFA franc | |
| **Adult literacy rate:** 60% | |
| **Life expectancy:** 50 years | |
| **People per doctor:** 10,000 | |
| **Televisions:** 18 per 1,000 people | |

*Many farmers have a vegetable garden where they grow food for their families.*

### AGRICULTURE

Lack of water and poor soil cause huge problems for Burkina's farmers. Before any crops can be planted, a farmer has to clear the land, burning the scrub and ploughing the ash into the ground to act as a fertilizer. The new field can only be used for four to five years before it is exhausted. Then it has to be left for at least another five years to recover.

*The Fulani carry many of their possessions in large bowls called calabashes, which are made from the dried fruit shells of the gourd.*

*The calabash rests on a roll of cloth.*

### THE FULANI

The Fulani are nomads who live by cattle herding. They travel wherever there is grazing land, pitching their huts or tents when they want to sleep. The Fulani live off the produce of their animals, eating mainly milk, butter, and cheese. Their wealth is measured by how many animals they own, so they rarely kill and eat them. Many Fulani have now abandoned this nomadic way of life and settled in one place.

*The Fulani's animals are mainly cattle, like these zebu, but they also keep goats, sheep, and, in the north of the region, camels.*

# TOGO

SANDWICHED BETWEEN GHANA and Benin, Togo is a former French colony that gained its independence in 1960. The population is a mix of about 30 different ethnic groups; the two largest are the Ewe in the south of the country and the Dagomba in the north. Phosphates – minerals used to make fertilizers – account for half of Togo's exports, but the economy has been badly affected by rises and falls in world phosphate prices. Togo's capital city, Lomé, is one of the major ports in West Africa.

### FARMING AND FISHING

Although Togo is a very poor country, it produces nearly all its own food. About two-thirds of the population live in the countryside and works there as farmers. They grow maize, yams, rice, and cassava to eat, and cocoa, coffee, and cotton to sell and export. Along the coast, many people make their living from fishing.

*Find out more*

FULANI: 207
PHOSPHATES: 210
RICH AND POOR : 278–279
SAHEL: 220, 222

# NIGERIA

NIGERIA IS HOME TO AN AMAZING mix of more than 250 different peoples. The largest groups are the Hausa-Fulani, in the north, the Yoruba in the west, and the Ibo in the east. Nigeria could be one of Africa's most successful economies. It has large reserves of oil, gas, and minerals, and abundant farmland. The population of 124 million is the largest of any African country, and one of the best educated. It has had a troubled history with a civil war in 1967 and a series of military coups. Today, Nigeria is struggling to pay off huge debts and to modernize its industry and agriculture.

| NIGERIA | |
|---|---|
| **Capital city:** Abuja | |
| **Area:** 923,770 sq km (356,668 sq miles) | |
| **Population:** 124,000,000 | |
| **Official language:** English | |
| **Major religions:** Muslim 50%, Christian 40%, traditional beliefs 10% | |
| **Government:** Military government | |
| **Currency:** Naira | |
| **Adult literacy rate:** 67% | |
| **Life expectancy:** 45 years | |
| **People per doctor:** 3,704 | |
| **Televisions:** 66 per 1,000 people | |

| BENIN | |
|---|---|
| **Capital city:** Porto-Novo | |
| **Area:** 112,620 sq km (43,480 sq miles) | |
| **Population:** 6,700,000 | |
| **Official language:** French | |
| **Major religions:** traditional beliefs 50%, Muslim 30%, Christian 20% | |
| **Government:** Multi-party democracy | |
| **Currency:** CFA franc | |
| **Adult literacy rate:** 40% | |
| **Life expectancy:** 53 years | |
| **People per doctor:** 10,000 | |
| **Televisions:** 10 per 1,000 people | |

**LAGOS**
The city of Lagos is situated on a coastal island in the southwest corner of Nigeria. The island was first settled in the 15th century by local Yoruba people. The town grew rapidly as a trading port used by European merchants, and became the capital of independent Nigeria in 1960. In 1992 the capital was moved to Abuja, in central Nigeria, but Lagos is still the biggest city.

## OIL

Oil was first produced in Nigeria in 1956 and within 20 years the new industry dominated the economy. Today it makes up about 95 per cent of the country's exports. Nigerian oil is high quality with a low sulphur content, making it ideal as aircraft fuel. However, it is dangerous for a country to rely on just one product. When world oil prices fell in the 1980s, Nigeria suffered badly. Efforts are now being made to develop other products so that the country is not so dependent on oil.

**Main exports**

Oil: 95%

Others: 5%

*The Niger Delta in the south of the country contains huge oil reserves, enough to last for at least another 25 years. Four huge refineries prepare the crude oil for export.*

## PLANTATIONS

In recent years huge plantations have been set up throughout Nigeria to produce crops in large quantities, mainly for export. Plantations make use of modern machinery to plant, grow, and process the crops, which include cotton, coffee, sugar, cocoa, and oil palms. Today Nigeria is one of the world's largest producers of palm oil. Oil from the fleshy fibre of the palm nut is used in cooking oil, margarine, soap, candles, and paint.

*Farmers clear and plough the land ready to plant crops.*

**SMALL FARMS**
Most Nigerian farmers work on their own small farms. They use hoes, ploughs, and other simple tools to grow food crops such as cassava, rice, yams, and maize to feed their families. They also grow crops such as cocoa, oil palms, rubber, and groundnuts (peanuts) to sell. These are known as cash crops. Despite the recent investment in plantations, most of Nigeria's cash crops are still grown on these small farms.

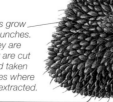

*Oil palm tree*

*Palm nuts grow in large bunches. When they are ripe, they are cut down and taken to factories where the oil is extracted.*

*Fleshy fibre*

*Kernel*

*Cross-section of a palm nut*

## VILLAGE LIFE

Most Nigerians are born and die in the same village and think of it as home even if they move to a big city for a while. Most of the villagers work as farmers, although each village usually has a traditional doctor, blacksmith, and carpenter. Villagers are almost self-sufficient, growing much of their own food, building their own houses, weaving cloth for clothes, and making pots for cooking. Anything they cannot make, they buy with money earned by selling goods in the local market.

*Firewood for cooking*

*Corrugated iron has replaced traditional building materials in many villages*

*Millet, an important part of the diet, is pounded in a clay pot to make flour.*

*Migrants add to the overcrowding in Nigeria's cities, and are often forced to live in shanty towns without proper drains or water supplies.*

*Villagers return from the market in the local town with chickens, cloth, and other goods.*

*In the south of Nigeria most meals include yams or other vegetables. Yams have to be peeled, boiled, and mashed before they can be eaten.*

*Women carry babies in slings made of cloth.*

### MOVING TO THE CITY

Many young Nigerians leave their villages for a few years and move to a city. They go to study, or to earn money that they can send back to their families when profits from farming are low. This money may be used to buy food, or sometimes it is spent on books for a child going to school. Once the migrants have finished their studies or saved up enough money, they return home to their villages.

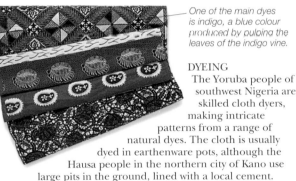

*One of the main dyes is indigo, a blue colour produced by pulping the leaves of the indigo vine.*

### DYEING

The Yoruba people of southwest Nigeria are skilled cloth dyers, making intricate patterns from a range of natural dyes. The cloth is usually dyed in earthenware pots, although the Hausa people in the northern city of Kano use large pits in the ground, lined with a local cement.

### RELIGION

Nigeria is divided in its religious beliefs. In the north, people follow Islam, which was introduced by Arab traders from across the Sahara Desert during the 11th century. Religious festivals, such as this Sallah procession to mark the end of Ramadan (the Islamic month of fasting), are important local events. Five hundred years later, European merchants brought Christianity into the south. Many Nigerians, however, still follow traditional African religions.

# BENIN

SQUASHED UP AGAINST THE WESTERN border of Nigeria, Benin is a long, thin country that stretches north from its narrow Atlantic Ocean coastline to the Niger River. Originally called Dahomey (it was renamed Benin in 1975), the country gained its independence from France in 1960. Since then Benin has had a series of military governments, and been a one-party state. In 1990 it became the first African nation to move from one-party rule to a multi-party democracy. Although it is a poor country, Benin has a growing economy based on agricultural products, such as cotton, cocoa, and coffee.

### COASTAL REGIONS

For centuries, the inhabitants of these stilt houses along the shores of Lake Ganvie have made their living from fishing in the lake. But many former lakes and lagoons have become partly silted up, and many of the fishermen have had to take up sea fishing or move to the towns to try to find work.

*Find out more*

AFRICAN CITIES: *206*
COCOA: *227, 228, 234*
OIL: *137, 152, 281*
RELIGION: *274–275*

# CENTRAL AFRICA

IN FERTILE CENTRAL AFRICA, steaming rainforests cluster around the Equator, and the mighty Congo River snakes its way through Congo and the Democratic Republic of the Congo. In the 1400s, Europeans began a cruel slave trade here; by the late 19th century, the region was colonized. Independence came in the 1960s, but democracy has been slow to arrive. The area has met with mixed fortunes. Countries range from stable, prosperous Cameroon to the Central African Republic, which has been crushed by poverty and harsh dictatorships.

**Faya, Chad**
Jan 21°C (69°F)
July 34°C (93°F)
Jan 0 mm (0 in)
July 0 mm (0 in)

CHAD

### THINGS TO LOOK FOR ON THE MAP

**Longest river:** Congo, Dem. Rep. of Congo 4,666 km (2,900 miles) *Map G10*

**Highest point:** Mt. Stanley, Dem. Rep. of Congo 5,110 m (16,765 ft) *Map K11*

**Largest lake:** L. Tanganyika, Dem. Rep. of Congo 32,893 sq km (12,700 sq miles) *Map K12*

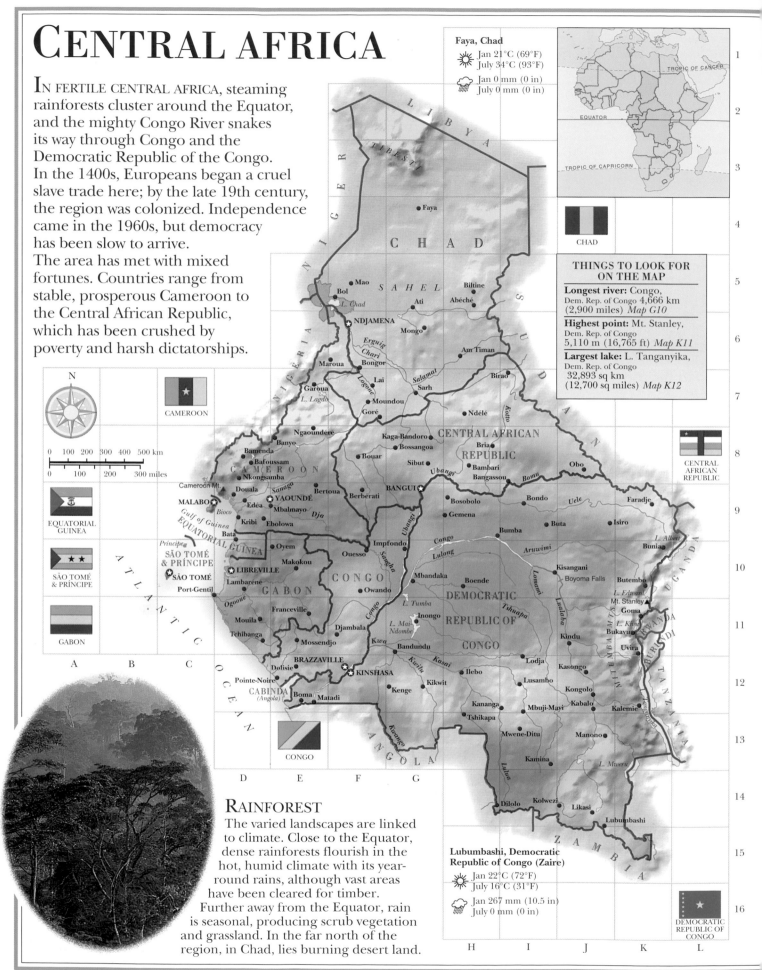

CAMEROON

0 100 200 300 400 500 km
0 100 200 300 miles

EQUATORIAL GUINEA

SÃO TOMÉ & PRÍNCIPE

GABON

CENTRAL AFRICAN REPUBLIC

CONGO

DEMOCRATIC REPUBLIC OF CONGO

## RAINFOREST

The varied landscapes are linked to climate. Close to the Equator, dense rainforests flourish in the hot, humid climate with its year-round rains, although vast areas have been cleared for timber. Further away from the Equator, rain is seasonal, producing scrub vegetation and grassland. In the far north of the region, in Chad, lies burning desert land.

**Lubumbashi, Democratic Republic of Congo (Zaire)**
Jan 22°C (72°F)
July 16°C (31°F)
Jan 267 mm (10.5 in)
July 0 mm (0 in)

# CAMEROON

IN AN AREA THAT HAS SEEN many troubles since independence, Cameroon is a relatively prosperous and stable success story, thanks to sensible government policies. Along with its southern neighbours, Gabon and Congo, the country has earned money from oil, and has used this to develop its economy. Many different peoples live in Cameroon, and its geography is just as varied. The humid coastal plain in the south gives way to a drier central plateau, while a finger of land points up to the marshes around Lake Chad.

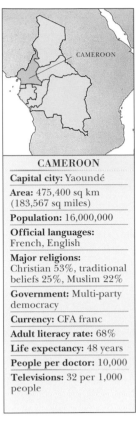

**CAMEROON**

**Capital city:** Yaoundé

**Area:** 475,400 sq km (183,567 sq miles)

**Population:** 16,000,000

**Official languages:** French, English

**Major religions:** Christian 53%, traditional beliefs 25%, Muslim 22%

**Government:** Multi-party democracy

**Currency:** CFA franc

**Adult literacy rate:** 68%

**Life expectancy:** 48 years

**People per doctor:** 10,000

**Televisions:** 32 per 1,000 people

Pearl millet grows to a height of 1.5–3 m (5–10 ft)

## PEOPLES

With more than 130 ethnic groups, Cameroon has one of the richest mixes of peoples and cultures in Africa. These range from the Fulani cattle herders, who live in the north and follow Islamic beliefs, to forest dwellers further south who practise traditional religions. Most people are settled farmers producing enough for their own needs, like this Hausa farmer tending his cattle.

Women grind and sieve the millet grains to make a coarse flour.

Millet can also be used to make beer. It is dried, pounded, and then brewed in large pots.

## GROWING MILLET

Most farmers in Cameroon grow crops, such as millet, for their own use (subsistence farming) and also produce crops to sell. Millet is cultivated widely in northern Cameroon, where there is less rainfall, because it grows well in poorer, drier soils. There has also been great investment in the production of commercial "cash" crops such as cocoa and coffee, oil palms, and bananas.

A stiff white porridge made from millet flour is a popular breakfast dish.

The gourds vibrate when the strings are plucked or a piece of wood is drawn across them.

This bow is basically a wooden stick with strings stretched down its length and dried, hollowed-out gourds placed at intervals.

## MUSIC

Traditional musical instruments of all shapes and sizes, such as this bow, can be heard in villages up and down the country. The most popular style of folk music in Cameroon is *makossa*, which mixes African sounds and soul music, and its lively rhythms are perfect to dance to. *Makossa* is widely enjoyed by people all over central Africa.

## INDUSTRY

Cameroon has an expanding timber industry. The country has extensive forests, and mahogany, ebony, and teak are all exported abroad. However, the industry is hampered by roads that are impassable during the rainy season. Much of the country's wealth is based on its reserves of oil, and other natural resources include bauxite, iron, and gold.

## FOOTBALL

Cameroon has won a place as one of Africa's most celebrated football (soccer) teams after some spectacular displays of skill on home territory and in the World Cup. The people of Cameroon love football, and at lunchtime and in the evenings informal matches spring up on any spare piece of open ground that they can find.

### Find out more

COCOA: *227, 228, 234*
LOGGING: *69, 227, 244*
OIL: *152, 230, 281*
OIL PALMS: *230*

# CENTRAL AFRICAN REPUBLIC

SITUATED AT THE CORE OF AFRICA, the north of the Central African Republic (CAR) is arid, while lush rainforest covers the south. Drought and political unrest have caused great problems. In 1965, Emperor Bokassa began a 14-year reign of terror, which was followed by military dictatorship. Today the country remains under military rule, although the government has pledged to introduce democracy.

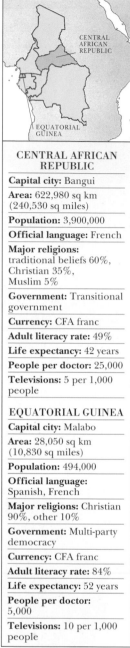

## CENTRAL AFRICAN REPUBLIC

**Capital city:** Bangui

**Area:** 622,980 sq km (240,530 sq miles)

**Population:** 3,900,000

**Official language:** French

**Major religions:** traditional beliefs 60%, Christian 35%, Muslim 5%

**Government:** Transitional government

**Currency:** CFA franc

**Adult literacy rate:** 49%

**Life expectancy:** 42 years

**People per doctor:** 25,000

**Televisions:** 5 per 1,000 people

## EQUATORIAL GUINEA

**Capital city:** Malabo

**Area:** 28,050 sq km (10,830 sq miles)

**Population:** 494,000

**Official language:** Spanish, French

**Major religions:** Christian 90%, other 10%

**Government:** Multi-party democracy

**Currency:** CFA franc

**Adult literacy rate:** 84%

**Life expectancy:** 52 years

**People per doctor:** 5,000

**Televisions:** 10 per 1,000 people

*This woman is sifting diamonds from a river bed.*

### INDUSTRY
A large part of the country's income comes from diamonds. There is potential for developing other industries, too, as gold, iron ore, copper, and uranium are also found here. Flooding caused by heavy seasonal rains, however, is a constant threat to any kind of mining.

### RIVER ROUTES
The CAR is totally surrounded by land, has no railway system and few well-surfaced roads, so its rivers are vital for transport and trade. Nearly three-quarters of trading goods are shipped down the 7,000 km (4,350 miles) of inland waterways. Many goods travel to Brazzaville in Congo. Here they are loaded on to trains and taken to the Atlantic coast.

### PYGMIES
Small huts made from banana leaves are found deep in the country's rainforests. These are the homes of a people known as pygmies, called this because they rarely grow taller than about 1.5 m (5 ft). Pygmies are hunter-gatherers, living on food collected from the rainforest. They are a shining example of people living in harmony with the natural world, without damaging the environment.

# EQUATORIAL GUINEA

THE ECONOMY AND PEOPLE of Equatorial Guinea have suffered badly because of brutal leadership. Macias Nguema ruled as a cruel dictator during the 1970s, but a more moderate government came to power in the 1990s. This tiny, beautiful country, which includes five islands, is now working hard to build its economy.

### FARMING
Although the hot climate and fertile volcanic soil of the largest island, Bioko, are perfect for growing crops, there are few good roads and the workforce is unskilled. Concentrating on growing cocoa for export has left little land for people to grow food for themselves.

*Hippopotamus tooth*

*Animal bone*

*Cowrie shell*

### TRADITIONAL MEDICINE
Traditional medicine is still widely practised in Africa. Animal bones, shells, and wooden sticks are used in public healing ceremonies. The healer will often sing and dance around the patient, using chants to cry out to the spirits for help.

*Tree root*

*Find out more*
COCOA: *227, 228*
DIAMONDS: *150, 226, 248*
HUNTER-GATHERERS: *201*
POLITICAL SYSTEMS: *270–271*

# CHAD

MUCH OF CHAD falls inside a wide belt of hot, dry grassland called the sahel, which extends across the African continent. Drought is a frequent occurence in the sahel. This has proved a disaster for the country because its economy is heavily dependent on agriculture. However, the recent discovery of oil has started to bring wealth into the country. Politically, Chad remains an unstable place.

| CHAD | |
|---|---|
| **Capital city:** Ndjamena | |
| **Area:** 1,284,000 sq km (495,752 sq miles) | |
| **Population:** 8,600,000 | |
| **Official language:** Arabic, French | |
| **Major religions:** Muslim 55%, traditional beliefs 35%, Christian 10% | |
| **Government:** Multi-party democracy | |
| **Currency:** CFA franc | |
| **Adult literacy rate:** 46% | |
| **Life expectancy:** 48 years | |
| **People per doctor:** 33,333 | |
| **Televisions:** 1 per 1,000 people | |

| SAO TOME AND PRINCIPE | |
|---|---|
| **Capital city:** São Tomé | |
| **Area:** 1,001 sq km (386 sq miles) | |
| **Population:** 175,883 | |
| **Official language:** Portuguese | |
| **Major religions:** Christian 84%, other 16% | |
| **Government:** Multi-party democracy | |
| **Currency:** Dobra | |
| **Adult literacy rate:** 83% | |
| **Life expectancy:** 66 years | |
| **People per doctor:** 2,000 | |
| **Televisions:** 163 per 1,000 people | |

THE KANIMBO
Chad's northern deserts stretch up into the Arab lands of North Africa, so the country is a mixture of Arabic and black African influences. More than 100 languages are spoken. One of Chad's many peoples is the Arabic and Muslim group, the Kanimbo, who live as nomads in the arid north.

*Camels being brought to drink at the waters of Lake Chad.*

## DISAPPEARING WATERS

Lake Chad was once a huge expanse of water that formed the meeting point of Chad, Cameroon, Niger, and Nigeria. In the past, water poured into Lake Chad from surrounding rivers, but as the climate has become drier (over the past 10,000 years), so the lake has dried up. The shrinking lake poses a serious problem for the local people, who rely on its fish for food.

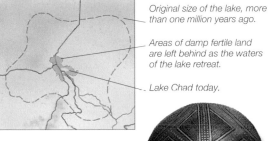

*Original size of the lake, more than one million years ago.*

*Areas of damp fertile land are left behind as the waters of the lake retreat.*

*Lake Chad today.*

*Gourds are one of the crops grown on the fertile land surrounding Lake Chad. When cut and dried, gourds can be carved and decorated.*

# SAO TOME AND PRINCIPE

THE VOLCANIC ISLANDS of São Tomé and Príncipe lie off the coast of Equatorial Guinea and Gabon. Dense tropical forest cloaks the upper slopes whilst lower down farms and large plantations growing cocoa and sugar can be found. The islands were ruled by Portugal until 1975. Today, the people make a living from farming and fishing, and cocoa remains a vital crop.

*The creole people of São Tomé and Príncipe are called filhos de terra, which is Portuguese for "sons of the earth".*

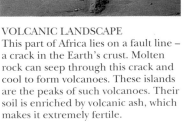

VOLCANIC LANDSCAPE
This part of Africa lies on a fault line – a crack in the Earth's crust. Molten rock can seep through this crack and cool to form volcanoes. These islands are the peaks of such volcanoes. Their soil is enriched by volcanic ash, which makes it extremely fertile.

## CREOLE CULTURE

No one was living on these islands when the Portuguese first landed in the 1400s. Soon most of the population was made up of slaves imported from the mainland. Today, one of the main groups of people are of both African and Portuguese ancestry, creating a creole culture with a distinctive language and style of building.

> **Find out more**
> COCOA: *227, 228, 234*
> PEOPLES OF AFRICA: *206–207*
> SAHEL: *220, 222*
> VOLCANOES: *13*

# GABON

SITTING ASTRIDE THE EQUATOR, and with plentiful rain all year round, three-quarters of Gabon is covered with tropical rainforest. Timber is an increasingly valuable resource, though Gabon's biggest earner is oil. This should have made Gabon a wealthy country, but most people are very poor. This is partly because after independence in 1960, a one-party state was created that wasted much of the wealth. In 1990, Gabon became a multi-party democracy.

**LIBREVILLE**
The capital city, Libreville, means "free town" in French, and was founded in 1849 as a haven for freed slaves. French influence is strong because Gabon was colonized by France during the 1880s. Libreville is a bustling modern city, where some people enjoy great wealth, in contrast to the poverty suffered by most people on the city streets.

## GABON

**Capital city:** Libreville

**Area:** 267,667 sq km (103,346 sq miles)

**Population:** 1,300,000

**Official language:** French

**Major religions:** Christian 55%, traditional beliefs 40%, other 5%

**Government:** Multi-party democracy

**Currency:** CFA franc

**Adult literacy rate:** 71%

**Life expectancy:** 53 years

**People per doctor:** 5,000

**Televisions:** 37 per 1,000 people

## CONGO

**Capital city:** Brazzaville

**Area:** 342,000 sq km (132,046 sq miles)

**Population:** 3,700,000

**Official language:** French

**Major religions:** Traditional beliefs 50%, Christian 48%, Muslim 2%

**Government:** Multi-party democracy

**Currency:** CFA franc

**Adult literacy rate:** 83%

**Life expectancy:** 52 years

**People per doctor:** 3,333

**Televisions:** 12 per 1,000 people

**PEOPLE**
Although just over 1 million people live in Gabon, there are around 40 different ethnic groups here, each speaking their own dialect. The largest group is the Fang, once famed as warriors and skilled wood carvers. Many people in Gabon moved here from other African countries in search of work.

## MINERAL RICH

Oil and manganese became important exports in the 1960s. This manganese mine is in southeast Gabon. The country is one of the world's biggest producers of the mineral, which is used to make paints, batteries, and steel. There are also plentiful reserves of iron ore and other metals, but these have yet to be properly developed.

# CONGO

CONGO'S EASTERN BORDER follows the course of the Congo River and the Ubangi, its main tributary, or offshoot. Oil reserves have boosted Congo's economy considerably in recent years. Although ordinary people have benefited from this more than those in Gabon, many scratch out a living from farming, producing just enough to feed themselves. Cassava, a starchy root vegetable, is the major food crop.

*Oil is of vital importance to Congo, bringing in 90 per cent of the country's export income.*

*Animal skin stretched across the top and fixed with pegs.*

**DRUM BEAT**
As in other parts of Africa, music is a vital part of life, and drum beats form the backbone of this music. Many drums are wooden, and the one shown here is almost as tall as its players. One popular style in the region is called Congo music, which is similar to soul music.

## OIL WEALTH

The government has wisely invested the money that comes from oil in the economy, in projects such as dams, paper mills, transport systems, and forest-planting. Though industry is limited, there is a skilled workforce. Most industries are found around the towns and cities, especially Congo's capital, Brazzaville.

### Find out more

CASSAVA: *221, 240*
OIL: *152, 230, 281*
POLITICAL SYSTEMS: *270–271*
RAINFORESTS: *15, 69, 204*

# DEMOCRATIC REPUBLIC OF THE CONGO

APART FROM A TINY FINGER of land that stretches to the coast, the vast country of the Democratic Republic of the Congo is landlocked. The Congo River snakes its way through the country, providing a watery lifeline for its people. The climate is warm and wet, and most people are farmers. Since independence from Belgium in 1960, the Democratic Republic of the Congo has suffered from civil war, a harsh dictator, and falling prices for its products. These problems have made it one of the world's poorest countries.

*Shells sewn onto material made from vegetable fibres.*

### AFRICAN ART
The Democratic Republic of the Congo is famous for its distinctive art. The Kuba people of the country's central region, whose ancestors date back many centuries, use shells, beads, and raffia (fibres from palm leaves) to create geometric patterns. A Kuba chief would have worn the haunting mask shown above in order to take on some of the power of a great spirit.

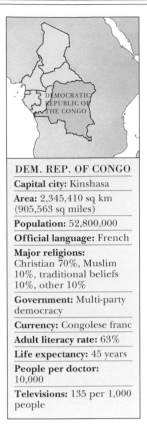

| DEM. REP. OF CONGO | |
|---|---|
| **Capital city:** Kinshasa | |
| **Area:** 2,345,410 sq km (905,563 sq miles) | |
| **Population:** 52,800,000 | |
| **Official language:** French | |
| **Major religions:** Christian 70%, Muslim 10%, traditional beliefs 10%, other 10% | |
| **Government:** Multi-party democracy | |
| **Currency:** Congolese franc | |
| **Adult literacy rate:** 63% | |
| **Life expectancy:** 45 years | |
| **People per doctor:** 10,000 | |
| **Televisions:** 135 per 1,000 people | |

*A hydro-electric dam has been built on the Congo at Inga. The dam harnesses the power of the water to create electricity.*

*Boats stop at river ports for repair work and to refuel.*

## CONGO RIVER
The people here call the Congo River the Zaire. One of the largest rivers in the world, this wide ribbon of water forms the nation's transport system as it cuts a great upside down "U" through miles of forest. People travelling from place to place crowd into motorized boats and dug-out canoes. Some large boats are even floating health clinics or bars. The river's fish provide vital food, while crops are grown on the fertile river banks.

**The course of the Congo River**

Kisangani
Mbandaka
EQUATOR
Kinshasa

*Traders taking their produce to a river market.*

*Tug-boat pushing logs along the river.*

*People travel downstream in dug-out canoes produced by local craftsmen or in passenger boats with outboard motors.*

*The curving Congo River crosses the Equator twice.*

## MINING WEALTH
The Democratic Republic of the Congo's mining industry seems to hold the key to greater wealth in the future. There are vast seams of copper, cobalt, gold, uranium, silver, and diamonds here, and reserves of oil lie just off the coast. Copper mining, shown below, is very important, but when the price of copper fell in the 1970s the economy virtually collapsed.

**Diamond production in Dem. Rep. of the Congo**

x 1,000 carats
25,000
20,000
15,000
10,000
5,000

1948  1970  1980  1990  2000

*The Democratic Republic of the Congo is one of the biggest producers of diamonds in the world. Together with copper and cobalt, they provide about 85% of the country's export earnings.*

### MARKETS
Colourful, bustling river ports are meeting points for trade and travel along the Congo River. Shops selling travel provisions or farming tools nestle alongside markets where people from riverside villages come to sell their goods. Markets are not only based on land. Traders often sell their fresh vegetables and fish direct from their dug-out canoes.

### Find out more
COPPER MINING: *73, 245*
DIAMONDS: *150, 226, 248*
HYDRO-ELECTRICITY: *108, 262*
POLITICAL SYSTEMS: *270–271*

# CENTRAL EAST AFRICA

A LINE OF DRAMATIC HIGHLANDS, volcanic mountains, gorges, and vast lakes runs through this region from Uganda in the north to Malawi in the south. This is part of a huge split in the Earth's crust, known as the Great Rift Valley. Much of the rest of the landscape is flat grassland, called savanna – the perfect environment for the big game animals which draw thousands of tourists to countries such as Kenya and Tanzania. Growing tea and coffee provides another important source of income for the seven countries of the region. Mining and small-scale farming have always been important, and other industries are now increasing.

## SAVANNA LANDSCAPE

Golden grasses that can grow up to 4 m (13 ft) tall cover the flat savanna. The rains come only once a year, so the grasses make the most of whatever water is available by spreading long roots deep into the soil. Needle-like leaves on acacia trees minimize water loss, while baobab trees can store water in their swollen trunks. To protect this landscape and its wildlife, vast areas have been turned into nature reserves, such as the Serengeti in Tanzania and the Masai Mara in Kenya.

### ANIMALS OF THE SAVANNA

Rhinoceroses, giraffes, elephants, antelopes, and zebras wander across the savanna in search of pasture and water. They are closely watched by cheetahs, lions, and leopards, waiting to kill any weak animals. Finally, jackals and vultures will move in to finish off the carcasses.

*Masai warriors and women wear jewellery – usually bead necklaces, large earrings, and copper bracelets.*

*Most Masai men have more than one wife. Each wife lives in a separate hut with her children.*

## FARMING IN THE HIGHLANDS

Most farmers in this region produce only enough food to feed their own families, either from small plots of land or from cattle herding. In the highland areas, which have a cool, moist climate, the volcanic soils are particularly fertile and companies own large farms where tea and coffee are grown for export. However, as the population has grown, many farms have been divided up into impossibly small units. The soil has begun to erode as farmers cultivate even the steepest slopes.

*Tea is made from the leaves of the tea bush. Pickers have to push their way into the bushes to reach the freshest shoots, so they wear rubber aprons to protect themselves.*

## THE RIFT VALLEY

The Great Rift Valley stretches 7,000 km (4,350 miles) from Syria in Asia to Mozambique. Over millions of years, movement between two of the plates that form the Earth's crust have created this dramatic landscape. In some places, this movement has formed steep-sided valleys such as Kenya's Mau Escarpment. Elsewhere, volcanic peaks have erupted and wide plateaux, such as the Athi Plains in Kenya, have formed where lava has seeped through the Earth's surface.

*Africa's tallest mountain is Mount Kilimanjaro, a dormant volcano in the Tanzanian part of the Rift Valley.*

### NOMADIC CATTLE FARMERS

In the lowland areas of central east Africa, where lack of rainfall makes growing crops difficult, nomadic people travel with herds of cattle, sheep, goats, and sometimes donkeys and camels in search of water and grazing. In Kenya, the Masai people herd humpbacked zebu cattle in the area south of Nairobi straddling the Tanzanian border. The Masai keep their cattle for milk and for blood, which they draw off from a vein through a thin reed to drink.

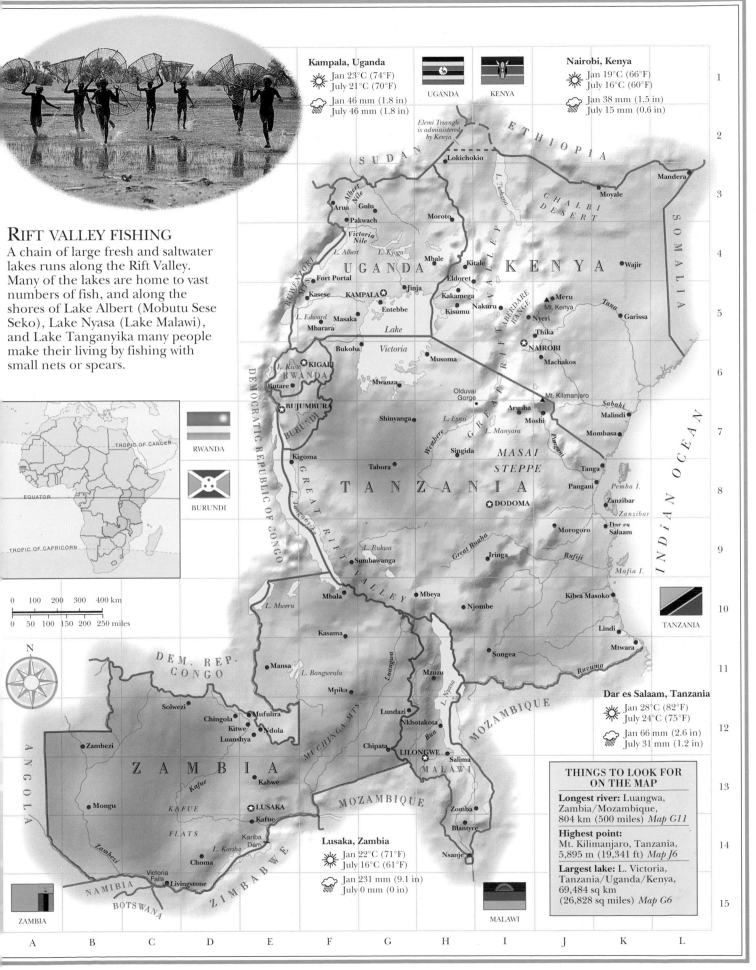

**Kampala, Uganda**
Jan 23°C (74°F)
July 21°C (70°F)
Jan 46 mm (1.8 in)
July 46 mm (1.8 in)

UGANDA  KENYA

**Nairobi, Kenya**
Jan 19°C (66°F)
July 16°C (60°F)
Jan 38 mm (1.5 in)
July 15 mm (0.6 in)

## RIFT VALLEY FISHING

A chain of large fresh and saltwater lakes runs along the Rift Valley. Many of the lakes are home to vast numbers of fish, and along the shores of Lake Albert (Mobutu Sese Seko), Lake Nyasa (Lake Malawi), and Lake Tanganyika many people make their living by fishing with small nets or spears.

RWANDA

BURUNDI

**Lusaka, Zambia**
Jan 22°C (71°F)
July 16°C (61°F)
Jan 231 mm (9.1 in)
July 0 mm (0 in)

**Dar es Salaam, Tanzania**
Jan 28°C (82°F)
July 24°C (75°F)
Jan 66 mm (2.6 in)
July 31 mm (1.2 in)

TANZANIA

ZAMBIA

MALAWI

### THINGS TO LOOK FOR ON THE MAP

**Longest river:** Luangwa, Zambia/Mozambique, 804 km (500 miles) *Map G11*

**Highest point:** Mt. Kilimanjaro, Tanzania, 5,895 m (19,341 ft) *Map J6*

**Largest lake:** L. Victoria, Tanzania/Uganda/Kenya, 69,484 sq km (26,828 sq miles) *Map G6*

0 100 200 300 400 km
0 50 100 150 200 250 miles

N

# UGANDA

BEFORE INDEPENDENCE, Uganda was a prosperous country, which Winston Churchill called the "Pearl of Africa". But by 1986, the country lay shattered and bankrupt. From 1971–79, President Idi Amin ruled Uganda as a dictator. During this period, thousands of people were persecuted or murdered, Europeans and Asians were expelled, and their property was seized. International aid was cut off when other countries realized how corrupt Amin's government was. In 1979, Amin was deposed, but the disruption continued until 1986, when President Yoweri Museveni came to power. His government restored peace and has begun to rebuild the economy.

**FISHING IN LAKE VICTORIA**
The vast, shallow Lake Victoria is shared by Uganda, Tanzania, and Kenya. Huge Nile perch fish were introduced to the lake 30 years ago to increase fish production and provide sport fishing for tourists. Since then the perch have spread to every corner of Lake Victoria and have devoured most of its original species.

| UGANDA |
| --- |
| **Capital city:** Kampala |
| **Area:** 236,040 sq km (91,135 sq miles) |
| **Population:** 25,800,000 |
| **Official language:** English |
| **Major religions:** Traditional beliefs 84%, Muslim 8%, other 8% |
| **Government:** Non-party government |
| **Currency:** New Uganda shilling |
| **Adult literacy rate:** 69% |
| **Life expectancy:** 43 years |
| **People per doctor:** 20,000 |
| **Televisions:** 27 per 1,000 people |

*The cassava plant grows up to 90 cm (3 ft) tall. It is grown for its roots, which can be eaten as a vegetable or ground to make flour.*

*Kampala is said to be built on seven hills. The city centre lies on just one of them – Nakasero Hill.*

## FARMING

Fertile, volcanic soil and high levels of rainfall make more than four-fifths of Uganda's land suitable for farming. Large plantations produce the coffee, cotton, and tea which make up 70 per cent of the country's exports. Although 80 per cent of employed Ugandans work on farms, most are involved in small-scale farming, growing crops such as maize, millet, cassava, and sweet potatoes for their own use or to sell in local markets.

*Sweet potato (left) and cassava (right) are common vegetables in this region.*

**KAMPALA**
People in Uganda's capital, Kampala, rarely go out without an umbrella, as most days see a heavy downpour in the afternoon. Kampala has an average of 242 days a year with violent thunderstorms. By evening, the rain has stopped and the air is cool. Kampala suffered much destruction during and immediately after Amin's period in power, but is now being restored with the help of foreign investment.

**What Have You Heard About AIDS?**

What Does It Mean?
How Does It Harm Us?
Who Can Get It?
What Causes It?
How Can We Stop It?

What Can We Do For People Who Have It?
How Can It Be Cured?
What Does It Look Like?
Which Of Us Has It?

**Don't GUESS the Answers!**
**LEARN THE TRUTH ABOUT AIDS!**

## AIDS AWARENESS

Uganda had one of the highest numbers of HIV and AIDS sufferers in the world. HIV (which can lead to AIDS) is a mainly sexually transmitted disease and as yet there is no known cure for it. Doctors are trying to teach people how to avoid contracting the disease. Special campaigns aimed at educating children, such as this UNICEF poster, have dramatically reduced the rate of infection.

**WILDLIFE**
In Ruwenzori National Park, tourists can take a boat trip down the Kazinga Channel to see thousands of hippos and pelicans. Much of Uganda's wildlife was wiped out during the years of conflict, and today there are not many places in Africa where you are likely to see so many hippos.

*Find out more*
COFFEE: 50, 62, 66
LAKE VICTORIA: 204
POLITICAL SYSTEMS: 270–271
TEA: 172, 238

# RWANDA

SINCE 1994, RWANDA HAS rarely been out of the news. War between the two main ethnic groups – the Tutsi and Hutu – has torn Rwanda apart and wrecked its economy, leaving it one of the poorest countries in the world. Before the war, Rwanda's main export was coffee. Today, although 95 per cent of the people still live off on the land, few crops are grown for export. The country's instability has also hindered attempts to develop manufacturing and mining industries.

| RWANDA | |
|---|---|
| **Capital city:** Kigali | |
| **Area:** 26,338 sq km (10,169 sq miles) | |
| **Population:** 8,400,000 | |
| **Official languages:** French and Kinyarwanda | |
| **Major religions:** Traditional beliefs 50%, Christian 45%, other 5% | |
| **Government:** Multi-party democracy | |
| **Currency:** Rwanda franc | |
| **Adult literacy rate:** 69% | |
| **Life expectancy:** 40 years | |
| **People per doctor:** 20,000 | |
| **Televisions:** No figures available | |

| BURUNDI | |
|---|---|
| **Capital city:** Bujumbura | |
| **Area:** 27,830 sq km (10,745 sq miles) | |
| **Population:** 6,800,000 | |
| **Official languages:** French and Kirundi | |
| **Major religions:** Christian 60%, traditional beliefs 39%, Muslim 1% | |
| **Government:** Transitional government | |
| **Currency:** Burundi franc | |
| **Adult literacy rate:** 50% | |
| **Life expectancy:** 42 years | |
| **People per doctor:** 10,000 | |
| **Televisions:** 4 per 1,000 people | |

## GENOCIDE

In 1994 centuries-old tensions between the majority Hutu and minority Tutsi populations boiled over into one of the world's worst acts of genocide (the murder of one ethnic group). About 800,000 of the previously dominant Tutsi were massacred alongside some of their Hutu supporters. Over one million Rwandans fled the country. Although peace has been restored, few people have been put on trial and tensions remain high.

### HEALTH
Rwanda is one of Africa's most densely populated countries, and the population continues to grow. Most Rwandan women have at least six children, compared to an average of only one or two in developed countries. However, few Rwandans live to be over 50. Diseases such as malaria and AIDS are common, and medical facilities are in short supply and are rarely free, so few people can afford them.

*There are only about 650 gorillas left in the world. The mountain gorilla is found only in this region of Africa.*

MOUNTAIN GORILLAS
One of the last known refuges for the mountain gorilla is the Volcanoes National Park in Rwanda. Even though the gorilla is protected here, it is still in danger of extinction by poachers, and its habitat is threatened by farming.

# BURUNDI

UNTIL INDEPENDENCE IN 1962, Burundi and neighbouring Rwanda formed one country. Like Rwanda, Burundi is home to Tutsi and Hutu people, and the wars between these tribes have been part of Burundi's history too. In 1972, about 10,000 Hutu were killed by Tutsis. Warfare continues today, although a peace agreement was reached in 2000. Burundi's problems are made worse by fighting in neighbouring Democratic Republic of the Congo.

### DRUMMING GROUPS
In Burundi, stories, songs, and music are passed down from generation to generation rather than written down in a formal way. Tutsi folk dancing is one of the highlights of traditional culture, as are the groups of 12 to 15 drummers who play together with no other instruments.

POPULATION PRESSURE
Most people in Burundi make their living from farming. So many people live in the most fertile areas that land is very scarce. Plots of land are usually just large enough to support a family in good years, but bad weather or disease can lead to widespread famine. In some areas, the land is so over-used that the soil has begun to erode.

*Find out more*
HEALTH: *276*
POPULATION: *16–17, 206*
REFUGEES: *207*
SOIL EROSION: *55, 244*

# KENYA

UNLIKE MANY AFRICAN countries, Kenya has been stable and relatively democratic since it gained its independence from Britain in 1963. Under British rule, large farms were created in many areas to produce cash crops, and a network of roads and railways were built to link ports and towns. Today, Kenya is one of Africa's richest countries, producing crops such as coffee and tea for export, and welcoming tourists to its vast game reserves. Side-by-side with this, many people still make their living from small farms or cattle herding. Kenya used to have one of the world's fastest growing populations, leaving it with increasing poverty, rivalry over land, and some ethnic violence.

### KENYA

**Capital city:** Nairobi

**Area:** 582,650 sq km (224,961 sq miles)

**Population:** 32,000,000

**Official language:** Kiswahili, English

**Major religions:** Christian 60%, traditional beliefs 25%, Muslim 6%, other 9%

**Government:** Multi-party democracy

**Currency:** Kenya shilling

**Adult literacy rate:** 84%

**Life expectancy:** 46 years

**People per doctor:** 10,000

## NAIROBI

Lions, giraffes, and cheetahs roam the plains which surround Kenya's capital, Nairobi, with the tower blocks of the modern city as a backdrop. This is the largest city in east Africa, with a population of about 3 million people. It developed after European colonization as a convenient stopping place on the railway from Uganda to Kenya's main port of Mombasa.

### Kenya's main crops

*The main farming area, shown enlarged on the map below, is in the southwest of the country.*

KENYA

*On game reserves such as Kenya's Masai Mara and Amboseli National Park, tourists can photograph wild animals close up.*

- Coffee
- Tea
- Sisal
- Sugarcane
- Rice
- Forest
- Other

Tea

Coffee beans

## FARMING AND THE ECONOMY

Farming is Kenya's chief export earner, but much of the country is far too dry to grow crops. In the highlands – where there is more rain – tea, coffee, wheat, maize, sisal, and sugarcane are grown. Where less water is available, dairy and meat cattle are farmed on large ranches. Dams and lakes provide water to irrigate land for growing market garden crops, such as green beans, which are exported by air to foreign supermarkets.

Green beans

## TOURISM

Tropical beaches and some of Africa's best game reserves attract thousands of tourists to Kenya. Tourism is vital to the country's economy, and the government has invested in roads, airports, and hotels to make Kenya one of the easiest and most comfortable African countries for tourists to visit. Because most people come to see the animals on game reserves, the government has placed a high priority on protecting wildlife and stamping out poaching.

### KENYAN PEOPLES

These villagers belong to Kenya's largest tribe, the Kikuyu, who live around Mount Kenya. The Kikuyu god, Ngai, is believed to live on the mountain, so the Kikuyu traditionally built their houses with the door facing the mountain. Like two-thirds of the country's 70 tribal groups, the Kikuyu speak Bantu. Small numbers of Asians, Arabs, and Europeans also live in Kenya.

### KENYAN ATHLETES

Athletes from Kenya's Rift Valley area excel at running long distances. They have won gold in the Olympic 3,000 m steeplechase events in five recent Olympic Games, and Kenyan Moses Kiptanui was the first man to run the 3,000 m steeplechase in under eight minutes. The runners' skill may stem from the high altitude they live and train in, or perhaps from years of running long distances to school.

### Find out more

AFRICAN CITIES: *206*
HIGHLAND FARMING: *238*
POPULATION: *16–17, 206*
RIFT VALLEY: *204*

# TANZANIA

TANZANIA WAS CREATED in 1964, when the mainland country of Tanganyika and the island of Zanzibar united. For its first 21 years, Tanzania had a socialist government, which tried to encourage people to work together on schemes such as state-run plantations. Although now it is expanding its range of exports, Tanzania is much poorer than neighbouring Kenya, and only about one third of people live in towns and cities. About 120 different peoples live here, most of whom speak Kiswahili, a language which developed as a means of communication between Africans and foreign traders.

## TANZANIA

**Capital city:** Dodoma

**Area:** 945,087 sq km (364,898 sq miles)

**Population:** 37,000,000

**Official languages:** Kiswahili, English

**Major religions:** Traditional beliefs 30%, Muslim 33%, Christian 33%, other 4%

**Government:** Multi-party democracy

**Currency:** Tanzanian shilling

**Adult literacy rate:** 77%

**Life expectancy:** 43 years

**People per doctor:** 25,000

**Televisions:** 21 per 1,000 people

OLDUVAI GORGE
The steep sides of Olduvai Gorge in northern Tanzania were carved out of the flat Serengeti Plain by the flow of water over millions of years. Here, archaeologists have unearthed fossils of the earliest humans, dating back 2 million years. Yet more ancient footprints of human-like creatures have been discovered too, left by two adults and a child walking across the still-soft lava that formed the plain, 3.5 million years ago.

**Making sisal fibre**

*The outer leaves of the sisal plant are cut off close to the stalk when they reach their full length.*

*The sisal fibre is usually obtained by crushing the leaves between rollers. The pulp is removed, leaving strands of white fibre over 1 m (3 ft) long.*

*The strands of fibre are washed and then hung out to dry.*

DAR ES SALAAM
Although Tanzania's capital is now the purpose-built inland city of Dodoma, the old capital Dar es Salaam remains the country's biggest city and port. It is also the end of the TanZam railway which carries goods from land-locked Zambia to the sea.

*The name Dar es Salaam means "Haven of Peace". The city is still fairly small, with few high-rise buildings and many low, red-tiled roofs.*

## SISAL
One of Tanzania's main crops is sisal, a plant with leaves that are used to make rope and twine, and also mats, brushes, hats, and baskets. Sisal ropes are particularly useful on board ships since they do not rot in sea-water. However, Tanzania's sisal trade is now under threat because many products made with sisal in the past can now be made with synthetic substitutes.

*String made from sisal.*

## TANZANIAN VILLAGES
The country's population used to be scattered in small villages. Then, in 1970, the government started a programme to resettle the population in larger villages of about 250 households. By grouping people together in this way, it is easier and more economic to provide schools, water, and other services, and to distribute fertilizers and seeds. Today, 66 per cent of Tanzanians live in villages in the countryside.

*The buildings and style of clothes reflect Zanzibar's continuing Arabic flavour.*

ZANZIBAR
Off Tanzania's coast lies the island of Zanzibar. In the 18th and 19th centuries, the port of Zanzibar, on the island's western side, was used as an Arab trading post. African slaves passed though here, en route to the Arab world. The island's main crop, cloves, was also shipped out of the port. The clove tree was only introduced to the island in 1818, but today Zanzibar is the world's third largest producer.

---

***Find out more***

EARLY PEOPLE: *206*
POLITICAL SYSTEMS: *270–271*
POPULATION DISTRIBUTION: *206*
TANZAM RAILWAY: *245*

---

# MALAWI

LYING ON A PLATEAU at the southern end of the Great Rift Valley, Malawi's six major tribal groups have lived together in relative peace. This was in part due to the harsh rule of the dictator Hastings Banda. However since democracy was introduced in 1994, there have been some open political tensions. Malawi's economy is based on agriculture, but the government is trying to encourage the growth of agricultural processing industries, such as food canning and cooking oil manufacture, as well as mining and other heavy industries. New mineral deposits were discovered in 2000.

**MALAWI**

**Capital city:** Lilongwe

**Area:** 118,480 sq km (45,745 sq miles)

**Population:** 12,100,000

**Official languages:** English

**Major religions:** Christian 75%, Muslim 20%, traditional beliefs 5%

**Government:** Multi-party democracy

**Currency:** Malawian kwacha

**Adult literacy rate:** 62%

**Life expectancy:** 38 years

**People per doctor:** 20,000

**Televisions:** 2 per 1,000 people

## LAKE NYASA

Over one-fifth of Malawi's total area is taken up by Lake Nyasa, one of the largest and deepest lakes in the world.

*Fishermen collect these brightly coloured fish, called cichlids, for export to aquariums around the world.*

A huge fishing industry has developed around the lake, which is home to more than 500 species of fish. A sardine-like fish called the usipa is one of the main catches. The fish are dried on the shore and sold throughout Malawi. However overfishing has meant that there are not enough fish left over anymore to export.

*Many people grow just enough food to feed themselves and their families. If there is any extra produce, they sell it in local markets like this one.*

## FARMING

Farming is the most important business in Malawi. Tobacco, tea, and sugar make up 85 per cent of exports, and more than 80 per cent of Malawi's population make their living by farming. To increase the land available to farm, swamps have been drained, and woodland has been cleared. Rivers have been dammed and wells dug to water dry grasslands. Poor harvests can lead to extreme hardship among Malawi's people.

**Soil erosion**

*Wind blows away soil on exposed areas.*

*Tree roots help to bind the soil together.*

*If the trees are cut down, wind and rain wear away the soil.*

*Water runs down the hillside, washing the soil away to form gulleys.*

**PEOPLE OF MALAWI**

Malawi is one of the least urbanized countries in the world, with 85 per cent of its population living in villages in the countryside, mostly near the seasonal wetlands, called *dambos*. Villages are small and are usually made up of people who are closely related. Unlike many other African countries, Malawi's main ethnic groups, the Chewas, Nyanja, Tumbuka, Tonga, Ngonis, and Yao, live together peacefully.

## FORESTS

Forests and woodlands cover nearly half the country, but huge areas have been cut down for fuel and to clear land for farming. Malawi has no oil and little coal, so the most popular fuel is charcoal, made by partially burning wood so that it becomes smokeless and slow-burning. Where more land is needed for farming, trees are cut down and burned, and then crops are grown in the ashes. Such land is fertile for only a short time, as the forest soil is quickly eroded.

**HASTINGS BANDA**

For 30 years after independence, Dr Hastings Banda was president of Malawi, and ruled the country virtually alone. His government helped the country to become strong and self-reliant, but other political opinions were not tolerated and many people were tortured or imprisoned. In 1994, democratic elections led to Banda's downfall.

*Find out more*

DEFORESTATION: 69, 227, 233
PEOPLES OF AFRICA: 206–207
POLITICAL SYSTEMS: 270–271
REFUGEES: 207

# ZAMBIA

ZAMBIA OCCUPIES A BROAD plateau scattered with mountains and deep valleys. After independence from Britain in 1963, political violence based on tribal differences rocked the country until 1972, when President Kenneth Kaunda declared a one-party state. In 1991, Kaunda was defeated in the first democratic election for 19 years. Today, the country is less affected by ethnic conflict than many African states, even though there are 14 main tribal groups. Zambia is the world's largest producer of copper, and also exports seasonal vegetables, flowers, and cotton.

## ZAMBIA

**Capital city:** Lusaka

**Area:** 752,614 sq km (290,584 sq miles)

**Population:** 10,800,000

**Official languages:** English

**Major religions:** Christian 63%, traditional beliefs 36%, other 1%

**Government:** Multi-party democracy

**Currency:** Zambian kwacha

**Adult literacy rate:** 80%

**Life expectancy:** 37 years

**People per doctor:** 10,000

**Televisions:** 137 per 1,000 people

**Mineral deposits in Zambia**

Copper

Cobalt

*TanZam railway*

Kasama

*The copperbelt*

ZAMBIA

Lusaka

Livingstone

**Zambia's exports**

Copper: 49%

Other: 33%

Cobalt: 18%

*Copper ore*

## CITIES

A chain of shanty towns lies along the railway linking Zambia's copperbelt with the capital Lusaka. The makeshift shacks have no water, power, or drains, and disease is widespread. Most people here have jobs in the copper industry. In fact, 40 per cent of Zambians live in the towns, making it the most urbanized country in the region. Many Zambian families have been city dwellers for three or four generations, which is rare for Africa.

### TANZAM RAILWAY

Landlocked Zambia has to rely on roads and railways through other countries to export copper and other products to ports, so good relations with its neighbours are important. Until the 1960s, most goods went through Rhodesia (now Zimbabwe), but relations between the two countries broke down. Today, the main trade route is the TanZam railway, through Tanzania.

*The TanZam railway links Zambia to the port of Dar es Salaam, in neighbouring Tanzania.*

## COPPER MINING

Seams of copper run through an area over 320 km (200 miles) long and 50 km (30 miles) wide in central Zambia, called the copperbelt. First developed commercially in the 1930s, copper mining has funded much of Zambia's development. Copper accounts for 50 per cent of the country's exports, and if the world price of copper were to fall, Zambia's economy could be wrecked. To add to this problem, the copper reserves are beginning to run out.

## ZAMBEZI RIVER

Forming Zambia's southern border, the Zambezi River is one of the country's main tourist attractions. Visitors can go white-water rafting on the river, take a wildlife safari in one of the area's game parks, and visit the magnificent Victoria Falls. A huge dam at Kariba provides power in the form of hydroelectricity for Zambia's copperbelt and for neighbouring Zimbabwe. Lake Kariba, the artificial lake formed by the dam, is a popular fishing destination for tourists.

### FISH EAGLE

National parks, set up to protect wildlife, take up more than one-third of the country's area. The fish eagle is Zambia's national symbol, and appears on the country's flag. It is common around open stretches of water, where it swoops down to snatch fish from the surface and rises up with a fish in its talons.

---

***Find out more***

EXPORT DEPENDENCY: *281*
HYDROELECTRICITY: *108, 262*
POLITICAL SYSTEMS: *270–271*
VICTORIA FALLS: *250*

# SOUTHERN AFRICA

THE EIGHT COUNTRIES THAT MAKE UP southern Africa have much in common. Once governed by European settlers, almost all of them had to struggle to achieve independence. Many endured years of vicious warfare. Today, all eight countries are independent, multi-racial democracies. Their climate ranges from warm and mild in the south to tropical in the north, while the landscape includes both deserts and rainforests, vast plains, and towering mountain ranges. The population varies in wealth from extremely rich industrialists and landowners in South Africa to hunter-gatherer Bushmen in the Kalahari Desert.

*Before 1994, demonstrations against apartheid were held throughout South Africa.*

*The magnificent Table Mountain towers above Cape Town in the Cape Peninsula, South Africa. The Cape is home to many unique species of plants and flowers.*

## POLITICS

Southern Africa is dominated by the politics of South Africa. After 1948, South Africa pursued a policy of separate development for white and black people known as apartheid. South Africa tried to weaken the neighbouring countries that opposed it. It supported rebels fighting the Angolan and Mozambique governments, and helped those resisting black rule in Zimbabwe and Namibia. The ending of white rule in 1994 led to better relations between South Africa and its neighbours.

## A LAND OF CONTRASTS

The landscape of Southern Africa varies from the Namib and Kalahari deserts in the west and centre to lush vegetation and tropical forests in the north. Inland, vast grassy savannas and woodlands are home to much of the region's wildlife, from the minute *dik-dik* (the world's smallest antelope) to the African elephant. Game reserves and national parks have been set up to protect endangered species. Tourists come from all over the world to visit the reserves and enjoy the dramatic scenery.

### OKAVANGO DELTA

Unlike most rivers, which run out to the sea, the Okavango River runs inland into a desert. The river begins in Angola, then flows southeast through Namibia into a delta in the Kalahari Desert in Botswana. The vast swamps and waterways of the river and its delta cover an area of more than 22,000 sq km (8,500 sq miles). This provides a haven for a wide variety of plants and animals. People travel into the swamps in dug-out canoes, called *mokoros*.

### KALAHARI BUSHMEN

The Bushmen, or San, of the Kalahari Desert are one of the few groups of hunter-gatherers left in Africa. These people live and work together in small, tightly knit communities. Traditionally they moved from place to place, searching for insects and edible plants and hunting small animals with poisonous arrows. Today, however, many of the San live a more settled existence.

## MINERAL RICHES

Southern Africa is rich in mineral resources. Much of the world's gold, diamonds, uranium, and copper come from the region, and have transformed the local economies. Botswana is the most dependent upon its mineral resources. Almost 80 per cent of the country's export earnings come from diamonds. South Africa is the world's leading producer of gold, and Namibia has one of the world's largest uranium mines. Coal is southern Africa's major source of energy. South Africa, Zimbabwe, Botswana, and Mozambique all have large coal reserves.

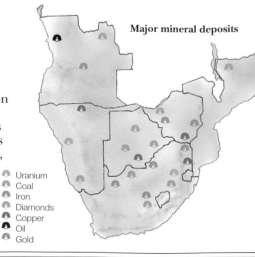

**Major mineral deposits**

- Uranium
- Coal
- Iron
- Diamonds
- Copper
- Oil
- Gold

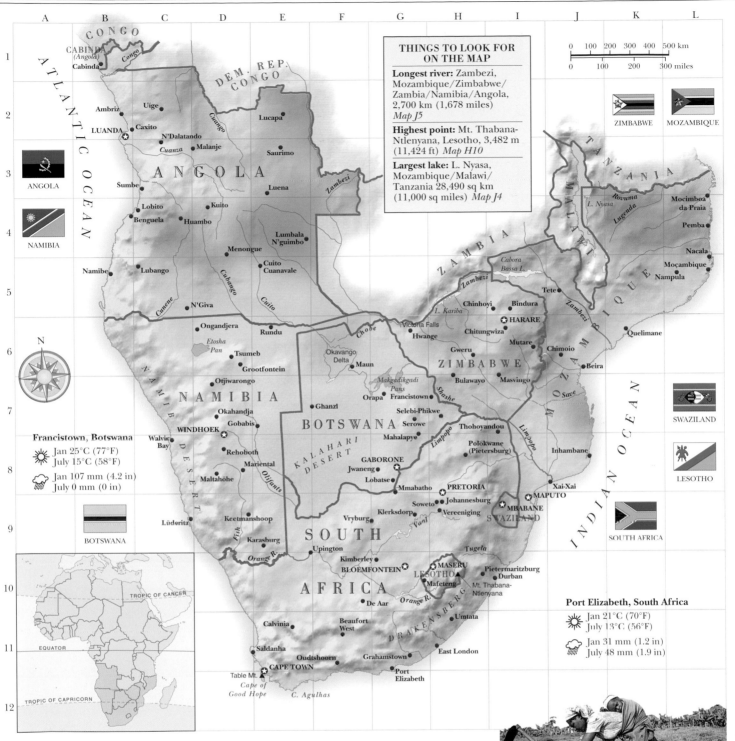

A B C D E F G H I J K L

### THINGS TO LOOK FOR ON THE MAP

**Longest river:** Zambezi, Mozambique/Zimbabwe/Zambia/Namibia/Angola, 2,700 km (1,678 miles) *Map J5*

**Highest point:** Mt. Thabana-Ntlenyana, Lesotho, 3,482 m (11,424 ft) *Map H10*

**Largest lake:** L. Nyasa, Mozambique/Malawi/Tanzania 28,490 sq km (11,000 sq miles) *Map J4*

0 100 200 300 400 500 km
0 100 200 300 miles

ZIMBABWE

MOZAMBIQUE

ANGOLA

NAMIBIA

**Francistown, Botswana**
Jan 25°C (77°F)
July 15°C (58°F)
Jan 107 mm (4.2 in)
July 0 mm (0 in)

BOTSWANA

SWAZILAND

LESOTHO

SOUTH AFRICA

**Port Elizabeth, South Africa**
Jan 21°C (70°F)
July 13°C (56°F)
Jan 31 mm (1.2 in)
July 48 mm (1.9 in)

TROPIC OF CANCER
EQUATOR
TROPIC OF CAPRICORN

## CITY GROWTH

Across southern Africa, people are leaving the countryside and moving to the cities in search of work. The outlying areas surrounding such cities as Johannesburg in South Africa are crammed with shanty towns which are now a permanent feature of the landscape. Maputo, the capital of Mozambique (right), doubled in size between 1975 and 1983, and now contains more than 1.5 million people.

### WOMEN'S ROLE

In traditional African society, women generally acted as wives and mothers and were responsible for routine household tasks and growing crops. Today, many African men work away from home in the mines and cities for one or two years at a time, leaving women to form the majority in their villages. This means that women are now taking on more responsibility in the households.

# ANGOLA

ANGOLA SHOULD BE ONE of the most successful countries in Africa. The land is largely fertile, with dense tropical forests in the north giving way to drier grasslands in the south. Farmers produce enough food to support the small population, while huge oil and mineral reserves bring wealth to the economy. However, Angola has been torn apart by a civil war that began in 1975. Few parts of the country have been left unaffected by the fighting, which has killed or injured thousands of people and reduced this potentially rich country to poverty.

| ANGOLA | |
|---|---|
| **Capital city:** Luanda | |
| **Area:** 1,246,700 sq km (481,351 sq miles) | |
| **Population:** 13,600,000 | |
| **Official language:** Portuguese | |
| **Major religions:** Christian 70%, other 30% | |
| **Government:** Transitional government | |
| **Currency:** New kwanza | |
| **Adult literacy rate:** 40% | |
| **Life expectancy:** 47 years | |
| **People per doctor:** 10,000 | |
| **Televisions:** 14 per 1,000 people | |

● Major towns
‥‥‥‥ Benguela railway

*The Benguela railway runs from the coastal ports of Benguela and Lobito in Angola, and heads eastwards across country until reaching Zaire.*

## CIVIL WAR

In 1975, Portuguese rule in Angola ended and civil war broke out. The conflict was between the Angolan People's Liberation Movement (MPLA), supported by the Soviet Union and Cuba, and the National Union for Total Angolan Independence (UNITA), supported by South Africa and the USA. After a ceasefire in 1991, the MPLA were elected into power, but fighting broke out again. A ceasefire in 2002 has now brought some peace to this shattered land.

LUANDA
The port of Luanda is Angola's capital and biggest city. Founded by the Portuguese in 1576, for centuries it was a centre for shipping slaves to the Portuguese colony of Brazil. The Portuguese built a fort and many other fine buildings which stand alongside modern skyscrapers. On the hills surrounding the city vast shanty towns house thousands of people.

## BENGUELA RAILWAY

Opened in 1931, the Benguela railway was built to transport copper and other minerals from the mines of landlocked Zambia and the Congo to the coastal ports of Lobito and Benguela for export round the world. The railway and ports provided work for many Angolans, who lost their jobs when the railway was destroyed in the civil war. After the ceasefire of 1991, engineers began to rebuild sections of the track, and plans have been made to reopen the railway.

## INDUSTRY

The tiny Angolan territory of Cabinda, to the north of the main part of the country, is one of the richest oil-producing regions in Africa. Offshore oil fields contain reserves of 1,500 million barrels of oil and vast quantities of natural gas. Some of the richest diamond deposits in the world are found in the northeast of the country, while iron and other minerals are mined further south. However, constant fighting has destroyed some mines and factories.

*A brace divides the bow string into two unequal lengths.*

MUSICAL BOW
The Humbi people of southwestern Angola use an ordinary hunting bow as a musical instrument. The musician supports the bow with one hand and holds it in his mouth. As he hits the string with a stick held in his other hand, he produces different notes by altering the shape of his lips.

*Find out more*
AFRICAN CITIES: *206*
DIAMONDS: *150, 226, 248*
OIL: *152, 230, 281*
RAILWAYS: *245*

# BOTSWANA

WITH ONE OF THE WORLD'S FASTEST growing economies, based on rich diamond supplies and large cattle ranches, Botswana was one of Africa's few real economic success stories. In recent years however it has become the most powerful symbol of Africa's greatest modern threat – HIV and AIDS. It has one of the highest proportions of sufferers in the world – 36 per cent of adults are infected.

GABORONE
When Botswana became independent, the country had no capital city, as it had previously been governed from Mafikeng in South Africa. The new country therefore built a new capital, called Gaborone. Today more than 200,000 people live in the city, which houses the national government and is the centre of communications and industry.

| BOTSWANA |
|---|
| **Capital city:** Gaborone |
| **Area:** 600,370 sq km (231,803 sq miles) |
| **Population:** 1,800,000 |
| **Official language:** English |
| **Major religions:** traditional beliefs 50%, Christian 30%, other 20% |
| **Government:** Multi-party democracy |
| **Currency:** Pula |
| **Adult literacy rate:** 79% |
| **Life expectancy:** 38 years |
| **People per doctor:** 3,333 |
| **Televisions:** 20 per 1,000 people |

| NAMIBIA |
|---|
| **Capital city:** Windhoek |
| **Area:** 825,418 sq km (318,694 sq miles) |
| **Population:** 2,000,000 |
| **Official language:** English |
| **Major religions:** Christian 90%, traditional beliefs 10% |
| **Government:** Multi-party democracy |
| **Currency:** Namibian dollar |
| **Adult literacy rate:** 83% |
| **Life expectancy:** 42 years |
| **People per doctor:** 3,333 |
| **Televisions:** 21 per 1,000 people |

*Parents and young children live in the main sleeping hut.*

*People cook, eat, and receive guests in the lolwapa.*

*Trees are valued for their shade.*

*Women are responsible for building and maintaining the huts.*

## TSWANA HOMES

The Tswana people, who make up most of the Botswana population, traditionally organize themselves into chiefdoms. Each chiefdom consists of a capital town, around which are a number of satellite villages. Families live in dwellings made up of three or four huts, each hut serving a particular purpose. The huts are arranged around a central courtyard, or *lolwapa*.

*The lolwapa is surrounded by a low wall.*

*The thatched roof is supported on poles which encircle the wall of the hut. The space between the wall and the roof gives ventilation.*

*The huts are decorated with finger markings in earth shades of brown, red, and orange.*

# NAMIBIA

ORIGINALLY A GERMAN COLONY, Namibia was governed by its neighbour, South Africa, from 1915 until independence in 1990. Rich in minerals and other natural resources, the country is dominated by the Namib Desert, which runs in a thin strip down the west of the country near the Atlantic Ocean, and the vast Kalahari Desert, which lies in the south.

*Copper*

MINING
Namibia is one of the four biggest mineral producers in Africa, with large deposits of copper, diamonds, tin, and other minerals. One of the world's largest uranium mines is located at Rössing, in the Namib Desert in the centre of the country. Namibia is also the largest producer of salt in Africa.

*To show that she is married, a Himba woman will lengthen her hair by adding hair cut from her brother's head.*

## RURAL LIFE

Most Namibian people live on the high plains in the north of the country. Here the Ovambo people build fenced-in enclosures known as *kraals*. The Himba people live further west in the rugged land bordering Angola. These semi-nomadic people make their living from tending cattle, which provide them with meat, milk, and clothing. The number of cattle owned is a reflection of wealth and status.

*Find out more*
COPPER MINING: *73, 237, 245*
DEMOCRACY: *270*
DESERTS: *15, 204*
DIAMONDS: *150, 226, 248*

# ZIMBABWE

ZIMBABWE WAS ONCE PART OF a great trading empire. Many centuries ago, central African merchants exported gold and copper to India and China. The centre of this empire was Great Zimbabwe ("house of the chief"), a huge stone palace, from which Zimbabwe took its name when it became independent in 1980. Today the country's great economic potential has been ruined by the corrupt rule of the president, Robert Mugabe. He has tried to oppress opposition supporters and his policy of encouraging illegal occupation of white-owned farm land by black settlers has caused food shortages and economic chaos.

### ZIMBABWE

**Capital city:** Harare

**Area:** 390,580 sq km (150,803 sq miles)

**Population:** 12,900,000

**Official language:** English

**Major religions:** Syncretic (part Christian, part traditional beliefs) 50%, Christian 25%, traditional beliefs 24%, other 1%

**Government:** Multi-party democracy

**Currency:** Zimbabwe dollar

**Adult literacy rate:** 90%

**Life expectancy:** 39 years

**People per doctor:** 10,000

**Televisions:** 30 per 1,000 people

## FIGHTING OPPRESSION
Robert Mugabe's Zanu-PF party has been in power since the country's independence in 1980. The harsh rule imposed by him, and widespread corruption of his party, led to the formation of the Movement for Democratic Change (MDC) in September 1999. This party campaigns for an end to political oppression, but supporters risk violent attacks by Mugabe supporters.

## VICTORIA FALLS
As the Zambezi River flows eastwards along the border between Zambia and Zimbabwe, it drops 128 m (420 ft) down into a narrow chasm. The thick mist and loud noise produced by the waterfall can be seen and heard up to 40 km (25 miles) away. Local people call the falls *Mosi-oa-tunya* ("the smoke that thunders"), but internationally they are known as the Victoria Falls.

## ECONOMIC CRISIS
A few years ago Zimbabwe had one of the most successful economies in Africa. During the Ethiopian drought in the 1980s it was the only country in the region to export food there. However, political uncertainty has had a destabilizing effect on the economy and jobs have been lost in all sectors. The country no longer has regular supplies of oil, as it does not have the foreign currency required to pay for them, and this has led to petrol shortages and long queues at filling stations.

## THE SHONA PEOPLES
The majority of Zimbabweans are Shona (or Mashona) peoples, who live in the centre and east of the country. Many make a living from farming or work in industry. Many Shona people are Christians, but they also believe in animism, that is that natural objects such as lakes and trees have spirits. The Shona are known for their pottery and sculpture.

## FARMING THE LAND
Zimbabwe is rich in fertile farm land, producing tobacco and other crops for selling (commercial farming). Until recently the best land was owned by a few thousand mainly white landowners, leaving the poorer areas to be farmed by about five million blacks, who grow enough to live on (subsistence farming). Mugabe's policy of seizing land from the whites has been violent, and has led to many thousands of black farm workers losing their jobs, while Mugabe supporters have been given the best land.

*Tobacco plant*

**How the land is farmed**

Commercial farming
Subsistence farming
Land unsuitable for farming
Tobacco
Cattle

*Find out more*

# MOZAMBIQUE

WHEN MOZAMBIQUE BECAME independent from Portugal in 1975, its former rulers fled the country, destroying transport and machinery as they left. Years of civil war, drought, and flooding have since reduced the country to one of the poorest in the world. Land mines left over from the war still litter the countryside, and few bridges remain standing. But Mozambique has the potential to overcome its disastrous recent history. The land is rich and fertile, and its mineral resources are largely untouched.

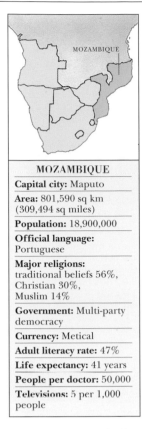

## MOZAMBIQUE

**Capital city:** Maputo

**Area:** 801,590 sq km (309,494 sq miles)

**Population:** 18,900,000

**Official language:** Portuguese

**Major religions:** traditional beliefs 56%, Christian 30%, Muslim 14%

**Government:** Multi-party democracy

**Currency:** Metical

**Adult literacy rate:** 47%

**Life expectancy:** 41 years

**People per doctor:** 50,000

**Televisions:** 5 per 1,000 people

BEIRA
The Indian Ocean port of Beira is the second city of Mozambique, and its major port. Most of neighbouring Zimbabwe's imports and exports pass through the port, using the rail, road, and pipeline links that run between Beira and the Zimbabwean capital of Harare. During the civil war, up to 10,000 Zimbabwean soldiers guarded this vital lifeline.

*During the civil war, millions of refugees fled the country or left villages to find safety in the towns.*

*Workers taking a health-care class in Mozambique.*

## HEALTH CARE

After independence, the Mozambique government brought all health services under national ownership and provided free health care for all. However, years of civil war have destroyed most rural hospitals and clinics, and diseases such as tuberculosis, malaria, and pneumonia continue to kill many people. Today, almost the entire population live in poverty, and more than half rely on food aid supplied from abroad. The situation is made worse by repeated flooding which wipes out homes and crops and spreads disease.

**Where the aid comes from**

Japan: 6.5%
Portugal: 7.1%
Italy: 7.6%
Germany: 8.5%
USA: 8.8%

## CIVIL WAR

After independence in 1975, civil war broke out between the communist Frelimo government and the Mozambique National Resistance (Renamo) rebels, supported by South Africa. The war led to the deaths of 900,000 people and to widespread starvation. Withdrawal of international support from Renamo and the decision of the Frelimo government to hold multi-party elections resulted in a peace treaty that was signed by the two sides in 1992, but tensions still persist.

## FARMING
More than 80 per cent of working Mozambicans are farmers. They grow crops such as sugar, cotton, tea, cashew nuts, and citrus fruits on the fertile coastal plains, and grow tobacco and herd cattle on the inland pastures. The seas are rich in fish, the export of shrimps, lobsters, and other seafoods providing much needed income for the national economy.

*Workers carrying bundles of sugarcane after the harvest.*

LOCAL MUSIC
The coastal Chopi people produce music based on the sound of the *timbila*, a type of xylophone. *Timbila* orchestras provide the music for poetic songs and elaborate *migodo* (dance suites) reflecting village life. *Timbila* music is the national music of Mozambique.

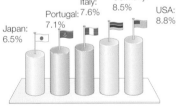

*Find out more*

HEALTH CARE: *276*
REFUGEES: *207*
RICH AND POOR: *278–279*
SUGAR: *52*

# SOUTH AFRICA

IN 1994 SOUTH AFRICA moved from minority rule by its white population to majority government under the multi-racial control of the African National Congress (ANC). Since 1948, the South African government had practised apartheid, keeping the different races apart and restricting power to white people. South Africa became isolated from the rest of the world and violence between the races grew. After the election of the ANC leader, Nelson Mandela, as president, the apartheid system was dismantled and South Africa has since resumed full international relations.

NELSON MANDELA
Jailed in 1964 as a senior member of the ANC, Nelson Mandela (shown above with F. W. de Klerk) spent 26 years in prison until he was released in 1990. This was a result of President de Klerk's decision to legalize black freedom groups, with a view to ending apartheid. Under Nelson Mandela's leadership, the ANC won political power in 1994, and Mandela became the first black president of South Africa.

### SOUTH AFRICA

**Capital cities:** Pretoria, Cape Town, Bloemfontein

**Area:** 1,219,912 sq km (471,008 sq miles)

**Population:** 45,000,000

**Official languages:** 9 African languages, English, Afrikaans

**Major religions:** Christian 68%, traditional beliefs 29%, Muslim 2%, Hindu 1%

**Government:** Multi-party democracy

**Currency:** Rand

**Adult literacy rate:** 86%

**Life expectancy:** 46 years

**People per doctor:** 1,667

**Televisions:** 125 per 1,000 people

### SWAZILAND

**Capital city:** Mbabane

**Area:** 17,363 sq km (6,704 sq miles)

**Population:** 1,100,000

**Official languages:** Siswati, English

**Major religions:** Christian 60%, traditional beliefs 40%

**Government:** Absolute monarchy

**Currency:** Lilangeni

**Adult literacy rate:** 81%

**Life expectancy:** 44 years

**People per doctor:** 5,000

### LESOTHO

**Capital city:** Maseru

**Area:** 30,355 sq km (11,720 sq miles)

**Population:** 1,800,000

**Official languages:** English, Sesotho

**Major religions:** Christian 90%, traditional beliefs 10%

**Government:** Multi-party democracy

**Currency:** Loti

**Adult literacy rate:** 81%

**Life expectancy:** 38 years

**People per doctor:** 10,000

**Televisions:** 25 per 1,000 people

## THE TOWNSHIPS

As part of South Africa's apartheid policies, black workers and their families were excluded from the main towns and forced to live in specially built townships a great distance from their work. The biggest and most famous of these townships is Soweto, home to more than 1 million people. Everyday, black workers leave Soweto and commute for many hours on over-crowded buses and trains to work in the mines and factories of neighbouring Johannesburg.

THE NDEBELE
South Africa is a multi-racial country, with many different ethnic groups and 11 official languages. One group, the Ndebele, are known for their distinctive houses, which are brightly decorated in strong, geometric shapes. Women are responsible for the upkeep of the huts and repaint the outer walls each spring.

*Grapefruit*

*Lime*        *Lemon*

FRUIT GROWING
South Africa is a major exporter of food, thanks to its warm, dry climate and fertile soil. Citrus fruits, apples, and grapes are grown and then exported around the world. South Africa is also known for its fine wines.

## THE GOLDEN CITY

South Africa has three capital cities, with the administration in Pretoria, the law courts in Bloemfontein, and the parliament in Cape Town. However, the financial and industrial heart of South Africa is Johannesburg (shown right), known as "the golden city". Gold mines deep beneath the surface have created enormous wealth, encouraging the development of a sprawling industrial area manufacturing cars, textiles, and hi-tech and heavy engineering products.

# DIGGING FOR GOLD

Over the last 100 years, the Witwatersrand gold field around Johannesburg has produced almost half the world's gold, and still accounts for more than 30 per cent of the world's total output each year. Diamonds and other minerals are also mined in huge quantities, and the country has a large manufacturing industry and financial sector. As a result, South Africa has the strongest and most advanced economy in Africa. However, population growth and rising unemployment are putting the economy under pressure.

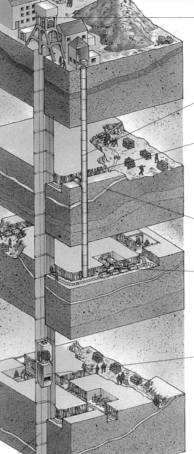

*In the reduction plant, gold ore is removed from its surrounding rock.*

*A ventilation shaft lets air into the mine.*

*Tunnels lead from the main shaft to the reef – the thin, slanting layer of rock which contains the gold.*

*Reef*

*Diesel trains take the gold ore to large containers called ore skips which carry the gold up to the surface.*

*Ore skip*

*Shafts may be more than 3 km (2 miles) deep.*

*Huge underground rooms known as stoped-out areas are created by drilling and blasting the surrounding rock.*

*The main shaft takes workers and supplies down into the mine.*

## What the gold is used for

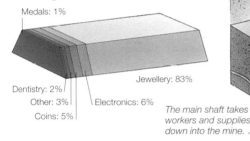

Medals: 1%
Dentistry: 2%
Other: 3%
Coins: 5%
Electronics: 6%
Jewellery: 83%

## SPORT

Under apartheid, sporting facilities were segregated and black and white players belonged to different teams. As a result, South Africa was banned from international sporting competition. With the ending of apartheid, sport became multi-racial and South African teams were allowed once more to compete in world sporting events. The national rugby team, the Springboks became the first team to win the Rugby World Cup twice in 1995 and 1999.

# SWAZILAND

THE KINGDOM OF SWAZILAND is dominated by its powerful neighbour, South Africa, relying on it for much of its wealth and energy supplies. Swaziland's main export is sugarcane, although it also exports wood pulp, coal, and asbestos. The king of Swaziland holds great power, running its affairs as head of government and appointing many members of its parliament. His power is reflected in his title, *Ngwenyama*, meaning "lion".

*The coronation of King Mswati III in 1986.*

# LESOTHO

ENTIRELY SURROUNDED BY South Africa, the mountainous kingdom of Lesotho is the only country in Africa where all the land is above 1,000 m (3,300 ft). Its main natural resource is water; a huge hydro-electric scheme currently being built will eventually supply all of Lesotho's energy needs and vast quantities of water for South Africa. Until then, Lesotho is economically dependent on its wealthy neighbour.

### MOHAIR SPINNING

The mountainous terrain of Lesotho is ideal for rearing goats, whose mohair wool is much prized. Using foot-powered treadle wheels, women spin the mohair into yarn to make finely woven material for clothes and other products.

*Find out more*

AFRICAN CITIES: *206*
HYDRO-ELECTRICITY: *108, 262*
POLITICAL SYSTEMS: *270–271*
SUGARCANE: *52*

# AUSTRALASIA AND OCEANIA

THIS VAST ISLAND REGION is spread over a huge area of the Pacific Ocean, to the south of southeast Asia. Australasia is made up of Australia, New Zealand, Papua New Guinea and several nearby islands. Australia is the only country which is also a continent in its own right, the smallest of the seven. Australasia is often linked with three groups of Pacific islands – Melanesia, Micronesia, and Polynesia – which form an even wider region, called Oceania. The climate and geography of Australasia and Oceania are as diverse as the region itself, ranging from the rainforests of northern Australia, and the glaciers of southern New Zealand, to the coral atolls and volcanoes which form many of the Pacific islands.

### PAPUA NEW GUINEA
Papua New Guinea is the eastern end of the island of New Guinea. The western end is Irian Jaya, part of Indonesia. Papua is a country of high mountains and thick forests. The highest peak, Mount Wilhelm, reaches 4,300 m (14,107 ft) and is often snow-capped, despite lying close to the Equator. Lower down, the climate is hot and humid, ideal for the growth of the rich, tropical rainforests which cover two-thirds of the island.

The frilled lizard lives in the deserts of the outback.

## THE AUSTRALIAN OUTBACK
Australia has four major deserts – the Simpson, Gibson, Great Sandy, and Great Victoria. Together, they cover most of the heart of the continent in a vast, barren area, known as the outback. Very few people live in the outback, though the dry conditions are good for raising sheep and cattle.

**Highest temperature:** Bourke, Australia, 53°C (128°F)

**Lowest temperature:** Canberra, Australia, -22°C (-8°F)

### THINGS TO LOOK FOR ON THE MAP
**Area:** 8,508,238 sq km (3,285,048 sq miles)

**Highest point:** Mt. Wilhelm, Papua New Guinea, 4,300 m (14,107 ft) *Map F7*

**Longest river:** Murray-Darling, Australia, 3,824 km (2,376 miles) *Map F12*

**Largest lake:** L. Eyre, Australia, maximum size 9,690 sq km (3,742 sq miles) *Map E11*

**Largest island:** New Guinea, 787,878 sq km (304,200 sq miles) *Map E7*

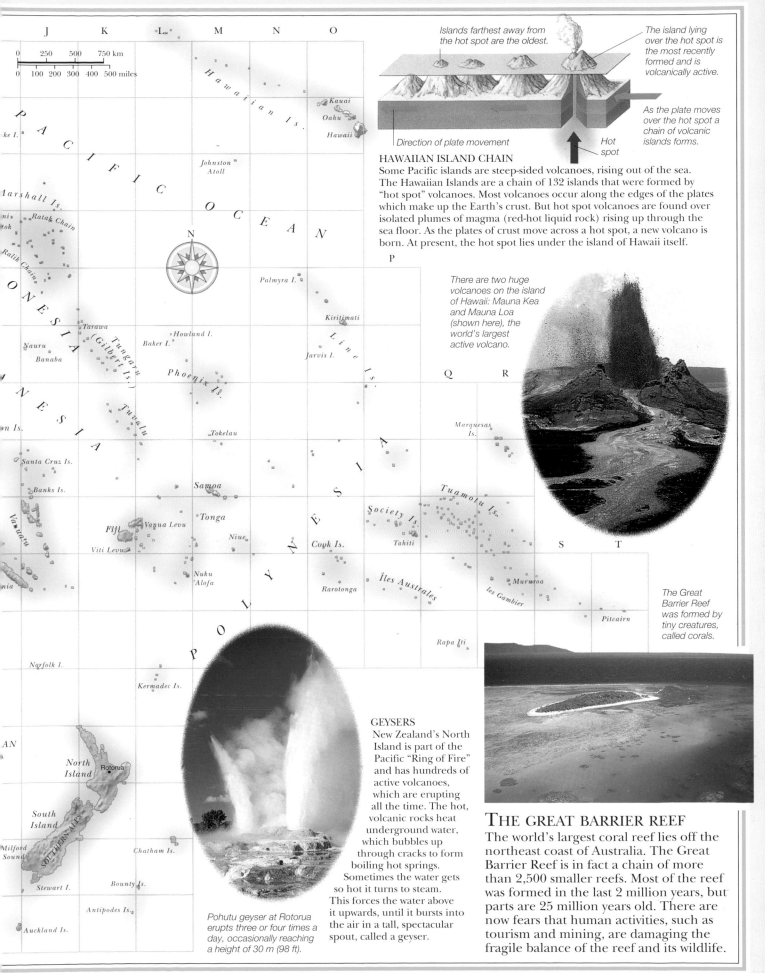

Islands farthest away from the hot spot are the oldest.

The island lying over the hot spot is the most recently formed and is volcanically active.

Direction of plate movement

Hot spot

As the plate moves over the hot spot a chain of volcanic islands forms.

## HAWAIIAN ISLAND CHAIN

Some Pacific islands are steep-sided volcanoes, rising out of the sea. The Hawaiian Islands are a chain of 132 islands that were formed by "hot spot" volcanoes. Most volcanoes occur along the edges of the plates which make up the Earth's crust. But hot spot volcanoes are found over isolated plumes of magma (red-hot liquid rock) rising up through the sea floor. As the plates of crust move across a hot spot, a new volcano is born. At present, the hot spot lies under the island of Hawaii itself.

There are two huge volcanoes on the island of Hawaii: Mauna Kea and Mauna Loa (shown here), the world's largest active volcano.

The Great Barrier Reef was formed by tiny creatures, called corals.

## GEYSERS

New Zealand's North Island is part of the Pacific "Ring of Fire" and has hundreds of active volcanoes, which are erupting all the time. The hot, volcanic rocks heat underground water, which bubbles up through cracks to form boiling hot springs. Sometimes the water gets so hot it turns to steam. This forces the water above it upwards, until it bursts into the air in a tall, spectacular spout, called a geyser.

*Pohutu geyser at Rotorua erupts three or four times a day, occasionally reaching a height of 30 m (98 ft).*

## THE GREAT BARRIER REEF

The world's largest coral reef lies off the northeast coast of Australia. The Great Barrier Reef is in fact a chain of more than 2,500 smaller reefs. Most of the reef was formed in the last 2 million years, but parts are 25 million years old. There are now fears that human activities, such as tourism and mining, are damaging the fragile balance of the reef and its wildlife.

# PEOPLES OF AUSTRALASIA AND OCEANIA

ISOLATED FROM THE REST of the world, parts of this region were among the last places on Earth to be settled. The first inhabitants came from Asia, and include the Aboriginals of Australia, the Maoris of New Zealand, and the peoples of the Pacific Islands. In the 18th century, settlers started to arrive from Europe, and both Australia and New Zealand became British colonies. Many Pacific Islands were European colonies. Today, links with the European colonizers are no longer so strong. In recent decades, people have migrated to Australia and New Zealand from the Middle East and southeast Asia, and they have both become multicultural societies with successful modern economies.

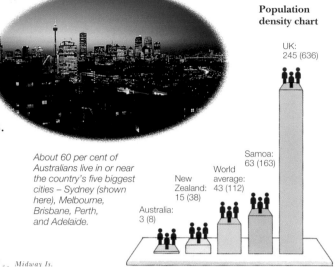

*About 60 per cent of Australians live in or near the country's five biggest cities – Sydney (shown here), Melbourne, Brisbane, Perth, and Adelaide.*

**Population density chart**

UK: 245 (636)

Samoa: 63 (163)

World average: 43 (112)

New Zealand: 15 (38)

Australia: 3 (8)

*The figures show the number of people per sq km, with per sq mile in brackets.*

## POPULATION DENSITY

With a population density of only three people per sq km (eight per sq mile), Australia is the most sparsely populated continent. Most Australians live in the cities around the coasts, away from the harsh climate of the interior. Many of the Pacific Islands are more densely populated, as relatively large numbers of people live on very small areas of land.

**Population:** approximately 31,400,000 people

**Number of countries:** 14

**Most densely populated country:** Nauru, 599 people per sq km (1,552 per sq mile)

**Largest country:** Australia, 7,686,850 sq km (2,967,893 sq miles)

**Least densely populated country:** Australia, 3 people per sq km (8 per sq mile)

**Smallest country:** Nauru, 21 sq km (8 sq miles)

*Midway Is. (USA)*

*Wake I. (USA)*

*Hawaii (USA)*

*Johnston Atoll (USA)*

Northern Mariana Is. (USA)

Guam (USA)

MARSHALL ISLANDS

*Kingman Reef (USA)*

MICRONESIA

*Palmyra Atoll (USA)*

PALAU

NAURU

*Howland I. (USA)*
*Baker I. (USA)*

*Jarvis I. (USA)*

PAPUA NEW GUINEA

K I R I B A T I

SOLOMON ISLANDS

TUVALU

*Tokelau (NZ)*

*Coral Sea Is. (Aus)*

VANUATU

*Wallis & Futuna (Fr)*

SAMOA

*American Samoa (USA)*

TONGA

FIJI

*Niue (NZ)*

*Cook Is. (NZ)*

*French Polynesia (Fr)*

*New Caledonia (Fr)*

*Pitcairn Is. (UK)*

AUSTRALIA

*Norfolk I. (Aus)*

*Kermadec Is. (NZ)*

*Lord Howe I. (Aus)*

*A protest against the use of vast drift nets which can kill dolphins.*

**BAN DRIFT NETS**

NEW ZEALAND

*Chatham I. (NZ)*

*Bounty I. (NZ)*

*Antipodes Is. (NZ)*

*Auckland Is. (NZ)*

*Campbell I. (NZ)*

CONSERVATION
Concern for the environment has become a common theme throughout the region. In Australia this has involved protecting wildlife and natural sites. Due to their isolation, some Pacific Islands have been used for nuclear testing, although there is much opposition from local people.

**Key to arrows**

| | |
|---|---|
| ➤ | 50,000–70,000 years ago |
| ➤ | 5000–1000 BC |
| ➤ | 1000–200 BC |
| ➤ | 200 BC – AD 1000 |

*Early peoples sailed from New Guinea to the nearest islands, known as Melanesia. Over the next few thousand years they settled other islands. To the north they arrived in the region known today as Micronesia.*

*The early settlers sailed in outrigger canoes. Today, similar canoes are still used by islanders for fishing.*

NEW GUINEA

AUSTRALIA

*Towards Hawaii*

*Towards Easter Island*

*The Maoris sailed to New Zealand in about AD 950.*

NEW ZEALAND

## EARLY SETTLERS

The first settlers were the Aboriginals, who arrived in Australia between 50,000 and 70,000 years ago, when the continent was still connected by a land bridge to New Guinea. The inhabitants of the Pacific Islands arrived next, when, about 7,000 years ago, people from southeast Asia began to settle the islands. Parts of this region have been settled for little more than 1,000 years – the Maoris, for example, arrived in New Zealand in about AD950.

*Australia's history as a British colony is reflected in its flag, which features the British flag, the Commonwealth Star, and the Southern Cross constellation.*

### POPULATION TODAY

As a legacy of their colonial past, most people in New Zealand and Australia today are of British descent. In the last few decades, however, new settlers have arrived in the region from throughout the world. For more than three million Australians, English is not their first language. The various groups of migrants have brought their own customs, traditions, festivals, and food, making Australia and New Zealand multicultural societies.

| AUSTRALIA'S EXPORT MARKETS | |
|---|---|
| 1  Japan | 18% of exports |
| 2  USA | 10% of exports |
| 3  South Korea | 8% of exports |
| 3  New Zealand | 7% of exports |
| 5  China | 7% of exports |

### TRADING PARTNERS

Traditionally, the UK was the main trading partner for both Australia and New Zealand. However, since the UK joined the European Union in 1973, Australia and New Zealand have had to look for new export markets. Both countries are now concentrating on the growing Asian market. In 1960, Asia accounted for only 25 per cent of Australia's exports. Today 60 per cent of Australia's trade is with Asia, and Japan is its most important market.

*Today, Aboriginals make up between 1 and 2 per cent of Australia's population.*

## ABORIGINAL RIGHTS

For many years, Aboriginal children in Australia and Maoris in New Zealand were taught only in English and were discouraged from learning their own languages. Today the situation is very different. The Maori language is officially recognized in New Zealand, and in Australia schoolchildren learn about Aboriginal culture and traditions. But many people feel that the future also depends on reclaiming the land and resources taken from the original peoples when European settlers first arrived.

*The England-Australia Test Matches are played every two years.*

### SPORT

In both Australia and New Zealand, sport has played an important role in creating a sense of national identity. Rugby is the national sport of New Zealand, while Australia's main sports are Australian Rules football, rugby, and cricket. Success in these sports is a great source of national pride.

# AUSTRALIA AND PAPUA NEW GUINEA

SURROUNDED BY THE INDIAN and Pacific oceans, Australia is the world's smallest continent. It is vast, nearly the size of the USA, and very dry. There is little rain, and arid desert stretches across about two-thirds of the land. Most of the people live in the big cities along the coasts. To the north, only 150 km (93 miles) across the Torres Strait, lies Papua New Guinea. An Australian colony until 1975, it consists of the eastern end of the island of New Guinea and more than 600 surrounding islands.

*Raggiana's bird of paradise – two-thirds of all birds of paradise live in the forests of Papua New Guinea.*

ISLAND OF MOUNTAINS AND FORESTS
Papua New Guinea lies entirely in the tropics and has a hot, wet climate. Running from west to east along the island is a range of high rugged mountains, covered with dense rainforest. These remote forests are home to a vast range of plants and animals, many of which are found nowhere else in the world. Mangrove swamps grow along many of the island's coasts.

## THE OUTBACK

Most of Australia is a flat plain without mountains, forests, or rivers. The huge central region, known as the outback, is one of the hottest and driest places on Earth. It has sandy or stony deserts, which can be baked by intense heat during the day, and frozen by extreme cold at night. In places where there is some vegetation, or the land has been irrigated, farmers raise cattle and sheep.

*When rains do come, there are flash floods, and plants like this Sturt's Desert Pea flower from seeds that have lain dormant for years.*

### ULURU (AYERS ROCK)
This massive block of sandstone stands almost in the middle of Australia. It measures 9.4 km (5.8 miles) around the base, and rises to 348 m (1,142 ft). To the Aboriginals, the first people of Australia, the rock is known as Uluru. It is a sacred site and features in their beliefs about the creation of the world. Once called Ayers Rock after a former premier of South Australia, the rock regained its Aboriginal name in 1985.

## GREAT BARRIER REEF

The Great Barrier Reef, the largest living thing on Earth, stretches for 2,000 km (1,243 miles) along the northeast coast of Australia. It is the world's largest coral reef and home to more than 2,000 species of fish. Its coral is made of layer upon layer of tiny anemone-like creatures called polyps. The Great Barrier Reef is a major tourist attraction, but swimmers and divers can easily pollute and damage it. To protect it, the reef has been made a World Heritage Area.

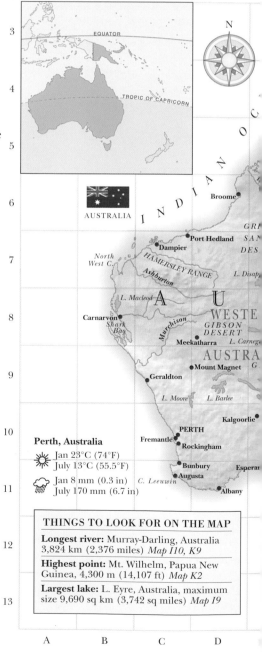

Perth, Australia
Jan 23°C (74°F)
July 13°C (55.5°F)
Jan 8 mm (0.3 in)
July 170 mm (6.7 in)

### THINGS TO LOOK FOR ON THE MAP

**Longest river:** Murray-Darling, Australia 3,824 km (2,376 miles) *Map I10, K9*

**Highest point:** Mt. Wilhelm, Papua New Guinea, 4,300 m (14,107 ft) *Map K2*

**Largest lake:** L. Eyre, Australia, maximum size 9,690 sq km (3,742 sq miles) *Map I9*

# PAPUA NEW GUINEA

Fewer than six million people live in Papua New Guinea, most of them in small, isolated villages. By western standards, many people are poor. Papua is rich in natural resources, especially minerals such as copper, gold, nickel, and cobalt. It also has extensive oil and natural gas reserves. Timber from the rainforests is another major export. The challenge is to develop these resources without damaging the environment.

### PAPUA NEW GUINEA

**Capital city:** Port Moresby

**Area:** 462,840 sq km (178,703 sq miles)

**Population:** 5,700,000

**Official language:** English

**Major religions:** Christian 62%, traditional beliefs 34%, other 4%

**Government:** Multi-party democracy

**Currency:** Kina

**Adult literacy rate:** 65%

**Life expectancy:** 57 years

**People per doctor:** 10,000

**Televisions:** 24 per 1,000 people

**BIG BUTTERFLY**
Queen Alexandra's Birdwing butterfly, with a wingspan of 25 cm (10 in), is the world's largest butterfly.

**Port Moresby, Papua New Guinea**
- Jan 28°C (82.5°F)
- July 25.5°C (78°F)
- Jan 178 mm (7 in)
- July 28 mm (1.1 in)

PAPUA NEW GUINEA

*Tribespeople from Mendi, wearing head-dresses made from bird of paradise feathers.*

## TRIBAL PEOPLE

The mountains and forests of Papua New Guinea have always restricted contact between the various groups of people who live there. As a result, the country is now home to about 1,000 tribes, speaking more than 700 different languages. Most of these people live off the land they farm.

**Alice Springs, Australia**
- Jan 28.5°C (83.5°F)
- July 11.5°C (53°F)
- Jan 43 mm (1.7 in)
- July 8 mm (0.3 in)

**Sydney, Australia**
- Jan 22°C (71.5°F)
- July 12°C (53°F)
- Jan 89 mm (3.5 in)
- July 117 mm (4.6 in)

PORT MORESBY
The capital, Port Moresby, is a sprawling city built around a natural harbour on the island's southern coast. Unlike the rest of the country, it is dry for much of the year. Port Moresby has grown rapidly in recent years, as people from remote regions have moved there to find work.

# AUSTRALIA

UNTIL ABOUT 200 YEARS AGO, the land that is now Australia was occupied only by Aboriginals. Then, in 1770, the British explorer James Cook arrived in Botany Bay and claimed it for Britain. In 1901, Australia became an independent commonwealth. Over the years settlers from overseas, firstly from Britain and Europe, but more recently from Asia, have shaped the culture of this huge country. Wool and wheat, as well as mineral resources of iron ore, coal, and copper have made Australia wealthy, and most people benefit from a high standard of living.

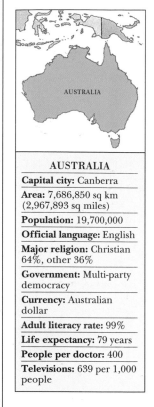

| AUSTRALIA | |
|---|---|
| **Capital city:** Canberra | |
| **Area:** 7,686,850 sq km (2,967,893 sq miles) | |
| **Population:** 19,700,000 | |
| **Official language:** English | |
| **Major religion:** Christian 64%, other 36% | |
| **Government:** Multi-party democracy | |
| **Currency:** Australian dollar | |
| **Adult literacy rate:** 99% | |
| **Life expectancy:** 79 years | |
| **People per doctor:** 400 | |
| **Televisions:** 639 per 1,000 people | |

### SETTLERS
In the 18th century, British prisons were overcrowded and criminals were often sent overseas. In 1778 the first ships arrived from Britain with 757 adult convicts, forming a settlement in what is now Sydney. By 1860 more than 160,000 convicts had been transported to Australia.

## LIVING ON THE COAST
About 85 per cent of Australians live in or around cities along the coast. Most of the schools, hospitals, offices, and factories are located here, and life is easier than in the remote towns and farms of the outback. Homes in the city are built of wood or brick, often with verandas, as well as a patio or backyard for the barbecue. The five largest cities contain 60 per cent of the population. One of these is Sydney, shown left, with its Opera House overlooking the harbour.

## ABORIGINAL BELIEFS
The word Aboriginal means "from the beginning", and Aboriginals believe they have occupied Australia since the beginning of time. They have a detailed knowledge of the land; women gathered fruits, nuts, and grubs, and men hunted animals such as kangaroos and possums. The Dreamtime, long ago when the land and all living things were made, is the basis of Aboriginal culture.

*Aboriginals act out their beliefs in their songs, ceremonies, and art. This group is from Queensland.*

| MAIN CITIES BY POPULATION | |
|---|---|
| Sydney | 4,200,000 |
| Melbourne | 3,488,750 |
| Brisbane | 1,770,000 |
| Perth | 1,433,200 |
| Adelaide | 1,072,600 |

*People in Sydney demonstrate for land rights. On the Aboriginal flag, black represents the people, yellow the Sun, and red the land.*

### VAST DISTANCES
Away from the coasts, much of Australia is dry and hot, with very few towns or settlements. Alice Springs, in the centre of the country, began as a station linking the telegraph line between Darwin and Adelaide. Separated by such large distances, many children cannot get to school and take lessons through the School of the Air learning scheme.

*The journey from Darwin to Sydney, via Adelaide, is 4,822 km (2,996 miles). This would take about 2.5 days and nights of non-stop driving.*

### LAND RIGHTS
The arrival of the British changed life for the Aboriginals. Many lost their lands and thousands died of European diseases. Today, they no longer live off the land in the traditional way, but work in factories or farms. Many suffer poor health and bad housing. In 1967, they were granted the right to vote. Since then a series of laws have given Aboriginals control over some of the land.

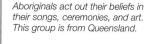

— Major roads
— Route shown below

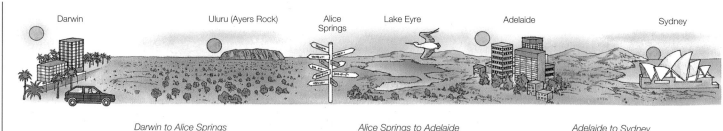

*Darwin to Alice Springs*
*1,508 km (937 miles)*

*Alice Springs to Adelaide*
*1,529 km (950 miles)*

*Adelaide to Sydney*
*1,785 km (1,109 miles)*

# SHEEP FARMING

Australia is the world's chief wool-producing country, with New South Wales the leading area. Most of Australia's sheep are Merinos which were brought from South Africa and England in the 1790s. Today, there are about 100 million sheep in Australia, most of them kept on farms, called stations. Some stations are huge and can cover 15,000 sq km (5,792 sq miles), which is half the size of Belgium. Motorbikes and four-wheel-drive vehicles are now used to control livestock over such wide areas.

*Sheep usually graze on grass, but eat hay or grain in the summer when pastures are dry.*

*Drovers ride horses to follow the flock.*

*There are usually about 3,000 sheep in a flock.*

*Merino sheep have fine, soft wool.*

*Shearers usually wear blue singlets. Some women work as shearers, although most shearers are men.*

*Farmers keep kelpie and border collie dogs to round up the sheep.*

*Some workers can shear more than 100 sheep in a day.*

*Merino sheep can survive the heat and still produce a heavy fleece of good wool.*

*Wool is graded and stored in bins.*

## RICHES FROM THE EARTH

In the 1850s, the discovery of gold in Victoria and New South Wales attracted people to Australia and helped boost the economy. Today, mining for coal, copper, and iron ore, shown above, is still big business. Australia is the world's largest coal exporter, and also has the world's most productive diamond mine, near Lake Argyle. However, modern mining relies more on machinery than on labour, and does not employ many people.

## LOOKING EAST

For many years, Australia traded mainly with Britain. However, since Britain joined the European Union in 1973, Australia has strengthened its trading links with the United States and Asian countries, such as Japan and China. Today, many foreign companies, including car manufacturers and computer businesses, have factories in Australia.

# THE NEW AUSTRALIANS

For many years, Australia allowed only white people to settle there: mostly people from Britain, Italy, and Greece. In 1972, this policy was changed and since then immigrants have arrived from all over the world. The "New Australians" include Vietnamese, Japanese, and Chinese. These groups have brought their own languages, festivals, and types of food.

*Many Australians have relatives in Britain.*

*This boy has parents who came from Vietnam.*

*Many Greek people live in the city of Melbourne.*

*This girl has parents who came from China.*

*Many Italians moved to Australia after World War II.*

## SPORTING LIFE

Australians love the outdoors, and sport is a major part of their lifestyle. Sandy beaches, warm water, and good surf make swimming, sailing, water-skiing, and surfing extremely popular. Australians also excel in international events at cricket, tennis, athletics, and rugby. In the year 2000 Sydney hosted the Olympic Games for the first time.

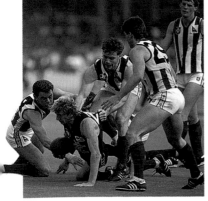

*In Australian Rules football, players can kick or punch the ball, but they must not throw it.*

***Find out more***

DIAMONDS: *150, 226, 248*
POPULATION DENSITY: *256*
SETTLING AUSTRALIA: *256–257*
TRADE (PACIFIC RIM): *257*

# NEW ZEALAND

Situated about 1,500 km (932 miles) from Australia, its nearest neighbour, New Zealand consists of two large islands – North and South Island – and several smaller ones. The North Island has a warm, mild climate and is volcanically active. The South Island is colder, with glaciers, high mountain peaks, and forests. From 1840 to 1907 New Zealand was a British colony, but gained full independence in 1947. The original inhabitants – the Maoris – still make up about 12 per cent of the population. New Zealand is a wealthy and progressive country, and was the first in the world to give women the vote.

## NEW ZEALAND

**Capital city:** Wellington

**Area:** 268,680 sq km (103,737 sq miles)

**Population:** 3,900,000

**Official language:** English, Maori

**Major religions:** Christian 62%, other 38%

**Government:** Multi-party democracy

**Currency:** New Zealand dollar

**Adult literacy rate:** 99%

**Life expectancy:** 78 years

**People per doctor:** 225

**Televisions:** 508 per 1,000 people

### PEOPLE AND CITIES
There are only about 3.9 million people in New Zealand – just over half the population of London or Paris. Nearly three-quarters of New Zealanders live on the North Island, and most of them live in the cities. Wellington (shown here) is New Zealand's capital city.

## FARMING
Large areas of grass and a warm, damp climate make New Zealand ideal for farming, especially raising sheep and cattle. There are about 40 million sheep (about 10 for every one person) and 10 million cattle. About half of New Zealand's exports are agricultural products. The country is one of the world's leading exporters of wool, frozen meat, and dairy products such as butter and cheese.

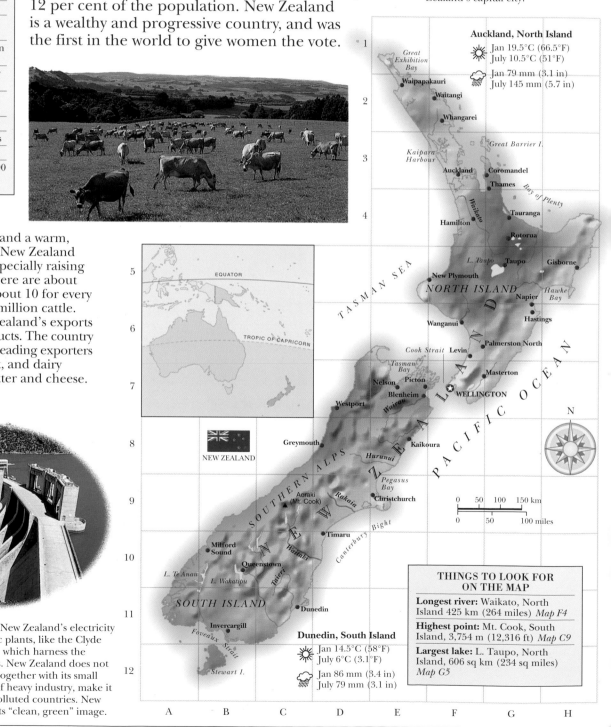

**Auckland, North Island**

☼ Jan 19.5°C (66.5°F)
July 10.5°C (51°F)

🌧 Jan 79 mm (3.1 in)
July 145 mm (5.7 in)

**Dunedin, South Island**

☼ Jan 14.5°C (58°F)
July 6°C (3.1°F)

🌧 Jan 86 mm (3.4 in)
July 79 mm (3.1 in)

### THINGS TO LOOK FOR ON THE MAP

**Longest river:** Waikato, North Island 425 km (264 miles) *Map F4*

**Highest point:** Mt. Cook, South Island, 3,754 m (12,316 ft) *Map C9*

**Largest lake:** L. Taupo, North Island, 606 sq km (234 sq miles) *Map G5*

## ENERGY
More than 60 per cent of New Zealand's electricity comes from hydro-electric plants, like the Clyde Dam on the South Island, which harness the power of its rushing rivers. New Zealand does not use nuclear power. This, together with its small population and the lack of heavy industry, make it one of the world's least polluted countries. New Zealand is very proud of its "clean, green" image.

## THE FIRST NEW ZEALANDERS

New Zealand was one of the last places on Earth to be inhabited by people. The first settlers, the Maori, arrived from Polynesia in about AD 950. Today, although most Maoris have adopted western lifestyles, their culture lives on in their language, art, and extended family groups. Maoris are represented in the government, and there are moves to ensure that they receive equal opportunities in health, education, and employment, which have been lacking in the past.

**MAORI ART**
This neck pendant represents Tiki, one of the Maori gods, and is worn to bring good luck. It is carved from greenstone, a kind of hard jade found on the South Island.

**OUTDOOR LIFE**
New Zealand's pleasant climate and beautiful countryside make it ideal for outdoor activities. New Zealanders enjoy sports of all kinds, from hiking and mountain climbing to canoeing, yachting, and rugby. The country's rugby team, the All Blacks, are shown in action above. Many tourists visit New Zealand for its outdoor lifestyle, and tourism is now a major source of income.

## KIWI FRUIT

The Chinese gooseberry was introduced into New Zealand in about 1900, and was later renamed the kiwi fruit after the country's famous bird. New Zealand is now the world's principal producer, and exports kiwi fruit worldwide. The fruit, known as a subtropical, needs a warm, sunny climate. It is grown in special orchards, divided into sections by fences or hedges.

*The orchards are divided into sections about 150 m by 40 m (492 ft x 131 ft).*

*Home of the orchard manager.*

*Strong supports hold the vines steady while the kiwi fruit grows.*

*Tall trees, or hedges, protect the vines from gusts of wind.*

*Pickers, wearing gloves to protect the fruit, pluck the kiwi fruit from the branch.*

*The fruit is placed in a special apron while the picker moves along the rows.*

*The kiwi fruit has a fuzzy, greenish-brown skin a little like the feathers of the bird after which it is named.*

*Pickers sort the fruit by size, then pack it in cardboard boxes.*

## ORCHARD FRUITS

Because New Zealand lies in the southern hemisphere, it can grow crops when its customers in the north are in the middle of their winter. The main types of fruit, with examples from each group shown below, are – pip fruit (apple), berry fruit (strawberry), stone fruit (peach), citrus fruit (orange), and subtropicals (tamarillo).

*Orange*

*Strawberry*

*Apple*

*Peach*

*Tamarillo*

### FLIGHTLESS BIRDS

New Zealand's isolated position has allowed many unique plants and animals to develop there. The most famous are the flightless birds, such as the kakapo and kiwi. These birds lost the ability to fly because they had no enemies and did not need to be able to fly away.

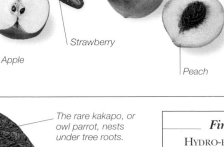

*The long-beaked kiwi is New Zealand's national emblem.*

*The rare kakapo, or owl parrot, nests under tree roots.*

***Find out more***
HYDRO-ELECTRICITY: *108*
SETTLING PACIFIC ISLANDS: *257*
SHEEP FARMING: *261*
VOLCANIC ACTIVITY: *13, 255*

# THE PACIFIC OCEAN

| MICRONESIA |
|---|
| **Capital city:** Palikir |
| **Area:** 702 sq km (291 sq miles) |
| **Population:** 108,143 |

| NAURU |
|---|
| **Capital city:** None |
| **Area:** 21 sq km (8.1 sq miles) |
| **Population:** 12,570 |

| PALAU |
|---|
| **Capital city:** Koror |
| **Area:** 458 sq km (177 sq miles) |
| **Population:** 19,717 |

| SOLOMON ISLANDS |
|---|
| **Capital city:** Honiara |
| **Area:** 28,450 sq km (10,985 sq miles) |
| **Population:** 477,000 |

| VANUATU |
|---|
| **Capital city:** Port Vila |
| **Area:** 12,200 sq km (4,710 sq miles) |
| **Population:** 212,000 |

| FIJI |
|---|
| **Capital city:** Suva |
| **Area:** 18,270 sq km (7,054 sq miles) |
| **Population:** 839,000 |

| TUVALU |
|---|
| **Capital city:** Fongafale |
| **Area:** 26 sq km (10 sq miles) |
| **Population:** 11,305 |

| TONGA |
|---|
| **Capital city:** Nuku'alofa |
| **Area:** 748 sq km (289 sq miles) |
| **Population:** 108,141 |

| SAMOA |
|---|
| **Capital city:** Apia |
| **Area:** 2,944 sq km (1,137 sq miles) |
| **Population:** 178,000 |

| KIRIBATI |
|---|
| **Capital city:** Bairiki |
| **Area:** 811 sq km (313 sq miles) |
| **Population:** 98,549 |

| MARSHALL ISLANDS |
|---|
| **Capital city:** Majuro |
| **Area:** 181 sq km (70 sq miles) |
| **Population:** 56,429 |

THE WORLD'S LARGEST, DEEPEST OCEAN, the Pacific covers one-third of the Earth's surface, stretching from the shores of Asia and Australia to the Americas and Antarctica. About 20,000 volcanic and coral islands lie scattered over its vast expanse, many covered with lush vegetation. Over much of the Pacific the climate is hot and moist. The native island peoples, who originally came from Southeast Asia, fall into three main groups, Polynesians, Melanesians, and Micronesians. Europeans began to arrive in the 1500s, and by the 1800s many islands were colonies of powerful countries overseas. Today, some of the islands are self-governing; in others foreign control is still strong.

*Coconut palms provide the islanders with food, milk, and fibre to make rope.*

*Large families of 10 or more live together under one roof.*

## PACIFIC PEOPLES

Some islanders live in towns, but many people continue the traditional farming way of life, growing crops such as yams and sweet potatoes, or fishing from the sea. The shape of homes varies from island to island but most, like this Fijian *bure*, are simply built using a large wooden frame topped with a thatch of plant fronds. Today, corrugated iron is often used as roofing because it lasts longer than thatch. Community life on the islands is important, with large extended families ruled by tribal chiefs. Property and personal objects belong to everybody.

*People often keep chickens and pigs.*

*Men wear a cloth skirt called a sulu.*

*A special meal might include fish, chicken, yams, vegetables, coconut, and bananas.*

*Boys learn to weave using green coconut leaves.*

*This area of the house is used for guests.*

## EXPORTS

Rich, volcanic soil and regular rainfall make these hot, sunny islands especially fertile. Some farmers produce surplus crops that they export. Sugar, ginger, black pepper, and copra (dried coconut) are among the main export crops. Fish, timber, livestock, and minerals are also important sources of income on certain islands.

*The green fruit of the black pepper plant is dried to make black peppercorns.*

*Ground pepper*

## NUCLEAR TESTING

Since the first experiments at Bikini Atoll in 1946, the USA, Britain and France have used the Pacific to test nuclear weapons. The islanders and groups such as Greenpeace campaigned to stop the testing. France carried out the last explosions in 1996. A treaty banning tests was signed in 1998, but some islands are still not safe to live on due to high radiation levels.

## THE EFFECT OF TOURISM

Many of the "island paradises" are fast becoming major tourist destinations – especially around Fiji, Tonga, and Samoa. Tourism brings in valuable income, but it can also damage the environment and affect the life of local people. For example, already limited water supplies may be diverted away from villages to hotel pools and showers.

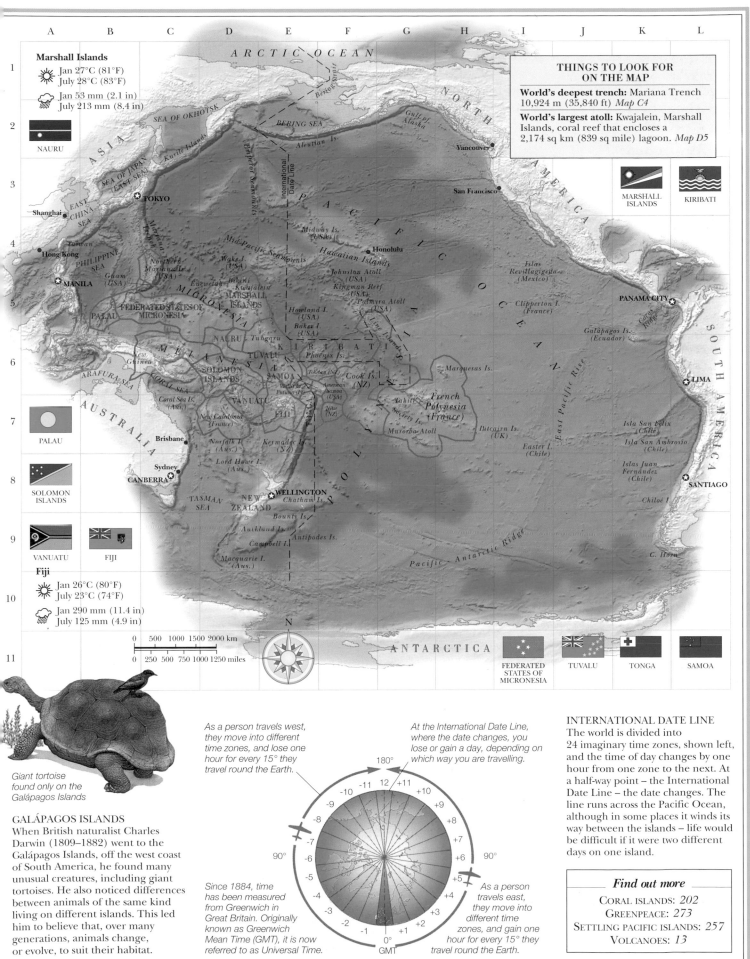

**Marshall Islands**
☀ Jan 27°C (81°F)
☀ July 28°C (83°F)
☁ Jan 53 mm (2.1 in)
🌧 July 213 mm (8.4 in)

NAURU

## THINGS TO LOOK FOR ON THE MAP

**World's deepest trench:** Mariana Trench 10,924 m (35,840 ft) *Map C4*

**World's largest atoll:** Kwajalein, Marshall Islands, coral reef that encloses a 2,174 sq km (839 sq mile) lagoon. *Map D5*

MARSHALL ISLANDS

KIRIBATI

PALAU

SOLOMON ISLANDS

VANUATU

FIJI

**Fiji**
☀ Jan 26°C (80°F)
☀ July 23°C (74°F)
☁ Jan 290 mm (11.4 in)
🌧 July 125 mm (4.9 in)

0  500 1000 1500 2000 km
0  250 500 750 1000 1250 miles

FEDERATED STATES OF MICRONESIA

TUVALU

TONGA

SAMOA

*Giant tortoise found only on the Galápagos Islands*

## GALÁPAGOS ISLANDS
When British naturalist Charles Darwin (1809–1882) went to the Galápagos Islands, off the west coast of South America, he found many unusual creatures, including giant tortoises. He also noticed differences between animals of the same kind living on different islands. This led him to believe that, over many generations, animals change, or evolve, to suit their habitat.

*As a person travels west, they move into different time zones, and lose one hour for every 15° they travel round the Earth.*

*At the International Date Line, where the date changes, you lose or gain a day, depending on which way you are travelling.*

*Since 1884, time has been measured from Greenwich in Great Britain. Originally known as Greenwich Mean Time (GMT), it is now referred to as Universal Time.*

*As a person travels east, they move into different time zones, and gain one hour for every 15° they travel round the Earth.*

## INTERNATIONAL DATE LINE
The world is divided into 24 imaginary time zones, shown left, and the time of day changes by one hour from one zone to the next. At a half-way point – the International Date Line – the date changes. The line runs across the Pacific Ocean, although in some places it winds its way between the islands – life would be difficult if it were two different days on one island.

### *Find out more*
CORAL ISLANDS: *202*
GREENPEACE: *273*
SETTLING PACIFIC ISLANDS: *257*
VOLCANOES: *13*

# THE ARCTIC

THE MOST NORTHERLY CONSTELLATION of stars, Arktos, or the Great Bear, gives its name to the icy ocean beneath it that surrounds the North Pole. One of the coldest places on Earth, the Arctic Ocean is bordered by the northernmost parts of Europe, Asia, and North America, including Greenland, the world's largest island. Most of the Arctic Ocean is covered by ice, although warmer currents from the Atlantic and Pacific flow northwards into it, warming the sea and air and clearing ice from the coasts in summer. Few people live in the Arctic, although the region is rich in minerals and wildlife.

## CLIMATE

During the long winter months, the Sun never rises over the horizon, and temperatures drop as low as -70°C (-94°F). In the summer, the Sun never sets, bathing the region in constant daylight and raising temperatures considerably. This is because the Earth rotates at an angle to the Sun, plunging the Arctic from total light to total darkness as the North Pole moves towards and away from the Sun. The dark polar skies are lit by the Aurora, wispy curtains of red and green light caused by electricity in the upper atmosphere.

*The polar bear is well adapted to Arctic life. It has acute senses, runs fast, swims well, and is camouflaged against the snow and ice by its white fur. Polar bears feed on seals and other animals, ranging far across the ice in search of prey.*

*Arctic terns breed in large colonies during the Arctic summer. When winter comes, they fly halfway around the world to take advantage of the daylight and rich food supply of the Antarctic summer.*

## NATURAL RESOURCES

The lands that surround the Arctic Ocean are rich in minerals. Vast oil and gas reserves lie under Alaska, while Norwegian and Russian companies are mining coal on the island of Svalbard (shown here). Smaller quantities of gold, iron, silver, tin, and other minerals are found throughout the region. Extracting these resources is expensive, but as supplies elsewhere begin to run out, oil and mining companies are turning their attention to the untapped wealth of the Arctic region.

## ARCTIC WILDLIFE

The Arctic Ocean teems with wildlife. Seals, walrus, and many species of whale thrive in the icy waters, protected from the cold by layers of thick blubber beneath their skins. On land, reindeer, musk ox, hares, Arctic foxes, and wolves scavenge for food, migrating south to avoid the worst of the winter. In the brief summer hardy plants bloom, providing food for millions of insects. Birds such as the Arctic tern and Brent goose take advantage of this abundant food supply to breed and raise their young.

## PEOPLE OF THE ARCTIC

The cold, inhospitable Arctic region is home to few people. The Sami of northern Scandinavia, the Yugyts and Nenets of Siberia, and the Inuit of Canada traditionally survived by hunting and trapping wild animals. Large herds of reindeer provided them with all their basic needs, such as food, clothing, tents, tools, and items to trade. Some native peoples still follow this nomadic lifestyle, but most now live in settled communities, like this one in Iqaluit in Canada.

*Traditional Inuit clothing is often lined with fur to keep out the cold.*

## TRAVEL IN THE ARCTIC

Transport on land has always been difficult in the Arctic. In the winter, thick snow covers the ground, while the summer thaw turns much of the land into a boggy marsh. Snowshoes and skis stop people sinking into the soft snow, while boots with rough or spiky soles grip well on icy ground. In the past, teams of huskies pulled sledges with supplies over great distances, but now the dogs have largely been replaced by snowmobiles. These small, motorized sledges on skis are easy to manoeuvre and can pull very heavy loads.

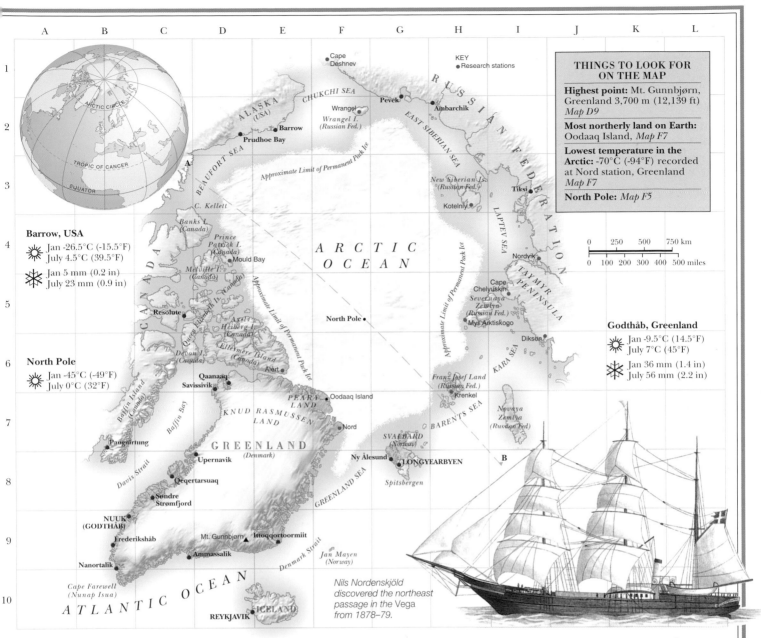

**THINGS TO LOOK FOR ON THE MAP**

**Highest point:** Mt. Gunnbjørn, Greenland 3,700 m (12,139 ft) *Map D9*

**Most northerly land on Earth:** Oodaaq Island, *Map F7*

**Lowest temperature in the Arctic:** -70°C (-94°F) recorded at Nord station, Greenland *Map F7*

**North Pole:** *Map F5*

**Barrow, USA**
- Jan -26.5°C (-15.5°F)
- July 4.5°C (39.5°F)
- Jan 5 mm (0.2 in)
- July 23 mm (0.9 in)

**North Pole**
- Jan -45°C (-49°F)
- July 0°C (32°F)

**Godthåb, Greenland**
- Jan -9.5°C (14.5°F)
- July 7°C (45°F)
- Jan 36 mm (1.4 in)
- July 56 mm (2.2 in)

KEY
● Research stations

*Nils Nordenskjöld discovered the northeast passage in the Vega from 1878–79.*

## ICE-BREAKERS

The Arctic sea ice is usually about 2 m (6 ft) thick. Ships called ice-breakers are specially constructed with reinforced hulls and bows shaped for ploughing through this icy obstacle. Their powerful engines push the bow on top of the ice until the weight of the ship breaks it and clears a passage for other ships.

## ARCTIC EXPLORATION

In the 16th century, European sailors first explored the Arctic seas in search of a new trade route to Asia. English sailors began to map the northwest passage around the top of Canada, while the Dutch explored the northeast passage around Siberia. By 1906, both routes had been successfully navigated. Three years later, the American, Robert Peary, claimed to have reached the North Pole itself. However the speed of his journey has led some explorers to doubt his achievement.

*Roald Amundsen sailed through the northwest passage in the Gjöa from 1903–06.*

*This cross-section follows the line A–B on the map above.*

## CROSS-SECTION THROUGH THE ARCTIC

For centuries, some Arctic explorers believed that the polar ice lay on top of a vast continent. In 1958, an American atomic-powered submarine, the USS *Nautilus*, demonstrated that this was untrue by sailing from Alaska to Svalbard underneath the ice. Subsequent exploration beneath the ice has revealed the ridges and basins of the seabed below.

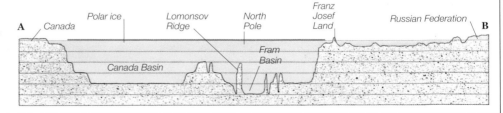

# THE ANTARCTIC

UNLIKE THE ARCTIC, which is an ocean surrounded by continents, the Antarctic is a continent surrounded by oceans. Antarctica is the remotest, most inhospitable place on Earth, and consists of a large land mass and numerous off-shore islands. Most of the mainland is covered by a vast ice-cap, which breaks up at the coastline, forming huge icebergs up to 200 km (125 miles) long. Antarctica is the only continent that has no permanent human population – the only inhabitants are visiting scientists studying the local environment. It is also unique in being governed by an international treaty that forbids countries from owning or exploiting the land.

*The hole in the ozone layer above Antarctica is the largest ever observed by scientists.*

## THE OZONE LAYER

The ozone layer is between 15–30 km (9–19 miles) up in the stratosphere. It protects the Earth from the sun's harmful rays by absorbing ultraviolet radiation. In recent years, scientists have observed a hole in the ozone layer above Antarctica. The hole is three times larger than the US and has caused huge concern about the production of ozone-destroying gases. These findings suggest Antarctica is much more fragile than was previously thought.

*The American-owned Amundsen-Scott base is situated at the South Pole.*

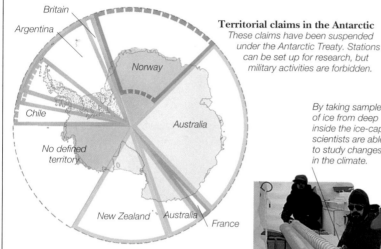

**Territorial claims in the Antarctic**
*These claims have been suspended under the Antarctic Treaty. Stations can be set up for research, but military activities are forbidden.*

Britain
Argentina
Norway
Chile
No defined territory
Australia
New Zealand
Australia
France

*By taking samples of ice from deep inside the ice-cap, scientists are able to study changes in the climate.*

## THE ANTARCTIC TREATY

In the first half of the 20th century, many countries claimed territory in Antarctica. In order to prevent future conflict, 12 countries signed the Antarctic Treaty in 1959, which suspended all national claims to the land. The treaty designated Antarctica as "a continent for science," and stated that it should be used for peaceful purposes only. Today, 45 countries have signed the treaty, which is one of the most successful examples of international cooperation.

### STUDYING ANTARCTICA

Scientists from all over the world come to Antarctica to study its unique climate, weather, geology, and wildlife. The age-old rocks tell them much about the development of the Earth, while analysis of the many meteorites that hit the ice-cap provides valuable information about the universe.

## RESEARCH STATIONS

Barely 1,000 people live in Antarctica in the winter, with another 3,000 joining them during the summer months. All are involved in scientific research and live on one of the 46 or so bases dotted around the continent. Each base is specially insulated against the intense cold and some have been constructed below the surface in order to conserve heat. Diesel fuel is used for heating and generating electricity, and enough fuel, food, and other supplies are kept to last an extra year in case the weather prevents new supplies being brought in.

*Captain Roald Amundsen taking sights at the South Pole in 1911.*

### ANTARCTIC EXPLORATION

It wasn't until 1820 that the shores of Antarctica were first sighted. From the 1840s onwards, explorers began to map the continent, but the South Pole remained unknown. In the summer of 1911–12, two expeditions – one from Norway led by Roald Amundsen, the other from Britain led by Robert Scott – set out to reach the Pole. Amundsen arrived on 14 December, followed by Scott a month later.

### TOURISM

Each year, a few intrepid tourists visit Antarctica, exploring the dramatic coastline in cruise ships or flying inland over the ice to land at the South Pole. So far, the small number of tourists has had little effect on the environment which was, however, under threat from the rubbish that was slowly accumulating around the older scientific bases.

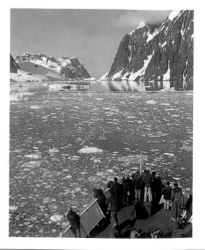

*Cruise liners have been bringing tourists to Antarctica since the 1950s, and now bring about 10,000 people each year.*

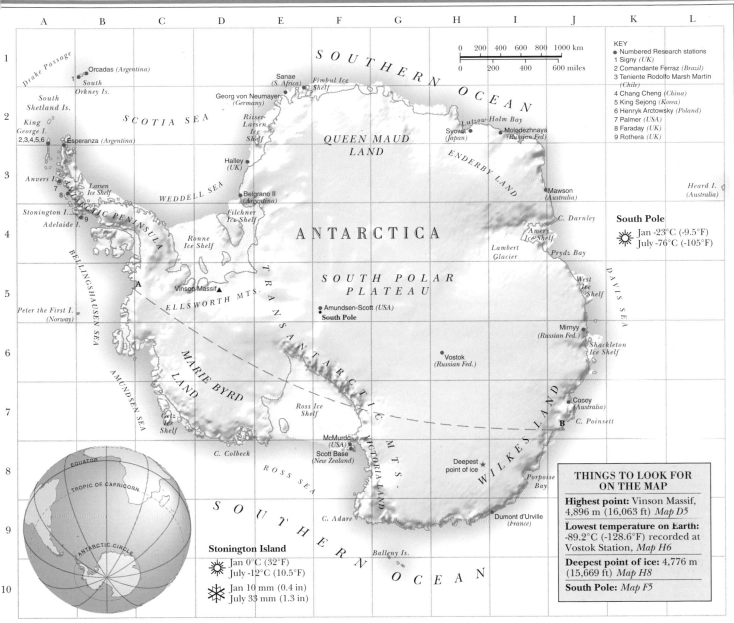

A B C D E F G H I J K L

**SOUTHERN OCEAN**

0 200 400 600 800 1000 km
0 200 400 600 miles

**KEY**
• Numbered Research stations
1 Signy *(UK)*
2 Comandante Ferraz *(Brazil)*
3 Teniente Rodolfo Marsh Martin *(Chile)*
4 Chang Cheng *(China)*
5 King Sejong *(Korea)*
6 Henryk Arctowsky *(Poland)*
7 Palmer *(USA)*
8 Faraday *(UK)*
9 Rothera *(UK)*

*Drake Passage*

Orcadas *(Argentina)*
*South Orkney Is.*
*South Shetland Is.*
*SCOTIA SEA*
*King George I.* 2,3,4,5,6
Esperanza *(Argentina)*
*Anvers I.*
*ANTARCTIC PENINSULA*
*Larsen Ice Shelf*
Stonington I.
*Adelaide I.* 9
*BELLINGSHAUSEN SEA*
Peter the First I. *(Norway)*

Sanae *(S. Africa)*
Georg von Neumayer *(Germany)*
*Fimbul Ice Shelf*
*Riiser-Larsen Ice Shelf*
Halley *(UK)*
Belgrano II *(Argentina)*
*Filchner Ice Shelf*
*WEDDELL SEA*
*Ronne Ice Shelf*

*QUEEN MAUD LAND*

Syowa *(Japan)*
*Lutzow-Holm Bay*
Molodezhnaya *(Russian Fed.)*
*ENDERBY LAND*
Mawson *(Australia)*
*C. Darnley*
*Amery Ice Shelf*
*Lambert Glacier*
*Prydz Bay*

*Heard I. (Australia)*

**South Pole**
☀ Jan -23°C (-9.5°F)
July -76°C (-105°F)

**ANTARCTICA**

*SOUTH POLAR PLATEAU*

Vinson Massif ▲
*ELLSWORTH MTS.*
*TRANSANTARCTIC MTS.*

Amundsen-Scott *(USA)*
**South Pole**

Vostok *(Russian Fed.)*

Mirnyy *(Russian Fed.)*
*West Ice Shelf*
*DAVIS SEA*
*Shackleton Ice Shelf*

*MARIE BYRD LAND*
*AMUNDSEN SEA*
*Getz Ice Shelf*
*Ross Ice Shelf*
C. Colbeck
*ROSS SEA*
McMurdo *(USA)*
Scott Base *(New Zealand)*
*VICTORIA LAND*
C. Adare
*Balleny Is.*

*WILKES LAND*
Casey *(Australia)*
*C. Poinsett*
Deepest point of ice ★
*Porpoise Bay*
Dumont d'Urville *(France)*

**SOUTHERN OCEAN**

*EQUATOR*
*TROPIC OF CAPRICORN*
*ANTARCTIC CIRCLE*

**Stonington Island**
☀ Jan 0°C (32°F)
July -12°C (10.5°F)
❄ Jan 10 mm (0.4 in)
July 33 mm (1.3 in)

**THINGS TO LOOK FOR ON THE MAP**
**Highest point:** Vinson Massif, 4,896 m (16,063 ft) *Map D5*
**Lowest temperature on Earth:** -89.2°C (-128.6°F) recorded at Vostok Station, *Map H6*
**Deepest point of ice:** 4,776 m (15,669 ft) *Map H8*
**South Pole:** *Map F5*

## CROSS-SECTION THROUGH THE ANTARCTIC

Antarctica is buried beneath an enormous ice-cap which covers 99.6 per cent of the land area. It has formed from the build up of snow compacted over 100,000 years. The ice-cap contains most of the fresh water on Earth, and 90 per cent of all the ice. If the ice were to melt, the oceans would rise by up to 64 m (210 ft). The ice weighs so much that it pushes much of Antarctica below sea level.

*This cross-section follows the line A–B on the map above.*

Sea level
Ross Ice Shelf
Transantarctic Mountains
Deepest point of ice
A
B

## ANTARCTIC WILDLIFE

Antarctica's severe climate and isolated position have greatly reduced the variety of its wildlife. The largest animal that lives on land all year round is a tiny insect. During the brief summer, however, seals, penguins, and many birds visit the continent to take advantage of the safe breeding sites and plentiful food supply to raise their young. At sea, a dozen species of whale feed off the many seals, fish, and krill that live in the icy waters.

### KRILL
Krill are shrimp-like crustaceans up to 5 cm (2 in) in length. They feed on plankton and other crustaceans and occur in such large numbers that they sometimes turn the oceans around Antarctica pink.

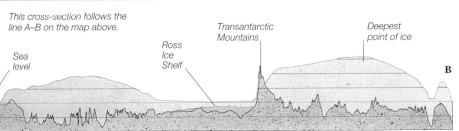

### EMPEROR PENGUINS
The majestic emperor penguin stands up to 1.15 m (4 ft) tall and can weigh 30 kg (66 lb). After spending most of the year at sea, the emperors come ashore in April to breed. The male alone then incubates the single egg during the icy winter, holding it on his feet to keep it warm. The female returns in July to feed the new-born chick.

# POLITICAL SYSTEMS

NO TWO COUNTRIES have identical political systems, as over the years each country has evolved a form that suits its history, culture, people and rulers. However, it is possible to group the political systems of the world into a few main categories. There can be variations within each category. Some countries have a system that is in transition from one category to another, such as Afghanistan, which is moving from theocracy to multi-party democracy, or Zimbabwe, which is being moved from democracy to dictatorship by its leader, Robert Mugabe.

Woman voting in elections in India – the world's most populous democracy.

## POLITICAL TERMS

**Alliance** A formal agreement between nations for economic, political, or military reasons.

**Apartheid** A policy of separating people by race.

**Capitalism** A system in which wealth and profit in the hands of a few people drives the country's economy.

**Communism** A system in which property and land are owned by the whole community and each person is paid according to their needs and abilities.

**Democracy** A system in which people vote for the government of their choice.

**Economy** The organization of a country's finances, exports, imports, industries, and services.

**Multi-party elections** More than one party standing for election.

**Nationalized** Industries or services owned by the state.

**Privatization** State-owned organizations taken over by private companies.

**Republic** A state where people elect the head of state and the government.

**Socialism** A system in which the economy is controlled by the whole community.

**Trade union** An organized group of workers united to protect their rights and interests.

**West, the** Countries in Europe and North America with capitalist economies and democratic governments that share similar cultural values.

## MULTI-PARTY DEMOCRACY

In a multi-party democracy, people are given a choice between several parties to elect. Because this allows different points of view to be expressed in public, and opposition to form against the elected government, not every country can make a multi-party democracy work. Some countries claim to be multi-party democracies, but real power is actually held by the president.

### CONSTITUTIONAL MONARCHY
In a constitutional monarchy, the head of the ruling royal family is head of state and is succeeded by his or her closest relative in hereditary succession. Japan, for example, is a constitutional monarchy whose head of state is the emperor. The monarch has no real power, but acts as a figurehead for the country. This is in the hands of the democratically elected government, led by the prime minister, the ruler of the largest party in parliament. Over the years, many countries have evolved from absolute to constitutional monarchies.

### FEDERAL REPUBLIC
Some nations, including Germany, are federal republics, with each state in the republic having considerable power and electing its own prime minister. In Germany, the federal assembly acts as an umbrella over the states, and elects a chancellor (prime minister) to rule the republic as a whole. The president is chosen by the states and assembly together.

Pro-democracy protesters are confronted by riot police in Indonesia.

## PRESIDENTIAL REPUBLIC
A presidential republic is a true democracy where voters choose both the head of state – the president – and elect representatives to parliament. It is the most common form of government in the world. In countries such as the USA and South Africa, the president is both the head of state and of government. In France and Russia, the president is elected head of state and chooses the prime minister to run the government, but retains considerable power in the running of the nation. In many countries, such as Ireland, India, and Israel, the president is a symbolic figurehead and real power is held by the prime minister and government.

Voters    Candidates
Candidates from several parties are elected into office.

## ONE-PARTY STATE

In a one-party state, only one political party is allowed to exist. All other parties are forbidden. All power in the state is held by the one party. The former communist states of eastern Europe and many of the African nations are now moving from being one-party states to establishing a multi-party democracy.

Soldiers on the streets in Indonesia

### THEOCRACY
In a theocracy, power is held by religious leaders who rule according to their scriptures. In Iran, the *mullahs* – Muslim scholars and priests – hold the real power, though the government is in non-religious hands. The Vatican

City, the world's smallest state, is a mixture of a theocracy and an elected monarchy. The head of state is the Pope, who is leader of the world's Roman Catholics. He is elected for life by cardinals, who are senior clergy.

### ONE-PARTY DOMINATED STATES
Some countries, such as Egypt and Tunisia, claim to be multi-party democracies, but are run by a single party that keeps a firm hold on power, often with the support of the army, as in Syria.

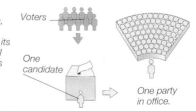
In an election, the party decides who its candidate will be and voters are only required to endorse that choice.

Voters

One candidate

One party in office.

# ABSOLUTE MONARCHY

In an absolute monarchy, power is held by the ruling monarch of the country and is handed down through the royal family to his or her successor. In the past, absolute monarchs kept all power to themselves, but today most appoint a small advisory council to help them rule.

## MONARCHY WITH A PARTIAL DEMOCRATIC SYSTEM

In some countries, the ruling monarch retains a strong grip on the government but allows some limited democracy. In Jordan, King Abdullah allows direct elections to the lower House of Representatives, but keeps strong control by appointing all 55 members of the upper house, or Senate.

# DICTATORSHIP

A number of countries around the world are ruled by single rulers, called dictators, who have absolute authority. Most dictators gain power either through military coups (an army takeover), by seizing leadership from an existing ruler, as in Iraq, or through direct elections and then banning opposition parties. Once in office, dictators rule in a personal, often brutal, fashion, eliminating all opposition to themselves.

*Dictator of the Central African Republic from 1965 to 1975, Jean-Bédel Boukassa crowned himself "emperor" in 1977.*

# MILITARY GOVERNMENT

Military governments are usually set up after the army has seized leadership from a weak or unpopular government. An example of a military government is Pakistan, where the military under Pervez Musharraf seized power. All power is held by senior military officers, usually drawn from the army. Elections and parliament are abolished and political parties are declared illegal. Military governments have often held power in South and Central America, Africa, and Asia.

# EMPIRE

Empire is when one country controls a number of other countries, usually under the control of one ruler or emperor. Empires have existed since ancient times, though the 18th and 19th centuries are often called "the Age of Empire," as this was when the European powers expanded their rule throughout the continents of South America, Africa, and Asia. Today, only small pockets of these European empires remain.

*Hong Kong was handed back to the Chinese after 157 years of British rule in 1997.*

# DEPENDENT TERRITORIES

Not every country rules itself. About 10 million people around the world live under the protection of either the UK, Denmark, Norway, France, the Netherlands, the USA, New Zealand, or Australia. Most dependent territories are relics of the colonial era that have remained attached to their former colonial rulers. Some territories have recently changed status. Hong Kong, for example, reverted from British to Chinese rule in 1997. Some territories are retained because of their strategic or economic importance, while others remain colonies because they are too small, remote, or weak to survive on their own.

**Examples of dependent territories**

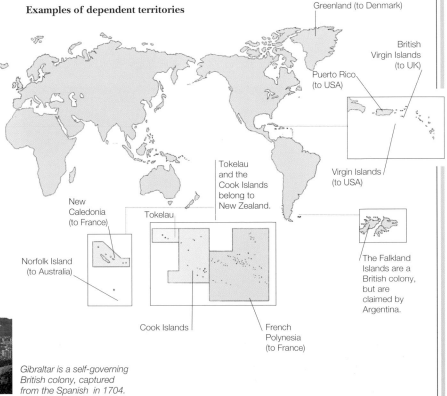

Greenland (to Denmark)

British Virgin Islands (to UK)

Puerto Rico (to USA)

Virgin Islands (to USA)

New Caledonia (to France)

Tokelau

Tokelau and the Cook Islands belong to New Zealand.

Norfolk Island (to Australia)

Cook Islands

French Polynesia (to France)

The Falkland Islands are a British colony, but are claimed by Argentina.

*Gibraltar is a self-governing British colony, captured from the Spanish in 1704.*

# NATURAL DISASTERS

NATURAL DISASTERS SHAPE both our landscape and human history. Since civilization began, mankind has had to cope with the the power unleashed by nature in the form of volcanoes, earthquakes, floods and fires. The immense forces nature unleashes affect all our lives and influence everything from the way we construct buildings to where we situate towns and cities. Though we can prepare in a limited way for natural disasters, no one knows when the next will strike and with what force. People also pollute the atmosphere, and this means that our climate and its destructive power is changing in ever more extreme and unpredictable ways.

*Kiribati in the Pacific will be one of the first countries to be totally submerged.*

## TROPICAL CYCLONES

Tropical cyclones, known as hurricanes in the the Caribbean and the USA, and typhoons in the west of the Pacific Ocean, are powerful, seasonal storms with high winds of over 113 km/h (70 mph). They originate in oceans over the equator and there are around 100 worldwide each year. Sometimes they do not reach land, but when they do, vast destruction is usual. Tropical cyclones are given names, such as Hurricane Katrina or Mitch, so people can identify them in forecasters' warnings. The thunder storms they generate can produce 25 cm (10 in) of rain each day and thus make huge amounts of energy, often equivalent in one day to as much power as the USA uses in one year.

EL NINO
The satellite image of Earth shows the temperature of the land and sea around Indonesia, the red and white colours indicating higher than average readings. Later sea temperatures dropped dramatically. The departure of the large mass of warm water affects where rain clouds come from, and brought drought to Indonesia. This is the weather disrupting phenomenon known as El Niño.

## GLOBAL WARMING

An ever increasing amount of so-called "natural disasters" are, in fact, the results of global warming, a heating up of the Earth's climate that scientists now believe is probably caused by atmospheric pollution. As countries' climates change, people must prepare for new weather situations they had not previously encountered, such as flooding and drought. The warmer temperatures are also melting polar ice caps, thus increasing sea levels. The result is that low-lying areas of some countries will revert back to the sea and some whole islands may be lost.

*A bush fire rages in Kakadu National Park, Australia.*

## FIRE

Bush, or forest, fires can be one of the most terrifying of all natural disasters. They destroy vast tracts of vegetation, kill large numbers of animals, and can do great damage to crops and property. They usually start after a dry season, and while fires may be set off spontaneously or through lightning, often they are caused by people. Once burning, the fire quickly grows in scale, becoming a huge wall of flame. Strong winds can drive the flames, spreading them at huge speed and across vast distances.

*Hurricane Mitch sustained winds of over 290 km/h (180 miles per hour) and caused huge destruction.*

# VOLCANOES

A volcano is a vent in the Earth's surface through which molten rock and hot gases escape. Volcanoes can lie dormant for many years before erupting suddenly, causing tremendous destruction as the poisonous gases are discharged and lava (molten rock) flows out. The word volcano comes from an island in the Mediterranean that the Romans called Volcano. This volcanic island had a crater that blew out smoke-like vapour, making the Romans believe that it was the home of Vulcan, their god of fire.

*Mount Ruapehu in New Zealand lights up the night sky as it erupts.*

*A mud slide in Nicaragua that killed over 1,000 people.*

## LANDSLIDES

When a hillside collapses, it is called a landslide. It can be both a natural or a man-made disaster. It can be caused by the ground becoming saturated with rain water and giving way, earthquakes, or volcanic eruptions, but can also be triggered by human activity weakening the hillside through deforestation, machinery vibration, or the weight of buildings.

# TORNADOES

Tornadoes, sometimes called twisters, are powerful whirling winds, accompanied by funnel-shaped clouds. The winds blow clockwise north of the equator and anti-clockwise south of the equator. It is thought that they form when cold polar air meets warm tropical air. These winds have tremendous power and can rip up everything in their path, including whole buildings. Tornadoes are most common in Australia and the Midwestern and Southern USA.

*A tornado approaches a corn field in Kansas, USA.*

# TSUNAMIS

A tsunami is a huge wave set off by an underwater earthquake, or by a volcanic eruption at or below sea level. Shockwaves from the earthquake create a tsunami that can travel at more than 700 km/h (435 mph). The tsunami gains height as it nears land. As the wave breaks, it causes devastation and loss of life in low lying coastal areas.

# MAJOR INTERNATIONAL AID ORGANIZATIONS

**CARE**
One of the world's largest private international relief and development organizations, it works in over 60 countries around the world. CARE reaches out to people whose lives are devastated by humanitarian emergencies, or who are struggling each day in poor communities to improve their lives.

**CARITIS INTERNATIONALIS**
A worldwide network of Catholic relief and development organizations, such as CAFOD in the United Kingdom, that spreads solidarity and social justice, without regard to creed, race, or gender.

**MEDECINS SANS FRONTIERS (DOCTORS WITHOUT BORDERS)**
Medecins Sans Frontiers (MSF) is an international humanitarian aid organization that provides emergency medical assistance to populations in danger in more than 80 countries. It provides medical aid wherever it is needed, regardless of race, religion, politics, or sex, and also raises awareness of the plight of the people in the developing world.

**MUSLIM AID**
Founded in 1985, it tries to improve the lives of people in the 44 poorest countries in the world through development programs such as the provision of clean water, health, shelter, and education.

**OXFAM INTERNATIONAL**
Working for an end to the waste and injustice of poverty, both in long-term development work and times of urgent need. A group of independent organizations that work together to achieve greater impact by collective efforts.

**SAVE THE CHILDREN**
Founded in the United Kingdom in 1919 by Eglantyne Jebb, Save the Children works to improve the lives of children who are faced with poverty, violence, and injustice around the world.

**UNITED NATIONS CHILDREN'S FUND (UNICEF)**
Founded in 1946, UNICEF works for the protection of children's rights, to help them meet their basic needs, and to expand their opportunities so that they can reach their full potential.

# WORLD RELIGIONS

THROUGHOUT HISTORY, people have asked about the meaning of life and death and have sought answers through religion. There are many faiths throughout the world, each with its own practice and belief. Some religions, such as Christianity, have spread over the world; others, such as traditional African beliefs, have stayed in one place. The world's major faiths roughly divide into two groups – the Western tradition and the Eastern tradition. The Western tradition originated in the Near and Middle East and includes Judaism, Christianity, and Islam. The Eastern tradition began in India and includes Hinduism and Buddhism.

The Ka'bah in Mecca is Islam's holiest site and the focus for the annual hajj (pilgrimage) made by millions of Muslims.

## CHRISTIANITY

Christianity was founded around 2,000 years ago by Jesus Christ, who was born in the town of Bethlehem, in present-day Israel. Jesus was born into the Jewish faith, but interpreted the Jewish Bible in a new way. After his death, his teachings were written down and collected together in the New Testament of the Bible. Christians believe in one God, that Jesus is the Son of God, that he rose from the dead, and that those who follow him will have eternal life. The Christian symbol is the cross on which Jesus was killed.

The cross is the most sacred symbol in the Christian religion.

## ISLAM

Muslims follow the Islamic faith, based on a belief in one God, Allah. Islam shares the same roots as Judaism and Christianity, all three recognizing certain prophets, such as Abraham. Followers believe the last and greatest of the Islamic prophets was Mohammed, who was born in Mecca, Saudi Arabia, in AD 570. The words revealed to Mohammed by Allah were later written down in the Koran. After Mohammed's death, Islam split into two branches: the traditional Sunnis, who follow Mohammed's original successors (the Caliphs), and the radical Shi'ites, who followed Mohammed's cousin and son-in-law, Ali. Shi'ites are the majority in Iran and Iraq, Sunnis the majority elsewhere.

The Western Wall in Jerusalem is Judaism's most holy place.

### DIVISIONS OF CHRISTIANITY

More than half of all Christians are Roman Catholics, who follow the leadership of the Pope in Rome. There are large numbers of Catholics in southern Europe, Central and South America, and the Philippines. One-quarter of Christians are Protestants, who split from the Catholic Church 500 years ago, and belong to a number of self-governing churches. The main areas of Protestantism are in northern Europe and North America. About one in ten Christians belong to one of the Eastern Orthodox Churches of eastern Europe and Russia; each national church has its own Patriarch, or leader.

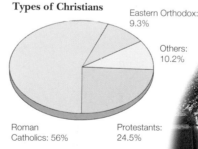
**Types of Christians**

Eastern Orthodox: 9.3%

Others: 10.2%

Roman Catholics: 56%

Protestants: 24.5%

## JUDAISM

Judaism, the religion of the Jews, began in about 2000 BC when the ancient Hebrew people settled in what is now mainly Israel. Judaism is the parent of the other two major monotheist (one-god) religions, Christianity and Islam. There is no single founder, but Abraham was the first leader. The scripture is the Jewish Bible, of which the Torah (the first five books) is the most important part. After persecution in Europe, the Jewish people established a homeland in Israel in 1948, although Jews are found in most countries of the world. The Jewish symbol is the six-pointed Star of David.

The Torah is a Jewish sacred scroll and is made up of the first five books of the Old Testament.

# BUDDHISM

Buddhism is based on the teachings of Buddha, the "Enlightened One", a prince who was born in India in about 563 BC. Buddha taught that suffering is always present in daily life and is caused by desiring things. Freedom from desire leads to the end of suffering and the attainment of perfect peace, or *nirvana*. Although Buddhism began in India, most Buddhists today are found elsewhere, in China, Sri Lanka, Tibet, and southeast Asia.

*Buddhist monks in Thailand in their traditional saffron coloured robes – Buddhism came to Thailand from India in around the first century BC.*

## OTHER FAITHS

**CONFUCIANISM** Often thought to be more like a philosophy than a religion, Confucianism was founded by Confucius, or K'ung Fu Tze, in around 500 BC. It is not based on the worship of a god but on following a moral code. Confucianism is practised in China and other parts of east Asia.

**TAOISM** This faith was founded in China by Lao Tzu around 300 BC. Taoists believe in many gods and aim to live in harmony with nature. Their symbol, *Yin Yang*, stands for balance and harmony. Taoism is followed in China and other parts of east Asia.

**SHINTOISM** The ancient religion of Japan is based on the worship of gods of nature and ancestor worship. Most Shinto shrines are in parks, gardens and on mountains.

**JAINISM** Jains do not believe in a god; their faith is based on non-violence to all living things and a belief in rebirth. Most of its followers live in India.

**ZEN BUDDHISM** Very important in Japan, this branch of Buddhism originated in China. It aims to harmony in living and stresses the need for meditation.

**TRADITIONAL BELIEFS** Around the world, there are numerous local religions handed down by word of mouth from generation to generation. Many share a belief that there are spirits living in the world – in the sky, stars, trees, lakes, and rivers. Many traditional faiths are found in Africa, where beliefs vary widely depending on the individual tribe. The ancient faith of Shamanism, found in parts of Asia, centres on a priest, or *shaman*, who goes into trances to enable people to leave their bodies and visit the spiritual world.

### ANGKOR WAT

Between AD 880 and 1228, a city called Angkor was built by the Khmer people in what is now northwestern Cambodia. One of the most impressive buildings was a temple called Angkor Wat (pictured). Originally dedicated to the Hindu god Vishnu, it is a fusion of Hindu and Khmer art, and is spread over 81 hectares (200 acres). It consists of five towers, each thought to represent Mount Meru, the home of the gods and centre of the Hindu universe. With the decline of the Khmer Empire and the rise of Buddhism in Cambodia, Angkor Wat became a Buddhist temple. Today, it is a World Heritage site, though rising numbers of tourists are causing increasing amounts of damage to it.

# HINDUISM

The world's third largest religion, Hinduism originated in India in about 1750 BC. The word "Hindu" comes from the Persian for "India". Today it is the dominant faith in India, Nepal, and among the Tamils of Sri Lanka. It has no single founder or scripture, though the earliest beliefs were written down in the *Vedas*, a collection of hymns and chants. Most Hindus believe in many gods but in one underlying reality (*Brahman*). They believe that when a person dies their soul is reborn in another body. People who live good lives are born again in a higher life; bad lives lead to a lower life. Devout Hindus aim to be free from the cycle of rebirth and become one with *Brahman*.

*A statue of the Hindu god Shiva, the destroyer. Shiva, Brahma, and Vishnu are three of the most important gods in Hinduism.*

*Varanasi in India stands on the banks of the River Ganges, a holy place for Hindus.*

# SIKHISM

This faith began in the Punjab region of India in the 1400s. Its founder was Guru Nanak. He was succeeded by nine other Gurus who all helped to develop Sikhism. The *Guru Granth Sahib* is the Sikh holy book. The religion is based on the worship of one God and on the cycle of human rebirth. Sikhs believe that God is found in all things, and that all people are equal in the eyes of God. Sikhism is mainly practised in India, but followers are also found throughout the world.

*The golden Palace at Amritsar, Punjab is a site sacred to Sikhs*

# HEALTH

OVER THE LAST 100 YEARS, the world has become a healthier place to live. Advances in medical science, improved diet, higher living standards, and better health education have all helped people live longer and healthier lives. However, many problems remain, especially in the less fortunate countries within Africa and Asia. While immunization has protected millions of children against disease, many illnesses remain common. Tuberculosis and malaria are widespread, AIDS is decimating the population in parts of Africa, and thousands of babies die each year of tetanus. In the world's richer continents, which include North America, Oceania, and Europe, cancer and heart disease plague many people.

*The Japanese generally live longer as they often have a high standard of living and a low-fat diet.*

| LOW LIFE EXPECTANCY | |
|---|---|
| Sierra Leone | 37 |
| Zambia | 37 |
| Malawi | 38 |
| Botswana | 38 |

## LIFE EXPECTANCY

Life expectancy is a measure of how long a person is likely to live. In 1950, the average person expected to live 40 years, but now most live to at least 63. This hides the differences between rich and poor countries, and the social groups within them. Wealthier people are generally healthier than the poor, and rich countries, like Andorra, with the world's highest life expectancy, are usually healthier places to live.

| HIGH LIFE EXPECTANCY | |
|---|---|
| Andorra | 83 |
| Japan | 82 |
| San Marino | 81 |
| Sweden | 80 |

*In wealthy countries, many premature babies survive because of good health facilities such as incubators.*

## PEOPLE PER DOCTOR

One way of measuring the provision of healthcare in a country is to count the number of people cared for by each doctor. Countries that are rich or have good welfare systems provide easy access to health services, and on average have one doctor for every 390 people. In contrast, there is only one doctor to every 50,000 people in the world's poorer countries, and over half the population lives more than 10 km (6 miles) from a doctor or medical centre.

### CHILD MORTALITY

The child mortality rate is the number of deaths of children under five years of age per 1,000 births. In some areas of the world, such as Afghanistan and parts of Africa, poor medical care and lack of nourishment lead to a high number of child deaths. The story is much better in Europe and North America, where less than 10 out of every 1,000 children under five die.

| HIGHEST CHILD MORTALITY | |
|---|---|
| *Country* | *per 1,000 births* |
| Sierra Leone | 390 |
| Niger | 354 |
| Liberia | 288 |
| Angola | 260 |
| Afghanistan | 257 |
| Somalia | 225 |

## PREVENTIVE MEDICINE

There are many ways of safeguarding against illness. Immunization protects people from catching diseases such as measles and tetanus. In rich countries most children are immunized, but in some poor countries only 30 per cent of children receive this care. Across the world, people are warned of the dangers of smoking, alcohol, and drugs. Governments also try to promote the idea of regular exercise to keep the population fit and healthy. Attention to water quality, food hygiene, sanitation, and good housing all play their part in keeping people well. In the countries that can afford it, campaigns in the media, schools, and clinics help to educate people in basic health care and issues such as hygiene.

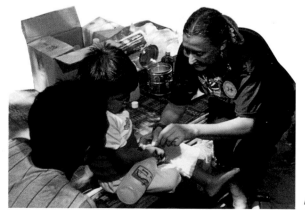

### CONTROLLING DISEASE

War has a devastating effect upon every country, but apart from the carnage and destruction it causes, the humanitarian crisis can be enormous. People fleeing from areas of conflict to live in refugee camps often have little food and fresh water and serious diseases spread quickly. Organizations such as the Red Cross (shown here at a refugee camp for Cambodians in Thailand) try to minimise suffering by providing food and medical supplies at the camps.

### HEALTHY EATING

People are known to live longer if they eat a healthy diet that is low in saturated fats and includes fresh fruit and vegetables. The diet eaten by people who live in Mediterranean countries, such as Italy and Spain, contains a variety of healthy food, such as fish, leafy vegetables, olive oil, and pulses. Regular exercise is also important for a healthy life.

*Food typically eaten in many Mediterranean countries.*

# EDUCATION

EDUCATION IS ONE OF the most important ways of creating a better world, for it enables people to improve their own lives. Most children receive a primary education up to the age of 11, which gives them the basic skills of reading, writing, and mathematics. About half the world's children also receive a secondary education up to the age of 16 or 18, and some go on to higher education. But education provision varies greatly. Children in rich countries generally receive a better education than those in poorer areas. One of the biggest problems for poor countries is that having fewer educated people, they are less capable of coping with the demands of the modern world.

## ADULT LITERACY

The adult literacy rate of a country shows how many adults over the age of 15 can read and write. The test involves asking a person to read and write a short, simple statement about their everyday life. In the USA, for example, the literacy rate is 99 per cent, which means that only one adult in 100 cannot read or write. In Niger in west Africa, however, the adult literacy rate is only 17 per cent, which means that 83 people in every 100 cannot read or write.

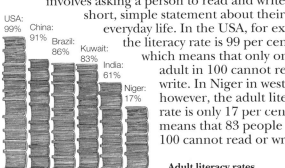

USA: 99%
China: 91%
Brazil: 86%
Kuwait: 83%
India: 61%
Niger: 17%

**Adult literacy rates**

## EDUCATION LEVELS

A country's ability to educate its people is related to its wealth. Rich countries can spend money on schools and teachers, as well as books and computers. In turn, a good education adds to that country's wealth by producing qualified people to work in its offices, factories, and farms. Better education supplies more teachers, trains farmers to be more productive, and office workers to be more efficient.

*In the USA over a quarter of all young people go on to higher education.*

*Children in Japan work hard to pass their exams. Many attend special classes on Saturdays or in the evenings.*

### EFFICIENT EDUCATION
Japan has one of the most efficient education systems in the world. Nearly all children attend a nursery before they are old enough to go to primary school, and one-third of children stay on for higher education. Japanese children do well in science and maths, which are subjects much in demand by industries.

### RURAL AND URBAN SCHOOLING
In the poorer countries of Africa and Asia, children who live in towns usually receive a better education than those who live in the countryside. This is because many country children are needed to stay at home to work the land and help in the family, and would have to travel long distances to get to school. However, educating rural children can bring great advantages, because they can develop skills to increase productivity in agriculture and local industry.

*These children are studying at a rural school in Haiti.*

### MALE AND FEMALE DIFFERENCES
In many countries, girls are not as well-educated as boys. Girls often leave school earlier and some are not educated at all. This might be for religious or economic reasons, because society thinks they should remain at home or because they are needed to work on the land. However, the situation is improving because educating women benefits the national economy.

*In some countries girls are forced to leave school early to help in the home.*

**Male and female differences in literacy rates**

In each case the female figure is a percentage of the male average, which is given as 100. The closer the figure to 100, the smaller the gap in literacy rates.

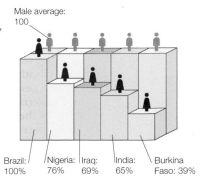

Male average: 100

Brazil: 100%
Nigeria: 76%
Iraq: 69%
India: 65%
Burkina Faso: 39%

# RICH AND POOR

THE DIFFERENCE IN WEALTH between the richest and poorest countries is vast. The average person in Mozambique earns one six-hundredth of the average person's wages in Switzerland. How wealthy a country is depends on its natural resources, industrial strength, population size, and political stability. Libya is much richer than its neighbour, Chad. Both are desert countries with small populations, but Libya has oil while Chad has few natural resources. Many poor countries borrow money from richer countries. Debt repayment is difficult, with the result that poor countries stay poor, while rich countries continue to grow richer.

| POOREST COUNTRIES (Based on real GDP per person) | |
|---|---|
| *Country* | *US$* |
| East Timor | 400 |
| Malawi | 600 |
| Sierra Leone | 600 |
| Somalia | 600 |
| Burundi | 600 |

| RICHEST COUNTRIES (Based on real GDP per person) | |
|---|---|
| *Country* | *US$* |
| Luxembourg | 58,900 |
| USA | 40,100 |
| Norway | 40,000 |
| San Marino | 34,600 |
| Switzerland | 33,800 |

## NATIONAL WEALTH

There are two official measures of national wealth. The Gross Domestic Product (GDP) measures the total value of finished goods and services produced by a national economy. The Gross National Product (GNP) measures GDP and the income from abroad that flows into the country. Both figures are usually expressed in US dollars. When the figures are divided by the total population of the country, they give an indication of how rich or poor that country is. The tables on the left show that the five richest countries are in Europe and the US, while the five poorest countries are in Africa and Asia.

## World distribution of wealth

The wealthiest areas of the world are North America, Japan, Australia, United Arab Emirates, and parts of Europe. The poorest areas are parts of Africa and Southern Asia. Figures are based on real GDP per person.

## Map key

Figures are in US$ and based on real GDP per person.

- Above 15,000
- 10,000–15,000
- 5,000–10,000
- 1,000–5,000
- Below 1,000
- Figures not available

## ABSOLUTE AND RELATIVE POVERTY

About a quarter of the world's population lives in "absolute poverty". This means that their basic needs for a healthy life are not met: they have little or no food to eat, no access to safe drinking water, and are often poorly clothed. The vast majority of these people live in southern and eastern Asia and the area south of the Sahara in Africa. Many more people live in "relative poverty", which means they are much poorer than the majority of people living in the same country.

Women washing clothes at a watering hole in Burkina Faso.

# SOCIAL POVERTY

In most countries, there are groups of people who are poorer than others. Women are usually poorer than men – they are often paid less (see chart right) or are housewives with no income. Also, women often have a lower standard of education, which means they are not qualified to obtain higher-paid jobs. Single mothers and elderly single women are particularly at risk from poverty. Older people on low pensions and the sick are also poorer than average. In some places, such as São Paulo in Brazil (shown left), children are forced to live on the streets because they have no families to support them or homes to live in. They often beg or turn to crime to survive.

*Favelas (slums) in Rio de Janeiro, Brazil, stand next to luxurious apartment buildings.*

**Male and female wages**

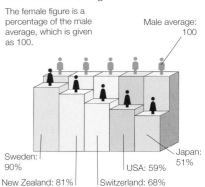

The female figure is a percentage of the male average, which is given as 100.

Male average: 100

Sweden: 90%

New Zealand: 81%

USA: 59%

Switzerland: 68%

Japan: 51%

WOMEN'S EQUALITY

In September 1893 New Zealand became the first country in the world to give women the right to vote. This marked a major step in the long, worldwide struggle by women in many countries for equal rights in all aspects of life, including education, divorce and equal opportunities at work.

# THE NEWLY RICH

Historically, the wealthy countries of the world have been in Europe and North America. With the discovery of oil reserves in the Middle East in the past 60 years, the desert states of the Arabian Peninsula are now among the richest nations in the world. Also, the spectacular growth of Asian economies, such as Hong Kong, Taiwan, South Korea, and China – which have all followed in the footsteps of Japan – means that these countries may soon join the world's wealthiest nations.

*Oil wealth has helped Dubai grow from a small trading post fifty years ago to a rich city with modern buildings.*

# EQUAL WEALTH DISTRIBUTION

Some countries strive for a more equal distribution of wealth among their citizens, so that there are few, if any, very rich or very poor people. Their governments spend a large proportion of national wealth on education, healthcare, social welfare, and job creation to help all levels of society. New Zealand was the first country in the world to introduce a full welfare state, while Scandinavian countries, such as Sweden concentrate on providing jobs for everyone. Today, they are among the most equal societies in the world.

*The Big Issue is one of 35 street papers sold round the world by the homeless, with proceeds from sales going to help the homeless.*

DIFFERENCES IN WEALTH

Within many countries there are great differences in income between rich and poor. In Europe and North America there are many homeless people on the streets or seeking refuge in cardboard shelters. In some poor countries, such as India, rich landowners and industrial managers flourish. In Brazil, the poorest 10 per cent of the people earn only 0.7 per cent of the total income, while the richest 10 per cent earn 48 per cent, a difference of 68 times. In comparison, the poorest 10 per cent in Hungary earn 4.1 per cent, while the richest 10 per cent earn 20.5 per cent, a difference of only 5 times.

*Rodeo Drive, Beverley Hills, USA, is one of the richest shopping streets in the world.*

## INTERNATIONAL AID

In order to help the world's poorest countries, the richer nations give them aid in the form of grants, loans, or, when a natural disaster such as an earthquake occurs, food, tents, and clothing. Some African countries, such as Mozambique, are dependent on aid for much of their income. The largest source of aid is the USA, which provides more than $13.3 billion per year, although this is only 0.13 per cent of its Gross National Product (GNP).

# WORLD TRADE

TRADE BETWEEN THE COUNTRIES of the world allows each nation to specialize in the goods it produces best. A country will sell its products abroad to buy goods that are produced more cheaply elsewhere. Trade creates wealth and jobs by encouraging countries to produce goods that can be sold abroad, or exported. However, the benefits of trade are not evenly spread across all countries – some produce a range of goods much more cheaply than others, and these gain the most from trading. Today, much of world trade is controlled by about 200 multinational companies, which have offices and factories across the globe.

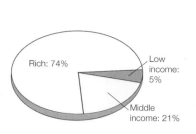

**SHARE OF WORLD TRADE**
The 23 richest countries in the world control 74 per cent of all world trade. The 40 poorest countries, such as Haiti and Laos, control only 5 per cent. The remaining 130 countries, such as the nations of eastern Europe and much of South America, control 21 per cent.

Rich: 74%
Low income: 5%
Middle income: 21%

## NORTH AND SOUTH

As shown on the map, there is a clear divide in the share of world trade between the rich economies of the "North" and the poor economies of the "South". In order to prosper, a country needs to have a positive balance of trade, that is, earn more from exports than it spends on imports. Many nations have a negative balance of trade – importing more than they export. To improve their trade balance, many have grouped together to form regional trading blocs.

**Percentages of world exports and imports by region**

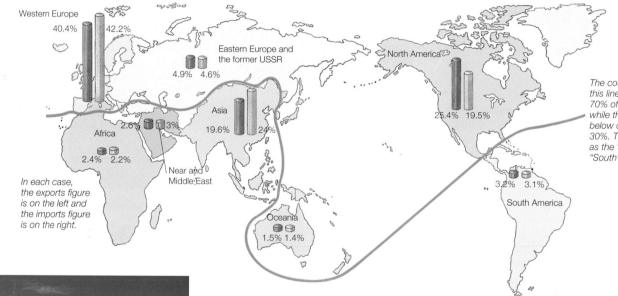

Western Europe
40.4%   42.2%

Eastern Europe and the former USSR
4.9%   4.6%

North America
25.4%   19.5%

The countries above this line control about 70% of world trade, while the countries below control about 30%. This is known as the "North" and "South" divide.

Africa
2.6%   3%

Asia
19.6%   24%

Africa
2.4%   2.2%

Near and Middle East

In each case, the exports figure is on the left and the imports figure is on the right.

South America
3.2%   3.1%

Oceania
1.5%   1.4%

**THE PACIFIC RIM**
Over the last 20 years, the centre of world trade has begun to shift from the USA and Europe to the USA and Asia, in particular those countries found around the edge of the Pacific Ocean, an area known as the Pacific Rim. Countries such as South Korea and Thailand, as well as the island states of Singapore and Taiwan, and the Chinese province of Hong Kong (above), have developed high-tech electronic industries, exporting their low-cost products around the world. Secure governments and encouragement of foreign investment have helped generate trade.

## TRADING BLOCS

Some countries form alliances, or trading blocs, which give companies easier access to foreign markets and make it more profitable for them to trade with countries that are also members of the bloc. Countries may try and harmonize the rules that govern buying and selling so that foreign firms can trade on an equal footing with local companies. Some trading blocs, such as the European Union (EU), also have political functions, while others, such as the North American Free Trade Association (NAFTA), are concerned solely with the buying and selling of goods.

**NORTH AMERICAN FREE TRADE AGREEMENT**
The North American Free Trade Agreement (NAFTA) was created in 1994 and is an agreement between the USA, Mexico (pictured) and Canada that removes many barriers to trade and investment between these countries. It is the largest free trade zone in the world, and there are plans to extend it to other countries on the American continent.

## OIL TRADE

Without oil, the world would grind to a halt. Industry and transport would stop. This is why oil is the most important product traded in the world today. Oil is produced and exported by a few countries, mostly in the Middle East, north and west Africa, and Central and South America. Because oil is not a renewable source of energy, and its use causes a lot of pollution, alternative sources of energy are being developed.

*All oil products start life as crude oil, a dark sticky liquid.*

## WHAT IS TRADED

World trade is dominated by manufactured goods, which include cars, televisions, and computers. Most of these products are made by rich countries. Poorer countries generally produce food and raw materials, known as primary products. This means that rich countries are growing richer, because bigger profits are made by exporting expensive manufactured goods than by exporting cheaper primary products.

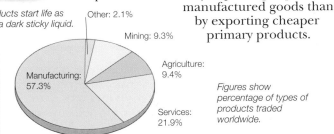

Other: 2.1%
Mining: 9.3%
Manufacturing: 57.3%
Agriculture: 9.4%
Services: 21.9%

*Figures show percentage of types of products traded worldwide.*

## INVISIBLE EXPORTS

In addition to goods, companies may also trade internationally in services. This trade is often referred to as 'invisible exports'. These exports cover a wide range of services and can include anything from banking and insurance to tourism and advertising. France (pictured above), for example, is the world's most popular tourist destination, while the United Kingdom is one of the world's most important financial centres.

## TRADE DEPENDENCY

Some countries rely almost entirely on one product to sell abroad. For example, many smaller countries in Central America and the Caribbean depend on bananas for a large percentage of their income. This dependency on one product can leave a country at the mercy of events beyond its control. If the price of a commodity rises around the world, the country will benefit, but if the price drops, or a natural disaster such as a hurricane destroys the harvest, the country can be plunged into economic hardship.

*Workers sort and pack bananas ready for distribution.*

FINANCIAL EXCHANGES
When money, stocks and shares, and other financial assets are traded, this is called a financial market. Stock exchanges are the best known type of financial market - here people buy and sell shares in companies. For example, if you own 500 shares in a firm that has issued 5 million shares, you would own a 1,000th part of the company. Share prices can go up and down. The futures market, such as the London International Financial Futures and Options Exchange (above), is a financial market where dealers speculate on what the price of stocks, shares and commodities will be in the future.

### CHILD LABOUR

In many countries in the developing world, children are forced to work, often for very little money. It is estimated that in some countries up to 20 per cent of children who are forced to work are under the age of 10. In Pakistan, for example, it is estimated that there are over 11 million children working in the country's factories, including 1 million working in the carpet weaving industry, such as these boys in Lahore, Punjab. Children are usually employed because factory owners do not have to pay them as much money as adults and sometimes because their fingers are more dextrous than those of an adult.

*Child labour is still very common in the economies of many poorer countries.*

# GLOSSARY

**Aboriginals:** the earliest known, original, inhabitants of a country; most often used to refer to the native peoples of Australia.

**Acid rain:** rain that has been polluted by gases from factories and traffic; when the rain falls it can damage crops, forests, and lakes.

**Apartheid:** the policy, developed in South Africa, of separating people according to their race.

**Archipelago:** a large group of islands

**Arid:** dry; with little rainfall.

**Barren:** lacking in vegetation; not able to produce fruit or crops.

**Bauxite:** the mineral ore from which aluminium is obtained.

**By-product:** a substance produced as a result of making something else.

**Capitalism:** an economic system based on private ownership of property, and on free and competitive conditions for business.

**Cash crops:** crops that are grown specifically to be sold for a profit.

**Cattle ranch:** a large farm where cattle are reared.

**Civil war:** a war between rival groups who live in the same country or region.

**Collective farm:** a farm owned and run by a group of people working together.

**Colonize:** to send a group of people to settle in another land and establish a colony.

**Colony:** a region or country that is controlled by another country; a group of people settled in a land outside their homeland but still ruled by its laws.

**Commercial farming:** raising crops or animals for sale and profit.

**Communism:** an economic and political system in which farms and factories and the goods they produce are owned by the state.

**Consumer goods:** goods such as cars, computers, and televisions, purchased by people for personal use.

**Co-operative farm:** see Collective farm

**Crude oil:** petroleum in its natural state, before it has been treated in any way.

**Culture:** the values, beliefs, and way of life of the people of a country or region.

**Deforestation:** the large-scale clearing of healthy trees, often to make room for cash crops or for cattle ranching.

**Delta:** the flat area (often triangular in shape) formed by material deposited at the mouth of some rivers where they enter the sea or a large lake; deltas usually have highly fertile soil.

**Democracy:** a form of government based on the rule of the people, usually through representatives who have been voted into office by the people.

**Dependency:** a land run by another, usually more powerful, country.

**Deposit:** a natural grouping of minerals, such as oil or coal, within the Earth.

**Dictatorship:** a system of government where the ruler, or dictator, has absolute power.

**Economy:** the system by which a society manages its resources, makes and distributes goods and services.

**Emigrant:** a person who leaves his or her native country to settle in another.

**Empire:** a country and the conquered lands which it rules.

**Environment:** the natural world around us.

**Ethnic group:** a group of people sharing a common racial, religious, or cultural background.

**Ethnic mix:** the mix of ethnic groups in a country or region.

**Export earnings:** the money a country earns from selling goods or services to other countries.

**Exports:** goods or services sold to another country.

**Extended family:** a family which may include grandparents and other relatives as well as their children.

**Favela:** name used in Brazil for a shanty town.

**Fertility rate:** the average number of children born to a woman of childbearing age.

**Fundamentalism:** the belief that all the teachings of a particular religion must be strictly obeyed.

**Guerilla:** a member of a small, military group fighting a stronger, official army, usually through surprise attacks.

**Gulf:** a large area of sea partly enclosed by land, such as the Persian Gulf or the Gulf of Mexico.

**Hardwood:** wood from broad-leaved trees, such as beech, oak, and mahogany.

**Health care:** medical services that diagnose and treat illness, and provide care for pregnant women, the elderly, and disabled.

**High-tech industries:** industries that use or make the most recently invented and technologically advanced products, such as computers.

**Hunter-gatherers:** people who feed themselves by hunting wild animals and gathering fruits, nuts, and berries.

**Hydroelectric power:** electricity created by capturing the power of running water.

**Immigrant:** a person who has come from another country to settle.

**Imports:** goods or services bought from another country.

**Indigenous people:** the first or native people of an area or country.

**Industry:** economic activity that is concerned with manufacturing goods or processing raw materials.

**Investment:** the provision of resources, usually money, for a business venture, with the aim of later making a profit from it.

**Irrigation:** supplying dry land with water through a system of canals or pipes so that crops will grow.

**Landlocked:** surrounded by land; with no access to the sea.

**Latin America:** those parts of the American continent where the official language is Spanish or Portuguese; often used to mean Mexico, Central and South America.

**Life expectancy:** the average number of years a person can expect to live.

**Literacy rate:** the percentage of people over the age of 15 who can read and write a simple sentence.

**Manufactured goods:** products made from raw materials using machines, or made by hand.

**Mestizo:** a person of mixed race with one parent European and the other native Indian.

**Migrant:** a person moving from one place or country to settle in another.

**Mineral:** a natural substance found in rocks of the Earth, such as a metal; removed by mining.

**Missionary:** a person who goes abroad trying to convert others to their particular religion.

**Monarchy:** a country ruled by a king or queen, who has usually inherited the position rather than been elected by the people.

**Monsoon:** a wind that changes direction with the change of seasons; it causes a rainy season from April to October in Southeast Asia.

**Multicultural:** a group of people or society made up of various different ethnic groups.

**Native peoples:** the people who belong by birth or origin to a place.

**Natural resources:** materials which occur naturally in an area, such as wood, coal, oil, or gas.

**Nomads:** people who move from place to place in search of food, water, and land to graze their animals.

**Northern hemisphere:** the half of the Earth which lies north of the Equator.

**Oasis:** a fertile place in the desert, where water lies near or on the surface.

**Ore:** a mineral or rock from which a valuable metal, such as iron, gold or copper, can be mined or extracted.

**Overfarming:** exhausting the soil by growing too many crops.

**Overgrazing:** exhausting the land by not moving animals around to graze in different places.

**Overpopulation:** when population growth exceeds economic growth and results in food shortages and lack of housing.

**Paddy field:** a flooded field where rice is grown.

**Peninsula:** a strip of land surrounded on three sides by water.

**Petrochemicals:** chemicals obtained from natural gas or petroleum.

**Phosphate:** a chemical compound used in fertilizers and detergents.

**Pilgrim:** a person who goes on a journey, or pilgrimage, to a sacred place.

**Plantation:** a large farm using hired workers to grow and harvest one main crop, such as coffee, sugarcane, rubber, or cotton.

**Plateau:** a high, flat area of land.

**Population density:** the number of people living in a given area of land.

**Racism:** the belief that one's own racial group is superior to others.

**Raw materials:** the basic materials used to make a product, such as minerals, or wood.

**Refined oil:** oil that has been treated to remove water, and other impurities, to separate out fuels such as petrol, diesel, and paraffin.

**Refugee:** a person who has fled to another country in search of safety because of war, or political or religious oppression.

**Regime:** a particular government, or system of government.

**Republic:** a country ruled by elected representatives of its people, with an elected president rather than a king or queen.

**Reserves:** the amount of a resource, such as copper, known to exist, but which has not yet been extracted.

**Revolution:** the overthrow of a government.

**Ring of fire:** the zone around the Pacific Ocean where there are many volcanoes and frequent earthquakes.

**Rural:** relating to the countryside.

**Sahel, the:** zone of semi-desert and dry grassland to the south of the Sahara in Africa.

**Sanctions:** penalties imposed by one or more countries to persuade another country to follow a certain course of action.

**Savanna:** open grassland in a tropical or sub-tropical region.

**Shanty town:** an area in or around a city where people live in temporary shacks, often without basic services such as running water.

**Silt:** tiny particles of earth deposited by a river or lake.

**Slash-and-burn agriculture:** a method of clearing land to create fields, by cutting down trees or bushes and then burning away any remaining roots.

**Social services:** welfare services provided by a state or local authority.

**Socialism:** a system of society in which goods are owned collectively and the whole community exercises political power.

**Softwood:** wood from cone-bearing trees, such as pine or cedar.

**Soil erosion:** the natural wearing away of the soil by wind or rain.

**Southern hemisphere:** the half of the Earth which lies south of the Equator.

**Standard of living:** the quality of life in a country, usually measured by income, possessions, and levels of health care and education.

**Staple crop or food:** a crop that provides the main food, such as rice, potatoes, or wheat.

**Steppe:** a vast grass-covered plain, that stretches from eastern Europe across central Asia.

**Stock exchange:** an international market for buying and selling the stocks or shares of a public company.

**Subsistence farming:** raising just enough crops or animals to feed the farmer's family.

**Technology:** the development of methods, materials, and tools used in doing work.

**Terrorist:** a person who uses violence, often against ordinary people or buildings, to win demands or influence the policies of a government.

**Third world:** the poorer, less developed parts of the world in Asia, Africa, Central and South America.

**Urban:** relating to a town or city.

**Vegetation:** the plant life of a region.

**Welfare system:** the way a government organizes assistance to its people, particularly the young, the elderly, the sick, and the unemployed.

**West, the:** the western, industrially advanced countries of the world, specifically North America and western Europe.

**Workforce:** all the people available to work in a country; all the workers employed by a particular factory or place of work.

# GAZETTEER

## HOW TO USE THE GAZETTEER

This gazetteer helps you to find places on the maps. For example, to find the city of Paris in France, look up its name in the gazetteer. The entry reads:

Paris *Town* France 97 F3

The first number, 97, tells you that Paris appears on the map on page 97. The second number, F3, shows that it is in square F3 of the grid printed over the map. Turn to page 97. Trace down from the letter F along the top of the grid and then across from the number 3 along the side of the grid. You will find Paris in the square where the letter and the number meet.

## A

Aachen *Town* Germany 95 D7
Aalborg *Town* Denmark 82 E10
Abadan *Town* Iran 153 F6
Abeokuta *Town* Nigeria 221 K12
Aberdeen *Town* UK 87 J5
Abha *Town* Saudi Arabia 153 C10
Abidjan *Town* Ivory Coast 21 H12
Abilene *Town* Texas, USA 35 H10
Abu Dhabi *Town* United Arab Emirates 153 H9
Abuja *Town* Nigeria 221 M11
Acapulco *Town* Mexico 39 G9
Accra *Town* Ghana 221 I12
Aconcagua, Mt. Argentina 41 F11, 71 F7
Ad Dammam *Town* Saudi Arabia 153 F8
Adamaoua, Massif d' *Region* Cameroon 205 E7
Adana *Town* Turkey 145 F8
Adapazari *Town* Turkey 145 C5
Addis Ababa *Town* Ethiopia 215 G9
Adelaide *Town* South Australia, Australia 259 I11
Aden *Town* Yemen 153 C12, 203 D3
Aden, Gulf of 10 F8, 132 C13, 203 D3, 215 J8
Adriatic Sea S. Europe 78 G11, 103 G6
Aegean Sea 78 H12, 131 H6
Afghanistan *Country* Central Asia 18 G6, 161 F9
Africa *Continent* 10 C7, 205
Agadir *Town* Morocco 208 F4
Agalega Islands Indian Ocean 10 F10, 18 F10
Agra *Town* India 167 F5
Aguascalientes *Town* Mexico 39 F7
Ahaggar Mts *Mountain range* Algeria 205 E4, 209 L8

Ahmadabad *Town* India 167 D6
Ahvaz *Town* Iran 153 F5
Ajaccio *Town* Corsica 97 L10
Akosombo Dam Ghana 221 J12
Akron *Town* Ohio, USA 37 F5
Al 'Amarah *Town* Iraq 153 F5
Al Hufuf *Town* Saudi Arabia 153 F8
Al Ladhiqiyah *Town* Syria 147 F3
Al Mukha *Town* Yemen 153 C12
Al' Aziziyah *Town* Libya 205 F2, 209 O4
Al-Hillah *Town* Iraq 153 E5
Alabama *State* USA 37 D10
Åland *Island group* Finland 82 I8
Alaska *State* USA 19 Q3, 33 C2, 267 E2
Alaska, Gulf of USA 11 Q4, 20 E6, 265 G2
Alaska Range *Mountain range* Alaska, USA 20 D4, 33 C2
Albania *Country* S.E. Europe 124 I10, 18 D5
Albany *Town* New York, USA 37 I5
Albany *Town* Western Australia, Australia 258 D11
Albert Canal Belgium 91 H9
Albert, Lake Uganda/Congo, Dem. Rep. 205 I8, 239 F4
Alberta *Province* Canada 27 E12
Albuquerque *Town* New Mexico, USA 35 E9
Aldabra Islands Indian Ocean 203 D6, 205 K10
Ålesund *Town* Norway 82 E7
Aleutian Islands Alaska, USA 11 O4, 20 B7, 33 B3, 265 E2
Alexandria *Town* Egypt 215 D1
Algeciras *Town* Spain 100 D9
Algeria *Country* N.W. Africa 18 B6, 209 J6
Algiers *Town* Algeria 209 K2
Aliákmonas *River* Greece 131 D3
Alicante *Town* Spain 100 I6
Alice Springs *Town* Northern Territory, Australia 259 H7
Allahabad *Town* India 167 G6
Allentown *Town* Pennsylvania, USA 37 H5
Alps *Mountain range* C. Europe 10 C5, 78 E11, 97 I7, 103 B3, 106 D8
Altai Mts. N. Asia 10 I5, 133 H7, 175 F5
Altiplano *Region* Bolivia 41 G9
Altun Mts. China 133 H9, 174 D9
Amarapura *Town* Burma 189 C4
Amarillo *Town* Texas, USA 35 G9
Amazon *River* Brazil/Peru 11 W9, 41 G6, 59 E5, 67 C4, G3
Amazon Basin *Region* S. America 11 W9, 41 G6, 59 E5, 67 E4
Ambato *Town* Ecuador 59 C5
Ambon *Town* Moluccas, Indonesia 197 O10
American Samoa *Dependent territory* Polynesia, Pacific Ocean 11 O10, 19 P10, 265 F6
Amherst *Town* Burma 189 D8
Amicante Islands Indian Ocean 203 E5
Amiens *Town* France 97 F2
Amman *Town* Jordan 147 F8
Amritsar *Town* India 167 E3
Amsterdam *Town* Netherlands 91 H6
Amsterdam Island Indian Ocean 18 H12, 203 G9
Amu Darya *River* Central Asia 132 E9, 161 F9
Amundsen Sea Pacific Ocean 269 B7

Amundsen-Scott *Research station* Antarctica 269 F5
Amur *River* China/Russian Federation 10 L4, 133 M7, 139 R10, 175 N2, Q3
An Nasiriyah *Town* Iraq 153 E5
An-Najaf *Town* Iraq 153 E5
Anchorage *Town* Alaska, USA 33 D2
Andalusia *Region* Spain 100 F8
Andaman Islands Indian Ocean 10 H8, 18 I8, 133 I13, 203 H3
Andaman Sea 189 C9, 203 I3
Andes *Mountain range* S. America 11 V9, W11, 41 E7, 59 D3, D9, 71 F6, G13
Andijon *Town* Uzbekistan 161 H7
Andorra *Country* Europe 18 B5, 97 F10, 100 J2
Andorra la Vella *Town* Andorra 97 F10
Angel Falls *Waterfall* Venezuela 41 G4, 59 H3
Angkor Wat *Ancient site* Cambodia 189 G9
Anglesey *Island* UK 87 H9
Angola *Country* Southern Africa 18 D10, 247 D3
Angola Basin Atlantic Ocean 77 I9
Ankara *Town* Turkey 145 E6
Annaba *Town* Algeria 209 M2
Annapolis *Town* Maryland, USA 37 H6
Anne Arbor *Town* Michigan, USA 37 E5
Anshan *Town* China 175 O7
Antakya *Town* Turkey 145 G9
Antalya *Town* Turkey 145 D8
Antarctic Peninsula Antarctic 269 B4
Antarctica *Continent* 265 I11, 269
Antigua and Barbuda *Country* West Indies 19 W7, 45 V11
Antipodes Islands New Zealand, Pacific Ocean 11 O13, 19 O13, 255 K16, 265 E9
Antofagasta *Town* Chile 41 E4
Antwerp *Town* Belgium 91 G9
Anvers Island Pacific Ocean 269 A3
Apeldoorn *Town* Netherlands 91 J6
Apennines *Mountain range* Italy 78 F11, 103 F6
Appalachian Mts. USA 11 V6, 21 M10, 37 G7
Apure *River* Venezuela 59 F2
Aqaba, Gulf of S.W. Asia 147 E11, 215 F2
Ar-Ramadi *Town* Iraq 153 E4
Arabian Peninsula S.W. Asia 10 E7
Arabian Sea 10 G7, 132 E12, 153 G12, 203 F3
Arad *Town* Romania 127 D6
Arafura Sea S.E. Asia 10 L9, 133 M16, 197 Q10, 265 B6
Arak *Town* Iran 153 G5
Aral Sea *Lake* Kazakhstan/Uzbekistan 10 G5, 132 E8, 161 D5, 258 E8
Ararat, Mt. Turkey 145 K6
Arauca *River* Colombia/Venezuela 59 E2
Arctic Bay *Town* Northwest Territories, Canada 27 H5
Arctic Circle 11 Z2
Arctic Ocean 10 K1, 267 F4
Ardabil *Town* Iran 153 G3
Ardennes *Region* Belgium 91 I11
Arequipa *Town* Peru 59 E10
Argentina *Country* S. America 19 W12, 71 G8

Argentine Basin Atlantic Ocean 77 F11
Århus *Town* Denmark 82 E11
Arica *Town* Chile 71 E2
Arizona *State* USA 33 K11
Arkansas *State* USA 35 K9
Arkhangel'sk *Town* Russian Federation 138 F4
Arlon *Town* Belgium 91 J12
Armenia *Country* S.W. Asia 18 E5, 121 P14
Armenia *Town* Colombia 59 D3
Arnhem *Town* Netherlands 91 J7
Arnhem Land *Region* Northern Territory, Australia 254 D8, 259 G4
Arno *River* Italy 103 D6
Ar Rub 'al Khali (Empty Quarter) *Desert region* Saudi Arabia 10 F7, 132 C12, 153 E10
As Sulaymaniyah *Town* Iraq 153 E4
Ascension Island *Dependent territory* Atlantic Ocean 10 A9, 18 A9, 77 H8
Ashgabat *Town* Turkmenistan 161 D7
Ashmore and Cartier Islands Indian Ocean 18 K10, 203 K6
Asia *Continent* 10 I4, 132
Asmara *Town* Eritrea 215 G7
Assad, Lake Syria 147 H3
Assen *Town* Netherlands 91 K4
Astana *Town* Kazakhstan 161 G3
Astrakhan' *Town* Russian Federation 138 B8
Asunción *Town* Paraguay 71 J4
Aswân *Town* Egypt 215 E4
Aswân High Dam Egypt 215 E4
Asyût *Town* Egypt 215 D2
Atacama Desert Chile 11 V11, 41 F10, 71 F4
Athabasca, Lake Alberta/Saskatchewan, Canada 21 J6, 27 F11
Athens *Town* Greece 131 F7
Atlanta *Town* Georgia, USA 37 E9
Atlantic Ocean 10 B10, 11 X5, 77
Atlantic-Indian Ridge 77 H7
Atlas Mts. *Mountain range* Morocco 10 B6, 205 D2, 208 H4
Auckland *Town* New Zealand 262 F3
Auckland Islands New Zealand, Pacific Ocean 11 N13, 19 N13, 255 I16, 265 D9
Augsburg *Town* Germany 95 H10
Augusta *Town* Maine 37 K4
Austin *Town* Texas, USA 35 I12
Australasia and Oceania 254-255
Australes, Iles French Polynesia, Pacific Ocean 11 Q11, 255 P10
Australia *Country and continent* 10 K10, 18 K11, 259 G8
Australian Capital Territory *Territory* Australia 259 L11
Austria *Country* Europe 18 C5, 106 J6
Ayacucho *Town* Peru 59 D9
Ayers Rock *see* Uluru
Ayutthaya *Town* Thailand 189 E9
Az Zarqa' *Town* Jordan 147 F7
Azerbaijan *Country* S.W. Asia 18 F5, 121 P15
Azores *Island group* Atlantic Ocean 11 Z5, 19 Y5, 77 G4
Azov, Sea of Russian Federation/ Ukraine 78 J10, 121 J9, 138 A7

# B

Babruysk *Town* Belorussia 111 J10
Babylon *Ancient site* Iraq 153 E4
Bacau *Town* Romania 127 I6
Bacolod *Town* Philippines 196 L4
Badgastein *Town* Austria 106 H7
Baden *Town* Austria 106 K5
Badlands *Region* North/South Dakota, USA 35 F3
Baffin Bay Canada/Greenland 11 W2, 21 O3, 27 I4, 267 C7
Baffin Island Northwest Territories, Canada 11 V2, 21 N4, 27 J6, 267 B7
Bafoussam *Town* Cameroon 232 D8
Baghdad *Town* Iraq 153 E4
Baguio *Town* Philippines 196 K2
Bahamas *Country* West Indies 11 V7, 19 V7, 45 M5
Bahía Blanca *Town* Argentina 71 I9
Bahrain *Country* S.W. Asia 18 F7, 153 F8
Baia Mare *Town* Romania 127 F4
Baikal, Lake Russian Federation 10 J4, 133 J6, 139 M10
Baja California *Peninsula* Mexico 39 B3
Baker Island *Dependent territory* Pacific Ocean 19 P9, 255 L6, 265 E5
Bakersfield *Town* California, USA 33 H11
Bakhtaran *Town* Iran 153 F4
Baku *Town* Azerbaijan 121 T13
Balaton, Lake Hungary 115 G11
Balearic Islands Spain 78 E12, 100 J5
Bali *Island* Indonesia 196 I12
Balikesir *Town* Turkey 145 B6
Balikpapan *Town* Borneo, Indonesia 196 J9
Balkan Mts. S.E. Europe 78 H11, 124 K7, 127 F11
Balkhash, Lake Kazakhstan 10 H5, 133 G8, 161 I5
Ballarat *Town* Victoria, Australia 259 J12
Baltic Sea N. Europe 10 D4, 78 G8, 82 I10, 111 E5
Baltimore *Town* Maryland, USA 37 H6
Bamako *Town* Mali 221 F9
Banda Sea S.E. Asia 133 M15, 196 M10
Bandar Seri Begawan *Town* Brunei 196 I7
Bandar-e 'Abbas *Town* Iran 153 H8
Bandar-e-Bushehr *Town* Iran 153 G7
Bandundu *Town* Congo, Dem. Rep. 232 G11
Bandung *Town* Java, Indonesia 196 F12
Bangalore *Town* India 187 E11
Bangkok *Town* Thailand 189 E9
Bangladesh *Country* S. Asia 18 H7, 167 J6
Bangui *Town* Central African Republic 232 G9
Banja Luka *Town* Bosnia and Herzegovina 124 F4
Banjarmasin *Town* Borneo, Indonesia 196 I10
Banjul *Town* Gambia 220 B8
Banks Island Northwest Territories, Canada 11 S2, 21 H3, 29 E5, 267 C4
Baotou *Town* China 178 K8
Baranavichy *Town* Belorussia 111 H10
Barbados *Country* Caribbean Sea 19 W8, 45 W14
Barbuda *Island* Antigua and Barbuda 45 V11
Barcelona *Town* Spain 100 K3
Barcelona *Town* Venezuela 59 G1
Bareilly *Town* India 167 G4
Barents Sea Arctic Ocean 10 E2, 78 K4, 138 G3, 267 H7
Bari *Town* Italy 103 J9
Barinas *Town* Venezuela 59 F2

Barisian Mts. Sumatra, Indonesia 196 C10
Barnaul *Town* Russian Federation 139 I10
Barquisemeto *Town* Venezuela 59 F1
Barranquilla *Town* Colombia 59 D1
Barysaw *Town* Belorussia 111 J9
Basra *Town* Iraq 153 F6
Basque Provinces Spain 100 F2
Bassein *Town* Burma 189 B7
Basseterre *Town* St Kitts and Nevis 45 U11
Batangas *Town* Philippines 196 K3
Batdâmbâng *Town* Cambodia 189 G10
Baton Rouge *Town* Louisiana, USA 35 K11
Bavarian Alps *Mountain range* Austria/Germany 95 I11
Bayamo *Town* Cuba 45 L7
Baykonur *Space centre* Kazakhstan 161 F5
Beagle Channel Argentina 71 I16
Bear Island *Island group* Russian Federation 139 Q3
Beaufort Sea Arctic Ocean 11 Q2, 20 F4, 27 C6, 33 C1, 267 D3
Beaumont *Town* Texas, USA 35 J12
Beersheba *Town* Israel 147 E8
Beijing *Town* China 175 M8
Beira *Town* Mozambique 247 J6
Beirut *Town* Lebanon 147 F5
Bejaia *Town* Algeria 209 L2
Belém *Town* Brazil 67 H3
Belfast *Town* UK 87 G7
Belgium *Country* Europe 18 C4, 91 G10
Belgrade *Town* Serbia & Montenegro 124 I4
Belize *Country* Central America 19 U7, 44 D8
Belle Île *Island* France 97 B5
Bellevue *Town* Washington, USA 33 G4
Bellinghausen Sea Pacific Ocean 269 B5
Bello *Town* Colombia 59 D2
Belmopan *Town* Belize 44 D8
Belo Horizonte *Town* Brazil 67 I9
Belorussia *Country* E. Europe 18 D4, 111 I10
Ben Nevis *Mountain* UK 87 H5
Bengal, Bay of India 10 H7, 133 H12, 167 H9, 203 H3
Benghazi *Town* Libya 209 R4
Benidorm *Town* Spain 100 I6
Benin *Country* W. Africa 18 C8, 221 K10
Berbera *Town* Somalia 215 I8
Berbérati *Town* Central African Republic 232 F9
Bergen *Town* Norway 82 D8
Bergen op Zoom *Town* Netherlands 91 G8
Bering Sea Pacific Ocean 11 O3, 20 B6, 33 A3, 139 T3, 265 E2
Bering Strait Arctic Ocean/Pacific Ocean 11 P3, 20 C5, 33 B2, 265 F1
Berlin *Town* Germany 95 J5
Bermuda *Dependent territory* Atlantic Ocean 11 W6, 19 W6
Bern *Town* Switzerland 106 C8
Bethlehem *Town* West Bank 147 E8
Bhopal *Town* India 167 F6
Bhutan *Country* S. Asia 18 I6, 167 J5
Bialystok *Town* Poland 115 K3
Bielefeld *Town* Germany 95 F5
Bien Hoa *Town* Vietnam 189 I11
Bihac *Town* Bosnia and Herzegovina 124 E4
Bikini Island Marshall Islands, Pacific Ocean 265 D5
Bila Tserkva *Town* Ukraine 120 F5
Bilbao *Town* Spain 100 G1
Birmingham *Town* Alabama, USA 37 D9

Birmingham *Town* UK 87 J10
Biscay, Bay of 10 B5, 78 D11, 100 G1
Bishkek *Town* Kyrgyzstan 161 I6
Bismarck *Town* North Dakota, USA 35 H3
Bismarck Archipelago *Island group* Papua New Guinea 10 L9, 254 G6, 259 L1
Bissau *Town* Guinea-Bissau 220 B9
Bitola *Town* Macedonia 124 J9
Biwa, Lake Japan 185 F9
Black Forest *Region* Germany 78 F10, 95 E10
Black Hills South Dakota, USA 35 G4
Black Rock Desert Nevada, USA 33 H8
Black Sea Asia/Europe 10 E5, 78 J11, 127 L10, 132 B8, 138 A7
Black Volta *River* W. Africa 205 C6, 221 H10
Blackpool *Town* UK 87 I8
Blantyre *Town* Malawi 239 H14
Blenheim *Town* New Zealand 262 E7
Blida *Town* Algeria 209 K2
Bloemfontein *Town* South Africa 247 G10
Blue Mts. Oregon/Washington, USA 33 H6
Blue Nile *River* E. Africa 205 I5, 215 E7
Bobo Dioulasso *Town* Burkina 221 G10
Bogor *Town* Java, Indonesia 196 F12
Bogota *Town* Colombia 59 D3
Bohemia *Region* Czech Republic 115 C8
Bohemian Forest *Region* Germany 95 J9
Boise *Town* Idaho, USA 33 H6
Bolivia *Country* S. America 19 W10, 59 G10
Bologna *Town* Italy 103 E5
Bombay *see* Mumbai
Bonin Islands Pacific Ocean 10 L6
Bonn *Town* Germany 95 E7
Borås *Town* Sweden 82 F10
Bordeaux *Town* France 97 D8
Borneo *Island* S.E. Asia 10 J9, 133 K14, 196 I8
Bornholm *Island* Denmark 78 G8, 82 G12
Borobudur *Ancient site* Java, Indonesia 196 G12
Bosnia and Herzegovina *Country* S.E. Europe 18 D5, 124 F4
Bosporus Channel Turkey 145 C5
Boston *Town* Massachusetts, USA 37 J5
Bothnia, Gulf of Finland/Sweden 78 H6, 82 I6
Botosani *Town* Romania 127 I4
Botrange *Mountain* Belgium 91 J10
Botswana *Country* Southern Africa 18 D11, 247 F7
Bounty Islands New Zealand, Pacific Ocean 11 O13, 19 N13, 255 L15, 265 E9
Bourke *Town* New South Wales, Australia 254 G12
Bournemouth *Town* UK 87 J12
Bouvet Island *Dependent territory* Atlantic Ocean 77 I12
Boyoma Falls *Waterfall* Congo, Dem. Rep. 205 H8, 232 J10
Bradford *Town* UK 87 J8
Brahmaputra (Yarlung Zangbo) *River* India/China 133 H10, 167 K5, 174 C11
Braila *Town* Romania 127 K7
Brasília *Town* Brazil 67 H8
Brasov *Town* Romania 127 H7
Bratislava *Town* Slovakia 115 F10
Braunschweig *Town* Germany 95 H5
Bravo del Norte *River* Mexico 39 E2
Brazil *Country* S. America 19 W9, 67 H6
Brazil Basin Atlantic Ocean 77 G8
Brazilian Highlands *Mountain range*

Brazil 41 J9, 67 I8
Brazzaville *Town* Congo 232 F12
Breda *Town* Netherlands 91 H8
Bremen *Town* Germany 95 F4
Brest *Town* Belorussia 111 F11
Bridgeport *Town* Connecticut, USA 37 I5
Bridgetown *Town* Barbados 45 W14
Brighton *Town* UK 87 K12
Brindisi *Town* Italy 103 K9
Brisbane *Town* Queensland, Australia 259 M8, 265 C7
Bristol *Town* UK 87 I11
British Columbia *Province* Canada 27 B12
British Indian Ocean Territory *Dependent territory* Indian Ocean 18 H9, 203 G5
British Isles *Country* Europe 10 B4, 78 C8, 87
British Virgin Islands *Dependent Territory* Caribbean Sea 45 T10
Brittany *Region* France 97 B4
Brno *Town* Czech Republic 115 F8
Broken Hill *Town* New South Wales, Australia 259 J10
Broken Ridge Indian Ocean 203 I9
Brooks Range *Mountain range* Alaska, USA 20 D4, 33 C1
Broome *Town* Western Australia, Australia 258 D6
Bruges *Town* Belgium 91 F9
Brunei *Country* Borneo, S.E. Asia 18 J8, 196 H7
Brussels *Town* Belgium 91 G9
Bucaramanga *Town* Colombia 59 D2
Bucharest *Town* Romania 127 I9
Budapest *Town* Hungary 115 H10
Buenaventura *Town* Colombia 59 C3
Buenos Aires *Town* Argentina 71 J8, 77 E10
Buenos Aires, Lake (Lake General Carrera) Argentina/Chile 41 F15, 71 G13
Buffalo *Town* New York, USA 37 G4
Bujumbura *Town* Burundi 239 E7
Bukavu *Town* Congo, Dem. Rep. 232 K11
Bukhara *Town* Uzbekistan 161 F7
Bulawayo *Town* Zimbabwe 247 H7
Bulgaria *Country* E. Europe 18 D5, 127 H11
Buon Ma Thuot *Town* Vietnam 189 I10
Buraydah *Town* Saudi Arabia 153 D7
Burgas *Town* Bulgaria 127 J11
Burgundy *Region* France 97 H5
Burkina *Country* W. Africa 18 B8, 221 I9
Burma *Country* S.E. Asia 18 I7, 189 C5
Bursa *Town* Turkey 145 C6
Burundi *Country* Africa 18 E9, 239 E7
Butuan *Town* Philippines 196 M5
Buzau *Town* Romania 127 I8
Bydgoszcz *Town* Poland 115 G3

# C

Cabanatuan *Town* Philippines 196 K2
Cabimas *Town* Venezuela 59 E1
Cabinda *Region* Angola 18 C9, 232 E12, 247 B1
Cabo da Roca *Cape* Portugal 78 C11, 100 A6
Cabot Strait Canada 29 J5
Cacak *Town* Serbia & Montenegro 124 I5
Cadiz *Town* Philippines 196 L4
Cádiz *Town* Spain 100 D8
Caen *Town* France 97 D3
Caernarfon *Town* UK 87 H9

**Cagayan de Oro** *Town* Philippines 196 M5

**Cagliari** *Town* Sardinia 103 C11

**Cairns** *Town* Queensland, Australia 259 K5

**Cairo** *Town* Egypt 215 D1

**Calabria** *Region* Italy 103 I12

**Calais** *Town* France 97 F1

**Calama** *Town* Chile 71 F4

**Calbayog** *Town* Philippines 196 M4

**Calcutta** *see* Kolkata

**Calgary** *Town* Alberta, Canada 27 E13

**Cali** *Town* Colombia 59 C3

**California** *State* USA 33 H10

**Callao** *Town* Peru 59 C8

**Camaguey** *Town* Cuba 45 L6

**Cambodia** *Country* S.E. Asia 18 I8, 189 H10

**Cambrian Mts.** UK 87 H10

**Cambridge** *Town* UK 87 K10

**Cameron Highlands** *Mountain range* Malaysia 189 E14

**Cameroon** *Country* Central Africa 18 C8, 232 D8

**Cameroon, Mt.** *Volcano* Cameroon 232 D9

**Campbell Island** New Zealand, Pacific Ocean 19 N13, 265 E9

**Campeche** *Town* Mexico 39 K8

**Campinas** *Town* Brazil 67 H10

**Can Tho** *Town* Vietnam 189 H11

**Canada** *Country* N. America 19 S3, 26–27, 28–29

**Canary Basin** Atlantic Ocean 77 G6

**Canary Islands** Atlantic Ocean 10 A6, 18 A6, 77 H5, 205 A3

**Canberra** *Town* Australian Capital Territory, Australia 254 G13, 259 L11, 265 C8

**Cancún** *Town* Mexico 39 L7

**Cannes** *Town* France 97 J9

**Canterbury** *Town* UK 87 L11

**Canton** *Town* China 175 N14

**Cape Basin** Atlantic Ocean 77 I10

**Cape Canaveral** *Peninsula* Florida, USA 37 G12

**Cape Cod** *Peninsula* Massachusetts, USA 21 N9, 37 K5

**Cape Horn** *Peninsula* Chile 11 off W13, 41 off G16, 71 I16, 77 D12

**Cape of Good Hope** *Peninsula* South Africa 10 D12, 77 J10, 203 B9, 205 G14, 247 E12

**Cape Town** *Town* South Africa 203 B9, 247 E11

**Cape Verde** *Peninsula* Senegal 205 A5, 220 A8

**Cape Verde Islands** Atlantic Ocean 10 A7, 18 A7, 77 G6, 205 A5

**Cape York** *Peninsula* Queensland, Australia 254 F9, 259 J4

**Cappadocia** *Region* Turkey 145 G7

**Capri** *Island* Italy 103 G9

**Caracas** *Town* Venezuela 59 G1

**Cardiff** *Town* UK 87 I11

**Caribbean Sea** 11 V8, 41 F2, 44 J10, 77 C6

**Caroline Islands** Federated States of Micronesia, Pacific Ocean 10 L8, 254 G5

**Carpathians** *Mountain range* Central Europe 10 C4, 78 H10, 115 I8, 120 B6, 127 F10, H8

**Carpentaria, Gulf of** Northern Territory/Queensland, Australia 254 E8, 259 I5

**Carson City** *Town* Nevada, USA 33 H9

**Cartagena** *Town* Colombia 59 D1

**Cartagena** *Town* Spain 100 H7

**Casablanca** *Town* Morocco 208 G3

**Cascade Range** *Mountain range* USA 21 H7, 33 G6

**Caspian Sea** *Lake* Central Asia 10 F5, 78 M11, 132 D8, 138 B9, 161 B6

**Castries** *Town* St Lucia 45 V14

**Catalonia** *Region* Spain 100 J3

**Catania** *Town* Sicily 103 H13

**Caucasus** *Mountain range* Europe/Asia 10 E5, 78 L11, 121 O12, 132 C8

**Cayenne** *Town* French Guiana 59 L3

**Cayman Islands** *Dependent territory* Caribbean Sea 44 I7

**Cebu** *Town* Philippines 196 M4

**Cedar Rapids** *Town* Iowa, USA 35 K5

**Celebes Sea** S.E. Asia 133 L14, 196 K8

**Central African Republic** *Country* Central Africa 18 D8, 232 H8

**Central America** *Region* 11 U7, 41, 44

**Central Siberian Plateau** Russian Federation 10 I2, 133 K3, 139 L6

**Ceuta** *Spanish enclave* Morocco 208 H2

**Cevennes** *Mountain range* France 97 G8

**Chad** *Country* Central Africa 18 D7, 232 G4

**Chad, Lake** Central Africa 205 F5, 221 P9, 232 F5

**Chagos Archipelago** *Island group* Indian Ocean 10 H9

**Chalbi Desert** Kenya 239 J3

**Chandigarh** *Town* India 167 F3

**Changchun** *Town* China 175 O5

**Changsha** *Town* China 175 M12

**Channel Islands** UK 18 B4, 78 D10, 87 I13, 97 C3

**Channel Tunnel** UK/France 87 L11, 97 F1

**Chapala, Lake** Mexico 39 E7

**Charleroi** *Town* Belgium 91 G11

**Charleston** *Town* South Carolina, USA 37 G10

**Charleston** *Town* West Virginia, USA 37 F7

**Charlotte** *Town* North Carolina, USA 37 F8

**Charlottetown** *Town* Prince Edward Island, Canada 29 J6

**Chatham Islands** New Zealand, Pacific Ocean 11 O13, 19 O13, 255 L15, 265 E8

**Chattanooga** *Town* Tennessee, USA 37 E8

**Cheju** *Town* South Korea 175 Q9

**Chelyabinsk** *Town* Russian Federation 138 F8

**Chemnitz** *Town* Germany 95 J7

**Chengdu** *Town* China 175 J11

**Chennai (Madras)** *Town* India 167 F11

**Chenonceaux** *Town* France 97 E5

**Cherbourg** *Town* France 97 C2

**Cherkasy** *Town* Ukraine 120 G6

**Chernihiv** *Town* Ukraine 120 G4

**Chernivtski** *Town* Ukraine 120 C6

**Chernobyl** *Town* Ukraine 120 F4

**Cheyenne** *Town* Wyoming, USA 35 F6

**Chiang Mai** *Town* Thailand 189 E6

**Chicago** *Town* Illinois, USA 37 C5

**Chichén Itzá** *Ancient site* Mexico 39 L7

**Chiclayo** *Town* Peru 59 B7

**Chihuahua** *Town* Mexico 39 E3

**Chile** *Country* S. America 19 V12, 71 F6, F14

**Chilka, Lake** India 167 H8

**Chillán** *Town* Chile 71 F9

**Chimbote** *Town* Peru 59 C7

**China** *Country* E. Asia 18 I6, 175 G8

**Chingola** *Town* Zambia 239 D12

**Chios** *Island* Greece 131 I7

**Chisinau** *Town* Moldavia 120 E8

**Chittagong** *Town* India 167 K7

**Chitungwiza** *Town* Zimbabwe 247 I6

**Chon Buri** *Town* Thailand 189 E9

**Ch'ongjin** *Town* North Korea 175 Q6

**Chongqing** *Town* China 175 K12

**Christchurch** *Town* New Zealand 262 E9

**Christmas Island** Indian Ocean 18 J10, 203 J6

**Chugoku Mts.** Japan 185 D10

**Chukchi Sea** Arctic Ocean 11 O2, 20 B4, 139 R1, 267 F1

**Churchill** *Town* Manitoba, Canada 27 I10

**Cincinnati** *Town* Ohio, USA 37 E6

**Citlaltépetl (Orizaba)** *Volcano* Mexico 39 H8

**Ciudad Bolívar** *Town* Venezuela 59 H2

**Ciudad Guayana** *Town* Venezuela 59 H2

**Ciudad Juárez** *Town* Mexico 39 E2

**Clermont-Ferrand** *Town* France 97 G6

**Cleveland** *Town* Ohio, USA 37 F5

**Clipperton Island** *Dependent territory* Pacific Ocean 19 T8, 265 I5

**Cluj-Napoca** *Town* Romania 127 F5

**Coast Mts.** Canada 11 R3, 20 G6

**Coast Ranges** *Mountain range* N. America 11 S5, 21 H9, 33 F8

**Cobán** *Town* Guatemala 44 C8

**Cochabamba** *Town* Bolivia 59 G10

**Cochin** *Town* India 167 E12

**Coco** *River* Honduras/Nicaragua 44 F10

**Cocos Islands** Indian Ocean 10 I10, 18 I10, 203 J6

**Coihaique** *Town* Chile 71 G13

**Coimbatore** *Town* India 167 E11

**Coimbra** *Town* Portugal 100 B4

**Cologne** *Town* Germany 95 E7

**Colombia** *Country* S. America 19 V8, 59 E3

**Colombo** *Town* Sri Lanka 167 F13, 203 H4

**Colón** *Town* Panama 44 H14

**Colorado** *River* Argentina 41 G13, 71 I10

**Colorado** *River* Mexico/USA 21 J9, 33 I12, 35 E6

**Colorado** *State* USA 35 E6

**Colorado Springs** *Town* Colorado, USA 35 F7

**Columbia** *River* Canada/USA 27 D13, 33 G5

**Columbia** *Town* South Carolina, USA 37 F9

**Columbus** *Town* Georgia, USA 37 E10

**Columbus** *Town* Ohio, USA 37 F6

**Communism Peak** *Mountain* Tajikistan 161 H7

**Como, Lake** Italy 103 C3

**Comodoro Rivadavia** *see* Rivadavia

**Comoros** *Country* Indian Ocean 10 E10, 18 E10, 203 D6

**Conakry** *Town* Guinea 220 C10

**Concepción** *Town* Chile 71 F9

**Concord** *Town* California, USA 33 G10

**Concord** *Town* New Hampshire, USA 37 J4

**Congo** *River* Central Africa 10 C9, 205 F9, G8, 232 F11, G10

**Congo** *Country* Central Africa 18 C9, 232 F10

**Congo, Dem. Rep** *Country* Central Africa 18 D9, 232 H11

**Congo Basin** *Region* Congo/Congo, Dem. Rep. 205 G8

**Connecticut** *State* USA 37 J6

**Constance, Lake** Switzerland/Austria/Germany 95 G12, 106 E7

**Constanta** *Town* Romania 127 K9

**Constantine** *Town* Algeria 209 M2

**Cook Islands** *Dependent territory* Polynesia, Pacific Ocean 11 P10, 19 P10, 255 O9, 265 F6

**Cook Strait** New Zealand 262 F7

**Cook, Mt.** New Zealand 262 C9

**Copenhagen** *Town* Denmark 82 F11

**Copiapó** *Town* Chile 71 F5

**Coral Sea** Pacific Ocean 10 M10, 254 G8, 259 L4, 265 C6

**Coral Sea Islands** *Dependent territory* Pacific Ocean 18 M10, 265 C7

**Córdoba** *Town* Argentina 71 H7

**Córdoba** *Town* Spain 100 E7

**Corfu** *Island* Greece 131 A5

**Corinth** *Town* Greece 131 E8

**Cork** *Town* Ireland 87 E10

**Coromandel** *Town* New Zealand 262 G3

**Coromandel Coast** India 167 G11

**Corpus Christi** *Town* Texas, USA 35 I13

**Corrib, Lough** *Lake* Ireland 87 E8

**Corrientes** *Town* Argentina 71 J5

**Corsica** *Island* France 78 E11, 97 L10

**Costa Blanca** *Coast* Spain 100 I7

**Costa Brava** *Coast* Spain 100 K3

**Costa del Sol** *Coast* Spain 100 F8

**Costa Rica** *Country* Central America 19 U8, 44 E13

**Côte d'Azur** *Coast* France 97 J9

**Coventry** *Town* UK 87 J10

**Craiova** *Town* Romania 127 F9

**Crete** *Island* Greece 78 H13, 131 H12

**Crimea** *Peninsula* Ukraine 121 H9

**Croatia** *Country* S.E. Europe 18 C5, 109 H4

**Crozet Islands** Indian Ocean 10 F13, 18 F13, 203 E10

**Cuba** *Country* Caribbean Sea 19 V7, 45 K6

**Cúcuta** *Town* Colombia 59 E2

**Cuenca** *Town* Ecuador 59 C5

**Culiacán** *Town* Mexico 39 D5

**Cumaná** *Town* Venezuela 59 H1

**Curitiba** *Town* Brazil 67 H10

**Cusco** *Town* Peru 59 E9

**Cyclades** *Island group* Greece 131 H9

**Cyprus** *Country* Europe 18 E6, 132 B10, 145 F10

**Czech Republic** *Country* Central Europe 18 C4, 115 E7

# D

**Da Lat** *Town* Vietnam 189 J10

**Da Nang** *Town* Vietnam 189 I8

**Dagupan** *Town* Philippines 196 K2

**Dakar** *Town* Senegal 220 A8

**Dalian** *Town* China 178 O8

**Dallas** *Town* Texas, USA 35 I10

**Dalmatia** *Region* Croatia 109 G7

**Damascus** *Town* Syria 147 F6

**Dampier** *Town* Western Australia, Australia 258 C7

**Danube** *River* Central Europe 10 D5, 78 G10, H11, 95 G11, J10, 106 K5, 109 K4, 115 G10, H11, J5, 127 F10, K8

**Danube Delta** Romania 127 L7

**Danzig, Gulf of** Poland/Russian Federation 115 H4

**Dar es Salaam** *Town* Tanzania 239 K9

**Dardanelles** *Channel* Turkey 145 A5

**Darling** *River* New South Wales, Australia 10 L11, 254 F12, 259 K9

**Dartmoor** *Region* UK 87 H12

**Darwin** *Town* Northern Territory, Australia 259 G4

**Dasoguz** *Town* Turkmenistan 161 D6

**Datong** *Town* China 175 L8

**Daugavpils** *Town* Latvia 111 H7

**Davao** *Town* Philippines 196 M6

**David** *Town* Panama 44 E14

**Davis Sea** Antarctica 269 K5

**Davis Strait** Canada/Greenland 11 W2, 21 O4, 27 L5, 267 B8

**Dayr az Zawr** *Town* Syria 147 J3

**Dayton** *Town* Ohio, USA 37 E6

**De Bilt** *Town* Netherlands 91 I6

**Dead Sea** *Lake* Israel/Jordan/West Bank 132 B10, 147 E8

**Death Valley** California, USA 21 I10

**Debrecen** *Town* Hungary 115 J10

**Deccan Plateau** *Region* India 10 H7, 167 E8

**Delaware** *State* USA 37 I7

**Delphi** *Ancient site* Greece 131 D7

**Denali** see *McKinley, Mt.*

**Denizli** *Town* Turkey 145 C7

**Denmark** *Country* Europe 18 C4, 82 E10

**Denmark Strait** Greenland/Iceland 10 A2, 267 E9

**Denver** *Town* Colorado, USA 35 F7

**Derby** *Town* UK 87 J9

**Des Moines** *Town* Iowa, USA 35 J6

**Detroit** *Town* Michigan, USA 37 E5

**Devon Island** Northwest Territories, Canada 11 U1, 27 H4, 267 C6

**Dezful** *Town* Iran 153 F5

**Dhaka** *Town* Bangladesh 167 J7

**Dhanbad** *Town* India 167 I6

**Dharwad** *Town* India 167 D10

**Dieppe** *Town* France 97 E2

**Dijon** *Town* France 97 H5

**Dimlang** *Mountain* Nigeria 221 O11

**Dinaric Alps** *Mountain range* Croatia 109 F6

**Dire Dawa** *Town* Ethiopia 215 H9

**Diyarbakir** *Town* Turkey 145 I7

**Djebel Toubkal** *Mountain* Morocco 208 G4

**Djibouti** *Country* E. Africa 18 F8 215 H8

**Djibouti** *Town* Djibouti 203 D3, 215 I8

**Dnieper** *River* E. Europe 10 E4, 78 I9, J10, 111 K12, 120 G5, I7

**Dniester** *River* Ukraine 78 I10, 120 C6

**Dnipropetrovs'k** *Town* Ukraine 121 I7

**Dobrich** *Town* Bulgaria 127 K10

**Dodecanese** *Island group* Greece 131 J9

**Dodoma** *Town* Tanzania 239 I8

**Doha** *Town* Qatar 153 G8

**Dolomites** *Mountain range* Italy 103 E3

**Dominica** *Country* Caribbean Sea 19 W7, 45 U13

**Dominican Republic** *Country* Caribbean Sea 19 W7, 45 P9

**Don** *River* Russian Federation 10 E4, 78 K9, K10

**Donbass** *Region* Ukraine 121 K7

**Donegal Bay** Ireland 87 E7

**Donets'k** *Town* Ukraine 121 K7

**Dongguan** *Town* China 175 N14

**Donostia–San Sebastián** *Town* Spain 100 G1

**Dordogne** *River* France 97 E7

**Dordrecht** *Town* Netherlands 91 H7

**Dortmund** *Town* Germany 95 E6

**Douglas** *Town* Isle of Man, UK 87 H8

**Douro (Duero)** *River* Portugal/Spain 78 C12, 100 D3, F3

**Dovala** *Town* Cameroon 232 D9

**Dover** *Town* Delaware, USA 37 H6

**Dover** *Town* UK 87 L11

**Drake Passage** *Channel* Atlantic Ocean/ Pacific Ocean 269 A1

**Drakensberg** *Mountain range* South Africa 205 H14, 247 G11

**Drava** *River* S.E. Europe 78 G10, 109 F2, K4

**Dresden** *Town* Germany 95 K7

**Drobeta-Turnu-Severin** *Town* Romania 127 E8

**Dubai** *Town* United Arab Emirates 153 H8

**Dublin** *Town* Ireland 87 G8

**Dubrovnik** *Town* Serbia & Montenegro 109 J9

**Dufourspitze, Mt.** Switzerland 106 C9

**Duisburg** *Town* Germany 95 D6

**Duluth** *Town* Minnesota, USA 35 K3

**Dumont d'Urville** *Research station* Antarctica 269 H9

**Dundee** *Town* UK 87 J5

**Dunedin** *Town* New Zealand 262 C11

**Dunkirk** *Town* France 97 F1

**Durango** *Town* Mexico 39 E5

**Durban** *Town* South Africa 247 I10

**Dushanbe** *Town* Tajikistan 161 G8

**Düsseldorf** *Town* Germany 95 D6

**Dvina (Northern, Western)** *River* Russian Federation 78 I8, L6, 111 G6, J8, 138 E5

**Dzhugdzhur Range** *Mountain range* Russian Federation 133 O6, 139 Q8

# E

**East China Sea** China 10 K6, 133 L10, 265 A3

**East Frisian Islands** Germany 95 E3

**East London** *Town* South Africa 247 H11

**East Sea** *see Japan, Sea of*

**East Siberian Sea**, Arctic Ocean 11 N2, 133 P3, 139 P3, 267 I12

**East Timor** *Country* S.E. Asia 18 K10, 197 N12

**Easter Island** *Dependent territory* Polynesia, Pacific Ocean 265 I7

**Eastern Ghats** *Mountain range* 167 G9

**Ebro** *River* Spain 78 D11, 100 H3

**Ecuador** *Country* S. America 19 V9, 59 C5

**Edinburgh** *Town* UK 87 I6

**Edmonton** *Town* Alberta, Canada 27 E13

**Egypt** *Country* N.E. Africa 18 D7, 147 D10, 215 D2

**Eindhoven** *Town* Netherlands 91 I8

**El Faiyúm** *Town* Egypt 215 D2

**El Mansûra** *Town* Egypt 215 D1

**El Minya** *Town* Egypt 215 D2

**El Obeid** *Town* Sudan 215 D7

**El Paso** *Town* Texas, USA 35 E11

**El Salvador** *Country* Central America 19 U8, 44 C10

**El'brus, Mt.** Russian Federation 78 K11

**Elat** *Town* Israel 147 E10

**Elâzig** *Town* Turkey 145 I7

**Elba** *Island* Italy 103 D7

**Elbe** *River* Germany 78 F9, 95 H3, J6

**Elbert, Mt.** Colorado, USA 35 E7

**Elburz Mts.** Iran 132 D9, 153 G4

**Ellesmere Island** Northwest Territories, Canada 21 N1, 27 H2

**Ellsworth Mts.** Antarctica 269 D5

**Emperor Seamounts** Pacific Ocean 265 D3

**Enderby Land** *Region* Antarctica 269 H3

**England** *Region* UK 87 K10

**English Channel** France/UK 78 D9, 87 J12

**Enschede** *Town* Netherlands 91 J6

**Entebbe** *Town* Uganda 239 G5

**Ephesus** *Ancient site* Turkey 145 A7

**Epidaurus** *Ancient site* Greece 131 E8

**Equator** 11 Z7

**Equatorial Guinea** *Country* Africa 18 C9, 232 C9

**Erfurt** *Town* Germany 95 H7

**Erg Tifernine** *Desert region* Algeria 209 M7

**Erie** *Town* Pennsylvania, USA 37 G4

**Erie, Lake** Canada/USA 21 M9, 29 F9, 37 F5

**Eritrea** *Country* E. Africa 215 G6

**Erzurum** *Town* Turkey 145 J6

**Esequibo** *River* Guyana 59 I3

**Esfahan** *Town* Iran 153 G5

**Eskisehir** *Town* Turkey 145 C6

**Esmeraldas** *Town* Ecuador 59 B4

**Essen** *Town* Germany 95 E6

**Estonia** *Country* E. Europe 18 D3, 111 H4

**Ethiopia** *Country* E. Africa 18 E8, 215 H9

**Ethiopian Highlands** *Mountain range* Ethiopia 10 E8, 205 I6, 215 G9

**Etna, Mt.** *Volcano* Sicily 78 G12, 103 H13

**Eugene** *Town* Washington, USA 33 F6

**Euphrates** *River* S.W. Asia 132 C9, 145 H8, 147 K4, 153 E5

**Europe** *Continent* 10 C4, 78–79

**Evansville** *Town* Indiana, USA 37 D7

**Everest, Mt.** China/Nepal 10 H6, 133 H11, 167 J5, 174 D12

**Everett** *Town* Washington, USA 33 G4

**Everglades Swamp** *Region* Florida, USA 21 M11, 37 F13

**Evvoia** *Island* Greece 131 F6

**Exeter** *Town* UK 87 H11

**Eyre, Lake** South Australia, Australia 10 L11, 254 E11, 259 I9

# F

**Faeroe Islands** *Dependent territory* Atlantic Ocean 10 B3, 18 B3, 77 H3, 78 C6

**Fairbanks** *Town* Alaska, USA 33 D2

**Faisalabad** *Town* Pakistan 167 D3

**Falkland Islands** *Dependent Territory* Atlantic Ocean 11 W13, 19 W13, 41 H16, 71 K15, 77 E11

**Famagusta** *Town* Cyprus 145 F9

**Farg'ona** *Town* Uzbekistan 161 H7

**Faro** *Town* Portugal 100 B8

**Fens, The** *Region* UK 87 K10

**Fernando de Noronho** *Island* Atlantic Ocean 19 J9, 77 G8

**Fez** *Town* Morocco 208 H3

**Fianarantsoa** *Town* Madagascar 203 D7

**Fiji** *Country* Melanesia, Pacific Ocean 11 O10, 19 O10, 255 K9, 265 E7

**Finland** *Country* Europe 18 D3, 82 K6

**Finland, Gulf of** 78 H7, 82 K9, 111 I3

**Fitzroy** *River* Western Australia, Australia 258 E6

**Flinders** *River* Queensland, Australia 259 J6

**Flinders Ranges** *Mountain range* South Australia, Australia 259 I10

**Flint** *Town* Michigan, USA 37 E4

**Florence** *Town* Italy 103 E6

**Flores** *Island* Indonesia 196 L12

**Florida** *State* USA 37 F11

**Focsani** *Town* Romania 127 J7

**Formentera** *Island* Balearic Islands, Spain 100 J6

**Formosa** *Town* Argentina 71 J4

**Fort Lauderdale** *Town* Florida, USA 37 G13

**Fort Wayne** *Town* Indiana, USA 37 E5

**Fort Worth** *Town* Texas, USA 35 I10

**Fortaleza** *Town* Brazil 67 K4

**Forth** *River* UK 87 I5

**Foxe Basin** Northwest Territories, Canada 21 M5, 27 J7

**France** *Country* Europe 18 B4, 97

**Francistown** *Town* Botswana 247 H7

**Franconian Jura** *Mountain range* Germany 95 I9

**Frankfort** *Town* Kentucky, USA 37 E7

**Frankfurt am Main** *Town* Germany 95 F8

**Franz Josef Land** *Island group* Russian Federation 10 F1, 139 J1, 267 H6

**Fray Bentos** *Town* Uruguay 71 J7

**Fredericton** *Town* New Brunswick, Canada 29 I6

**Frederikshavn** *Town* Denmark 82 E10

**Freeport** *Town* Bahamas 45 L3

**Freetown** *Town* Sierra Leone 220 C11

**Fremantle** *Town* Western Australia, Australia 203 K9, 258 C10

**French Guiana** *Country* S. America 19 X8, 59 K3

**French Polynesia** *Dependent territory* Pacific Ocean 19 Q10, 265 G6

**Fresno** *Town* California, USA 33 G10

**Fribourg** *Town* Switzerland 106 B8

**Frobisher Bay** Baffin Island, Northwest Territories, Canada 27 L7

**Fuji, Mt.** *Volcano* Japan 185 H9

**Fundy, Bay of** Canada 29 I7, 77 D4

**Fushun** *Town* China 175 O6

**Fuzhou** *Town* China 175 O12

# G

**Gabon** *Country* Central Africa 18 C9, 232 F10

**Gaborone** *Town* Botswana 247 H8

**Gaizin Kalns** *Mountain* Latvia 111 H6

**Galápagos Islands** Pacific Ocean 11 V9, 19 V9, 265 J5

**Galati** *Town* Romania 127 K7

**Galdhøppigen, Mt.** Norway 82 E7

**Galicia** *Region* Poland 115 I8

**Galicia** *Region* Spain 100 C2

**Galway Bay** Ireland 78 B9

**Gambia** *Country* W. Africa 18 A8, 220 B8

**Gäncä** *Town* Azerbaijan 121 Q13

**Gander** *Town* Newfoundland, Canada 29 K4

**Ganges** *River* India 10 H7, 133 H11, 167 G5, I6, J7

**Ganges Delta** *River mouth* Bangladesh 167 J7

**Garda, Lake** Italy 103 D3

**Garova** *Town* Cameroon 232 E7

**Gary** *Town* Indiana, USA 37 D5

**Gaza Strip** *Region* 147 D8

**Gaziantep** *Town* Turkey 145 H8

**Gdansk** *Town* Poland 115 G2

**Geelong** *Town* Victoria, Australia 259 J12

**Gelsenkirchen** *Town* Germany 95 E6

**General Santos** *Town* Philippines 196 M6

**Geneva** *Town* Switzerland 106 A9

**Geneva, Lake** France/Switzerland 97 I6, 106 B9

**Genoa** *Town* Italy 103 C5

**George Town** *Town* Malaysia 189 E14

**Georgetown** *Town* Guyana 59 J1

**Georgia** *Country* S.W. Asia 18 E5, 121 O12

**Georgia** *State* USA 37 E9

**Gerlachovka** *Mountain* Slovakia 115 I8

**Germany** *Country* Europe 18 C4, 95

**Ghana** *Country* W. Africa 18 B8, 221 I11

**Gharyan** *Town* Libya 209 O4

**Ghawar Oilfield** Saudi Arabia 153 F8

**Ghent** *Town* Belgium 91 F9

**Gibraltar** *Dependent territory*

Mediterranean Sea 18 B6 100 E9
**Gibraltar, Strait of** 78 C13, 100 D9
**Gibson Desert** Western Australia, Australia 10 K11, 254 C11, 258 D8
**Gilbert Islands** *see* Tungaru
**Gisborne** *Town* New Zealand 262 H5
**Giza** *Town* Egypt 215 D1
**Glana** *River* Norway 82 F7
**Glasgow** *Town* UK 87 I6
**Gobi** *Desert* Central Asia 10 IS, 133 I8, 175 I7
**Godavari** *River* India 167 F8
**Godoy Cruz** *Town* Argentina 71 G8
**Godthab (Nuuk)** *Town* Greenland 267 B9
**Goiânia** *Town* Brazil 67 H8
**Golan Heights** *Region occupied by Israel* Syria 147 F6
**Gold Coast** *Region* Queensland, Australia 259 M9
**Gonder** *Town* Ethiopia 215 G8
**Goose Lake** California/Oregon, USA 33 G7
**Gostivar** *Town* Macedonia 124 J8
**Gothenburg** *Town* Sweden 82 F10
**Gotland** *Island* Sweden 82 H11
**Gough Island** Atlantic Ocean 10 B12, 18 B12, 77 H10
**Gozo** *Island* Malta 103 G15
**Grampian Mts.** UK 87 I5
**Gran Chaco** *Region* Argentina 41 G11, 71 H4
**Granada** *Town* Spain 100 F8
**Grand Banks** *Sea shelf* Atlantic Ocean 29 L4, 77 E4
**Grand Canal** China 178 O10
**Grand Canyon** Arizona, USA 21 I10, 33 J10
**Grand Cayman** *Island* Cayman Islands 44 F7
**Grand Forks** *Town* North Dakota, USA 35 I2
**Grand Junction** *Town* Colorado, USA 35 D7
**Grand Rapids** *Town* Michigan, USA 37 D4
**Grasse** *Town* France 97 J8
**Graz** *Town* Austria 106 K7
**Great Australian Bight** Australia 10 K12, 254 D13, 259 G10
**Great Barrier Reef** Australia 254 G9, 259 L6
**Great Basin** *Region* USA 21 I9
**Great Bear Lake** *Northwest Territories,* Canada 11 S2, 21 H5, 27 D8
**Great Dividing Range** *Mountain range* Queensland, Australia 10 M11, 254 G11, 259 L8
**Great Eastern Erg** *Desert region* Algeria 205 D3, 209 L5
**Great Lakes** Canada/USA 11 V4, 21 M8, 37 E2
**Great Plain of China** 10 J6, 133 K10
**Great Plains** USA 11 T5, 21 J8, 35 G6
**Great Rift Valley** E. Africa 10 D9, 205 H9, I9, 239 F9, I6
**Great Salt Lake** Utah, USA 21 I9, 33 J8
**Great Salt Lake Desert** Utah, USA 33 J8
**Great Sandy Desert** Western Australia, Australia 10 K11, 254 C10, 258 E7
**Great Slave Lake** Northwest Territories, Canada 11 S3, 21 I6, 27 E10
**Great Victoria Desert** Western/South Australia, Australia 10 K11, 254 C11, 258 F9
**Great Wall** *Ancient site* China 175 H8, I8, J9, K9, M7
**Great Western Erg** *Desert region* Algeria 205 C3, 209 J5
**Greater Antilles** *Island group* Caribbean

Sea 11 V7, 41 E1, 45 M10
**Greater Khingan Range** *Mountain range* China 175 N5
**Greece** *Country* Europe 18 D5, 131
**Green River** W. USA 33 K9
**Greenland** *Dependent territory* Arctic Ocean 11 X1, 19 X1, 21 R3, 77 F2, 267 D7
**Greenland Sea** Arctic Ocean 11 Z2, 77 H2, 267 F8
**Greensboro** *Town* North Carolina, USA 37 G8
**Grenada** *Country* Caribbean Sea 19 W8, 45 U15
**Greymouth** *Town* New Zealand 262 D8
**Groningen** *Town* Netherlands 91 K4
**Groznyy** *Town* Russian Federation 138 B9
**Guadalajara** *Town* Mexico 39 E7
**Guadalquivir** *River* Spain 100 D7
**Guadeloupe** *Dependent territory* Caribbean Sea 45 V12
**Guadiana** *River* Portugal/Spain 100 C6,E6
**Guam** *Dependent territory* Micronesia, Pacific Ocean 18 L8, 254 F3, 265 B5
**Guantánamo** *Town* Cuba 45 M8
**Guatemala** *Country* Central America 19 U8, 44 B8
**Guatemala City** *Town* Guatemala 44 B9
**Guayaquil** *Town* Ecuador 59 B5
**Guernsey** *Island/Dependent territory* UK 87 I13
**Guiana Highlands** *Mountain range* S. America 41 G4
**Guinea** *Country* W. Africa 18 B8, 220 C10
**Guinea Highlands** *Region* W. Africa 205 C6, 221 E11
**Guinea, Gulf of** Atlantic Ocean 10 B8, 77 I7
**Guinea-Bissau** *Country* W. Africa 18 A8, 220 B9
**Guiyang** *Town* China 175 K13
**Gujranwala** *Town* Pakistan 167 E3
**Gulf, The** S.W. Asia 10 F6
**Gunnbjørn, Mt.** Greenland 267 D9
**Guri** *Reservoir* Venezuela 59 H
**Guyana** *Country* S. America 19 W8, 59 I4
**Guyana Basin** Atlantic Ocean 77 F7
**Gwalior** *Town* India 167 F5
**Gyda Peninsula** Russian Federation 133 G3, 139 J5
**Gyumri** *Town* Armenia 121 P14

# H

**Ha Long Bay** Vietnam 189 I5
**Haarlem** *Town* Netherlands 91 H6
**Hagen** *Town* Germany 95 E6
**Hai Phong** *Town* Vietnam 189 I5
**Haifa** *Town* Israel 147 E6
**Haikou** *Town* China 175 M15
**Hainan** *Island* China 175 L16
**Haiti** *Country* Caribbean Sea 19 V7, 45 O9
**Hakodate** *Town* Japan 185 H4
**Halab** *Town* Syria 147 G2
**Halifax** *Town* Nova Scotia, Canada 29 J6
**Halle** *Town* Germany 95 F6
**Hamada** *Town* Japan 185 D10
**Hamadan** *Town* Iran 153 F4
**Hamah** *Town* Syria 147 G4
**Hamburg** *Town* Germany 95 G3
**Hamersley Range** *Mountain range* Australia 254 B10, 258 C7
**Hamilton** *Town* New Zealand 262 F4
**Hamilton** *Town* Ontario, Canada 29 F6

**Hammar, Lake al-** Iraq 153 E4
**Handan** *Town* China 175 M9
**Hangzhou** *Town* China 175 O11
**Hanoi** *Town* Vietnam 189 H9
**Hanover** *Town* Germany 95 G5
**Harad** *Town* Saudi Arabia 153 F8
**Harare** *Town* Zimbabwe 247 I6
**Harbin** *Town* China 175 P5
**Hardanger Fjord** Norway 82 D8
**Hargeysa** *Town* Somalia 215 I9
**Harrisburg** *Town* Pennsylvania, USA 37 H6
**Hartford** *Town* Connecticut, USA 37 J5
**Hasselt** *Town* Belgium 91 I9
**Hastings** *Town* New Zealand 262 G6
**Hat Yai** *Town* Thailand 189 E13
**Havana** *Town* Cuba 44 I5
**Hawaii** *Island* USA 33 H15, 255 O2
**Hawaii** *State* USA 19 P7, 33 G14
**Hawaiian Islands** Polynesia, Pacific Ocean 11 P7, 255 M1, 265 F4
**Heard Island** Indian Ocean 203 G11
**Hefei** *Town* China 175 N10
**Helena** *Town* Montana, USA 35 C3
**Helsingborg** *Town* Sweden 82 F11
**Helsinki** *Town* Finland 82 J9
**Helwân** *Town* Egypt 215 D2
**Henzada** *Town* Burma 189 C7
**Herat** *Town* Afghanistan 161 E9
**Hilo** *Town* Hawaii, USA 33 H14
**Himalayas** *Mountain range* S. Asia 10 H6, 133 G10, 167 H4, 174 D12
**Hims** *Town* Syria 147 G4
**Hindu Kush** *Mountain range* Central Asia 10 G6, 132 F9, 161 G9
**Hiroshima** *Town* Japan 185 D10
**Hispaniola** *Island* Caribbean Sea 41 F1
**Hitachi** *Town* Japan 185 I8
**Hkakabo Razi** *Mountain* Burma 189 D1
**Ho Chi Minh** *Town* Vietnam 189 I11
**Hobart** *Town* Tasmania, Australia 259 K13
**Hodeida** *Town* Yemen 153 C11
**Hohhot** *Town* China 175 L7
**Hokkaido** *Island* Japan 10 L5, 133 N8, 185 I2
**Holguín** *Town* Cuba 45 M7
**Holon** *Town* Israel 147 E7
**Holyhead** *Town* UK 87 H9
**Homyel'** *Town* Belorussia 111 K11
**Honduras** *Country* Central America 19 U7, 44 E9
**Hong Gai** *Town* Vietnam 189 I5
**Hong Kong** *Town* China E. Asia 18 J7, 175 N14, 285 A4
**Honolulu** *Town* Hawaii, USA 33 G14, 265 F4
**Honshu** *Island* Japan 10 L6, 133 N9, 185 H8
**Horlivka** *Town* Ukraine 121 K7
**Hormus, Strait of** Iran/Oman 153 I8
**Horn of Africa** *Region* Somalia 205 K6, 215 K8
**Houston** *Town* Texas, USA 35 J12
**Howland Island** *Dependent territory* Polynesia, Pacific Ocean 19P9, 255 L6, 265 E5
**Hrodna** *Town* Belorussia 111 F9
**Huainan** *Town* China 175 N10
**Huancayo** *Town* Peru 59 D8
**Huang He,** *see* Yellow River
**Huascarán** *Volcano* Peru 59 C7
**Hudson** *River* New York, USA 37 I5
**Hudson Bay** Canada 11 U3, 21 L6, 27 I10, 29 D4
**Hudson Strait** Northwest Territories, Canada 27 K8
**Hue** *Town* Vietnam 189 I8

**Hungary** *Country* Central Europe 18 D5, 115 G11
**Huntsville** *Town* Alabama, USA 37 D9
**Huron, Lake** Canada/USA 21 M8, 29 F8, 37 E3
**Hyderabad** *Town* India 167 F9
**Hyderabad** *Town* Pakistan 167 C5

# I

**Iasi** *Town* Romania 127 J5
**Ibadan** *Town* Nigeria 221 K11
**Ibiza** *Island* Balearic Islands, Spain 100 J6
**Ica** *Town* Peru 59 D9
**Iceland** *Country* Atlantic Ocean 10 A3, 18 B44, 77 H2, 78 A5, 267 E10
**Idaho** *State* USA 33 H6
**Iguaçu Falls** *Waterfall* Brazil 41 I10, 67 F10
**Ijsselmeer** *Lake* Netherlands 91 C5
**Île d'Ouessant** *Island* France 97 A4
**Ilebo** *Town* Congo, Dem. Rep. 232 H12
**Iligan** *Town* Philippines 196 M5
**Illinois** *State* USA 37 C6
**Iloilo** *Town* Philippines 196 L4
**Ilorin** *Town* Nigeria 221 L11
**In Salah** *Town* Algeria 209 K6
**Inari** *Lake* Finland 78 I4, 82 K3
**Inch'on** *Town* South Korea 175 Q8
**Independence** *Town* Missouri, USA 35 J7
**India** *Country* S. Asia 18 H7, 167 F6
**Indian Ocean** 18 H9, 203
**Indiana** *State* USA 37 D6
**Indianapolis** *Town* Indiana, USA 37 D6
**Indonesia** *Country* S.E. Asia 18 J9, 196 K11, 203 J5
**Indore** *Town* India 167 E7
**Indus** *River* Pakistan 132 F11, 167 B6, C4
**Inner Hebrides** *Island group* UK 78 C7, 87 G5
**Innsbruck** *Town* Austria 106 G7
**Insein** *Town* Burma 189 C7
**International Date Line** 265 E3
**Invercargill** *Town* New Zealand 262 B11
**Ionian Islands** Greece 131 A6
**Ionian Sea** Greece/Italy 103 J12, 131 A6
**Ios** *Island* Greece 131 H10
**Iowa** *State* USA 35 J5
**Ipoh** *Town* Malaysia 189 E14
**Ipswich** *Town* UK 87 L10
**Iquique** *Town* Chile 71 E3
**Iquitos** *Town* Peru 59 D5
**Irakleio** *Town* Crete 131 H12
**Iran** *Country* S.W. Asia 18 F6, 153 H5
**Iranian Plateau** S.W. Asia 10 G6, 132 D10
**Iraq** *Country* S.W. Asia 18 E6, 153 E4
**Irbid** *Town* Jordan 147 F7
**Irbil** *Town* Iraq 153 E3
**Ireland** *Country* Europe 18 34, 87 F8
**Irian Jaya** *see* Papua
**Irish Sea** Ireland/UK 87 H8
**Irkutsk** *Town* Russian Federation 139 M10
**Irrawaddy** *River* Burma 133 I12, 189 C4
**Irtysh** *River* N./Central Asia 10 H4, 133 G2, 138 H7, H8, 161 I2, 174 E5
**Ischia** *Island* Italy 103 G9
**Ishim** *River* Kazakhstan/Russian Federation 161 F2
**Iskenderun** *Town* Turkey 145 G8
**Islamabad** *Town* Pakistan 167 D2
**Ismâ'iliya** *Town* Egypt 215 E1
**Isparta** *Town* Turkey 145 D7
**Israel** *Country* S.W. Asia 18 E6, 147 E9

Istanbul *Town* Turkey 145 C5
Itaipú Dam Paraguay 71 K4
Italy *Country* Europe 18 C5, 103 E7
Ivano-Frankivs'k *Town* Ukraine 120 C6
Ivory Coast *Country* W. Africa 18 B8, 221 I11
Izabal, Lake Guatemala 44 C9
Izhersk *Town* Russian Federation 138 E7
Izmir *Town* Turkey 145 A7
Izmit *Town* Turkey 145 C5

# J

Jabalpur *Town* India 167 G7
Jackson *Town* Mississippi, USA 37 C10
Jacksonville *Town* Florida, USA 37 F11
Jacques Cartier, Mt. Quebec, Canada 29 I5
Jaipur *Town* India 167 E5
Jakarta *Town* Java, Indonesia 196 F11
Jalandhar *Town* India 167 E3
Jamaica *Country* Caribbean Sea 18 V7, 46 K9
Jambi *Town* Sumatra, Indonesia 196 D9
Jan Mayen *Island* Norway 18 B2, 267 F9
Japan *Country* E. Asia 18 L6, 185
Japan, Sea of (East Sea) E. Asia 10 L5, 133 M9, 139 S11, 185 G7, 265 B3
Japanese Alps *Mountain range* Japan 185 G9
Jarris *Island* Pacific Ocean 19 Q9
Java *Island* Indonesia 133 K16, 196 G12
Java Sea Indonesia 10 J9, 196 F11
Jayapura *Town* Irian Jaya, Indonesia 197 T9
Jaz Murian *Salt Lake* Iran 153 J8
Jedda *Town* Saudi Arabia 153 B8
Jefferson City *Town* Missouri, USA 35 K7
Jember *Town* Java, Indonesia 196 I12
Jerez de la Frontera *Town* Spain 100 D8
Jericho *Town* Israel 147 E8
Jersey *Island/Dependent territory* UK 87 I13
Jerusalem *Town* Israel 147 E8
Jilin *Town* China 175 P5
Jinan *Town* China 175 N9
Jingdezhen *Town* China 175 N11
Jingzhou *Town* China 175 M11
Jodhpur *Town* India 167 D5
Johannesburg *Town* South Africa 247 H9
John Day *River* Oregon/Washington, USA 33 H6
Johnston Atoll *Dependent territory* Polynesia, Pacific Ocean 19 P8, 255 M3, 265 F4
Johor Baharu *Town* Malaysia 189 G16
Jönköping *Town* Sweden 82 G10
Jordan *Country* S.W. Asia 18 E6, 147 G8
Jordan *River* S.W. Asia 147 E7
Juan Fernández, Islas *Island group* Pacific Ocean 11 U12, 19 V12, 265 K8
Juliaca *Town* Peru 59 E10
Juneau *Town* Alaska, USA 33 E3
Jura *Mountain range* Switzerland/France 97 I5, 106 B8
Jutland *Peninsula* Denmark 78 F8, 82 E11

# K

K'ut'aisi *Town* Georgia 121 O12
Kabalebo Reservoir Surinam 59 J3
Kabul *Town* Afghanistan 161 G9
Kabwe *Town* Zambia 239 E13
Kaduna *Town* Nigeria 221 M10
Kafue Flats *Region* Zambia 239 C13

Kagoshima *Town* Japan 185 C12
Kahramanmaras *Town* Turkey 145 G8
Kaikoura *Town* New Zealand 262 E8
Kalahari Desert Botswana 10 D11, 205 G12, 247 F8
Kalemie *Town* Congo, Dem. Rep. 232 K12
Kalgoorlie *Town* Western Australia, Australia 258 E10
Kalimantan *Region* Borneo Indonesia 196 I9
Kaliningrad *Town* Russian Federation 111 D8
Kamchatka Peninsula Russian Federation 10 M4, 133 P6, 139 T6
Kampala *Town* Uganda 239 G5
Kâmpóng Cham *Town* Cambodia 189 H10
Kananga *Town* Congo, Dem. Rep. 232 I12
Kandahar *Town* Afghanistan 161 E10
Kandi *Town* Benin 221 K10
Kano *Town* Nigeria 221 N9
Kanpur *Town* India 167 G5
Kansas *State* USA 35 H7
Kansas City *Town* Kansas, USA 35 J7
Kaohsiung *Town* Taiwan 175 P14
Kapuas *River* Borneo, Indonesia 196 G9
Kara *Sea* Russian Federation 10 G2, 79 O3, 133 G2, 138 H4
Kara *Town* Togo 221 J10
Kara Kum *Desert* Kazakhstan 10 F5, 132 F9, 161 J4
Karachi *Town* Pakistan 167 B5, 203 F2
Karaganda *Town* Kazakhstan 161 H3
Karaj *Town* Iran 153 G4
Karakoram Range Central Asia 133 G10, 174 A8
Karakum Canal Turkmenistan 161 E8
Karbala *Town* Iraq 153 E5
Karlsruhe *Town* Germany 95 F10
Karpathos *Island* Greece 131 K12
Karshi *Town* Uzbekistan 161 F7
Kashmir *Region* India/Pakistan 167 F2
Kathmandu *Town* Nepal 167 I5
Katowice *Town* Poland 115 H7
Kattegat *Channel* Denmark/Sweden 82 F10
Kauai *Island* Hawaii, USA 33 G14, 255 O2
Kaunas *Town* Lithuania 111 G8
Kawasaki *Town* Japan 185 H9
Kayseri *Town* Turkey 145 G7
Kazakh Uplands *Region* Kazakhstan 133 G7, 161 H3
Kazakhstan *Country* Central Asia 18 G4, 161 F4
Kazan' *Town* Russian Federation 138 E7
Kefallonia *Island* Greece 131 B7
Kemerovo *Town* Russian Federation 139 J9
Kemijoki *River* Finland 82 J5, K4
Kendari *Town* Celebes, Indonesia 196 L10
Kénitra *Town* Morocco 208 G3
Kentucky *State* USA 37 E7
Kenya *Country* Africa 18 E9, 239 J4
Kenya, Mt. Kenya 239 J5
Kerguelen *Island group* Indian Ocean 18 G13, 203 G11
Kermadec Islands Polynesia, Pacific Ocean 19 O11, 255 L12, 265 E7
Kerman *Town* Iran 153 I7
Kerulen *River* Mongolia/China 175 L5
Khabarovsk *Town* Russian Federation 139 R10
Kharkiv *Town* Ukraine 121 J5
Khartoum *Town* Sudan 215 E7
Kherson *Town* Ukraine 121 H8

Khmel'nyts'kyy *Town* Ukraine 120 D5
Khon Kaen *Town* Thailand 189 G8
Khujand *Town* Tajikistan 161 G7
Khulna *Town* Bangladesh 167 J7
Khyber Pass *Mountain pass* Afghanistan/Pakistan 161 G9
Kiel *Town* Germany 95 G2
Kiel Canal Germany 95 G2
Kiev *Town* Ukraine 120 F5
Kigali *Town* Rwanda 239 F6
Kigoma *Town* Tanzania 239 E8
Kikwit *Town* Congo, Dem. Rep. 232 G12
Kilimanjaro, Mt. Tanzania 205 I9, 239 J6
Kimberley *Town* South Africa 247 G10
Kimberley Plateau *Region* Western Australia, Australia 254 C9, 259 F5
Kingman Reef *Dependent territory* Polynesia, Pacific Ocean 19 P8, 265 F5
Kingston *Town* Jamaica 45 L9
Kingston *Town* St Vincent and the Grenadines 45 V14
Kingston upon Hull *Town* UK 87 K8
Kinshasa *Town* Congo, Dem. Rep. 232 F12
Kirghiz Steppe *Region* Kazakhstan 10 F4, 132 D7, 161 D3
Kiribati *Country* Micronesia/Polynesia, Pacific Ocean 19 P9, 265 F6
Kirkuk *Town* Iraq 153 E4
Kirov *Town* Russian Federation 138 E6
Kirovohrad *Town* Ukraine 120 G7
Kisangani *Town* Congo, Dem. Rep. 232 I10
Kismaayo *Town* Somalia 215 I12
Kisumu *Town* Kenya 239 H5
Kitwe *Town* Zambia 239 E12
Kitzbühel *Town* Austria 106 G7
Kizil Irmak *River* Turkey 145 F5, G6
Kjølen Mts. Norway/Sweden 78 G5, 82 G5
Klagenfurt *Town* Austria 106 I8
Klaipeda *Town* Lithuania 111 E7
Klang *Town* Malaysia 189 E15
Klerksdorp *Town* South Africa 247 G9
Klyuchevsk *Volcano* Russian Federation 139 I5
Knossos *Ancient site* Crete 131 H12
Knoxville *Town* Tennessee, USA 37 E8
Knud Rasmussen Land *Region* Greenland 21 O2, 267 E7
Kobe *Town* Japan 185 F10
Kodiak Island Alaska, USA 20 E7, 33 C3
Kola Peninsula Russian Federation 78 J5, 138 F3
Kolkata (Calcutta) *Town* India 167 J7
Kolyma Range *Mountain range* Russian Federation 133 P5, 139 S5
Konya *Town* Turkey 145 E7
Koryak Range *Mountain range* Russian Federation 133 Q5, 139 T3
Kos *Island* Greece 131 K9
Kosciusko, Mt. New South Wales, Australia 259 K11
Kosovo *Province* Serbia & Montenegro 124 J7
Kosovska Mitrovica *Town* Serbia & Montenegro 124 J6
Kota *Town* India 167 E6
Kota Bharu *Town* Malaysia 189 F13
Kota Kinabalu *Town* Borneo, Malaysia 196 K6
Kowloon *Town* Hong Kong China 175 N14
Kragujevac *Town* Serbia & Montenegro 124 J5
Kraljevo *Town* Serbia & Montenegro 124 J5
Kramators'k *Town* Ukraine 121 K6
Krasnodar *Town* Russian Federation 138 A7

Krasnoyarsk *Town* Russian Federation 139 K9
Krefeld *Town* Germany 95 D6
Kremenchuk *Town* Ukraine 121 H6
Krusevac *Town* Serbia & Montenegro 124 J6
Kryvyy Rih *Town* Ukraine 121 H7
Kuala Lumpur *Town* Malaysia 189 F15
Kuala Terengganu *Town* Malaysia 189 F14
Kuantan *Town* Malaysia 189 F15
Kuching *Town* Borneo, Malaysia 196 G8
Kujawy *Region* Poland 115 G4
Kumamoto *Town* Japan 185 C12
Kumanovo *Town* Macedonia 124 K8
Kumasi *Town* Ghana 221 I12
Kunlun Mts. China 10 H6, 133 H9, 174 D9
Kunming *Town* China 175 J14
Kupang *Town* Timor, Indonesia 196 M13
Kurile Islands *Disputed territory* E. Asia 10 M5, 133 O8, 139 U9, 185 K1, 265 C2
Kütahya *Town* Turkey 145 C6
Kuwait *Country* S.W. Asia 18 F6, 153 F6
Kuwait *Town* Kuwait 153 F6, 203 E1
Kwajalein Atoll Marshall Islands, Pacific Ocean 265 D5
Kyoto *Town* Japan 185 F10
Kyrgyzstan *Country* Central Asia 18 G5, 161 H6
Kythira *Island* Greece 131 E11
Kyushu *Island* Japan 133 M10, 185 C11

# L

L'viv *Town* Ukraine 120 B5
Laâyoune *Town* Western Sahara 208 D5
La Paz *Town* Bolivia 59 F10
La Plata *Town* Argentina 71 J8
La Serena *Town* Chile 71 F7
Labrador *Region* Newfoundland, Canada 29 I3
Labrador Sea Canada/Greenland 11 W3, 21 P6, 29 H2, 77 F3
Laccadive Islands Indian Ocean 203 G3
Laccadive Sea Indian Ocean 10 G8
Ladoga, Lake Russian Federation 10 E3, 78 J7
Lagao dos Patos *Lagoon* Brazil 67 G12
Lagos *Town* Nigeria 221 K12
Lahore *Town* Pakistan 167 E3
Lake District *Region* UK 78 D8, 87 I7
Lakshadweep *Island group* Indian Ocean 18 G8, 132 E13
Lambert Glacier Antarctica 269 I4
Lanai *Island* Hawaii, USA 33 G14
Land's End *Cape* UK 87 G12
Lansing *Town* Michigan, USA 37 E4
Lanzhou *Town* China 175 J9
Laos *Country* S.W. Asia 18 I7, 189 F6
Lapland *Region* N. Europe 78 H4, 82 I4
Laptev Sea Arctic Ocean 10 K1, 133 L2, 139 M4, 267 I4
Laredo *Town* Texas, USA 35 H13
Larisa *Town* Greece 131 D5
Larnaca *Town* Cyprus 145 E10
Larsen Ice Shelf Antarctica 269 B3
Las Vegas *Town* Nevada, USA 33 I11
Latvia *Country* E. Europe 18 D4, 111 G6
Lausanne *Town* Switzerland 106 B9
Laval *Town* Québec, Canada 29 H7
Le Havre *Town* France 97 E2
Le Mans *Town* France 97 E4
Lebanon *Country* S.W. Asia 18 E6, 147 F5
Leeds *Town* UK 87 J8
Leeward Islands Caribbean Sea 45 U10
Lefkada *Island* Greece 131 B6

**Legaspi** *Town* Philippines 196 L3
**Leicester** *Town* UK 87 J10
**Leiden** *Town* Netherlands 91 H6
**Leipzig** *Town* Germany 95 I6
**Leiria** *Town* Portugal 100 B5
**Lelystad** *Town* Netherlands 91 I5
**Lena** *River* Russian Federation 10 K2, 133 K5, L4, 139 N6, N8
**León** *Town* Mexico 39 F7
**León** *Town* Nicaragua 44 D11
**Leskovac** *Town* Serbia & Montenegro 124 K6
**Lesotho** *Country* Southern Africa 18 D11, 247 H10
**Lesser Antilles** *Island group* Caribbean Sea 11 W8, 41 G3, 45 R14, T12
**Lesser Khingan Mts.** N.E. Asia 175 O3
**Lesvos** *Island* Greece 131 I5
**Leuuwarden** *Town* Netherlands 91 J4
**Levin** *Town* New Zealand 262 F6
**Lexington** *Town* Kentucky, USA 37 E7
**Lhasa** *Town* China 175 F12
**Liberia** *Country* W. Africa 18 B8, 221 E12
**Libreville** *Town* Gabon 232 D10
**Libya** *Country* N. Africa 18 D6, 209 Q6
**Libyan Desert** Egypt/Libya/Sudan 10 D6, 205 G3, 209 T7, 215 C3
**Liechtenstein** *Country* Europe 18 C5, 106 E7
**Liège** *Town* Belgium 91 I10
**Liepaja** *Town* Latvia 111 E6
**Ligurian Sea** Italy 103 C6
**Likasi** *Town* Congo, Dem. Rep. 232 J14
**Lille** *Town* France 97 F1
**Lillehammer** *Town* Norway 82 F8
**Lilongwe** *Town* Malawi 239 H13
**Lima** *Town* Peru 59 C8, 265 L6
**Limassol** *Town* Cyprus 145 E10
**Limoges** *Town* France 97 E6
**Limpopo** *River* Southern Africa 205 I12, 247 I8
**Lincoln** *Town* Nebraska, USA 35 I6
**Lincoln Sea** Arctic Ocean 21 O1
**Line Islands** Kiribati, Pacific Ocean 11 P8, 255 O6, 265 F5
**Linz** *Town* Austria 106 I5
**Lisbon** *Town* Portugal 100 B6
**Lithuania** *Country* E. Europe 18 D4, 111 F7
**Little Rock** *Town* Arkansas, USA 35 K9
**Liverpool** *Town* UK 87 I9
**Ljubljana** *Town* Slovenia 109 E3
**Llanos** *Region* Colombia/Venezuela 11 V8
**Locarno** *Town* Switzerland 106 D9
**Lódz** *Town* Poland 115 H5
**Lofoten** *Island group* Norway 78 G4, 82 G3
**Logan, Mt.** Yukon Territory, Canada 27 A9
**Logroño** *Town* Spain 100 G2
**Loire** *River* France 78 D10, 97 D5, H6
**Lombardy** *Region* Italy 103 D4
**Lombok** *Island* Indonesia 196 J12
**Lomé** *Town* Togo 221 J12
**Lomond, Loch** *Lake* UK 87 H5
**London** *Town* Ontario, Canada 29 F6
**London** *Town* UK 87 K11
**Londonderry** *Town* UK 87 G6
**Long Beach** *Town* California, USA 33 H12
**Long Island** New York, USA 37 I5
**Long Xuyen** *Town* Vietnam 189 H11
**Longyearbyen** *Town* Svalbard 267 G8
**Lop Nur** *Lake* China 175 F8
**Lord Howe Island** *Dependent territory* Pacific Ocean 19 N11, 265 D8
**Los Angeles** *Town* California, USA 33 H12

**Los Ángeles** *Town* Chile 71 F10
**Louangphabang** *Town* Laos 189 F6
**Louise, Lake** Alberta, Canada 27 E13
**Louisiana** *State* USA 35 K11
**Louisville** *Town* Kentucky, USA 37 D7
**Lowell** *Town* Massachusetts, USA 37 J4
**Loyalty Islands** Pacific Ocean 11 N10
**Luanda** *Town* Angola 247 B2
**Luanshya** *Town* Zambia 239 E12
**Lubbock** *Town* Texas, USA 35 G10
**Lübeck** *Town* Germany 95 H3
**Lublin** *Town* Poland 115 K6
**Lubumbashi** *Town* Congo, Dem. Rep. 232 J14
**Lucena** *Town* Philippines 196 L3
**Lucerne** *Town* Switzerland 106 C8
**Lucknow** *Town* India 167 G5
**Ludhiana** *Town* India 167 E3
**Lugano** *Town* Switzerland 106 D9
**Luhans'k** *Town* Ukraine 121 L6
**Lundy** *Island* UK 87 H11
**Luoyang** *Town* China 175 L10
**Lusaka** *Town* Zambia 239 E13
**Luts'k** *Town* Ukraine 120 C4
**Luxembourg** *Country* Europe 18 C4, 91 J12
**Luxembourg** *Town* Luxembourg 91 J13
**Luxor** *Town* Egypt 215 E3
**Luzon** *Island* Philippines 133 L12, 196 L2
**Lyon** *Town* France 97 H6

# M

**Maastricht** *Town* Netherlands 91 I10
**Macao** *Town* China, S.E. Asia 175 N14
**MacDonnell Ranges** *Mountain range* Northern Territory, Australia 254 D10, 259 G7
**Macedonia** *Country* S.E. Europe 18 D5, 124 J8
**Maceió** *Town* Brazil 67 L6
**Machala** *Town* Ecuador 59 B6
**Machu Picchu** *Ancient site* Peru 59 E9
**Mackenzie** *River* Northwest Territories, Canada 11 S3, 21 H5, 27 D9
**Mackenzie Mts.** Northwest Territories, Canada 20 G5, 27 C9
**Macon** *Town* Georgia, USA 37 E10
**Macquarie Island** *Dependent territory* Pacific Ocean 265 D9
**Madagascar** *Country* Indian Ocean 10 F11, 18 F11, 203 D7, 205 K12
**Madeira** *Island* Atlantic Ocean 10 A6, 18 A6, 77 H5, 205 A2
**Madgeburg** *Town* Germany 95 I5
**Madison** *Town* Wisconsin, USA 37 C4
**Madras** *see* Chennai
**Madre de Dios** *River* Bolivia/Peru 59 F8
**Madrid** *Town* Spain 100 F4
**Madurai** *Town* India 167 F12
**Magellan, Strait of** *Channel* Chile 41 G16, 71 H16
**Maggiore, Lake** Italy/Switzerland 103 C3, 106 D9
**Mahajanga** *Town* Madagascar 203 D7
**Mahalapye** *Town* Botswana 247 G8
**Mahé** *Island* Seychelles 203 E6, 205 L9
**Mahilyow** *Town* Belorussia 111 K9
**Maine** *State* USA 37 K3
**Mainz** *Town* Germany 95 F8
**Majorca** *Island* Balearic Islands, Spain 100 L5
**Makassar** *Town* Celebes, Indonesia 196 K11
**Makiyivka** *Town* Ukraine 121 K7
**Malabar Coast** India 167 D11
**Malabo** *Town* Equatorial Guinea 232 C9
**Malacca, Strait of** S.E. Asia 203 I4

**Málaga** *Town* Spain 100 E8
**Malang** *Town* Java, Indonesia 196 H12
**Malatya** *Town* Turkey 145 H7
**Malawi** *Country* Africa 18 E10, 239 H13
**Malaysia** *Country* S.E. Asia 189 F15, 196 G7
**Maldive Ridge** Indian Ocean 203 G5
**Maldives** *Country* Indian Ocean 10 G8, 18 H9, 203 G4
**Male** *Town* Maldives 203 G5
**Mali** *Country* W. Africa 221 H6
**Malmö** *Town* Sweden 82 F11
**Malopolska** *Region* Poland 115 I7
**Malta** *Country* Europe 18 C6, 103 H15
**Mammoth Caves** Kentucky, USA 37 D7
**Man, Isle of** *Dependent territory* UK 87 H7
**Manado** *Town* Celebes, Indonesia 196 M8
**Managua** *Town* Nicaragua 44 E11
**Manama** *Town* Bahrain 153 F8
**Manaus** *Town* Brazil 67 E4
**Manchester** *Town* New Hampshire, USA 37 J4
**Manchester** *Town* UK 87 J9
**Manchuria** *Region* China 175 P5
**Manchurian Plain** *Region* China 10 K5, 133 L8
**Mandalay** *Town* Burma 189 C4
**Manila** *Town* Philippines 196 K3, 265 A5
**Manisa** *Town* Turkey 145 B7
**Manitoba** *Province* Canada 27 H11
**Manizales** *Town* Colombia 59 D3
**Mannheim** *Town* Germany 95 F9
**Maputo** *Town* Mozambique 247 I9
**Mar del Plata** *Town* Argentina 71 K9
**Maracaibo** *Town* Venezuela 59 E1
**Maracaibo, Lake** Venezuela 41 F3, 59 E1
**Marañón** *River* Peru 41 E6, 59 D6
**Marathon** *Ancient site* Greece 131 F7
**Marbella** *Town* Spain 100 E8
**Mariana Trench** Pacific Ocean 10 L8, 265 C4
**Maribor** *Town* Slovenia 109 G2
**Marie Byrd Land** *Region* Antarctica 269 D6
**Maritsa** *River* Bulgaria 127 I12
**Mariupol'** *Town* Ukraine 121 K8
**Marka** *Town* Somalia 215 I11
**Marmara, Sea of** Turkey 145 B5
**Maroua** *Town* Cameroon 232 F6
**Marquesas Islands** French Polynesia, Pacific Ocean 11 Q9, 255 R7, 265 H6
**Marrakesh** *Town* Morocco 208 G4
**Marseille** *Town* France 97 I9
**Marshall Islands** *Country* Micronesia, Pacific Ocean 11 N8, 19 N8, 255 J3, 265 D5
**Martinique** *Dependent territory* Caribbean Sea 45 V13
**Maryland** *State* USA 37 H7
**Masai Steppe** *Region* Tanzania 239 I7
**Maseru** *Town* Lesotho 247 H10
**Mashhad** *Town* Iran 153 J4
**Massachusetts** *State* USA 37 J5
**Massif Central** *Region* France 78 E11, 97 G7
**Masterton** *Town* New Zealand 262 F7
**Matadi** *Town* Congo, Dem. Rep. 232 E12
**Matanzas** *Town* Cuba 44 J5
**Mato Grosso, Plateau of** Brazil 11 W10, 41 H8, 67 F6
**Maturín** *Town* Venezuela 59 H1
**Maui** *Island* Hawaii, USA 33 G14
**Mauritania** *Country* W. Africa 18 B7, 220 D5
**Mauritius** *Country* Indian Ocean 18 F10, 203 E7, 205 L12
**Mayagüez** *Town* Puerto Rico 45 R10

**Mayotte** *Dependent territory* 18 E10, 203 D7, 205 J10
**Mazar-e-Sharif** *Town* Afghanistan 161 F8
**Mazyr** *Town* Belorussia 111 J11
**Mbabane** *Town* Swaziland 247 I9
**Mbandaka** *Town* Congo, Dem. Rep. 232 G10
**Mbeya** *Town* Tanzania 239 H10
**Mbuji-Mayi** *Town* Congo, Dem. Rep. 232 I12
**McKinley, Mt. (Denali)** *Mountain* Alaska, USA 20 E5, 33 C2
**McMurdo** *Research station* Antarctica 269 F8
**Mead, Lake** Arizona/Nevada, USA 33 J11
**Mecca** *Town* Saudi Arabia 153 B8
**Medan** *Town* Sumatra, Indonesia 196 B7
**Medellín** *Town* Colombia 59 D2
**Medina** *Town* Saudi Arabia 15 C7
**Mediterranean Sea** 10 C5, 77 J5, 78 G13, 103 F14, 131 H13
**Meerut** *Town* India 167 F4
**Meknès** *Town* Morocco 208 H3
**Mekong** *River* Asia 10 J7, 133 J12, 175 G11, I15, 189 E5, F6, H8
**Melaka** *Town* Malaysia 189 F16
**Melanesia** *Region* Pacific Ocean 255 I7, 265 D6
**Melbourne** *Town* Victoria, Australia 259 K12
**Melilla** *Spanish enclave* Morocco 209 I2
**Melville Island** Northwest Territories, Canada 11 TI, 21 I3, 27 F5, 267 D4
**Memphis** *Town* Tennessee, USA 37 C8
**Mendoza** *Town* Argentina 71 G7
**Mérida** *Town* Mexico 39 K7
**Mérida** *Town* Spain 100 D6
**Mérida** *Town* Venezuela 59 E2
**Mersin** *Town* Turkey 145 F8
**Mesa** *Town* Arizona, USA 33 K12
**Meseta** *Region* Spain 78 D12
**Messina** *Town* Italy 103 I12
**Mestre** *Town* Italy 103 F4
**Meuse** *River* W. Europe 78 E9, 91 H11, J8, 97 H2
**Mexicali** *Town* Mexico 39 A1
**Mexico** *Country* N. America 19 T7, 39 E5
**Mexico City** *Town* Mexico 39 G8
**Mexico, Gulf of** 11 U7, 21 L11, 39 I7
**Miami** *Town* Florida, USA 37 G13
**Michigan** *State* USA 37 E3
**Michigan, Lake** USA 21 L9, 37 D4
**Micronesia, Federated States of** *Country* Pacific Ocean 18 I8, 255 I5, 265 C5
**Mid-Atlantic Ridge** Atlantic Ocean 77 F5, F7, H10
**Mid-Indian Ridge** Atlantic Ocean 203 G3
**Mid-Pacific Seamounts** Pacific Ocean 265 D4
**Middelburg** *Town* Netherlands 91 F8
**Middleburg** *Town* Netherlands 91 F8
**Midway Island** *Dependent territory* Polynesia, Pacific Ocean 11 O6, 19 O6, 265 E4
**Milan** *Town* Italy 103 C3
**Milford Sound** *Town* New Zealand 255 I15, 262 B10
**Milwaukee** *Town* Wisconsin, USA 35 D4
**Minbu** *Town* Burma 189 B5
**Mindanao** *Island* Philippines 133 L14, 196 L5
**Mindoro** *Island* Philippines 196 K3
**Minneapolis** *Town* Minnesota, USA 35 J4
**Minnesota** *State* USA 35 J2
**Minorca** *Island* Balearic Islands, Spain 100 L5
**Minsk** *Town* Belorussia 111 I9

**Mississippi** *River* USA 11 U6, 21 L9, 35 K4, K10, 37 B3, B9
**Mississippi** *State* USA 37 C10
**Missouri** *River* USA 10 U5, 21 J8, 35 F2, I5, K7
**Missouri** *State* USA 35 K8
**Mitchell, Mt.** Tennessee, USA 37 E8
**Mitumba Mts.** Congo, Dem. Rep. 232 J12
**Mobile** *Town* Alabama, USA 37 C11
**Mogadishu** *Town* Somalia 215 J11
**Mojave Desert** California, USA 33 H11
**Moldova** *Country* E. Europe 18 D5, 120 E7
**Moluccas** *Island group* Indonesia 10 K9, 197 N9
**Mombasa** *Town* Kenya 239 K7
**Monaco** *Country* Europe 97 J8
**Mongolia** *Country* E. Asia 18 I5, 175 I5
**Monrovia** *Town* Liberia 220 D12
**Mons** *Town* Belgium 91 G10
**Mont Blanc** *Mountain* France 78 E11, 97 J6
**Montana** *State* USA 35 D2
**Monte Albán** *Ancient site* Mexico 39 H9
**Montería** *Town* Colombia 59 D1
**Monterrey** *Town* Mexico 39 G5
**Montevideo** *Town* Uruguay 71 K8
**Montgomery** *Town* Alabama, USA 37 D10
**Montpelier** *Town* Vermont, USA 37 J4
**Montpellier** *Town* France 97 H9
**Montréal** *Town* Québec, Canada 29 H7
**Monywa** *Town* Burma 189 C4
**Morar, Loch** *Reservoir* UK 87 H4
**Moravia** *Region* Czech Republic 115 F8
**Morocco** *Country* N.W. Africa 18 B6, 208 G3
**Moroni** *Town* Comoros 203 D6
**Moscow** *Town* Russian Federation 138 C5
**Mosel (Moselle)** *River* W. Europe 91 K13, 95 E8, 97 I3
**Mosquito Coast** Panama 41 D2
**Mostar** *Town* Bosnia and Herzegovina 124 G6
**Mosul** *Town* Iraq 153 E3
**Moulmein** *Town* Burma 189 D7
**Mozambique** *Country* Southern Africa 18 E10, 247 J6
**Mozambique Channel** Madagascar/ Mozambique 10 E10, 205 J12
**Muang Phitsanulok** *Town* Thailand 189 E7
**Muchinga Mts.** Zambia 239 F12
**Mufulira** *Town* Zambia 239 E12
**Mulhacén** *Mountain* Spain 100 F8
**Multan** *Town* Pakistan 167 D4
**Mumbai (Bombay)** *Town* India 167 D8, 203 G3
**Munich** *Town* Germany 95 I11
**Münitz** *Lake* Germany 95 J3
**Münster** *Town* Germany 95 E5
**Murcia** *Town* Spain 100 H7
**Murmansk** *Town* Russian Federation 138 F3
**Murray** *River* New South Wales/South Australia, Australia 10 L12, 254 F13, 259 I10
**Mururoa Atoll** *Island* French Polynesia, Pacific Ocean 255 R10, 265 G7
**Musala** *Mountain* Bulgaria 127 F12
**Muscarene Islands** Indian Ocean 10 F10, 203 F8
**Muscat** *Town* Oman 153 I9
**Mwanza** *Town* Tanzania 239 G6
**Mycenae** *Ancient site* Greece 131 E8
**Mykolayiv** *Town* Ukraine 120 G8
**Mykonos** *Island* Greece 131 H8
**Mysore** *Town* India 167 E11

# N

**Ndjamena** *Town* Chad 232 F6
**Naberezhnyye Chelny** *Town* Russian Federation 138 E7
**Nacala** *Town* Mozambique 247 L5
**Naga** *Town* Philippines 196 L3
**Nagasaki** *Town* Japan 185 B12
**Nagorno Karabakh** *Region* Azerbaijan 121 R14
**Nagoya** *Town* Japan 185 G9
**Nagpur** *Town* India 167 F7
**Nahik** *Town* India 167 D8
**Nairobi** *Town* Kenya 239 I6
**Nakhon Ratchasima** *Town* Thailand 189 F8
**Nakhon Sawan** *Town* Thailand 189 E8
**Nakhon Si Thammarat** *Town* Thailand 189 E12
**Nakuru** *Town* Kenya 239 I5
**Nam Dinh** *Town* Vietnam 189 H5
**Namib Desert** *Namibia* 10 C10, 205 F12, 247 C7
**Namibia** *Country* Southern Africa 18 D11, 247 D7
**Namp'o** *Town* North Korea 175 P7
**Nampula** *Town* Mozambique 247 L5
**Namur** *Town* Belgium 91 H10
**Nanchang** *Town* China 175 N12
**Nancy** *Town* France 97 I3
**Nanjing** *Town* China 175 O10
**Nanning** *Town* China 175 L14
**Nantes** *Town* France 97 C5
**Napier** *Town* New Zealand 262 G5
**Naples** *Town* Italy 103 G9
**Nashville** *Town* Tennessee, USA 37 D8
**Nassau** *Town* Bahamas 45 M4
**Nasser, Lake** Egypt 215 E4
**Natal** *Region* South Africa 247 I9
**Natal** *Town* Brazil 67 L5
**Nauru** *Country* Micronesia, Pacific Ocean 19 N9, 255 J6, 265 D6
**Navoiy** *Town* Uzbekistan 161 F7
**Naxos** *Island* Greece 131 I9
**Nazareth** *Town* Israel 147 E7
**Nazca** *Ancient site* Peru 59 D9
**Ndola** *Town* Zambia 239 E12
**Neagh, Lough** *Lake* UK 87 G7
**Nebraska** *State* USA 35 H5
**Negev Desert** Israel 147 E10
**Neiva** *Town* Colombia 59 D4
**Nelson** *Town* New Zealand 262 E7
**Nepal** *Country* S. Asia 18 H6, 167 H5
**Ness, Loch** *Lake* UK 87 I4
**Netherlands** *Country* Europe 18 C4, 91 I7
**Nevada** *State* USA 33 I9
**New Brunswick** *Province* Canada 29 I6
**New Caledonia** *Dependent territory* Melanesia, Pacific Ocean 19 N11, 255 I9, 265 D7
**New Delhi** *Town* India 167 F4
**New Guinea** *Island* Indonesia/Papua New Guinea 10 L9, 133 N15, 254 E7, 265 B6
**New Hampshire** *State* USA 37 K4
**New Jersey** *State* USA 37 I6
**New Mexico** *State* USA 35 E9
**New Orleans** *Town* Louisiana, USA 35 L12
**New Plymouth** *Town* New Zealand 262 F5
**New Siberian Islands** Russian Federation 10 L1, 133 N2, 139 O3, 267 H3
**New South Wales** *State* Australia 259 K10
**New York** *State* USA 37 I4
**New York** *Town* New York, USA 37 I6

**New Zealand** *Country* Australasia 11 N12, 19 N12, 262 E8
**Newark** *Town* New Jersey, USA 37 I6
**Newcastle** *Town* New South Wales, Australia 259 L10
**Newcastle upon Tyne** *Town* UK 87 J7
**Newfoundland** *Island* Canada 10 X4, 21 P8, 29 K4
**Newfoundland** *Province* Canada 29 J3
**Newfoundland Basin** Atlantic Ocean 77 F5
**Nha Trang** *Town* Vietnam 189 J10
**Niagara Falls** *Waterfall* Canada/USA 21 M9, 29 G9, 37 G4
**Niamey** *Town* Niger 221 K8
**Nicaragua** *Country* Central America 19 U3, 44 F11
**Nicaragua, Lake** Nicaragua 41 D3, 44 E12
**Nice** *Town* France 97 J8
**Nicobar Islands** Indian Ocean 10 H8, 18 H8, 133 I13, 203 I4
**Nicosia** *Town* Cyprus 145 E9
**Niger** *Country* W. Africa 18 C7, 221 O7
**Niger** *River* W. Africa 10 B8, 205 C5, E6, 221 E9, G8, K9, Mll
**Niger Delta** *River mouth* Nigeria 205 E7, 221 L13
**Nigeria** *Country* W. Africa 18 C8, 221 M10
**Niihau** *Island* Pacific Ocean 33 F14
**Nijmegen** *Town* Netherlands 91 J7
**Nile** *River* N.E. Africa 10 E7, 205 H3, I5, 215 E3, E5
**Ninety East Ridge** Indian Ocean 203 H7
**Ningbo** *Town* China 175 P11
**Nis** *Town* Serbia & Montenegro 124 K6
**Niue** *Dependent territory* Polynesia, Pacific Ocean 19 P10, 265 F7
**Nizhniy Novgorod** *Town* Russian Federation 138 D6
**Nkongsamba** *Town* Cameroon 232 D8
**Nome** *Town* Alaska, USA 33 B2
**Nord** *Research station* Greenland 267 F7
**Norfolk** *Town* Virginia, USA 37 H8
**Norfolk Island** *Dependent territory* Pacific Ocean 19 N11, 255 J11, 265 D7
**Normandy** *Region* France 97 D3
**North Albanian Alps** *Mountain range* Albania/Serbia & Montenegro 124 H7
**North America** *Continent* 11 T4, 20–21
**North American Basin** Atlantic Ocean 77 F5
**North Cape** Norway 78 H4, 82 J1
**North Carolina** *State* USA 37 G8
**North Dakota** *State* USA 35 G2
**North European Plain** Europe 78 G9
**North Frisian Islands** Denmark/ Germany 95 F1
**North Island** New Zealand 255 J13, 262 F5
**North Korea** *Country* E. Asia 18 K5, 175 P6
**North Pole** Arctic Ocean 267 F5
**North Sea** Atlantic Ocean 10 C4, 77 I3, 78 E8, 91 F7
**North-Eastern Atlantic Basin** Atlantic Ocean 77 H4
**Northampton** *Town* UK 87 K10
**Northern Dvina** *see* Dvina
**Northern Ireland** *Region* UK 87 G7
**Northern Mariana Islands** *Dependent territory* Micronesia, Pacific Ocean 10 L8, 18 L7, 254 F3, 265 C4
**Northern Territory** *Territory* Australia 259 G6
**Northwest Territories** *Province* Canada 27 F8
**Norway** *Country* Europe 18 C3, 82 G6

**Norwegian Sea** Atlantic Ocean 10 C3, 78 E5, 82 F5
**Norwich** *Town* UK 87 L10
**Nottingham** *Town* UK 87 J9
**Nouakchott** *Town* Mauritania 220 B6
**Nova Scotia** *Province* Canada 29 J6
**Novaya Zemlya** *Island group* Russian Federation 10 F2, 79 N2, 138 H3, 267 I7
**Novi Sad** *Town* Serbia & Montenegro 124 I3
**Novokuznetsk** *Town* Russian Federation 139 J10
**Novosibirsk** *Town* Russian Federation 139 I9
**Nubian Desert** Sudan 205 I4, 215 E5
**Nukus** *Town* Uzbekistan 161 D6
**Nullarbor Plain** *Region* South Western Australia, Australia 256 F10
**Nuremberg** *Town* Germany 95 H9
**Nuuk** *see* Godthåb
**Nyasa, Lake** Southern Africa 10 E10, 205 I10, 239 H11, 247 J4

# O

**Oahu** *Island* Pacific Ocean 33 G14, 255 O2
**Oakland** *Town* California, USA 33 G10
**Oaxaca** *Town* Mexico 39 H9
**Ob'** *River* Russian Federation 10 G3, 132 F4, 133 G6, 138 H6, 139 I8
**Oban** *Town* UK 87 H5
**Odense** *Town* Denmark 82 E11
**Oder** *River* Germany 78 G9, 95 K4
**Odesa** *Town* Ukraine 120 F8
**Odra** *River* Central Europe 115 D4, F6
**Ogbomosho** *Town* Nigeria 221 L11
**Ohio** *River* USA 37 C7, F6
**Ohio** *State* USA 37 F6
**Okavango** *River* Southern Africa 205 H12, 247 D3
**Okavango Delta** Botswana 247 F6
**Okayama** *Town* Japan 185 E10
**Okhotsk, Sea of** Japan/Russian Federation 10 L4, 133 O6, 139 S7, 185 J1, 265 C2
**Okinawa** *Island* Japan 185 A16
**Oklahoma** *State* USA 35 I9
**Oklahoma City** *Town* Oklahoma, USA 35 I9
**Öland** *Island* Sweden 82 H11
**Olduvai Gorge** Tanzania 239 I7
**Oloy Range** *Mountain range* Russian Federation 133 Q4, 139 R4
**Olympia** *Ancient site* Greece 131 C8
**Olympia** *Town* Washington, USA 33 F5
**Olympus, Mt.** Greece 131 E14
**Omaha** *Town* Nebraska, USA 35 I6
**Oman** *Country* S.W. Asia 18 F7, 153 G11
**Oman, Gulf of** Arabia/Iran 10 G7, 132 E11, 203 F2
**Omdurman** *Town* Sudan 215 E7
**Omsk** *Town* Russian Federation 138 H9
**Onega, Lake** Russian Federation 10 E3, 78 K6, 138 E4
**Onitsha** *Town* Nigeria 221 M12
**Ontario** *Province* Canada 29 D6
**Ontario, Lake** Canada/USA 21 M9, 29 G8, 37 G4
**Oodaaq Island** Arctic Ocean 267 F7
**Oporto (Porto)** *Town* Portugal 100 B3
**Oradea** *Town* Romania 127 E5
**Oran** *Town* Algeria 209 J2
**Orange River** Southern Africa 10 D11, 205 G13, 247 E10, G10
**Ore Mountains** Czech Republic/ Germany 95 I7, 115 C6
**Örebro** *Town* Sweden 82 G9

**Oregon** *State* USA 33 G6
**Orenburg** *Town* Russian Federation 138 E8
**Orinoco** *River* Venezuela 41 G4, 59 H2, F3, G3
**Orizaba** *see* Citlaltépetl
**Orkneys** *Island group* UK 78 D7, 87 J2
**Orlando** *Town* Florida, USA 37 F12
**Orléans** *Town* France 97 F4
**Orsha** *Town* Russian Federation 111 K8
**Orumiyeh** *Town* Iran 153 F3
**Oruro** *Town* Bolivia 59 F10
**Osaka** *Town* Japan 185 F10
**Osh** *Town* Kyrgyzstan 161 H7
**Oshogbo** *Town* Nigeria 221 L11
**Osijek** *Town* Croatia 109 K4
**Oslo** *Town* Norway 82 F8
**Osmaniye** *Town* Turkey 145 G8
**Osorno** *Town* Chile 71 F11
**Ostend** *Town* Belgium 91 E9
**Ottawa** *River* Ontario/Quebec, Canada 29 F7
**Ottawa** *Town* Ontario, Canada 29 G8
**Ouagadougou** *Town* Burkina 221 I9
**Oued Chelif** *River* Algeria 209 K2
**Oujda** *Town* Morocco 209 I3
**Oulu** *Town* Finland 82 J5
**Outer Hebrides** *Island group* UK 78 C7, 87 G3
**Oviedo** *Town* Spain 100 D1
**Oxford** *Town* UK 87 J10
**Oxnard** *Town* California, USA 33 H12

# P

**Pa-an** *Town* Burma 189 D7
**Pacific Ocean** 11 Q7, 255 L3, 265 H4
**Padang** *Town* Sumatra, Indonesia 196 C9
**Padua** *Town* Italy 103 E4
**Pagan** *Ancient site* Burma 189 C5
**Painted Desert** Arizona, USA 33 K11
**Pakistan** *Country* S. Asia 18 G6, 167 B4
**Pakokku** *Town* Burma 189 C5
**Pakxé** *Town* Laos 189 H9
**Palau** *Country* Micronesia, Pacific Ocean 18 L8, 254 D5, 265 B5
**Palembang** *Town* Sumatra, Indonesia 196 E10
**Palenque** *Ancient site* Mexico 39 J9
**Palermo** *Town* Italy 103 G12
**Palmerston North** *Town* New Zealand 262 F6
**Palmyra Atoll** *Dependent territory* Polynesia, Pacific Ocean 19 P8, 255 N5, 265 F5
**Palu** *Town* Celebes, Indonesia 196 K9
**Pamir** *River* Afghanistan/Tajikistan 161 H8
**Pamirs** *Mountain range* Tajikistan 133 G9, 161 H8
**Pampas** *Region* Argentina 11 W12, 41 G13, 71 H9
**Pamplona** *Town* Spain 100 H2
**Panama** *Country* Central America 19 V8, 44 G15
**Panama Canal** Panama 41 E3, 44 H15
**Panama City** *Town* Panama 44 I15, 77 C7, 265 L5
**Panama, Isthmus of** Panama 41 D4
**Pancevo** *Town* Serbia & Montenegro 124 J4
**Panevezys** *Town* Lithuania 111 G7
**Pantelleria** *Island* Italy 103 E14
**Papua (Irian Jaya)** *Region* Indonesia 197 R10
**Papua New Guinea** *Country* Australasia 18 M9, 259 L2

**Paraguay** *Country* S. America 19 W11, 71 I3
**Paraguay** *River* S. America 41 H9, 71 J4
**Paramaribo** *Town* Surinam 59 K3
**Paraná** *River* Argentina/Paraguay/Brazil 11 W11, 41 H11, 67 G9, 71 J5, J7
**Paranaíba** *River* Brazil 41 I9
**Paris** *Town* France 97 F3
**Parma** *Town* Italy 103 D5
**Parry Islands** Northwest Territories, Canada 21 K3, 27 F4
**Pasto** *Town* Colombia 59 C4
**Patagonia** *Region* Argentina 11 V13, 41 F14, 71 H13
**Patna** *Town* India 167 H6
**Patras** *Town* Greece 131 C7
**Peary Land** *Region* Greenland 21 R1, 267 E7
**Pec** *Town* Serbia & Montenegro 124 I7
**Pegu** *Town* Burma 189 C7
**Peipus, Lake** Estonia/Russian Federation 111 I4
**Pekanbaru** *Town* Sumatra, Indonesia 196 C9
**Pelagie Islands** Italy 103 F15
**Pelée, Mt.** *Volcano* Martinique 41 H2
**Peloponnese** *Island group* Greece 131 D8
**Pematangsiantar** *Town* Sumatra, Indonesia 196 B8
**Pennines** *Mountain range* UK 87 J7
**Pennsylvania** *State* USA 37 G5
**Penza** *Town* Russian Federation 138 C7
**Penzance** *Town* UK 87 G12
**Peoria** *Town* Illinois, USA 37 C6
**Perm'** *Town* Russian Federation 138 F7
**Persian Gulf** Saudi Arabia/Iran 132 D11, 153 F7, 203 E2
**Perth** *Town* UK 87 I5
**Perth** *Town* Western Australia, Australia 258 C10
**Peru** *Country* S. America 19 V10, 59 C6
**Perugia** *Town* Italy 103 F7
**Peshawar** *Town* Pakistan 167 D2
**Petah-Tiqwa** *Town* Israel 147 E7
**Petra** *Ancient site* Jordan 147 E10
**Philadelphia** *Town* Pennsylvania, USA 37 I6
**Philippine Sea** Philippines 10 K7, 196 L2, 254 C5, 265 B4
**Philippines** *Country* S.E. Asia 10 K8, 18 K8, 196 K5
**Phnom Penh** *Town* Cambodia 189 H11
**Phoenix** *Town* Arizona, USA 33 J12
**Phoenix Islands** Kiribati, Pacific Ocean 11 P9, 255 L6, 265 E6
**Phuket** *Town* Thailand 189 D12
**Piatra-Neamt** *Town* Romania 127 I5
**Pico da Neblina** *Mountain* Brazil 67 C3
**Picton** *Town* New Zealand 262 E7
**Pierre** *Town* South Dakota, USA 35 H4
**Pietermaritzburg** *Town* South Africa 247 H10
**Pietersburg** *see* Polokwane
**Pinar del Rio** *Town* Cuba 44 H5
**Pinatubo, Mt.** *Volcano* Philippines 196 K2
**Pindus Mountains** Greece 131 C5
**Pingxiang** *Town* China 175 M12
**Pinsk** *Town* Belarus 111 H11
**Piraeus** *Town* Greece 131 E8
**Pisa** *Town* Italy 103 D6
**Pitcairn Islands** *Dependent territory* Polynesia, Pacific Ocean 19 S11, 255 T11, 265 H7
**Pitesti** *Town* Romania 127 G8
**Pittsburgh** *Town* Pennsylvania, USA 37 G6
**Piura** *Town* Peru 59 B6
**Pleven** *Town* Bulgaria 127 G10

**Ploiesti** *Town* Romania 127 I8
**Plovdiv** *Town* Bulgaria 127 G12
**Plymouth** *Town* UK 87 H12
**Po** *River* Italy 78 F11, 103 B4, E4
**Podgorica** *Town* Serbia & Montenegro 124 H7
**Podlasie** *Region* Poland 115 K4
**Pointe-Noire** *Town* Congo 232 E12
**Poitiers** *Town* France 97 E6
**Poland** *Country* Central Europe 18 D4, 115 H4
**Polokwane (Pietersburg)** *Town* South Africa 247 H10
**Poltava** *Town* Ukraine 121 I6
**Polynesia** *Region* Pacific Ocean 255 N9, 265 F7
**Pomerania** *Region* Germany/Poland 115 E2
**Ponce** *Town* Puerto Rico 45 S10
**Pontchartrain, Lake** Louisiana, USA 35 L12
**Pontianak** *Town* Borneo, Indonesia 196 G9
**Pontic Mountains** Turkey 145 G5
**Poopó, Lake** Bolivia 41 G9, 59 F11
**Popayán** *Town* Colombia 59 C4
**Popocatépetl** *Volcano* Mexico 39 G8
**Port Elizabeth** *Town* South Africa 247 G11
**Port Harcourt** *Town* Nigeria 221 M13
**Port Hedland** *Town* Western Australia, Australia 258 C7
**Port Louis** *Town* Mauritius 203 E7
**Port Moresby** *Town* Papua New Guinea 259 K3
**Port of Spain** *Town* Trinidad & Tobago 45 U16
**Port Said** *Town* Egypt 203 C1, 215 E1
**Port Sudan** *Town* Sudan 215 F5
**Port-au-Prince** *Town* Haiti 45 O9
**Port-Gentil** *Town* Gabon 232 D10
**Portland** *Town* Oregon, USA 33 F5
**Porto** *see* Oporto
**Pôrto Alegre** *Town* Brazil 67 G12
**Porto-Novo** *Town* Benin 221 K12
**Portoviejo** *Town* Ecuador 59 B5
**Portsmouth** *Town* UK 87 J12
**Portugal** *Country* Europe 18 B5, 100 B6
**Posadas** *Town* Argentina 71 K5
**Potosí** *Town* Bolivia 59 G11
**Potsdam** *Town* Germany 95 J5
**Poznán** *Town* Poland 115 F4
**Prague** *Town* Czech Republic 115 D7
**Praia** *Town* Cape Verde 77 G6
**Pravets** *Town* Bulgaria 127 G11
**Prespa, Lake** Albania/Macedonia/Greece 124 J9, 131 B2
**Preston** *Town* UK 87 I8
**Pretoria** *Town* South Africa 247 H8
**Prijedor** *Town* Bosnia and Herzegovina 124 F3
**Prince Edward Island** *Province* Canada 29 J6
**Prince Edward Islands** Indian Ocean 10 E13, 18 E13, 203 E10
**Pristina** *Town* Serbia & Montenegro 124 J7
**Prizren** *Town* Serbia & Montenegro 124 J7
**Prome** *Town* Burma 189 C6
**Provence** *Region* France 97 I9
**Providence** *Town* Rhode Island, USA 37 J5
**Pucallpa** *Town* Peru 59 D7
**Puebla** *Town* Mexico 39 H8
**Puerto Barrios** *Town* Guatemala 44 D9
**Puerto Montt** *Town* Chile 71 F11
**Puerto Natales** *Town* Chile 71 G15
**Puerto Rico** *Dependent territory* Caribbean Sea 45 S10

**Puerto Rico Trench** Atlantic Ocean 77 D6
**Puerto Santa Cruz** *Town* Argentina 71 H14
**Puncak Jaya** *Mountain* Irian Jaya, Indonesia 197 R10
**Pune** *Town* India 167 D8
**Punjab** *Region* India 167 E3
**Punta Arenas** *Town* Chile 71 H15
**Pusan** *Town* South Korea 175 Q8
**Putorana Mts.** Russian Federation 139 L5
**Putrajaya** *Town* Malaysia 189 F15
**Pyinmana** *Town* Burma 189 C6
**Pyongyang** *Town* North Korea 175 P7
**Pyrenees** *Mountain range* S.W. Europe 78 D11, 97 E10, 100 I2

# Q

**Qatar** *Country* S.W. Asia 18 F7, 153 G8
**Qazvin** *Town* Iran 153 G4
**Qena** *Town* Egypt 215 E3
**Qingdao** *Town* China 175 O9
**Qinghai Hu** *Lake* China 175 H9
**Qiqihar** *Town* China 175 O4
**Qolleh-ye-Damavand** *Mountain* Iran 153 H4
**Qom** *Town* Iran 153 G4
**Qornet es Saouda** *Mountain* Lebanon 147 F5
**Quang Ngai** *Town* Vietnam 189 J8
**Québec** *Province* Canada 29 G6
**Québec** *Town* Québec, Canada 29 H7
**Queen Charlotte Island** British Columbia, Canada 20 G7, 27 A12
**Queen Elizabeth Islands** Northwest Territories, Canada 21 L2, 27 G4, 267 D5
**Queen Maud Land** *Region* Antarctica 269 F2
**Queensland** *State* Australia 259 J7
**Queenstown** *Town* New Zealand 262 B10
**Querétaro** *Town* Mexico 39 G7
**Quezaltenango** *Town* Guatemala 44 B9
**Quito** *Town* Ecuador 59 C5
**Quy Nhon** *Town* Vietnam 189 J9

# R

**Rabat** *Town* Morocco 208 G3
**Rach Gia** *Town* Vietnam 189 H11
**Rajkot** *Town* India 167 C7
**Rajshahi** *Town* Bangladesh 167 J6
**Raleigh** *Town* North Carolina, USA 37 G8
**Ramlat As Sab'Atayn** *Desert region* Saudi Arabia/Yemen 153 D11
**Râmnia Vâlcea** *Town* Romania 127 G8
**Rancagua** *Town* Chile 71 F8
**Ranchi** *Town* India 167 I7
**Rangoon** *Town* Burma 189 C7
**Rangpur** *Town* Bangladesh 167 J6
**Ras Dashen, Mt.** Ethiopia 215 G7
**Rasht** *Town* Iran 153 G3
**Ratchaburi** *Town* Thailand 189 E9
**Ravenna** *Town* Italy 103 F5
**Rawalpindi** *Town* Pakistan 167 D2
**Razim** *Lake* Romania 127 L8
**Reading** *Town* UK 87 J11
**Recife** *Town* Brazil 67 L5
**Red River** USA 21 K10, 35 H9
**Red Sea** 10 E7, 132 B11, 153 A7, 203 D2, 205 J4, 215 F3
**Red Volta** *River* W. Africa 221 I9
**Regina** *Town* Saskatchewan, Canada 27 G14

Reni *Town* Ukraine 120 E9
Rennes *Town* France 97 C4
Reno *Town* Nevada, USA 33 H9
Resistencia *Town* Argentina 71 J5
Resita *Town* Romania 127 D7
Resolute *Town* Northwest Territories, Canada 27 C5, 267 C5
Réunion *Dependent territory* Indian Ocean 18 F11, 203 E7, 205 L12
Revillagigedo Is. *Island group* Mexico 19 S7, 265 I4
Reykjavik *Town* Iceland 77 G3, 267 D10
Rheims *Town* France 97 G3
Rhine *River* W. Europe 10 C4, 78 E9, 91 J7, 95 D6, E10, 97 J3, 106 E7
Rhineland *Region* Germany 95 D8
Rhode Island *State* USA 37 J5
Rhodes *Island* Greece 131 L11
Rhodope Mts. *Mts.* Bulgaria/Greece 78 H11, 127 F12
Rhône *River* Switzerland/France 97 H8, 106 C9
Richmond *Town* Virginia, USA 37 H7
Riga *Town* Latvia 111 G6
Rijeka *Town* Croatia 109 E4
Rimini *Town* Italy 103 F5
Rio Cuarte *Town* Argentina 71 H7
Rio de Janeiro *Town* Brazil 67 I10
Rio Grande *River* Mexico/USA 11 T6, 21 J11, 35 F11, 39 G4
Rio Grande de Santiago *River* Mexico 39 E7
Riobamba *Town* Ecuador 59 C5
Rivadavia *Town* Argentina 41 G10, 71 H12
River Plate *River* Argentina/ Uruguay 41 H12, 71 J8
Rivne *Town* Ukraine 120 D4
Riyadh *Town* Saudi Arabia 153 E8
Rochester *Town* Minnesota, USA 35 K4
Rochester *Town* New York, USA 37 H4
Rockall *Island* UK, Atlantic Ocean 77 H3
Rockford *Town* Illinois, USA 37 C5
Rocky Mountains *N.* America 11 S4, 21 I7, 27 C11, 33 H5, 35 D6
Romania *Country* E. Europe 18 D5, 127 G6
Rome *Town* Italy 103, F8
Ronne Ice Shelf *Antarctica* 269 D4
Rosario *Town* Argentina 71 I7
Roseau *Town* Dominica 45 V13
Ross Ice Shelf *Antarctica* 269 E7
Ross Sea *Antarctica* 269 E8
Rostock *Town* Germany 95 I2
Rostov-na-Donu *Town* Russian Federation 138 B7
Rotorua *Town* New Zealand 255 K13, 262 G4
Rotterdam *Town* Netherlands 91 H7
Rouen *Town* France 97 E2
Rudolf, Lake *see* Turkana, Lake
Ruhr *River* Germany 95 F6
Ruse *Town* Bulgaria 127 I10
Russian Federation *Country* E. Europe/ N. Asia 18 D4, I3, 111 E8, 138–139
Ruwenzori Mts. *Uganda/Congo, Dem. Rep.* 205 H8, 239 E5
Rwanda *Country* Africa 18 D9, 239 F6
Ryazan *Town* Russian Federation 138 C6
Ryukyu Islands *E.* Asia 10 K7, 185 C15

# S

Saarbrücken *Town* Germany 95 D9
Sabac *Town* Serbia & Montenegro 124 I4
Sabah *Region* Borneo, Malaysia 196 J7
Sacramento *Town* California, USA 33 G9

Safi *Town* Morocco 208 F3
Sagaing *Town* Burma 189 C4
Sahara Desert *N.* Africa 10 C7, 205 D4, 209 M8, 221 H5
Sahel *Region* W. Africa 205 D6, 221 I7, 232 G5
Saimaa *Lake* Finland 10 D3, 78 I6, 82 K8
St Étienne *Town* France 97 H7
St George's *Town* Grenada 45 U15
St George's Channel *Ireland/UK* 87 G10
St Helena *Dependent territory* Atlantic Ocean 10 B10, 77 I9, 18 B10
St John's *Town* Newfoundland, Canada 29 L4
St Johns *Town* Antigua & Barbuda 45 V11
St Kitts and Nevis *Country* West Indies 19 V7, 45 U11
St Lawrence *River* Canada 21 N8, 29 H6
St Lawrence Seaway *Canal* Ontario, Canada 29 G8
St Lawrence, Gulf of *Canada* 21 O8, 29 I5
St Louis *Town* Missouri, USA 35 L7
St Lucia *Country* Caribbean Sea 19 W8, 45 V14
St Malo *Town* France 97 C3
St Paul *Island* Indian Ocean 18 H12, 203 G9
St Paul *Town* Minnesota, USA 35 K4
St Petersburg *Town* Florida, USA 37 F12
St Petersburg *Town* Russian Federation 138 D4
St Pierre *Town* St. Pierre and Miquelon 29 K5
St Pierre and Miquelon *Dependent territory* 19 W5, 29 K5
St Vincent and the Grenadines *Country* Caribbean Sea 18 V8, 45 V14
Sakhalin *Island* Russian Federation 133 N7, 139 S8
Salamanca *Town* Spain 100 D4
Salem *Town* Washington, USA 33 F6
Salisbury *Town* UK 87 J11
Salt Lake City *Town* Utah, USA 33 K8
Salta *Town* Argentina 71 G4
Salvador *Town* Brazil 67 K7
Salween *River* Burma/China 175 G11, H14, 189 D5
Salzburg *Town* Austria 106 H6
Samara *Town* Russian Federation 138 D7
Samarinda *Town* Borneo, Indonesia 196 J9
Samarqand *Town* Uzbekistan 161 F7
Samoa *Island* Pacific Ocean 255 M8
Samos *Island* Greece 131 J8
Samothraki *Island* Greece 131 I3
Samsun *Town* Turkey 145 G5
San Agustin *Ancient site* Colombia 59 C4
San Ambrosio Isla *Island* Chile 19 V11, 265 K7
San Antonio *Town* Texas, USA 35 I12
San Bernardino *Town* California, USA 33 H14
San Cristóbal *Town* Venezuela 59 E2
San Diego *Town* California, USA 33 H12
San Felix Isla *Island* Chile 19 V11, 265 K7
San Francisco *Town* California, USA 21 H10, 33 F10, 265 I3
San Jose *Town* California, USA 33 G10
San José *Town* Costa Rica 44 F13
San Juan *River* Utah, USA 33 K10
San Juan *Town* Argentina 71 G7
San Juan *Town* Peru 59 D10
San Juan *Town* Puerto Rico 45 S10
San Luis Potosí *Town* Mexico 39 F6

San Marino *Country* Europe 18 C5, 103 F6
San Miguel *Town* E1 Salvador 44 D10
San Miguel de Tucumán *Town* Argentina 71 H5
San Pedro Sula *Town* Honduras 44 D9
San Remo *Town* Italy 103 B6
San Salvador *Town* El Salvador 44 C10
San Salvador de Jujuy *Town* Argentina 71 G4
San'a *Town* Yemen 153 C11
Sanandaj *Town* Iran 153 F4
Sandoway *Town* Burma 189 B6
Sankt Gallen *Town* Switzerland 106 D7
Sankt Pölten *Town* Austria 106 J5
Sanliurfa *Town* Turkey 145 I8
Santa Ana *Town* California, USA 33 H12
Santa Ana *Town* El Salvador 44 C10
Santa Clara *Town* Cuba 45 K6
Santa Cruz *Town* Bolivia 59 G10
Santa Fe *Town* Argentina 71 I7
Santa Fe *Town* New Mexico, USA 35 E9
Santa Marta *Town* Colombia 59 D1
Santander *Town* Spain 100 F1
Santiago *Town* Chile 71 F8, 265 L8
Santiago *Town* Dominican Republic 45 P9
Santiago *Town* Spain 100 B2
Santiago de Cuba *Town* Cuba 45 M8
Santiago del Estero *Town* Argentina 71 H5
Santo Domingo *Town* Dominican Republic 45 P10
São Francisco *River* Brazil 11 X10, 41 K7, 67 I7
São Luís *Town* Brazil 67 I4
São Paulo *Town* Brazil 67 I10
São Tomé *Town* São Tomé and Príncipe 232 C10
São Tomé and Príncipe *Country* Central Africa 18 C9, 232 C10
Sapporo *Town* Japan 185 H3
Sarajevo *Town* Bosnia and Herzegovina 194 G5
Saratov
Sarawak *Region* Borneo, Malaysia 196 H8
Sarawak Chamber *Cave* Borneo, Indonesia 196 I7
Sardinia *Island* Italy 78 F12, 103 C10
Sargasso Sea *Atlantic Ocean* 77 E6
Sarh *Town* Chad 232 G7
Sari *Town* Iran 153 H4
Sarmiento *Town* Argentina 41 F14
Saskatchewan *Province* Canada 27 F12
Saskatoon *Town* Saskatchewan, Canada 27 F13
Satu Mare *Town* Romania 127 E4
Saudi Arabia *Country* S.W. Asia 18 E7, 153 D8
Sava *River* S.E. Europe 78 G11, 109 F3, I4, 124 G4
Savannah *Town* Georgia, USA 37 F10
Savannakhét *Town* Laos 189 H8
Scandinavia *Region* N. Europe 82
Schwerin *Town* Germany 95 H3
Scilly, Isles of *UK* 87 F12
Scotia Sea *Atlantic Ocean* 77 E12, 269 C2
Scotland *Region* UK 87 I5
Scott Base *Research station* Antarctica 269 F8
Scutari, Lake *Serbia & Montenegro/ Albania* 124 H7
Seattle *Town* Washington, USA 33 G4
Seikan Tunnel *Undersea rail tunnel* Japan 185 H4
Seine *River* France 78 D10, 97 F3, G3
Selvas *Region* Brazil 41 G7

Semarang *Town* Java, Indonesia 196 G12
Semnan *Town* Iran 153 H4
Sendai *Town* Japan 185 I7
Senegal *Country* W. Africa 18 A8, 220 C8
Seoul *Town* South Korea 175 Q8
Serbia & Montenegro *Country* S.E. Europe 18 D5, 124 I6
Seremban *Town* Malaysia 189 F15
Serengeti Plain *Region* Tanzania 205 I9
Sétif *Town* Algeria 209 L2
Sevan *Lake* Armenia 121 Q14
Sevastopol' *Town* Ukraine 119 H10
Severn *River* UK 87 I10
Severnaya Zemlya *Island group* Russian Federation 111 I1, 139 L2, 267 H5
Seville *Town* Spain 78 C13, 100 D7
Seward Peninsula *Alaska, USA* 20 C5
Seychelles *Country* Indian Ocean 10 F9, 18 F9, 203 E6, 205 K9
Sfax *Town* Tunisia 209 N3
Shackleton Ice Shelf *Antarctica* 269 J6
Shamiyah Desert *Syria* 147 I5
Shandong Peninsula *China* 175 O8
Shanghai *Town* China 175 P10, 265 A3
Shannon *River* Ireland 87 F8
Shaoxing *Town* China 175 O11
Shaoyang *Town* China 175 M12
Sheffield *Town* UK 87 J9
Shenyang *Town* China 175 O6
's-Hertogenbosch *Town* Netherlands 91 I7
Shetlands *Island group* UK 78 D7, 87 K1
Shijiazhuang *Town* China 175 M8
Shikoku *Island* Japan 185 D11
Shinano *River* Japan 185 C8
Shiraz *Town* Iran 153 G6
Shkhara *Mountain* Georgia 121 O12
Shreveport *Town* Louisiana, USA 35 J10
Shumen *Town* Bulgaria 127 J10
Siauliai *Town* Lithuania 111 F7
Siberia *Region* Russian Federation 10 J3, 133 K5, 139 M7
Sibiu *Town* Romania 127 G7
Sicily *Island* Italy 78 G13, 103 G13
Sidi Bel Abbès *Town* Algeria 209 J2
Siena *Town* Italy 103 E6
Sierra Leone *Country* W. Africa 18 A8, 220 D10
Sierra Madre Del Sur *Mountain range* Mexico 39 G9
Sierra Madre Occidental *Mountain range* Mexico 21 J11, 39 D5
Sierra Madre Oriental *Mountain range* Mexico 11 T7, 21 J11, 39 F5
Sierra Nevada *Mountain range* California, USA 33 G9
Sierra Nevada *Mountain range* Spain 78 C12, 100 F8
Silesia *Region* Czech Republic/Poland 115 F6
Simferopol' *Town* Ukraine 121 I10
Simpson Desert *Northern Territory/ South Australia, Australia* 254 D11, 259 H8
Sinai Desert *Egypt* 147 C11, 215 E2
Sincelejo *Town* Colombia 59 D1
Sindh *Region* Pakistan 167 B5
Singapore *Country* S.E. Asia 18 J9, 189 G16
Sinuiju *Town* North Korea 175 P7
Sioux Falls *Town* South Dakota, USA 35 I4
Sistan, Lake *Iran* 153 J6
Sittwe *Town* Burma 189 A5
Sivas *Town* Turkey 145 G6
Skagerrak *Channel* Denmark/Norway 78 F7, 82 E10
Skiáthos *Island* Greece 131 F6

**Skiros** *Island* Greece 131 G6
**Skopje** *Town* Macedonia 124 J8
**Skye** *Island* UK 87 H4
**Slavonski Brod** *Town* Croatia 109 J5
**Sliven** *Town* Bulgaria 127 I11
**Slovakia** *Country* Central Europe 18 D4, 115 H9
**Slovenia** *Country* S.E. Europe 18 C5, 109 E3
**Smederevo** *Town* Serbia & Montenegro 124 J4
**Smolensk** *Town* Russian Federation 138 C5
**Snake** *River* Washington/Idaho, USA 21 I9, 33 H5
**Society Islands** French Polynesia, Pacific Ocean 11 P10, 255 P9, 265 G7
**Socotra** *Island* Yemen 133 E13, 203 E3
**Sofia** *Town* Bulgaria 127 F11
**Sohâg** *Town* Egypt 215 E3
**Solapur** *Town* India 167 E9
**Solomon Islands** *Country* Pacific Ocean 10 M9, 19 N10, 255 J7, 265 D6
**Solway Firth** *Gulf* UK 87 I7
**Somalia** *Country* E. Africa 18 F8, 215 J10
**Somme** *River* France 97 F2
**Songkhla** *Town* Thailand 189 E13
**Sonoran Desert** Arizona, USA/Mexico 11 T6, 21 I10, 33 J12, 39 A1
**Sosnowiec** *Town* Poland 115 H7
**South Africa** *Country* Southern Africa 18 D11, 247 F9
**South America** *Continent* 11 W9, 41
**South Australia** *State* Australia 259 H9
**South Bend** *Town* Indiana, USA 37 D5
**South Carolina** *State* USA 37 F9
**South China Sea** 10 J7, 133 K13, 189 H12
**South Dakota** *State* USA 35 G4
**South East Cape** Tasmania, Australia 10 L13, 254 F15, 259 K13
**South Georgia** *Island group* Atlantic Ocean 77 G12
**South Island** New Zealand 255 J14, 262 B11
**South Korea** *Country* S.E. Asia 18 K6, 175 Q8
**South Orkney Islands** Pacific Ocean 77 F12, 269 B1
**South Polar Plateau** *Region* Antarctica 269 G5
**South Pole** Antarctica 269 F5
**South Sandwich Islands** *Dependent territory* Atlantic Ocean 77 G12
**South Shetland Islands** Atlantic Ocean 77 E12, 269 A1
**Southampton** *Town* UK 87 J11
**Southeast Indian Ridge** Indian Ocean 203 J10
**Southend-on-Sea** *Town* UK 87 K11
**Southern Alps** *Mountain range* New Zealand 255 J15, 262 C9
**Southern Ocean** 265 G10, 269 G1, F9
**Southwest Indian Ridge** Indian Ocean 203 E9
**Soweto** *Town* South Africa 247 H9
**Spain** *Country* Europe 18 B5, 100 E5
**Spitsbergen** *Island* Norway 267 G8
**Split** *Town* Croatia 109 H8
**Spokane** *Town* Washington, USA 33 H4
**Sporades** *Island group* Greece 131 F5
**Springfield** *Town* Illinois, USA 37 C6
**Springfield** *Town* Missouri, USA 35 K8
**Srebrenica** *Town* Bosnia and Herzegovina 124 H5
**Sri Lanka** *Country* S. Asia 10 H8, 18 H8, 133 G14, 167 F13
**Srinagar** *Town* India 167 E2
**Stanley, Mt.** Congo, Dem. Rep. 232 K11
**Stanovoy Range** *Mountain range* Russian Federation 133 K6, 139 N9

**Stara Zagora** *Town* Bulgaria 127 H12
**Stavanger** *Town* Norway 82 D9
**Stewart Island** *New Zealand* 255 J15, 262 B12
**Stockholm** *Town* Sweden 82 H9
**Stockton** *Town* California, USA 33 G10
**Stoke-on-Trent** *Town* UK 87 J9
**Stonington Island** Antarctica 269 B4
**Strasbourg** *Town* France 97 J3
**Stratford-upon-Avon** *Town* UK 87 J10
**Stromboli** *Volcano* Lipari Islands, Italy 103 H11
**Stuttgart** *Town* Germany 95 F10
**Subotica** *Town* Serbia & Montenegro 124 I2
**Suceava** *Town* Romania 127 I4
**Sucre** *Town* Bolivia 59 G11
**Sudan** *Country* N.E. Africa 18 D7, 215 D6
**Sudd** *Region* Sudan 215 D9
**Sudeten Mountains** Czech Republic/Poland 115 F7
**Suez** *Town* Egypt 203 C1, 215 E1
**Suez Canal** Egypt 203 C1, 215 E1
**Suez, Gulf of** Egypt 147 C11, 215 E2
**Sumatra** *Island* Indonesia 10 I9, 133 J15, 196 C8
**Sumbawa** *Island* Indonesia 196 J12
**Sumy** *Town* Ukraine 121 I4
**Sun City** *Tourist resort* South Africa 247 G8
**Superior, Lake** Canada/USA 21 L8, 29 D8, 37 D2
**Surabaya** *Town* Java, Indonesia 196 H12
**Surat** *Town* India 167 D7
**Surinam** *Country* S. America 19 W8, 59 J3
**Suzhou** *Town* China 175 O11
**Svalbard** *Island group* Arctic Ocean 10 C1, 18 C1, 267 G7
**Swabian Jura** *Mountain range* Germany 95 F11
**Swansea** *Town* UK 87 H10
**Swaziland** *Country* Southern Africa 18 E11, 247 I9
**Sweden** *Country* Europe 18 C3, 82 G7
**Switzerland** *Country* Europe 18 C5, 106 D8
**Sydney** *Town* New South Wales, Australia 259 L10, 265 C8
**Syracuse** *Town* New York, USA 37 H4
**Syria** *Country* S.W. Asia 18 E6, 147 I4
**Syrian Desert** S.W. Asia 10 E6, 132 C10, 147 H6, 153 D5

# T

**Ta'if** *Town* Saudi Arabia 153 B9
**Ta'izz** *Town* Yemen 153 C12
**Table Mt.** South Africa 247 E12
**Tabora** *Town* Tanzania 239 G8
**Tabriz** *Town* Iran 153 F3
**Tacloban** *Town* Philippines 196 L4
**Tacna** *Town* Peru 59 E10
**Tacoma** *Town* Washington, USA 33 F4
**Taegu** *Town* South Korea 175 Q8
**Tagus** *River* Spain/Portugal 78 C12, 100 C5, E5
**Tahiti** *Island* French Polynesia, Pacific Ocean 11 Q10, 255 P9, 265 G7
**Tahoe, Lake** California/Nevada, USA 33 G9
**Tai'an** *Town* China 175 N9
**Taipei** *Town* Taiwan 175 P13
**Taiping** *Town* Malaysia 189 E14
**Taiwan** *Country* E. Asia 18 K7, 133 L11, 175 P13, 265 A4
**Taiyuan** *Town* China 175 L8
**Tajikistan** *Country* Central Asia 18 GS, 161 G7
**Tajumulco** *Mountain* Guatemala 44 A8

**Takla Makan** *Desert* China 10 H5, 133 G9, 174 C8
**Talca** *Town* Chile 71 F9
**Tallahassee** *Town* Florida, USA 37 E11
**Tallinn** *Town* Estonia 111 H3
**Tamale** *Town* Ghana 221 I10
**Tampa** *Town* Florida, USA 37 F12
**Tampere** *Town* Finland 82 J8
**Tana, Lake** Ethiopia 215 G8
**Tanami Desert** Australia 254 D9
**Tanga** *Town* Tanzania 239 K8
**Tanganyika, Lake** Central Africa 10 E9, 205 I9, 232 K12, 239 F8
**Tanggula Mts.** China 175 F11
**Tangier** *Town* Morocco 208 H2
**Tangshan** *Town* China 175 N8
**Tanjungkarang** *Town* Sumatra, Indonesia 196 E11
**Tanta** *Town* Egypt 215 D1
**Tanzania** *Country* Africa 18 E9, 239 H8
**Taranto** *Town* Italy 103 J9
**Târgoviste** *Town* Romania 127 H8
**Târgu Mure** *Town* Romania 127 G6
**Tarragona** *Town* Spain 100 J4
**Tartu** *Town* Estonia 111 I4
**Tashkent** *Town* Uzbekistan 161 G6
**Tasman Sea** Australia/New Zealand 10 M12, 255 I13, 262 D6, 265 D8
**Tasmania** *Island/State* Australia 254 F14, 259 K13
**Tassili n'Ajjer** *Mountain range* Algeria 205 E3, 209 M7
**Tatar Strait** Russian Federation 139 S9
**Taunggyi** *Town* Burma 189 D5
**Taupo** *Town* New Zealand 262 G5
**Taupo, Lake** New Zealand 262 G5
**Tauranga** *Town* New Zealand 262 G4
**Taurus Mts.** Turkey 10 E5, 145 E8
**Tavoy** *Town* Burma 189 D9
**Taymyr Peninsula** Russian Federation 133 I2, 139 K4, 267 I5
**Tbilisi** *Town* Georgia 121 P13
**Te Anau, Lake** New Zealand 262 B10
**Tegucigalpa** *Town* Honduras 44 D10
**Tehran** *Town* Iran 153 H4
**Tel Aviv-Yafo** *Town* Israel 147 E7
**Tema** *Town* Ghana 221 J12
**Temuco** *Town* Chile 71 F10
**Tennessee** *State* USA 37 D8
**Tenochtitlán** *see* Mexico City
**Teotihuacán** *Ancient site* Mexico 39 G8
**Teresina** *Town* Brazil 67 J4
**Ternopil'** *Town* Ukraine 120 C5
**Tétovan** *Town* Morocco 208 H2
**Tetovo** *Town* Macedonia 124 J8
**Texas** *State* USA 35 H11
**Texcoco, Lake** Mexico 39 G8
**Thabana-Ntlenyana, Mt.** Lesotho 247 H10
**Thai Nguyen** *Town* Vietnam 189 H5
**Thailand** *Country* S.E. Asia 18 I7, 189 F8
**Thailand, Gulf of** 10 I8, 189 E10
**Thames** *River* UK 78 D9, 87 J11
**Thames** *Town* New Zealand 262 G3
**Thane** *Town* India 167 D8
**Thanh Hoa** *Town* Vietnam 189 H6
**Thar Desert** India/Pakistan 10 G6, 133 G11, 167 C5
**Tharthar, Lake** Iraq 153 E4
**Thasos** *Island* Greece 131 G3
**Thaton** *Town* Burma 189 D7
**The Hague** *Town* Netherlands 91 G6
**Thessaloniki** *Town* Greece 131 E3
**Thimphu** *Town* Bhutan 167 J5
**Thunder Bay** *Town* Ontario, Canada 29 E7
**Thuringian Forest** *Region* Germany 95 H7
**Tianjin** *Town* China 175 N8
**Tiber** *River* Italy 103 F7
**Tiberias, Lake** Israel 149 E6

**Tibesti** *Mountain range* Chad/Libya 232 G3
**Tibet, Plateau of** Asia 10 H6, 133 H10
**Tibetan Autonomous Region** China 174 D10
**Tien Shan** *Mountain range* Kyrgyzstan/China 10 H5, 133 H8, 161 I6, 174 C7
**Tierra del Fuego** *Island* Argentina/Chile 41 F16, 71 H16
**Tigris** *River* S.W. Asia 132 C10, 145 I7, 153 E3
**Tijuana** *Town* Mexico 39 A1
**Tikal** *Ancient site* Guatemala 44 C7
**Tilburg** *Town* Netherlands 91 H8
**Timaru** *Town* New Zealand 262 D10
**Timbuktu** *Town* Mali 221 H7
**Timisoara** *Town* Romania 127 D7
**Timor** *Island* Indonesia 133 L16, 196 M12
**Timor Sea** Australia/Indonesia 10 K10, 197 N13, 254 C8
**Tirana** *Town* Albania 124 I9
**Tisza** *River* Hungary 78 H10
**Titicaca, Lake** Bolivia/Peru 11 W10, 41 F8, 59 F10
**Toamasina** *Town* Madagascar 203 E7
**Toba** *Volcanic Crater* Sumatra, Indonesia 196 B8
**Togo** *Country* W. Africa 18 C8, 221 J11
**Tokelau** *Dependent territory* Polynesia, Pacific Ocean 19 P9, 255 M7, 265 E6
**Tokyo** *Town* Japan 185 H9, 265 B3
**Tol'yatti** *Town* Russian Federation 138 D7
**Toledo** *Town* Ohio, USA 37 E5
**Toledo** *Town* Spain 100 F5
**Tomsk** *Town* Russian Federation 139 J4
**Tonga** *Country* Polynesia, Pacific Ocean 11 O10, 19 O10, 255 M9, 265 E7
**Tongking, Gulf of** China/Vietnam 175 L15
**Tónlé Sap** *Lake* Cambodia 189 G10
**Topeka** *Town* Kansas, USA 35 J7
**Torkestan Mts.** Afghanistan 161 F9
**Toronto** *Town* Ontario, Canada 29 F9
**Torres Strait** *Channel* Australia/Papua New Guinea 259 J3
**Toulouse** *Town* France 97 F9
**Townsville** *Town* Queensland, Australia 259 L6
**Trabzon** *Town* Turkey 145 I5
**Transantarctic Mts.** Antarctica 269 F6
**Transvaal** *Region* South Africa 247 H8
**Transylvania** *Region* Romania 127 F6
**Trenton** *Town* New Jersey, USA 37 I6
**Trier** *Town* Germany 95 D8
**Trieste** *Town* Italy 103 G3
**Triglav** *Mountain* Slovenia 109 D2
**Trinidad and Tobago** *Country* Caribbean Sea 19 W8, 45 U16
**Trinidade** *Island* Atlantic Ocean 19 Y10, 77 G9
**Tripoli** *Town* Lebanon 147 F4
**Tripoli** *Town* Libya 209 O4
**Tristan Da Cunha** *Dependent territory* Atlantic Ocean 10 A12, 18 B12, 77 H10
**Trivandrum** *Town* India 167 E12
**Tromsø** *Town* Norway 82 I2
**Trondheim** *Town* Norway 82 F6
**Tropic of Cancer** 11 Z7
**Tropic of Capricorn** 11 Y11
**Troy** *Ancient site* Turkey 145 A6
**Trujillo** *Town* Peru 59 C7
**Tuamotu** *Island group* French Polynesia, Pacific Ocean 11 Q10, 255 Q8
**Tucson** *Town* Arizona, USA 33 K13
**Tula** *Town* Russian Federation 138 C5
**Tulsa** *Town* Oklahoma, USA 35 I8
**Tungaru (Gilbert Is.)** Kiribati, Pacific Ocean 11 N9, 255 K6, 265 D6

**Tunis** *Town* Tunisia 209 N2
**Tunisia** *Country* N. Africa 18 C6, 209 N3
**Turin** *Town* Italy 103 B4
**Turkana, Lake** Ethiopia/Kenya 205 J7, 215 F11, 239 I3
**Turkey** *Country* W. Asia 18 E5, 145 E6
**Turkmenabat** *Town* Turkmenistan 161 E7
**Türkmenbasy** *Town* Turkmenistan 161 B6
**Turkmenistan** *Country* Central Asia 18 F5, 161 D7
**Turks and Caicos Islands** *Dependent territory* West Indies 45 P8
**Turku** *Town* Finland 82 I8
**Tuscany** *Region* Italy 103 D6
**Tuvalu** *Country* Pacific Ocean 11 N9, 19 O9, 255 L7, 265 E6
**Tuzla** *Town* Bosnia and Herzegovina 124 H4
**Tyrrhenian Sea** S. Europe 103 E9

# U

**Ubon Ratchathani** *Town* Thailand 189 H8
**Ucayali** *River* Peru 59 D7
**Udon Thani** *Town* Thailand 189 G7
**Ufa** *Town* Russian Federation 138 E8
**Uganda** *Country* Africa 18 E9, 239 G4
**Ukraine** *Country* E. Europe 18 D4, 121 H6
**Ul'yanovsk** *Town* Russian Federation 138 D7
**Ulan Bator** *Town* Mongolia 175 J5
**Uluru (Ayers Rock)** *Sacred site* Northern Territory, Australia 259 G8
**Ungava Peninsula** Québec, Canada 21 N6
**United Arab Emirates** *Country* S.W. Asia 18 F7, 153 G9
**United Kingdom** *Country* Europe 18 B4, 87 H7
**United States of America** *Country* N. America 19 T5, 33, 35, 37
**Uppsala** *Town* Sweden 82
**Ural** *River* Kazakhstan 161 B3
**Ural Mountains** Russian Federation 10 F3, 79 N6, 132 E5, 138 F7
**Uralsk** *Town* Kazakhstan 161 C2
**Urganch** *Town* Uzbekistan 161 D6
**Urmia, Lake** Iran 153 F3
**Urosevac** *Town* Serbia & Montenegro 124 J7
**Uruguay** *Country* S. America 19 W11, 71 K7
**Uruguay** *River* S. America 41 H11, 71 J6
**Ürümqi** *Town* China 74 E6
**Utah** *State* USA 33 K9
**Utrecht** *Town* Netherlands 91 I6
**Uxmal** *Ancient site* Mexico 39 K7
**Uzbekistan** *Country* Central Asia 18 G5, 161 E6

# V

**Vadodara** *Town* India 167 D7
**Vaduz** *Town* Liechtenstein 106 E7
**Valdez** *Town* Alaska, USA 33 D2
**Valdéz Peninsula** Argentina 41 G14, 71 I11
**Valdivia** *Town* Chile 71 F10
**Valencia** *Region* Spain 100 H5
**Valencia** *Town* Spain 100 I5
**Valencia** *Town* Venezuela 59 F1
**Valladolid** *Town* Spain 100 F3
**Valletta** *Town* Malta 103 H15
**Valparaiso** *Town* Chile 71 F8
**Van** *Town* Turkey 145 K7
**Van, Lake** Turkey 145 K6

**Vanadzor** *Town* Armenia 121 P13
**Vancouver** *Town* British Columbia, Canada 27 C14, 265 H2
**Vancouver Island** British Columbia, Canada 21 H8, 27 B14
**Vänern, Lake** Sweden 78 G7, 82 G9
**Vanuatu** *Country* Melanesia, Pacific Ocean 11 N10, 19 N10, 255 I9, 265 D6
**Varanasi** *Town* India 167 H6
**Varna** *Town* Bulgaria 127 K10
**Västerås** *Town* Sweden 82 H9
**Vatican City** *Country* Rome, Italy 18 C5, 103 F8
**Vatter, Lake** Sweden 78 G7, 82 G10
**Velikiy Novgorod** *Town* Russian Federation 138 C4
**Venezuela** *Country* S. America 19 W8, 59 G2
**Venice** *Town* Italy 103 F4
**Vereeniging** *Town* South Africa 247 H9
**Verkhoyansk** *Town* Russian Federation 133 M4, 139 P5
**Verkhoyansk Range** *Mountain range* Russian Federation 133 M4, 139 O6
**Vermont** *State* USA 37 J4
**Verona** *Town* Italy 103 E4
**Versailles** *Town* France 97 F3
**Vesterålen** *Island group* Norway 78 G4, 82 H3
**Viareggio** *Town* Italy 103 D6
**Victoria** *River* Northern Territory, Australia 259 G5
**Victoria** *State* Australia 259 J11
**Victoria** *Town* Seychelles 203 E5
**Victoria** *Town* Vancouver Island, British Columbia, Canada 27 B14
**Victoria Falls** *Waterfall* Zambia/ Zimbabwe 205 H11, 239 C14, 247 G6
**Victoria Island** Northwest Territories, Canada 11 T2, 21 I4, 27 F6
**Victoria, Lake** Tanzania/Uganda/Kenya 10 E9, 205 I8, 239 G5
**Victoria Land** *Region* Antarctica 269 G8 Columbia, Canada 27 C14
**Vienna** *Town* Austria 106 K5
**Vientiane** *Town* Laos 189 G7
**Viet Tri** *Town* Vietnam 189 H5
**Vietnam** *Country* S.E. Asia 18 J8, 189 H7
**Villavicencio** *Town* Colombia 59 E3
**Vilnius** *Town* Lithuania 111 G8
**Viña del Mar** *Town* Chile 71 F8
**Vinh** *Town* Vietnam 189 H6
**Vinnytsya** *Town* Ukraine 120 E6
**Vinson Massif** *Mountain* Antarctica 269 D5
**Virgin Islands** *Dependent territory* Caribbean Sea 45 T10
**Virginia** *State* USA 37 H7
**Visby** *Town* Sweden 82 H10
**Vishakhapatnam** *Town* India 167 H9
**Vistula** *River* Poland 78 H9, 115 H2, J5, I7
**Vitava, Lake** Czech Republic 115 D8
**Vitoria** *Town* Spain 100 G2
**Vitsyebsk** *Town* Belarus 111 K8
**Vladivostok** *Town* Russian Federation 139 S11
**Vojvodina** *Province* Serbia & Montenegro 124 H3
**Volga** *River* Russian Federation 10 E3, 78 L8, L10
**Volgograd** *Town* Russian Federation 138 B7
**Volta, Lake** Ghana 205 D7, 221 I11
**Voronezh** *Town* Russian Federation 138 B6
**Vosges** *Mountain range* France 97 I4
**Vostok** *Research station* Antarctica 269 H8
**Vukovar** *Town* Croatia 109 K4

# W

**Waco** *Town* Texas, USA 35 I11
**Wad Medani** *Town* Sudan 215 E7
**Waddenzee** *Sea* Netherlands 91 I4
**Waikato** *River* New Zealand 262 F4
**Waipapakauri** *Town* New Zealand 262 E2
**Wairau** *River* New Zealand 262 E7
**Waitaki** *River* New Zealand 262 C10
**Waitangi** *Town* New Zealand 262 F2
**Wakatipu, Lake** New Zealand 262 B10
**Wake Island** *Dependent territory* Micronesia, Pacific Ocean 19 N7, 255 J2, 265 D4
**Wales** *Region* UK 87 H10
**Wallis and Futuna** *Dependent territory* Polynesia, Pacific Ocean 19 O10, 265 E6
**Walvis Bay** Namibia 205 F10
**Walvis Ridge** Atlantic Ocean 77 I10
**Wanganui** *Town* New Zealand 262 F6
**Warsaw** *Town* Poland 115 I4
**Wash, The** *North Sea* UK 87 K9
**Washington** *State* USA 33 G4
**Washington D.C.** *Town* District of Columbia, USA 21 N10, 37 H6
**Weddell Sea** Antarctica 77 F13, 269 C3
**Wellington** *Town* New Zealand 262 F7, 265 E8
**West Bank** *Region* Near East 147 E7
**West Frisian Islands** Netherlands 91 I3
**West Indies** *Island group* Atlantic Ocean 41 G1, 77 C6
**West Siberian Plain** Russian Federation 132 E5, 138 H6
**West Virginia** *State* USA 37 F7
**Western Australia** *State* Australia 258 D8
**Western Dvina** *see* Dvina
**Western Ghats** *Mountain range* India 167 D10
**Western Sahara** *Disputed territory* N.W. Africa 18 A7, 208 C7, 220
**Samoa** *Country* Polynesia, Pacific Ocean 11 O10, 19 O10, 265 F6
**Westport** *Town* New Zealand 262 D7
**Whangarei** *Town* New Zealand 262 F2
**White Nile** *River* E. Africa 205 I6, 215 E7
**White Sea** Russian Federation 78 J5, 138 F4
**White Volta** *River* W. Africa 221 I10
**Whitehorse** *Town* Yukon Territory, Canada 27 B9
**Wichita** *Town* Kansas, USA 35 I8
**Wicklow Mts.** Ireland 87 G9
**Wiesbaden** *Town* Germany 95 F8
**Wight, Isle of** UK 87 J12
**Wilhelm, Mt.** Papua New Guinea 254 F7
**Wilkes Land** *Region* Antarctica 269 I8
**Windhoek** *Town* Namibia 247 D7
**Windsor** *Town* Ontario, Canada 29 F6
**Windward Islands** Caribbean Sea 45 U13
**Winnipeg** *Town* Manitoba, Canada 27 I14
**Wisconsin** *State* USA 37 C3
**Wollongong** *Town* New South Wales, Australia 259 L10
**Wolverhampton** *Town* UK 87 J10
**Wrangel Island** Russian Federation 133 S3, 139 Q1, 267 F2
**Wroclaw** *Town* Poland 115 F6
**Wuhan** *Town* China 175 M11
**Wuppertal** *Town* Germany 95 E6
**Wuxi** *Town* China 175 O10
**Wyoming** *State* USA 35 E5

# X

**Xi'an** *Town* China 175 K10

**Xiamen** *Town* China 175 O13
**Xiangfan** *Town* China 175 L11
**Xining** *Town* China 175 I9
**Xinjiang Uyghur** *Autonomous Region* China 174 D6
**Xinyang** *Town* China 175 M11

# Y

**Yalta** *Town* Ukraine 121 I10
**Yamoussoukro** *Town* Ivory Coast 221 G12
**Yangtze** *River* China 10 J6, 133 K10, 175 L11, N11
**Yaounde** *Town* Cameroon 232 E9
**Yarlung Zangbo** *see* Brahmaputra
**Yaroslavl'** *Town* Russian Federation 138 D5
**Yasuj** *Town* Iran 153 G6
**Yazd** *Town* Iran 153 H6
**Yekaterinburg** *Town* Russian Federation 138 F7
**Yellow River** China 10 I5, 133 J9, 175 L8, M9
**Yellow Sea** China 10 K6, 133 L9, 175 O8
**Yellowknife** *Town* Northwest Territories, Canada 27 E9
**Yellowstone** *River* Montana/Wyoming, USA 21 J8, 35 F2
**Yemen** *Country* S.W. Asia 18 F7, 153 D11
**Yenisey** *River* Russian Federation 10 H2, 139 K8
**Yerevan** *Town* Armenia 121 P14
**Yichang** *Town* China 175 L11
**Yinchuan** *Town* China 175 J8
**Yogyakarta** *Town* Java, Indonesia 196 G12
**Yokohama** *Town* Japan 185 H9
**York** *Town* UK 87 J8
**Yuan** *River* China 175 L13
**Yucatán Peninsula** Mexico 39 K8, 41 C1
**Yueyang** *Town* China 175 M12
**Yukon** *River* Canada/USA 11 Q3, 20 E5, 27 A8, 33 D2
**Yukon Territory** *Province* Canada 27 B8

# Z

**Zadar** *Town* Croatia 109 F6
**Zagreb** *Town* Croatia 109 G3
**Zagros Mts.** Iran 10 F6, 132 D10, 153 G6
**Zahedan** *Town* Iran 153 J7
**Zakynthos** *Island* Greece 131 B8
**Zambezi** *River* Southern Africa 10 D10, 205 G11, I11, 239 H4, H5, J5
**Zambia** *Country* Africa 18 D10, 239 D13
**Zamboanga** *Town* Philippines 196 L6
**Zanjan** *Town* Iran 153 G3
**Zanzibar** *Town* Zanzibar, Tanzania 239 K8
**Zanzibar** *Island* Tanzania 205 J9, 239 K8
**Zaozhuang** *Town* China 175 N9
**Zaporizhzhya** *Town* Ukraine 121 I7
**Zaragoza** *Town* Spain 100 H3
**Zaria** *Town* Nigeria 221 M10
**Zenica** *Town* Bosnia and Herzegovina 124 G5
**Zhengzhou** *Town* China 175 M10
**Zhytomyr** *Town* Ukraine 120 E5
**Zibo** *Town* China 175 N9
**Zimbabwe** *Country* Southern Africa 18 D10, 247 H6
**Zonguldak** *Town* Turkey 145 D5
**Zrenjanin** *Town* Serbia & Montenegro 124 I3
**Zugspitze** *Mountain* Germany 95 H12
**Zurich** *Town* Switzerland 106 D7
**Zwolle** *Town* Netherlands 91 J5

# INDEX

# PICTURE SOURCES

The publisher would like to thank the following for their kind permission to reproduce the photographs.

t = top, b = bottom, c = centre, l = left, r= right, a = above

**Ace Photo Agency:** Chris Middlebrook 89cl.

**akg-images:** 84br.

**Alamy Images:** Index Stock 273cr; Network Photographers 154c.

**Allsport:** Shaun Botterill 253tr, 257bc, Clive Brunskill 96tr, 242bc, Adrian Murrell 56tr, Pascal Rondeao 28tr.

**Ancient Art & Architecture collection:** 181tr.

**Andes Press Agency:** Carlos Reynes Manzo 66cr.

**ArenaPAL:** 84bc.

**Art Directors:** 71cl.

**Asia Images:** John Molloy 188tc.

**Bridgeman Art Library:** By courtesy of the board of trustees of the V&A 155br.

**British Antarctic Survey:** R. Mulvaney 268c.

**Camera Press:** 64br, 154cl, 146tr, 168cr, Thierry Charlier 184c, J Allan Cash: 20bl, 75tr, 81tr, 96cla, 105br, 108clb, 108cr, 110tr, 110cr, 114ca, 144bl, 153br, 162bl, 195tl, 205clb, 219br, 220tc, 229bc, 230cr, 230br, 231c.David Rubinger 156tr.

**Lester Cheeseman:** 171bl, 172cl.

**Cephas Picture Library:** Mick Rock 119bc.

**Churches Ministry Among the Jews:** 150cb.

**Stephanie Colasanti:** 103br, 104cra.

**Bruce Coleman:** 53tr, 184cr, 239tl, 268br, Thomas Buchholz 81bc, 83clb, R. Campbell 206cl, Rob P. Carr 20bc, Brian J. Coates 197tl, 254cl, Alain Compost 133br, Raimund Cramm 21br, Gerald Cubitt 248cr, 250tr, Peter Davey 243tr, Keith Gunnor 63bl, Udo Hirsch 64cr, Harold Lange 24br, 94cr, Luiz Claudio Marigo 40bl, 69br, John Murray 204clb, Dr. Norman Myers 46bl, 228c, Carl Roessler 258bl, Jan Taylor 258cla.

**Collections:** Liba Taylor 88tr.

**Colorific:** Linda Bartlett 36cl, 124bl, M. Clark 90tr, Matrix /Robert Caputo 237cb /Sarah Leen 19tl, Claus Meyer 68clb, Kay Muldoon 219tr, Francois Perri 234tr, /Black Star: Peter Turnley 123tr, 123br.

**Comstock:** John Bulmer 61tr, Georg Gerster 2tl, 223tr.

**Michael Copsey:** 36tr, 37bc.

**Corbis:** 271cra; Tony Amuza 277cl; Adrian Arbib 281clb; Dave Bartruff 276tc; Yann Arthus-Bertrand 271cc, Bettmann / Reuter: 271tr; Jan Butchofsky-Houser 89bl; Ric Ergenbright 165crb; Macduff Everton 179cb; Franz-Marc Frei 54bc, Phillip Gould 277clb; Marc Granger 120br; Aaron Horowitz 273clb; Robbis Jack 74tr; Reed Kaestner 280clb; Stephanie Maze 279tl; Kelly-Mooney Photography 179tr; Yuriko Nakao/Reuters 197cra; Carmen Redondo 118c; Reuters 75tc; Vince Streano 277crb; Arthur Thevenart 279cra; David & Peter Tumley 276cl; David Turnley 121cra, 155cr, 277bc; Patrick Ward 271bl; Nik Wheeler 112crb; Janet Wishnesky 160tr; 272bl.

**Corbis-Bettmann / Reuter:** 271tr; /UPI: 228tr.

**James Davis Travel Photography:** 50tr, 57cr, 81tl, 100cb, 101tr, 101crb, 105tr, 110crb, 132cl, 132br, 140tr, 158bl, 260c, 262tr.

**Ecoscene:** Anthony Cooper 280br.

**Empics:** Stellan Danielsson 48br. 96tr; Tony Marshall 253tr.

**Environmental Picture Library:** Bob Edwards 141cla.
**European Space Agency:** 61bl.

**Mary Evans Picture Library:** 50cr, 65tr, 260 tr.

**Eye Ubiquitous:** David Cummings 101clb, 114cl, 138cb, 140br, Patrick Field 186cl, Steve Lindridge 91 bl, Steve Miller 70tr.

**Ffotograff:** Charles Aithie 152tr, Patricia Aithie 159tr.

**Martyn Foote:** 256tr, 258ca, 258c, 260cl

**Frederick Foster:** 26cb.

**Sir Norman Foster and Partners:** Ian Lambot 179tr.

**The Gambia Experience:** 224bc.

**Getty Images:** The Image Bank 108tr.

**Greenpeace:** Green 256br, Morgan 264br.

**Sonia Halliday Photography:** T.C. Rising 134tr, 144tr.

**Robert Harding Picture Library:** 22tc, 23cla, 26cr, 28cr, 33cl, 42cb, 49bl, 57tl, 60cr, 60c, 74bl, 81crb, 85bl, 89cb, 92c, 98cl, 99cb, 102bl, 128tr, 129cr, 132cb, 142cr, 144cr, 147bc, 154tr, 155tl, 155bl, 163bl, 170tr, 172 cr, 179br, 183bc, 185bc, 190tr, 190c, 195cb, 198tr, 198cl, 198bl, 203bc, 207clb, 208ca, 209tr, 220bc, 222tr, 223cra, 225c, 230tr, 242tr, 245tr, 248bl, 249tr, 253bc, 267cb, 275bc, Felix. A, 219cr, J.R. Ashford 63tr, C. Bowman 73cl, Jeremy Bright 105ca, G. Corrigan 177br, Rob Cousins 23tc, Alain Evrard 191cb, 201cl, 201crb, Robert Francis 151clb, Odyssey, Chicago / Robert Frerck 23tr, Robert Frerck 38tr, K. Gillingham 51cl, Gavin Hellier 119cr, Wally Herbert 86tr, Paulo Koch 149bl, 176cr, David Lomax 22br, C. Martin 95br, Robert McLeod 194tr, H.P. Merten 95bl, Louise Murray 129crb, Gary Norman 61ca, Roy Rainford 93tr, Geoff Renner 204tr, 246cb, Christopher Rennie 141cr, Riffet 233cb, John G. Ross 70br, Sassoon 123ca, Michael Short 124tr, E. Simanor 148bl, James Strachan 47c, Luca Invernizzi Tettoni 189br, 190br, 198cr, Adam Woolfitt 31cb, 62br, 76bl, 79tr, 79 br, 127bl, 129cl, 216tr, Earl Young 47 cr.

**Holt Studios International:** 214tr, Mary Cherry 229cl, Inga Spence 32bc, 51br.

**Jeremy Horner:** 62cr, 62bl.

**Hulton/Getty:** /Reuter 252tr, 268bl.

**Hutchison Library:** 17br, 29clb, 52 cla, 58tl, 68bc, 157cr, 162cr, 164cl, 164bl, 172tr, 210 bl, 214cr, 214cr, 217ca, 217cl, 226crb, 226bl, 228clb, 234cla, 236cr, 247br, 249bl, Robert Aberman 144cl, Christina Dodwell 142tc, John G. Egan 81tr,138clb, Sarah Errington 17tl, 55tr, 235tr, 237bl, Andrew Evans 130bl, Robert Francis 73br, Norman Froggatt 115 bl, Réne-Nicolas Guidicelli 179ca, Maurice Harvey 227cr, 245cr, John Hatt 148tr, Jeremy Horner 62tl, Chris Johnson 229cr, R.Ian Lloyd 188bl, 191tr, M. Macintyre 201cr, Brian Moser 65br, 193bl, B. Régent 227tr, P.W.Rippon 155cl, Trevor Page 219cla, Christine Pemberton 178tl, Stephen Pern 43cr, 70bl, 156cl, 240tr, Bernard Régent 202bc, 236cla, Kerstin Rodgers 65bl, T. Souter 150br, Isabella Tree 259cr, Anna Tully 48tr, 230clb, Philip Wolmuth 54bl, 55bl.

**ICCE:** Robert Carlson 50bl, Glyn Davies 197tr

**The Image Bank:** 93br, 113tr, 180bl, 194bl, Luis Castaneda 72bl, 274bl, Michael Coyne 259br, L.D. Gordon 39cb, Burton Mc Neely 32cr, Morrin E. Newman 36cr, Terje Rakke 83tr, J. Schmitt 38cr.

**Images Colour Library:** 98br, 106bl /AGE Fotostock: 101cr.

**Impact:** Christophe Bluntzer 164tr, Piers Cavendish 49cr, 76cr, 146bl /Clic Clap 45tc, 122cb, Sergio Doranles 39bl, Alain Evrard 136bl, Pilar Fernandez 37crb, Alain Le Garsmeur 49c, 49tr, 53cl, Robert Gibbs 42clb, Philip Gordon 182tr, Mark Henley Back cover cb, 2cb, 107br, 137cl, 192br, 195cl, Erol Houssein 126bl, Javed A. Jaffererji 136tr, Colin Jones 21bl, 51cb, 204cr, Alan Keohane 14bc, Geraint Lewis 114tr, M. Milivojevic 119cla, Vitaly Orlot 161br, Gary Parker 243bl, Caroline Penn 158tr, 213tr, 240cr, Christopher Pillitz 70cr, David Reed 225cr, 225tr, Ray Roberts 85tr, James Willis 157trb.

**International Coffee Organisation:** 66cb.

**Japan Information and Cultural Centre:** 184tr.

**John R. Jones:** 159cb, 188cra, 189tr, 192cl, 193tl, 193cr.

**Katz:** Rea Bellavia 180tr, Boisseaux-Chical 223bl, Bruno Hadjih 72cr, Randy G. Taylor 53br.

**Kodia:** I. Modic 109bl.

**Link Picture Library:** Orde Eliason 85bc

**Roger Kohn:** 75cra; **Korean Tourist Office:** 183bl.

**Luxner News Inc:** Larry Luxner 75cla.

**Magnum Photos:** Bruno Barbey 236tr, Steve McCurry 99cl.

**NASA:** 268tr.

**National Cotton Council:** 36crb.

**Nature Photographers:** Andrew Cleave 266cla.

**New Zealand Tourist Board:** 263tl.

**NHPA:** Hellio and Van Ingen 132tc.

**Novosti:** 162tr, 162crb.

**Christine Osborne Pictures:** 148bc.

**Oxford Scientific Films:** Johnny Johnson 26crb.

**Panos:** M. Adler 235crb, 235bl, Trygve Bolstad 166bl, 251tr, Katri Burri 217tr, Neil Cooper 169cr, 169bl, 218tr, Jean-Léo Dugast 135clb,191cl, Mark Mc Evoy 149c, Alain le Garsmeur 137bl, 173bl, 178bl, Ron Giling 200cr, 200br, 222crb, Jeremy Hartley 115br, 207tr, 226cr, 224cr, Chris Johnson 251c, Rhodri Jones 121tc, Barbara Klass 169cr, N.Durrell McKenna 73bl, Micheal J O'Brien 122tr, Trevor Page 163cr, Bruce Paton 231tl, 246bl, 251bl, Betty Press 207cr, 241tr, 241c, Dominic Sansoni 202tr, Paul Smith 47tr, 251cr, Jon Spaull 136bc, Sean Sprague 48bl, 66tc, 128bl, 143cb, 218cr, 234bl, 241crb, Chris Stowers 144ca, 168bc, 170br, Penny Tweedie 208bl, 210bc, 244c, 244cr, 260cr, 68c.

**Pearson Group:** 74cl.

**Performance Arts Library:** Clive Barda 88cr.

**Piaggio Veicoli Europei Spa:** 104cr.

**Pictor International Ltd:** 23bl, 24tr, 25cb, 36bl, 41clb, 54c, 56cr, 56br, 59cr, 67bl, 68tr, 74br, 76br, 81c, 84tr, 93bc, 109tr, 116cb, 118br, 119cr, 129c, 130cr, 135br, 137tr, 186tr, 186bl, 190cb, 206br, 207tc, 209tl, 210tr, 212crb, 227br, 238bl, 243cl, 264bl.

302

**Pictures Colour Library**: 25br, 52tr, 52bl, 58br, 60tr, 168tr, 246cla.
**Planet Earth Pictures**: Andre Bartschi 43tl, Dave Lyons 78tc, Nigel Tucker 47br.

**Popperfoto**: 152cb/EPA, 48cb, Andrew Winning 273cla; Elio Ciol 275bl; Enny Nuraheni/Reuters 270cb; Kaz Nagasayu/Reuters 199bc; Muzammil/Reuters 281br; Patrick de Noirmont 137tc; Paul Cadenhead 250tr; Peter Morgan/Reuters 36cra; Reuters 270tr, 273tr, 274tr; Rueters/Sayed Salahuddin 165tr; STR/Reuters/Popperfoto 250cra; TOPEX/Poseidon satellite/NASA/Reuters 272ca.

**Zev Radovan**: 146br. **Railway Gazette**: 248c.

**Rex Features Ltd.**: 31cl, 94tr, 121bl, 125bl, 125br, 126c, 183cr, 200c, 213cra, 213cl, 244bc, 247bc, Argas 182br, David Frazier 54br, Basile Grigorie 141tr, Tom Haley 125tr, Sylvain Julienne 119cb, Juhan Kuus 246tr, Laine 123cr, Anatoly Lolis 139bl, V. Miladinovic 137cr, Tim Rooke 252c, S. Tazana 13clb, Today 140bl, 152br,116ca; David Browne 227cl; Frank Monaco 171tl; Joel Nito 201tc.

**Royal Geographical Society**: Chris Caldicott 223cl, Sitting Images /David Constantine 193cl, Ian McWilliam 168c.

**Peter Saunders Photography**: 156c, 157 br, 158cl, 243bc.

**Science Photo Library**: Gregory Dimijian 14cr, Simon Fraser 13tc, Martin Land 13br, Peter Menzel 17cr, Dr. David Miller 268cra, Micheal Morten 79cr, David Parker 13cr, David Simson: 92 cb.

**South American Pictures**: Kimball Morrison 60br, Tony Morrison 1c, 40cl, 40tr, 40br, 72ca,72clb.

**Jon Spaull**: 165c.

**Spectrum Colour Library**: D & J Heaton 39br.

**Frank Spooner Picture Library**: Gamma: 270c, F. Apesteguy 271ca, Baitel 150bl, Bar 192cr, David Barritt 253bl, Borrilson 255cr, Boudin 225bl, Eric Bouvet 149tr, Laurent Maousiz 236bl, Noel Quidu 151cl, Renault 24bc, Vlastimir Shone 111br, Sidali 211bc, L.Van Der Stockt 157tr, Testelin 26bl, Torregano /Figaro Magazine 235cla /Liaison: 14br, Andy Bernandez 141bl, Engle 47tl, Giacomoni 53c, Kinch 26tl, © Peterson 271tc, Ken Ross 193br, Sallaz 34c.

**Sporting Pictures**: 66br, 261bl, Graeme Bachop 263tr, Greg Crisp 31bl.
**Still Pictures**: 194c, 272cr. 278bl, Nigel Dickinson 196c, Mark Edwards 43cl, 43c, 69bl, 84cr, 278br Julio Etchart 71cla; Herbert Giradet 60cla; Michel Gunther 232bl, Paul Harrison 43bc, 274br; T. Hornbeck 276cb; Yves Lefevre 272cr Andre Maslennikov 117c, Heine Pederson 273cra; Stephen Pern 181bc; Thomas Raupach 94cb, 96 ca, Hartmut Schwarzbach 207cla, Jorgen Schytte 135tl, 222c. Hartmut Schwarzbach 275cla; Jorgen Schytte 228tr Asia St George 116tr.

**Tony Stone Images**: 2ca, 17clb, 45cr, 54tr, 74c, 82bl, 113cr, 166br, 167br, 171 tr, 173cl, 173cr, 180br, 185tl, 187tl, 187cr, 208tr, 233crb, 234cr, 242cr, 248tr, Jerry Alexander 122cl, Doug Armand Front Flap bl, 57cl, 216bl, Oliver Benn 100tr, 107tr, Kathy Bushue Front cover crb, 266c, Paul Chesley 184clb, 192tr, Tony Craddock 107c, Nicholas Devore 104bc, Chad Ehlers 82br, David Endersbee 88c, 92tr, Robert Everts 102tr, Robert Frerck 210c, John Garrett 202cr, Susanne & Nick Geary Front cover cr, 80tr, David Hanson 86crb, Bruno de Hooves 241bl, Cris Haigh 56cl, Warren Jacobs 211c, 233tr, Chris Kapolka 51tr, John Lamb 204br, 255cr, Matt Lambert 89 tr, Nadia MacKenzie 255crb, Ian Murphy 250bl, 250cl, Nicholas Parfitt 204cl, Jean Pragen 117clb, Colin Raw 79ca, Ed Rooney 60bl, Andrew Sacks 34cr, Hugh Sitton 83crb, Don Smetzer 23cr, Aldo Torelli 32cr, Terry Vine 30tr, Tom Walker 266tr.

**Telegraph Colour Library**: 24bl, 25tr, 25cl, L.L.T. Rhodes 67br.

**The Big Issue**: 279cb

**John Tramper**: 176tr, 177cr.

**Trip Photographic Library**: 156br, M. Barlow 110cl, 118tr, 128cl, 252br, J. Batten 174ca, 178tr, A. Bloomfield 91br, 99bl, M. Both 244tr, D. Davis 245cb, Dinodia 166tr, M. Dubin 145br, R. Graham 126crb, G. Gunnarsson 76tr, J. Highet 158br, W. Jacobs 98cra, 231bc, 262c. P. Joynson-Hicks 240bc, V. Kolpakov 111bl, A. Kuznetsov 143tc, Janet Pugh 20c, Hélène Rogers 151cr, 158c, 215br, 217cr, V. Shuba 112tr, 112bl, V. Slapinia 120cl, Eric Smith 102cr, 202clb, G. Spenceley 126rc, A. Tjagny-Rjadno 113br, 141bc, B. Turner 142bl, E. Wedd 238cl, M. Wilson 238tr, Peter Wilson: 93c, 127tc.

**World Pictures**: 38cl, 79bc, 99c, 106tl, 150tr, 200tr.

**Zefa**: 28cl, 28bl, 44cla, 55c, 61cr, 86c, 86clb, 87cb, 89tl, 89crb, 90bl, 130tr, 131bc, 145bl, 151bl, 153bl, 160cl, 160bc, 163tr, 170c, 173tr, 177tr, 183tr, 187cl, 212cb, 213bl, 224tr, 252cr, 254cr, 257tr, 261tr, 261cr, 281c, / Australian Picture Library: J. Carnemolla 257c, J. Bitsch 181bc, Bramaz 50c, Brockhaus 130c, Damm 20crb, 159bl, 216c, E. Earp 242bl, Engen 105crb, V. Englebert 222bl, Enrico 49br, Enzinger 94cla, Goebel 195cr, Gunter Heil Back cover bl, Heilman 34br, Janoud 64tl, Helbig K 196tr, K. Kerth 41cla, Lagerway 180cr, O. Luz 46br, Messerschmi 83cb, / Orion Press: 180c, M. Pitner 32 bl, Kurt Scholz 211tr, Smith 179bl, Robin Smith 262bl, / Starfoto: 148 cr, Steenmans 35bl, I. Steinhoff 218bl, H. Sunak 46tr, Surpress 59br.

Every effort has been made to trace the copyright holders. Dorling Kindersley apologises for any unintentional omissions and would be pleased, in such cases, to add an acknowledgement in future editions.

**ADDITIONAL PHOTOGRAPHY BY:**
Geoff Brightling; Peter Chadwick; Joe Cornish; Geoff Dann; Philip Dowell; Andreas von Einsiedel; Neil Fletcher; Frank Greenaway; Stephen Hayward; Alan Hills; Colin Keates (Natural History Museum); Gary Kevin; Barnabas Kindersley; Dave King; Cyril Laubscher; Bill Ling; Andrew McRobb; Neil Mersh; Ray Moller; David Murray; Martin Norris; Roger Phillips; Martin Plomer; Tim Ridley; Kim Sayer; J Selmes; Karl Shone; Clive Streeter; Joel Sussman; Harry Taylor (Natural History Museum); Kim Taylor; Matthew Ward; Alan Williams; Jerry Young; Michel Zabe.

**Dorling Kindersley would like to thank the following museums and organizations:**
The British Library: early bible, p96; The Churches Ministry Among The Jews: Jewish prayer shawl and phylactery, p150; The Natural History Museum: copper p2, beryl and cut emerald p62, cinchona plant p69, gold p164, cut and alluvial diamonds p226, copper p249, krill p269; The Pitt Rivers Museum: tikki charm p263; The Wallace Collection: Ashante mask p228.

# ILLUSTRATORS

t = top, b = bottom, c = centre, l = left, r= right

**David Ashby**: 26 cl 38 bl, 46 c, 62 c, 75 cl, bc, 86 b, 90 bc, br, 99 tr, 102 c, 130 br, bc, 140 c, 148 c, 150 c, 156 b, 168 br, 171 c, 174 b, 183 cl, 213 br, 218 c, 219 cr, 223 br, 261 c.

**Andrew Beckett**: 13 c, 60 cl, 69 c, 92 bl, 108 c, 114 c, 117 cr, 162 c, 166 c, 172 b, 184 b, 187 b, 214 b, 220 l, 243 cr, 244 bl, 267 cr.

**Fiona Bell Currie**: 69 bc, 225 br, 230 bc.

**Evelyn Binns**: 110 br.

**Richard Bonson**: 96 bl.

**Peter Bull**: 11 tr, 12 c, 13 br, 14 tr, cl, 16 tr, 17 tr, c, 22 tr, bl, 23 br, 25 cr, 28 c, 31 tr, 32 cl, 40 cr, 42 br, 43 tl, tr, br, 44 bl, 54 cr, 55 br, 57 tc, tr, 58 bl, 60 cr, 66 bl, br, 69 cl, 70 cl, br, 73 r, 76 c, 80 br, 81 bl, 85 cr, 86 cl, 88 cl, bl, 93 cl, 94 cr, 96 cr, 101 bc, 108 cl, 116 cr, 118 cl, 120 b, 125 c, b, 126 bc, 129 bc, 130 c, 132 bl, 135 tr, bc, 136 c, 137 c, br, 140 cr, 141 c, 142 c, 143 br, 146 bc, 149 cl, 164 cr, 165 br, 166 bc, 168 cl, 169 c, 170 cr, 177 bc, 180 br, 181 c, 183 cr, 186 cl, 198 bc, 199 cr, 200 cl, bl, 207 cr, br, 211 cr, 212 cl, 213 c, 216 c, br, 220 c, 222 cr, 227 b, 230 cr, 235 c, 237 c, br, 242 c, 245 c, cl, 246 br, 248 cl, 250 br, 251 c, 253 cl, 256 tr, 257 t, 265 bc, 267 b, 268 cl, 269 br, 270 c, bl, 271 t, cr, br, 274 tr, 275 cl, cr, 277 tr, 279 br, bc, 280 tc, br, 281 br.

**Martin Camm**: 77 br.

**Luciano Corbella**: 76 br.

**Brian Delf**: 15 b.

**Peter Dennis**: 48 c, 83 c, 85 c, 143 br, 144 br, 149 cr, 155 c, 159 c, 160 br, 165 cr, 176 b, 178 c, 187 tr, 217 b, 233 c, 237 c, 248 br, 249 c, 251 br.

**Bill Donahoe**: 9 tl, 146 c, 253 tc, 260 b.

**Richard Draper**: 30 b.

**Michael Fisher**: 88 br.

**Eugene Fleury**: 47 cr, 50 c, 51 c, 149 c, 151 br, 152 bc, 154 tr, 152 bc, 191 cr, 194 br, 280 c, 281 t.

**Chris Forsey**: 29 b, 34 cl, 63 cr, 64 c, bl, 84 c, 112 c, 128 c, 152 bl, 182 cl, 188 b, 263 c.

**Adam Hook**: 229 cr, 231 tr.

**Aziz Khan**
All country locator maps.

**Kenneth Lily**: 33 bl, 58 tr, 61 br, 67 bl, 71 bc, 79 c, 111 bc, 132 c, 139 br, 143 b, 173 br, 197 tl, 209 tc, 238 tc, 254 bc,258 tr, 259 tr, 265 bl, 266 c.

**David More**: 102 cl.

**Peter Morter**: 152 c, 154 b, 188 c, 194 c, 195 tr, 199 tr, cl, cr.

**David Mure**: p102 c.

**Sue Oldfield**: 26 cl.

**Richard Orr**: 40 c, 204 bc, 245 br, 263 b.

**Gill Platt**: 201 bl, 228 b, 264 t.

**Catharine Slade**: 58 c, 104 cl, 106 br, 185 t, 211 cl, 230 bl, 240 c.

**Peter Visscher**: 24 c, 202 c.

**Richard Ward**: 204 c, 255 tr.

**Debra Woodward**: 52 c.

# ACKNOWLEDGEMENTS

**Additional editorial assistance:**
Bernadette Crowley, Christiane Gunzi, Terry Martin

**Additional design assistance:** Diane Clouting

**Index and gazetteer:** Lynn Bresler

**Additional picture research:** Giselle Harvey

**DK Picture Researchers:** Sarah Mills and Rose Horridge

**Additional DTP assistance:** Nicky Studdart

**Film outputting**: Brightside, London


**Dorling Kindersley would like to thank the following people and organizations
for their help in the production of this book.**

Action Aid; The Algerian Embassy, London; The Arab British Centre, London; The
Argentinian Embassy, London; The Australian High Commission, London; The Australian
Tourist Commission, London; BP Exploration, London; The Belguim Embassy, London;
The Brazilian Embassy, London; Bridgestone Corporation, Belgium; British Airways
Holidays, West Sussex; The British Consulate General, Rio De Janeiro; The British Embassy,
Argentina; The British Embassy, Philippines; The British Museum Education Service,
London; The Bulgarian Embassy, London; C. P. Rail System, Montreal, Canada; Chamber
of Mines of South Africa, Johannesburg, South Africa; China National Tourist
Administration, London; Coal World Magazine; The Coffee Museum, London; Cotton
Council International, London; The Council for the Advancement of Arab-British
Understanding, London; Cyprus Olive Products, Cyprus; The Cyprus Tourist Board,
London; The Danish Embassy, London; De Beers, London; The Embassy of Ecuador,
London; The Embassy of Jordan, London; The Embassy of Mexico, London; The Embassy
of the Republic of Estonia, London; The Embassy of the Republic of Yemen, London; The
Embassy of the Syrian Arab Republic, London; Farmers Weekly; The Financial Times,
London; The Finnish Embassy, London; The Football Association, London; Sir Norman
Foster and Partners, London; Fyffes Group Ireland Ltd; Joss Graham; I. Hennig and Co
Ltd, London; Hong Kong Government Office, London; The Indonesian Trade Centre,
London; Institute of Civil Engineers, London; International Cocoa Organisation, London;
International Coffee Organisation, London; International Cotton Advisory Committee,
Washington, USA; Israeli Government Tourist Board, London; The Jordan Information
Bureau, London; Kew Gardens, London; Kibbutz Representatives, London; The Latvian
Embassy, London; The Lithuanian Embassy, London; The Luxembourg Embassy, London;
The Macau Tourist Information Bureau, London; The Malaysian Rubber Research and
Development Board; Menelik Restaurant, London; The Ministry of Agriculture, Grenada;
The Ministry of Tourism, Mexico; The Moroccan Embassy, London; Moss and Co, Timber
Importers, London; The Museum of Mankind, London; The National Cotton Council of
America, Memphis, USA; Neal Street East, London; Northern Territory House, London;
The Royal Norweigan Embassy, London; Oxfam, Oxford; Pilsner Urquell, Czech Republic;
Portuguese Trade and Tourism Office, London; The Queensland Tourist and Travel
Corporation, London; Railway Gazette International; The Romanian Embassy, London;
The School of African and Oriental Studies, University of London; Science Museum
Library, London; The Swedish Embassy, London; The Swiss Embassy, London; The Taipei
Representative's Office, London; The Trade Delegation of the Russian Federation in the
United Kingdom; The Tunisian Embassy, London; The Turkish Information Office,
London; Marion Turnock; Joan Twelves; UNICEF, Kampala; United Nations High
Commissioner for Refugees, London; Valley of the Kings Restaurant, London;
Wine and Spirit Education Trust, London.